Islamic Finance and Global Capitalism

James Simon Watkins

Islamic Finance and Global Capitalism

An Alternative to the Market Economy

palgrave
macmillan

James Simon Watkins
Regent's University London
London, UK

ISBN 978-3-030-59839-6   ISBN 978-3-030-59840-2 (eBook)
https://doi.org/10.1007/978-3-030-59840-2

This Palgrave Macmillan imprint is published by the registered company Springer Nature Switzerland AG
The registered company address is: Gewerbestrasse 11, 6330 Cham, Switzerland

Dedicated to Rachelle Delarosa—my wonderful mother, singer, poet and thinker who did so much to inspire me, who did so much to support others and who was so happy for me that I was writing this book—Thank you

Preface

As I write, the global economy is in lockdown—as am I.

Typing this preface at home under UK Government restrictions, this book was being prepared at a special time in global history—when the power of Governments trumped the dominance of the 'titans' of global markets by responding to a series of public health emergencies roiling across the world.

I am confident that by the time you have picked up this book, we will be in the recovery room for the global economy.

But what has the early months of the 2020s taught us about political economy?

Is it really the case that laissez-faire markets are essential for peoples' well-being or does the COVID-19 outbreak tell us that, when it comes to the crunch, free trade and market economics are footloose and ephemeral without the bulwark of nation states?

It could be argued that either of these statements is not contradictory—that free markets combined with the steadying influence of Governments conforms with the thinking of Adam Smith and successive economists.

However, the 2020 COVID-19 crisis has led to a debate as to whether the traditional economic model has led to short-term decision-making which is against the public good. For example, although we could not have predicted when the pandemic would occur, the coronavirus threat had been known for many years. The SARS (2002) and MERS (2012) outbreaks meant public funds were used to help develop a potential coronavirus vaccine but this was abandoned by pharmaceutical companies due to a lack of a guaranteed financial return in the short term.

One of the most striking comments at the start of the decade was from the Allianz Chief Economic Adviser, Mohamed El-Erian who spoke of the discord between "*Wall Street and Main Street*":

With markets focusing on the improvement in the "second derivative", that is a reduction in the rate of labour force dislocation, U.S. stocks rose. This widens an already considerable decoupling from the real economy and will fuel the debates on Wall Street versus Main Street, companies versus people and the well-off versus the marginalised.[1]

Advocates of Islamic finance argue that the risk sharing nature of this model would mean that the disconnect between markets and the real economy that can occur in conventional finance, cannot practically happen in Islamic finance.

It is not just COVID-19 that has led to the reappraisal of assumptions that has belied the Washington Consensus for the workings of the global economy.

When Margaret Thatcher declared that "*there is no alternative*" to free market economics, most commentators in the 1980s and 1990s accepted this comment as a statement of the obvious.

For the then UK Prime Minister was speaking at a time when communism was collapsing and free markets were seen not just as an economic system but as a guarantor of liberty against the collectivist demands of the State.

However, in the first few decades of the twenty-first century, following the 2008 global financial crisis and the 2020 coronavirus outbreak, questions were being asked as to whether there is an alternative to business as usual.

Consequently, the proponents of a stronger role for nation states in national economies cite the 2008 financial crisis to argue for a more enhanced economic role for the State whilst laissez-faire advocates can revert to Adam Smith's infamous 'invisible hand' to rebut such arguments.

But is there an economic system that enables a market economy to be effective whilst protecting the long-term interests of Governments, regulators and consumers?

Could Islamic finance really be seen as that alternative?

Islamic finance has a rich structure and robust set of values which, at first glance, seems almost utopian. It embraces the profit motive but prohibits investment in sectors that are deemed unethical such as selling arms and gambling.

It encourages long-term investment but prohibits short selling (borrowing shares of a company from an existing owner through her/his brokerage, selling those borrowed shares at the current market price and pocketing the cash).

It focuses on returns to investors from the success of the business but rules out returns that are based on interest.

In short, Islamic finance is a fundamental challenge to business as usual. It embraces the positive nature of investing for long-term growth whilst stopping businesses being obliged to pay interest-based loans that may have no bearing on the current performance of the company.

There is also no conflict between ethics and enhancing profits as can be seen with conventional finance. In addition, Islamic finance is structured in such a way that it encourages long-term investment rather than making money at the potential strategic expense of a company or a nation.

On the surface, this utopian system of ethical capitalism also seems to be highly profitable. The industry's total worth was estimated to be US$ 2.05 trillion in 2017. Global Sukuk (Islamic finance bonds) surged by a record 25.6% to close at US$399.9 billion as of 2017.[2]

Islamic finance is now visible across the world. From the Persian Gulf to Malaysia and from London to New York to Tokyo, Islamic finance is now a key feature of the global economy.

However, is Islamic finance as utopian in practice as it is in theory?

This book will examine the highs and lows of Islamic finance. Whilst this model can be structured for long-term investment, in a number of markets the sector is largely focused on short-term financing. Why is this and are there inherent weaknesses in broadening the scope of Islamic finance to meet all of a nation's needs?

The richness of Islamic finance with its differences in contract structures is seen by its critics as a complex maze that could lead, eventually, to an Islamic finance bust. Other critics argue that Islamic finance is based on a false premise and is a ruse to pursue an ideological agenda.

Whilst this book takes cognisance of the critics, the structured nature of Islamic finance—preserving the profit motive whilst avoiding the depredations of interest-based loans—is a unique form that offers a route through the boom and bust economics that all of us have got used to—often with tragic results for left behind communities.

Islamic finance—as a model of capitalism—has proven to be profitable for investors. There is hardly a bank or a consultancy which is not involved—in one way or the other—in the sector.

But as the industry grows, can it really offer an alternative to conventional finance?

The answers may surprise you—for by the time you finish reading this book—you may question whether Margaret Thatcher's dictum that "*there is no alternative*" really does hold true for the 2020s.

Birmingham, UK James Simon Watkins
May 2020

Notes

1. Mohamed Al-Erin (7 May 2020), *The Market Keeps Distancing Itself from the Economy*, Bloomberg website.
2. Global Islamic Finance Market—Growth, Trends, and Forecast (2018–2024), (July 2019) Mordor Intelligence.

Contents

List of Arabic Terms and List of Acronyms

Common era (CE) chronology will be used throughout this book instead of Anno Hegirae (in the year of the Hijra—AH) chronology unless otherwise stated.

There are some Arabic terms that are used repeatedly throughout the book.

For ease of reference these terms are:

Allah—God
Fatwa—Ruling or judgement
Fiqh—Islamic jurisprudence
Gharar—Uncertainty
Hadith—Sayings of the Prophet
Hajj—One of the five pillars of Islam with the pilgrimage to Mecca and its environs
Halal—Allowed
Haram—Forbidden
Istisn'a—Long-term project finance contract
Ijara—Financial and operational lease contract
Ijtihad—Reasoning
Ijma—Consensus
Maqasid al shari'a—Objectives of shari'a law
Maysir—Speculation
Mudaraba—Direct equity investment contract. Losses borne by one party to the contract

Musharaka—Direct equity investment contract. Losses borne by all parties to the contract
Sunnah—Customs and practices of the Muslim community which has been codified
Qimar—Gambling
Qiyas—Analogy
Qur'ran—Holy Book of Islam; revelation as communicated from God to the Prophet
Riba—This term primarily relates to interest payments
Salam—Short-term finance forward (non-tradeable)
Shari'a—Framework of Islamic law
Sukuk—Islamic finance bond
Takaful—Islamic insurance
Ulama—Muslim scholars who have specialist knowledge of shari'a law and theology
Ummah—Muslim community
Wakala—Agency (as in an agency contract)
Zakat—One of the five pillars of Islam with part of an individual Muslim's discretionary spend being allocated for charitable purposes

Some acronyms are also used repeatedly. These are:
AAOIFI—Accounting and Auditing Organisation for Islamic Financial Institutions
ASEAN—Association of South East Asian Nations
GCC—Gulf Cooperation Council
IFIs—Islamic Financial Institutions
IFSB—Islamic Financial Standards Board
IRTI—Islamic Research and Training Institute (part of the IsDB)
IsDB—Islamic Development Bank
OIC—Organisation for Islamic Co-operation
UAE—United Arab Emirates

List of Figures

CHAPTER 1

Introduction: Is There an Alternative?

There is no alternative.

As the shock of the 2008 global financial crisis reverberated across continents, pundits stubbornly argued that the excesses of capitalism were something we all had to grin and bear.

Whether it was the seventeenth-century craze for tulip bulbs or the 2001 dot com bubble, finance ministers through to brokers patiently explained to shocked consumers that capitalism's many upsides do come with occasional downside risks.

Even respected observers of the global markets—years after the 2008 financial crisis—felt that it was all too complicated to change how global capitalism works, including in the world's number one economy:

> Does the United States really know how to build a financial system that is the servant, not the master, of the economy? Sadly, the answer is probably no; at present it is hard to imagine what this would even look like.[1]

The immediate responses, during the 2020 coronavirus crisis, as to the future of capitalism was far more mixed. Mariana Mazzucato argued that the 2020 crisis meant capitalism as we know it had to change:

> We desperately need entrepreneurial states that will invest more in innovation – from artificial intelligence to public health to renewables. But as

J. S. Watkins, *Islamic Finance and Global Capitalism*,
https://doi.org/10.1007/978-3-030-59840-2_1

> this crisis reminds us, we also need states that know how to negotiate, so that the benefits of public investment return to the public.[2]

Other commentators saw the impact on capitalism from the 2020 crisis very differently. Allister Heath argued, instead, that a more laissez-faire approach to the economy will have to be adopted once the crisis was over:

> Hurting the rich for populist reasons is something that governments can afford to do in the good years, not when they are desperate to attract entrepreneurs, capital and talent.[3]

The well-rehearsed left/right paradigm as to the future of capitalism is playing itself out again.

However, there is an economic model that does not fit neatly within this dynamic and which may contain important lessons for the future of the global economy.

For there was one financial services sector that continued to grow through the 2008 financial crisis and beyond—Islamic finance. The sector had double digit growth during the crisis achieving a compound annual growth rate of 16.94% between 2009 to 2013.[4]

How was this possible?

The answer is that the very restrictions which govern the space in which Islamic finance operates within also help guide the sector's success.

Monem Salam from the shari'a compliant investment firm, Saturna Capital, has argued that as it is forbidden to invest in key sectors such as conventional banking and gambling as well as avoiding investing in over-leveraged companies, the sector weathered the 2008 economic storm. Salam has argued that the Islamic finance industry is also performing well, as compared to conventional finance, during the 2020 COVID-19 crisis, for the very same reasons.[5]

But many free market thinkers did not take on board the strength of Islamic finance. Instead the focus has been on conventional forms of capitalism. Had not the race to economic and social recovery from the devastation of the Second World War through the Cold War and up to the final collapse of the Soviet Union clearly demonstrated the sclerotic growth of Communist states as compared to the dynamism of Western capitalist countries?

Divided Cold War Germany became the textbook example of how free market capitalism, despite its faults, was the greatest guarantor of liberty and success. Whilst people were trying to escape the poverty of East Germany's state economy in order to live and thrive in capitalist West Berlin there was no such desire for people to risk their lives to escape the other way.

But when the employees of Lehman Brothers had to carry away their office belongings in boxes after the collapse of the bank in 2008—with markets and Governments going haywire in their efforts to avoid the default of the market economy, it seemed for a moment that Karl Marx's prediction of the coming collapse of bourgeois capitalism may have been closer to the mark than we ever could have thought.

However, the assumptions that the capitalist system must remain with its ups and downs persisted into the 2010s. Even with the rise of populist politicians, from Marine Le Pen's xenophobic messaging helping her party gain a third of the vote in the 2017 French Presidential election through to US President Donald Trump railing against international global financial institutions, for many contemporary thinkers it was assumed that there was not much that could really change in economic thinking to avoid such populist pitfalls.

In fact, a number of free market thinkers did not blame the decline of living standards and the impact this has had with the rise of populist politics with faults within capitalism. Instead, failures within the structure of the State were blamed:

> The current weakness of much of the western world isn't rooted in capitalism but in fundamental weaknesses of the State – including its structural fiscal deficits, complex and burdensome regulation, and world-trailing public services, where even some gains in public health are being reversed.[6]

Ayn Rand (1905–1982) was the supreme communicator for championing free markets whilst warning against the depredations of the State. Rand argued that each person is an end in and of her or himself. Each individual must exist for their own sake, neither sacrificing themselves to others nor sacrificing others for their own ends. The pursuit of rational self-interest and of individual happiness was described as the highest moral purpose of life:

> Collectivism holds that man must be chained to a collective and collective thought for the sake of what is called 'the common good'.[7]

But even arch adherents of Rand's work eventually began to have their doubts. For example the former US Federal Reserve Chairman, Alan Greenspan said he found Rand's arguments "*compelling*" but when the 2008 financial crisis finally occurred, his belief in a reduced role for the state and freedom of the markets collided with the facts that were presented before him:

> I made a mistake in presuming that the self-interests of organisations, specifically banks and others, were such that they were best capable of protecting their own shareholders and their equity in the firms.[8]

So, do existing financial models remain fit for purpose in a global economy or is there space for new financial structures which take account of wider ethical and investment needs?

Let's take microfinance as one example. In developing countries, this form of finance is critical to achieving any kind of sustainable growth. However, conventional microfinance institutions can charge comparatively high interest rates on loans to poor people. These high rates are justified as an outcome of high transaction costs.

However, if you have virtually no assets or a bank account, can you really cope with these levels of interest or could it lead to an invidious cycle of debt?

As we will discuss later in this book, Islamic microfinance would operate on a very different basis as compared to conventional microfinance.

Another criticism of the capitalist model, particularly in countries such as the United States and the United Kingdom, is that the desire for short-term rewards negates the need for long-term "patient capital" to invest in technologies which can address systemic issues impacting societies such as the challenge of climate change. Even the cradle of innovation that is California's Silicon Valley has not fully risen to the challenge of funding clean tech with the focus remaining, instead, on meeting short-term consumer demands.

Is this too negative a view as to the operation of the capitalist system? After all, as the old expression goes, money attracts money—but that is not necessarily good news for national economies. As Stephane Garelli has argued "*the big tech companies in the US and China have a strategy to buy out all the very good start-ups*" but:

> If you look at the competitiveness of a nation like the UK or Switzerland, for example, then you have to ask yourself where the large companies of tomorrow in those countries are going to come from if all the start-ups are suddenly being bought out.[9]

This is where the need for long-term or patient capital comes in—but are traditional finance structures fixated on short-term growth—or are the long-term Islamic finance models part of the answer to end the patient capital gap?

To be fair, the model of 'developmental capitalism' does exist in the Asia-Pacific with the incorporation of long-term finance structures which has contributed to the transformation of economies across the region. Concerns remain, however, that there is no getting around the booms and busts of conventional economics as the 1997 Asian Financial Crisis clearly demonstrated.

But what if there is an economic model that does embrace the market economy—but also has a collectivist approach towards supporting society rather than the individual. Could there be a capitalist structure that embraces the profit motive—but encourages investment for the long term? Could there be an approach that supports entrepreneurs but has a strong ethical underpinning towards supporting society?

Maybe Islamic finance could be part of this answer.

Some would posit the view that Islamic finance is just a cover for continuing conventional finance by other means. Umar Ibrahim Vadillo, for instance, is connected to the relatively small Murabitun World Movement which argues, amongst other matters, that the regular practice of one of the five pillars of Islam, zakat (using discretionary income for charitable giving) is not in compliance with the faith. In respect of Islamic finance, Vadillo has been scathing about its very existence:

> The so-called 'Islamic bank' is a usurious institution contrary to Islam. The 'Islamic bank' is an absurd attempt to resolve, as was done in the case of Christianity, the unswerving opposition of Islam to usury for fourteen centuries. Since its origins, the 'Islamic bank' has been patronised and promoted by usurers.[10]

By the time you finish reading this book, this claim should be effectively debunked. However, the vehemence of the language does reflect the debates which have occurred as to the future direction of Islam, particularly from the late nineteenth and early twentieth centuries.

The attraction of Islamic finance, for me, was down to the promise of a sustainable funding model which could meet the needs of societies whilst avoiding the depredations of the conventional money markets.

In truth, though, I came across Islamic finance completely by accident.

I had been on the centre left of politics for a very long time and was a former European Parliamentary candidate for the UK Labour Party. I recall seeing some of my contemporaries knocked for six when the communist model finally collapsed in the early 1990s. Was the collectivist approach of the left really a fantasy which could never operate in the real world of human needs and desires?

Later I led a regional business group in the West Midlands of the United Kingdom where the demand for patient capital was strong but, despite the warm words of the banks, the provision of patient capital was weak.

In my desire for more investment to flow into the West Midlands, I invited the Lord Mayor of the City of London to visit Birmingham. I thought it was time to get some of the success of the Square Mile to be reflected 120 miles away in the Midlands.

The Lord Mayor, Sir David Brewer, though, had an agenda I admit I knew nothing about at the time—Islamic finance.

It emerged that outside of London, Birmingham was (and remains today) one of Europe's leading centres for Islamic finance. As part of the Lord Mayor's itinerary, I heard how Islamic finance, though at an early stage of development, was beginning to meet the ethical, social and patient capital concerns that had occupied so many of us for so long.

Islamic finance has already begun to shape the British economy. Just look at the imposing glass tower that is the Shard in central London, paid for by a consortium of Qatari investors, through to the initial rescuing of the Aston Martin car business by a group of Kuwaiti companies (though, at the time of writing, the firm is facing new challenges) and onto plans to redevelop part of Birmingham city centre.

The City of London now rivals Dubai as an international hub for Islamic finance. A 2011 US Embassy report—leaked to Wikileaks—expressed concern that "*should London successfully position itself as a leading Islamic finance center, it could gain an edge on New York, when the global financial markets recover*".[11]

Since that report was leaked, the UK government has worked on two Sukuks (Islamic finance bonds) which has received much interest in the City of London whilst the growth of Islamic finance investment funds based in the Square Mile has continued apace.

Islamic finance is about much more than high finance and diplomatic cables. As it prohibits earning money from interest and is based on investing in businesses and assets—where speculation, such as short selling, is not allowed—it prioritises long-term investment over short-term gains.

Above all, it promotes ethical investment. Buying shares in tobacco companies or weapon manufacturers is prohibited. The principles of Islamic finance can be found in the Qur'ran but the industry that we see today only began to take shape from the 1960s.

This early period saw specially designed funds to assist Malaysian pilgrims to travel to Mecca. The model has since grown to high levels of sophistication to meet the needs of a dynamic economy. From Dow Jones screening shares of FTSE companies to assess ethical investment standards through to finance professionals from all backgrounds gaining qualifications in Islamic finance, the industry is coming of age.

If Islamic finance was used for long-term growth, this could be a tried and tested way to meet the patient capital gap and to address the weaknesses of more conventional finance structures which encourage short-term returns at the expense of the wider community.

The variety of risk sharing contracts in Islamic finance further provides opportunities for borrowers as they do not have to bear all risks associated with engaging with conventional financial services. Implicitly, this could lower the cost of financing.

There is also the tantalising possibility that a fully compliant Islamic finance system would end the two basic reasons for company bankruptcies—legally binding liabilities of firms to service their debts outstanding according to predetermined interest rates and excessive leveraging beyond their economic value as uncertainty and gambling on outcomes is strictly prohibited within Islamic finance.

Islamic finance promotes risk sharing in financial transactions and a financial system based on risk sharing offers various advantages over conventional finance that is based on risk shifting.

However, the fact that Islamic finance has not yet offered that long-term support in many countries indicates there are some hurdles holding back the development of the sector.

One of these hurdles is Islamophobia. I recall one Chamber of Commerce official in the United Kingdom advising me to rename Islamic finance at a time when open prejudice against Muslims and Islam was widely prevalent. In Turkey, Islamic finance can be called "participation finance" but whether a rebranding that denies the Islamic basis for this form of finance is the right thing to do is an ethical dilemma in and of itself which will be explored further in this book.

In addition, is it realistic for such rebranding to occur - in any case - with the number of regulatory structures that already exist internationally to support the growth and efficacy of the Islamic finance market?

There is also the issue that Islamic finance, in a number of countries, focuses to a large extent either on Sukuks or Islamic finance mortgages. This is despite the fact that other Islamic finance structures could be especially pertinent for small and medium sized businesses who are in need of patient finance.

This book will consider why a number of Islamic financial institutions are holding back from patient finance in a range of countries despite the very nature of the sector seemingly designed to provide this very form of support.

We will begin by considering the historical and theological underpinning of Islamic finance—a set of values that is shared within Judaism, Christianity and the world's other great religions. We will also discover how the sector has grown from a niche market in the 1960s to high finance in the 2020s.

We will explore the controversies within Islamic finance. Are Islamic derivatives really compliant with the sector's values when uncertainty seems to be at the heart of these products and trading on uncertainty is forbidden under shari'a law.

How are the complex structures of Islamic finance being developed and could the industry's very complexity lead to consumer confusion and so become the harbinger of a future bust in the Islamic finance market.

Are the international institutions who regulate the industry really fit for purpose and should there be an Islamic monetary policy?

Is Islamic finance shaping the political economic structures of nations in Africa, Asia and the Middle East? What lessons can we draw from the debate regarding Islamic finance and its place within the larger context of Islamic economics?

We will also look at the specific structures and incentives of Islamic finance which lends it the potential to be the leading vehicle for developmental finance in wealthy nations and developing economies.

Along the way, we will observe the role of Islamic scholars in corporate boardrooms, how the London Metals Exchange plays an unexpected role in some forms of short-term Islamic financing and how gaining a uniform regulatory approach for the industry across international borders may be easier said than done.

For many reading this book, Islamic finance may seem a strange and hard to grasp concept. How can you invest without interest? Why is uncertainty seen as bad when investing in and of itself is an inherently uncertain activity? Can you really focus on profit, ethics and long-term finance all at the same time?

The answers to these questions will be found in this book as Islamic finance has so much to offer to the global economy—but its contribution in meeting the needs of communities has only just begun.

Notes

1. Gillian Tett (July 2019), Faith Based Finance, *Foreign Policy Review*.
2. Mariana Mazzucato (30 March 2020), *Capitalism's Triple Crisis*, Mariana Mazzucato website
3. Allister Heath (1 April 2020), The Coronavirus Recession will Shift British Politics—But Not to the Left, *The Telegraph*.
4. Asian Development Bank/Islamic Financial Services Board (2015), *Islamic Finance for Asia: Development, Prospects and Inclusive Growth*, page 19.
5. Islamic Markets webinar, 3 June 2020.
6. Neil Ferguson, *The Ascent of Money: A Financial History of the World*.
7. "The Only Path to Tomorrow," *Reader's Digest*, Jan, 1944, 8.
8. Alan Greenspan, October 2008.
9. As cited in *Business Life* (December 2018), British Airways.
10. As quoted in *Islamic Finance in the Global Economy*, Ibrahim Warde, page 20 (Edinburgh University Press).
11. Leaked US diplomatic cable dated 14 February 2011 (Wikileaks).

CHAPTER 2

The Emergence of Islamic Finance

> Nobody can hope to understand the economic phenomena of any, including the present epoch, who has not an adequate command of the historical facts and an adequate amount of historical sense or of what may be described as historical experience.[1]

Islamic finance cannot be understood in a vacuum.

The sophisticated legal structures and the vibrancy of the contemporary Islamic finance market is based upon the wider history and faith of Islam.

It is this history and the understanding of religion that enables us not only to ascertain the very genesis of Islamic finance but also how the sector has changed and grown since its modern incarnation in the 1960s.

The American economist, Joseph Schumpeter recognised that historical factors impacted upon economic trends. Consequently, when we consider the future direction of Islamic finance through the 2020s and beyond, we would be at a loss of analysing this trend without a clear historical and theological understanding of the premises which lie behind Islamic finance.

This is not to say that Islamic finance does not have wider significance for businesses and consumers from all nations and for people of all backgrounds. We will consider the role of Islamic finance as part of the wider mutual economy debate and how adherents to laissez-faire economics as

J. S. Watkins, *Islamic Finance and Global Capitalism*,
https://doi.org/10.1007/978-3-030-59840-2_2

well as supporters of social democracy can connect to different aspects of Islamic finance to advance their theoretical perspectives.

Though Islamic finance is viewed as a niche product by many participants in the global money markets, in countries such as Saudi Arabia, Iran, Pakistan and Malaysia, Islamic finance plays a significant role in the operation of the political economy.

In other countries such as my own—the United Kingdom—where Islamic finance is seen as a specialist area when compared to the larger conventional investment and retail banking institutions, the sector has a number of lessons which can help nations attract patient capital and invest in technologies which require long-term finance.

As Schumpeter rightly observed, the "*fundamental phenomenon of economic development*" can disrupt the "*circular flow of economic life as conditioned by given circumstances*" to transform how an economy operates and performs.

Islamic finance has that potential to change the "*business as usual*" approach at a time, following the 2008 global financial crisis and the economic implications flowing from the 2020 COVID-19 outbreak, where national and multilateral institutions are seeking new ways to jump start business activity and to engender sustainable economic growth.

Islamic finance is a subset of Islamic economics where a whole system of economics has been devised whereby monetary, trade, fiscal and financing policies are designed to serve the wider good. It is Islamic finance, though, in our era which is the most successful branch of Islamic economics in terms of successfully reaching out to consumers across the globe.

However, before we jump to the lessons that Islamic economics and Islamic finance afford all of us, let us first consider the very earliest basis of this model—the revelation as received by the Prophet.

Formation of the Faith

The seventh-century desert plains of Arabia may not seem the obvious starting point to consider the complexities of urban-based twenty-first-century capitalism.

However, the Prophet Muhammed had much to say on the economy whether it was to do with taxes, trade or prices policy. The holy Qur'ran contains a range of business-related stipulations.

It would be wrong to presuppose that the world's other great religions do not refer to economic themes as well. In fact, as this and the next chapter will demonstrate, from Judaism to Christianity and from Hinduism to Buddhism to Sikhism, religions do stipulate proper conduct when it comes to business affairs.

Mahatma Gandhi (1869–1948) famously called for a "*true economics*" as part of his non-violent struggle against British colonialism in India. Speaking from a Hindu perspective, individuals were urged to live a "*decent life*" based on dharma (righteousness), artha (material wealth), kaam (happiness) and moksha (spiritual enlightenment).[2]

However, it could be argued that Islam has a particular focus upon economic issues. The Prophet was a trader and his wife, Khadija, was an investor in various trade missions. The revelation that the Prophet received from Allah and the experiences of the Prophet is imbued with this socio-economic understanding.

There are five pillars of Islam (which literally means "submission to God") which Muslims (literally means "one to submit to the faith") should adhere to. One of these is zakat—whereby a believer with discretionary resources would provide a percentage of these funds for charitable good works. Therefore, the very basis of Islam reflects the economic responsibilities which individuals should adopt.

With interest banned in all Islamic finance practices, it could seem that there is a disconnect between Islamic finance and conventional macroeconomic practices. However, I will posit the approach that in a number of crucial areas, Islamic finance has distinct synergies with laissez-faire economics whilst, with some of its legal constructs, Islamic finance shares some of its thinking with social democracy and East Asian developmental capitalism.

The Prophet and the Emergence of Islamic Economics

Mecca had always been an important centre of trade and pilgrimage before the advent of Islam. Worshippers performed the rite of tawaf or circumambulation around the holy Kaa'ba with its sacred stone and the Well of Zamzam. The city was home to a range of businesses and various belief systems coexisted within Mecca.

The Prophet was born in the city at around 570 and was part of the Quraysh tribe, which earned its living through trade. Commercial caravans travelled across the desert with camels laden up with goods. These traders connected the cities to the various ports in the Red Sea and Persian Gulf.

The business of the Quraysh is specifically referred to in the Qur'ran:

> To bring harmony to Quraysh,
> Their harmony being the journey of winter and summer.
> So let them worship the Lord of this House,
> Who fed them against hunger,
> And secured them against fear.[3]

At the age of 25, the Prophet married Khadija who was a widow and a businesswoman. When the Prophet reached the age of 40, he experienced a revelation in the hillside cave of Hira near Mecca. Over time, the Prophet received a series of messages which were codified, after the Prophet's death, in the Qur'ran.[4] Khadija was the first adherent of Islam after listening to the words uttered by the Prophet.

With the Prophet's call to believe in one God, this monotheistic faith was seen by vested interests in Mecca as a threat to their business model of attracting pilgrims who believed in a range of deities. The Prophet and his followers eventually left Mecca and the first Muslims settled in the oasis city of Yathrib—now known as Medina ("City of the Prophet").

This moment in 622 marks the Hijra (Separation) and the starting point of Muslim chronology.

It was in Medina that the Prophet established institutional structures and regulations which engendered a vibrant market economy. Consequently, the conduct of business and the concept of an ethical macroeconomic system was witnessed at the very emergence of the faith:

> Muhammed's economic policy promoted entrepreneurial initiative, efficient distribution of resources, and wealth creation, a framework for creating wealth that lasted for centuries. To Muhammed's followers his attention to the practicalities of business and to regulations for trading and tax came as no surprise; they would have expected no less from a successful businessman who came from a family with a long tradition of entrepreneurial drive.[5]

Koehler argued that the Prophet adopted a position on prices policy which, centuries later, concurred with the influential laissez-faire economist, Fredrich von Hayek (1899–1992). Koehler referred to a period when there were concerns regarding high food prices and the Prophet was asked to agree to a price cap. The Prophet refused and later said "*Prices are in the hand of God*".[6]

This statement has synergies with the thought of the Scottish Enlightenment thinker, Adam Smith (1723–1790) who spoke, in a non-religious context, of the ***invisible hand*** of the profit motive which helps guide the provision of goods and services whilst Hayek argued that if the price mechanism "***were the result of deliberate human design, it would have been acclaimed as one of the greatest triumphs of the human mind***".[7]

Not only was this early period in Islam dedicated to a free market in prices policy but free competition—specifically preventing the emergence of monopolies and price fixing—were additional key platforms of Islamic economics. This was demonstrated by the writings of Islamic thinkers who came after the Prophet.

Ibn Taymiyyah (1263–1328), a major thinker within the Hanbalite school of Islamic jurisprudence, expounded on why monopolies were counter-intuitive for economic growth:

> A more serious matter than this is where certain people have a monopoly of particular commodities, such that foodstuffs or other goods are sold only to them and then retailed by them, any would be competitor being restrained either harshly, by imposition, or by gentler means less open to abuse. In this situation prices must be controlled so that the monopolists sell only for value and buy people's goods only for fair value.[8]

This insight opened up the possibility that business regulation is required to avoid monopolies distorting the operation of the real economy.

This thought, as it happens, was reflected centuries later in 2018 when the US Senator, Lindsey Graham, accused Facebook Group CEO, Mark Zuckerberg, of being in charge of a monopoly.[9]

It could be argued, to slightly misquote Ibn Taymiyyah, that Facebook had gained a monopoly via "*some gentler means less open to abuse*". Nonetheless we can see, even at this early stage in our discussion, that in some core economic areas there are distinct synergies between what is known as Islamic economics and conventional free market practices.

This also includes the need to combat price fixing. As Ibn Taymiyyah had put it:

> When a group who buy or sell a certain type of commodity conspire to depreciate what they buy and so buy for less than the customary fair price while promoting what they sell above the customary price, and to malign what they buy ... they will have conspired to wrong people so that they would have to sell their goods (for less) and to buy for more than the fair price.[10]

It should be noted that Ibn Taymiyyah was controversial in his day due to the literalist approach to Islam which he adopted which led one scholar from this early period to declare:

> Ibn Taymiyya is a servant whom God has forsaken, led astray, made blind and deaf, and degraded. Such is the explicit verdict of the leading scholars who have exposed the rottenness of his ways and the errors of his statements.[11]

Today, Ibn Taymiyya is viewed as one of the leading figures who contributed to the eventual emergence of Wahhabi thinking which is prevalent in contemporary Saudi Arabia. In turn, Wahhabism has been condemned by some modern commentators for encouraging terrorist acts. We will consider throughout this book the wider theological tensions in Islam and how this relates to modern Islamic finance practices.

Another synergy between Islamic economics and free markets relates to cluster theory. The words of the twelfth-century trader and Muslim economic thinker, Al-Dimashqi, presaged Adam Smith's *invisible hand* theory as well as pre-empting the concept of cluster theory as championed by the American academic, Michael Porter, in 1990.

Cluster theory is defined as a geographic concentration of related companies, organisations and institutions in a particular field which can be present in a region, state or nation. Clusters arise because they raise business productivity which is influenced by local assets and the presence of similar firms, institutions and infrastructure which surround it.

Abu al-Fadl Al-Dimashqi wrote:

> No individual can, because of the shortness of his life span, burden himself with all industries. If he does, he may not be able to master the skills of all of them from the first to the last. Industries are all interdependent.

> Construction needs the carpenter and the carpenter needs the ironsmith and the ironsmith needs the miner, and all these industries need premises. People are, therefore, necessitated by force of circumstances to be clustered in cities to help each other in fulfilling their mutual needs.[12]

The Emergence of Tax Policy

The Prophet pioneered tax policy for Muslims and people of other faiths in Medina. Tax exemptions existed for non-Muslims and tax rates were progressive for people of other religions depending upon the income of the individual.

However, controversy regarding the interrelationship between Islam and tax policy occurred from time to time. For instance, Schama noted there was an aggressive stance on tax for non-Muslims in Egypt (part of the Islamic caliphate) during the twelfth century:

> Collectors were supposed to keep their payers waiting, then shout at them, seize them by the scruff of the neck and even slap their faces.[13]

Centuries later, in April 2020, the Houthi administration in war-torn Yemen decided that the income generated from a 20% 'zakat tax' on utilising natural resources such as oil, gas and fishing would support poor people and the Hashemites who are considered to be the descendants of the Prophet. The rival Yemeni Government compared the tax change to the apartheid measures which had existed in South Africa.[14]

Many of the early Islamic thinkers, though, pioneered ideas that would now be defined as progressive taxation. Abu Yusuf (735 or 739–789 or 800) advanced Islamic thinking in respect of the economic benefits of progressive taxation. A key thinker from the Hanafi jurisprudence school, he argued that progressive taxation strengthened entrepreneurship and increased the tax take for the State.

This analysis did not always reflect the day to day actions as witnessed in the early Islamic caliphate. Caliph Uthman ibn Affan (579–656) was said, according to one account, to have been so heartened by the tax take from Egypt that he used the analogy that "*the camel has given more milk*" to which the Governor of Egypt, Amr al As (585–664) apparently responded with the quip that the camel may have given more milk but the camel's young had died.[15]

In Abu Yusuf's work *Kitab al kharaj* (Book of Taxation or Book of Land Taxation), which was prepared at the instigation of Caliph Hārūn al-Rashīd (763 or 766–809), it was demonstrated that progressive taxation, where taxes are raised on the individual ability to pay rather than a uniform tax band for all income groups, encouraged people to develop their businesses which led to greater economic growth and a high tax take for the State.

Consequently, the then practice of collecting taxes from farmers in the form of cash, if there had been a bad harvest or in the form of crops if there had been a good harvest, was condemned by Abu Yusuf as it discouraged business activity:

> The two alternating modes of fixed rates, in kind or in cash, are also detrimental to the taxpayers because of the opportunities they provide for unjust distribution of the taxes and the oppression of the weak by the strong.[16]

The analysis of Abu Yusuf would be more familiar to many people today with the Laffer Curve which was developed by the supply-side economist, Arthur Laffer. The theory is intended to show the relationship between tax rates and the amount of tax revenue collected by governments. The American economist first publicly presented this concept to senior aides of US President Gerald Ford on the back of a napkin.

Since then the curve has been used to illustrate Laffer's argument that sometimes cutting tax rates can increase total tax revenue (though arguments continue as to whether the premise of the theory takes into account a wide range of variables that are inherent in contemporary societies). Again, we can see the synergies between early Islamic economic thinking and contemporary laissez-faire economics.

Ibn Khaldun (1332–1406) was a scholar whose influence in economic theory is felt today. Like a number of other early Islamic thinkers, he presaged Adam Smith's analysis of the division of labour and argued that this social stratification created surplus value:

> Thus, he cannot do without a combination of many powers from among his fellow beings, if he is to obtain food for himself and for them. Through cooperation, the needs of a number of persons, many times greater than their own *(number)*, can be satisfied.[17]

Khaldun's thinking also has parallels with supply-side economics where he argued against excessive taxation:

> It should be known that at the beginning of the dynasty, taxation yields a large revenue from small assessments. At the end of the dynasty, taxation yields a small revenue from large assessments.[18]

Khaldun also praised the free market and argued that when Governments try to own many assets this is counter-intuitive to realising a sustainable income base to fund public services:

> Curtailment of allowances given by the ruler implies curtailment of the tax revenue ... Now, if the ruler holds on to property and revenue ... then the property in the possession of the ruler's entourage will be small. ... *(When they stop spending)*, business slumps and commercial profits decline because of the shortage of capital. Revenues from the land tax decrease, because the land tax and taxation depend on cultural activity and commercial transactions, business prosperity and the people's demand for gain and profit ... The dynasty is the greatest market, the mother and base of all trade, the substance of income and expenditure. If government business slumps and the volume of trade is small, the dependent markets will naturally show the same symptoms, and to a greater degree.[19]

With this early thinking on supply-side economics, it may not have been too surprising that Ronald Reagan, in the 1980s, quoted Ibn Khaldun to justify his determination for the United States to pursue such policies.[20]

Risk Sharing and the Concept of Interest Rates

The differences really emerge between conventional finance and Islamic finance when it comes to risk sharing and banning interest. The perceived banning of interest from the time of the Prophet is a cornerstone of modern Islamic finance structures.[21]

Caliph Ali ibn Abi Talib (who was a cousin and son-in-law to the Prophet and is considered by Shi'a Muslims to have been the legitimate successor to lead the caliphate after the death of the Prophet) succinctly defined profit and loss without the role of interest:

> Profit follows the conditions agreed upon, loss follows the capital.[22]

Therefore, there was a need for a legal structure for this business relationship to develop. The concept of qirads emerged.

Muhammad Ahmad Abi Sahl Abu Bakr al-Sarakhsi (died 1096) was a key theorist in the Hanafi school of Islam. Al-Sarakhsi defined qirads as a model which has some similarities to the contemporary Islamic finance contract of mudaraba:

> For the possessor of capital may not find it possible to engage in profitable trading activity, and the person who can find it possible to engage in such activity may not possess the capital. And profit cannot be attained except by means of both of these, that is, capital and trading activity. By operating this contract, the goal of both parties is attained.[23]

Consequently, profit shares, salary and bonuses for the manager of the trade mission were all agreed upon in advance. As we will also see in Chapter 5 with contemporary Islamic finance practices, there could still be complications:

> A manager could act on account of two separate qirads with profits accruing to a distinct line of business, say, one for trading in wool and another for trading in silk. Thus, there was an incentive to book losses to one qirad and profits to another, thereby excluding losses from bonus calculations. A case was brought before a qadi *(shari'a law judge)* where investors sued a manager who exploited this loophole to maximise his bonus; the qadi imposed on the manager a duty to set off losses from profits and calculate his bonus on the residual balance.[24]

The actions of Caliph Umar (584–644) set a legal precedent for Governments to be engaged in Islamic finance. Umar's sons, Abdullah and Ubaidullah, used public funds to invest in a successful business venture. When Umar became aware of this, he objected to what had happened and said his sons had exploited their privileged positions as his offspring to use public money for their own private gain.

However, Abdullah and Ubaidullah objected to the stance of their father and said they had taken a risk that had worked out so they should keep the profits which had accrued—for if the business venture had failed both men would have been personally liable for the losses.

Upon taking advice, Umar treated what had occurred as a qirad with the state having been a notional equity partner and the sons, consequently, were entitled to half the profits. This precedent is remembered today with Governments involved in Islamic finance projects such as, to take just one random example, the funding for the development of Dubai airport.

Following the death of the Prophet at the age of 61 or 62 in the year 632 there were various developments in monetary policy during the early decades of the Islamic caliphate which will be explored in Chapter 8.

Islamic belief and culture during these centuries shaped our modern world. For example, when we think, today, of algorithmic trading on global exchanges, we can acknowledge that the Islamic scholar al-Khwarizmi (died 850) lent his name to the term ‘algorithm’.

It was this Islamic legacy to global culture and economy that the US President, Barack Obama tried, in 2009, to tap into when he attempted to reset relations between the United States and Muslim majority nations:

> It was Islam – at places like Al-Azhar *(University in Cairo)* – that carried the light of learning through so many centuries, paving the way for Europe’s Renaissance and Enlightenment. It was innovation in Muslim communities – *(applause)* – it was innovation in Muslim communities that developed the order of algebra; our magnetic compass and tools of navigation; our mastery of pens and printing; our understanding of how disease spreads and how it can be healed. Islamic culture has given us majestic arches and soaring spires; timeless poetry and cherished music; elegant calligraphy and places of peaceful contemplation. And throughout history, Islam has demonstrated through words and deeds the possibilities of religious tolerance and racial equality. *(Applause)*[25]

There were also new developments in banking with merchants being able to pay money into accounts in one city and draw money in another. These drafts had several names and one of them in Persian was cak which is the linguistic basis for today’s word—cheque.

Other initiatives from these times also reflect practices undertaken today. For example, Islamic charitable foundations funded by endowments and known as waqfs had its genesis in this early period.

However, the Sunni–Shi’a divide changed the shape of Islam and has impacted on contemporary Islamic finance practices.

Sunni/Shi’a Divide

One of the key themes throughout this book is how Islamic finance legal structures enable the facilitation of long-term funding for small and medium sized enterprises combined with these very same contract models enabling investment not to be curtailed in the chase for short-term profits.

Instead, I will argue, some of the practices of Islamic finance can help engender longer-term business strategies which, in turn, encourages economic growth and job creation.

These legal structures find their genesis in Islamic jurisprudence. For Islam, as compared to some religions, is focused on doctrinal and, therefore, legal analysis. Koehler argued that this was due to the stance of the Prophet:

> Muhammad had set the direction of Islamic jurisprudence through his pronouncement that Islam should have no priestly caste. The ramifications of that decree were far-reaching, because in the absence of priests, debates over the direction of Islam were conducted in terms that were legal rather than theological.[26]

However, theological disagreements did emerge within the faith with the division between Sunni Islam (sunni derives from sunna—the traditions and customs of Islam) and Shi'a Islam (Shi'a is the contraction of the phrase 'Shiat Ali', meaning 'partisans of Ali').

It is outside of the purview of this book to provide a detailed history of this Sunni/Shi'a divide but a brief overview would be beneficial to readers who are not fully acquainted with this theme in order to understand what has led to the differences, as well as the similarities, in the practice and theory of contemporary Islamic finance within Iran, a Shi'a majority country and Saudi Arabia and the Gulf States which are primarily Sunni majority countries.

When the Prophet died in 632, he was succeeded as leader or caliph of the Muslim community by his close companion, Abu Bakr. However, there was a group, at the time, who argued that the Prophet's cousin and son-in-law, Ali, should have been appointed instead.

After the assassination of Caliph Uthman, Ali was finally recognised by all as Caliph. However, Aisha, the wife of the Prophet and daughter of Abu Bakr accused Ali of being lax in bringing Uthman's murderers to justice. These tensions eventually led to the Battle of the Camel in 656 in Basra where Aisha's forces were defeated. Aisha later apologised to Ali.

However, the Governor of Damascus, Mu'awiya, also said Ali should do more to bring to account the assassins of Uthman. This led to the indecisive Battle of Siffin in 657. Mu'awiya and Ali agreed to reach some kind of agreement through arbitration but a small group of Ali's followers objected to this approach and in 661 Ali was murdered while he was praying within the mosque at Kufa.

Mu'awiya then became caliph. In 680 on the death of Mu'awiya, his son, Yazid, succeeded his father as caliph. By this time, Ali's son, Hussein, was invited by people in Kufa to lead their Muslim community but this opening to Hussein was opposed by Yazid. Consequently, Yazid's forces took action in the Battle of Karbala where Hussein was killed—a moment in history that is remembered with much solemnity by Shi'a Muslims each year on the Day of Ashura.

This very brief account does not give full justice to the initial emergence of the Sunni/Shi'a divide—but it does indicate a division in view as to who was the appropriate person to succeed the Prophet in his separate role as Caliph and this led to wider consequences:

> … the conflict between Sunnis and Shi'a was never just a mere quarrel over the prophet of Islam's succession. For it immediately raised essential questions as to the nature of legitimate political authority. What sort of qualities should be possessed by the Muslim head of state? Could he be an ordinary human being or should there be something of the divine about him? How was he to be chosen and, by extension, what was the most legitimate type of political regime?[27]

There are also doctrinal differences between Sunni and Shi'a Islam. In particular, we should take particular note of Twelver Shi'a belief as it is now the largest Shi'a group and Twelver Shi'a Islam is reflected within the theocracy of the Islamic Republic of Iran.

The Twelfth Iman, Muḥammad ibn al-Ḥasan, was understood to have been born in around 870 but to have gone into occultation—a state of concealment by God—in around 874. The "Hidden Imam", as he is sometimes called, is believed to be alive and will return when God determines it to be appropriate and safe. As the Rightly Guided One (mahdī), upon his return he will inaugurate the processes associated with the last days and the Day of Judgement.

Consequently, the doctrine of the Imam's occultation meant a clergy was necessary to guide people in advance of the return of the Hidden Iman whilst in Sunni Islam the emphasis is on the direct relationship between the believer and God. In Twelver Shi'a Islam there is a greater focus on considering the spiritual example of holy men whilst Sunni Islam has a clear focus on various schools of textual Islamic jurisprudence.

However, as Louer has recognised, it is a relatively modern phenomenon that the division of Shi'a and Sunni has caused such violence and discord compared to occasional efforts over the centuries at Islamic concord:

> Whilst the pan-Islamic ideal continues to be seen as a desirable goal, the project of establishing a unified Islamic state across national borders is no longer on the agenda, having been swept aside in order to focus on the national framework. A number of ideologues, Sunni and Shi'a alike, have theorised the legitimate existence of citizenship-based belonging in the national framework.[28]

The modern tensions are on show in Saudi Arabia where its Eastern Province has a Shi'a majority whilst Saudi Arabia, as a whole, has a majority Sunni population. This has led some members of the governing Al Saud family to claim that Shi'a Muslims are not fully patriotic to the Saudi state. For example, in April 2015, the Governor of the Eastern Province, Prince Saud bin Nayef Al Saud, said:

> While our country is going through what it is going through and standing together as one bloc, we find the descendants of the fickle Safavid Abdullah Ibn Saba who try to divide that bloc.[29]

This is, in fact, a derogatory comment in referencing a seventh-century Yemeni Jew who ostensibly converted to Shi'a Islam. It is disputed whether such a person ever existed.

Schools of Islamic Jurisprudence

Islamic schools of thought have proven to be a pivotal factor as to the practical applicability and marketing of Islamic financial products. This is due to financial institutions being heavily reliant on the advice and fatwas (rulings) of religious scholars, based on Islamic jurisprudence (fiqh) to ascertain whether particular Islamic finance products are shari'a compliant and so can be marketed to consumers.

Depending upon which school of thought a scholar is from, this can have a bearing as to how a financial product is approved and considered.

This is critical to appreciate in Islamic finance as shari'a law (shari'a literally means 'the way') is not a corpus of legal texts, as would be found in common law in England and Wales, to take just one example.

In fact, the Qur'ran, sunna and hadiths provide a framework for judgements to be discerned, debated and analysed. Therefore, interpretations of shari'a law can be fluid depending upon which scholar from which school of thought is analysing a particular matter.

The framework approach of shari'a law is often misunderstood and, as we shall see in Chapter 11, even the European Court of Human Rights did not grasp the very nature and context of shari'a law in a judgement it reached in 2004.

Whilst the Zaidi, Zahiri, Sufian Al'thawree, Sufian bin O'yayna, Layth bin Sa'ad, Tabari and Qurtubi schools of thought do exist, within Sunni Islam there are four main schools of jurisprudence. These are:

- Hanafi (commonly found in Turkey, Pakistan, Balkans, Central Asia, India, Bangladesh, Afghanistan, China and Egypt)
- Maliki (commonly found in North Africa, West Africa and the Persian Gulf region)
- Shafi'i (commonly found in Arabia, Indonesia, Malaysia, Maldives, Egypt, Somalia, Eritrea, Ethiopia, Yemen and southern parts of India)
- Hanbali (commonly found in Arabia).

The Hanafi school stems from Abu Hanifa (699–767), a silk merchant from Kufa. Hanafites assume that God is rational so seek to discern the underlying purpose of texts from the holy Qur'ran via reasoning with the use of qiyas (analogy). This school of thought has developed forms of logic and questioning which has profoundly shaped modern Islam.

The Hanafi school, at an early stage in its history, developed the concept of hila (plural—hiyal) which means escape or, critics would argue, it could be translated as 'loophole'. Therefore, it allowed philanthropists to create charitable trusts which would seem, on the face of it, to be in violation of the inheritance rules as stipulated within the Qur'ran. Hanafi thinking also enabled the development of a money economy with the utilisation of paper cash, cheques and letters of credit.

Malik ibn Anas (718–796) took a different approach to doctrinal matters. Whilst the Hanafi school considered qiyas to develop their understanding of the faith, the Maliki school focused on ijma or scholarly consensus. This, in part, reflected Malik's background living in Medina. Malik was also an interesting figure for whilst he was a Sunni, he had supported the failed opposition against Caliph al-Mansur which was led by Shi'a Muslims.

In Malik's work *al-Muwatta* (The Smooth Path), it described how the scholars of Medina used ijma to address questions of ritual, etiquette and civic duty. There was also an element of considering legal precedents when reaching judgements. As Malik once stated:

> When there is a clear practice in Medina and people follow it, I do not see room for anyone to go against it. This is because the people of Medina have in their hands the inherited tradition that no one else can claim or falsely attribute to themselves.[30]

One of Malik's students, Muhammad al-Shafi'i from Cairo (767–820) was instrumental in founding the Shafi'i school. Al-Shafi'i agreed with Malik on the concept of ijma and he also agreed with Hanafi on qiyas. Al-Shaf'i went one stage further by setting down systemic ideas as to how to exercise a discretion where no clear rule governed the case that was being considered—arguably Islam's first theory of judgement.

In addition, Al-Shafi'i argued that hadiths could have as much legal force as the Qur'ran if the hadith in question could be directly sourced to the Prophet or an isnad—a supporting chain of named transmitters whose authenticity can vouch for the accuracy of the reported statements.

Al-Shafi'i also considered the thorny issue of naskh—a theory developed to resolve seemingly contradictory rulings of revelation by superseding or cancelling the earlier revelation. Al-Shafi'i contended that God's responses to changing circumstances meant some older verses of the Qur'ran could be legally ineffective. The Prophet also adjusted his behaviour so some hadiths may have succeeded over other hadiths. Therefore, detailed study was required, including study of various verses and hadiths by chronological order.

Hanbali thought took around 200 years to develop into a school of jurisprudence but, today, it is a particularly important doctrinal area of analysis for the Hanbalite tradition is rooted in Saudi Arabia where a number of key decisions for the development of the Islamic finance industry was made, such as the seminal 1976 Islamic economics conference in Mecca (which will be elaborated further in Chapter 10).

Ibn Hanbal (780–855) was influenced by the Hanafi jurist, Abu Yusuf, whose work in analysing tax policy was considered earlier in this chapter. Ibn Hanbal developed over time a literalist approach to faith.

Sometime after Ibn Hanbal's death, this stance was further refined in respect of the debate regarding verses in the Qur'ran which refers to the face of God and God being present on a throne. Some scholars argued that such matters can never be fully known but Hanbalites argued that these verses meant a literal understanding of the appearance of God could be sought. As Kadri observed:

> And though that might sound like a theological irrelevance, such things did not exist in tenth century Baghdad. Comprehending the attributes of God was a matter of salvation and damnation - and in a fraught political climate, the nature of His throne could, and occasionally did, become a matter of life and death.[31]

By the fourteenth century, the Hanbalite school was respected for producing thoughtful and impartial judges, including in Islamic finance matters, as a decree issued by the Baybars Sultan, An-Nasir Muhammad, in 1322 indicated:

> The people of Damascus are often in need of a judge from the Hanbalite school in most contracts of sale and lease, in certain sharecropping contracts, in assessing settlements when contracts are frustrated by natural disasters, in marrying off a male slave to a free woman with the permission of his master, in stipulating that a bride should not be relocated from her home town, in dissolving the marriage of a husband who deserted his wife without maintenance, and in the sale of an irreparable and dilapidated endowment that is of no use to its beneficiaries.[32]

In respect of Shi'a fiqh, this is reflected in the Jafari school, which is named after the sixth Imam, Jafar al-Sadiq (died 748).

Jafari thought recognises the Qur'ran, the sunna and ijma when reaching judgements. In that sense, Jafari thought shares some similarities with differing Sunni schools of fiqh. However, the Jafari school also recognises rational intellect (aql) as a source of reaching judgements under shari'a law. This reflected an earlier theological school in Islamic history, the Mut'taziltes which also argued that the meaning of shari'a can change over time based on changes in society and technology.

Therefore, aql was capable of inferring judgments drawn from both pure and practical reason. Whatever is judged necessary by reason is also judged necessary by revelation. This correlation between reason and revelation has allowed Shi'a jurists to derive religious rulings on many issues not covered in normative sources such as the *Qur'ran* and Sunna.

In a period where attempts were made to bring together the Shi'a and Sunni communities, Azhar University in Cairo, which has a very long history of Islamic scholarship stemming from 970 or 972, decided in 1959, to afford the Jafari school the status of the "*fifth school*" alongside the four main Sunni schools.

Today, Jafari fiqh has a direct bearing on society in Iran, including with the key role of Islamic finance in Iranian society, and influenced the thinking of the leader of the 1979 Iranian Revolution, Ayatollah Khomeini:

> Shi'a seminaries in Iraq and Iran still turn out more emotional ayatollahs *(high ranking Twelver Shi'a clerics)* than anyone could safely shake a stick at, but they retain an interest in Islam's encounter with Greek philosophy that Sunni jurisprudence has lost. Ayatollah Khomeini was particularly keen on the writings of a polymath named Abu Nasr al-Farabi (870–950/1), whose many works included a Muslim version of Plato's Republic - the Virtuous City - and he so liked the notion of an ideal state led by rational and virtuous men that he borrowed it to create the Islamic Republic of Iran.[33]

It was in the swinging 1960s that the Islamic finance industry—as we know it today—really began. It was the era of the Beatles, Carnaby Street, the Mary Quant dress and breaking away from long held cultural norms.

It was also the era of Nasser, anti-colonial struggles, the rise of nationalism in east Asia and the Middle East, the foundation of the Non-Aligned Movement and the Cold War. This desire for change in the '60s also led to the emergence of the modern Islamic finance industry.

In Chapter 10, we will see how the historical development of Islamic finance over the nineteenth and twentieth centuries also shaped the political economic models of countries in Africa, Asia and the Middle East.

Before we explore in depth the wider political implications of the industry, we need to first consider what are the overriding principles of Islamic finance which impinges upon the very operation of the industry which has led one ratings agency to describe such conditions as "*constraining*".[34]

Note

1. Joseph Schumpeter (1954: 12–13).
2. O P Misra (1995), *Economic Thought of Gandhi and Nehru: A Comprehensive Analysis* (M D Publications Pvt Ltd), page 104.
3. Qu'ran, 106:4.
4. The derivation of the word, Qur'ran, may be from an Arabic noun meaning "to read". However, this etymology continues to be the subject of academic debate.
5. Benedickt Koehler, *Early Islam and the Birth of Capitalism*, page 16.
6. Abu Yusuf, *Kitab al kharaj*, page 102.
7. Ibid., page 11.
8. Ibn Taymiyah, *Public Duties in Islam*, page 36.
9. The transcript of the questioning of Mr Zuckerberg in the US Senate on 10 April 2018 reflects ijtihad (process of legal reasoning) which is found in contemporary Islamic finance:

GRAHAM:	Who is your biggest competitor?
ZUCKERBERG:	We have a lot of competitors.
GRAHAM:	Who is the biggest?
ZUCKERBERG:	Do you want just one? I don't know that I can give one, but I can give a bunch.
GRAHAM:	Yes.
ZUCKERBERG:	There are three categories I focus on, platforms like Google, Apple, Amazon and Microsoft.
GRAHAM:	Do they provide the same service you provide?
ZUCKERBERG:	In different ways, in different parts, yes.
GRAHAM:	If I buy a Ford, it doesn't work well, I don't like it; I buy a Chevy. If I'm upset with Facebook, what's the equivalent product I can go and sign up for?
ZUCKERBERG:	The second category that I was going to talk about—
GRAHAM:	I'm not talking about categories; is there real competition you face? Car companies face a lot of competition: they make a defective car, it gets out in the world, people stop buying that car and buy another one. Is there an alternative to Facebook in the private sector?
ZUCKERBERG:	Yes, Senator. The average American uses eight apps to communicate with friends and stay in touch with people.

GRAHAM:	The same service you provide?
ZUCKERBERG:	We provide a number of services.
GRAHAM:	Is Twitter the same thing you do?
ZUCKERBERG:	It overlaps with what we do.
GRAHAM:	You don't think you have a monopoly?
ZUCKERBERG:	Doesn't feel like that to me. (Audience laughter)
GRAHAM:	It doesn't? You bought Instagram. Why did you buy Instagram?
ZUCKERBERG:	They were very talented app developers who were making good use of our platform and understood our values.
GRAHAM:	It was a good business decision. My point is that one way to regulate a company is through competition, through government regulation.

10. Ibn Taymiyyah, *Public Duties in Islam*, page 47.
11. Ibn Hajar al Haytami (1503–1566) as quoted by Rapoport, Yossef; Ahmed, Shahab (2010-01-01). *Ibn Taymiyya and His Times* (Oxford University Press), page 271.
12. Umer Chapra (2010), *EH.net: Encyclopedia of Economic and Business History*, edited by Robert Whaples.
13. Simon Schama, *The Story of the Jews—Finding the Words—1000 BCE–1492 CE*, page 246.
14. Bloomberg (10 June 2020), *Yemen's Houthis Slammed for 'Descent from Prophet' Tax Change.*
15. Benedict Koehler, *Early Islam and the Birth of Capitalism*, page 142.
16. Abu Yusuf, *Kitab al kharaj*, page 101.
17. Ibn Khaldun (1377), *The Muqaddimah: An Introduction to History*, translated by Franz Rosenthal, page 87.
18. Ibid., page 352.
19. Ibn Khaldun, *The Mugaddimah*, 3 vols., translated by Franz Rosenthal (New York: Pantheon Books, 1958), pages 279–280.
20. Reagan cites Islamic scholar, *New York Times*, 2 October 1981.
21. There is a theological debate as to whether the doctrines of Islam really do ban the use of interest and this debate is referred to in Chapter 3. However, the primary purpose of this book is to consider the practical application of contemporary Islamic finance practices upon political economy rather than consider the efficacy of these doctrinal disputes.
22. Udovitch, *Partnership and Profit in Early Islam*, page 129.
23. Al-Sarakhsi quoted in Ray, *The Medieval Islamic System of Credit and Banking*, pages 45–46.
24. Benedikt Koehler, *Early Islam and the Birth of Capitalism*, page 126.

25. Speech by then US President, Barack Obama (4 June 2009), Cairo University.
26. Benedikt Koehler, *Early Islam and the Birth of Capitalism*, page 137.
27. Laurence Louer, *Sunnis and Shi'a: A Political History*, page 1.
28. Ibid., page 80.
29. Human Rights Watch (24 August 2017), *Anti Shia Bias Driving Saudi Arabia Unrest*.
30. Abdul-Jabbar, *Bukhari*, page 67.
31. Sadakat Kadri, *Heaven on Earth—A Journey Through Shari'a Law*, page 70.
32. Ibid., page 105.
33. Ibid., page 77.
34. Fitch Ratings (17 June 2020), *Islamic Derivatives Increasingly Necessary but Constrains Remain*.

CHAPTER 3

In the Beginning …

Sometimes the law is not held in high regard as the fictional Mr Bumble expounded upon in *Oliver Twist*:

> The law is an ass - a idiot. If that's the eye of the law, the law is a bachelor; and the worst I wish the law is, that his eye may be opened by experience - by experience.[1]

As was witnessed during the 2008 global financial crisis, Mr Bumble's dictum was echoed across the world when regulatory failure was blamed—in part—for banks over-leveraging and for risky securities being sold without proper oversight, allowing the crisis to fester and eventually lead to financial ruin for far too many people.

Therefore, the values that underpin an economic model is critical to ascertain whether the model can be sustainable in and of itself.

Some of you reading this book may disagree with this and instead cite Adam Smith's ***invisible hand*** where markets self-regulate in the public interest and the goods and services we receive is thanks to the profit motive rather than an overarching set of ethical and/or religiously based values.

Smith also observed this invisible hand when it came to banking:

> This free competition too obliges all bankers to be more liberal in their dealings with their customers, lest their rivals should carry them away. In

J. S. Watkins, *Islamic Finance and Global Capitalism*,
https://doi.org/10.1007/978-3-030-59840-2_3

> general, if any branch or trade, or any division of labour, be advantageous to the public, the freer and more general the competition, it will always be the more so.[2]

However, contemporary regional disparities tell another story as to the effectiveness of Smithian thought where free markets are supposed to enable equality of opportunities. Examples include inequities within nation states such as the north–south divide within the United Kingdom, the success of the metropolitan east and west coasts in the United States as compared to the 'rust belt' states or the economic dynamism around China's Guangdong province compared to poorer provinces in the west of the country such as Xinjiang province.

The British centre right politician, Jesse Norman, has argued that Smith's ideas have yet to be fully implemented to enable free markets to spread wealth across populations:

> From a Smithian viewpoint, then, the case for freely trading markets is overwhelming, but the idea that the modern world has enjoyed a glorious history of free trade over the past two centuries, in Britain, continental Europe or the USA, is largely a myth. The West enjoyed the benefits of commercial society, but it also continued to deploy the weapons of mercantilism or crony capitalism to extract value from other countries. This is quite at odds with the radical critique of Smith as the supposed originator of the ills of global capitalism.[3]

Nonetheless, with the complexities of investment banking slipping into the realm of retail banking—with the impact the 2008 crisis and the 1997 Asian Financial Crisis had on consumers—this may indeed validate the argument that markets left to an invisible hand still require a sounder ethical basis for the financial services industry to operate within.

For though we can condemn regulatory failure for the bouts of financial crises that we have all weathered, it is the endeavour to establish a strong ethical basis for market operations that may be the best preventive cure for further instability.

Islamic finance claims it has this sound foundation for growth—with its very values flowing from the holy Qur'ran, the Sunna and the hadiths.

It is Islam that questions the very foundation of open markets—the role of money itself.

The Role of Money

As a fan of antique programmes on television, I always enjoy seeing the expert describing how the beautiful eighteenth-century Wedgewood ceramic plate was made or how the exciting appeal of the art deco patterns of Clarisse Cliff transformed the world of design.

However, if truth be told, I also relish the moment when the expert tells the owner of a precious item how much their cherished antique is really worth. Sometimes the recipient of the good news is genuinely shocked and sometimes, I suspect, the odd person is feigning surprise.

Often, though, the owner of an antique responds to the good news by declaring "I saw this in a charity shop. I knew it must be worth something and I only bought it for £1". At this, the expert and TV presenter congratulates the owner for their astuteness and invites the television audience to join in with the congratulations.

At first, I did praise these savvy bargain hunters but, as I grew older, I wondered whether the purchasers of these pricey antiques had really—from a moral sense—defrauded the charity shops who were selling the items to raise money for desperately needed good causes.

The founder of the Hanafi jurisprudence school would have probably told me that, indeed, the savvy bargain hunter was committing fraud. The story goes that Abu Hanifa took a singular approach when offered a bargain by a stall holder:

> The lady offered to sell the garment to Abu Hanifa for 100 dirhams, but Abu Hanifa would not buy it. 'It is worth more than a hundred', he told the surprised woman. 'How much?' he asked her again. She offered to sell it for 200 dirhams, and he turned her down. Then she asked for 300, then 400, at which point the exasperated woman scolded him. 'You are mocking me', she declared, and prepared to walk away from the deal to try her luck elsewhere. So, they summoned another merchant and he solemnly valued the garment at 500 dirhams. Rather than profit from the woman's ignorance, Abu Hanifa had opted to settle for a fair trade, a principle he would abide by all his life – that the greedy should be regulated from taking advantage of the vulnerable.[4]

It is this ideal of fairness and transparency that underlies the very foundation of Islamic finance. In that sense, Islamic finance could be described as a utopian ideal—where ethics and long-term investment comes before short-term business desires and indebtedness linked to interest rates.

In many ways, Islamic finance concepts express concerns as to the role of money in an economy.

The sixteenth-century author of *Utopia*, Sir Thomas More, shared these very same worries. More coined the word 'utopia' from the Greek ou-topos meaning 'no place' or 'nowhere'. This was a pun. The almost identical Greek word eu-topos means a good place.

In the 1516 work, More wrote:

> Whereas to gold and silver nature hath given no use that we may not well lack if that folly of men had not set it in higher estimation for the rareness' sake. But of the contrary part, nature, as a most tender and loving mother, hath placed the best and most necessary things open abroad, as the air, the water, and the earth itself, and hath removed and hid farthest from us vain and unprofitable things.[5]

The fetishisation of money was therefore condemned by More as it is also condemned within Islam. More's own journey to seek utopia, though, was never realised as he was one of a long line of people who fell out with the infamous English King, Henry VIII, and was subsequently executed.

Centuries before More, Al-Farabi (872–950) wrote of the ideal of a "*virtuous city*" where cooperation across society could be attained:

> ... in which people aim through association at co-operating for the things by which felicity in its real and true sense can be attained, is the excellent city, and the society in which there is a co-operation to acquire felicity is the excellent society.[6]

We can see the synergies between the concerns of Al-Farabi and More. These insights were also reflected at the seminal International Conference of Islamic Economics held in Mecca in 1976 (which is discussed further in chapter nine). One of the papers tabled for the conference ridiculed the position of money in conventional economics:

> In the so-called free-economy or capitalist economy, money has acquired a privileged status over all other commodities. By the definition arbitrarily given to it, it has become superior to man himself, it implies some qualifications that are not supposed to be within its jurisdiction and which have evolved and become as if they were genuine, despite the fact that they have no physical existence.[7]

The French socialist thinker, Pierre-Joseph Proudhon (1809–1865) also mocked the concept of money:

> Why are we short of housing, machinery and ships? He answered: because money is a sentinel posted at the entrance to the markets with orders to let no-one pass. Money, you imagine, is the key that opens the gates to the market (by which term is meant the exchange of products); that is not true - money is the bolt that bars them.[8]

The analysis presented by some Islamic scholars who claim that advocates of laissez-faire capitalism see money as an end in and of itself is not entirely fair. For whilst some market participants may have adopted this mindset, some of the key thinkers who advocated for this form of capitalism also saw money as a means—and not as an end.

Scottish philosopher, David Hume (1711–1776), for instance, described money in the following way:

> Money is not, properly speaking, one of the subjects of commerce; but only the instrument which men have agreed upon to facilitate the exchange of one commodity for another. It is none of the wheels of trade: It is the oil which renders the motion of the wheels more smooth and easy. If we consider any one kingdom by itself, it is evident, that the greater or less plenty of money is of no consequence; since the prices of commodities are always proportioned to the plenty of money.[9]

Islamic finance emerges from the philosophical position that whilst investors who risk capital should be rewarded if returns are delivered, the over-emphasis on the concept of money as an object in and of itself distorts the real economy with the trade in goods and services.

It is a view that has echoes with the thoughts of the British economist, J A Hobson (1858–1940) who argued that the cartels and monopolies of his era was leading to excessive profits due to the lack of competition. There was an imbalance between spending and saving and the excess savings was becoming unearned income held by wealthy businessmen rather than the funds being used for further economic activity. Hobson argued that other economists did not recognise that it was this phenomenon that led to the vagaries in the economic modelling of his time.

Indeed, there is a very graphic verse in the Qur'an which urges the use rather than the storage of money:

> And those who hoard gold and silver, and do not spend them in the cause of God – warn them of a most painful punishment, upon a Day when the fire of hell shall be stoked, and with it shall be scorched their foreheads, sides and backs. 'This is what you hoarded for yourselves, so taste what you used to hoard!'[10]

There is a minority view held in academia that money could be viewed as a commodity within Islam[11]:

> Cash waqf *(endowment)* is the best means of income generation and capital growth for a waqf. It is therefore instrumental in the creation of sustainable communities. However, for some reasons, it has remained controversial throughout centuries. This is because of the fact there is no express text in the Quran or sunnah enjoining or prohibiting cash waqf. The lack of express text in the two main sources of Islamic law, therefore, has moved the early scholars to allow or prohibit cash waqf based on principles of analogical reasoning (qiyas). This paper relies on the opinions of those who permitted cash waqf, considering cash as moveable property, categorised as comparable (mithai) asset and used for lending and trade.

The vast majority of the Islamic finance industry and the scholars who operate within the industry maintain a very firm stance that cash or money is not property or a commodity. Islamic finance is, fundamentally, an asset-based finance model.

This theological stance could arguably make it difficult for a shari'a compliant monetary policy to be developed as monetary theory focuses upon the concept of money as the key medium to revitalise and support national economies.

With the actions of central banks having been essential to stabilising national economies after the 2008 and 2020 crises, this is a challenge for Islamic economics to address. As we shall see in chapter seven, innovative solutions have been put forward to advance a fully formed Islamic monetary policy.

Religion and Interest Rates

The concept of banning interest rates had been a mainstay of Jewish and Christian belief:

> If you lend money to any of my people with you who is poor, you shall not be like a moneylender to him, and you shall not exact interest from

> him. If ever you take your neighbour's cloak in pledge, you shall return it to him before the sun goes down, for that is his only covering, and it is his cloak for his body; in what else shall he sleep? And if he cries to me, I will hear, for I am compassionate.[12]

Another part of the Bible is clear as to why interest is seen as an evil:

> Who does not put out his money at interest and does not take a bribe against the innocent. He who does these things shall never be moved.[13]

Interest was compared to extortion:

> In you they take bribes to shed blood; you take interest and profit and make gain of your neighbours by extortion; but me you have forgotten, declares the Lord God.[14]

It has been argued that a careful reading of these texts could indicate that the abuse of interest, rather than interest itself, is prohibited. A study of Judaic practices by Levine, though, has shown that Jewish law forbade the exaction of interest by a creditor and the payment of interest by a debtor in a loan between Jews.

Levine argued that this was not to the advantage to the creditor as if a value of the asset, which was the subject of a commodity loan, increased by the time the transaction occurred, then this appreciation in value cannot be passed on to the creditor as the value at the time of the loan agreement must be adhered to.[15]

Concerns regarding interest have also been reflected in the world's other great religions. In the Hindu *Sutra* (700-100 BCE) as well as in the Buddhist *Jatakas* (600-400 BCE) there are many references to the payment of interest, along with expressions of disdain for the practice. Whilst in Sikhism, there is a concern at the abuse of interest rather than condemnation of the principle itself:

> The shopkeeper who visited the Guru, had deserved to die by an impaling stake for the sins of deceit and usury, but, as he continued to progress in virtue, the impaling stake was reduced in size till it became merely a thorn. Having been pierced by it, he had fully expiated the sins of a former birth. Thus, may the decree of destiny be altered by the practice of virtue.[16]

In 1745 Pope Benedict XIV promulgated the encyclical *Vix Pervenit* which condemned the principle of interest. This encyclical was emphasised by Pope Gregory XVI in 1836:

> The nature of the sin called usury has its proper place and origin in a loan contract. This financial contract between consenting parties demands, by its very nature, that one return to another only as much as he has received. The sin rests on the fact that sometimes the creditor desires more than he have given. Therefore, he contends some gain is owed him beyond that which he loaned, but any gain which exceeds the amount he gave is illicit and usurious.

Many people were caught by surprise when this viewpoint was expressed again in 2009 in the pages of the Vatican newspaper, *Osservatore Romano.* Not only was usury condemned but Islamic finance was praised as a model that needed to be supported:

> The ethical principles on which Islamic finance is based may bring banks closer to their clients and to the true spirit which should mark every financial service. Western banks could use tools such as the Islamic bonds, known as sukuk, as collateral.

The newspaper went on to argue that Sukuk financing could be used to fund the "*car industry or the next Olympic Games in London*". This was another indication that the Islamic finance industry was appealing to people beyond its core consumer base by placing an emphasis upon core ethical values.

Interest Rates: The Economic Arguments

> Unfortunately, the attempts to prohibit interest were often illogical. The effect of outlawing loans at interest was generally to restrict certain types of investment and certain categories of commercial or financial activity that the political or religious authorities deemed less legitimate or worthy than others.[17]

So said Thomas Piketty whose book, *Capital*, when published in English in 2017, was greeted by luminaries such as Robert Reich, US Labour Secretary under President Bill Clinton, as "*breath taking*".

However, despite the voluminous material contained in Piketty's book, only a couple of pages briefly referred to the debate as to whether the role of interest distorts the workings of the real economy. Instead, Piketty dismissed the idea of ending interest as a conceit for the benefit of "*the political or religious authorities*".

Piketty argued that interest helps to gauge the true value of money. It is a view that has its antecedents in the Scottish Enlightenment. David Hume succinctly wrote of the relationship between interest rates and the value of money:

> High interest rates arises from three circumstances: A great demand for borrowing; little riches to supply that demand; and great profits arising from commerce: And these circumstances are a clear proof of the small advance of commerce and industry, not of the scarcity of gold and silver. Low interest, on the other hand, proceeds from the three opposite circumstances: A small demand for borrowing, great riches to supply that demand; and small profits arising from commerce: And these circumstances are all connected together, and proceed from encrease of industry and commerce, not of gold and silver.[18]

Islamic finance, though, turns this traditional perspective of interest on its head and removes the idea of interest, known by the Arabic term of riba, in one fell swoop. In many ways, this is one of the most radical aspects of this form of economics.

How, though, do the advocates of Islamic finance address the key point made by many economists that interest is required to gauge the value of money at any particular time?

Various economic perspectives have been presented by academics in the Islamic finance field to provide an economic rationale for not using the interest principle in financial affairs.

It has been argued that interest, as a predetermined cost of production, can prevent further growth in employment levels. The role of interest, it has been stated, has contributed to trade imbalances and booms and busts in monetary cycles. Others have questioned the efficacy of the rate of interest as a key determinant of savings and investment.

However, the concept of zero interest for many economists equates to zero demand to accumulate savings, infinite demand for money, no equilibrium in the financial system and massive capital flight out of any country adopting such policies.

However, Islamic finance advocates argue that the emphasis should be placed on the risk-based model of Islamic economics. The economy would operate according to different market signals which would not accord with the distorting actions which interest rates pose.

As Ariff observed:

> The question of erosion in the value of money and hence the need for indexation is an interesting one. But Islamic jurists have ruled out compensation for erosion in the value of money, or according to Hadith, a fungible good must be returned by its like: 'gold for gold, silver for silver, dates for dates, salt for salt, like for like, equal for equal, and hand to hand'.[19]

As will be seen in chapter seven, thinkers ranging from Karl Marx to Milton Friedman have, from very different perspectives, questioned the role of interest rates in the real economy.

It is an intellectual challenge to the world of conventional finance which cannot easily be ignored.

Islam and Riba

Interest is said to be condemned in the Qur'ran as it has no value. Money must be earned instead of accepting the illusory concept of treating money as a commodity:

> O believers, do not consume usury, multiplied many times over. Fear God and perhaps you may be saved.[20]

The specific problems with interest are spelt out in another passage from the Qur'ran:

> So, render to kinsmen what is their due, as also to the poor and needy wayfarer. This is best for those who seek the face of God and they shall prevail. What usury you practice, seeking thereby to multiply the wealth of people, shall not multiply with God. But the alms you render, seeking the face of God – these shall multiply their reward.[21]

Critics of Islamic finance argue that the interpretation of the Qur'ran against interest is a deliberate misreading of the term 'usury'. Instead, the prohibition, it is claimed, related to a doubling of the debt when there is a default and doubling again if the loan remained unpaid.[22]

The respected Egyptian jurist, Mohammed Abduh (1849–1905) also held the view that interest, under certain conditions, was allowed within Islam. In his work *Risālat al-tawḥīd* (Treatise on the Oneness of God), Abduh sought to establish the harmony of reason and revelation, the freedom of the will, and the primacy of the ethical implications of religious faith over ritual and dogma. In this sense, Abduh reflected the early period of Islamic thought with the Mu'tazilites school.

It was in that context that Abduh issued a fatwa allowing Muslims to be involved in business transactions involving interest. He based this ruling on the fiqh principle that dire necessity makes the forbidden allowable.

Critics of this fatwa argue that fiqh specifically defines dire necessity as involving matters of life and death or loss of limb and this would not be the case where business transactions were concerned.

In the sixteenth century, the Mufti of Istanbul, Ebusuud Efendi, argued that the taking of interest by awqaf or pious foundations was an act of necessity. Islamic scholars at that time vehemently disputed the Mufti's judgement and this controversy has echoes of the contentious debates of 1989 when the Grand Mufti of Egypt, Sheikh Muhammad Sayid Tantawi also defended the use of interest.

Tantawi (1928–2010) who bravely tried to bridge religious divides, including by meeting the Chief Rabbi of Israel in 1997, declared in 1989 that interest was halal.

Interest on some Government investments were allowed, Tantawi ruled, as the gain was little different from the sharing of the Government's profits from the use of funds. On another occasion Tantawi argued that interest-bearing bank deposits were more acceptable than some Islamic finance products due to some of the disadvantageous terms Islamic finance consumers had to weather.

In response, Tantawi faced fierce opposition for his fatwa and the Muslim Brotherhood opposition accused the Grand Mufti of being too cosy with the then Egyptian President, Hosni Mubarak.

The prohibition of interest is now an accepted part of the Islamic finance industry particularly following the seminal 1976 International Conference of Islamic Economics held in Mecca which enshrined this principle.

In 1985, the OIC's Fiqh Academy went further and defined riba as not just interest charged on a loan, but as excess profits made from a loan which would be viewed as another form of usury:

> Any excess or profit on a loan for a deferred payment when the borrower is unable to repay it after the fixed period and similarly any excess or profit on a loan at the time of contract are both forbidden as riba in the Shari' ah.

This ruling could make this form of finance more affordable for customers who may be reassured that they do not need to worry about hidden costs. However, how the word "*excess*" is interpreted remains a matter of debate. At the very least, a framework exists for the criteria of loan affordability to be debated.

Consequently, riba can be defined into two broad categories. Riba al-Naseeyah which is also known as Riba al-Qur'ran and Riba al-Jahiliyyah can be defined as the equivalence of interest that is paid on loans in conventional finance.

Riba al-Fadl which is also known as Riba al-Hadith and Riba al-Byuoo defines an excess compensation to one party resulting from both an exchange or sale of certain homogeneous goods and the deferred sale of certain homogenous goods.

Therefore, this categorisation relates to when the value of the assets offered by one party is in excess of the value of those goods offered by another party. There is a famous hadith which best sums up the need for just and fair valuations in assessing loan arrangements pertaining to business transactions:

> The Messenger of Allah (Peace Be Upon Him) said, 'Gold for gold, silver for silver, wheat for wheat, barley for barley, dates for dates, salt for salt, like for like, in equal weights, from hand to hand. If these species differ, then sell as you like, as long as it is from hand to hand.[23]

The very fact that financial institutions exist successfully today by not accepting the principle of interest is, in and of itself, a defining challenge for conventional finance. The very idea of a financial services industry which ignored the idea of interest would have been viewed as an anathema by market participants just 40 years ago.

Professor Mirakhor Abbas, in his analysis of the Qur'ranic verses banning interest has highlighted a wider meaning in one of the verses that has had a direct bearing on the development of the contemporary Islamic finance industry. The verse reads:

> Those who gorge themselves on riba behave but as he might behave whom Satan has confounded with his touch; for they say, 'Exchange is but a kind of riba while Allah has made exchange lawful and riba unlawful.[24]

Abbas argued that there is a wider meaning to this verse than simply the prohibition of interest:

> Up to the early 1980s most of the literature concentrated on the latter part of the verse— wa harrama ar-riba —but in contemporary finance, it is the first part of this rule prescribed by Allah, that is about the need for exchange to involve complete transfer of property rights titles between the two sides of a transaction that is crucial. However, the focus was placed on the second rule only, 'no riba.' Hence at that time, if you asked what Islamic finance was about, the response would have been 'no riba'.[25]

As we shall see in the next chapter, the legal forms that have been constructed to address the ownership of the title of assets is now a pillar of the Islamic finance industry.

Avoiding Detriment

One of the key tenets of Islam is to avoid causing detriment (darar) to others. The words of the Prophet directly reference the need for people to be responsible to each other:

> Abu Sa'id al-Khudri reported: The Messenger of Allah, peace and blessings be upon him, said, "Do not cause harm or return harm. Whoever harms others, Allah will harm him. Whoever is harsh with others, Allah will be harsh with him."[26]

Therefore if a person was selling their car but they deliberately omitted to tell the buyer how often the car had been driven on the road, then this could be to the detriment of the buyer and would not be allowed within the strictures of Islamic economics.

This is at variance to the concept of caveat emptor—which is prevalent in many jurisdictions—where the buyer alone is responsible for checking the quality and suitability of goods before a purchase is made.

It is also stated in the Qur'ran:

> Annoy them not, so as to restrict them.[27]

This statement is often cited to avoid an abusive relationship occurring within a marriage. It also, though, has validity in a business context where a contract between two parties must be based upon transparency and equity.

Therefore, the need to avoid darar in all its forms is intrinsic to the values system which underpins the operation of Islamic finance.

Avoidance of Gharar (Unnecessary Uncertainty or Ambiguity)

For many of us the idea of removing uncertainty from the concept of investment would be absurd—and with good reason.

In the 1980s, investing in shares in the photography business, Kodak, would have been recognised as a secure investment. It was a multi-million-dollar global conglomerate with fantastic name recognition—it even sponsored the Olympics! Today, most young people have never heard of Kodak—which is now a shadow of its former self.

Uncertainty is at the heart of business valuations as the decisions taken by shareholders and management in a fast-changing global economy can radically alter company valuations in a relatively short period of time.

In fact, some form of uncertainty or risk is accepted within Islamic finance. The key Islamic finance contracts are built on risk sharing between the contracting parties relying on profit and loss principles.

Dr Abdul Razaaq Al Sanhuri (1895–1971) a jurist who shaped Egyptian law and had a defining impact upon Arabic jurisprudence, defined gharar as:

> The contract in which any party to the agreement at the time of execution of the agreement, cannot decide as to how much it would give or take.

Therefore, in modern Islamic finance if there is any form of ambiguity or haziness in a contract this would not be allowed and would be defined as gharar.

Clearly deliberate misrepresentation in a contract is prohibited but would a vaguely worded section in a contract, if both parties were aware of this and agreed to its inclusion, also be gharar?

Ignorance of key features of a contract, with the Arabic term of jahalah being adopted for ignorance, would be recognised as gharar. Therefore, in modern business practices where a document is designed for some form of 'constructive ambiguity' for certain sections of the agreement, this would be prohibited in Islamic finance as gharar.

There are some references in the Qur'ran that would appear to support this prohibition. For example, there is a reference to Satan providing:

> false hopes – but what Satan promises is nothing but illusion.[28]

There are also various hadiths which relate to different forms of gharar. For instance, the sale of fish which was still in the sea was prohibited.[29]

The Prophet also said, "*do not sell what you do not own*".[30]

The prohibition of gharar helps people avoid excessive risk which would cause loss and damage to the contracting parties. In the hadiths, the Prophet is quoted as prohibiting the exchange of dates with raisins as this would cause excessive financial loss.[31]

However, would the sale of a home that was yet to be built but with building contractors working on site be gharar? Or would selling carrots be gharar if the contract had been agreed before the produce was harvested?

Generally speaking, most Islamic financial institutions would say this was not gharar—as there was some certainty the house would be built or the carrots would be harvested even if these events had not yet happened at the time the contract of sale was agreed to.

But when it comes to the futures market, would this be gharar?

The answer is yes. One hadith makes this position very clear:

> Do not sell what you do not possess.[32]

Futures markets are where financial products are bought and sold for delivery at some agreed-upon date in the future with a price fixed at the time of the deal. Futures markets are far more than simply agricultural contracts and involve the buying, selling and hedging of financial products and future values of interest rates.

Arguably, the first futures market originated in the United Provinces of the Netherlands in the seventeenth century. This was a time when the Netherlands had some form of democracy whilst other European states were still governed by monarchs.

Dutch trade was vibrant, culture was in its ascendency with the exquisite paintings of Vermeer and Rembrandt and there was, of course, the tulip craze which climaxed in just two short months—December 1636 and January 1637.

It was an era when a Dutch merchant paid 6650 guilders for a few dozen tulip bulbs when, at that time, a whole family could live for a year on around 300 guilders.[33] One of the key drivers of the craze to invest in tulip bulbs was the nascent futures market:

> Tulips were an unusually volatile commodity, even by the elastic standard of the futures trade. A merchant who dealt in timber knew precisely what he was buying. A florist purchasing a tulip for delivery at lifting time had no idea. He was gambling on a living thing. To be successful, he needed not just a shrewd understanding of the price his bulb might command in several months' time, but some idea of what was happening to it while it was still in the ground.[34]

However, when the end came, it was brutal for many investors who ended up in the workhouse or facing severe hunger or even an early death:

> Like a sun, tulip mania burned brightly and steadily while there was still fuel to feed it in the shape of a steady supply of bulbs. But during the winter of 1636-7, demand for tulips comprehensively outstripped supply and the mania then began, in effect, to consume everything around it.[35]

The high level of uncertainty, from an Islamic perspective, would mean that the futures trading in Dutch tulip bulbs would have been classed as gharar.

The Iraqi Shi'a cleric, Mohammed Baqir al-Sadr (1935–1980) discussed this very concept of gharar in his seminal work, Iqtisaduna (Our Economics):

> In the opinion of a number of jurists like al-'Umānī as-Sadūq, al-Shahīd ath-Thānī and others: If a merchant, for example, buys wheat but has not taken it in his possession; it will not be permissible for him to make a profit through selling of it at a higher price, but it will be permissible for him after he takes it into his possession even though the legal transfer is completed in the Islamic jurisprudence with the execution of the contract and does not depend on any positive work thereafter. The merchant becomes the owner of wheat even if he did not take possession of it yet, in spite of that it is not permissible for the merchant to do so and acquire profit in respect of it by selling it at a higher price as long as he does not take the goods

> into his possession, the desire being that the profit should be linked with work as also to exclude letting more trades being a legal transaction as a cover of profit.[36]

Whilst this analysis was not made in the context of considering the ethical basis of the futures market, we can see how receipt of commodities within Islam is viewed within a business context so that there is some surety about the terms of trade and the knock-on impact this form of security is said to have for enabling public confidence to continue in the operation of commercial transactions.

Therefore when, in the 2000s, so-called shari'a compliant derivatives were introduced to the market, this rang alarm bells across the Islamic finance community. How could conventional derivatives, inherently based on gharar and riba, ever be compatible when applied in an Islamic finance context.

It was a challenge, which, as we shall see in chapter three, led to some intriguing solutions being devised to ensure shari'a compliance was maintained.

Prohibition of Gambling (Qimar)

As well as gharar and riba, there are two further types of activity that are prohibited within Islamic finance—gambling, known as Qimar and speculation, known as Maysir.

In respect of gambling there is a verse in the Qur'ran which stipulates this prohibition:

> Follow not what you have no knowledge of: hearing, sight and the heart – all of these a person shall be questioned about.[37]

The prohibition against gambling and drinking alcohol is taken together in another passage from the Qur'ran:

> O believers, wine and gambling, idols and divining arrows are an abhorrence, the work of Satan. So keep away from it, that you may prevail. Satan only desires to arouse discord and hatred among you with wine and gambling, and to deter you from the mention of God and from prayer. Will you desist? Obey God and obey the Messenger and be on your guard.[38]

Arguably, this prohibition against gambling is not seen in Christianity. There are various references in the Bible that could refer to the implied risks of gambling. For instance, there is the reference to the danger of love of money:

> For the love of money is a root of all kinds of evil. Some people, eager for money, have wandered from the faith and pierced themselves with many griefs.[39]

This could be read as prohibiting excessive gambling rather than a demand to stop the occasional flutter at the bookmakers.

Prohibition on Speculation (Maysir)

It is the prohibition on speculation that is particularly radical—for the global economy operates to a large extent on speculation. The foreign exchange market has a daily global turnover of about £2.5 trillion. London, for example, accounts for 36.5% of this global market.

The Bank for International Settlements estimates that London generates 46% of daily global revenue in the interest rate derivative market. Whilst the Bank for International Settlements report that foreign exchange trading in New York amounts to an average of $5.3 trillion a day or $220 billion per hour. The New York Stock Exchange has $200 billion traded daily and there are dozens of other exchanges across the world.

How can Islamic finance ever be considered viable in a global economy when it is based on different forms of speculation? The short answer is speculation is tightly defined within Islamic finance which prohibits, for example, short selling but allows regular trading in company shares.

How have the practitioners of Islamic finance reached this conclusion? The answer lies in the assessment that entrepreneurialism entails legitimate risk, and this is not only allowed for but encouraged in Islam. As we noted in chapter one, the Prophet was a trader who encouraged an entrepreneurial economy when the Prophet and his followers established the first autonomous Muslim community in Medina in 622.

Therefore assessed risk in business is legitimate and if a person risks their capital and is successful then that person should benefit from the profits that have been accrued but if a loss is made on that business venture then the investor is bound to accept the loss rather than try and insure against any losses incurred.

The concept of insurance is more complex than this statement might indicate for there is now insurance in Islamic finance, known as takaful, which is judged to be shari'a compliant. How this has come about when, a superficial reading of the holy Qur'ran would indicate that insuring against uncertainty is haram, will be considered further in chapter eight.

As we return to maysir, how would we define the difference between maysir and qimar? Ayub has a concise description to describe maysir as opposed to qimar:

> 'Maisir' derived from 'Yusr' means wishing something valuable with ease and without paying an equivalent compensation ('Iwad) for it or without working for it, or without undertaking any liability against it, by way of a game of chance.[40]

Ayub went on to give an example of an investor in a scheme who gains a prize without any effort being made. There may not have been an active gambling activity that was being promulgated by the investor but she/he gained the prize by mere chance rather than by any work or any form of effort so this would be classed as maysir. Another example of maysir could be the uncertainty of timing in claiming benefits from a conventional life insurance policy.

The position of Islamic finance in respect of speculation is at variance with Jewish law. There are some similarities between Jewish law and Islamic finance. Jewish law (halakha) prohibits the interest rate mechanism playing a role in commercial transactions between Jews (the Arabic term for interest is riba which bears linguistic similarities to the Jewish term for interest being ribbit).

When it comes to speculation in the money markets the variance between the two faiths do differ as it is only when fraud may be involved when speculation is prohibited under Jewish law:

> Our investigation of the phenomenon of short selling has demonstrated that Jewish law generally finds no moral issue with this type of trade in the financial markets. The key here is that the short seller accomplishes the sale by first borrowing the shares that he sells, hoping to make a profit by buying them back at a lower price. Nonetheless, when motivated by the seller's desire to capitalise on the discovery of fraud in the company whose stock is sold short, the short sale is unethical because it

amounts to selling the defective merchandise without apprising the buyer upfront of the defects in the merchandise. Disgorgement of ill-gotten gains is indicated in that case.[41]

Consequently, the prohibition of maysir and gharar marks out Islamic finance amongst the three Abrahamic religions of Judaism, Christianity and Islam. This, alongside the ban on interest and that money cannot be viewed as a commodity, are key features of the values system which underpins Islamic finance which makes this model distinctive and at variance with conventional finance.

It is, though, the subtlety, if not beauty, of Islamic finance which is really on show when the different contract types are examined. It is these legal structures that have ensured there is a profitable Islamic finance industry in existence—and it challenges the norms and beliefs of many participants in global markets who claim that the fundamentals of the market economy can never change.

Notes

1. Charles Dickens (1839), *Oliver Twist*, page 489.
2. Adam Smith (1776), *An Inquiry into the Nature and Causes of the Wealth of Nations*, page 359.
3. Jesse Norman MP (2018), *Adam Smith—What He Thought and Why It Matters*, page 254.
4. Harris Irfan, *Heaven's Bankers: Inside the Hidden World of Islamic Finance*, page 23.
5. Sir Thomas More (1516), *Second Book of Utopia.*
6. Al Farabi, *Perfect State* V, 15, 3: 231.
7. Professor Dr Mahmud Abu Saud (1976), *Money, Interest and Qirad*, International Conference on Islamic Economics.
8. Quotation from Silvio Gesell (1929), *The Natural Economic Order*, translated by Philip Pye (Neo Verlang, Berlin, Frohman), page 7.
9.. David Hume (1752), *Of Money*, page 33.
10. Qur'ran, 9.35.
11. Mohammad Tahir Sabit Haji Mohammad (2015), Theoretical and Trustees' Perspectives on the Establishment of an Islamic Social (Waqf) Bank, *Humanomics*, vol. 31, no. 1, pp. 37–73.
12. Exodus 22:25.
13. Psalm 15:5.
14. Ezekiel 22:12.
15. Arron Levine, *Economic Morality and Jewish Law*, page 223.

16. Life of Guru Nanak: Chapter V, sec IV.
17. Thomas Piketty (2017), *Capital in the Twenty-First Century*, pages 685–686.
18. David Hume, *Of Interest*, page 49.
19. Mohamed Ariff (September 1988), *Islamic Banking*, Asian-Pacific Economic Literature, page 50.
20. Qur'ran, 3:129.
21. Qur'ran, 30.37.
22. Timur Kuran, *Islam & Mammon*, page 14.
23. Hadith narrated by Ubida ibn al-Samit.
24. Qur'ran, Sura Al Baqara, verse 275.
25. As quoted by Emmy Abdul Alim, *Global Leaders in Islamic Finance*, page 117.
26. al-Sunan al-Kubrá 11070.
27. Qur'ran, Al Talaq: 6.
28. Qur'ran, 4.121.
29. Al Shawkani, ND, page 230.
30. An-Nawawi (1987), page 156.
31. Al Bukhari (1987), page 839.
32. Related by Ahmad. Hadith No 15311; Abu Dawud hadith No 3503; al-Tirmidhi hadith No 1232; al Nassa'I hadith No 4613; Ibn Majah hadith No 2187.
33. Mike Dash, *Tulipmania* (1999), page xv.
34. Ibid., page 136.
35. Ibid.
36. Mohammed Baqir al-Sadr, Iqtisaduna, Vol 2, Part 2.
37. Qu'ran, 17.36.
38. Qu'ran, 5:90.
39. Timothy 6:1.
40. Muhammed Ayub, *Understanding Islamic Finance*, page 62.
41. Aaron Levine, *Economic Morality and Jewish Law*, page 229.

CHAPTER 4

The Beauty of Islamic Finance Contracts

The Alhambra is one of the wonders of the world.

Situated in Granada, the grandiose structure was built by the Nasrid Dynasty (1232–1492)—the last Muslim dynasty to rule Spain.

The greatest concern of the architects of the Alhambra was to cover every single space with decoration. Most of the interior arches are false arches which are there solely for decorative purposes. Walls are covered with beautiful and extremely rich ceramics and plasterwork and the coverings have wooden frames that have been exquisitely carved.

One of the most striking aspects of the Alhambra, perched over the Sierra Nevada, is how precise mathematical design patterns with subtle differentiation creates a sense of awe and wonder in the observer. The sophistication of Islamic art also reflects the strictures of the faith which ordains that representations of the Prophet or God is forbidden to avoid idolatry.

Therefore, from this precise religious framework a range of beautiful design features and imagery was developed within Islamic art.

There are synergies between the development of Islamic art with the emergence of Islamic finance. Out of the framework of the religion, a range of sophisticated contract models has developed to comply with the value system (as outlined in Chapter 3) and to enable investors and wider retail banking consumers to benefit from a range of financial products that are relevant and apposite for twenty-first-century living.

J. S. Watkins, *Islamic Finance and Global Capitalism*,
https://doi.org/10.1007/978-3-030-59840-2_4

The adaptability of Islamic finance to adjust to changing situations whilst remaining true to its underlying principles is a hallmark of the industry. In fact, the agile nature of Islamic finance to respond to contemporary requirements was highlighted by scholars during the early history of the faith.

Even one of the critics of Islamic finance, El-Gamal, whilst disparaging some of the pre-occupations of the industry has also, in essence, acknowledged the very flexibility of the sector:

> … the great Hanafi jurist, Al Sarakhsi wrote in Al Mabsut the general principle that "establishment (of rights etc.) by customary practice is akin to establishment by canonical texts". In addition, recognising that conventions change from one historical period to another, the 39th article of Majallat Al Ahkam Al Aldiyya[1] stated that juristic rulings must keep up with the times.[2]

El-Gamal drew the conclusion that the "*bias*" in the industry to focus on alternatives to conventional finance models is misplaced. I would contend that this is the wrong conclusion to draw. In fact, it can be argued that the development of jurisprudence where a framework has developed for contract models demonstrates the very agility of the industry rather than a stubbornness to engage with conventional finance.

In fact, some of the critics of Islamic finance, from a religious perspective, criticise the industry for tying itself too closely to conventional finance. In practice, the sector is recognising the needs of consumers whilst challenging established conventions in conventional finance for ethics and efficacy to be combined.

In practice, there have always been calls for changes to the conventional finance model, from Robert Owen's New Lanark model from 1800 to 1825 through to the social market economy that was championed in West Germany following the end of the Second World War.

The benefit of the Islamic finance model is that it may have a greater ability to engage positively with conventional finance institutions in order to evince societal and economic change as compared to other forms for mutual finance that were developed over the last 200 years. This theme will be explored in greater depth in Chapter 9.

The Qur'ran emphasises the need for written contracts:

> When you deal with each other, in transactions involving future obligations in a fixed period of time, reduce them to nothing … It is more just in the sight of God, more suitable as evidence and more convenient to prevent doubts amongst yourselves.[3]

Wealth creation is directly connected, in the Qur'ran, to contractual agreements:

> O believers, consume not the wealth you trade among yourselves dishonestly, unless it be a commercial deal resulting from mutual agreement.[4]

The Qur'ran also directs believers to adhere to contracts as part of the wider setting of a person's spiritual growth and responsibilities:

> It is not righteousness that ye turn your faces toward East or West; but it is righteousness to believe in Allah and the Last Day, and the Angels, and the Book and the Messengers; to spend of your substance, out of love for Him, for your kin, for orphans, for the needy, for the wayfarer, for those who ask, and for the ransom of slaves; to be steadfast in prayer, and practice regular charity, to fulfil the contracts which we have made; and to be firm and patient, in pain (or suffering) and adversity, and throughout all periods of panic. Such are the people of truth, God fearing.[5]

Despite this Qur'ranic emphasis on the primacy of contracts, Professor Amin El-Gamal has argued that the complex nature of the Islamic finance contracts in the modern era are so complicated as it:

> implies some level of inefficiency is intrinsic to this industry, taking the forms of transaction costs, additional legal costs and fees for Islamic jurists.[6]

From a different perspective, Irfan has expressed fears that some Islamic finance contracts are merely ruses to get around the ban on interest. Irfan recalled the reaction of bankers to the comments of the Islamic finance consultant, Tarek El Diwany, when he spoke of attempts by bankers in medieval Europe to get around the then Christian ban on usury:

> 'Imagine I made an investment of money into your business and we agree to share profits', he suggested. 'Then I agree to sell to you future profits on the investment for a price we agree today. Finally you agree to insure

> me for a loss on my investment. In the end, you have ended up paying a fee to me for money which I "invested" in you.' Thus three contracts – the contractum trinius – are combined, leaving a loan with interest. Many in the audience shifted nervously as they recognised the parallels with the modern Islamic finance industry.[7]

When it comes to long-term investment finance, it could be argued that the models that have been developed provide surety for investors, support for businesses and provides stability for long-term economic growth.

Islamic finance contracts can be applied in all markets. As the shari'a scholar, Sheikh Nizam Yaquby has argued it is how the contract adjusts to the structure of the law in a given country that has to be carefully considered. Yaquby has praised the common law of England and Wales for being flexible enough to accommodate shari'a compliant contracts:

> Common law is a precedent law and implements what has been contracted between the parties. So if you and I do business and sign a contract, it doesn't need to be explicitly stated that it is Islamic or shari'ah. Islamic law of contracts says that everything is permissible unless there is a specific prohibition. So if you use common law, we have to make sure there are no specific prohibitions involved, and we eliminate three things— riba, maysir and gharar.[8]

This analysis reflects the views of conventional finance participants who cite the use of common law as one of the reasons they prefer London as a base for global financial operations as it is said to be easier to develop innovative financial products within the framework structure of common law as compared to the more prescriptive state and federal legal structures in New York.

However, it should be noted that Michael McMillen, an experienced Islamic finance lawyer, has argued that US law is suited for the development and implementation of contract law within the Islamic finance space:

> … the focus of many United States laws (such as tax laws) is the economic substance of the transaction: the economic essence. How the transaction is dressed up is largely irrelevant. Which also means that the law does not really care if the transaction is structured to be compliant with the shari'ah. What U.S. law does care about as a legal matter is the economic substance. So every time we've tried to get a tax ruling in the United States, like New

> York State or Office of Control of Currency or the Federal Reserve Bank, the regulators have said, in essence: fine, no problem; we don't care if it's structured to be compliant with the shari'ah.[9]

Another key aspect of Islamic finance contracts is the certainty of timescales or project timelines, in respect of project financing such as via the istisn'a contract. As was discussed in the last chapter, any uncertainty is prohibited in Islamic finance. The Organisation for Islamic Co-operation's Fiqh Academy made this point clearly in a judgement reached in June 2006 at a meeting held in Amman:

> *First*: The basic principle of dating from both parties is that it is bound by religion and is not obligated to make a judgment.
> *Second*: Dating from both parties on a contract that circumvents usury, such as collusion over the sample or dating on the sale and advances prohibited by law.
> *Third*: In cases where it is not possible to complete the sales contract because there is no sale in the seller's property with a general need to compel each of the parties to complete a contract in the future by law or otherwise, or by virtue of international commercial norms, as in opening a documentary credit to import the goods, it is permissible to make dating binding for both parties, either by legalisation by the government, or by agreement by both parties to a text in the agreement that makes dating binding for both parties.
> *Fourth*: The obligatory dating in the case mentioned in Clause Three does not take the ruling of the added sale to the future. The property of the sale is not transferred to the buyer, and the price does not become a debt against him, and the sale does not take place except on the date agreed upon positively and acceptably.
> *Fifth*: If one of the two dating parties fails, in the cases mentioned in Clause Three, from what he promised, then he is forced to eliminate the fulfilment of the contract, or to bear the actual damage that the other party caused due to his failure to promise (without the lost opportunity).

Against this context of the primacy of contracts within the ethical framework of Islam, is a myriad of contract structures. This chapter will provide an overview of the following contract types:

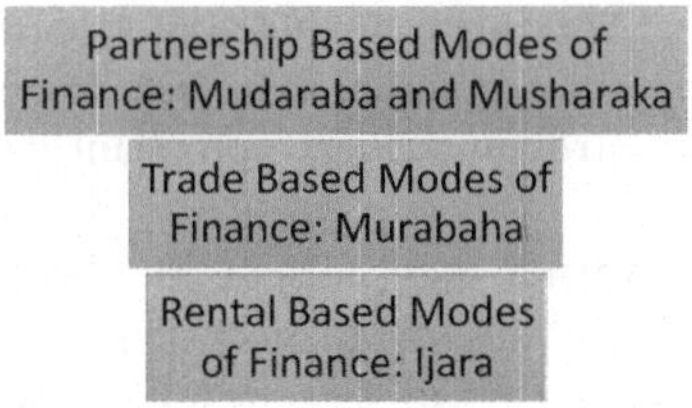

Fig. 4.1 Islamic finance contracts

- Mudaraba—Profit and loss sharing partnership agreement (material loss is bourne by one party to the agreement unless negligence is proven)
- Musharaka—Profit and loss sharing partnership agreement (partners have unlimited liability) and a related contract type, Bai Bithaman Ajil
- Murabaha—Sale at cost plus profit mark-up
- Salam—Contract for the manufacture of a product in which the payment is at spot price against delivery of the items at a future date
- Istisn'a—Contract for the manufacturing of a product in which payment is made progressively during the life span of the project
- Ijara—Leasing in which the lessee pays rental to the lessor
- Sukuk—Islamic finance bond
- Islamic finance derivatives
- Islamic personal finance products such as shari'a compliant "credit cards"
- 'Islamic pawnbroking'.

It should be noted that a variant of Islamic finance contract types is promoted in Iran and this will be addressed in Chapter 10.

We will discuss takaful (Islamic finance insurance) in Chapter 9 (Fig. 4.1).

Liquidity Financing and Conventional Banking

Fred doesn't do small talk and so we sat down and got straight to the point. I could see him becoming increasingly anxious, although this wasn't new - I'd noted that the more I spoke to bankers around this time, the more anxious they became. His message for me was clear: unless the Bank

> of England put more liquidity into the system, quickly, it would seize up, inevitably leading to another bank failure.[10]

This was the recollection of Alistair Darling when he was the UK's Chancellor of the Exchequer (Finance Minister) when he met the then Chief Executive of the Royal Bank of Scotland during the 2008 financial crisis.

Liquidity financing is critical to keep banks operating, as we can see from this vivid example, and without banks providing finance support for businesses and consumers, the whole economy seizes up.

The need to keep banks operating to support the wider economy in the face of the global lockdown that faced national economies during the 2020 COVID-19 outbreak was demonstrated by the US Federal Reserve deciding in March 2020 to purchase at least $700 billion of securities and this added to the liquidity available by increasing the $14.5 trillion of deposits held by American banks by about 5%. In addition, the Federal Reserve launched a primary dealer credit facility and encouraged banks to borrow from the discount window.

In March and April 2020, to take another example, the Central Bank of the United Arab Emirates provided liquidity support to the value of AED256bn (US$70 billion) whilst the European Central Bank (ECB) decided in March 2020 to implement additional longer-term refinancing operations (LTROs) to provide immediate liquidity support to banks. The operations were conducted as fixed rate tender procedures with full allotment. The rate in these operations were fixed at the average of the deposit facility rate over the life of the respective operation. Interest was paid when the respective operation matured in late June 2020.

Therefore, liquidity in conventional banking refers to the ability of a bank to meet its financial obligations as they come due. It can come from direct cash holdings in currency or on account at a central bank. More frequently, it comes from acquiring securities that can be sold quickly with minimal loss.

A bank's liquidity condition, particularly in a crisis, will be affected by much more than just the reserve of cash and highly liquid securities. The maturity of its less liquid of assets would also matter.

For Islamic finance banks, whilst liquidity support is fundamental to provide ongoing support for businesses and consumers and to remain operational, the same liquidity models used by conventional banks are clearly not available for Islamic finance banks as interest or riba is forbidden.

Subsequently the Murabaha and Tawarruq models are used to provide liquidity for Islamic finance banks—which can involve the active involvement of the London Metals Exchange.

Murabaha and Tawarruq Explained

Murabaha comes from the Arabic word meaning profit. This contract type refers to a sale transaction where a seller sells an asset to a buyer at cost plus profit mark-up. The cost price and mark-up are known to both the buyer and the seller. For example, the price that A will agree to in order to buy 150 kilograms of pears from B will be £110 where the cost of the pears to B was £100. B has added £10 of profit.

Consequently, the payment in a murabaha transaction can be at spot price. What is very important in this contract type is not just the avoidance of riba but also the need for certainty in advance of an agreement being formalised between the buyer and the seller for, as we discussed in Chapter 3, gharar (uncertainty) is forbidden (haram).

In a non-bank liquidity scenario, murabaha can be used as a method of finance when a consumer or business requires funds to purchase goods. In a non-banking context, there has been some debate amongst shari'a scholars as to the role and benefits of murabaha.

This debate, whether in respect of murabaha or other contract models, is linked in part to the different jurisprudence schools which exist within this faith. As we will discuss in Chapter 5, financial institutions engage with particular religious scholars to decide whether the launch of a particular financial product is in compliance with the requirements of Islam.

The Maliki school of thought (linked to Sunni Islam) has had concerns about murabaha as a number of conditions has to be met to ensure it is shari'a compliant and so there are difficulties in meeting this high standard. Nonetheless this fiqh school does not oppose Murabaha per se.[11] Whilst a Jafari jurist (Shi'a Islam) has argued that the consumer gains some protection from unfair trading practices via this contract type.[12]

In 1979, the Dubai Investment Bank played a key role in organising the world's first Islamic banking conference in the emirate where the concept of wa'ad (promise) was analysed as part of the wider murabaha offer. Scholars present at the conference eventually issued a fatwa which approved the murabaha offer.

It should be noted that gold, silver, barley, salt, wheat and dates cannot be used in murabaha and tawarruq contracts. This is linked to a hadith which goes as follows:

> Sell gold in exchange of equivalent gold, sell silver in exchange of equivalent silver, sell dates in exchange of equivalent dates, sell wheat in exchange of equivalent wheat, sell salt in exchange of equivalent salt, sell barley in exchange of equivalent barley, but if a person transacts in excess, it will be usury (Riba). However, sell gold for silver anyway you please on the condition it is hand-to-hand (spot) and sell barley for date anyway you please on the condition it is hand-to-hand (spot).

Therefore, these like for like sales in respect of gold, silver, barley, salt, wheat and dates would not be able to address short-term bank liquidity issues where overnight finance, for instance, would be the more relevant issue.

Murabaha does not just need to entail a relationship between a buyer and a seller. In fact, a more common form of murabaha contract would involve a bank as the key intermediary. The following steps would involve all parties in such an agreement:

Step 1:
The buyer promises to buy the goods from the bank. The Accounting and Auditing Organisation for Islamic Financial Institutions (AAOIFI) has decided that the commitment from the buyer would be deemed as legally binding. Upon signing the contract, the down payment becomes a part of the agreed price.
Step 2:
The bank enters into a sales contract with the seller. Usually the bank would appoint the buyer as the agent to pay for the goods from the seller.
Step 3:
The seller delivers the goods to the bank.
Step 4:
The bank enters into a murabaha agreement with the buyer and sells the goods to the buyer at a higher price as this would comprise the price plus the mark-up. Therefore, this second sale can be seen as a deferred payment sale or an instalment credit sale.
Step 5:

The buyer pays the bank the agreed amount on the specified future date. The date must be clear. Ambiguity in this or any other matter is not allowed for in Islamic finance (Fig. 4.2).

A slight variation of murabaha is Murabaha to the Purchase Orderer where the bank acquires an asset to meet the customer's order and the bank could face a loss if the customer fails to take delivery of the item. To guard against such losses, Hamish Jeddiyah ('earnest money') is retained in part or in whole to cover any such loss or arbun (non-returnable down payment).

Hamish Jeddiyah applies at the time of the wa'ad to purchase but before the parties enter into the murabaha contract. Arbun is provided by the purchaser after the contract is signed.

The practical steps that are followed in this variation of murabaha is as follows:

Step 1:
The purchaser makes a binding promise (wa'ad) to purchase the item from the bank and this may involve Hamish Jeddiyah;
Step 2:
The bank via its agent buys the asset at spot price from the supplier;

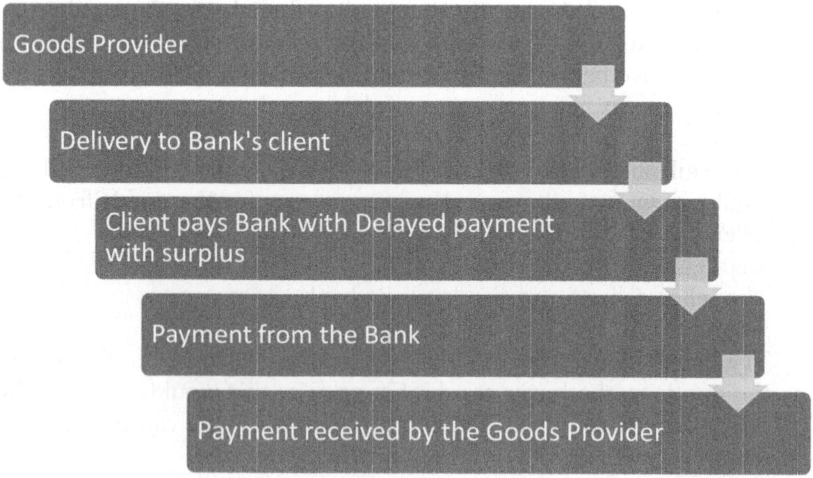

Fig. 4.2 Murabaha

Step 3:
The bank enters into a murabaha agreement with the purchaser of the goods at spot price plus margin. The asset is delivered to the purchaser;
Step 4:
Purchaser sends money in instalments to the bank.

The murabaha model has been tested in the Dubai courts during the 1980s and this has helped, in part, to establish this practice as a key plank of the Islamic finance industry.

For example, in 1984, a buyer had requested to a bank to buy a car according to his description and promised that he would buy it from the bank according to the murabaha contract. The bank imported the car and handed it over to the customer. After driving around in the car for a while, the customer complained that the specifications of the car were not as agreed. The Dubai First Instance Court agreed that the bank had acted properly as the buyer accepted the car at the time of delivery.

In another case that was heard at the Dubai High Appeal Court in 1986, it was stated that a bank, at the insistence of a ship buyer, changed the year that the ship had been built from 1967 to 1980 to allow the buyer to register the ship in Saudi Arabia. The court ruled that the bank should not have been a party to recording false information.

It is Commodity Murabaha and Tawarruq that is used for short-term bank liquidity purposes. A Commodity Murabaha is very similar to the murabaha structure that has already been described.

However, in this case, a deferred payment sale involves metals—and the London Metals Exchange is actively involved in Commodity Murabaha contracts. The whole process can be described as follows:

Step 1:
The bank buys a warrant from a metals broker. The ownership of the warrant transfers from the broker to the bank. The bank agrees to buy the warrants for the value of the deposit—let's say for £2 million.
Step 2:
The bank pays the spot price and it initiates payment of £2 million to the broker in return for the warrant.
Step 3:

The bank sells the warrant to a counterparty on a deferred payment basis and agrees that the counterparty will pay for the warrant in three months' time for £2.05 million.
Step 4:
The counterparty asks the bank to act as its agent to sell the warrant on its behalf. The bank sells the warrant at spot price of £2 million to the broker.
Step 5:
The broker pays the counterparty the spot price of £2 million in return for the warrant, using the bank as the agent. The counterparty receives £2 million and does not have to pay the bank until three months later when the counterparty will then pay £2.05 million to the bank.
Step 6:
The payment takes place at the agreed time and comprises the principal of the original purchase (£2 million) plus the pre-agreed mark-up of £0.05 million.

As we can see from this example, liquidity flows avoid the effect of interest and enables the ownership structure of the metal to be clear throughout this process.

Tawarruq (which means "to buy on credit and sell at spot value") is very similar to Commodity Murabaha. In this case the commodity, using a metal, is sold straight away to obtain the required funds. As the aim is not to own the commodity but to use it for liquidity purposes, therefore some interest (riba) is seen to be involved.

Some scholars argue that this structure is not shari'a compliant. Specifically, the Hanbali and Shafi'i schools do approve Tawarruq:

> Majority of scholars argue that its permissibility relies on the fact that: the Muwarriq (seller/financier) does not get involved in the resale of the commodity, no pre-arrangement between Muwarriq and the end buyer and that the Mutawarriq (buyer) receives cash directly from the end buyer.[13]

The Hanafi school would argue that Tawarruq is not permissible as it is viewed as a forced sale and such an exploitative condition is prohibited in Islam. The contract, the Hanafis argue, is undertaken by someone who is forced to seek liquidity, and the counterparty is not willing to provide a loan but, instead, sells the commodity with a profit.

Cost is also a concern with tawarruq:

> According to Bouheraoua (2013), the Islamic finance institutes which adopt the concept of tawarruq often exaggerate the charges and expenses due to a series of interrelated binding agreement such as Murabaha profit and agency fee. Hence, it becomes the arguments to oppose the proponent scholars who base the legality of tawarruq on the legal maxim that is "transactions are permissible unless a transaction is specifically prohibited by the Shari'ah".[14]

The use of Tawarruq started with the Saudi British Bank in October 2000 followed by Al-Jazeera Bank in 2002. Tawarruq has become popular in Saudi Arabia and other Gulf Cooperation Council (GCC) member states. The National Commercial Bank in Saudi Arabia has been using Tawarruq as a financial product under the brand of Taysir since 2000. The Abu Dhabi Islamic Bank launched a Tawarruq product called Al Khair.

As earlier discussed, whether in respect of Commodity Murabaha or Tawarruq, gold, silver, barley, salt, wheat and dates are not used as commodities due to the strictures in the hadiths. Other metals are used and the London Metals Exchange and the Bursa Suq-al Sila in Kuala Lumpur are engaged to facilitate these agreements with brokers.

The value system within Islam which is linked to changes in Malaysian law means that the Reverse Tawarruq is an additional technique used by banks.

The Islamic Financial Service Act 2013 classified Islamic bank deposits in Malaysia as a principal guaranteed and investment account.

Consequently, murabaha is deemed to be unsuitable for deposit accounts since its essence is a non-guaranteed principal. The application of a Tawarruq term deposit, however, would be supported by wakala (agency) where the bank is appointed as an agent of the customer to purchase a commodity from the supplier.

Therefore, in summary, Reverse Tawarruq is a method where the financial institution, either directly or indirectly, will buy an asset and immediately sell it to a customer on a deferred payment basis. The customer then sells the same asset to a third party for immediate delivery and payment; the end result being that the customer receives a cash amount and has a deferred payment obligation for the marked-up price to the financial institution.

Ijara: The Islamic Mortgages Market

The US sub-prime mortgage defaults, which directly contributed to the 2008 financial crisis, could not have happened within Islamic finance.

This may sound like a bold claim but if we consider what happened in the period leading up to 2008, then we will see that each set of decisions made by mortgage companies and investment banks would have been in conflict with shari'a compliance requirements.

In the early 2000s in the United States the dream of buying your own home seemed to be in everyone's grasp and the rise of so-called sub-prime mortgages for lower income earners looked too good to be true.

As it later turned out, the reality of this market was hard for the home-owners to bear with repossessions rising in 2006, 2007 and 2008 due, in part, to changes in interest rates.

However, before the crisis fully came into its own with the collapse of Lehman Brothers, the techniques that were adopted to provide mortgages and its link to market trades was detrimental to the health of the American economy. These practices were subsequently laid bare by a US official investigation:

> When originators made loans to hold through maturity - an approach known as originate to hold - they had a clear incentive to underwrite carefully and consider the risks. However, when they originated mortgages to sell, for securitisation or otherwise - known as originate to distribute - they no longer risked losses if the loan defaulted. As long as they made accurate representations and warranties, the only risk was to their reputations if a lot of loans went bad - but during the boom, loans were not going bad. In total, this originate to distribute pipeline carried more than half of all mortgages before the crisis....[15]

This form of speculation would not be allowed within Islamic finance. As was discussed in Chapter 3 the element of gharar (uncertainty) would mean that speculating on monetary variables which involve the value of money and the rate of interest (both of which are prohibited within Islamic finance) simply would not occur.

In addition, the rise in interest rates which led to mortgagees defaulting, who did not meet the affordability criteria due to the decisions being made, which were directly linked to the securitisation process, are also factors that could not arise in Islamic finance.

But Islamic mortgages do exist and the market flourishes in the Persian Gulf, south east Asia and other key markets where Islamic finance is playing an increasingly dominant role in national economies.

In addition, shari'a compliant mortgages also have a growing presence in the mortgage market in the United States and in the United Kingdom. In the mid-1990s the US Office of the Comptroller of the Currency (OCC) recognised the ijarah and the murabaha models as being valid for transactions involving residential property purchases. Whilst this is still a niche product in the United States, interest in shari'a compliant mortgages has meant this is a sustainable sector in the US marketplace.

When it comes to the United Kingdom, Islamic mortgages play a very significant role as a proportion of all Islamic finance activity in the UK. Islamic retail banking began in the United Kingdom in the 1990s when Gulf Cooperation Council (GCC) based businesses introduced Islamic mortgages (based on the murabaha principle) and offered mortgage financing (based on the ijarah principle) shortly thereafter.

These instruments were expensive due to the double stamp duty which were applicable (first, when a bank purchases a house, and, second, when a buyer/client purchases this house from the bank). The abolition of the double taxation regime in 2004 paved the way for increased demand for Islamic home financing.

Murabaha, as previously discussed, is a form of bridge funding which is used in a variety of settings including interbank liquidity requirements. There is also the Diminishing Musharaka mortgage which will be considered later in this chapter.

Ijara, on the other hand, is equivalent to a leasing arrangement. Ijara is the Arabic word for providing goods or services on a temporary basis against a wage. Ijara can be seen as being similar to an operating lease but redemption features can be structured into the agreement so that it acts as a lease.

In reality, most ijara contracts contain redemption features where the lessee takes possession of the object at the end of the lease. This is the basic structure of most Islamic finance mortgages. This is known as Ijara wa Iqtina (lease with acquisition).

Ijara wa Iqtina can be seen in operation—step by step.

Step 1:
The purchaser negotiates and agrees to buy the property from the asset owner.

Step 2:
The purchaser negotiates and agrees with the bank the terms of the financing of the acquisition.
Step 3:
The bank buys the asset from the seller by using the purchaser as the bank's agent.
Step 4:
The bank leases the property to the purchaser.
Step 5:
At maturity of the contract, the ownership of the property is transferred by the bank to the purchaser.
(Fig. 4.3)

There is another form of ijara which, in conventional finance, would be viewed as a forward contract.

Ijara Mawsoofa Bil Thimma (forward lease) can occur in the construction industry when properties are being built for onward purchase. The uncertainty principle which is prohibited in Islamic finance does not apply here as scholars have deemed there is a high level of certainty that as there is a construction process then, once work has begun, it is highly likely to be completed.

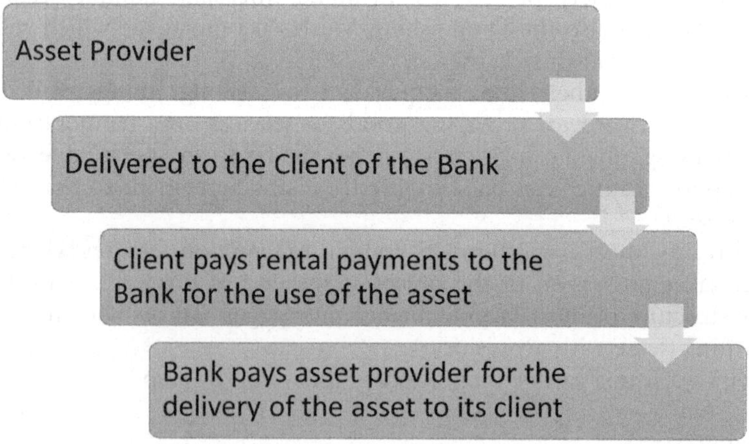

Fig. 4.3 Ijara

Clearly unexpected circumstances can get in the way which is where takaful (Islamic insurance) would be considered. Takaful will be considered in Chapter 7.

Salam

Salam (literally means payment in advance) is when a spot payment is made in advance for future delivery of goods. Superficially, this mechanism may seem to contradict the very essence of Islamic finance for uncertainty or gharar is prohibited and surely if you pay for an item that has yet to be delivered there must be an element of uncertainty in the item never arriving.

However, gharar would cover a whole range of uncertainties which cannot be easily discerned such as short selling and the futures market. However, in the case of a house being built or crops being harvested there is some certainty as to when the purchase can be completed. Scholars refer to one of the hadiths where the Prophet said:

> Whoever pays money in advance (for fruit) (to be delivered later) should pay it for a known quantity, specified measure and weight of course along with the price and time of delivery.[16]

According to the sunna, the Prophet also referred to the nature and composition of a salam contract:

> Whoever wishes to enter into a contract of salam, he must effect the salam according to the specified measure and the specified weight and the specified date of delivery.[17]

For bank liquidity purposes, a concept known as Parallel Salam exists. The purpose of Parallel Salam is similar to the murabaha contract we discussed earlier which is to ensure the regular liquidity needs of banks are met whilst meeting shari'a compliance requirements in order to avoid speculation.

It can best be summed up by examining the following example:

Step 1:
Bank enters into a Salam contract and buys $200,000 of commodities. The commodities are to be delivered in a month's time. The

bank can appoint an agent—such as a metals broker—to execute the contract.
Step 2:
The agent, on behalf of the bank, agrees to sell back the commodities to the original seller for $220,000.

Salam can be used for Mergers and Acquisitions (M&A). One such example was in 2007 when Abraaj Capital wanted to buy Egyptian Fertilisers Company (EFC). A lease and buy-back model (ijara) was considered but the timescale for the deal as well as the need to meet Egyptian regulatory requirements meant this option was not seen as viable. The option of a murabaha contract was then vetoed by the scholar employed by Deutsche Bank:

> The default option of the ubiquitous commodity murabaha structure had been vetoed by the conservative Sheikh Hussain for looking too much like a conventional loan. If it looks like a loan, smells like a loan and acts like a loan, it is a loan, he reasoned – it doesn't matter what fancy Arabic words you attach to the finance documents.[18]

Deutsche Bank executives then proposed to the scholar that the fertiliser product could be bought as a forward contract, under a salam arrangement, which would act as a form of debt financing for the acquisition to go ahead:

> 'As the bank, we buy the urea from EFC for $850 million on day one', we suggested to Sheikh Hussain, 'and they deliver the product to us for selling on into the market over a period of eight years, the term of the equivalent debt financing.' This would be a real economy transaction, one where the bank acts as a merchant, buying and selling on a product – an Islamic transaction. Sheikh Hussain paused, smiled and slowly nodded his head. 'Praise be to Allah', he affirmed in Arabic in a low voice, as if speaking to himself. 'You have learnt well.'

The Forex Dilemma

Salam covers commodities but not currencies as, due to exchange rates, there cannot be any certainty or a like for like process in currency transactions. One study has summed up why currencies cannot be part of a salam contract:

> It is not permissible to pay one of them as Salam principal for the other because Salam requires payment of only one of the two exchanged objects of the contract at the time of signing the contract, while the currency exchange requires simultaneous payment of both the exchanged amounts.[19]

Consequently, the difficulties in foreign currencies exchange or Forex could be seen as, arguably, one of the biggest challenges for the future growth of the Islamic finance industry. Being able to change Saudi rial into US dollars, for example, is clearly fundamental to advance international business transactions.

However, exchange rates are governed by conventional speculation which is gharar (uncertainty) and it will always be difficult in all periods of any business cycle to be certain of the exchange rate between different currencies. At the same time, currencies cannot be exchanged on a like for like basis as the speculative nature of the international money markets would preclude such an approach under the ethical framework which underpins Islamic finance.

As we will see in our discussion of a potential Islamic monetary policy in Chapter 7, some scholars and former Malaysian Prime Minister, Mahathir Mohammed would like an Islamic monetary system to be based on the gold standard—a monetary structure that has not existed since US President Richard Nixon ended the link between the US dollar and the gold price in 1971. This concept of a new gold standard, as we will discover, creates its own economic dilemmas.

However, in advance of any potential ideal outcome being established in the realm of Islamic monetary policy, how can businesses engage in forex and also be shari'a compliant?

Various conventional forex options cannot be considered because of gharar and maysir (speculation).

This would include Contract for Differences (CFD). This method is offered by brokers for individual investors in the retail market for speculation. No real currency is bought or sold in the retail market.

As was discussed in Chapter 3, the futures market and spread betting is considered not to be shari'a compliant so this would rule out FX futures and FX spread betting.

FX options are also seen as speculative. This is a type of foreign exchange derivative contract that confers to its holder the right, but not the obligation, to engage in a forex transaction. In general, buying such an option would allow a trader to elect to purchase one currency against another in a specified amount or on a specified date for an upfront cost.

This leaves the spot forex option which has been seen as shari'a compliant. This would see the currency trade as a loan. We can take the example of buying yen and converting yen into US dollars. The yen can be borrowed at the overnight lending rate, converting the yen into dollars then depositing the dollars at the US dollar overnight deposit rate. In that way the person is paying the difference between what a person would pay on the loan and what the person subsequently receives with the deposit.

Another shari'a compliant forex deal can occur during the working day.

The broker debits the client's account and transfers the amount to the counterparty. The counterparty receives the funds in real time into their account. The buy currency is settled and delivered the very same day. In this case, there is no trading in currencies, as such, as the client is paying the broker a simple fee for gaining access to a currency.

This arrangement has also been confirmed as shari'a compliant by the Accounting and Auditing Organisation for Islamic Financial Institutions (AAOIFI):

> To credit a sum of money to the account of the customer in the following situations:
>
> ....
>
> When the customer enters into a spot contract of currency exchange between himself and the Institution, in the case of the purchase of a currency against another currency already deposited in the account of the customer.[20]

Istisn'a: Long-Term Project Financing

Poverty cannot be eradicated in East Asia without a significant change as to how project financing is structured and delivered.

These were the startling conclusions of reports from the Asian Development Bank (ADB) and Marsh & McLennon Companies.

In March 2017, the Asian Development Bank stated that East Asia required US$1.7 trillion of project financing to maintain a growth trajectory that would sufficiently eradicate poverty. This is double the estimate of funding the ADB had assumed for the region when it made its calculations in 2009.

A 2017 report went further and stated that the very mechanisms adopted by investors to assess and agree to infrastructure financing is the key to understanding the project funding gap in east Asia:

> Across much of Asia, there is an insufficient pipeline of infrastructure projects that meet the bankability requirements of international investors. This issue is a key driver of the infrastructure financing gap in the region and needs to be resolved for a meaningful level of international private sector investment to be channelled towards Asia.

This report from Marsh & McLennon highlighted how current project financing structures were hindering economic growth across the Asia-Pacific:

> There have been instances of project failures due to cash flow and liquidity challenges, largely driven by slow ramp-up of demand or traffic flow. Examples include the pre-IPO greenfield construction of the BTS Sky Train project in Thailand, as well as the Brisbane Airport Link.

The solutions offered within the report went against long established conventional project financing mechanisms:

> In instances where there are no minimum revenue guarantees or availability pay-outs, financing repayment should be structured to allow for flexibility in the payment amortization schedule (or even use of deferred interest or Payment in Kind structures), while additional financial headroom should be allowed for if the private player takes on significant volume risks, with the government entity also potentially undertaking a "first loss" guarantee on behalf of the SPV *(Special Purpose Vehicle).*
>
> In other sectors, where there could be a single offtake agreement, the financiers should also expect the project entity to take on some form of non-payment insurance which is covered next in "presence of legal and economic recourse".

The report also commented on the additional complications of project financing which could lead to lengthy litigation:

> The construction of large-scale projects is often met with delays, disruptions or even cancellations. As such, all stakeholders in an infrastructure deal will both put in place appropriate risk mitigants as well as further escalation (terms of settlement, litigation) procedures. In such instances,

> players will first seek economic settlement (out of court, through insurance or contractual claims), before escalating to forms of legal recourse.[21]

The issues identified in this analysis could be significantly addressed by the istisn'a contract model. It provides for certainty for the investor and the business and guards against unexpected developments such as a sudden change in interest rates. Whilst legal action can clearly occur in any context, the istisn'a model provides a surety of purpose that is not fully provided for in conventional forms of project financing.

So, what makes istisn'a such a good model for project financing?

Istisn'a is a derivative from the Arabic root word 'Sa na'a', which means to manufacture or to construct something.

It takes the form of a sales transaction where the manufacture, construction or processing of an item is required before it is sold. Due to the detailed specification within the contract, gharar can be largely avoided.

Therefore, under the istisn'a model, there is a staged process towards financing which is linked to each stage of the production process. This contract type could work in areas such as the Black Country in the West Midlands region of the United Kingdom. This area is known for its many engineering businesses who cry out for project financing for upscaling projects or for meeting tailor made orders for key clients.

Normally, the costs involved for these businesses are front ended such as insurance, due diligence, potential legal costs and so on. Whilst it is fair to say not all of these costs are removed in istisn'a (for example, due diligence will always be required), each stage of the work would be linked to a payment structure.

Whilst similar models do exist in conventional finance, the other variables such as deferred interest would not be there. A greater understanding of istisn'a can be gained by looking at a practical istisn'a agreement via a step by step process:

> Step 1:
> The ultimate buyer enters into an istisn'a agreement with the construction company.
> Step 2:
> A bank may provide financing to the buyer and so the buyer would act as the agent of the bank where a separate contract between the buyer and the bank would be agreed.

Step 3:
The buyer receives money to pay the construction company under the terms of the istisn'a agreement. This would be paid on an instalment basis according to the work being progressed.
Step 4:
The manufacturer enters into a forward lease agreement with the ultimate buyer who pays a rental cost during the construction period.
Step 5:
At maturity of the agreement which coincides with the construction work being completed, the asset is transferred to the ultimate buyer.

Therefore, whilst in conventional finance, there is the issue of security to insure against risk for the investor, in the istisn'a model the lease element provides some element of security for the investor combined with the staged process of payment dependent upon work undertaken.

Whilst problems can occur, as in any contractual arrangement, the scope for such disagreements are reduced as compared to conventional project financing.

There can also be complications if, with the involvement of a bank, it wants to guard against the risk of holding a property once it is constructed due to the potential, as in any commercial agreement, with a default by the ultimate buyer. In such a situation, the parallel istisn'a model could be used.

In this structure, the bank enters into two separate contracts with the same product specifications. The difference in price between the two contracts can relate to the margin earned by the bank.

It should be noted that neither contract is dependent on the other. Otherwise this would take us back to the principles of avoiding uncertainty and funding being linked directly to assets rather than the concept of money. Therefore, if the construction company fails to deliver according to the specification then the bank is at risk of defaulting.

To explain this further, let us consider parallel istisn'a by the use of a step by step process.

Step 1:
Bill Bloggs Limited needs to meet an order to supply 100 drink vending machines to the local rail terminus and needs finance from the bank to meet his immediate liquidity needs.

Step 2:
The bank decides it will pay the vending machine manufacturer and it will profit from a mark-up arrangement from Bill Bloggs Limited.
Step 3:
The bank agrees to ensure the vending machines are manufactured and delivered by 1 October.
Step 4:
The bank enters into an istisn'a contract with the vending machine manufacturer agreeing to the same price and delivery terms as was agreed with the separate contract with Bill Bloggs Limited.
Step 5:
Therefore, on 1 October, under one of the agreements the vending machines are delivered to Bill Bloggs Limited under the agreement between the manufacturer and the bank. At the same time, Bill Bloggs Limited—once delivery is confirmed—would pay the margin mark-up to the bank for completion of this whole arrangement.

The parallel istisn'a model may sound trickier as compared to the istisn'a model, but it does work and compared to the covenants in many conventional project funding agreements, is not as complex (Fig. 4.4).

Alfadhli, Alghoussein and Alarifi examined the use of a parallel Istisn'a Sukuk (Islamic bond) with the supply of solar panels to Kuwait:

> The parallel istisn'a structure requires a buyer, a seller and a third party contractor, In this case, the buyer will be the Kuwaiti Ministry of Energy, the seller will be an Islamic bank and the third party contractor will be a

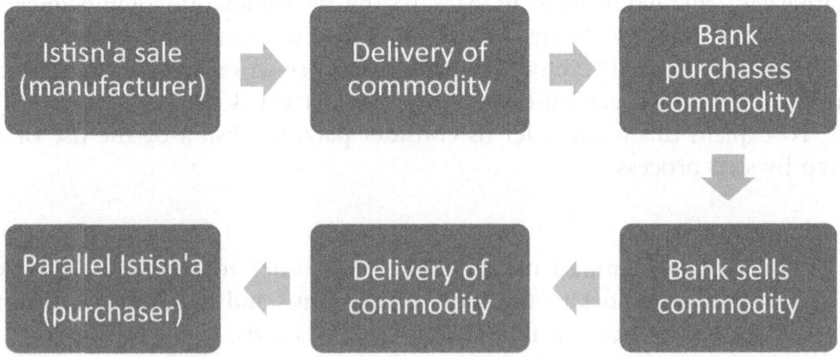

Fig. 4.4 Parallel Istisn'a

manufacturer that Kuwait's bordering countries are using, the Electricite de France company (EDF).

As the authors put it:

> The key part of parallel istisna'a, and the differentiating factor from regular istisn'a, is the third party, that is, in this case, the Islamic bank. As mentioned, the party will be the Islamic bank. They will be responsible for making the payment and purchasing the asset from the manufacturer once the asset is physically ready for the transfer of ownership.
>
> The manufacturer, the Electricite de France company, will be responsible for delivery of the asset which, of course, will be enough solar panels capable of producing the energy required and already specified for this project.
>
> Once the asset and ownership thereof has been fully 100% transferred to the bank, the bank is then responsible for providing the asset to the customer, who will be the Kuwait Ministry of Energy and will be responsible … for the payment to the Islamic bank.
>
> As such, the Islamic bank will act as the intermediary between the customer and manufacturer.[22]

With corporate businesses and the public sector amending their procurement and public–private partnership structures, the istisn'a model is particularly relevant for the current business environment.

To take just one example, the US space agency, NASA, since 2006, has established fixed-price contracts within public-private partnerships, where NASA does not exclusively own the resulting technology. Commercial partners can sell their services and technology to other customers. Costs are shared, and NASA pays for milestones reached.

Instead of detailed specifications within a tender being issued by NASA, the agency instead specifies high level goals (the what), leaving the how to the commercial partners. The innovators can then exploit these technologies commercially as they see fit, further fuelling the development of space technology and enhancing the value of the industry overall.

The istisn'a model would fit with this form of public–private partnership (PPP) due to the staged process of funding linked to technological delivery of a contract and the contract type has the in-built flexibility to bring in other investment partners for more complex financing arrangements.

The potential for this model of finance to be widened to meet a range of business financing opportunities is significant and whilst there are conventional finance models that can be adjusted to address innovative PPP arrangements, the ready-made istisn'a contract type is already ready to go to meet these market opportunities.

Profit Sharing and Patient Finance: The Islamic Finance Offer

> The first investment primer was delivered in around 600 BC by Aesop who, you will remember, said 'a bird in the hand is worth two in the bush' .... now Aesop was on to something but he didn't finish it because there are a couple of other questions that go along with that. It is an investment equation that a bird in the hand is worth two in the bush. He forgot to say exactly when you would get the two in the bush and he forgot to say what interest rates were that you had to measure this against but if he had given those two factors he would have defined investment for the next 2600 years.
>
> You'll trade a bird in the hand, you lay out cash today, and the question is, as an investment decision you'll have to evaluate how many birds are in the bush .... now if interest rates are at 5% and you'll going to get two birds in the bush in five years versus one now, two birds in the bush are much better than a bird in the hand now because if you trade your bird in the hand with two in the bush, well, in five years that's roughly 14% compounded annually and interest rates at only 5%. But if interest rates were at 20% you would decline to take two birds in the bush by five years from now. You would say "that's not good enough because at 20% if I just keep this bird in the hand and compound it I would have more birds in the bush in five years.[23]

This was the analysis from the legendary American investor, Warren Buffett, equating Aesop's fable with an investment equation. This argument exemplifies why so many investors do not consider Islamic finance as a sustainable proposition as interest rates would not be used to gauge the true value of money.

Consequently, the need for Islamic finance to develop legal models so that investments can still be assessed for true monetary value without resorting to interest was a significant bar that the industry had to meet. It did so, in part, with the mudaraba and musharaka models.

These models have also been cited as helping to address the patient capital gap which plagues businesses in developed as well as developing countries. Former UK Business Secretary, Vince Cable, has spent many years analysing the issues that stem from the patient capital gap:

> In the UK … there is a serious market failure in the provision of capital for small, growing companies and social enterprises in the form of 'patient capital', which produces decent returns over a long time period.[24]

Cable later gained immense popularity when his unexpected ballroom dancing skills were exposed on prime-time television. Cable, though, has never danced around the need for more support for small and medium sized businesses and he made a contribution to addressing this requirement when, during the 2010–2015 UK coalition government, he championed patient finance. As Business Secretary, he established the British Business Bank and the Green Investment Bank. However, the Green Investment Bank was later privatised by the subsequent majority Conservative Government—much to Cable's chagrin.

Musharaka and Mudaraba contract models can help address this patient capital gap. The contract types are based upon risk sharing and therefore profit sharing. The way these contract types have been devised enable long-term investment to take place whilst providing some security for investors.

Critics of this model would argue that these very contract structures inhibit economic growth. For example, one journalist stated:

> The most significant of the sharia-rooted economic liabilities was the Islamic partnership, which proved no match for the Western world's joint-stock company. Partnerships were short-lived, dissolving with the death of any of the partners, and they tended to be small, often formed among family members. Joint-stock companies, which sharia prohibited, had much greater reach and risk-hedging power.[25]

As it happens, later in the article the journalist contradicts himself and states that joint-stock companies are allowed in Islamic finance. However, on the broader point, is it true that risk sharing contract types as envisaged in Islamic finance is inherently weak and woolly. The answer is a resounding no.

To demonstrate how, in fact, these contract types are effective we will first consider mudaraba.

Mudaraba

Mudaraba is a partnership contract model and the very structure and nature of this contract goes back to the Prophet's business arrangement with Khadija before they were married.

Banks use the mudaraba model on a regular basis when customers deposit their money via an investment account structure with the customer having an expectation that there will be a return on their investment.

However, this contract type can be used in a variety of different ways such as Islamic finance bonds (Sukuks) and direct business financing. In the case of an investment account, the step by step process is as follows:

> Step 1:
> The bank, when receiving the funds, would act as the mudarib –in other words the entrepreneurial partner with the customer investing the funds.
> Step 2:
> Customers will be offered the choice of the funds being invested in an unrestricted investment account (UIA) or a restricted investment account (RIA). The choice the customer makes depends upon the level of risk the customer is willing to take. There is a range of variables in this decision-making process.

For instance, in a UIA, a customer's money can be mixed with the normal investment capital of the bank therefore reducing the risk of loss. On the other hand, an RIA that stipulates that funds will only be invested in a three-month commodity murabaha is likely to carry less risk than a UIA which may contain a medium risk.

Let us now consider mudaraba from the point of view of a straightforward contract from a step by step perspective:

> Step 1:
> When a business enters into a mudaraba contract with a bank, the bank would act as the Rab al Mal (an investor who provides capital).

The business is the Mudarib (the entrepreneur who has the expertise to deliver a return on the investment).
Step 2:
If profits are made, they are shared between the business and the bank based upon the agreed ratio as stipulated in the contract.

It is from this simple structure that we move to the next iteration of this model—the two tier mudaraba contract. This is seen as an exemplar by Islamic scholars—and for good reason. It marries the need for generating a return for customers investing in a bank with the requirements of a business which requires funds for business development.

The two tier mudaraba contract concerns, as the name suggests, two contracts. The first contract concerns investors to a bank or an investment fund. The second contract concerns the bank or fund's links to an entrepreneur.

It can be described using a step by step process.

Step 1:
Investors deposit £300,000 with a bank under a mudaraba contract for a period of 12 months with a profit allocation set out in the contract with 80% to the investors (the term being Arbab al Mal) and 20% to the bank (Mudarib). The investors would receive certificates in return for the deposit of funds.
Step 2:
The bank (as the capital provider—Rab al Mal) would invest £300,000 with Bill Bloggs Limited (the Mudarib) to develop a piece of machinery. Whilst Bill Bloggs Limited is not providing any funding from company funds for this project, it can charge a management fee—known as a Mudarib fee—as it is the company's expertise that will help ensure the project is a commercial success.
Step 3:
At the end of the second contract, when the machinery is manufactured and then sold for £320,000, the bank recovers its initial £300,000.
Step 4:
The profit is allocated as follows in respect of the second contract:

- £4000 (20%) to Bill Bloggs Limited (as the Mudarib—the management fee)
- £16,000 (80%) to the bank (Rab al Mal—the capital provider).

Step Five:
The £16,000 is allocated to the investors under the first contract in the following way:

- £12,800 to the investors
- £3200 to the bank (as the Mudarib—the entrepreneur) (Fig. 4.5).

This is an ideal risk sharing model in the sense that timescales can be agreed in the contract. There is an element of risk, as in any business venture, but this is mitigated by the staged approach that is reflected in both contracts. The bank can act as a facilitator of finance for a business which may find it difficult to raise funds via lots of investors (though, admittedly, this contract type was developed before the concept of crowd-funding was formed. Shari'a complaint crowdfunding is discussed in Chapter 7).

The benefits of mudaraba was highlighted by the Hanafi jurist, Al Sarakhsi (1009–1090):

> Because people have a need for this contract. For the owner of capital may not find his way to profitable trading activity and the person who can find his way to such activity may not have the capital. And profit cannot be attained except by means of both of these, that is, capital and trading activity. By permitting this contract, the goal of both parties is attained.[26]

It therefore provides confidence to the business, the investors and to the bank.

With all of these advantages, what could go wrong?

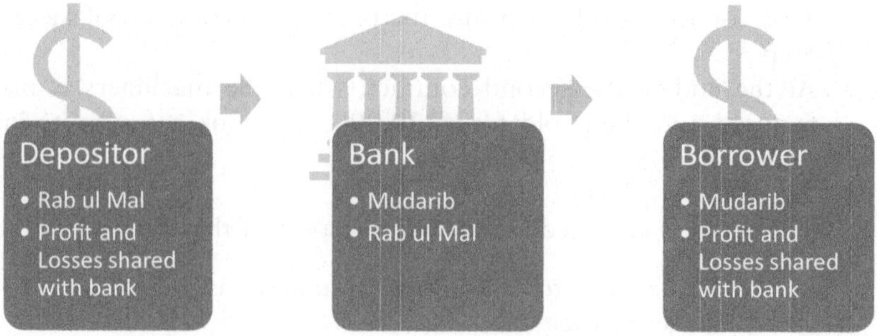

Fig. 4.5 Two Tier Mudaraba

In practice, a number of financial institutions are not keen on the two tier mudaraba contract. At the end of the day, investors could lose all their money and for bank customers who are used to conventional investment accounts, this would be quite a shock. Arsalan has summed up well the reticence to utilise this model:

> The pursuit to offer smoothened, market tracking returns to the IAH (Investment Account Holder) has implications on the overall risk appetite, product and tenor of the financing assets on the books of an IB (Islamic Bank) - justifying IBs logical preference for short term, debt based and blue-chip lending to manage the asset liability mismatch and the subsequent liquidity risk. The challenge here is that of the overall asset-liability management and rate of return risk, wherein it is a fixed term and fixed returns asset side funded by on-demand PLS *(profit and loss sharing)* deposit base offering a market tracking varying returns. This situation is further exacerbated by the lack of liquidity instruments, inter-banks and Lender of last resort facilities which burdens the efficiency of the IBs.[27]

However, it was the mudaraba model that inspired many of the early initiatives to form an Islamic finance industry in the first place. The early caliphs of Umar and Uthman used mudaraba to invest charitable funds. As was discussed in Chapter 2, the medieval financial practice of qirads is an antecedent of today's mudaraba contract model.

Al-Sarakhsi was an early champion of mudaraba whose advocacy of this contract model included reference to Caliph Uthman:

> The people of Medina call this contract Muqaradah, and that is based on a tradition concerning Uthman (Gbpwh), who entrusted funds to a man in the form of a Maqarada. This is derived from al-Qard (loan), which signifies cutting; for, in this contract, the investor cuts off the disposition of a sum of money from himself and transfers its disposition to the agent. It is therefore designated accordingly. We, however, have preferred the first term because it corresponds to that which is found in the book of Almighty Allah. He said: 'while others travel in the land (yadribuna fil-ard) in search of Allah's bounty,' that is to say, travel for the purposes of trade.[28]

Mudaraba was also included as Article 1404 in the Mejelle:

> A partnership of capital and labour is a type of partnership where one party supplies the capital and the other the labour. The person who owns the

> capital is called the owner of the capital and the person who performs the work is called the workman.[29]

The Mejelle was the civil code of the Ottoman Caliphate and is considered to be the first attempt to codify Islamic law. The Mejelle was elaborated between 1869 and 1875 as part of the legislative purpose of the tanzimat or reorganisation of the law. The Mejelle was based on Hanafi fiqh.

In 1964, Irshad developed a clear mudaraba model which inspired others to follow his lead in establishing an Islamic finance industry:

> Irshad (1964) also spoke of mudarabah as the basis of Islamic banking, but his concept of mudarabah was quite different from the traditional one in that he thought of capital and labour (including entrepreneurship) as having equal shares in output, thus sharing the losses and profits equally. This actually means that the owner of capital and the entrepreneur have a fifty-fifty share in the profit or loss as the case may be, which runs against the Shariah rulings. Irshad (1964) further suggested two kinds of deposit accounts. The first sounded like current deposits in the sense that it would be payable on demand, but the money kept in this deposit would be used for social welfare projects, as the depositors would get zero return. The second one amounted to term deposits which would entitle the depositors to a share in the profits at the end of the year proportionately to the size and duration of the deposits. He recommended the setting up of a Reserve Fund which would absorb all losses so that no depositor would have to bear any loss. According to Irshad (1964), all losses would be either recovered from the Reserve Fund or borne by the shareholders of the bank.[30]

More recently, mudaraba is defined within Article 693 up to Article 707 of the UAE's Civil Transaction Act. However, an example of the reticence of Islamic financial institutions to fully engaged with mudaraba can be seen from the example of the Dubai Investment Bank. It was essentially the very first Islamic bank ever established in 1975 following the short-lived Mit Ghamr Bank in Egypt but it only began to use mudaraba from 1987.[31]

Arguably, attitudes are changing as consumers are more open to a higher risk appetite to gain rewards in what was a bull market until the first half of 2020 when the COVID-19 crisis began. Whilst attitudes are changing from consumers and banks with the use of mudarabah, the model is also used via Sukuks which will be examined later in this chapter.

We should also consider another risk sharing contract—Musharaka.

Musharaka

Continuous Musharaka

Musharaka literally means sharing and this is, essentially, a partnership contract. This contract model fits within two broad categories. There is permanent or continuous musharaka which concerns business financing and then there is diminishing musharaka which is suited for property transactions.

With continuous musharaka, each partner to the contract retain their share in the capital until the project has been completed. A partner could sell their musharaka share to a third party. The profit ratio is stipulated within the contract.

Within continuous musharaka are two subcategories—Shirkat al Milk and Shirkat al Aqd. Shirkat al Milk is a partnership of two or more owners who hold a shared asset. The aim of this form of agreement is that the asset, often a property, is not divided in any way and it can be used for inheritance purposes.

Shirkat al Aqd is a partnership contract for business financing purposes. Contributions from partners with Shirkat al Aqd contracts can be in kind services or of monetary value.

One example of an in-kind service is a business using the commodities of one partner which can then be used by the other partner to manufacture a product. The senior Islamic scholar, Sheikh Muhammed Taqi Usmani has confirmed this stance:

> We may, therefore, conclude that the share capital in a Musharaka can be contributed either in cash or in the form of commodities. In the latter case, the market value of the commodities shall determine the share of the partner in the capital.[32]

Banks may decide to reduce their risk profile in musharaka contracts by advising clients as to their assessment for when a liquidation should occur. As in conventional finance, a formal notice of bankruptcy would meet such requirements.

Let us consider continuous musharaka via a step by step process:

Step 1:
Investors place their funds with the bank and, in return, they receive Notes of Participation to fund a musharaka agreement with Bill Bloggs Limited to buy a property which would be rented out.

Step 2:
The bank provides £400,000 (80% of the funds) and Bill Bloggs Limited provides £100,000 (20% of the funds). The property is bought and a tenant is found who pays rent for the property. The rental income is shared, in this instance, with 60% to the bank and 40% to Bill Bloggs Limited.
Step 3:
If it is decided to sell the property and the selling price is £400,000 then there would be a loss of £100,000. The loss would be shared on the ratio of the initial 80%/20% split when the investment agreement was first entered into. So once the property is sold for £400,000 the bank would receive £320,000 and Bill Bloggs Limited would receive £80,000.

This is a good partnership model where there is certainty in terms of timescales, investment structure, the proportion of profits or losses and is project based. It can also be used to supply lines of credit to businesses.

Using musharaka to provide such lines of credit can be controversial from an Islamic perspective as there is a debate as to whether an element of interest is essentially inherent within this process.

To consider this matter in some depth, we can consider how a musharka line of credit could work in Pakistan. As will be been discussed in Chapter 10, Islamic finance plays a key role in that nation's political economy.

The central bank of Pakistan had established an export refinance scheme on a musharaka basis where a business seeking credit is charged the bank's average profit rate based on the rate earned on financing offered to a number of the bank's corporate businesses. Guidance from the State Bank of Pakistan stipulates the following:

> The Islamic Commercial banks shall have to ensure that the effective cost of funds to the exporters does not exceed the rate declared by the State Bank under its Export finance scheme, besides ensuring that there is no negative spread on their portfolio under the Scheme.[33]

Khan has been scathing as to the true implications of this scheme:

> That is, the State Bank of Pakistan sets the rate charged by Islamic Banks so the 'musharaka pool' and 'setting profit rates' is simply rigmarole designed

to give a semblance of Islamic risk sharing on what is effectively a straight interest based, conventional finance transaction since the 'pool' has to equal the refinance lending rate set by the State Bank of Pakistan.[34]

Diminishing Musharaka

Diminishing musharaka enables one of the partners over time to purchase units in the venture from one or more of the other partners. As more units are bought the greater the stake the partner has in the venture.

It works on a step by step basis as follows:

> Step 1:
> Julie wants to buy a house and so enters into a diminishing musharaka contract with the bank. The bank then buys the house and leases the house to Julie at £700 per month for 25 years. Julie would buy the house at the end of the term.
> Step 2:
> After ten years, payments from Julie ceases. The bank can amend the lease or adjust the ownership share to reflect Julie's past payments or evict Julie.

A more nuanced form of diminishing musharaka can be seen when differing stakes in a property is considered:

> Step 1:
> Julie enters into a diminishing musharaka contract with the bank where it is agreed that Julie will initially buy 20% of the property and the bank will purchase 80% of the property.
> Step 2:
> Arrangements can be made as to when and how Julie intends to buy the units to gain the final 80% of the property over a given period of time.
> Step 3:
> Julie pays the agreed rental payments to the bank and the rental payments can include a proportion of funds to buy the property.

There is a concern amongst many in the legal profession in England and Wales that the complex structure of a diminishing musharaka in the property sector can lead to conflicts of interest for lawyers who are engaged in this field:

> With Ijara and Diminishing Musharaka schemes some of the terms of the mortgage may be negotiated between the parties which will bring the mortgage within the definition of an individual mortgage. In addition, as both of these schemes operate on the basis that the lender sells the property over a period of time, a solicitor acting for both parties may be in breach of Chapter 3 SRA (Solicitors Regulatory Authority) Code of Conduct 2011 (Conflict of Interests).[35]

In a business context, a diminishing musharaka would occur when one of the partners gradually buys out the other partner's shares until the whole of the partnership is transferred to one of the partners.

An example would be for a client and a bank to enter into a musharaka agreement for a project or business, which is divided into equity units. The client, aiming to have full ownership of the project, would purchase the bank's equity over time at a fixed or progressive rate. In this type of joint venture, the profit and loss sharing can be revised after each period that the client repurchases the bank's equity.

The bank has the advantage of deriving income in the transaction in two ways—firstly, by the profits of the business and secondly, through receiving cash from the client for the bank's equity.

Whilst diminishing musharaka is an agile vehicle for business transactions where such flexibility could not be so easily found in conventional finance, debates continue as to whether diminishing musharaka, in the property market, is a ruse to charge interest by another name.

Nonetheless, diminishing musharaka is seen as a very flexible option for buyers who may have limited liquidity, in the first instance, to get onto the property ladder. Arguably, for these consumers the diminishing musharaka contract provides some space to acquire a valuable asset.

Bai Bithaman Ajil

There is a slight variation to the diminishing musharaka contract which is Bai Bithaman Ajil which literally means a deferred payment sale. This contract type for buying property is particularly prevalent in Malaysia, Indonesia and Brunei Darussalam.

Unlike diminishing musharaka, which has a rental element as part of the purchase of the property, this is not the case in Bai Bithaman Ajil. Instead, the focus is on paying for the property via regular deferred instalments:

> Step 1:
> The customer identifies the property and normally pays 20% of the selling price and asks the bank to finance the remaining 80%.
> Step 2:
> The customer then signs an agreement with the bank. The bank will buy the property from the customer at a price equal to the financing amount required. The bank will pay the remaining 80% to the developer.
> Step 3:
> The customer then agrees to buy back the asset at a price equal to the financing amount plus profit charged by the bank. The amount will be paid on deferred terms based on the tenor agreed.

A practical example of how Bai Bithaman Ajil works can be discerned by the legal action that a Malaysian bank took against a customer who had defaulted on paying the regular instalments:

> … the customer bought a house for a sum of RM 346.000 and the loans was to be repaid over an 18-year tenure or 216 monthly instalments and charge was registered against the title. At the end of December 1997, the defendant resigned from the agreement at his request, the loan facility was restructured … over a period of 25 years. There was no fresh set of documents executed. After making several payments in total of RM 33,454.19 and the last was in June 2001, the defendant defaulted again. The two actions were filed, namely an order for sale and an order to recover such sums in the event of a deficiency in the proceeds of sale.[36]

Sukuks and Conventional Bonds

Sukuks are often termed as Islamic bonds but, in reality, there is a very real difference between Sukuks and conventional bonds.

Conventional bonds relate to investors buying into a package of loans whilst Sukuk concerns investment in assets—a very different proposition. Both conventional bonds and Sukuk have a multiple of investors and their outward looking structure has similarities but their underlying purpose is fundamentally different.

A conventional bond can be described as a fixed income instrument which represents a loan made by an investor to a borrower. A bond is an agreement between the lender and borrower that includes the details of the loan and its payments.

Bonds are used by companies and governments to finance projects. Owners of bonds are creditors of the issuer. Bond details include the end date when the principal of the loan is due to be paid to the bond owner and usually includes the terms for variable or fixed interest payments made by the borrower.

It was bonds that were at the heart of the 2008 global financial crisis. A number of housing loans were brought together in bonds. It was felt in the period leading up to the crisis that there were a limited number of defaults within the bonds and so the overall value of the bonds should remain profitable:

> Securitisation was designed to benefit lenders, investment bankers and investors. Lenders earned fees for originating and selling loans. Investment banks earned fees for issuing mortgage backed securities. These securities fetched a higher price that if the underlying loans were sold individually, because the securities were customised to investors' needs, were more diversified and could be easily traded.[37]

An official inquiry commissioned by President Barack Obama and the US Congress found severe deficiencies as to how these bonds operated with the operation of a specific bond model known as collateralised debt obligations (CDOs). The weaknesses were identified by one member of the inquiry panel:

> Mortgage originators took advantage of these lower credit quality securitisation standards and the easy flow of credit to relax the underwriting discipline in the loans they issued. As long as they could resell a mortgage to the secondary market, they didn't care about its quality.
>
> Borrowers, originators, securitisers, rating agencies and the ultimate buyers of the securities into which the risky mortgages were packaged all failed to exercise prudence and perform due diligence in their respective transactions. In particular, CDO buyers who were, in theory, sophisticated investors relied too heavily on credit ratings.[38]

What happened to bonds in 2008 could not happen to Sukuks as Sukuks are asset-based. That does not mean that an investment in a Sukuk cannot fail. Any business investment, by its very nature, contains an element of risk. However, the elements of interest and uncertainty that are features of conventional bonds are not the same risks as contained in Sukuk investments.

By investing in a Sukuk it is a participation in the ownership of the company issuing the Sukuk. This entitles the Sukuk holder to appreciation (or depreciation) of the underlying assets. As would be expected in Islamic finance, Sukuk holders have the right to the profits but they also have to bear the losses.

From a financial perspective it would seem, superficially, that the holders of conventional bonds mitigate against risk more effectively than Sukuk holders as bond holders do not incur the damages and losses suffered by the company since their rights are not linked to the assets of the company. Instead, conventional securities represent a loan against interest payable by the issuer plus the face value on maturity.

However, as was observed during the 2008 crisis, there can be systemic risks in bond financing. The advantage of Sukuks is that it encourages medium- to long-term investment. By having a multiple of investors in one Sukuk this enables greater investment collaboration to occur within a secure bond like framework rather than incurring the complexity and costs of using a multiple of mudaraba or musharaka contracts to meet the same objective.

To see how Sukuks operate in practice, we will consider the operation of the following Sukuk models:

- Mudaraba Sukuk
- Musharaka Sukuk
- Ijara Sukuk
- Salam Sukuk
- Istisn'a Sukuk

It would be helpful if you reference this section with the earlier descriptions, in this chapter, of the operation of the mudaraba, musharaka, ijara, salam and istisn'a contract types, to fully gain an understanding as to how their respective features have been incorporated within the Sukuk structure.

Mudaraba Sukuk

Mudaraba Sukuk represent common ownership and entitle the holders of this Sukuk to the share of the profits of the underlying assets as contained within the Sukuk.

Let us look at the operation of a Mudaraba Sukuk using a step by step process.

> Step 1:
> A special purpose vehicle (SPV) or trust could be established to issue the Mudaraba Sukuk. The SPV, in the name of the Sukuk holders, owns shares which equates to the percentage of the profit generated from the project as specified in the agreement.
> Step 2:
> The SPV issues the Mudaraba Sukuk with a fixed maturity.
> Step 3:
> The SPV enters into a mudaraba agreement with the company which will drive the project forward. The SPV, on behalf of the Sukuk holders, provide the funds and the company provides their time and effort.

Musharaka Sukuk

Mudaraba Sukuks and Musharaka Sukuks are very similar. The primary difference is that along with musharaka contracts, one or more of the holders of the Musharaka Sukuk do not just invest their capital but also their in kind support for the project such as the use of commodities for the project. Consequently, those Sukuk holders who have invested capital and in-kind services would gain a greater percentage of the profits as compared to a Sukuk holder who has solely invested in the project by utilising their capital.

Ijara Sukuk

An Ijara Sukuk relates to a bond like structure which holds the title deeds in a leasing project, such as equipment or property, thereby giving the Sukuk holders the right to own shares, receive rental fees and dispose of their properties without affecting the lessee's rights.

The holders of an Ijara Sukuk incur the leased property's costs such as maintenance. Such outlays are incorporated into the rental fee so it is covered by the owner through the receipt of periodic rents.

The operation of an Ijara Sukuk can be seen in this step by step process:

Step 1:
An SPV may be established for the issuance and operation of the Ijara Sukuk;
Step 2:
The SPV buys the title ownership of the assets from an obligor;
Step 3:
The SPV issues the Ijara Sukuk with a mixed maturity date;
Step 4:
The SPV leases the asset to the obligor;
Step 5:
At the same time as the issuance of the Ijara Sukuk, the obligor signs a purchase undertaking to buy back, at the maturity of the Sukuk, the title ownership of the asset at an agreed value;
Step 6:
The obligor pays periodic rent and the proceeds of the receipt of these rents is distributed to the Sukuk holders.

Salam Sukuk

The Salam Sukuk is designed for spot price transactions and the advantage of this model is the affordability process by collecting funds from a multiple of investors.

The step by step process of a Salam Sukuk is as follows:

Step 1:
The SPV collects the funds from the investors;
Step 2:
The obligor agrees to deliver in the future specific assets at a predetermined spot price.

However, the Sukuk holders are unlikely to want to own assets as a consequence of a spot price agreement. It then arranges a third stage process—which turns this Salam Sukuk into a parallel Salam Sukuk;

Step Three:
An underwriter agrees to buy at maturity the asset at a predetermined price from the Sukuk holders. This stage three action transforms a Salam Sukuk into a parallel Salam Sukuk.

The Central Bank of Bahrain, since June 2001, has issued short-term Salam Sukuks.

Istisn'a Sukuk

As Istisn'a is a project financing contract then when the model is applied to a Sukuk it means the returns for Sukuk holders is also linked to when investment capital is directed to the company managing a project's life cycle.

A step by step process to illustrate the workings of an Istisn'a Sukuk can be found below:

Step 1:
The SPV and the obligator enter into an Istisn'a agreement with the manufacturer to manufacture the assets.
Step 2:
The SPV issues Sukuk certificates to the investors.
Step 3:
The Sukuk holders' funds are transferred by the SPV to the obligor.
Step 4:
These funds are then transferred to the manufacturer in line with the agreed payment schedule.
Step 5:
When the work is completed the manufacturer delivers the assets.
Step 6:
Title to the assets is passed to the SPV and the physical assets are delivered to the obligator. Therefore, the SPV is now acting as the lessor and the obligator is now acting as the lessee.
Step 7:
Now that both parties have entered into a lease agreement, this arrangement will end on the day that the Istisn'a Sukuk matures. The periodic rents paid by the lessee would be distributed to the Sukuk holders.

Step 8:
At maturity of the Sukuk the SPV sells the assets to the lessee.
Step 9:
SPV reimburses the proceeds from the sale of the asset to the investors who had been the Sukuk holders.

The Scope of the Global Sukuk Market

The global Sukuk market, as of 2018, was valued at US$123.2 billion.[39] It is one of the most successful Islamic finance models in operation and, as the constant references throughout this book will demonstrate, Sukuks are used for a wide range of purposes—from airport developments through to vaccine research.

This does not mean that abuses cannot occur within the Sukuk market. Some Sukuk issuances could be seen as no more as a ruse to pay interest by hidden means. There is a technique, for instance, called Bai al Inah where the borrower sells an item to the seller and then buys it pack for a higher price on credit. This is really a loan with interest.

It is such a blatant abuse that the Islamic finance specialist, Muhammad Ayub, has called such practices "*disgusting*".[40] This practice has similarities to what is called sale and buy back in the United Kingdom. At street markets across Britain, there are traders buying mobile phones from teenagers and letting these customers buy back their phones at high rates several weeks later. Whilst this is a legal practice, there have been some murmurings in the UK as to whether regulation of this sector was now required.

The success of the Sukuk market flowed from a decision of the OIC's Fiqh Academy, in February 1988, to allow the concept of Sukuk to become operational. In April 2009, the Fiqh Academy endorsed the operation of the Sukuk market:

> Based on the fact that Islamic law is able to absorb new developments, including the solution to everything that occurs and judge everything that arises, and based on the fact that Islamic Sukuk is an innovation of a legal financing instrument that accommodates large economic capabilities, the areas of application of the Sukuk have multiplied, including using it as an effective tool of monetary policy tools or in financing Resources of Islamic banks or investing excess liquidity, in the construction of endowment properties, financing of government projects, and the possibility of using these

> sukuk in temporary privatisation provided that the return of all these sukuk results from the income-generating assets.[41]

The commercial success of the Sukuk market stemmed from Malaysia.

Wan Rahim Kamil is credited as the Bank Islam official who structured the world's very first Sukuk—the 1990 Shell MDS Sdn Bhd RM125 million (US$33 million) Sukuk. Wan Rahim has stated that it was HSBC who, later, promoted the idea of Sukuk to the Malaysian Government which led, in 2002, to the issuance of the world's first sovereign wealth Sukuk.

The complexities of devising Sukuks that are fit for purpose has been vividly described by the former banker, Harris Irfan. Irfan recounted how Deutsche Bank worked on a Mudaraba Sukuk to finance the construction of the seven towers that now surround the Masjid Al-Haram which houses the Kaaba in Mecca—the geographical heart of Islam.

It involved a series of detailed requirements linked, in part, to the operation of the supply chain. There was a surprising end to this story:

> Despite concluding the contractual structure and receiving all relevant regulatory and Sharia approvals, the Bin Ladins *(the construction company)* lost patience and sold the whole tower in one go to a single buyer. Strangely, it did not matter to Deutsche – such a wealth of goodwill had been generated in the structuring and marketing phases of this unprecedented financial instrument that Islamic investors and the competition were in awe of Deutsche's boldness and capabilities. A Western investment bank had been allowed into Makkah and imagined possibilities of which others had dared not dream.[42]

The United Kingdom became the first jurisdiction, outside of countries with majority Muslim populations, to be engaged in the Sukuk market.

In January 2007, the then UK Treasury (finance) Minister, Ed Balls, said the UK's Labour Government wanted the country to be "*a global centre for Islamic Finance*". That government had already made significant steps to facilitate Islamic finance when, in 2003, it removed double stamp duty on murabaha- and ijara-based mortgages.

This commitment to Islamic finance in the United Kingdom continued under the Conservative and Liberal Democrat coalition Government when, in 2014, the Government issued a £200 million Sukuk set at 2.036% in line with the yield on gilts of similar maturity. The value of the Sukuk was realised in July 2019.

Then under a majority Conservative Government, the then Chancellor of the Exchequer, Philip Hammond, announced plans in June 2019 for the United Kingdom to issue another sovereign Sukuk.

As will be seen in Chapter 5, the ruling by Sheikh Taqi Usmani in 2007 to clean up the structures and operation of the Sukuk market was an initial shock to investors and led to banner headlines in the financial press.

However, the Sukuk market is now stronger today than it ever was—and the demand for Sukuks to finance economic development projects in the post-pandemic world is likely to grow.

Islamic Derivatives

The very term, 'Islamic derivatives' will raise the ire of some of you studying this book as the term will be seen as an oxymoron.

Derivatives have been associated with gharar, riba and maysir and so the idea that the concept can be adjusted to meet the underlying principles which are inherent in the Islamic finance industry would be a hard sell to many people.

Before considering the concept of Islamic derivatives, let us first look at conventional derivatives.

Conventional derivatives are financial contracts where prices are derived from the value of an underlying asset or financial construct such as interest rates. Derivatives can be used by a company to hedge against price risk by entering into a derivatives contract which can be offset against the effect of price movements. Losses suffered by a company with price movements can be regained in the derivatives market.

We can see how this can work by considering the two key products in the conventional derivatives market—options and futures.[43]

Traded options grant the buyer the right—but not the obligation—to buy or sell financial instruments at a price and date in the future. If, for instance, the share price of Bill Bloggs PLC is £1.49, you could believe the share price will go up to £1.55 in the next three months. If the share price does go up to £1.55 you would exercise the option (before or at expiry) and purchase the shares. Say the shares were £1.75—you would exercise the option to buy at £1.55, making a profit of 20 pence minus the price of the option itself.

A similar approach would be adopted if you believed the share price would fall by a set amount in, say, three months' time. Therefore, a call option is the right to buy the financial product and the put option is the right to sell the financial product.

Call and Put options go beyond share prices and cover a range of areas including currencies, bonds and interest rates.

This is a very basic summary of the derivatives market which also includes swaps. Swaps are where one party exchanges or swaps the values or cash flows of one asset for another. Of the two cash flows, one value is fixed and one is variable and based on an index price, interest rate or currency exchange rate.

There are also credit default swaps (CDS) where the seller of the CDS will compensate the buyer in the event of a debt default or other credit event.

The conventional derivatives market was in the spotlight with the aftermath of the 2008 global financial crisis. A joint US Government/Congress report expressed particular concerns as to what it saw as the complex nature of this market:

> When the nation's biggest financial institutions were teetering on the edge of failure in 2008, everyone watched the derivatives markets. What were the institutions' holdings? Who were the counterparties? How would they fare? Market participants and regulators would find themselves straining to understand an unknown battlefield shaped by unseen exposures and interconnections as they fought to keep the financial system from collapsing.[44]

The US report targeted CDS as a contributory factor as to the causation and severity of the downturn. It went on to lambast the overall contribution of the derivatives market to the crisis:

> … when the housing bubble popped and crisis followed, derivatives were in the centre of the storm. AIG, which had not been required to put aside capital reserves as a cushion for the protection it was selling, was bailed out when it could not meet its obligations. The government ultimately committed more than $180 billion because of concerns that AIG's collapse would trigger cascading losses throughout the global financial system. In addition, the existence of millions of derivatives contracts of all types between systemically important financial institutions – unseen and unknown in this unregulated market – added to the uncertainty and escalated panic, helping to precipitate government assistance to those institutions.[45]

How, then, when conventional derivatives are based on uncertainty and speculation—which are both prohibited in Islamic finance—can there be any such concept as Islamic derivatives?

Contentious Developments During the 2000s

Various products marketed as shari'a compliant derivative structures were developed over the 2000s. This included the Primary (Term) Murabaha. In this case a bank sourced commodities from a commodity broker at a cost price and sold these commodities to the swap counterparty.

Payment by the counterparty for the commodities purchased under the Primary Murabaha was on a deferred basis with instalments payable on pre-agreed payment dates. This would be undertaken in one currency.

Each instalment represents a portion of the pre-agreed profit element, with the exception of the final instalment, which also included payment in full of the cost price.

The commodities were delivered on the agreed date. On receipt of the commodities, the counterparty promptly sold the commodities to a different commodity broker to generate another currency.

The aim of this model was to develop a shari'a compliant version of a cross-currency swap. The model has also been used to closely align with (but not tied to) interest rate movements by the use of the buying and selling of commodities to different brokers. Examples of such models in practice include, in October 2006, Standard Chartered Saadiq who entered into a US$150 million three-year primary term murabaha with Kuwait-based Aref Investment Group SAK.

These so-called shari'a compliant derivatives were condemned as mimicking conventional derivatives such as a total return swap structure which claimed to be based on commodity sales but were closely aligned with a similar conventional model that was focused on interest rate movements. The Islamic finance scholar, Sheikh Yusuf Talal De Lorenzo condemned this concept by saying it was a "*wrap up of a non-Shari'a compliant underlying into a Shari'a compliant structure*".[46]

Shari'a Compliant Derivative Products and the International Islamic Financial Market

With new derivative products entering the market there was a need to address these concerns about the validity of claims of shari'a compliance. The International Islamic Financial Markets (IIFM) was successful in developing a template for Islamic derivative products in partnership with the International Swaps and Derivatives Association (ISDA).

Manama-based IIFM is the global standard setting body for the Islamic capital and money markets.

After a long period of consultation and with the help of a range of specialists, such as Priya Uberoi of law firm, Clifford Chance, it was agreed, in 2010, that the following key principles would govern the operation of this market:

- Transactions should be entered into only for the purpose of hedging actual risks of the relevant party.
- Transactions should not be entered into for purposes of speculation, i.e. actual settlements of assets and payments must take place. Cash settlement should relate to actual transactions involving a deliverable asset.
- The asset must be halal.
- No interest (whether called interest or an alternative name but which represents interest) is to be chargeable under a Transaction.

The subsequent Tahawwut (a term which relates to financial hedging) documentation was based, in part, on standard derivative documentation developed by the ISDA in 1992.

Consequently, the IIFM and ISDA agreed a template that could be used in the industry which would enable shari'a compliant products to emerge which would have parallels to a fixed rates swap and a floating rates swap. A slight variant of the Primary (Term) Murabaha was adopted that meant that the buying and reselling of commodities can mirror price movements which may have some synergy with interest rate movements.

A similar structure for the buying and selling of commodities but, this time, buying the commodities in one currency and selling the commodities in another currency helped to align this structure with a cross-currency swap.

Another structure was aligned with a conventional foreign currencies (FX) forward. The Islamic Foreign Exchange Forward (IFX) is based on the concept of Wa‘ad. Wa’ad is defined as a legally binding promise. The OIC's Fiqh Academy defined Wa'ad as:

> … a promise (made unilaterally by the purchase orderer or the seller), is morally binding on the promisor, unless there is a valid excuse. It is however legally binding if made conditional upon the fulfilment of an obligation, and the promisee has already incurred expenses on the basis of such a promise. The binding nature of the promise means that it should be either fulfilled or a compensation be paid for damages caused due to the unjustifiable non fulfilling of the promise.[47]

Consequently, an IFX requires a party to promise to buy the relevant currency for settlement on a forward value date at the rate and amount agreed today. Whilst this may remove uncertainty, the fact that money is being bought and sold would make money a commodity and, as discussed in Chapter 3, money cannot be treated as a commodity in Islamic finance. At the same time, we also considered how innovative solutions were found to meet shari'a compliance requirements with regular foreign exchange transactions.

As we discussed earlier in this chapter, the Accounting and Auditing Organisation for Islamic Financial Institutions (AAOIFI) made the following ruling:

> A bilateral promise to purchase and sell currencies is forbidden if the promise is binding, even for the purpose of hedging against currency devaluation risk. However, a promise from one party is permissible even if the promise is binding.[48]

By this AAOIFI ruling, the ban on the buying and selling of currencies is preserved as the agreement is based on the promise from one party alone. Whilst this is a technical solution to help ensure global businesses can operate across borders on a shari'a compliant basis, there will be other Islamic scholars who would condemn this practice as pedantry as, ultimately, two parties are tied to an agreement even if only one party is making the promise.

The development of the Islamic derivatives market is a recognition of the need for Islamic financial operations to operate across the global economy where currency risk linked to interest rate movements are live issues. To ensure that the underlying principles of Islamic finance are adhered to the use of commodities at set prices and at defined time lines is required to ensure that gharar (uncertainty), maysir (gambling) and riba (interest) are not incurred in these arrangements.

According to the credit ratings agency, Fitch, this product range was required more than ever due to the COVID-19 pandemic as the "*oil price fall and cuts in central banks repo rates highlights the need to use effective sharia-compliant derivatives as hedging tools (tahawwut)*".[49]

The development of the concept of Islamic derivatives is also a recognition that the scholars who work in the Islamic finance industry have shifted their stance over the years to allow businesses to hedge against currency moves, credit exposures and interest rate movements in the recognition that shari'a compliant businesses need to compete across borders.

There is potential for the market to grow. An example of this potential is the valuation of the daily average of shari'a compliant derivatives which align to conventional interest rate derivatives in the UAE, Malaysia, Saudi Arabia, Indonesia, Turkey and Bahrain. This combined value, as of April 2019, amounted to US$3 billion.[50] This shows promise for further growth prospects. UAE has a shari'a compliant exchange traded derivatives market and Saudi Arabia announced plans to establish such a market.

Whilst some scholars may continue to object to the concept of shari'a compliant derivatives, the safeguards which IIFM have been able to enshrine in the Tahawwut Master Agreement, have prevented the abuses of the term 'shari'a complaint' which were beginning to occur in the 2000s.

They have also ensured the key principles of Islamic finance remain intact—though arrangements linked to currency trading is likely to remain contentious for some time due to shari'a requirements that money should not be treated as a commodity.

The very existence of the market has a wider benefit. It can be seen as a gateway for a wider range of Islamic finance products to be made available to a broader consumer base.

From that point of view alone, the primary advantage of Islamic derivatives could be their role as a gateway to the wider Islamic finance marketplace.

Personal Finance

So far in our discussion we have considered Islamic finance from two key perspectives—business finance and the buying and selling of property.

In part this is because the early development of the Islamic finance industry referred to the hadiths where the Prophet spoke of the need for ethical business conduct. As Islamic finance is based on the utilisation of assets, this model is particularly well suited to trade finance.

In addition, the focus of the early advocates of Islamic finance in the nineteenth and twentieth centuries was upon positing an alternative approach to the laissez-faire capitalist model (as will be discussed in Chapter 9). This meant a particular analysis was adopted to consider the conduct of business operations to enable the realisation of wider Islamic economic objectives.

However, the flip side of enabling businesses to access finance is for their customers to have the wherewithal to access goods and services. Consequently, over recent decades, the focus on serving the needs of individuals has gone beyond shari'a compliant mortgages to the provision of shari'a compliant credit cards.

A shari'a compliant credit card, literally speaking, would be a misnomer. Money cannot be treated as a commodity and clearly interest is prohibited. Nonetheless a credit card like product now exists alongside other personal loan services which are geared towards consumers. Even pawnbroking whose very essence was the interest rate element now has branched out into so-called shari'a compliant operations.

The growth of these personal finance instruments demonstrates another step forward for the industry in embedding itself in key markets, such as Malaysia and the Gulf states.

This trend necessitates a re-evaluation of the state of the industry. No more can Islamic finance be classed as a niche product when, in different parts of the world, shari'a compliant and conventional finance products are competing head to head in mainstream markets. All finance needs are being addressed for an individual—from meeting trade finance requirements to splashing out in the local department store.

How, then, does shari'a compliant personal finance work?

> Take advantage of our Personal Finance facilities to buy a range of goods and services. Whether you are thinking of furnishing your home, buying the latest electronic gadget, need financing for travel, a wedding, education

> or house rent, our finance solutions give you the flexibility you need. Using the Islamic principles of Murabaha and Ijarah, the bank buys the service you need directly from the provider and resells it to you. This gives you the convenience of making your payments in easy monthly instalments.[51]

This is the offer as presented by Emirates Finance in the UAE. This basis of personal finance options is focused on ijarah and murabaha. Within these two contract types are three categories of personal finance:

- Service Ijarah
- Murabaha Line of Credit
- Murabaha/Service Ijarah Credit Card

In addition, there is also the emergence of what is known as shari'a compliant pawnbroking.

We will look at each one of these categories in turn.

Service Ijarah

As we discovered earlier in this chapter, ijarah is a leasing contract model. To adapt this model for personal finance terms, a personal loan is predicated on the payment of rent rather than interest as would be witnessed in a conventional personal loan.

Rent, in this case, would relate to renting out the use of an object such as a flat screen TV or a dishwasher. It can also involve accessing services such as paying for an education course at the local college.

The UAE's Ajam Bank described Service Ijarah to its customers in the following way[52]:

> … a transaction where the Bank will purchase the service as requested by the customer and allow the customer the right to use it and the benefits of the service for a predetermined period of time and in return the customer will pay a pre-determined agreed rent.

An understanding of service ijarah can be seen via a step by step process:

Step 1:
The customer submits an application for financing a specific service to the bank.

Step 2:
The bank leases the service or item from the service provider under the Service Ijarah contract.
Step 3:
The bank subleases the service or item to the customer under the Service Ijarah contract which determines the fees, method of payment, length of service and related terms and conditions.

Murabaha Line of Credit

If a customer needs money in a hurry to meet cashflow problems, then the murabaha line of credit could be the answer.

Initially this technique was used by central banks to assist with the liquidity requirements of Islamic banks, but it has been adapted for the personal finance market. Unlike conventional finance, money cannot be treated as a commodity.

Therefore the murabaha line of credit is linked to the service ijarah so that customers do not need to worry about buying an item or service upfront and they can access funds to pay the rent to enable access to the goods or services.

The agreement between the bank and the customer sets out sets the terms and conditions for the funding facility including payment of a mark-up to the bank. The agreement would also include the maturity date, maximum amount of each murabaha transaction, conditions of payments, the use of collaterals and the types of goods and services which are being purchased.

Murabaha/Service Ijarah Credit Card

In essence the credit card is the vehicle for bringing together the murabaha line of credit and service ijarah in an easy to use credit card format. The emphasis is on the purchase and rent of assets to avoid interest and to also prohibit treating money as a commodity:

> Murabahah credit card structure is based on the same concept of Murabahah line-of-credit agreement except that it is implemented through a credit card. The cardholder acts as the issuing IB's *(Islamic Bank)* agent and executes transactions on its behalf. It gives the customer, as agent of the Bank, the right to execute several transactions and can be used for all

permissible goods purchases. Service Ijarah can be added in the same card (Service Ijarah and Murabahah combined in one credit card and one agreement) because the transaction is similar to Murabahah with the exception that it is based on the concept of services and usufruct facility. There will be an agreement with a Wakalah *(agency)* assigning the customer as agent to purchase/hire services, goods and usufructs for the IB, take delivery for the IB and on its behalf, and then sell/lease to itself and take delivery of this last sale.[53]

Shari'a Compliant Pawnbroking and Conventional Pawnbroking: Is There a Difference?

In 1751, William Hogarth's caricature of poverty-stricken London was published with the title "*Gin Lane*". It showed fights, poverty and a mother so drunk on gin that she does not realise she had just dropped her baby into the River Thames.

This dystopian image was designed to encourage British lawmakers to legislate against the perils of addiction to gin. One aspect of the cartoon is also worth noting—it shows a crowd of people desperate for credit at the local pawnbrokers.

This is how pawnbroking was seen for many years—an unscrupulous profession exploiting the neediest in society.

The novelist, Charles Dickens, in his role as a journalist, condemned the industry in the early nineteenth century:

> Of the numerous receptacles for misery and distress with which the streets of London unhappily abound, there are, perhaps, none which present such striking scenes as the pawnbrokers' shops. The very nature and description of these places occasions their being but little known, except to the unfortunate beings whose profligacy or misfortune drives them to seek the temporary relief they offer.[54]

However, today, pawnbroking has seen a renaissance in a number of international markets with some pawnbroking businesses being seen as so responsible that they are listed on stock markets.

The success of the sector has also led to a number of businesspeople claiming that they have established shari'a compliant pawnbroking. The question is, though, can pawnbroking—that is based on the principle of interest—be amended to such an extent that it can be in compliance with Islamic ethics?

With conventional pawnbroking, a pawnbroker earns income on the interest that is charged on the loan secured by a pledged item. In order to accept goods into pawn a pawnbroker makes an on-the-spot valuation of the goods. The customer and the pawnbroker will agree the sum to be advanced and various contractual documents are signed by the customer. The agreement is usually for a period of six or seven months.

When the loan and the interest are paid, the goods are returned to the customer. If the customer has not repaid the loan during this time, the customer will receive notice that the property is due to be sold. If the customer does not renew or respond to the notice served, the pawnbroker may take steps to dispose of the goods. Having served the notice of the intention to sell the goods the pawnbroker must obtain the true market value on the date of sale which ensures a fair price is obtained for the customer. Where the proceeds of sale are greater than the amount due to the pawnbroker, the balance is sent to the customer.

From 1992, pawnbrokers described as Islamic compliant first made their mark in Malaysia. Razak described the shari'a compliant pawnbroking process in the following way:

> Principally, Islamic pawnbrokers would prefer the customer to redeem their collateral within six months. However, if there is no repayment, there is an extension period of three months after which the client is informed that the item will be sold by auction within a further two months period. Based on the Manual of Islamic Pawnbroking of Bank Kerjasama Rakyat Malaysia Berhad, any surplus from the sale of the gold over the amount owed to the pawnbroker, including accumulated deposit fee and any costs related to the sale, has to be returned to the customer.[55]

There is, therefore, virtually no difference between conventional pawnbroking and Islamic pawnbroking. However, in conventional pawnbroking, the pawnbroker makes their money via the interest charged on the loan. As Razak describes, there is a different criteria in a shari'a compliant pawnbroking loan:

> The loan granted is based on four concepts, i.e. al-qardhul hassan (loan without interest), al-wadiah yad dhammanah (keeping valuable goods by guarantee), al-ujrah (storage fees) and ar-rahn (collateral). The storage fee is based on the value of gold and not on the amount of the loan.

As we can see, the money made from what is described as shari'a compliant pawnbroking includes a range of factors which does not include interest. There is extensive legislation in Malaysia covering this sector and the concept is growing in other markets (I recall a pawnbrokers in London's Edgware Road claiming that they were shari'a compliant).

You may think that this is interest by another name—though this is hotly disputed by pawnbrokers working in this space.

What is clear is that the concept of Islamic finance informing every aspect of a person's financial life has even gone as far as pawnbroking. In a sense, it is a good example of how the concept of Islamic finance is moving from being seen as a niche area to becoming a mainstream brand.

The Chief Executive of HSBC Amanah, Arsalaan Ahmed, commented that one of the first things many Malaysians did when COVID-19 lockdown restrictions were lifted in 2020 was to seek financial help from pawnbrokers—again demonstrating the growing role of this financial services product in key markets.[56]

Whether, though, so-called shari'a compliant pawnbroking is more than just a branding exercise is another matter. However, for those customers who are concerned about any product involving riba, this may be the answer—though whether there is a difference between the range of fees in what is called Islamic pawnbroking and interest as in conventional pawnbroking—will be a matter of scholarly debate for some years to come.

This chapter has considered some of the main vehicles used in Islamic finance—Mudaraba, Musharaka, Murabaha, Salam, Istisn'a, Ijrara, Bai Bithaman Ajil, Sukuk as well as the more controversial concepts of Islamic derivatives and Islamic pawnbroking.

All these structures, though, may count for nothing if full compliance procedures within the Islamic finance industry are not in place.

As we shall see, ensuring full compliance within the industry can be easier said than done.

Notes

1. Codified legal code during the Ottoman Caliphate.
2. Mahmoud A. *El-Gamal, Islamic Finance: Law, Economics, and Practice*, page 30.
3. Qur'ran, Sura 2:282.
4. Qur'ran, 4.29.
5. Qur'ran, 2:177.

6. As quoted in the *Financial Times*, 8 December 2009.
7. Harris Irfan, *Heaven's Bankers: Inside the Hidden World of Islamic Finance*, page 75.
8. As quoted by Emmy Abdul Alim, *Global Leaders in Islamic Finance*, page 149.
9. Ibid., page 168.
10. Alistair Darling, *Back from the Brink: 1000 days at Number 11*, page 61.
11. Muhammad Ayub, *Understanding Islamic Finance*, page 216.
12. Ibid., pages, 216–217.
13. Ellida Fauziah Ahmad, Mariyam Shihama, NurSulaim Ashikin bt Mohamad Tarmizi, Saidu Mudi Jibril, Samia Ibrahim Djama, Aishath Muneeza, *Tawarruq as a Product for Financing Within the Islamic Banking System*.
14. Ibid.
15. US National Commission on the Causes of the Financial and Economic Crisis in the United States (2011), *The Financial Crisis Inquiry Report*, page 89.
16. Iman Bukhari (810–870) is the source of this hadith. Iman Bukhari who was from Bukhara (in modern Uzbekistan) is considered by Sunni Islam to be a reliable source for hadiths.
17. al-Bukhari. No. 2240. Muslim. No. 1604.
18. Harris Irfan, *Heaven's Bankers: Inside the Hidden World of Islamic Finance*, page 61.
19. Islamic Research and Training Institute of the Islamic Development Bank (1995), Umar, page 39.
20. AAIOFI Standard No. 1.
21. Marsh & McLennon Companies (2017), *Closing the Financing Gap: Infrastructure Project Bankability in Asia*.
22. Mohammad M Alfadhl, Sami Alghoussein, Faisal Alarifi (November 2019), The Use of Parallel Istisn'a Sukuk in Financing Solar Energy Project in Kuwait, *International Academic Journal of Economics and Finance*, vol. 3, no. 4, pp. 204–217.
23. Warren Buffett speaking at the 2000 Berkshire Hathaway annual meeting.
24. Vince Cable, *After the Storm*.
25. Guy Sorman (2011), Is Islam Compatible with Capitalism, *City Journal*.
26. Al Sarakhsi, *Al-Mabsut* and AAIOFI 2004–2005a, Standard on Mudaraba, clause 4, pages 240–241.
27. Muhammed Arslan Aqeeq, *Islamic Finance from the Ideal of 'Two Tier Mudaraba' to a Fixed Returns Model—Rationalising the Blatant Divergence* (University of Newcastle, Australia), October 2015.
28. Al Sarakhsi, *Al-Mabsut* and AAIOFI 2004–2005a, Standard on Mudaraba, clause 4, page 231.

29. C A Hooper (1989), The Mejelle: Book X: Joint Ownership, *Arab Law Quarterly*, vol. 4, no. 2, pp. 157–171.
30. Abdul Ghafar Ismail (June 2011), The Theory of Islamic Finance: Look Back to the Original Idea, *Journal of Islamic Economics*, vol. 7, no 3.
31. Mehmet Asutay (2010), "Islamic Banking and Finance and Its Role in the GCC-EU Relationship: Principles, Developments and the Bridge Role of Islamic Finance." In *The EU and the GCC: Challenges and Prospects Under the Swedish EU Presidency*, edited by Leif Stenberg and Christian Koch, pp. 35–58. Dubai: Gulf Research Centre.
32. Usmani, 2000a, pages 38–41.
33. State Bank of Pakistan, 2005, page 2.
34. Feisal Khan, *Islamic Banking in Pakistan: Shariah Compliant Finance and the Quest to Make Pakistan More Islamic*, page 105.
35. Edited by Frances Silverman, *Conveyancing Handbook*, 9.13.
36. Rininta Nurrachmi, Hamida Mohamed, Nawalin Nazah (28 January 2013), *Dispute Between Bank and Customer in Bai Bithaman Ajil (BBA): Case in Malaysia* (International Islamic University Malaysia).
37. US National Commission on the Causes of the Financial and Economic Crisis in the United States (2011), *The Financial Crisis: Inquiry Report*, page 42.
38. Ibid., pages 425–426.
39. https://www.iifm.net/iifm-publishes-its-annual-sukuk-report-2019-usd-123-2-billion-sukuk-issued-globally-in-2018/.
40. Muhammad Ayub, *Understanding Islamic Finance*, page 396.
41. Resolution 178 (4/19).
42. Harris Irfan, *Heaven's Bankers: Inside the Hidden World of Islamic Finance*, page 53.
43. The futures market is also discussed in Chapter 3.
44. US National Commission on the Causes of the Financial and Economic Crisis in the United States, *The Financial Crisis: Inquiry Report*, page 51.
45. Ibid., page xxv.
46. Cambridge Institute of Islamic Finance, *Global Islamic Finance Report 2010*, page 138.
47. Resolution N. 40-41 (2/5 & 3/5) Concerning Discharging of Promise and Murabaha for the Orderer of Purchase (December 1988), OIC Fiqh Academy.
48. Shari'a Standard No. 1: Trading in Currencies, AAOIFI.
49. *Islamic Derivatives Increasingly Necessary, but Constraints Remain*, Fitch Ratings, 17 June 2020.
50. Ibid.
51. Emirates Finance website.
52. Ajman Bank (2017).

53. Monzer Kahf, Amiirah Nubec Mohomed (2017), *Islamic Personal Financing: An Attempt to Engineer Shari'ah-Compliant Instruments* (Hamad bin Khalifa University, Doha).
54. Charles Dickens (June 1835), Sketches of London No. 35, Evening Standard.
55. Azila Abdul Razak, *Malaysian Practice of Ar-Rahnu Scheme: Trends and Development*.
56. Islamic Markets webinar, 24 June 2020.

CHAPTER 5

Compliance

Compliance is the critical requirement for all investors and consumers in order to trust the veracity of any financial product.

In the case of conventional finance, there are regulators such as central banks overseeing the markets and regulators to protect consumers from unscrupulous lenders. Examples include the Consumer Financial Protection Bureau in the United States which was championed by US Senator Elizabeth Warren or the British regulations to stop pay day lenders exploiting deprived communities as advocated by the Labour Party Member of Parliament, Stella Creasy.

As the Islamic finance industry only came into its own from the mid-1970s, the need to reassure the markets and to ascertain products are genuinely shari'a compliant meant that the whole compliance regime at a national and international level had to be brought together in just a few decades whilst in conventional finance, regulatory structures had taken centuries to evolve.

As the Islamic compliance regime has developed, questions have been raised as to whether the compliance structures really are fit for purpose.

As this chapter will demonstrate, despite the many questions that have arisen out of the actions—or even inactions—of some compliance actors over the decades, by the time we reach the 2020s an increasingly robust compliance regime had been established.

J. S. Watkins, *Islamic Finance and Global Capitalism*,
https://doi.org/10.1007/978-3-030-59840-2_5

One of the key issues, though, that has dogged the Islamic finance industry is whether market participants are just paying lip service to the prohibition on interest and, if so, what could the courts do about this.

This debate was shown in stark relief during a contentious court case in London.

Is Interest Really Banned in Practice?

> … it is not uncommon for banks, in their enthusiasm to make profitable loans, to use a Morabaha Agreement to disguise what is, as a matter of commercial reality, an interest-bearing loan. That is precisely what happened in the present case and both the Claimant and the Defendants were quite content that this should happen. Neither was under any illusion as to the commercial realities of the transactions, and the claimant was happy to dress the loan transactions up as Morabaha sales (or Ijarah leases), whilst taking no interest in whether the proper formalities of such a sale or lease were actually complied with.[1]

This was the statement of a businessman to the Court of Appeal of England and Wales when he and other defendants were seeking to nullify murabaha and ijara contracts which had been agreed with the Shamil Bank of Bahrain.

These comments reflect criticism that is directed at the Islamic finance industry from time to time that the ban on interest is more apparent than real.

Similar claims were made during the medieval period when interest was prohibited in Europe due to Christian teaching at that time—but it was said that ways were found to get round the ban:

> The investor would simultaneously enter into three contracts with an entrepreneur: to invest money as a sleeping partner; to insure himself against any loss; and to sell any profits over and above a year.[2]

This form of contract, Contractum trinius, was said to have met the terms of the ban but was really introducing interest via the back door. The question that has been posed in recent years is whether some Islamic finance contracts are really being used as a cover for hiking up interest payments.

In 2002, the Shari'at Appellate Bench of the Supreme Court of Pakistan heard representations that a number of Islamic finance practitioners were not just charging riba in hidden forms within Islamic finance contracts but that the practices adopted were more onerous for consumers than conventional interest loan repayments:

> Mr Gilani argued that all the Islamic banking system suggested in the judgement under review is a misnomer and except Musharika all other modes of finance are nothing but Heela, i.e. devices to avoid which is otherwise Riba which are in fact more harsh and oppressive having the element of 'zulm' (*oppression*) and are worst in consequences as compared to the various forms of interest prevalent in the present day banking system ....[3]

The argument as to what was or was not riba was also heard in London in 2004. On that occasion, the High Court of England and Wales ruled in favour of Shamil Bank of Bahrain which was seeking debts to be recouped from Beximco Pharmaceuticals Limited and a number of Beximco company directors who acted as guarantors for the company.

At stake during this court case was not just the millions of pounds that the bank was seeking but also whether murabaha and ijara contracts were being used to get around the ban on interest and whether secular courts can take Islamic fiqh (jurisprudence) into consideration when considering Islamic finance disputes.

The story began in 1995 when two Bangladeshi companies, Beximco Pharmaceuticals Limited and Bangladesh Export Import Co Limited, which were both part of the Beximco group, sought working capital from the Shamil Bank of Bahrain to acquire goods. Consequently a US$15 million murabaha contract was entered into.

Then in 1996 the Bangladesh Export Import Co Limited gained an additional US$15 million murabaha contract from this bank. However, by 1999, the bank expressed concerns that the repayment schedule was not being adhered to so new repayment terms were entered into—by which a number of Beximco company directors would act as guarantors.

The repayment schedules were expressed in a number of 'Exchange in Satisfaction and User Agreements' (ESUAs). However, the defaults continued and so the bank sued the parties concerned for the following sums:

1. US $ 25,207,000 being the amount due under the first ESUA relating to the 1995 Murabaha Agreement;
2. US $ 21,472,800 being the amount due under the second ESUA relating to the 1996 Murabaha Agreement;
3. US $ 1,147,540.76 being accrued compensation due under clause 4.2.4 of the first ESUA;
4. US $ 1,884,169.75 being accrued compensation due under clause 4.2.4 of the second ESUA.

So, in 2004, the Court of Appeal was the setting for a debate which went beyond the immediate demand for financial redress as it also reflected wider academic discussions as to the operation of modern Islamic finance practices.

The questions posed included:

- Was the use of murabaha and ijara contracts a ruse to charge interest?
- Were the values system of Islam being reflected in the day-to-day operations of Islamic financial institutions?
- Can secular courts judge Islamic finance matters?

Mr Justice Khan, the former Chairman of the Shari'a Appellate Bench of the Supreme Court of Pakistan appeared as an expert witness for the defendants and proceeded to try to dismantle the shari'a basis for the bank's actions:

> Mr Justice Khan acknowledged that the Sharia recognises two modes of financing as permissible, namely Morabaha and Ijarah agreements, but asserted that, for such transactions to be valid, the requirements prescribed and provided for in the agreement must be fulfilled, failing which the transaction as a whole will be void according to the principles and rules of Sharia. On the basis of the (uncontradicted) assertion of the defendants that the advances were never applied or intended to be applied in the purchase or lease of any property, the relevant agreements were void. The ESUAs were similarly void and unenforceable on the basis of a number of arguments advanced, the principal one of which was that, irrespective of their form as purported Ijarah leases of assets, the ESUAs simply constituted a rescheduling or roll-over of the 1995 and 1996 Morabaha Agreements, the bank charging interest or an additional amount over and

> above the sums due in consideration of the giving of time. This too was Riba and accordingly prohibited and void.[4]

The bank defended itself against the charge that it was not fulfilling its Islamic responsibilities:

> The Bank's expert, Dr Lau, the former director of the Centre of Islamic and Middle Eastern Law, stated that the precise scope and content of Islamic law in general, and Islamic banking in particular, are marked by a degree of controversy within the Islamic world, best exemplified by the fact that the actual practice of Islamic banking differs widely within the Islamic world. Even within particular jurisdictions such as Pakistan, which are committed and constitutionally obliged to introduce Islamic financial systems, the issue is subject to on-going debate and a high degree of uncertainty. In the absence of any agreement on the boundaries of 'Islamic banking' or, indeed, on what ought to be the precise ingredients of a Morabaha agreement, it is in practice up to individual banks to determine the issue. In the absence of any legal prescription as to what does and what does not constitute Islamic banking or finance, most Islamic banks, including those in Bahrain, seek the advice of Islamic scholars who examine and approve particular agreements and forms of agreement, the role of the Religious Supervisory Committee being to formulate the bank's interpretation of the Sharia.[5]

What is striking as to the bank's position is that the concept of a general uniformity of approach as to the framework within which the Islamic finance industry operates within was rejected.

As we will see later in this chapter, attempts to ensure a regulatory framework was accepted by all market participants is now a core objective for central banks.

The emphasis on religious scholars to ascertain whether products and practices are shari'a compliant was also emphasised by the bank's stance—an issue that we shall shortly return to.

The Court of Appeal hearing also considered how robust the Qur'ran, sunna and hadiths were to ascertain precise Islamic finance practices. The Shamil Bank of Bahrain told the court that a reliance on religious sources could not be relied upon:

> … most of the classical Islamic law on financial transactions is not contained as 'rules' or 'law' in the Qur'an and Sunnah but is based on

> the often divergent views held by established schools of law formed in a period roughly between 700 and 850 CE. The particular form and content of Morabaha agreements varies. If a bank's Religious Supervisory Board is satisfied that the bank's activities are in accordance with Sharia law, that concludes the matter, there being no provision in Bahrain law, or Islamic law generally, for an appeal by a customer of the bank against the Board's rulings and certifications. Finally, even if the relevant agreements amounted to agreements to pay Riba, the principal sums advanced could be validly claimed.[6]

The barrister for the bank argued that though the hearing was being held under the common law of England and Wales, it was within the remit of the court to consider whether shari'a requirements had been breached and he cited case law in England and Wales to justify this contention. However, it was ruled that though the court took cognisance of the law from other jurisdictions, the common law of England and Wales would be the governing framework for any decision that would be reached.

This, the Court of Appeal added, was helpful in this case as the debate within Islamic finance meant there was not a common understanding of shari'a requirements, so the common law had to be relied upon in any case:

> ... so far as the "principles of ... Sharia" are concerned, it was the evidence of both experts that there are indeed areas of considerable controversy and difficulty arising not only from the need to translate into propositions of modern law texts which centuries ago were set out as religious and moral codes, but because of the existence of a variety of schools of thought with which the court may have to concern itself in any given case before reaching a conclusion upon the principle or rule in dispute. The fact that there may be general consensus upon the proscription of Riba and the essentials of a valid Morabaha agreement does no more than indicate that, if the Sharia law proviso were sufficient to incorporate the principles of Sharia law into the parties' agreements, the defendants would have been likely to succeed. However, since I would hold that the proviso is plainly inadequate for that purpose, the validity of the contract and the defendants' obligations thereunder fall to be decided according to English law.[7]

Consequently, the bank won the case.

This test case was fascinating for many different reasons. The case enabled the tensions which exist in the Islamic finance industry to be exposed and for the arguments for and against certain practices to be played out in the open arena of the court.

The court case also showed how non-Islamic jurisdictions can consider Islamic finance issues. The United Kingdom is one of the most welcoming markets in the world for the sector. The regulatory framework has been adapted to accommodate Islamic finance—though Islamic market participants in the United Kingdom say that more could still be achieved.

Nonetheless, the 2004 Court of Appeal hearing highlighted the debate within academic circles as to the comparison between theory and practice within the Islamic finance sector.

It also demonstrated the tensions between doctrinal understanding and contemporary commercial realities as the Court of Appeal decreed that that though it recognised that riba was prohibited within the Islamic finance industry, it implicitly stated that both the claimant and the defendants never really took the prohibition that seriously as "*the proviso* (within the agreement between the bank and the defendants) *is plainly inadequate for that purpose*". This judgement can be seen, within a wider context, as a direct challenge for the whole of the Islamic finance industry as to how to put principles into practice.

Ultimately, the case demonstrated how critical religious scholars are within the Islamic finance compliance regime.

It was, though, the shock at the collapse of a conventional bank in the 1980s which provided a further spur to improve Islamic finance compliance practices.

Bank of Credit and Commerce International (BCCI) and Egyptian Islamic Finance Scandals

When a group of BCCI executives gathered together, in 1988, to attend a wedding reception amidst the balmy skies and palm trees of Tampa, life seemed good.

BCCI had global operations and the bank was becoming a household name for many consumers.

However, in reality, the executives were not going to witness any nuptials that afternoon as they were about to be arrested in an FBI sting operation.

BCCI was a conventional finance institution established in 1972 by the Pakistani businessman, Agha Hassan Abedi. The bank was incorporated in Luxembourg and in 1980 it received a licence to operate in the United Kingdom.

However, this respectable looking bank was a front for widespread criminality:

> BCCI's criminality included fraud by BCCI and BCCI customers involving billions of dollars; money laundering in Europe, Africa, Asia, and the Americas; BCCI's bribery of officials in most of those locations; support of terrorism, arms trafficking, and the sale of nuclear technologies; management of prostitution; the commission and facilitation of income tax evasion, smuggling, and illegal immigration; illicit purchases of banks and real estate; and a panoply of financial crimes limited only by the imagination of its officers and customers.[8]

The liabilities of the collapsed bank were around US$20 billion.

This whole affair, whilst it did concern a conventional bank, also embroiled the Islamic finance industry as BCCI had opened an Islamic finance 'window' in 1984. This enabled shari'a compliant operations to take place which was not directly linked to BCCI's wider operations.

Faisal Islamic Bank of Egypt, Dubai Investment Bank, Khartoum-based Tadamon Islamic Bank, Qatar Islamic Bank and Kuwait Finance House invested funds in BCCI which should have been allocated to murabaha commodity contracts. When the Bank was liquidated in 1991 it emerged that these murabaha contracts had not been recorded. As Alim had put it:

> While Islamic financial institutions were not BCCI's only victims, the extent of the fraud shone an unflattering light on the Islamic sector.[9]

This was not the first banking scandal to affect the fledging industry in the 1980s:

> The emergence of Islamic banks in Egypt … paved the way for a proliferation of Islamic money management companies from the mid-1980s. There were nearly 200 of them, all touting shari'ah compliance and baiting Egyptians with returns of up to 26 percent at a time when both conventional and Islamic banks could not offer more than 11 percent. Some commentators estimate a million Egyptians had invested in these companies, but no accurate figures for their assets are available. The Egyptian central bank began trying to audit the companies from around late 1986. Most of them

> collapsed in May 1988, a month before the enactment of a new investment law. With the collapse of these companies, Egyptian depositors instigated a run on the banks as they tried to withdraw their money out of fear that the authorities would clamp Islamic investment companies, public confidence in Islamic banking and finance sank.[10]

US media reports at the time stated that the Government of President Hosni Mubarak attempted to censor domestic newspaper reports of the scandal whilst the victims were often low-paid people who could not afford to lose even a small amount of funds. One Egyptian Government official seemed to blame the consumers for the scandal:

> "Islam promises a sensuous heaven," an Egyptian official said. "These people were anticipating heaven."

However, it was the lack of regulation from the Egyptian Government until it was nearly too late, that was largely to blame for the corruption:

> "They left these companies to grow and grow without moving to stop them or even investigate," Bahaa el-Din, a respected columnist, wrote in the Government-owned newspaper Al Ahram.
>
> When the laws came into force, the Islamic companies were obliged to stop taking deposits. Small savers responded with angry demonstrations and demands that they be repaid. But most funds stopped paying dividends, too.[11]

Consequently, the 1980s Egyptian bank run and the BCCI scandal was a spur for regulatory action which included the examination of the pivotal role of religious scholars within the compliance regime.

Role of Religious Scholars

Unlike many of the world's great religions, Sunni Islam does not rely on clerics.

In fact, there is not an intermediary between God and the believer. For readers who are not acquainted with Islam this may seem to be a surprising statement as media images of Islam often show worshippers following the every word of the Imam.

However, the Imam in a mosque is a learned scholar whose understanding of the faith and shari'a is respected by others. That is not to say there cannot be lively debates between an Imam and worshippers as to the discussions regarding moral dilemmas which is part and parcel of everyday life.

Due to the reliance on scholars to help gauge a full understanding of Islam, financial institutions employ scholars to help decide whether a product is shari'a compliant.

One such scholar, UAE based Mufti Aziz ur Rehman, outlined the process he follows when working within a financial institution:

> First of all a Shariah Board and adviser has to be appointed.
>
> 2. The Shariah Board needs to know about the questions raised and doubts created regarding an issue and they have to convince people on the same.
>
> 3. The Shariah Board also needs to confirm the auditing set up and fund uses.
>
> 4. This Shariah Board will come to the conclusion approval/refusal/alternative and will pronounce an official Fatwa.[12]

Scholars were not integral in the early period of the modern Islamic finance industry. The much heralded Mit Ghamr Bank and the Malaysian Pilgrims Fund, both from the 1960s, did not employ religious scholars as part of their respective regulatory regimes.[13]

1976 was the year when the use of a shari'a board of scholars were first employed by Islamic financial institutions. Faisal Islamic Bank of Egypt set up a shari'a board which was shortly followed by shari'a boards being formed for the Jordan Islamic Bank and the Sudanese Faisal Islamic Bank in 1978 and for the Kuwait House of Finance in 1979.[14]

Today, the role of scholars is critically important to the very health of the industry. Clients can be reassured that the products they are investing in are shari'a compliant and it provides the credibility that a young industry desperately seeks.

However, as the following case study will illustrate, when the industry and scholars are out of sync, this can lead to lost orders and a financial shock to global markets.

Usmani and Sukuks

Mufti Muhammad Taqi Usmani is one of the most respected scholars operating in the contemporary Islamic finance industry. At the same time, he is seen by many people—outside of the Islamic finance world—as a controversial figure.

In April 2020, the Mufti was one of a group of senior religious leaders who defied the orders of Pakistani Prime Minister, Imran Khan to impose "social distancing"—a policy adopted at that time in many countries to stop people being too close to each other in order to stem the spread of the COVID-19 virus.

"*Restriction of three or five people at mosques is not proving practical, those who are sick, elderly should not come to mosques*" Mufti Taqi Usmani declared on 15 April 2020[15] before talks with President Arif Alvi led to a compromise agreement.

Usmani welcomed the understanding reached with the Pakistani Government when he said, on 19 April 2020 that "*the distance of six feet between the lines for prayers and between the namazis* (persons at prayer) *was discussed, however, WHO (World Health Organisation) called for three feet distance between the two persons. Three-foot distance would be maintained between two namazis while a six-foot distance in the lines would be maintained*".[16]

This was not the first time that Usmani's actions caused consternation as he was closely associated with Pakistan's Council of Islamic Ideology from 1977 to 1981. This body helped draft the contentious Hudood Ordinances.

General Zia ul Haq was transforming the country after a military coup brought him to power in 1977. As part of his vision to embed Islamic values in Pakistan, Zia asked the Council of Islamic Ideology to examine a range of criminal justice measures which could be introduced.

As part of the implementation of this policy, the Zina Ordinance included a series of offences with corresponding punishments which included stoning to death, public whipping and imprisonment for adultery.

However, whilst Usmani was technically a member of the Council from 1977 to 1981 he did not attend its proceedings. Zaman described Usmani's equivocal stance:

> He did not go out of his way to discredit the work of the committee, as he would in the case of the Protection of Women Act of 2006. Yet in refusing to take any part in the committee's work, he had made clear what he thought of it.[17]

In 1995, Amnesty International reported that these ordinances were responsible for horrendous human rights abuses:

> The Zina Ordinance is an enormous obstacle inhibiting women from pursuing cases against police officers who have raped them. It has also been exploited by police officers in order to get their own way. Amnesty International knows of a number of instances where women were threatened with being charged with zina if they did not comply with police demands. Police have also bribed women who have been raped in custody to persuade them not to pursue complaints or have threatened them with violence or with false criminal charges.[18]

In 2006, the Women's Protection Act was enacted which substantially changed parts of the Hudood and Zina Ordinances though the United Nations Special Rapporteur on Freedom of Religion or Belief, Asman Jahangir, declared that Pakistan still had "*a long way to go*" in attaining full rights for women. Around the same time, in December 2006, there were strikes in Karachi against this law being introduced at all as it was viewed by conservative Muslims as a weakening of religious strictures.

In 2016, Usmani tried to justify the Hudood Ordinances by placing them within a much wider context of engendering an Islamic society:

> It should be clear that Hudud Laws are just a small part of Islamic teachings. They do not make up the 'whole Islam'. Enforcement of these laws is a stage in the process of Islamising society, not the final aim. Thus, there is a need to introduce comprehensive and well co-ordinated reforms in other sectors of society, including education, economy, civil administration, enforcement of law, and the role of courts.[19]

In the field of Islamic finance, Mufti Muhammad Taqi Usmani has played an instrumental role in the development of the industry.

In his book, *Causes & Remedies of the Present Financial Crisis*, in reference to the 2008 financial crisis, Usmani gave a carefully worded critique as to the value of Islamic finance from religious, ethical and economic perspectives:

> When thinking about an economy as a whole, it is not enough to concentrate on its numerical growth only, nor on the wheel of production running with full vigour and with the best possible speed. It is of much more importance to make the system of distribution of wealth really equitable

> to accommodate the economic needs of all segments of the society on fair basis. It required some conceptual restrictions on market operations, which were not given serious consideration.

The power of Usmani's statements were felt in 2007. By this time, Usmani was not just a respected jurist but was also Chairman of the Shari'a Council of the international *Accounting and Auditing Organisation for Islamic Financial Institutions* (*AAOIFI*). Consequently, the stance of Usmani carried much weight in the Sukuk market.

At that time the Sukuk sector was going from strength to strength and it was worth US$51.5 billion in 2007.[20]

Usmani shocked these market participants when he issued a ruling which decreed that a significant proportion of the Sukuk market was not shari'a complaint:

> Quite recently, the market has witnessed a number of Sukuk in which there is doubt regarding their representation of ownership. For example, the assets in the Sukuk may be shares of companies that do not confer true ownership but which merely offer Sukuk holders a right to returns. Such Sukuk are no more than the purchase of returns from shares; and this is not lawful from a Shariah perspective. Likewise, there has been a proliferation of certain Sukuk that are based on a mix of ijarah, istisna' and murabahah contracts undertaken by Islamic banks or institutions such that these are packaged and sold to Sukuk holders who hope to obtain the returns from these operations. The inclusion of murabahah contracts into such Sukuk, however, cannot but bring into question the issue of the sale of debt, even if the percentage of the murabahah contracts may be considerably less than that of the ijarah, musharakah and istisna' contracts.[21]

Usmani also referred to some Sukuk issuers guaranteeing returns for investors:

> From the perspective of the higher purposes of Islamic economics, such "incentives" in today's Sukuk actually defeat the purpose of an Islamic economic system in which wealth is equitably distributed among investors.
>
> Sukuk that are based on such "incentives" distribute profits to investors on the basis of prevalent interest rates, and not on the basis of actual returns from an enterprise. If Shariah supervisory boards have tolerated such irregularities (mafasid) when Sukuk began to be issued, the time has now come to revisit the matter and to rid Sukuk from now on from such blemishes.

> Either Sukuk should be free of all such "incentives" or these should be based on the enterprise's expected profits. These should certainly not be based on prevalent interest rates. This will then become a truly distinguishing characteristic of Islamic financial institutions, and one that sets them apart from their conventional, interest-based counterparts.[22]

With these observations, Usmani was rightly identifying systemic abuses which were occurring in the Sukuk marketplace. Instead of Sukuks being asset based, the structures were instead being designed to mirror conventional bonds. By calling out these abuses, Usmani and the AAOIFI were aiming to ensure that Sukuks return to the asset-based model that was always intended for this financial model.

The Sukuk market was, at that time, still in its infancy with the first sovereign wealth Sukuk issued by the Malaysian Government in 2002 and this intervention by such a prominent scholar was required in order to ensure the distinctiveness of the Sukuk product. As we discussed in Chapter 4, there are a number of advantages of Sukuks in terms of facilitating long term finance which does not relate in any way to conventional bond financing.

Usmani's actions demonstrate how a prominent scholar can completely change the direction of the market. After Usmani had issued his statement in November 2007, between that month and February 2008 not one sizeable international or US dollar denominated Sukuk was issued. However, the market adapted and other forms of Sukuks such as the ijara Sukuk continued.

What is also noticeable about the actions of Usmani was that the industry, according to Islamic finance lawyer, Michael McMillen, was ignoring Usmani's entreaties a year in advance of this statement being made:

> More than a year before [the AAOIFI clarification], Sheikh Taqi had alerted the law firms, the bankers, and the industry as a whole, including those directly involved, of what he considered to be matters that were not in compliance with shari'ah principles pertaining to certain sukuk al musharaka structures. The matter was not addressed by the practitioners. So he circulated his memo and conducted open meetings to discuss these matters. And still necessary adjustments were not made. Hence the AAOIFI statement. If you look at the statement, towards the end there is a paragraph directed, rather forcefully, at shari'ah scholars that approve and oversee these structures. It doesn't name anybody, but if you

> are in the industry you'd know who it was directed at. It basically said to these scholars that you can't just approve something and then walk away. Scholars have an obligation to monitor how the whole transaction is implemented; it is an ongoing obligation and an ongoing process.[23]

In essence the industry which was still in the very early stage of its' development, especially as far as the Sukuk market was concerned, was willing to ride roughshod over shari'a requirements until Usmani's statement was issued.

Religious Scholars: Will There Need to Be Greater Accountability?

Tensions can exist between the industry and the scholars for whilst the industry wants to develop products that are competitive with conventional finance products, this can create strains with the need for these same products to be shari'a compliant.

Nonetheless, Islamic finance is structured for religious scholars to be at the core of the industry's decision-making processes:

> This deference to scholars is rooted in the Qur'ran which reminds people to seek knowledge from its possessors. The idea of remembrance in the verse refers to the scholars' knowledge of the rules, regulations, and philosophical bases of relevant Qur'ranic and Sunnatic injunctions, all designed to condition the affairs of humanity in accordance with the Divine Guidance in public and in private. These injunctions extend far and wide covering such issues as worship and piety, conduct with family, neighbours, and society at large, and business and political relationships.[24]

This reliance on scholars can lead to a lack of scruples by some market participants. According to a BBC report in 2009 some financial institutions were going to extremes to ensure they can bring products to market whilst seeking compliant scholars to nod the approval of the products through. This practice is often dubbed as "*fatwa shopping*":

> As one investment banker based in Dubai, working for a major Western financial organisation explains:
>
> "We create the same type of products that we do for the conventional markets. We then phone up a Sharia scholar for a Fatwa. If he doesn't give it to us, we phone up another scholar, offer him a sum of money

> for his services and ask him for a Fatwa. We do this until we get Sharia compliance. Then we are free to distribute the product as Islamic."[25]

From a religious perspective, it has been claimed that shari'a scholars are too busy focusing on the needs of meeting clients' compliance requirements rather than addressing the longer-term objectives of Islamic economics. This argument has been presented within the context of Maqasid.

Maqasid is a core Islamic concept that was ably elucidated upon by the influential scholar, Al-Ghazali (1058–1111). As will be discussed further in Chapter 6, maqasid relates to the belief that Islamic jurisprudence is critical to the safeguarding of human well-being: religion, life, intellect, lineage and property. There are distinct synergies to the secular economic debate as to the need to attain social welfare and environmental objectives.

Saudi businessman and founder of the Al Baraka Bank, Saleh Abdullah Kamel, also known as Sheikh Saleh, argued that too many scholars in the Islamic finance space are missing the very objectives of maqasid and are too enmeshed in the intricacies of specific finance contracts:

> Before, we saw that the shari'ah scholars didn't understand the economy and economics. Now I can say that some of them don't understand shari'ah either. I wouldn't say all shari'ah scholars, but certainly some of them don't look to the maqasid, they only look to the mechanism. If they do this it means that they don't understand shari'ah.[26]

As Alim has stated:

> For Sheikh Saleh, Islamic banking and finance must first gain a solid maqasid foothold within Islamic communities. Muslims must be the first to develop the system closely aligned with maqasid al shari'ah and champion the cause if there is any hope the Islamic financial and economic system can present itself as the definitively better alternative to the interest-based system.[27]

Alim claimed that two unnamed Malaysian bankers had told her that maqasid was being abandoned by the industry as the focus on profitability remained paramount.[28]

There has been an increase in the number of scholars engaged with the Islamic finance market. The ICD-Refinitiv Islamic Finance Development

Report 2019 reported that there were 1166 specialist Shari'a scholars in 2018. This was up slightly from 952 in 2014 as reported by ISRA and Thomson Reuters in the Islamic Commercial Law Report 2016.

In 2018, 659 out of 1166 scholars were based in Malaysia, Bangladesh, Indonesia, Sudan and Bahrain, according to the IFDI 2019 report. This is 65% of all Shari'a scholars practising in Islamic finance based in just five countries. This trend has contributed to stymying the growth of the industry. The Central Bank of the Philippines stated in June 2020 that the lack of qualified scholars in the country was one of the reasons that the sector had not developed further.

Maya Marissa Malek, Executive Director of Global Shariah Advisory, and CEO of Amanie Advisors Global Office has argued that the industry has a lack of qualified scholars whose skills-set includes a good understanding of shari'a and the financial services industry. Malek has also commented on the small number of women shari'a scholars in the industry as a whole though progress in increasing the number of women scholars is being made in Malaysia and Indonesia.[29]

Overall, though, there is a still a limited number of scholars who cater for the sector. In 2011 German-based Funds@Work released a report that found that just two scholars, Sheikh Nizam Yaquby and Sheikh Dr Abdul Sattar Abdul Karim Abu Ghuddah each sat on the most boards: 85. The report also indicated that the top 20 scholars have 621 board memberships between them while the remaining 260 scholars held 520 board memberships between them.

Leading Islamic finance lawyer, Michael McMillen, rebutted claims from some commentators that the small number of scholars holding so many positions on Boards would inevitably lead to conflicts of interest. McMillen made the telling point that controversies regarding the role of senior scholars is almost unheard of and the overall small number of scholars is inevitable in an industry that is young but growing. Over time, McMillen argued, this discrepancy between the number of scholars and the number of Board positions would naturally be equalised.[30]

Despite such observations, this has not stopped the criticisms levelled against the sector regarding conflicts of interest and a lack of transparency. One media outlet, *AsiaMoney*, even suggested the scholars were acting like a cartel. The fees being charged by this small number of senior scholars was also highlighted:

> The Egyptian scholar Sheikh Hussain Hamid Hassan, now the most prominent scholar in Dubai, made waves recently when he suggested that US$300,000 was not an unusual fee for advice on a complex transaction. Others suggest that the retainer for an international bank would be in the region of US$150,000 to $250,000, and one source says he was quoted US$100,000 just to get shariah approval on a fund, after all the product development had taken place.[31]

For Sheikh Nizam Yaquby, the very idea of having to publicly declare the level of fees that scholars are paid was unacceptable:

> Do the banks disclose what they pay for lawyers, or for auditors, or for high management? If the law of the country says they must disclose everything they pay to everyone, then why not. But if these things are not there, why should we only insist on it when it comes to the shariah? It is a contractual matter between the bank and the shariah scholars. They should disclose there is a contract, that's enough.[32]

With the likelihood of a greater focus on the sector, as the industry transitions from being seen as a niche product to a mainstream player in global markets, the pressure to address disclosure and conflict of interest requirements may become too great to resist from regulators and a growing pool of investors.

Philosophical approaches can differ between senior scholars as to how to work with and for the Islamic finance industry. Yaquby has said, for instance, that taking on board the actions of the conventional finance industry and applying these actions in an Islamic context can be the right approach to take. In fact, in 2003, Yaquby ruled that there could be a shari'a equivalent of conventional hedge funds if key conditions were met:

> Now, imitating good things is okay; we are not against that, because we seek wisdom everywhere. We know conventional banking has a long experience of some 500 years, and there are certain norms and things that we have to learn. However, if we see that any of these is against our principles, we should not be reluctant or hesitant to say so. Take, for example, derivatives—there are some things we might be able to do but not the full-fledged derivatives as in the interest-based system. We don't want to trade in assets which do not exist, which are fictitious. This is dangerous and not good for society. So we must have the courage to say no and to point out when something is haram.[33]

Usmani adopted a very different approach.

> There are two approaches. One is that whatever is available in conventional financial institutions should be available in Islamic institutions as well, with certain modifications. I do not adhere to that approach. The Islamic banking system has its own philosophy, and because of it we cannot bring about an alternative for all the products that are being used. I do not fully agree with the concept that the hedge funds must have some alternative in Islamic finance. Many things that are not fully compliant with the basic philosophy of Islamic economics, we do not need to bring about alternatives for. That's the second approach. I subscribe to it.[34]

In 2010, the regulatory body, the International Islamic Financial Markets (IIFM) announced global standards were now in place for shari'a compliant derivative products, which is discussed in further detail in Chapter 4.

The Malaysian scholar, Dr Mohammed Daud Bakar, has argued that there is a clear need to improve training for scholars who wish to operate in the industry:

> Shari'a scholars should be guided and trained to ask the relevant questions at the right time.

Dr Bakar has also been scathing about the quality of work provided by some scholars:

> I have come across examples of when shari'a scholars take things easy without reading through the documentation. If you read the documentation it can be rubbish from a shari'a perspective.

Bakar argued that conventional banks who operate with Islamic finance "windows" or Islamic finance operations which are run separately from the core bank, can be more meticulous in assessing shari'a compliance than some Islamic financial institutions. One of the core issues that Bakar has found in respect of shari'a non-compliance is that banks:

> tend to forget to update terms and conditions with the shari'a committee.[35]

Khalid Howladar, Head of Credit and Sukuk Advisory at R J Fleming also expressed severe doubts as to how some scholars operate:

> The shari'a scholar, in many cases, doesn't read a thousand pages of legal documentation though, maybe, you might argue that they should. They will receive the commercial terms, someone will summarise it and it will be translated and in many cases there is a translation error between what a person thinks they're providing a fatwa for and what they are. And as someone who has read tens of thousands of pages of legal docs (*sic*) and seen some of the fatwas I can see a disconnect ....[36]

This situation, combined with the current lack of scholars meeting the needs of a fast-growing Islamic finance industry, has accentuated the need for the multilateral regulatory organisations to oversee the industry.

A significant step forward was made in 1998 when one of the international multilateral organisations, Accounting and Auditing Organisation for Islamic Financial Institutions (AAOIFI), established a shari'a board of scholars to oversee global standards and practices.

Some analysts of the Islamic finance industry, though, have even gone as far as to imagine an Islamic finance industry without the need for any shari'a scholars. Orhan argued that the (arguably) first ever Islamic finance institution in the modern era,[37] Mit Ghamr, did not contain a shari'a board. As Orhan posited:

> ... in today's conditions, shariah boards are seen as the places where such legitimacy can be attained. But, in the future, if the locus of legitimacy changes –for instance towards more centralised authorities, Mit Ghamr and similar institutions can be a role model in developing alternative sources of legitimacy.[38]

Howladar has also questioned whether the use of scholars is required in all circumstances:

> .... with fatwa shopping there is a lot of controversy and this idea that everything seems to need a fatwa suddenly. I sort of step back a bit ... I see technology as a tool that implements a purpose ... It is not so much the tool that is relevant as the purpose.

Howladar went on to argue that a scholar could "*validate the purpose is halal*" whilst the processes of a commercial arrangement could be left to technology such as blockchain software.

Howladar's concept of a scholar validating the purpose but not the structure of a financial product would be opposed by other scholars as not providing the full due diligence that is required though Howladar's argument is in sync with Bakar who has also called for the greater use of artificial intelligence in shari'a compliant processes.

As for Orfan's idea to end shari'a boards, this is difficult to envisage in current circumstances but as the sector enters new markets and targets consumers who may be from other religions or of no religion at all, then, depending upon the credibility of the industry at that stage, such a scenario could be imagined.

Dr Mohammed Daud Baker has elucidated upon the need to focus on Artificial Intelligence (AI):

> Most of the cases of shari'a non-compliance I have seen is due to human error, human negligence.

Bakar believes AI could be the game changer that the sector needs:

> AI can make shari'a compliance cheaper, easier and smarter. AI can guide you to the right fatwa to issue as AI can analyse thousands of books.

The use of AI would:

> let the humans focus more on leadership and innovation as we come to the second part of the first 100 years of the industry.[39]

How, though, could AI work when compliance can vary depending upon which school of fiqh is being relied upon to judge compliance requirements?

Bakar had a good response to this challenge:

> I would put all standards in one go and pick the standard that has been endorsed by the (*respective*) shari'a board to select the algorithm with the respective institution.[40]

It has been argued that global standards first need to be established to attain some form of regulatory alignment across the industry. This aim can be achieved via multilateral institutions. If these organisations were successful in setting standards it is hoped this could end the conflicting fatwas from differing scholars on key financial products which has the potential to cause confusion in the markets.

As we will see, there are complications in attaining any form of regulatory alignment.

Multilateral Institutions

> I think now is the time to systemise. Western banking, riba banking, they have developed a system that is universally applied. We have to follow that route in putting the principles into a form that can be accepted, and the implementation of them becomes professional.

So said Prince Mohamed Al Faisal Al Saud, a key player in the Islamic finance industry. However, when it came to the means to attain this universal approach, the Prince shied away from centralising such standards:

> No, you cannot [have a centralised shari'ah body for the industry] because you'll put yourself in a straitjacket. On the contrary, the more differences there are the better because it will allow you to have different approaches. The central tenets should be the same because they stem from shari'ah and the same Islamic principles. I mean, you cannot have different interpretations of riba. Riba is riba, that's all there is to it. But you can have different interpretations of the mudaraba, for instance, or the murabaha. There could be some differences.[41]

This dichotomy lies at the heart of the role and purpose of the Islamic finance multilateral institutions that have been established to ensure there is adequate quality control and also to enable financial institutions to innovate within an international regulatory framework.

There are a number of multilateral organisations that have been formed to provide consistency of approach, quality control and the smooth operation of Islamic finance across different markets. The primary institutions are:

- Organisation of Islamic Cooperation's Fiqh Academy—Provides judgements in relation to jurisprudence on a number of themes including Islamic finance;
- Accounting and Auditing Organisation for Islamic Financial Organisations (AAOIFI) -Responsible for the formulation and issuance of accounting, auditing, ethics, governance and shari'a standards;
- Islamic Financial Services Board (IFSB)—Issues prudential standards and guiding principles for the banking, capital markets and insurance sectors.

There are other relevant multilateral organisations to consider such as the International Islamic Financial Markets which aims for the standardisation of products, documentation and related processes and whose role was discussed in Chapter 4. The International Islamic Rating Agency is a credit rating agency for the Islamic finance industry.

In addition, there is the General Council for Islamic Banks and Financial Institutions which is a trade association. The Islamic Research and Training Institute is an arm of the Islamic Development Bank (IsDB). The role of the IsDB will be considered in detail in Chapter 7 when we explore the theme of Islamic microfinance.

OIC's Fiqh Academy

The formation of the Organisation for Islamic Co-operation (OIC) occurred following an arson attack on the Al-Aqsa mosque in Jerusalem in 1969. As we will see in Chapter 10, King Faisal of Saudi Arabia had worked diligently to prepare the ground for the OIC's founding.

The first Prime Minister of Malaysia, Tunku Abdul Rahman, also played a key role in the establishment of the OIC:

> It started off in a miraculous way. A mad Australian attempted to burn down the holy mosque, the Al-Aqsa of Jerusalem and this caused great excitement among Muslims throughout the world. At the time I was holidaying in Hong Kong and received a message from His Majesty the late King Feisal of Saudi Arabia to attend a conference which he and the king of Morocco were holding in Rabat, Morocco.... There was much talk and much excitement at the conference and in the end it was resolved to form a united Muslim organisation. I was asked to head it.[42]

The OIC subsequently established the Fiqh Academy which is based in Jeddah. The Academy considers jurisprudence issues on a range of ethical issues including in the realm of Islamic finance. It has played an important role in establishing some firm foundations for the Islamic finance industry.

This included the decision reached in May 1992 for the approval of a limited liability company structure combined with the ability to buy and sell shares. At the same time it was also agreed to allow shari'a compliant investment firms to exist.[43] These were integral steps that has helped establish the credibility of the industry.

Further examples of the Fiqh Academy's work included the decision reached in November 2019, when meeting in Dubai, that *Fédération Internationale Des Ingénieurs-Conseils* (FIDC) engineering contracts were sharia'a compliant:

> The Synod considers that these contracts are permissible according to Sharia, if there is compliance with the legal provisions and controls, as a measure for it on the contracts of Istisna'a, leasing and contracting, and what may arise in it from disputes and disputes, then it is permissible to resort to arbitration, according to the Council's Resolution No. 91 (9/8) and it is permissible in the event that Delaying implementation by the specified date, applying the penal clause in accordance with the council's decision 109 (3/12). As for what is increased in price due to changing conditions of implementation or amendment of the location of the contract, it is compensation for the damage.

Accounting and Auditing Organisation for Islamic Financial Organisations (AAOIFI)

AAOIFI is a critically important organisation as it ensures some form of uniformity and best practice for everyday Islamic finance accounting and auditing procedures. Over a relatively short period of time, AAOIFI has established itself as a well-respected organisation providing practical advice and support to ensure that contract practices in the multi billion-dollar industry meets the highest of professional standards.

The genesis for AAOIFI began in 1987 when one of the external auditors of the Islamic Development Bank (IsDB), Abdulaziz Al Rashed proposed the need for an AAOIFI type organisation to ensure that practitioners who operate in a range of jurisdictions had a common approach to core auditing and accounting practices.

The concept was discussed at an IsDB meeting held in Istanbul in 1987. As a result of a decision reached at that meeting a steering group was set up which led, in February 1990, to a group of Islamic financial institutions signing a memorandum of understanding. The next step, in 1991, was for the Financial Accounting Organisation for Islamic Banks and Financial Institutions to be registered in Bahrain. In 1995 it changed its name to AAOIFI to reflect its enhanced auditing function and AAOIFI continues to be based in Manama.

To ensure Islamic banks had the same high standards of capital reserves as conventional banks (as reflected by the Basel accords as issued by the Bank of International Settlements) a similar standard was published by AAOIFI in 1999.

AAOIFI established a sharia'a board of scholars in 1998. This helped to enhance the credibility and reputation of Islamic finance as a sector with standards, ethics and a focus on shari'a compliance.

Despite the excellent work of AAOIFI, it should be recognised that AAOIFI provides best practice advice and guidance—it is not a regulator of the international Islamic finance industry. Nonetheless, its standards are respected in a number of jurisdictions such as Bahrain, Dubai, Jordan, Lebanon and Qatar and AAOIFI standards were said to be respected in Sudan[42] as well as in Syria before the Syrian civil war began in 2011.

The Geneva based accountant, Anthony Travis, who played a role in the work of AAOIFI and the IFSB has argued that the work of AAOIFI was sorely needed:

> As we went along, there were things called acceptable accounting standards, generally accepted accounting standards, and international accounting standards. The latter were, I think, either insufficiently well developed or they were insufficiently focused to take into account the activities of an Islamic financial institution. I can say that the reaction and the action that was taken by AAOIFI in the first place and IFSB [with its disclosure standard IFSB-4 that sets guidelines for transparency and market discipline for Islamic financial institutions] have been exemplary in my view.[44]

Islamic Financial Services Board (IFSB)

The formation of the Islamic Financial Services Board came out of the work of AAOIFI. The focus of the IFSB is to ensure best practice and high standards for central banks and other regulators responsible for supervising the Islamic finance market in their respective jurisdictions.

The IFSB was finally established in Kuala Lumpur in 2002 despite Bahrain arguing that Manama should host IFSB as well as AAOIFI.

Its full members reflects regulators from many jurisdictions—Oman, Sudan, Iran, Kazakhstan, Brunei Darussalam, Bangladesh, Morocco, Indonesia, Qatar, United Arab Emirates, Singapore, Mauritania, Nigeria, Malaysia, Mauritius, Turkey, Djibouti, Saudi Arabia, Bahrain, Iraq, Jordan, Kuwait, Libya and Egypt. With its other classes of membership including regulators such as the Bank of England, its breadth of membership reflects the growing strength, relevance and vibrancy of the Islamic finance industry.

It has been claimed that IFSB are so efficient that they came up with capital adequacy requirements before the Bank of International Settlements.[45] As the former IFSB Deputy Secretary General, Abdullah Haron, has argued, the IFSB continues to play a vital role:

> Regulators would regulate in different ways. For example, with capital adequacy, jurisdictions would apply risk weights differently. IFSB helps the industry to have a consistent approach to these types of issues. It also provides technical assistance to member countries and to other countries. The organisation provides technical assistance to countries that request advice on Islamic finance from the IMF, the World Bank and the Islamic Development Bank, for example, because they don't have the necessary specialised expertise.[46]

The Future of the Multilateral Organisations

An intervention by the United Arab Emirates may change the direction and role of these organisation as, in May 2020, the UAE Ministry of Finance, the Islamic Development Bank (IsDB) and the Dubai Islamic Economy Development Centre (DIEDC) announced plans for a global legislative framework in order to attain improved standardisation within the sector.

A memorandum of understanding was signed between DIEDC and AAOIFI, enabling DIEDC to use AAOIFI's standards as a reference point in building this international legal framework with the guidance of the UAE Ministry of Finance and IsDB.

Whether this will further support the work of AAIOFI, IFSB and the OIC's Fiqh Academy is hard to judge. A uniformity of approach is required in the industry, despite the excellent work of these three organisations, to address continuing concerns regarding quality control and practices across the industry.

However, national interests can play a role in setting global standards. At the moment with the Fiqh Academy based in Jeddah, AAOIFI and IIFM based in Manama and the IFSB based in Kuala Lumpur, different national interests are balanced by the location and operation of these institutions.

The UAE initiative could be seen in a cooperative light with the core aim to enhance common standards across the industry. Another potential scenario is that this initiative will be seen as an attempt by Dubai, in particular, to take some of the glory in setting international norms which may upset the fine balance that has been achieved thus far between setting international standards and reflecting and balancing national interests.

Only time will tell which scenario will win out.

Dow Jones Islamic Markets Index

Despite the many strengths of Islamic finance, this industry could have remained as an interesting niche area of study with no real potential for growth and with the very notion of this model being confined to the odd arcane publication.

For how could Islamic finance operate in a global economy that was not shari'a compliant? With the concept of interest seen as a given by central banks and most financial institutions and a range of products and services, from gambling to conventional insurance products being haram could Islamic finance ever develop beyond the intellectual concept?

One hadith is crystal clear as to how profits should not be made from haram items:

> If Allah forbids people to eat something, He also forbids them to take its price.[47]

It was, though, the decision of leading scholars that enabled a step change to occur and helped to embed Islamic finance as a key part of the political economic models of Malaysia, Indonesia, Brunei and across the Middle East.

In 1998, Sheikh Muhammad Taqi Usmani, Sheikh Mohamed A Elgari, Sheikh Abdul Sattar Aby Ghudah, Sheikh Nizam Yaquby and Sheikh Yusuf Talal DeLorenzo made a seminal judgement call that enabled Islamic finance to be part of the global money markets.

Instead of arguing that all investments had to be shari'a compliant, the fatwa issued by these scholars stated that the majority of the investments had to be compliant. By this one significant step, funds from the wealthy Gulf States and from other sources could be realised within shari'a investment models whilst ensuring the core principles which underpin Islamic finance was maintained:

> It was clear to the Shari'ah Board that an Islamic equity index and investments in equity securities were not possible if the applicable criteria preclude, as an absolute matter, investment in a company that has any interest income or expense, direct or indirect, or engages in any impermissible business activity. Virtually every company had some degree of impermissible interest income or expense, primarily as a result of direct or indirect deposits, investments or indebtedness. Some companies engaged primarily in permissible business activities but had limited involvement in impermissible business activities. Consider, as examples, an automobile and truck manufacturing company that also owned a credit company that financed purchases of its vehicles, a grocery purveyor that sold pork products or beer, or the business composition of various multinational conglomerates. The question, generally posed, was whether the Shari'ah was absolutely preclusive and intolerant of even slight impurities. The debate was, and remains, spirited.[48]

A pragmatic approach was adopted so that the investment criteria considered the core focus of the business rather than dwelling upon peripheral activity which would be classified as haram.

To achieve this objective, the fatwa set out two tests that should be met for shari'a compliant investments:

> The first test had two branches: (a) whether the subject security is itself impermissible because, say, it is a fixed income instrument (such as preferred stock) with an impermissibly stipulated or guaranteed return; and (b) whether the "core" business of the subject entity (as opposed to "any" business) is halal and impermissible (because it entails dealings in alcohol, tobacco, pork products, interest-based financial services, non-takaful insurance, defence and weapons, casinos/gambling, pornography, or other inappropriate elements). If those threshold tests do not preclude

> investment, the inquiry turns to whether the entity has an impermissible degree of ribā or haram income as determined pursuant to a series of financial tests.[49]

This fatwa was prepared within the context of the decision of Dow Jones who wanted to reach out to clients who would only invest on a shari'a compliant basis.

Consequently, the fatwa had a methodical structure to enable suitable investment strategies to be developed and enabled the Dow Jones software to assess the percentage of permissible and impermissible activities in order to assess which shares could be acquired. AAOIFI took until 2004 to concur with this fatwa.

The Dow Jones screening process is careful with its use of scholars in overseeing the screening process:

> Since the Shari'ah is by no means entirely monolithic and differences of opinion must be respected, the members of the DJIM Shari'ah Supervisory Board are from a spectrum of six countries to allow for both diversity of scholarly opinion and greater acceptance of Shari'ah authenticity internationally. Thus, Shari'ah scholars act as gatekeepers for what is permissible (halal), thus ensuring continued Shari'ah compliance of the index methodology and the index constituents. Shari'ah scholars also act as consumer advocates for (minority) shareholders and depositors (investment account holders).

The screening aims to exclude investments in the following sectors:

- Alcohol;
- Tobacco;
- Pork products;
- Conventional banking products;
- Defence/arms manufacturing;
- Entertainment (gambling, pornography and related business interests)

In practice, though, excluding investments that cover all of these sectors is not practical due to the nature of traditional investment structures and corporate structures covering a wide range of business sectors:

> Thus, we are today in a state of interim tolerance, where a little impermissibility, as interpreted by the Shari'ah scholars, is accepted as long as the Islamic finance community continues to strive for Shari'ah purity. Put differently, today we have Shari'ah compliance (tolerating a little impermissibility) and tomorrow we should reach the new paradigm: Shari'ah enabling (Shari'ah purity).[50]

Consequently:

> The Shari'ah allows investing in shares of companies in which the primary business activity is deemed lawful if the accounts receivable do not represent the majority (more than 50 percent) of the total assets. Thus, if the primary business of the company is halal, and the sale methodology for obtaining corporate revenue is through instalment payments, which may be deemed incidental if the accounts receivable do not exceed 33 percent of market capitalization, then investment in such a company will be permissible. It should be noted in this regard that if the receivables total more than 50 percent of the assets, the majority of the company's dealings will actually be in money, and not in goods, services, and assets. Thus, this position is consistent with the established and recognized Islamic juristic rule cited in many contemporary fatwas stating that what is not permitted independently may be permitted subordinately.[51]

For some scholars, there is a feeling of queasiness by engaging with conventional finance structures. In a 2011 book, Masudul Alam Choudhury condemned the use of DJIMI as well as the comments of Mufti Taqi Usmani who had said that the London Interbank Offered Rate (LIBOR) rate (which calculates the daily interest rate for borrowing between conventional banks) could be used as a benchmark in murabaha transactions:

> This is a deplorable apologetic statement, in the same way as debt is being legitimated on fiqi grounds up to one third of the asset value of an enterprise.[52]

Since this book was published an Islamic interbank rate has been established in Kuala Lumpur.

What is striking about the Dow Jones Islamic Markets Index is not only that it has worked in enticing new clients to invest in the markets but, more significantly for the long term credibility and viability of the Islamic finance industry, it demonstrates that financing based on these ethical constructs delivers long term returns—the ultimate win—win for investors and ethical financing:

> When compared with other markets and regions, the Islamic indexes still outperform conventional indexes. Across nearly every region, Islamic indexes perform better over the long run.[53]

Al Rifai has argued that this record of performance is directly linked to the screening process excluding highly leveraged companies with the focus being maintained on healthcare, technology and energy stocks. This is a by-product of the ethical considerations which means the screening normally excludes media, entertainment and hospitality firms from consideration. Consequently, stable and financially robust sectors can receive shari'a compliant funding.

One of the scholars involved in drafting the 1998 fatwa, Sheikh Yusuf Talal De Lorenzo, argued in 2009, that the screening process meant that businesses which were attractive to conventional investors, such as Enron, WorldCom and Tyco, were excluded months before these firms collapsed in specular style.[54]

When the industry moved into the 2020s a new question was posed to Islamic finance participants—is conventional finance overtaking Islamic finance in embracing ethical standards?

From CSR to ESG: The Challenge for Islamic Finance

Kofi Annan (1938–2018) was seen by some diplomats as unassuming and self- effacing but his gentlemanly manner and his hushed speaking voice belied a strength of character that contributed to transforming international law and, to a limited extent, helped change the very operation of global capitalism itself.

Annan was born in what was then called the Gold Coast by the British colonial authorities but is now Ghana. After working studiously through the United Nations (UN) bureaucracy, Annan was appointed UN Secretary General in 1997 where his tenure in office continued until 2006.

However, Annan's career was marked by one of the most horrific massacres ever to occur during the post Second World War era. In January 1994, the head of UN peacekeepers in Rwanda, General Romeo Dallaire informed the UN in New York of reports that a Hutu group were planning to massacre Tutsis and moderate Hutus. The General sought permission to destroy an arms cache to pre-empt this violence.

Kofi Annan was the UN official who responded to Dallaire's request. Annan refused to provide this authorisation and he justified the decision when he told Dallaire "*the overriding consideration is the need to avoid entering into a course of action that might lead to the use of force and unanticipated consequences*".

However, after the Rwandan President, Juvenal Habyarimana, died in an unexplained plane crash in April 1994, extremist Hutu groups began a massacre of Tutsis where an estimated 800,000 people were killed. Eventually, in July 1994, a new UN peacekeeping operation, Operation Turquoise, contributed to ending the violence.

Annan was profoundly affected by this tragedy and, as UN Secretary General, he led initiatives to change international law. In 2005, it was agreed that under the concept of Responsibility to Protect (R2P) outside military action can intervene in a country to prevent any attempts at genocide.

Whilst arguments continue to this day as to the validity and practicality of R2P in contemporary geopolitics, this was an indication of Annan's belief that change for the better can be achieved through multilateralism.

Annan also saw this potential for change when it came to the operation of the global economy. At the start of his term of office as UN Secretary General, the global economy was rocked by the 1997 Asian Financial Crisis. In July of that year, speculators lost confidence in the Thai Baht currency which triggered a wider regionwide currency crisis which inevitably flowed into a financial crisis affecting a broad range of asset classes. It was, at the time, the biggest economic shock to hit East Asia since the end of the Second World War.[55]

The crisis led to a trend in academic circles to condemn the abuses of the market. This was exemplified by Professor Lee Phil-Sang when examining the impact of speculation on daily living conditions in Seoul:

> The economy, already suffering from unemployment and fluctuating prices, is now being plagued by rampant real estate speculation. This real estate speculation boom is an arch-fiend wielding terrible power, capable of blowing out the flickering signs of a hopeful economic recovery. In the Kangnam area, south of the Han River, outright acts of apartment purchase speculation bear an uncanny resemblance to speculation in action at a

> bustling, lively gambling table. Dealers and owners are colluding to buy up purchase rights of newly built apartments in order to boost apartment prices after which they will walk away with enormous profits from trading.[56]

In September 1997, the then Malaysian Prime Minister, Mahathir Mohamad, hit out against the speculators:

> For them wealth must come from impoverishing others, from taking what others have in order to enrich themselves. Their weapon is their wealth against the poverty of others.[57]

1997 was also the year when the first international treaty was agreed to reduce carbon emissions to help tackle climate change with the signing of the Kyoto Protocol.

Therefore, with global capitalism being blamed in the same year for causing economic chaos and hardship in East Asia and whose practices were condemned for threatening the very viability of the planet, attention was focused on what should happen to address the perceived weaknesses of conventional finance as it related to indices of global well-being.

Supporters of laissez faire economics pointed out that growth rates in the United States and Western Europe were robust throughout the late 1990s and so change was not required. Nonetheless, Annan took on board the critique that improvements were required in the operation of the global economy.

In January 2004, Annan wrote to over fifty CEOs of major financial institutions inviting them to participate in a joint initiative under the auspices of the UN Global Compact and with the support of the International Finance Corporation and the Swiss Government. The goal of the initiative was to find ways to integrate what is now known as ESG objectives into capital markets.

ESG stands for environmental, social and governance factors which should be considered as part of everyday business practices. This objective seemed at the time by some commentators as utopian bearing in mind the pressures on financial institutions and businesses due to the cyclical pressures of the markets. Many corporates pointed to the fact that they were already involved in corporate social responsibility (CSR).

CSR has been defined in slightly different ways. Carroll argued in 1979 that CSR could be defined as firms having responsibilities to societies including economic, legal, ethical and discretionary (or philanthropic).[58] Donaldson and Dunfee, in 1999, wrote of a "*social contract*" between the firm and society; the contract bestows certain rights in exchange for certain responsibilities. Whilst Freeman's Stakeholder Theory, defined in 1984, is now part of everyday business language with the concept of a stakeholder being any group or individual who can affect or is affected by the achievement of an organisation's purpose. Freeman argued that it was in the company's strategic interest to respect the interests of all its stakeholders.

However, despite this analytical framework, CSR was seen by many people as just a form of public relations and not a real attempt to embed the activities of businesses in the service of wider society.[59] Annan went beyond the commonly defined voluntarist approach of CSR and argued that ESG goals should be embedded in the business plans of multinational enterprises (MNEs).

In 2005, the *Who Cares Win* report was published where it made the case that embedding environmental, social and governance factors in capital markets made good business sense and would lead to more sustainable markets and better outcomes for societies. It described the following win–win scenario for businesses and societies:

> Companies that perform better with regard to these issues can increase shareholder value by, for example, properly managing risks, anticipating regulatory action or accessing new markets, while at the same time contributing to the sustainable development of the societies in which they operate. Moreover, these issues can have a strong impact on reputation and brands, an increasingly important part of company value.

Also in 2005, the United Nations Environment Programme was instrumental with the production of the so-called Freshfield Report which demonstrated that ESG issues are relevant for valuation purposes. This report was clear, for instance, that far from investment decision-making being based on mathematical calculations, investment judgements were also based upon subjective analysis:

> Like many professional activities, investment decision-making is an art rather than a science: there is no formula that guarantees a particular outcome. It is important to distinguish therefore between optimal decision-making and optimal decisions. The law is concerned with the former, as the latter can be arrived at only with hindsight. The oft-repeated caveat

that 'past returns are no indication of future performance' is reflected in the legal duties imposed on investment decision-makers.[60]

It was also stated within the report that an analysis of businesses meeting ESG requirements can lead to long term economic growth, whilst the moral considerations of trustees on pension boards, for example, should not be sidelined in the chase for immediate profit:

> … the links between ESG factors and financial performance are increasingly being recognised. On that basis, integrating ESG considerations into an investment analysis so as to more reliably predict financial performance is clearly permissible and is arguably required in all jurisdictions. It is also arguable that ESG considerations must be integrated into an investment decision where a consensus (express or in certain circumstances implied) amongst the beneficiaries mandates a particular investment strategy and may be integrated into an investment decision where a decision-maker is required to decide between a number of value-neutral alternatives.

These two reports were the foundation for the launch of the Principles for Responsible Investment (PRI) at the New York Stock Exchange (NYSE) in 2006 encouraging businesses to embed ESG aims in their everyday activity. As Kofi Annan rang the NYSE's Opening Bell, it was still felt by many commentators that the concept of ESG would not last long in the rough and tumble of the money markets.

However, Annan persisted and in 2007, shortly after Annan had stepped down as Secretary General, the UN launched the Sustainable Stock Exchange Initiative (SSEI). The SSEI enables stock exchanges to track the performance of share capital as it relates to meeting ESG objectives. The United Nations Conference on Trade and Development continues to ensure that the SSEI is a live index assessing the role of meeting ESG targets around the world. As for the PRI, it now has over 1600 members representing over US$70 trillion assets under management.

Cynics could argue that Annan's initiatives did not prevent the 2008 global financial crisis from occurring. A contrary view is that the growth of the ESG initiatives, which had little time to be embedded before the 2008 crisis, was influenced by consumers who supported the overall aims of meeting ESG ends, especially after the lack of due diligence and the culture of short-termism was exposed by the global financial crisis.

Following this crisis, the Bank of International Settlements produced its Basel III guidance for capital and reserve requirements to mitigate against the future risk of the contagion of systemic credit failure caused by deficiencies in the operation of the banks. The guidance, which was finalised in 2011, has been described by an Islamic Development Bank official as "*looking like a book on Islamic finance*".[61]

Consequently, the trend for conventional banks to take on board wider sustainability objectives is becoming a regulatory requirement.

Public perception of banks may still be rooted in the regulatory loosening of regulations, such as in the UK with the "Big Bang" reforms of 1987. This, combined with general global monetary loosening in the 1980s led to negative portrayals of capitalism during this decade such as the British comedian, Harry Enfield, playing a speculator whose catchphrase was "*loads of money*" through to the speech of the fictional character, Gordon Gekko (played by Michael Douglas) in the 1987 film, *Wall Street,* where the character declares to an audience of investors that "*greed is good*".

Since the end of Kofi Annan's tenure as UN Secretary General and the chastening of global markets by the 2008 crisis, the emphasis on sustainability has grown in the conventional banking industry.

On a macro level, the United Nations agreed in 2015 to set seventeen overall objectives for the sustainable development goals as part of the UN's 2030 Agenda for Sustainable Development. These objectives include "*No Poverty*", "*Zero Hunger*" and "*Gender Equality*". Behind each goal are detailed targets. For instance, under the "*No Poverty*" heading it includes the target:

> By 2030, eradicate extreme poverty for all people everywhere, currently measured as people living on less than $1.25 a day.

The widespread support amongst UN member states for these Sustainable Development Goals has also led to an enhanced focus on ESG. With ESG gaining further credence with multi-national enterprises it has enabled a number of corporate businesses to find their role in helping to reduce carbon emissions further to the 2015 Paris Climate Change Agreement. Businesses now had the infrastructure within their firms to contribute to these aims and so also meet consumer expectations.

In April 2020, French businesses were part of an advisory group, established by President Emmanuel Macron, which called for investment in green technologies as part of the post COVID-19 recovery plan[62]—an approach endorsed by Macron and German Chancellor, Angela Merkel, the following month.[63] This was yet another indication that even in the midst of a crisis, the concept of long-term economic sustainability had embedded itself in the psyche of decision-makers.

The economic advantages of meeting ESG targets was also exemplified by a 2020 study by AXA Investment Management which studied the impact of the COVID-19 outbreak on firms who took on board the need to address ESG targets and those firms who either paid lip service or were not concerned about ESG.

AXA found that companies with the highest ESG ratings were proven to be more resilient in the coronavirus market crash than those with the lowest ESG ratings. In addition, AXA concluded that a basket of stocks consisting of ESG Leaders outperformed ESG Laggards by 16.8 percentage points in Q1 2020 whilst a basket of bonds consisting of ESG Leaders outperformed ESG Laggards by 5.2 percentage points in the same period.[64]

How, then, does Islamic finance compare with the growth of ESG targets in conventional finance?

From 1998, the practical operation of Islamic finance in respect of its engagement with global markets related to the permissibility criteria of the Dow Jones Islamic Markets Index (DJIMI). Whilst this approach did reflect a breakthrough for ethical financing at that time compared with conventional finance, the climate has now changed and the 2020s could become the era when—at least on paper—conventional finance has higher ethical targets as compared to the strategy adopted by the Islamic finance industry.

However, in 2019, the Bank Negara Malaysia (the central bank of Malaysia), introduced guidance for Islamic financial institutions (IFIs) known as Value Based Intermediation (VBI). This was a values-based document which advised IFIs as to how to develop key performance indicators to meet shari'a standards of good conduct in terms of societal impact:

> The customers' businesses, if not run properly, can be a source of negative impact such as climate risk, biodiversity loss and deforestation, labour and human rights abuse, pollution, corruption etc. either directly or through their supply chain. If not managed well, the issues presented above can contribute to the degradation and depletion of natural and social capital,

> which presents a significant threat to the long-term resilience and growth of businesses and wider economy and society with ramifications on financial institutions.[65]

Dr Ziyood Mahomed of the Malaysian based International Centre for Education in Islamic Finance has expressed concern that the guidance may be seen as a "*philosophical document*"[66] rather than a plan for action. However, once a central bank issues guidance, the need for financial institutions to maintain good relations with that central bank, can lead to its guidance having a discernible impact on financial institutions' daily operations.

Dr Ziyood Mahomed has also stated that "*we need to move from shari'a compliance to substance compliance or shari'a best practice*".[67] The permissibility criteria of Islamic finance would be in danger of being overtaken by the proactive ESG criteria of conventional banks if this advice was not followed.

How this transition is to be achieved is difficult to discern. Monem Salam, the Executive Vice President of the shari'a compliant Saturna Capital has said, for instance, that for his company the "*next step is for our shari'a scholars to consider what it is we want to promote*".[68]

The VBI approach that has been introduced by the Bank Negara Malaysia is a significant step forward in addressing this challenge for the industry. If other jurisdictions which play an important role in Islamic finance, such as in the Gulf, also adopt ESG style criteria for Islamic finance practitioners then these steps—combined with the innovative contract structures which help support patient and project financing—could give the industry a winning edge.

The question, to paraphrase Ziyood, is whether the industry will "*focus on the letter of the law, not the spirit of the law*".[69]

Notes

1. Shamil Bank of Bahrain v Beximco Pharmaceuticals Ltd. (2004) EWCA Civ 1.
2. Harris Irfan, *Heaven's Bankers: Inside the Hidden World of Islamic Finance.*
3. "Review Judgement on Ribā: The Supreme Court of Pakistan (Sharī'at Appellate Bench)." (2002) *Islamic Studies*, vol. 41, no. 4, pp. 705–724.
4. Shamil Bank of Bahrain v Beximco Pharmaceuticals Ltd. (2004) EWCA Civ 1.

5. Ibid.
6. Ibid.
7. Ibid.
8. Senator John Kerry, Senator Hank Brown (December 1992), *The BCCI Affair.*
9. Emmy Abdul Alim, *Global Leaders in Islamic finance*, page 61.
10. Ibid., page 59.
11. *New York Times* (5 January 1989), Cairo Journal; Finance and Islam Mix, Igniting a Mighty Scandal.
12. Islamic Finance News, 15 May 2013.
13. Mit Ghamr Bank is discussed in Chapter 7 and the Malaysian Pilgrims Fund is discussed in Chapter 10.
14. Monzer Kahf, *Islamic Banks: The Rise of a New Power Alliance of Wealth and Shari'ah Scholarship* (2001).
15. Gulf News, 15 April 2020, https://gulfnews.com/world/asia/pakistan/covid-19-pakistan-clerics-call-for-lifting-of-congregational-prayer-limits-1.70988562.
16. https://www.thenews.com.pk/latest/646682-renowed-scholar-mufti-taqi-usmani-welcomes-agreement-on-prayers-during-ramazan.
17. Muhammad Qasim Zaman, *Islam in Pakistan: A History* (Princeton University Press), page 119.
18. Amnesty International, 1995 report, https://www.amnesty.org/download/Documents/172000/asa330231995en.pdf.
19. Sheikh Mufti Taqi Usmani, *The Case of Hudood Ordinances*, January 2016, page 16.
20. Information from the Islamic Finance Information Service.
21. Mufi Muhammad Taqi Usmani, *Sukuk and Their Contemporary Applications*, page 6.
22. Ibid., pages 12–13.
23. As quoted by Emmy Abdul Alim, *Global Leaders in Islamic Finance*, page 175.
24. Rushdi Siddiqui (2007), Shari'ah Compliance, Performance, and Conversion: The Case of the Dow Jones Islamic Market Index, *Chicago Journal of International Law*, vol. 7, no. 2.
25. BBC (11 December 2009), *How Sharia-compliant Is Islamic Banking?*
26. As quoted by Emmy Abdul Alim, *Global Leaders in Islamic Finance*, page 90.
27. Ibid.
28. Ibid.
29. Salaam Gateway, 29 March 2020, https://salaamgateway.com/story/qa-with-amanies-maya-marisa-malek-when-it-comes-to-islamic-finance-women-are-clearly-and-woefully-un.
30. Ibid.

31. AsiaMoney (September 2006), *The Shariah Scholar Cartel*, September 2006.
32. Ibid.
33. As quoted by Emmy Abdul Alim, *Global Leaders in Islamic Finance*, page 151.
34. AsiaMoney (September 2006), *Shariah Scholar Cartel.*
35. Islamic Markets webinar, 12 May 2020.
36. As stated in an Islamic Markets webinar, 6 August 2020.
37. Mit Ghamr is discussed in Chapter 7.
38. Zeyneb Hafsa Orhan, Mitt Ghamr Savings Bank: A Role Model or a Irreplicable Utopia? *Journal of Humanity and Society*, April 2018
39. In this statement, Bakar is dating the start of the contemporary Islamic finance industry with the establishment of Islamic finance in 1975 in the United Arab Emirates (UAE). Further detail regarding the pivotal role of the UAE in the sector can be found in Chapter 10.
40. Islamic Markets webinar, 12 May 2020.
41. As quoted by Emmy Abdul Alim, *Global Leaders in Islamic Finance*, page 66.
42. Abdul Rahman (1983), Putra Al-Haj Something to Remember (Selangor: Malaysia: Eastern Universities Press) page 144.
43. Resolution No 63/1/7 (May 1992), 7th session of the Fiqh Academy, Jeddah.
44. For more on the Sudanese Islamic finance industry please refer to Chapter 10
45. As quoted by Emmy Abdul Alim, *Global Leaders in Islamic Finance*, page 143.
46. Ibid., page 138.
47. Ibid., page 143.
48. Related by Ahmad, hadith No 2221; Abu Dawud, hadith No: 3488; al-Bayhaqi in Al-Sunan al-Kubra, hadith No 11051.
49. Michael McMillan, *Sequelae of the Dow Jones Fatwa and Evolution in Islamic Finance: The Real Estate Investment.*
50. Ibid.
51. Rusdi Siddiqui (2007), Shari'ah Compliance, Performance and Conversion: The case of the Dow Jones Islamic Markets Index, *Chicago Journal of International Law*, vol. 7, no. 2.
52. Ibid.
53. Masudul Alam Choudhury, *Islamic Economics and Finance: An Epistemological Inquiry*, page 134.
54. Tariq Al Rifai as cited in *Contemporary Islamic finance: Innovations, Applications and Best Practice*, edited By Karen Hunt-Ahmed, pages 199–200.
55. Comments made to the National Council for US—Arab Relations, 17 February 2009.

56. The 1997 Asian Financial Crisis and how it impacted the development of the Islamic finance industry is discussed in Chapter 9.
57. Lee, Phil-Sang (31 January 2001), Nightmarish Real Estate Speculation and Currency Crisis. *Korea Times*.
58. Premier of Malaysia Spars with Currency Dealer (22 September 1997), *New York Times*.
59. DeGeorge (1999), *Myth of the Amoral Firm*.
60. Jessica Robinson of Abu Dhabi Global Markets has, for instance, expressed this view, from a personal perspective, during an Islamic Markets webinar as of 19 May 2020.
61. United Nations Environment Programme/Freshfield Bruckhaus Deringer (October 2005), *A Legal Framework for the Integration of Environmental, Social and Governance Issues into Institutional Investment*.
62. Comments were featured in an Islamic Markets webinar of 6 May 2020 by Dr Sami Al Sulwaliem, Director General of the Islamic Research and Training Institute (part of the Islamic Development Bank).
63. Haut Conseil pour le Climat (April 2020), *CLIMAT, SANTÉ : MIEUX PRÉVENIR, MIEUX GUÉRIR*.
64. Joint statement by the French President and German Chancellor, 19 May 2020.
65. AXA Investment Management (April 2020), *Coronavirus: How ESG Scores Equalled Resilience in the Q1 Market Downturn*.
66. Bank Negara Malaysia (November 2019), *Value-Based Intermediation Financing and Investment Impact Assessment Framework*.
67. Islamic Markets webinar, 19 May 2020.
68. Islamic Markets webinar, 3 June 2020.
69. Islamic Markets webinar, 19 May 2020.

CHAPTER 6

Faith and Capitalism

The Role of Faith in Economic Thought

The fictional detective, Sherlock Holmes astounded the flat-footed policemen of New Scotland Yard with his brilliance when he caught the cunning criminals and outsmarted his arch nemesis, Moriarty.

The secret of Holmes' success was, apparently, his ignorance for when told by his faithful assistant, Dr Watson, that the Earth orbits the Sun, Holmes declared:

> Now that I do know it I shall do my best to forget it.
>
> You see … I consider that a man's brain originally is like a little empty attic, and you have to stock it with such furniture as you choose. A fool takes in all the lumber of every sort that he comes across, so that the knowledge which might be useful to him gets crowded out, or at best is jumbled up with a lot of other things, so that he has a difficulty in laying his hands upon it.
>
> Now the skilful workman is very careful indeed as to what he takes into his brain-attic. He will have nothing but the tools which may help him in doing his work, but of these he has a large assortment, and all in the most perfect order. It is a mistake to think that that little room has elastic walls and can distend to any extent. Depend upon it there comes a time when for every addition of knowledge, you forget something that you knew before. It is of the highest importance, therefore, not to have useless facts elbowing out the useful ones.
>
> "But the Solar System!" I protested.

J. S. Watkins, *Islamic Finance and Global Capitalism*,
https://doi.org/10.1007/978-3-030-59840-2_6

> "What the deuce is it to me?" he interrupted impatiently: "you say that we go round the sun. If we went round the moon it would not make a pennyworth of difference to me or to my work."[1]

This fictional conversation can be viewed as a parody of the growing nineteenth-century secularism within Europe and North America. The very idea that understanding the place of humanity in the universe could be considered as unimportant was a mirror to the changing social mores.

Though the United Kingdom was, then, a devoutly Christian country, opinions were being transformed from the old accepted ways of thinking. According to a survey carried out in England and Wales in March 1851, out of a total population of 17,927,609, only 7,261,032 had attended church on any Sunday that month.[2]

During the nineteenth century, Jeremy Bentham and John Stuart Mill spoke of utilitarianism where the utility of any policy is whether it is useful in bringing about the greatest happiness of the greatest number of people. The focus was shifting away from doing good works to claim spiritual salvation in the afterlife to enhancing life chances for the living as a good in and of itself.

Later in the century Nietzche had declared that "*God is dead*" whilst Lenin was on the verge of leading the world's first Communist secular state. Even that arch nineteenth-century capitalist, the American financier, Andrew Carnegie had his doubts about religion and when challenged as to why he was endowing churches with organs, he said he hoped "*the music would distract the audience from the rest of the service*".

Ayn Rand, who as we shall see later in this chapter, critiqued the role of religion as it related to capitalism, could see how the connection sprang up between faith and political economy—whilst ridiculing the connection at the same time:

> No social system can stand for long without a moral base. Project a magnificent skyscraper being built on quick sands: while men are struggling upward to add the hundredth and two-hundredth stories, the tenth and twentieth are vanishing, sucked under by the muck. That is the history of capitalism, of its swaying, tottering attempt to stand erect on the foundation of the altruist morality.[3]

Clearly, the dictum of Sherlock Holmes would have no place in Islamic economics. The belief in faith and its relationship to space and time is the very foundation of Islam and informs the development of Islamic finance concepts.

For instance, when Al-Farabi (872–950) wrote of an ideal city, he saw that an understanding of the stars had as much relevance for daily life as the understanding of a bank account:

> The things in common which all the people of the excellent city ought to know are: (1) In the first place to know the First Cause and all its qualities; (2) then the immaterial existents …; (3) the celestial substances …; (4) then the natural bodies which are beneath them, and how they come to be and pass away …; (5) then the generation of man; (6) then the first ruler …; (7) then the rulers who have to take his place …; (8) then the excellent city and its people and the felicity which their souls ultimately reach ….[4]

However, the difference between the Holmes dictum and Islamic doctrine goes way beyond this for concepts inherent within Islamic economics is ultimately based on the theological conception of the Tawhid.

Tawhid literally means the oneness of God and belief in this concept does not just inform Islamic theological thought but also an understanding as to how the spiritual meaning of life informs everyday conduct.

As for Sherlock Holmes not wanting to know about the universe, far from this helping Holmes in his everyday life, Islamic thought would indicate that an understanding of daily life cannot be fully attained without a learned spiritual dimension.

The acclaimed American novelist and essayist, Marilynne Robinson, made a similar point where not just faith but also culture and history are said to be required to fully understand economic processes:

> We have been optimised by competition and environment, we are shaped by economic forces and means of production, we are inheritors of a primal guilt, we are moulded by experiences of frustration and reinforcement. These are all assertions that have shaped modern thought. But they are not to be reconciled with one another. The Freudian neurasthenic is not the Darwinian primate, who is not the Marxist proletarian, who is not the behaviourists' organism available to being moulded by a regime of positive and negative sensory experience. To acknowledge an element of truth in each of these models is to reject the claims of descriptive sufficiency made by all of them. What they do have in common, beside the claim to sufficiency, is an exclusion of the testimonies of culture and history.[5]

There are some sweeping assertions as articulated by Robinson, for commonalities of thought have been analysed between the works of Freud, Darwin and Marx. However, Robinson was able to ridicule the concept that full understanding can be attained without recourse to religion, culture and history.

From a completely different perspective, the accounting specialist, Professor Trevor Gambling, also argued that culture cannot be discounted when analysing economic processes:

> Accounting theory and culture are not readily separable and that accounting theory is culture, at least in the anthropological sense.[6]

This takes us back to the concept of Tawhid.

Within the concept of the oneness of God are a series of layered concepts. Tawhid al-Rububiyyah refers to Allah being the sole creator. Tawhid al-Uluhiyyah relates to only Allah being worshipped and not any other deity or series of deities. Finally, in Sunni Islam, there is asma al-husna where Allah's meaning cannot be extended by rational human thought.

However, as we discussed in Chapter 2, the different jurisprudence schools within Islam approach the issue of human rationality and the oneness of God in similar but in differentiated ways whilst with Shi'a Islam, in particular, there is also a focus on the role of the intellect (aql).

A number of Shi'a scholars during the period of the Safavid dynasty, particularly during the seventeenth century, argued that God had the ability to change His mind (bada) as God could respond to human events which had occurred due to people having free will. This concept was embraced by the theocratic regime which gained power in Iran following the 1979 revolution.

Ayatollah Morteza Motahhari (1920–1979) argued that bada enabled a greater understanding of free will:

> In Islam there is an issue called bada' (revision). The concept of bada' has an apparent meaning which few would regard as acceptable. Some have even criticised the Shi'a for believing in bada'. The meaning of bada' is revision in Divine Destiny (qada'), meaning that God has not fixed a definite and final form for the course of human history. In other words, God Says to man: "You yourselves are in charge of the fulfilment of Divine Destiny, and it is you who can advance, stop or reverse the course of

> history." There is no blind determinism either on the part of nature or the means of life or from the viewpoint of Divine Destiny, to rule over history.[7]

Therefore, Tawhid—through the concept of the oneness of God—enables a broader understanding of human free will and humanity's place in the university. This enables our daily individual actions to be informed by a higher good. It is in that context that Islamic economics and the practical applicability of Islamic finance has been viewed.

Islam, in many ways, is a very disciplined faith in the sense that there is a clear framework of worship which relates to daily life such as prayer directed towards the holy city of Mecca five times a day, fasting during the daytime during the holy month of Ramadan (if a person's health allows this), the obligation to spend discretionary income for charitable purposes (zakat) and, if a person can afford to do so and has the health to undertake such a task, to pay homage to God on the pilgrimage to Mecca at least once in their life (Hajj).

Islamic finance fits within this credo of religion informing all aspects of life—from prayer to parity ratios. Islamic finance scholars have emphasised the point that outward prayer is not enough to fully fulfil the requirements of the faith.

As we have already learnt from earlier chapters in this book, the subtleties and flexibilities of Islamic finance, whilst operating within the religious framework, demonstrates the faith and the practice of Islamic finance to be open and inclusive.

This openness contradicts the "*clash of civilisations*" narrative which the American political scientist, Samuel Huntington derived when referring to Western thought and how it related to Islam.[8] In fact, we can see in Islamic finance, for instance, considerable synergies between Islamic finance and mutualism in financial services (this theme is explored further in Chapter 9).

Far from Islam being an inward-looking faith, as Huntington claimed, the very essence of the religion is based upon continual learning. One verse of the Qur'ran reflects this very concept:

> Had We sent down this Qur'ran on a mountain, you would surely have seen it humbling itself and rent asunder by the fear of Allah. Such are the parables which We put forward to mankind that they may reflect.[9]

This verse, whilst pointing to an underlying truth, encourages an openness of debate and learning, which is reflected in the scholarly debates which takes place within contemporary Islamic finance and which contradicts rival narratives of the religion as not being open to outside influences and studious learning.

Al-Ghazali (1058–1111) can assist our understanding further as to how the concept of Tawhid impacts on the underlying philosophical tenets in Islamic finance.

Al-Ghazali was born in Persia (modern Iran) and is known as a Mujjaddid—an individual who helped renew the faith with the growth in the number of adherents and a growing acceptance of the spirituality of Islam.

Al-Ghazali was a senior adviser to the vizier of the Islamic caliphate, Nizam al-Mulik. However, in around 1095, Al-Ghazali left the Royal Court at Baghdad, ostensibly to go on pilgrimage to Mecca. In reality, Al-Ghazali was reassessing his core beliefs and for many years he led an ascetic life where he reflected and developed concepts as an Islamic scholar. His legacy, today, is reflected in the Shafi'i school of fiqh (jurisprudence).

One of the key insights that Al-Ghazali developed, which resonates with the emergence of Islamic finance, is the idea of the interdependence between God and the world. Al-Ghazali rejected the notion held by other Islamic scholars at that time that God was a cause ('illa) of the world and no more.

Al-Ghazali went beyond this idea and argued that God uses knowledge which becomes the blueprint of creation. This leads to causes and effects. The nature of a fire means it emits light and if a fire did not emit light then, in turn, it is not a fire. What would now be considered a Cartesian turn of thought was prefigured by Al-Ghazali.

In fact, Al-Ghazali enlarges the potential for human understanding. This can be seen in response to Aristotle's understanding of the modalities as to what is deemed necessary, possible or impossible.

Aristotle argued there were clear suppositions that had to be accepted in order to make sense of the world:

> Whatever is and always will be true is necessarily true … once we grant … the highly plausible principle that if something is true, then it can be false if and only if it can come to be false. For example, assume it true that the sun is and always will be hot. No proposition of this form can ever come to be false. Hence this proposition cannot be false. Hence it is

> necessarily true, and so too is anything that follows from it. In particular, it is necessarily true that the sun is hot. Moreover, if the sun not only is and always will be hot, but also always has been, it follows by similar reasoning that the sun not only cannot now fail to be hot, but also never could have failed. Anything everlastingly true is therefore, in the strictest sense of the term, necessarily true.[10]

Al-Ghazali's response to this reasoning is to enlarge the possibilities which really exist:

> Anything whose existence the mind supposes, (nothing) preventing its supposing it possible, we call 'possible', and if it is prevented we call it 'impossible'. If (the mind) is unable to suppose its non-existence, we name it 'necessary'. For these are rational propositions that do not require an existent so as to be rendered a description thereof.[11]

As we now know, Al-Ghazali's reasoning in challenging Aristotle's propositions of modalities was correct. Physicists have demonstrated that far from the Sun always being a constant, as Aristotle implied, it will in fact cease to exist—in 5 billion years' time. If we consider another example, the concept of quantum mechanics in science is blowing away established preconceptions.

Consequently, Al-Ghazali has shown how religious thought can help to expand the mind's horizons whilst, he would have argued, operate within the ethical and disciplined framework of Islam. This brings us back again to Tawhid where the development of practical concepts, such as Islamic finance, also fits within this broader perspective. For Al-Ghazali also made the following observation between the practical and theoretical:

> Whoever combines both virtues, the epistemological and the practical, is the worshipping 'knower', the absolutely blissful one. Whoever has the epistemological virtue but not the practical is the knowledgeable (believing) sinner who will be tormented for a period, which (torment) will not last because his soul had been perfected through knowledge but bodily occurrences had tarnished (it) in an accidental manner opposed to the substance of the soul ... He who has practical virtue but not epistemological is saved and delivered but does not attain perfect bliss.[12]

This leads to the conclusions that writers, such as Choudhury, has reached when it is argued that learning, including in the field of Islamic finance, helps inform spiritual growth:

> The Hereafter is the only 'optimal' state of the events and knowledge – time – space relationships that can be attained out of the endless labyrinth of evolutionary learning experiences. Such learning experiences arise as processes of advancing consciousness from, and moving toward, Tawhid in the 'End as in the Beginning'.[13]

Vice-Regency (khalifah): The Islamic Perspective of the Position of Humanity

When HSBC Bank named its Islamic finance 'window', Amanah, a superficial reading of this branding would relate to the translation of this Arabic word to meant trust. So, is not the brand of HSBC Amanah simply encouraging customers to trust the bank?

In fact, the term Amanah has a deeper theological meaning which relates to the concept that humanity acts as the vice-regency for God.

The concept of vice-regency or khalifah can be seen in the Qur'ran with the story of the first human on Earth, Adam. It is made clear that this concept of vice-regency is a central tenet for humanity.

It is worth considering in full the verses which addresses Adam as a vice-regent on Earth before we analyse the implications of these verses:

> And remember when God said to the angels: 'I shall appoint a deputy on earth,' and they answered: 'Will you place therein one who sows discord and sheds blood while we chant Your praises and proclaim Your holiness?'.
>
> God said: 'I know what you do not'.
>
> He taught Adam the names of all things. Then He displayed them to the angels and said: 'Tell me the names of these things, if you are truthful'.
>
> They said: 'Glory be to You! We have no knowledge except what You taught us. You! You are All-Knowing, All-Wise'.
>
> God said: 'O Adam, reveal to them their names'. When Adam revealed their names, God said: 'Did I not tell you that I know the Unseen of the heavens and earth? That I know what you make public and what you hide?'.[14]

These verses speak directly to the concept of free will including the potential for individuals to do harm as well as to fulfil good deeds. The verses also relate to the concepts of the oneness of God whilst humanity is given responsibility over the material realm to act in a trusteeship position on Earth.

The concept of free will continues in the story of Adam when we consider the description of Satan enticing Adam and his wife to breach God's strictures:

> We said: 'O Adam, inhabit the Garden, you and your wife. Eat from it in comfort and ease, wherever you wish. But do not come near this tree, or else you will transgress'. Satan seduced them away from it and caused them to leave their earlier abode.
>
> We said: 'Go down, an enemy each to each! On earth you will find habitation and a certain term of life'.
>
> And Adam obeyed the words of his Lord, and his Lord pardoned him. He is Ever-Ready to pardon; He is compassionate to each.[15]

This, again, emphasises the concept of free will and God's forgiveness for sins transgressed if individuals seek redemption through God. Therefore, the Fall from the Garden of Eden is transformed into the concept of vice-regency or trusteeship of humanity on Earth.

This is in contrast to the Christian story of Adam and Eve as, instead of forgiveness, the Christian concept of original sin is derived:

> The LORD God said, "Who told you that you were naked? Have you eaten fruit from the tree I commanded you not to eat from?"
>
> The man said, "It's the fault of the woman you put here with me. She gave me some fruit from the tree. And I ate it."
>
> Then the LORD God said to the woman, "What have you done?"
>
> The woman said, "The serpent tricked me. That's why I ate the fruit."
>
> So the LORD God spoke to the serpent. He said, "Because you have done this,"
>
> "You are set apart from all livestock
> and all wild animals.
> I am putting a curse on you.
> You will crawl on your belly.
> You will eat dust
> all the days of your life.
> I will make you and the woman hate each other.
> Your children and her children will be enemies.
> Her son will crush your head.

> And you will bite his heel."
>
> The LORD God said to the woman,
>
> "I will increase your pain when you give birth.
> You will be in great pain when you have children.
> You will long for your husband.
> And he will rule over you."
>
> The LORD God said to Adam, You listened to your wife's suggestion. You ate fruit from the tree I warned you about. I said, 'You must not eat its fruit.'
>
> "So I am putting a curse on the ground because of what you did.
> All the days of your life you will have to work hard.
> It will be painful for you to get food from the ground. You will eat plants from the field,
> even though the ground produces thorns and prickly weeds.
> You will have to work hard and sweat a lot
> to produce the food you eat.
> You were made out of the ground.
> You will return to it when you die.
> You are dust,
> and you will return to dust."
>
> Adam named his wife Eve. She would become the mother of every living person.[16]

It is necessary to elucidate the differences between the Muslim and Christian narratives of Adam and Eve as we can see that in the Muslim version, the concept of free will, God's pardon through individuals seeking forgiveness for sins committed and the trusteeship of humanity on Earth has contributed to the concept of khalifah.

Within Christianity there continues to be a debate as to the consequences of the belief in original sin. Pelagius (360–420) argued that the sins of Adam and Eve did not impact on all of humanity except in the sense that Adam and Eve had set a bad example. Saint Augustine (354–430) stressed that humanity was seminally present in Adam and Eve and all of humanity sinned accordingly. This was a view that was later endorsed by the French Protestant reformer, Jean Calvin (1509–1564).

Catholicism, on the other hand, had put forward the belief that original righteousness was lost in that moment in the Garden of Eden thereby leaving humanity in its natural state but that salvation can be gained by the actions of individuals.

Jonathan Edwards (1703–1758), whose theological work was part of the religious movement subsequently known as the Great Awakening, which shaped the American practices of Christianity, argued that individuals were born free—a view at odds with Calvin. In his final work, which was prepared months before his death, Edwards articulated the view that individuals were born free by reverting back to the story of Adam and Eve:

> And I am persuaded, no solid reason can be given, why God, who constitutes all other created union or oneness, according to his pleasures … may not establish a constitution whereby the natural posterity of Adam, proceeding from him, much as the buds or branches from the stock or root of a tree, shall be treated as one with him.[17]

However, the Augustinian perspective was popularised by the English poet, John Milton (1608–1674) in his seminal work, *Paradise Lost*:

> Of Man's first disobedience, and the fruit
> Of that forbidden tree, whose mortal taste
> Brought death into the world, and all our
> woe,
> With loss of Eden …

The Augustinian concept of original sin was ridiculed by Ayn Rand (1905–1982)—seen by many as the intellectual eminence grise of contemporary American capitalism:

> What is the nature of the guilt that your teachers call Original Sin? What are the evils man acquired when he fell from a state they consider perfection? Their myth declares that he ate the fruit of the tree of knowledge — he acquired a mind and became a rational being. It was the knowledge of good and evil — he became a moral being. He was sentenced to earn his bread by his labour — he became a productive being. He was sentenced to experience desire — he acquired the capacity of sexual enjoyment. The evils for which they damn him are reason, morality, creativeness, joy — all the cardinal values of his existence. It is not his vices that their myth of

> man's fall is designed to explain and condemn, it is not his errors that they hold as his guilt, but the essence of his nature as man. Whatever he was — that robot in the Garden of Eden, who existed without mind, without values, without labour, without love — he was not man.[18]

As we will explore further, Rand's opposition to established religion shaped her view as to the ideal form of capitalism.

Whilst Christianity's version of the Adam and Eve narrative has led to internal introspection as to the meaning and consequences of original sin, the khalifah concept can be seen as more outward facing by projecting a trusteeship model for humanity.

Consequently, khalifah has been cited as being instrumental as to how the Islamic finance industry should conduct itself. For example, in 2019, the central bank of Malaysia issued guidance to Islamic finance institutions (IFIs) as to good conduct which has synergies with the concept of environmental, social and governance key performance indicators in conventional finance.

In the Malaysian central bank guidance, it specifically referred to the concept of vice-regency for IFIs to be fully cognisant of:

> Any financing and investment activities undertaken by the IFI would be evaluated against this premise of benefit and harm. This premise is entrenched in the requirements of Islam and is reflected in the application of Shariah. The concept of "vicegerency" on the earth is well articulated in the Quran and the teachings of Islam, which has explicitly entrusted to humankind (the believers) the custodianship of all resources of the earth (water, food, land, energy, animals and etc.) and prescribed certain rights and rules regarding the social interactions between humans and their activities. This is very much in line with the concept of sustainability and triple bottom-line (people, planet and profit).[19]

Abul A'la Maududi (1903–1979)[20] highlighted the concept of khalifah whilst he also spoke of the '*popular vice-regency*' concept where governments gain support for their trusteeship role via the support of the people. As Bannerman stated, this was

> .... an attempt to assimilate the principles of Western democratic representative government which does little more than add a little flesh to the bones of earlier formulations.[20]

If we go back to our earlier discussion of the term, Amanah, we can now see that it is inherently linked to khalifah as God had placed trust in humanity to act responsibly:

> We did indeed offer the trust *(amanah)* to the heavens and the earth and the mountains. But they refused to undertake it, being afraid thereof; but man undertook it – he was indeed unjust and foolish (ignorant that some may betray it).[21]

The Sudanese scholar, Jaafar Sheikh Idris, has argued that incorrect interpretations of khalifah has taken hold that has led some people to interpret this concept as less of a trusteeship role and more as a "*master of this world*".[22] This is an intriguing thought which may influence future debates as to how best practice in the Islamic finance industry should be viewed and how Islamic economics relates to concepts pertaining to environmental sustainability. As we shall see in Chapter 9 the concept of khalifah is shaping—to some extent—contemporary business practices in the Islamic finance industry.

Islamic Finance: Faith and Its Critics

A note of caution is required at this stage in our discussion. Though Islamic finance has so much to offer in terms of lessons and practices that can be adopted in the wider financial services space, and whilst Islamic finance is developing into a political economic structure in its own right in a number of countries in the Persian Gulf, east Africa, south Asia and south east Asia, it would be wrong to ignore the synergies that Islamic finance has with other financial models across the world.[23]

For the purposes of this chapter, we should also not take for granted the statements from Islamic scholars that Islamic economics and Islamic finance is uniquely best placed to challenge the concepts of conventional capitalism.

Despite the claims by scholars, such as Taqi Usmani and Khurshid Ahmad, for example, that Islamic economics is a direct challenge to contemporary capitalism, these statements seem to be predicated on the belief that there is only one form of capitalism that is dominant in the world. In fact, there are communitarian forms of capitalism that has been highly successful in countries such as the city state of Singapore or the economic giant that is Japan.

However, a number of Islamic scholars do not seem to recognise this variety in capitalist structures but instead focus on capitalism as an atavistic activity with the emphasis on the here and now and the selfish needs of the individual but with no focus on the long term needs of the economy and the community as a whole.

Choudhury summed up this thinking when he wrote despairingly of what he called the 'liberal world-system':

> Among the kind of artifacts influenced by rationalism and economic rationalism are markets (micro), economy (macro), institutions (policy) and the political economy (world-system). In all such artifacts, competing behaviour, marginality concepts and scarcity of resources silence the process dynamics of real forms of social reconstruction. The result is that morality, ethics and values cannot be introduced as endogenous forces to explain exchange relations and the inherent decision-making.[24]

A number of commentators in Europe and North America, who are not familiar with the concepts of Islamic economics and Islamic finance, would have concurred with at least part of this analysis. Whilst there would be a difference of view as to the benefits of a liberal approach to society, the concept of the rapacious capitalist would be a shared motif. This characterisation is also portrayed in cultural settings.

J B Priestley's play, *An Inspector Calls*, for example, mocks the aloof attitudes of capitalists:

> Well it's my duty to keep labour costs down, and if I'd agreed to this demand for a new rate we'd have added about twelve per cent to our labour costs. Does that satisfy you? So I refused. Said I couldn't consider it. We were paying the usual rates and if they didn't like those rates, they could go and work somewhere else. It's a free country, I told them.

So spoke the businessman, Mr Birling who showed scant interest in the desperate living conditions of his workers when speaking to the mysterious inspector.

Priestley was writing in 1945 with the United Kingdom having been devastated with the impact on lives, homes and infrastructure—as well as victorious—with the end of the Second World War and the election of a socialist Labour Government replacing the wartime leadership of Winston Churchill.

The play is an allegory of the ethical socialist values of the inspector and the selfish capitalist values of the businessman. This is a perspective that is shared by some on the Left of politics and by some Islamic scholars.

However with a proper analysis of political economy, the nature of capitalism across the world is far more complex than this. In the United States, we could describe a form of laissez-faire capitalism where, despite the debate between Republicans and Democrats on health care, the role of the state is limited in the economy, as compared to European style capitalism where the state's role in national life is more significant, and the focus is geared towards shareholder value.

In Europe we could define the form of capitalism as stakeholder capitalism with the emphasis on long term investment, a role for stakeholders such as trade union representatives on works councils and a significant role for the state in the economy. It is within this context that that the European Union has propagated the concept of a "*Social Europe*" where workplace rights have significant prominence alongside the liberalisation of markets.

Whether, in fact, social rights have as much significance as there is with the focus on free markets within the EU is another story and is outside the purview of this book. Nonetheless, as the 2019 *gilet jaune* or yellow vest demonstrations have shown in France, any move towards liberalisation, as was being propagated by President Emmanuel Macron, would face severe public opposition.

It has been argued by some on the Left and by some Islamic scholars that laissez-faire capitalism is merely informed by concepts of efficiency. For instance, Ibrahim M Abu-Rabi (1956–2011) argued that there was a distinct difference between religious identity and culture as compared to Western forms of capitalism:

> We cannot compare a normative civilization (Islamic worldview) to a concrete and historically present civilization; that is, the global capitalist civilization. That is to say that it is impossible to fathom modern global identity outside the rubric of capitalism. We cannot view religious identity outside the domination of the capitalist system. Capitalists (proponents of a capitalist civilization) can be found all over the world, including the Muslim world, and class conflict still defines social relations. Furthermore, the Muslim world, unlike Europe, has failed to develop its capitalist system in the modern period and has thus become dependent on the world capitalist system, which has been pioneered by the West. The Muslim world has culture but lacks its own distinctive civilization.[25]

For some of the left and for a number of people inspired by Islamic economics, the concept of this form of laissez-faire capitalism may have been exemplified by the words of one its leading advocates—Margaret Thatcher (1925–2013). As the UK Prime Minister, Thatcher not only championed laissez-faire economics and relished the fight against the Left but also spoke against the idea of society:

> There is no such thing as society. There are individual men and women, and there are families. And no government can do anything except through people, and people must look to themselves first.[26]

One of Thatcher's successors as Conservative Party leader and UK Prime Minister, Boris Johnson, distanced himself from this infamous statement when, speaking at the height of the 2020 COVID-19 outbreak (with a focus on the integral role of public sector and retail workers) Johnson declared "*there really is such a thing as society*".[27]

It should be noted, though, that Thatcher's belief in individualism was not just based on an economic premise but was also based on religion. This may seem surprising to some as during her time as Prime Minister, Thatcher was in conflict with the Bishop of Durham, David Jenkins, who condemned "*trickle down*" economics in 1984 and later in 1985 when the Church of England produced a report that stated that poverty was a factor in the 1981 urban riots. One of Thatcher's Cabinet Ministers told the media at that time that the report was "*pure Marxist theology*".[28]

It would be wrong to suppose that laissez-faire economics, as has been suggested, is not informed by faith. In fact, the contrary is the case. Thatcher referred to the influence of faith on her politics:

> Although I have always resisted the argument that a Christian has to be a Conservative, I have never lost my conviction that there is a deep and providential harmony between the kind of political economy I favour and the insights of Christianity.[29]

Therefore, the concept of faith shaping political economy goes beyond the concept of Islamic economics and Islamic finance and impinges on the operation of conventional models of market economics.

Far from the idea that Thatcher's belief that "*there is no such thing as society*" was purely driven by economic concepts, in fact, the laissez-faire approach to economics was informed directly by faith.

As discussed in Chapter 2, there are synergies between the supply side economics of Thatcher and Reagan, as adopted in the 1980s, with the thought of the early Islamic thinkers such as Ibn Taymiyyah, Abu Yusuf, Al-Dimashqi and Ibn Khaldun—with the latter being quoted approvingly by Ronald Reagan.[30]

Nonetheless, the focus of Thatcher and Reagan on the primacy of the individual, whilst based upon religious thought, is clearly distinct from the communitarian principles which underpin Islamic finance.

Margaret Thatcher acknowledged her gratitude to her father, Alfred Roberts, for the development of her political thought. Roberts was a Methodist Christian lay preacher and this form of Christianity emphasises the need for self-reliance, belief in faith and good works to attain salvation (Methodism also inspired financial mutual models).

The Church of England, meanwhile, in the late twentieth century and early twenty-first century had a more ecumenical approach towards society and faith. As the current Archbishop of Canterbury, Justin Welby, has put it:

> It's my belief that the values we find in our Christian heritage – compassion, generosity and solidarity, to name a few – offer a source of hope and wisdom for Britain in the 21st century, even as we rightly embrace who we are becoming as a multi-faith and multi-cultural society.[31]

In particular, Welby praised the liberal economist, John Maynard Keynes, as an example to guide nations away from the path that led to the 2008 financial crisis:

> Now we must find an approach to economic justice that works in fair weather and foul, but that will require brilliance, vision and political leadership. Another Keynes is needed. It is only within such a global system that it is possible for individuals, businesses and societies to dethrone Mammon, and to give all for the pearl of great price.[32]

One can only imagine how Margaret Thatcher, who helped to end the Keynesian political consensus in the UK, would have responded to this statement.

Thatcher, during her premiership, was influenced by the American Catholic thinker, Michael Novak. In his 1982 book, *The Spirit of Democratic Capitalism,* Novak argued that spiritual growth and liberty was connected to the freedom of the market:

> three dynamic and converging systems functioning as one: a democratic polity, an economy based on markets and incentives, and a moral-cultural system which is pluralistic and, in the largest sense, liberal.[33]

Consequently, Novak argued, free markets enabled liberty to flourish:

> The spirit of democratic capitalism is the spirit of development, experiment, adventure. It surrenders present security for future betterment. In differentiating the economic system from the state, it introduced a novel pluralism into the very centre of the social system.

As for the spiritual dimension of laissez-faire economics, Novak argued that other forms of political economy create unwieldy bureaucracies where the individual loses control and is not able to strive to meet their spiritual needs:

> To look upon history as love-infused by a Creator who values others as others... is to glimpse a world in which the political economy of democratic capitalism makes sense.[34]

However, it should be noted there was another intellectual tradition which informed the nature of contemporary American capitalism. Ayn Rand's seminal work, *Atlas Shrugged*, spoke to the moral benefits of individualism. Rand argued that each individual is an end in her/himself and each person must exist for their own sake, neither sacrificing individuality to others nor sacrificing others to an individual. The pursuit of a person's own rational self-interest and of their own happiness is the highest moral purpose of a person's life.

This concept of objectivism led Rand to advocate for laissez-faire capitalism as the ideal form of political economy when it comes to attaining liberty and freedom.

Rand argued that religion led people to give up their individuality:

> The good, say the mystics of spirit, is God, a being whose only definition is that he is beyond man's power to conceive — a definition that invalidates

> man's consciousness and nullifies his concepts of existence. ... Man's mind, say the mystics of spirit, must be subordinated to the will of God. ... Man's standard of value, say the mystics of spirit, is the pleasure of God, whose standards are beyond man's power of comprehension and must be accepted on faith ... The purpose of man's life ... is to become an abject zombie who serves a purpose he does not know, for reasons he is not to question.[35]

Interestingly, the Iraqi Shi'a cleric, Mohammed Baqir Al Sadr (1935–1980), who may not have been aware of Rand's work, also identified the desire for freedom in 'Western' forms of capitalism:

> Freedom has played a major role in the European economy. It has been possible for the process of development to benefit from the deep rooted feeling for freedom, independence and individuality pervading the Europeans in the success of the free economy, as a device which is compatible with the deep rooted inclinations and ideas of the European peoples.[36]

Despite these seemingly warm words, Al Sadr saw moral decay in this approach towards the economy:

> The absence of any feeling of moral responsibility was a basic precondition in many of the activities which were part of the process of development. And all of us know that it was the deep feeling of freedom which prepared the ground for the fulfilment of this precondition.[37]

It is fascinating to see the symmetry and the disconnect between Rand and Al Sadr. Both speak of the economic benefits of individuality but whilst Rand reached the conclusion that this was a moral good, Al Sadr reached the conclusion that individuality was the flip side of the coin which equated to selfishness.

Al Sadr also wrote that European forms of capitalism was not informed by religion—a statement which, as we have discovered in this chapter, is far from the case. It is this misconception combined with the collectivist approach that is inherent in Islam, as it is in many of the world's great religions, that may have led Al Sadr to reach the conclusions that he did. As we will see in Chapter 10, Al Sadr's approach to the economy, when reflected within the Iranian context, turned out to be incremental rather than radical.

As for Ayn Rand, her work influenced a generation of American public figures. For example, Alan Greenspan, Chairman of the Federal Reserve from 1987 to 2006 said that he had found Rand's analysis to be "*compelling*" but indicated he subsequently questioned some of the underlying assumptions. Paul Ryan, Speaker of the US House of Representatives from 2015 to 2019 argued that "*in almost every fight we are involved in here, on Capitol Hill .... it is a fight that usually comes down to one conflict: individualism versus collectivism*".[38]

Therefore for the Islamic finance industry, whose values are based not just on religion but on a form of collectivism and mutual responsibility, the ideas of Rand would seem to be contradictory to Islamic economics and is a philosophical challenge as to whether political economic models should foster a sense of community—or whether the term 'community' is really a front for collectivism thereby inhibiting individual liberty.

The concept of asabiyya challenges the Rand critique of collectivism. Asabiyya, which means to bind or tie together, is a concept that emphasises how individuals within the collective can effectively fulfil their personal objectives. Ibn Khaldun (1332–1406) wrote that asabiyya as a concept described the ability for peoples to advance their ambitions through a shared collective effort.

Ibn Khaldun recognised how such trends can lead to the successful dominant group detaching itself from the original motivating force for success leading to a more sedentary approach towards life. Nonetheless, asabiyyah can also motivate individual growth within the solidarity of a wider community.

A hadith states that the Prophet described the term asabiyyah in a holistic fashion:

> It was reported by Ibn Majah from the father of Fusaylah, that the Prophet, peace be upon him, was asked whether the love for one's own qawm (group, tribe or nation) constituted under the meaning of 'asabiyah. He replied: "No! 'asabiyah is rather the helping of one's qawm in *(facing)* zulm (injustice)."[39]

It could be argued that asabiyyah has synergies with the concept of social capital, particularly as articulated by the American political scientist, Robert Putnam:

> Whereas physical capital refers to physical objects and human capital refers to the properties of individuals, social capital refers to connections among individuals – social networks and the norms of reciprocity and trustworthiness that arise from them. In that sense social capital is closely related to what some have called "civic virtue." The difference is that "social capital" calls attention to the fact that civic virtue is most powerful when embedded in a sense network of reciprocal social relations. A society of many virtuous but isolated individuals is not necessarily rich in social capital.[40]

The advantage of the asabiyyah concept, from the branding perspective, is that as there are synergies between the concepts of asabiyyah and social capital, this can lever in investors who want to invest their funds in a socially responsible way, whilst having a positive impact on the world. For instance, the Hong Kong tycoon, Li Ka-shing, who has described his family office which invests in goods works, as his "*third son*" has praised the concept of social capital:

> Social capital is the key. Its assets of empathy, compassion, trust, shared values, community involvement, volunteerism, social networks and citizenship have quantifiable value. These assets can be measured.[41]

Therefore, the reach that Islamic finance can have in terms of actively championing the assabiyah concept could be very significant.

Al Khaldun's analysis of asabiyyah has been considered in the context of realist thought in international relations where there is a framework to analyse why countries grow in power and a decline in that nation's fortunes is later witnessed.

From a political economy perspective, Al Khaldun's insight would indicate that a collectivist approach is required for economic advancement—a repudiation of the individualist construct as advocated by Rand and other laissez-faire thinkers.

Faith and Conventional Finance

Thatcher's nemesis when it came to economics, John Maynard Keynes (whose theory of interest is discussed in Chapter 8) was also influenced by faith. Keynes' father was a Dissenter (a Christian Protestant belief which had broken away from the established Church of England) and whilst working at Cambridge University, the ethos of the campus was shaped by Christian Anglicanism.

It was G E Moore's *Principia Ethica* which is said to have informed Keynes' formative years particularly between 1903 and 1906. The book was based on Christian teaching and examined philosophy from a communitarian perspective. Keynes used biblical language to describe the impact the book had on his thinking:

> It was exciting, exhilarating, the beginning of a new renaissance, the opening of a new heaven on earth.[42]

Therefore when questions are raised regarding the linkage of Islam to Islamic finance, we can see that faith has always influenced a wide range of contemporary economic debates—including the ongoing political debates in Europe and North America regarding the merits or otherwise of Keynesian economics as opposed to monetarism.

The concept of free markets and individual freedom being endowed with faith has also been reflected by the Australian philosopher, J L Mackie (1917–1981) who argued that God ensured individual freedom to realise each person could reach their full spiritual potential. Mackie made this insight in the context of the debate within and between religions as to why evil exists in the world:

> If there is no logical impossibility in a man's freely choosing the good on one, or on several occasions, there cannot be a logical impossibility in his freely choosing the good on every occasion. God was not, then, faced with a choice between making innocent automata and making beings who in acting freely, would sometimes go wrong: there was open to him the obviously better possibility of making beings who would act freely but always go right. Clearly his failure to avail himself of this possibility is inconsistent with his being both omnipotent and wholly good.[43]

Therefore, the link was inherently made between the concept of open markets and morality via the religious concept that God has given people the freedom to make moral and just decisions and choices.

However, this understanding amongst a number of Christian thinkers seemingly conflicted with the thoughts of Saint Thomas Aquinas (1225–1274). The Catholic Church respected Aquinas' analysis for centuries as the bridge between Catholic teaching and ancient Greek philosophical thought until the science of physics challenged many of the underlying scientific assumptions made by Aristotle.

Aquinas argued that people were totally reliant on the existence of God:

> Just as God not only gave being to things when they first began, but is also - as the conserving cause of being - the cause of their being as long as they last … so he not only gave things their operative powers when they were first created, but is also always the cause of these in things. Hence if this divine influence stopped, every operation would stop. Every operation, therefore, of anything is traced back to him as its cause.[44]

This statement by Aquinas caused some pause for thought. For if God is accountable for all human actions does that mean that God is responsible for all evil actions as well as all good actions? In a market economy, are selfish actions from some market participants at the expense of enabling a sustainable economy to flourish really part of God's plan?

Saint Paul seemed perplexed as to this dichotomy:

> Oh, the depth of the riches both of the wisdom and knowledge of God! How unsearchable are his judgements and his ways past finding out.[45]

The Catholic theologian, Herbert McCabe (1926–2001) did address this issue by arguing that God enabled people to make choices—not that God made the choices in and of Himself:

> The creative causal power of God does not operate on me from outside, as an alternative to me; it is the creative causal power of God that makes me me.

McCabe emphasised this very point with the pithy statement:

> We are not free in spite of God, but because of God.[46]

Greenstone considered this debate by examining the religious and ethical motivations of the founding fathers of the United States and how there was a tension as to how to develop a society and economy that enabled the individual to flourish, as was forcefully advocated by Thomas Jefferson (1743–1826), or whether an economic and constitutional structure should be established to help enable citizens to reach their full potential, as argued for by John Adams (1735–1826):

> Given Jefferson's belief in negative liberty and tranquillity, the Virginian placed less emphasis than Adams on the possibilities for fundamental changes in individuals. On Jefferson's humanist liberal view, education and experience would surely help the individual to pursue his or her goals more effectively. Even without assistance, however, all normal individuals could be trusted to identify their own goals - that is, to define happiness for themselves - but also act altruistically where appropriate. For Adams, however, his belief in a positive side of liberty did not just allow but required the active improvement of oneself and others through assiduous emancipation from the passions and systematic cultivation of the faculties.[47]

Therefore in the United States, seen by many commentators as the home of free markets, the categorisation of capitalism as a selfish creed does not pass muster when we consider the debates that took place and continue to take place in the United States on the nature of the state and the future direction of capitalism. The differences between Adams and Jefferson on the empowering role of the individual reflected these religious and philosophical tensions within the early body politic of the United States.

It should be noted, though, that the debate between Jefferson and Adams on liberty and economic efficacy was taken within a context where thousands of African American people were bound into slavery. Though slavery was formally abolished following the end of the American Civil War in 1865, institutional discrimination continued for decades afterwards. Debate was revived around the existence of institutional discrimination in the United States and across the world following the death of George Floyd in Minneapolis in May 2020.

The different perspectives of the Founding Fathers of the United States highlight how it would be wrong to stereotype American capitalism, let alone other forms of capitalism, as an established economic system purely focused on the individual with no thought offered as to the consequences for society.

There has been changes in economic direction from the communitarian *New Deal* of President Franklin Delano Roosevelt in the 1930s through to the influence of the economist, Milton Friedman, shaping the reduction of the size of the state and a focus on individual liberty and entrepreneurship under President Ronald Reagan during the 1980s.

Religion, though, was also a factor in shaping Reagan's thinking. When President Reagan, in 1980, spoke of the United States as a "*shining city*" on a hill to inspire the world this was a direct reference to the parable of Salt and Light in Jesus' Sermon on the Mount from the Gospel of Matthew.

The concept of linking faith to economic constructs, therefore, predates the modern emergence of Islamic finance from the 1960s and debates regarding capitalist models and the relationship towards religion should be examined in that context.

However, as we shall see next, arguments against faith has contributed to a religious revival that has significantly contributed towards the contemporary evolution of the Islamic finance industry.

Arguments Against Faith

> God is dead. God remains dead. And we have killed him. How shall we comfort ourselves, the murderers of all murderers? What was holiest and mightiest of all that the world has yet owned has bled to death under our knives: who will wipe this blood off us? What water is there for us to clean ourselves? What festivals of atonement, what sacred games shall we have to invent? Is not the greatness of this deed too great for us? Must we ourselves not become gods simply to appear worthy of it?[48]

Nietzsche's declamation came at a time when there was a conflict between belief, science and a changing industrial Germany. For some in German society, this led to Romanticism, embracing emotion as the true reality of being. For Nietzche it was the cold headed reality, as he saw it, that God was a notion that did not relate to analysis, comprehension and individual liberty.

However, there is no automaticity in the concept of rationalism and not believing in God. Descartes (1596–1650) used Cartesian logic to argue that the existence of God can be ascertained by thought:

> I saw quite well that assuming a triangle, its three angles must be equal to two right angles; but for all that, I saw nothing that assured me that there was any triangle in the real world. On the other hand, going back to an examination of my idea of a perfect Being, I found that this included the existence of such a Being; in the same way as the idea of a triangle includes the equality of its three angles to two right angles … Consequently, it is at least as certain that God, the perfect Being in question, is or exists, as any proof in geometry can be.[49]

It is the institution of religion, rather than the debate as to whether or not God exists, which causes much animus. The argument goes that institutionalised religions hold back freedom of thought and ties people in mental knots rather than enabling people to explore ideas free of preconceived conceptions.

The biologist, Richard Dawkins, whilst expressing the view that God does not exist, really directs his ire against religions and how, as he sees it, belief in faith holds back rational thinking. An example of his approach can be found in his book, *The God Delusion*, where he ridiculed what he saw as the inherent inconsistencies in religion:

> Deists differ from theists in that their God does not answer prayers, is not interested in sins or confessions, does not read our thoughts and does not intervene with capricious miracles.
>
> Deists differ from pantheists in that the deist God is some kind of cosmic intelligence, rather than the pantheist's metaphoric or poetic synonym for the laws of the universe. Pantheism is sexed-up atheism. Deism is watered-down theism.[50]

The British philosopher, Bertrand Russell, in the 1920s, had argued that established religion was harming the progress of society:

> Religion prevents our children from having a rational education; religion prevents us removing the fundamental causes of war; religion prevents us from teaching the ethic of scientific co-operation in place of the old fierce doctrines of sin and punishment. It is possible that mankind is on the threshold of a golden age; but if so, it will be necessary first to slay the dragon that guards the door, and this dragon is religion.[51]

Al-Farabi had a singular role in the early Islamic period where he saw religion not as an end in itself but as a means to an end:

> Religion is opinions and actions, determined and restricted with stipulations and prescribed for a community by their first ruler, who seeks to obtain through their practicing it a specific purpose with respect to them or by means of them. .... If the first ruler is excellent and his rulership truly excellent, then in what he prescribes he seeks only to obtain, for himself and for everyone under his rulership, the ultimate happiness that is truly happiness; and that religion will be the excellent religion.[52]

This approach to religion is different from the adherents of many of the great religions who see faith not as a process but as an all-embracing theology representing the divine. It is not on a par with Al-Farabi who saw religion as "*opinions and actions*" linked to contemporary political circumstances.

Karl Marx (1818–1883) may have had some sympathy with the analysis of Al-Farabi if he had been aware of his thought. Marx, instead, lambasted religion for holding back the prospects of millions of people and so was the "*opium of the people*".

The Iranian academic, Ali Shiriati (1933–1977), who played a significant role in the immediate period leading up to the 1979 Iranian Revolution, directly referenced Marx's analysis and argued that this statement was true—but not for the reasons that Marx espoused. Instead, Shariati said it was the Shi'a clerics in Iran who were maintaining the hierarchical status quo but religion should really be radical and transformative:

> Our mission is to continue the mission of the divinely appointed prophets who were the rightful prophets, who had arisen from the fabric of the people ... who confronted the pseudo-priests who were attached, affiliated to and dependent upon the rich aristocrats.[53]

Shariati was unusual, as a leading figure imbued in Islamic thought, to see some merit in Communist condemnation of religion. In fact, the series of Communist thinkers condemning religion had, as we shall see, a direct bearing on schools of thoughts within Islam.

Paul Lafargue (1842–1911), the French thinker and Karl Marx's son in law argued that as people extend their control over nature, belief in religion will decline until the communist revolution finally ended religious belief as people will be able to control the conditions of their own existence.

Nikolai Bukharin (1888–1938) was one of the first Communist leaders to undertake a detailed study of the relationship between philosophy and Communist thought in his work *The Theory of Historical Materialism: A Popular Manual of Marxist Sociology* (1921). Despite his commitment to the cause, Bukharin lost his life in one of Stalin's show trials.

Bukharin referred to a form of Christian belief where people did not have free will and all human actions are causally determined. Consequently, there is also no concept of chance in any real sense. Bukharin's description of Christianity is not fully accurate, as we have already discussed with a significant number of Christian adherents of laissez-faire economics.

It does reflect the concept of predestination which is prevalent in some Christian orders as well as in Islam. This related to the belief that God has a foreknowledge of what a person will do in their life and so will know which soul will enter Heaven. However, this Christian concept is refined by the caveat that a person must fulfil the accomplishments as set for this individual by God.

Sayyid Jamāl al-Dīn al-Afghānī (1838–1897) viewed the concept of predestination within Islam as a positive doctrine. From a Shi'a perspective he argued that "*Islam was the religion of free will*". When it came to the concept of predestination, Al-Afghānī stated that this belief would encourage Muslims to be active rather than passive as believers would know that God was with them when good actions were being committed.

The German philosopher, Ernst Bloch (1885–1977) continued the theme developed by Marx and Bukharin and argued that all religions are linked to a desire for a nostalgic era that never existed as compared to the future orientated approach of Communism:

> Throughout Judeo-Christian philosophy, from Philo and Augustine to Hegel, the Ultimum is related only to the Primum and not to the Novum, so that what finally comes about is only a repetition of what was in the beginning - something already fulfilled, which has meanwhile become lost or alienated.[54]

As Bloch further argued, religious salvation was represented as the return to a lost paradise and not to fulfilling a new destiny.

Those who argue against the denial of religion as postulated by Communist thinkers highlighted the flaws in the arguments that were being presented. The Russian writer, Mikhail Bulgakov (1891–1940) argued that communist thought denied the concept of chance as a determinative understanding of the world. This, in and of itself was a repudiation of Bukharin who claimed that chance did not exist within a religious context.

The Communist experiment proved, though, not to be a success with the end of the Cold War in 1989 to 1991. The deterministic form that Communism had developed led to a sclerotic and bureaucratic system where the transitional stage of the dictatorship of the proletariat before full emancipation was attained remained static at the level of bureaucratic control and this, therefore, hindered innovation and economic growth.

One of the early Communist leaders prefigured this development despite his adherence to the cause. Leon Trotsky had been close to attaining power following Lenin's death in 1924. The successful back room manoeuvrings of Stalin, however, eventually obliged Trotsky to flee the Soviet Union and he was finally murdered by one of Stalin's assassins in Mexico City in 1940.

In his book, *The Revolution Betrayed*, Trotsky saw how bureaucratic control was able to flourish in the Communist system:

> The basis of bureaucratic rule is the poverty of society in objects of consumption, with the resulting struggle of each against all. When there are enough goods in a store, the purchasers can come whenever they want to. When there are few goods, the purchasers are compelled to stand in line. When the lines are very long, it is necessary to appoint a policeman to keep order. Such is the starting point of the power of the Soviet bureaucracy. It 'knows' who is to get something and who has to wait.[55]

Easterly and Fischer went further in an analysis published just a few years after the end of the Cold War. They argued that the very structures of communism mitigated against the objectives of meeting Soviet growth targets by limiting the availability of resources which are essential to sustaining economic growth:

> Some forms of physical or human capital that were missing would have been market orientated entrepreneurial skills, marketing and distributional skills and information intensive physical and human capital (because of the restrictions on information flow). It is more difficult to substitute more and more drill presses for a labourer than it is to substitute a drill press plus a computerised inventory and distribution system for a labourer.[56]

Therefore, whilst some of the reasoned arguments against the very concept of religion came from those advocating a communist approach towards society and the economy, it emerged that the very hierarchies which existed within the "*dictatorship of the proletariat*" contained the inflexibilities which prevented the elasticity of the economy. It was these same Communist thinkers, though, who were condemning the rigidities of the structures within faith communities.

There were arguments in the 1920s and 1930s amongst Muslim scholars and Muslim politicians in British controlled India as to whether there were some synergies between Communism and Islam—but as we shall see in Chapter 9, the denial of spirituality within Communism was seen as not just morally wrong but also logistically impractical when implementing an egalitarian economic system.

This denial of religion from a range of perspectives contributed to post-modernism which, some Islamic scholars have argued, led to a revival of the idea of an Islamic society which, in part, forms ideas which impinge upon Islamic finance.

Postmodernism does not accept there is such a thing as an objective reality and that the very nature of language itself can lead to assumed patterns of understanding based on an objective reality that does not exist. Postmodernism is seen by its adherents as a liberating process. As the Belgian artist, Erik Pevernagie, has argued:

> Man may feel like a feeble and powerless pawn, at some moment in his life. This apprehension can come out of the blue, in the middle of the day, at the centre of a public place, like a cerebral attack. Checkmated by 'daily routine', he may feel trapped in a smothering set of circumstances and only a deconstruction of all impeding barriers can bring about a vital mental deliverance. ("Check and mate")

As the Turkish writer, Mustafa Armagan argued, postmodernism enabled Islamic ideas of society to flourish:

> postmodernism is attractive to Islamists because: (1) it shows the failures and limitations of modernism; (2) given the exhaustion of modernism, the postmodernist search for alternatives opens up an opportunity for Islam; (3) in their rejection of the secular uniformity of modernism, postmodernists freely borrow from tradition and religion which Islamists advocate; (4) the postmodernist emphasis on diversity and (5) the announcement of the death of "meta-narratives" strengthens the hand of Islam in its struggle against modern "isms" such as socialism, positivism, or Darwinism.[57]

As Felipe Fernandez-Armesto observed:

> It was a common mistake of twentieth century intellectuals to suppose that God was dead and that religion must wither. The godly of every faith colluded in affirming the onset of a crisis by denouncing the growth and

spread of unbelief; for nothing so stimulates religious reaction as the fear of pagan revanche.[58]

This reaction to postmodernism was reflected in the arguments regarding consumerism as postulated by, amongst others, the Algerian writer, Malik Bennabi (1905–1973). Mohamed El-Tahir El-Mesawi summed up Bennabi's consumerist stance:

> In the wake of modernity's struggle against tradition and religion, man was left without heart and soul, but at least it was said that reason and its time-honoured ally science, would take care of him. Now post-modernity is cutting up his head and stripping him of his mind. What is then left is a soulless and mindless body that is being pampered by a sweeping culture of consumerism and nihilism.[59]

This characterisation of consumerism would seem to suggest that consumerism as a concept had not been critiqued in other societies. However, the analysis of the adverse impact of consumerism is prevalent within the academic literature and has helped to inform the global movement to tackle climate change as exemplified by the anti-consumerist comments of the Swedish climate change campaigner, Greta Thunberg.

The American sociologist, Thorstein Veblen (1857–1929), observed, with his identification of the term '***conspicuous consumption***', the honorific form of consumption which had become a normative feature in shaping the economy:

> The leisure class lives by the industrial community rather than in it. Its relations to industry are of a pecuniary rather than an industrial kind. Admission to the class is gained by exercise of the pecuniary aptitudes; aptitudes for acquisition rather than for serviceability.

Veblen later added:

> Since the consumption of these more excellent goods is an evidence of wealth, it becomes honorific; and conversely, the failure to consume in due quantity and quality becomes a mark of inferiority and demerit.[60]

French sociologist, Pierre Bourdieu (1930–2002) reached a similar conclusion as to the societal consequences of consumerism:

> Consumption is … a stage in the process of communication, that is, an art of deciphering, decoding, which presupposes practical or explicit mastery of a cipher or code.[61]

Despite Bennabi's characterisation of consumerism as a "Western" phenomenon, this stance does not sustain itself under scrutiny. In fact, the very promotion of the central tenets of Islam was, in part, a response to the societal impact which trade and the desire for goods had on communities.

However, this reaction to postmodernism via the prism of consumerism continued to be felt following the establishment of the Islamic Republic of Iran in 1979. The theocratic government had accepted some form of consumerism, though this led to its own set of tensions:

> Advances of consumerism in Iran … brought loud protests not only from traditionalists but also from nationalists, often in the middle class itself, who continued to see the emblems of consumerism as foreign without connection to the regional culture. The advance of commercial television drew some into greater awareness of consumer attractions but showed others how repulsive consumerism could appear. Advertising taught rural and working class viewers about the gulf in wealth and attitudes between a limited cosmopolitan upper class and the bulk of the Iranian population. Mixed sentiments of envy and outrage, of cultural inferiority and cultural pollution grew among the traditional majority. Here was a context in which, even toward the end of the twentieth century, an astonishing anti consumerist outcry could still emerge.[62]

Nonetheless, the very existence of consumerism in Iran, whose international trade links were hampered by severe economic sanctions, would indicate that consumerism was far being a "Western" import as a reflection of postmodernism. The very nature and context of consumerism is, in fact, linked to endogenous societal influences and the workings of an economy in terms of supply and demand.

However, the fact that consumerism can be seen through the prism of a reaction against postmodernism has contributed to debates about the nature of identity in the Middle East:

> Egypt remained a centre for genuinely Middle Eastern but also consumerist film production with impact throughout the region. It was the ongoing

> division that was striking as each side fed the other. Consumers knew they were making a statement of values, beyond their interest in specific fashions or goods. Fundamentalists knew that while their power was considerable, they had not definitely won the day. A debate over identity continued and the forces of what the fundamentalists viewed as 'cultural pollution' remained strong.[63]

Identifying Egyptian cinema as a 'Western' import when its basis is in Arab culture is not a sustainable position to hold and therefore such debates reflects wider societal tensions. Different strands of Islam have emerged from a range of theological, political and societal factors which have impinged on the development and on-going evolution of Islamic economics, and consequently, on Islamic finance itself.

The impact of the denial of religion in a number of societies is part of this wider narrative in setting the stage for the emergence of Islamic economics. As we will see next, it was the dynamics of religion itself which shaped the form and structure of Islamic finance.

Religion and the Economy

The need to recognise the role of religion in analysing and understanding how the economy works was one of the key insights of Karl Polanyi (1886–1964). With the theory of embeddedness, Polanyi argued that religion and social institutions were naturally part of an economic structure but, from the eighteenth century onwards, the need to place a commercial value to assess validity had caused dissent in societies and was destined to cause social disturbances as a consequence:

> The human economy, then, is embedded and enmeshed in institutions, economic and non-economic. The inclusion of the non-economic is vital. For religion or government may be as important for the structure or the availability of tools and machines themselves that lighten the toil of labour.[64]

Dr Muhammad Yunus, who won the 2006 Nobel Peace Prize for his Grameen microfinance fund in Bangladesh, echoed this concept that ideas as to how people should live their lives is predicated upon the underlying assumptions which underpin the operation of the markets:

> We have remained so impressed by the success of the free market that we never dared to express any doubt about our basic assumption. To make it worse, we worked extra hard to transform ourselves, as closely as possible, into one dimensional human beings as conceptualised in the theory to allow the smooth functioning of the free market mechanism.
>
> By defining 'entrepreneur' in a broader way we can change the character of capitalism radically and solve many of the unresolved social and economic problems within the scope of the free market. Let us suppose an entrepreneur, instead of having a single source of motivation, which are mutually exclusive, but equally compelling – a) maximisation of profit and b) doing good to people and the world.
>
> Each type of motivation will lead to a separate kind of business. Let us call the first type of business a profit maximisation business and the second type of business a social business.[65]

This analysis reflects the debate amongst scholars regarding Islamic economics where conventional capitalist structures are seen as antithetical to human needs whilst Islamic finance is designed to be part of a system where the economy is people centred rather than profit centred for the owners of capital.

This leads to the wider debate as to the role of morality in conventional finance and Islamic finance.

The German philosopher, Immanuel Kant (1724–1804), argued that the existence of the concept of morality presupposed, via a series of deductive steps, the existence of God:

> The acting rational being in the world is not at the same time the cause of the world and of nature itself. Hence there is not the slightest ground in the moral law for a necessary connection between the morality and proportionate happiness of a being which belongs to the world as one of its parts and as thus dependent on it. Not being nature's cause, his will cannot of its own strength bring nature, as it touches on his happiness, into complete harmony with his practical principles.
>
> Nevertheless … in the necessary endeavour after the highest good, such a connection is postulated as necessary: we should seek to further the highest good (which therefore must at least be possible). Therefore, the existence is postulated of a cause of the whole of nature, itself distinct from nature, which contains the ground of the exact coincidence of happiness with morality …
>
> As a consequence the possibility of a highest derived good (the best world) is at the same time the postulate of the reality of the highest original

> good, namely the existence of God … Therefore, it is morally necessary to assume the existence of God.[66]

Whilst sceptics such as Dawkins would pour scorn on Kant's deductive reasoning, the analysis presented by Kant has echoes in the theological underpinning which contributed to the emergence of Islamic finance.

If we accept Kant's analysis that there is a connection between a belief in God, and therefore in faith, and how this is intrinsically linked to morality, this is just a short hop to the development of a more defined understanding of the relationship between religion and capitalism. It was an intellectual challenge that the German thinker, Max Weber, embraced.

Weber (1864–1920) argued that the belief in Protestant Christianity was directly linked to enhanced capitalist productivity and entrepreneurship. Weber's approach fits within his larger sociological body of work which included his analysis of elite theory. Unlike other elite theory thinkers such as the Italian thinker, Vilfredo Pareto, Weber did believe that the concept of mass democracy was not necessarily distorted by business interests.

However, Weber argued, the complex nature of mass democratic societies meant that elite groups competed for mass support within the electoral process. Weber argued that this realisation was not an argument against electoral democracy but an understanding as to how specialist elites are formed to compete for power in complex industrialised societies. Weber looked at the British and American leaders of his own time to support his analysis:

> David Lloyd George, Theodore Roosevelt and Woodrow Wilson - political leaders praised by Weber as modern charismatic 'great statesmen' - all played a central role in successful elite integration and nation building. They also strengthened mass democracy by cultivating mass trust, public confidence and national support. By contrast, Germany was criticised as a laggard in the modernisation stakes and as 'leaderless'.[67]

When it came to the relationship between religious thought and capitalism, he did see the concept of salvation-based religious thought as being disruptive to the running of societies as the focus appeared to Weber to be a hankering for the hereafter rather than making a success of life on Earth. Weber did praise Confucianism (which is not a religion but can be seen as a guide to living) arguing that it "*knew no radical evil or salvation*".

It is his work, *The Protestant Ethic and the Spirit of Capitalism*, that is unequivocal about the link between religion and economic productivity:

> A glance at the occupation statistics of any country of mixed religious composition brings to light with remarkable frequency a situation which has several times provoked discussion in the Catholic press and literature, and in Catholic congresses in Germany, namely the fact that business leaders and owners of capital, as well as the higher grades of skilled labour, and even more the higher technically and commercially trained personnel of modern enterprises, are overwhelmingly Protestant.

Weber argued that Protestantism encouraged individualism which, in turn, encouraged freedom of thought that has a direct correlation to entrepreneurship. Weber claimed that Catholicism, on the other hand, was collectively minded and did not allow the freedom to lead and be different from the collective. Martin Luther who effectively kick-started the Christian Reformation when he nailed, in 1517, his Ninety Five Theses to the door of All Saints' Church in Wittenberg, can be seen as emblematic of Protestant individualism with the apocryphal cry—"*Here I stand; I can do no other*".

Whilst Weber put forward an interesting hypothesis, it can be criticised for Protestantism contains a series of beliefs which do not necessarily favour individualism. The entrepreneurialism of the Venetian merchants occurred within a Catholic setting thereby contradicting Weber's claim that Catholicism militated against individualism. MacCulloch has gone further in undermining Weber's central thesis:

> Certainly Protestants disrupted some forms of community, the structures created by medieval Catholicism, but they did so precisely because they considered them harmful to the community, just like witches or images. They then rebuilt those communities and did so most successfully where Reformed Protestantism was at its most effective and thoroughgoing: Scotland, Hungary and New England. Such places were not at the forefront of the birth either of modern individualism or of modern capitalism.[68]

Robert Lucas also poured cold water on Weber's ideas. In his seminal 1988 article on macroeconomics, Lucas could not see how such a concept could ever be substantiated:

> ... we can no more directly measure the amount of human capital has, or the rate at which it is growing, than we can measure the degree to which a society is imbued with the Protestant ethic.[69]

Despite the ability to dismantle Weber's hypothesis, there is some merit in Weber's work as it reminds all of us as to how faith can drive business growth and economic prosperity. In Chapter 2 we considered how the Prophet was from a business background and how the Qur'ran and the hadiths frequently refer to business ethics and the ability to align ethical conduct with enhanced productivity.

A 2011 study of the attitudes of Malaysian managers who work in the Islamic finance industry also may help to demonstrate that there may be some validity in Weber's analysis, though a more empirical approach may be required to fully test the hypothesis in contemporary conditions as to the strength of the link between adherence to a faith and business productivity.

When considering the attitudes of Malaysian managers, Sloane-White saw the similar motivating factors for commercial success which Weber claimed he saw with German Protestants:

> Clearly there are parallels in these perspectives on Islamic business activity to that of Calvinist businessmen described by Weber, in which work provides rewards to capitalists in both this world and the next.[70]

We will return to this study in Chapter 9.

Religion, Party Politics and the Economy

Religion can shape societal responses to economic upheavals and we could argue that Islamic finance reflects a growing trend for new ways to finance business growth which is sustainable and takes account of ethical considerations.

In Europe, this approach to marrying religion with the need to find solutions in addressing the needs of daily life emerged in a party political form with the formation of Christian democratic parties. Though such parties did exist in Europe in the early part of the twentieth century, it was the end of the Second World War which helped to relaunch this movement with the rise of the Christian Democratic Union (CDU) in Germany.

It was seen as an attempt to overcome the fascist era when, for example, Hitler had denied the existence of the soul with all the ramifications which could follow if this denial is linked to fascist ideology.[71] It was also intended to bridge the Catholic–Protestant divide in West Germany whilst also opposing Communism when Germany was at the very crossroads of the Cold War.

The CDU has morphed into a mainstream centre right political party though echoes of its Christian heritage continued into the twenty-first century when CDU leader and German Chancellor, Angela Merkel, was challenged as to the rise of Islamophobia after thousands of mainly Muslim refugees sought sanctuary in Germany in 2015. Merkel, in response to the critics, argued that Germany suffered not from "*too much Islam*" but from "*too little Christianity*".[72]

The Muslim Brotherhood established political parties in the Middle East to compete for political power. Whilst it is fair to say there is no true comparison between the CDU and the Muslim Brotherhood on many levels, different branches of the Muslim Brotherhood organised national political parties with faith being at the forefront of the party's platform combined with a broad range of manifesto commitments to appeal to the electorate.

One common theme within the Muslim Brotherhood's thinking is its concern with the direction of global capitalism. Hasan al-Banna, the driving force of the movement, wrote to the sixteen-year old King of Egypt, Farouk, in 1936 where he lambasted the impact of capitalism and proposed an alternative economic model:

> The pursuit of comfort and worldly goods has shaken the foundations of Europe. Be the first to offer in the name of God's Prophet (May God bless and save him), the Qur'ran's medicine to save this sick and tormented world.[73]

Banna argued for a government accountable to the people and therefore opposed a theocratic state. As part of the reforms that he proposed, it included a policy for the "*oppression of monopolistic companies*"—a reference to foreign control over the Suez Canal.

Banna's struggle eventually led to his assassination in Cairo in 1949—possibly by elements within the Egyptian Government.

Today, Banna's legacy is a source of contention and for understandable reasons. Banna was able to mobilise millions of Egyptians in a display of populist democracy but was opposed to freedoms for women and uttered anti-Semitic rhetoric. At times, he seemed to support conciliatory moves to aid political progress by working with the Egyptian and American governments and, during other periods, engaged in violence to achieve his ends.

In 2012, the Muslim Brotherhood's candidate, Mohamed Morsi, briefly gained power by winning the Egyptian Presidential election. This was a challenging time for Morsi as a rentier economy existed in Egypt where the military was the primary economic actor.

Such an unsustainable economic model clearly needed reform after decades of economic stasis under the rule of President Hosni Mubarak. However, how to transition the economy of the Middle East's most populous nation became a matter of lively debate within the Muslim Brotherhood. For Abdel Hafez el Sawy, he indicated a move towards the wholesale adoption of Islamic economics:

> Speculative instruments have caused great trouble for the Egyptian economy. We will start off by communicating that some of these acts are not in compliance with Sharia. But if we feel that these acts are harming the economy, they will be clearly prohibited.[74]

For economists outside the Muslim Brotherhood, such a shift in direction, when the economy was so reliant on global markets, could cause an economic crisis on top of the political crisis. For instance, Dr Magda Kandil of the Egyptian Centre for Economic Studies said in response to Sawy's plans:

> I thought they would be a little more mainstream. There is a downside risk to a more isolationist approach to the economy that closes doors to investors and alienates it from the international financial markets.[75]

Key figures within the Muslim Brotherhood were also at odds with Sawy. Khairat al-Shater was released from prison once Morsi became President. Having been a leading businessman before his incarceration, he argued for a move away from the rentier economy towards a liberal market economy which would encourage private sector investment.

However, before a conclusion could be reached in this internal party debate, the Morsi Presidency collapsed via a military coup led by Abdel

Fattah el-Sisi and aided by mass demonstrations against the Morsi government. Morsi was imprisoned where he maintained that he remained the legitimate President of Egypt up to his unexpected death in 2019. As for Al-Shater, he is back in prison.

This short interlude in Egyptian history gave a brief insight as to the potential for a change of direction in Egypt's economic model under a Muslim Brotherhood led Government.

Over recent years, Saudi Arabia has led criticisms against the Muslim Brotherhood's influential scholar, Yusuf al-Qaradawi, who has been accused of using inflammatory language to encourage terrorism. Saudi Arabia and other neighbouring countries have condemned Qatar for sheltering Qaradawi.

Al-Qaradawi has spoken out on Islamic economics and his perspective has gained some traction in shaping the debate around this discipline. Al-Qaradawi has said economic success is a means to an end and not an end in and of itself and has claimed that some systems of thought is purely focused to "*make bread their goal and give the economy the highest priority*". This view, as discussed earlier, can be disputed if we consider the faith-based reasons which supporters of different economic models cite. Al-Qaradawi later added:

> ... an Islamic one *(economic system)* will give importance to these things only as a means. The main goal remains the enhancement of man and his rescue from the injustice of materialism by lifting his moral and spiritual being.[76]

As we will consider in Chapter 10, the influence of the Muslim Brotherhood contributed to Islamic economics being heralded as the political economic model of Sudan. When President Omar al-Bashir was finally toppled in 2019, it became all too clear that crony capitalism really reflected the Sudanese economic experience.

The Muslim Brotherhood was accused in 2020 of helping to entice Turkish proxy forces to fight in the Libyan civil war[77] whilst others argued that the presence of the Muslim Brotherhood in Libya was very limited and mention of the organisation is used as a bogeyman to buttress the fake credentials of Khalifa Haftar, who is opposing the United Nations backed Libyan Government of National Accord.[78]

During this same period, a US lobbying company working on behalf of the UAE sent an email to American politicians where the role of

Turkish forces in Libya was objected to by discussing the stance of Libya's neighbour—Egypt:

> Egypt will NOT allow a Muslim brotherhood -supporting country to set up shop on its border. That is an existential threat to them. That would be the equivalent of having China in place of Canada, and Russia in place of Mexico. (Email sent by Hagir Elawad of Akin Gump to US politicians, 22 June 2020)

Whilst the very existence of the Muslim Brotherhood remains a contentious issue in the Middle East, it should be acknowledged that the formation of the Muslim Brotherhood played a role—limited though it may be—in the overall history of Islamic finance.

Maqasid al-Shari'a

One of the key concepts of Islamic thought, which has informed the development of Islamic finance, relates to the concept of maqasid or, to be precise, maqasid al-shari'a. It can be defined as meeting the overall objectives of shari'a law thereby meeting the requirements of well-being and attaining happiness for all people now and for the hereafter.

Ibrahim ibn Musa al-Shatibi (died 1388) was a scholar from the Maliki school of jurisprudence and was based in Granada. His work *al-Muwafaqat* (Reconciliation of the Fundamentals of Islamic Law) elucidated the concept of maqasid al-shari'a by considering the concept by analysing five underlying themes:

- the fundamental concepts of the discipline of religion;
- the aḥkam (rules) and what is related to them;
- the legal purposes of the shari'a and the aḥkam related to them;
- the comprehensive treatment of the adilla (evidences);
- the rules of ijtihad (legal reasoning) and taqlid (conformity of one person to the teaching of another).

The Tunisian scholar, Muhammad ibn Ashur (1879–1973) and Yusuf al-Qaradawi promoted Al-Shatibi's ideas to new audiences. Qaradawi delineated from this work the concept of fiqh al-awlawiyyat (jurisprudence of priorities) as a juristic basis for setting social policies. Consequently, the controversial hudud, where there are fixed punishments for various criminal offences, would not necessarily be a priority compared to more pressing issues for contemporary societies.

Maqasid al-shari'a meets six primary objectives which are the protection and preservation of:

- Religion
- Life
- Progeny or the family
- Property
- Intellect
- Honour

The secondary objectives can be defined as:

- Justice and equity in society;
- Mutual help and solidarity particularly with the most vulnerable people in society;
- Peace and security;
- Promote good acts and prevent evil deeds;
- Promote universal moral values and ensure the preservation of the environment.

From an Islamic finance perspective, the actions of market participants help achieve the wider ethical and social objectives which is defined within the overall objectives of shari'a law.

Muhammad Umar Chapra, an economist at the Islamic Development Bank, has described how the concept of maqasid has impacted the industry:

> ... if well-being were to be defined in a way that rises above the materialist and hedonist sense and incorporates humanitarian and spiritual goals, then economics may not be able to avoid a discussion of what these goals are and how they may be realised.[79]

Al-Ghazali wrote of sustaining knowledge in the light of the inner surrender to the conscious oneness. Spiritual inner reflection and attaining market objectives are not seen as a conflict between spiritual and secular goals. Instead it is the ability of maqasid to define a deeper meaning of spiritual life within an individual's daily activity:

Development of sustainable moral self, society and the Islamic world system was cast in the generalised framework of explaining the interrelationships that exist between these areas of expertise. The maqasid al shari'ah was thus seen as the comprehensive understanding of the Islamic law in addressing the time-bound problems of human society.[80]

Maqasid al-Shari'a and Maslaha

From the concept of maqasid flows the corresponding theme of maslaha which can be translated as individuals working in the public interest or achieving benefits for the public weal.

From this innocuous sounding term, a series of profound implications can be drawn as to the interpretations of the Qur'ran, hadiths and sunna and how such interpretations shape the understanding and implementation of shari'a law. Maslaha is a concept that has a direct bearing on the conduct of the scholarly decision-making processes within the Islamic finance industry.

Maslaha is studied in connection with istislah which can be interpreted as juristic preference. Therefore, there are various routes that jurists can follow from the concept of maslaha which is dependent on which school of fiqh a scholar may be from.

As is often the case in the story of Islamic finance, we go back to the insights of al-Ghazali.

Al-Ghazali saw maslaha as God's purpose in revealing the divine law and how, for humanity, this meant the preservation of religion, life, intellect, descendants and property.

Al-Ghazali, with this analysis, intended to bring together the rationalist and subjective stances. The rationalist stance argued that the human mind can decide via reasoning (ijtihad) what actions are right or wrong. The subjectivist stance would contend that our understanding of right and wrong is informed by the revelation from God and therefore when seeking judgements reference to divine law must always come first.

Al-Ghazali's understanding of maslaha meant that the divine law could be used to reach judgements on new cases whilst being able to amend the law in the light of new circumstances being displayed in particular cases.

As can be seen, there is a tension between the rationalist and subjectivist stances, for can the role of the intellect still be seen as helping jurists reach judgements that should be predicated on the revelation from God or has not God endowed individuals with the intellect to make rational decisions. Al-Ghazali attempted to bridge this divide with his analysis and by promoting the use of analogy (qiyas) to reach judgements.

Shihāb al-Dīn Abu 'l-Abbās Aḥmad ibn Abi 'l-ʿAlāʾ Idrīs ibn ʿAbd al-Raḥmān ibn ʿAbd Allāh ibn Yallīn al-Ṣanhājī al-Ṣaʿīdī al-Bahfashīmī al-Būshī al-Bahnasī al-Miṣrī al-Mālikī also known as Shihāb al-Dīn al-Qarāfī (1228–1285) developed further the concept of maslaha.

Al-Qarafi, a Maliki jurist, also supported the use of analogy but he went further with the idea of using precepts to define what is legally right or wrong. His work eliminated a number of legal precepts which, he argued, were merely pretexts for committing illegal actions. Maslaha, by the use of correct legal precepts, acted as an independent standard by which rulings could be deemed to be valid.

Najm ad-Dīn Abū r-Rabīʿ Sulaimān ibn ʿAbd al-Qawī at-Tūfī (1276–1316) was a Hanbali jurist who took a different approach towards the concept of maslaha. Al-Tufi argued that anything that brought about maslaha and averted harm was commensurate with the purposes of the law. Therefore, a ruling that achieved some form of maslaha outcome should receive priority over a contradictory ruling. Al-Tufi's ideas were endorsed by subsequent jurists such as Jamal al-Din al Qasimi (1866–1914) and Muhammad Rashid Rida (1865–1935).

Abu Ishaq al-Shatibi (1320–1388), also a Maliki jurist, argued that a case that lacked reference to textual evidence could be judged by its conformity to the law by consideration of its maslaha implications. Maslaha considerations were given priority over most matters though exceptions existed such as stipulations surrounding the act of worship. Al-Shatibi's ideas were embraced by subsequent jurists such as Subhi Rajab Mahmasani (1909–1986), Allal al Fasi (1910–1974) and Mahmud Muhammad Taha (1909 or 1911–1985).

Abū ʿAlī Ḥasan ibn ʿAlī ibn Isḥāq al-Ṭūsī who became known as Niẓām al-Mulk (1018/19–1092) popularised the concept of maslaha as the overriding principle as it pertained to the good conduct of effective governance. Niẓām al-Mulk (literally 'Order of the Kingdom) was the Persian vizier of the Turkish Seljuk sultans.

In his work, *Seyāsat-nāmeh* (The Book of Government or Rules for Kings), he wrote about a just king who would serve in the public interest. His work was the polar opposite of Niccolò Machiavelli's *The Prince* which took a far more cynical view as to the principles of kingship. Niẓām al-Mulk's advocacy of Sunni Islam at the expense of Shi'a Islam was also a key feature of his book.

Whilst the concept of maslaha was popularised by the words of Niẓām al-Mulk, his ideas fell out of favour with Sultan Malik-Shāh who became envious of the powers of his de facto Chief Minister. In 1092, Niẓām al-Mulk was assassinated on the road from Eṣfahān to Baghdad, with the Sultan possibly conniving in the murder of his servant.

This is a very brief summary of some of the key historical themes in maslaha and how it impacts upon scholarly decision-making. Approaches to maslaha explain, to some extent, how scholars can reach differing conclusions in the Islamic finance industry dependent upon which juristic path is chosen.

However, this should not be seen as a weakness for the efficient running of the sector. On the contrary, the fact that the need to reach general well-being is a goal for the industry confirms how this model is theoretically geared to go beyond the profit motive and reaching bonus performance targets and, instead, examines how an ideal political economy can serve the wider public good.

Maqasid al-Shari'a and the Future of the Islamic Finance Industry

Maqasid objectives place a great onus on the Islamic finance industry to not just be profitable and to grow the sector but to meet these core values as an intrinsic part of its work.

Can such idealism really shape the daily actions of Islamic finance participants?

The founder of Al Baraka Bank, the Saudi businessman, Saleh Abdullah Kamel, also known as Sheikh Saleh, blamed the scholars who were active in Islamic finance for not taking seriously enough masaqid objectives when advising on the direction and conduct of the industry:

> Before, we saw that the shari'ah scholars didn't understand the economy and economics. Now I can say that some of them don't understand shari'ah either. I wouldn't say all shari'ah scholars, but certainly some of them don't look to the maqasid, they only look to the mechanism. If they do this it means that they don't understand shari'ah.[81]

One of the scholars who is very active in the Islamic finance industry, Sheikh Nizam Yaquby, has argued that expectations for the sector is far too high and a more realistic perspective as to the contribution it can make needs to be adopted:

> We are not claiming that this sector, the Islamic banking sector, is going to solve all the problems in the matters of economics. No, no bank will claim this. No bank says 'I want to solve the world's poverty problems.' Nobody says this, although it is one of our goals to help poor people.[82]

The issue of maqasid and the consequent role of Islamic finance was hotly debated during the height of the 2020 COVID-19 crisis. During a live webinar, Harris Irfan of Gatehouse Global LLP argued that it is at times of crisis that the sector can demonstrate its worth by highlighting how Islamic finance is a sustainable business model compared to conventional finance strategies:

> Perhaps Islamic finance banks ignored the opportunities offered by the 2008 financial crisis and with the COVID-19 crisis this opportunity has come round again.[83]

However, during this same event, the Director General of the Islamic Research and Training Institute (part of the Islamic Development Bank), Dr Sami Al-Sulwaliem, echoed the comments of Sheikh Nizam Yaquby where he argued that critics:

> are being unfair to the Islamic finance sector. We are expecting them to do everything. That is impossible. Banks are doing an essential function but banks by their very nature are risk averse.[84]

Islamic finance lawyer, Michael McMillen, has argued that maqasid objectives within Islamic finance can sometimes not be fully addressed.

This, McMillen said, is not because of the lack of willingness to engage in this moral outlook by the banks. In fact, he argued, it is the actions of the bank's clients that lead to a distortion in meeting these objectives:

> I have had experiences in a number of funds on which I work, where, if returns dip, the investors, very prominent Middle Eastern investors, demand to get their money out at the level of returns they were getting before the returns dropped. That's just contrary to the contracts and is often in conflict with the applicable shari'ah principles. As a practical

> matter, some of these funds are administered by big international institutions. And these institutions will sometimes accommodate these people. It depends on how 'important' they are, and I use that term reluctantly. I've seen it enough times. It's not a one-off thing.[85]

The challenge for the industry, then, is how to ensure the ethical and sustainable economic structures that has been developed within the sector are implemented in practice.

The institutional and cultural tensions to achieve such a step change clearly exists—but the opportunities to realise patient capital resources and ensure real and tangible sustainable growth is there.

As will be discussed in the next chapter, the question is not whether we should attain these wider social objectives of Islamic finance—but how.

Notes

1. Sir Arthur Conan-Doyle, *A Study in Scarlet.*
2. Humanists, UK.
3. Ayn Rand, *Capitalism: The Unknown Ideal*, page 316.
4. Al Farabi, *Perfect State* V, 17, 1: 277–279.
5. Marilynne Robinson, *Absence of Mind*, page xvi.
6. Trevor Gambling, *Societal Accounting* (London: Allen & Unwin, 1974). Trevor Gambling, *Beyond the Conventions of Accounting* (London: Macmillan, 1978).
7. Murtada Mutahhari, *IMAM REZA (A.S.) NETWORK: History and Human Evolution: The Problem of Bada'*.
8. Huntington's thesis is explored further in Chapter 11.
9. Qur'ran, 59:21.
10. Aristotle, *De Caelo,* 1: 11–12.
11. Al-Ghazali, *Tahafut*, 42.
12. Al Ghazali, *The Incoherence of the Philosophers*, as translated by Michael E Marmura (1997), page 217.
13. Masudul Alam Choudhury, *Islamic Economic and Finance: An Epistemological Inquiry*, page 22.
14. Qur'ran, 2.29–2.33.
15. Qur'ran, 2.33–2.39.
16. Genesis, 11–20.
17. Quoted in *A History of the American People*, Paul Johnson, page 96.
18. Ayn Rand, *For the New Intellectual*, page 137.
19. Bank Negara Malaysia, *Value Based Intermediation Financing and Investment Impact Assessment Framework*, November 2019.
20. Patrick Bannerman, *Islam in Perspective*, page 126.

21. Qur'ran, al-Ahzab 72.
22. Jaafar Sheikh Idris (1990), pages 109–110.
23. This theme of links between different forms of political economy is explored in Chapter 9.
24. Jaafar Sheikh Idris, pages 109–110 (1990).
25. This theme of links between different forms of political economy is explored in Chapter 9.
26. Masudul Alam Choudhury, *Islamic Economics and Finance: An Epistemological Inquiry*, pages 234–235.
27. *Blackwell Companion to Contemporary Islamic Thought*, page 16.
28. Margaret Thatcher, *The Downing Street Years*, page 626.
29. UK Prime Minister's office, 29 March 2020.
30. This is believed to have been the then Employment Secretary, Norman Tebbit—now Lord Tebbit.
31. Margaret Thatcher, *The Path to Power*, pages 554–555.
32. Further analysis between supply chain economics and early Islamic thought can be found in Chapter 2.
33. Justin Welby, *Reimagining Britain* (2018).
34. Justin Welby, *Dethroning Mammon*, page 18 (2016).
35. Michael Novak, *The Spirit of Democratic Capitalism*, page 14.
36. Ibid., page 355.
37. Ayn Rand, *For the New Intellectual.*
38. Mohammed Baqir al-Sadr, *Iqtisaaduna* (Iranian Government translation), page xxxvi.
39. Ibid.
40. Paul Ryan, April 2012.
41. Quoted by the IsDB's IRTI and Universiti Brunei Darussalam (2008), *Islamic Finance for Micro and Medium Enterprises.*
42. Putnam, 2000, page 19.
43. As quoted in *FT Wealth*, October 2015.
44. John Maynard Keynes (1949), *My Early Beliefs* as published in volume x, *Collected Writings* (1949).
45. Romans 11:33.
46. Aquinas, *Summa contra Gentiles*, III, 67.
47. J David Greenstone, *The Lincoln Persuasion: Remaking American Liberalism*, page 112.
48. Friedrich Nietzche (1883), *Thus Spoke Zarathustra.*
49. Rene Descartes, *Discourse on Method* (AT VI.36; CSMK 1.129).
50. Richard Dawkins, *The God Delusion.*
51. Bertrand Russell, *Why I Am Not a Christian* (1927), page 37.
52. Al Farabi, *Book of Religion*, 1:93.
53. As quoted by Elizabeth F Thompson, *Justice Interrupted: The Struggle for Constitutional Government in the Middle East*, page 289.

54. Ernst Bloch (1968), *Atheismus im Christentum* (1968), page 233.
55. Leon Trotsky, *The Revolution Betrayed*, page 112.
56. William Easterly, Stanley Fischer, *The Soviet Economic Decline*, National Bureau of Economic Research (May 1994).
57. Felipe Fernandez-Armesto (1995), *Millennium*, page 554.
58. Cited in: Gulap, "Globalizing Postmodernism," 429.
59. As quoted in *Blackwell Companion to Contemporary Islamic Thought*, page 218.
60. Thorstein Veblen (1899), *Theory of the Leisure Class*.
61. Pierre Bourdieu (1984).
62. Peter N Stearns, *Consumerism in World History: The Global Transformation of Desire*, page 134.
63. Ibid., page 135.
64. K Polanyi (1968), The Economy as Instituted Process. In *Economic Anthropology*, edited by E LeClair and H Schneider (New York: Holt, Rinehart and Winston), page. 126.
65. Muhammad Yunus, 2006, page 5–6.
66. Immanuel Kant, *Critique of Practical Reason*, translated Thomas Kingsmill Abbott (1909), page 129.
67. Jan Pakulski (2012), The Weberian Foundations of Modern Elite Theory and Democratic Elitism, *Historical Social Research/Historische Sozialforschung*, vol. 37, no. 1 (139), pp. 38–56.
68. Diarmaid MacCulloch, *Reformation: Europe's House Divided 1490–1700*, page 606.
69. Robert E Lucas (1988), On the Mechanics of Economic Development, *Journal of Monetary Economics*, vol. 22.
70. A 2011 study by Patricia Sloane- White led to the following observation: "Clearly there are parallels in these perspectives on Islamic business activity to that of Calvinist businessmen described by Weber, in which work provides rewards to capitalists in both this world and the next"—Working in the Islamic Economy, *Journal of Social Issues in Southeast Asia*, vol. 26, no. 2.
71. Hitler, for instance, once said "To the Christian concept of the infinite significance of the individual soul … I oppose with ice clarity the saving doctrine of the nothingness and insignificance of the human being" as quoted Craig Baxter (1955), Germany's Christian Democratic Party, *Social Science*, vol. 30, no. 1, pp. 17–22.
72. https://www.christiantoday.com/article/angela-merkel-how-germanys-iron-chancellor-is-shaped-by-her-christianity/75803.htm.
73. As quoted by Mitchell, *The Society of the Muslim Brothers*, pages 193–194.
74. As quoted by *The National*, 4 July 2011.
75. Ibid.

76. As cited by Raymond William Baker, *Islam Without Fear: Egypt and the New Islamists*, page 132.
77. Anchal Vohra (5 May 2020), It's Syrian v Syrian in Libya, *Foreign Policy Review*.
78. Dr. Karim Mezran of the Atlantic Council, at an event at the Brooking's Institution, 24 February 2020.
79. Chapra, *Journal of Socio-Economics*, vol. 29, pages 21–37.
80. Masudul Alam Choudhury, *Islamic Economics and Finance: An Epistemological Inquiry*, page 125.
81. As quoted by Emmy Abdul Alim, *Global Leaders in Islamic finance*, page 90.
82. Ibid., page 151.
83. Islamic Markets webinar, 6 May 2020.
84. Ibid.
85. As quoted by Emmy Abdul Alim, *Global Leaders in Islamic Finance*, page 178.

CHAPTER 7

Ethical and Business Finance

Venture Capital and Islamic Finance

For a time, I worked in leafy Oxfordshire.

Just a few miles away from the dreaming spires of the University of Oxford is Harwell Technology Park. Located close to the railway junction of Didcot, Harwell is a centre for pharmaceutical and space research.

It is such an impressive centre for cutting edge scientific research, that it brings together the European Space Agency, RAL Space, Satellite Applications Catapult and UK Space Agency (part of the UK Government), Airbus Defence & Space, Lockheed Martin and Thales Alenia Space.

There are also smaller space related businesses on site such as Oxford Space Systems, Deimos Space UK, Rezatec and NDA. Harwell is home to the Science & Technology Facilities Council (part of the UK Government), with over £2 billion of infrastructure for both public and private research and development.

However, when I attended events there in the early 2010s, a number of the start-up space related businesses were heard complaining that they could not get hold of long-term finance! With space businesses contributing £5.1 billion to UK GDP the question that must be asked is how this can be so?

A number of these businesses were courted every so often by venture capital funds but these start-ups were in it for the long haul and they did not want to lose significant equity stakes in businesses they had risked

J. S. Watkins, *Islamic Finance and Global Capitalism*,
https://doi.org/10.1007/978-3-030-59840-2_7

their mental well-being and their homes (mortgaging their only asset to realise their dream).

There have been repeated warnings that there is a need for a mechanism to finally fix the patient capital gap. For instance, in September 2012, the then UK Secretary of State for Business, Vince Cable, said:

> There is a real shortage of long-term 'patient' capital for businesses. Try and secure a loan for more than five years of venture capital and options are very limited especially for innovative, high-growth potential firms.

The economist, Stephane Garelli, has highlighted the risks to national economies if the patient capital funding gap is not properly addressed:

> ... if you look at the competitiveness of a nation like the UK or Switzerland, for example, then you have to ask yourself where the large companies of tomorrow in those countries are going to come from if all the start-ups are suddenly being bought up.[1]

Patient capital is characterised by a long-term investment profile and greater risk tolerance. These financiers typically stay with their investments through good times and bad. They are willing to incur uncertainty today in hopes of a more substantial return later in the term of the investment programme.

It seemed to me that Islamic finance could have a role to play in addressing this patient finance gap. The very structures of Islamic finance, as discussed in chapter three, are geared towards project financing and patient capital investment.

I recall mentioning to a market participant in the Islamic finance space about these opportunities and how meeting these needs could also assist the growth of the Islamic finance sector. I remember the far-off look and an off-hand reference to the potential of Sukuks one day meeting such requirements.

We discussed the risk averse approach in the Islamic finance industry in chapter four and we will come back to this theme again in the conclusion to this book. As for Sukuks, this could be a vehicle for meeting long-term investment needs as we will soon discover.

Different governments have used the tax system to encourage patient capital formation. In the United Kingdom, in November 2017, the Government introduced a principles-based test on tax reliefs to encourage patient capital investment. This was intended to ensure funding is focused on investment into companies seeking long-term growth and employment. There was a 'risk to capital' condition, which has two effects for HM Revenue & Customs to assess which are—first—does the company have the objective to grow and develop over the longer term and—second—is there significant risk to investors' capital that could potentially result in investors losing capital that is greater than their net subscription.

Despite similar tax incentive schemes introduced in various international jurisdictions, it would seem that the real solution to the patient capital gap would be innovative custom-built design options which the financial services sector could adopt.

Islamic finance could be a significant part of that offer.

It could be argued that funding already exists for technology start-ups by looking at the exemplar that is Silicon Valley. This small geographical area of San Francisco only covers 46 square miles but within this small area—no bigger than the English Channel island of Jersey—lies the technology firms that continue to shape our lives—Facebook, Intel, Microsoft, Google …. the list goes on.

The Silicon Valley model of investing in start-ups may be the answer for technologically savvy firms, particularly if we consider the investments which has led to multi-billion dollar valuations for businesses such as Uber, Airbnb and Slack.

The success of Silicon Valley has centred on high technology firms that have been launched on the basis of potential growth. The opportunities to establish technologically based start-ups can emanate from research and development (R&D) created within the organisational context of an incumbent firm or organisation, such as a university.

An abundance of new ideas can drive a flourishing start-up environment. However, only a subset of entrepreneurial ventures survives by actualising innovative activity and generating vigorous growth rates, while the remainder stagnate and ultimately exit from the industry.

Despite the image of Silicon Valley being primarily a success story due to entrepreneurialism, in fact, US federal funding and legislation in the form of the Bayh-Dole Act of 1980 was integral to Silicon Valley becoming the success story that it is today.

The Bayh–Dole Act or Patent and Trademark Law Amendments Act addresses intellectual property funded research. Bayh-Dole permits universities or non-profit organisations which receive federal funding to elect to pursue ownership of an invention, rather than obliging inventors to assign inventions to the federal government.

It could be argued that whilst US Government support has been integral to the flourishing of business start-ups in Silicon Valley, the symbiosis between venture capital (VC) investors and start-ups has also been key to Silicon Valley's growth story.

However, there are weaknesses within the VC model which militates against the kind of long-term financial support that many business sectors require. It is in this context that Islamic finance can meet the funding gaps that VC and other funding mechanisms are missing. To gain a greater understanding of this theme, we will first consider the strengths of the VC market before we move on to an analysis of the sector's deficiencies.

Comparative Analysis: Strengths of the Venture Capital Market

The Chief Executive of Softbank, Masayoshi Son and Crown Prince Mohammed bin Salman of Saudi Arabia were beaming from ear to ear when they signed a multi-billion-dollar deal at the New York Plaza Hotel in March 2018.

That deal was a US$200 billion agreement to provide what was described as the largest solar power project in the world by 2030. The Crown Prince described the signing ceremony and all that it represented as "*a huge step in human history*".[2]

The relationship between Saudi Arabia and Softbank has been positive with the kingdom having provided nearly half the money for SoftBank's US$93 billion tech-focused Vision Fund, which has made significant investments in start-ups such as WeWork (which had a hesitant start) and Slack (which was very successful). The sovereign wealth fund of the United Arab Emirates is also funding the Vision Fund.

Whilst venture capital is often cited as one of the key vehicles to deliver the emergence of high growth firms, this financing model is geared towards realising a return in a relatively short time period, as the record of most VC funds in Silicon Valley have indicated.

The ride-hailing platform Lyft and the shared-office business WeWork secured some of the largest venture capital funding deals in the United States, receiving $3 billion and $1.5 billion, respectively.

Those businesses who are successful due to VC funding are known as unicorns; private companies valued at more than $1 billion.

The US venture capital industry was established in the 1960s which gave it a head start of a couple of decades over the European Venture Capital sector. As Jones and Wadhwani have described venture capital it:

> ... occupies a unique place in the financial system by specialising in relatively risky long term financing of entrepreneurs with little in the way of assets to collaterise.[3]

Venture capital firms in the United States invested $84 billion to 8000 technology start-ups and companies in 2017, the highest amount of capital seen since the early 2000s, according to an annual industry report from PitchBook and the US National Venture Capital Association.

The amount of invested venture capital in the US has seen a near-consistent rise since 2009 and more than doubled since 2012—though venture capital dipped in 2016 to $72.4 billion from $79.3 billion in 2015, according to Bloomberg.

More than half of European VC firms have been active for over 12 years, meaning there is now a wealth of experienced fund managers who have seen multiple cycles and developed track records and sector-specific knowledge. This presents investors with a far more compelling investment proposition than might have been the case 10 years previously. In 2016 Europe's venture capital funds raised €6.4 billion—a nine-year high.[4]

Previously, European funds had been significantly smaller than those seen in the United States, but larger funds are now gaining momentum. Nearly 30% of funds raised in 2016 were over €100 million.

The European Commission and the European Investment Fund announced in 2017 a €1.6 billion VC fund-of-funds programme to further increase fund sizes and attract larger global institutional investors to the market.

Meanwhile, the Commission has amended the European venture capital regulation, as part of its Capital Markets Union action plan. This move was intended to help VC firms more easily make cross-border investments within the European Union and increase the breadth of companies that they can invest with this regime.

VC funds are sought after and have been instrumental in advancing technology development, such as US venture capital firm Andreessen Horowitz supporting companies in the United States that apply artificial intelligence to areas such as healthcare and food science. However, the expectations on return for investment plus the fact that the founder of a start-up will lose a significant proportion of equity in their own business means this option is not welcomed by all technology businesses.

VC fund managers would argue that along with a diminishing stake for entrepreneurs in their own companies, there is an improvement in efficiency as professional management can be brought into commercialise products. However, as Garelli has stated, the impact on the growth of endogenous firms and the knock on impact on national economies by such practices is another matter.

To provide an illustration of the expectations that are sought for in the VC industry, let us assume the average "win" returns to the Fund 5 times the amount invested. In our example, the $20 million becomes $100 million:

Venture partners fund

Capital commitments: 400
Winning investments

Company	*Amount invested*	*% ownership*	*Return multiple*	*Investment value at harvest*	*Value of company*
1	20	50	5	100	200
2	20	50	5	100	200
3	20	50	5	100	200
4	20	50	5	100	200
5	20	50	5	100	200
	100			500	

If the Fund owns 50% of a company then the value of the company at harvest has to be $200 million in order for the Fund to receive five times its investment.

Most Funds have a 10-year life. At the end of 10 years they are liquidated. Funds plan to harvest winners in 5 to 7 years or less.

For Early Stage Funds it is typical for the Fund to reserve $2–$3 for every $1 invested. For example, if the Fund invests $2 million in Round 1 they will reserve another $4 million–6 million for follow-on rounds. So, a $400 million Fund might invest $100 million in the first rounds of portfolio companies and $300 million in follow-on rounds.

A Fund usually makes its initial investments in the first 3 years of the Fund life cycle. During the remaining life of the Fund follow-on investments are made and the portfolio companies are positioned for "harvest".

Management fees can also be a significant proportion within the VC investment offering. The General Partners receive an annual Management Fee, which is usually a percentage of the Capital Commitments to the Fund.

A typical fee is 2.5%. On a $400 million fund this is $10 million per year.

It would be fair to observe that management fees are a function of all banking operations, including in Islamic finance.

In the 5, 7 or 10 year time horizon, the aim can be to sell the invested company to a larger established company with publicly listed shares or by an initial public offering (IPO) such as on the NASDAQ Small Cap Market whose requirements for listing is less severe as compared to the New York Stock Exchange and other leading stock markets.

Nonetheless, as we are about to see there are wider systemic issues within VC which militate against funding for long-term growth for critical business sectors where exponential growth in the short term cannot be realised.

Comparative Analysis: Deficiencies of the Venture Capital Market

There is no doubt that the venture capital market has been transformative. It has helped realise businesses that many of us now take for granted when accessing apps on our mobile phones. Venture capital has made possible further advances in the digital interconnectedness of our world.

However, such a model may not be helpful for sectors that need the time to grow and meet long-term challenges such as climate change adaptability. Remarkable as venture capital funds have been, such as Combinator Y, to support household brands like Airbnb and Dropbox, the focus is on platform orientated technologies that can be applied to real world settings in order to deliver exponential growth in a relatively short period of time.

Away from platform-based technologies, this model is not geared towards addressing patient capital gaps. As one investor, Alex Lazarow, has put it:

> In Silicon Valley, the quest for growth all too often trumps sustainable unit economics and profitability. It is not unusual for start-ups to burn through millions of VC dollars a month as they chase ambitious growth targets, often subsidizing user costs to drive acquisition numbers. The hope is that in highly competitive winner-take-all markets, a firm's revenue will increase exponentially as it dominates its market, and profitability will eventually sneak past zero and then grow rapidly. This strategy works well for start-ups that successfully make it through to the other side: If the number of users takes off, start-ups can indeed become very large, very fast.[5]

Colli and Rose, though, would argue that the very nature of most Silicon Valley start-ups is about meeting short-term objectives rather than longer term goals:

> In hi-tech clusters, such as Silicon Valley, ventures are set up to exploit a temporary competitive advantage based upon technological creativity, rather than as long-term ventures.[6]

Lazarow also notes how Silicon Valley's focus is not upon sustainable technology solutions to systemic issues such as health and energy:

> A study by Village Capital determined that out of the nearly 300 unicorn start-ups in the United States, only 18% were focused on health, food, education, energy, financial services, or housing. Conversely, my analysis of leading start-ups in Latin America, sub-Saharan Africa, and Southeast Asia reveals that far more (up to 60% of a sample in sub-Saharan Africa) target those basic human needs.

To see how Islamic finance could address these basic human needs we will first look at healthcare.

Healthcare and the Potential Role of Islamic Finance

Could there have been a vaccine for COVID-19 before the virus outbreak in Wuhan was first observed in December 2019?

According to Dr Peter Hotez, the co-director of the Center for Vaccine Development at Texas Children's Hospital and Dean of the National School of Tropical Medicine at the Baylor College of Medicine in Houston the answer was yes.

Dr Hotez told the US Congress in March 2020 that in 2016 his team was in the advanced stage for developing a vaccine for a form of coronavirus—but the work could not be completed:

> We tried like heck to see if we could get investors or grants to move this into the clinic. But we just could not generate much interest.

The comment from Dr Hotez did not surprise Professor Jason Schwartz of the Yale School of Public Health. Professor Schwartz told US media that the global response to COVID-19 exposed broader flaws in the way medical research was funded which, he said, was tended to be market-driven and reactive rather than proactive.[7]

This an extreme example—but an example nonetheless—as to how the aim of realising short-term returns combined with the lack of patient capital can hold back economic growth. In the case of the novel coronavirus, as Dr Hotez had put it:

> There is a problem with the ecosystem in vaccine development, and we've got to fix this.[8]

Having just read this example, you may think this is not a good case study to cite when considering the lack of long-term or patient capital for research and development (R&D). For how could pharmaceutical companies predict that such an unprecedented pandemic would occur and so invest accordingly?

Putting aside the comments of specialists such as Dr Susan Murray, programme director of the Smithsonian Global Health Programme who also told the US Congress that COVID-19 was "*not a surprise*" to experts who had been researching the spread of similar infectious diseases in recent years,[9] the fact that financial returns were expected in the pharmaceutical sector in relatively short time frames is an illustration of how markets can operate, particularly in North America and Europe.[10]

Venture capital had been attracted to the pharmaceutical sector due to the defined income streams that can be realised in relatively short time frames combined with low labour costs. These returns are linked in part to the intellectual property (IP) or patenting process. Large research-based corporations tend to invest heavily in the identification of new product candidates.

Most proposals do not end up on the market, as the drug could prove ineffective during trials, or to have severe side effects, or to be non-compliant with numerous regulatory stipulations. When a medicine does end up on the market, however, the patent system guarantees that the company responsible for its discovery and development retains exclusive rights to commercialisation. As soon as the patent expires (typically after 10–12 years), the drug may be replicated by generic pharmaceutical developers.

It is typically costly, time-consuming and risky for a research-based firm to bring a drug to market as generic pharmaceutical products are comparatively cheaper and less risky to operate. Although generic pharmaceutical firms engage in process-oriented R&D, they do typically incur lower product R&D costs.

Producers of generic medicines know more in advance about whether a particular drug has been shown to be valuable and commercially successful. Demand is better understood, and the product has commonly been well-established in the market, when the drug comes off patent, so marketing costs tend to be lower as well.

As Kuisch has observed:

> the number of FDA *(United States Food and Drug Administration)*-approved drugs per billion US dollars of R&D spending has halved roughly every 9 years since 1950 (adjusted for inflation). This steady decline in R&D productivity, dubbed Eroom's Law (note: Moore's Law, backwards) is particularly remarkable in light of the massive strides that have been made in terms of the scientific understanding of particular diseases and technologies (e.g. combinatorial chemistry, high-throughput compound screening, and three-dimensional protein structure mapping).[11]

Investors in this field, it has been argued, have a risk averse approach to the pharmaceutical sector which inhibits long-term finance in R&D. In 2012, a group of academics tried to explain this phenomenon by using the analogy of the music industry:

> Imagine how hard it would be to achieve commercial success with new pop songs if any new song had to be better than the Beatles, if the entire Beatles catalogue was available for free, and if people did not get bored with old Beatles records. Yesterday's blockbuster is today's generic.[12]

Therefore, the long-term Islamic finance investment model would, on the face of it, seem a good fit for long-term R&D research which could lead to commercial returns over a longer term profile.

There have been some tentative steps from the Islamic finance industry to support long-term pharmaceutical research. In December 2014 an immunisation programme secured a US$500 million issuance of Sukuk. At that time this was the largest issuance ever by a global non-profit organisation, International Finance Facility for Immunisation Co (IFFIm).

The Sukuk as issued by the IFFIm had been part of the World Bank's efforts to adapt Sukuk for use in a variety of ethical pursuits, including advising the Dubai government on a funding strategy for the emirate's green investment programme. Two further vaccine Sukuks from the IFFIm followed—in September 2015 the vaccine Sukuk raised US$200 million and in April 2019 the vaccine Sukuk raised US$50 million.

The money raised by these Sukuk issuances supported Gavi, the public–private partnership Vaccine Alliance. Since its inception in 2000 to the end of 2017, Gavi has helped to immunise more than 288 million children in 33 Organisation of Islamic Cooperation (OIC) member states. Gavi's financial support to these countries totals more than US$6 billion as of the end of September 2018. This represented 50% of Gavi's overall disbursements worldwide.

It is interesting to note that—other than the use of Sukuks—direct investment via musharaka and mudaraba vehicles does not seem to have been adopted and that the project financing vehicle of istisn'a has also—it seems—not been utilised. This could be a reflection of wider concerns across the whole of the investment community of the risks of supporting groundbreaking pharmaceutical research.

Sukuks may be seen as helping to mitigate this risk by utilising a bond like structure.

However, an official at the World Bank has argued that the use of Sukuks to support such work helps to lever in not just investors who want to ensure their funds are part of a shari'a compliant vehicle but also engages the wider conventional investor base:

> This high level of demand from both traditional Sukuk investors and conventional investors, including those with a socially responsible investment focus, proves the convergence of Islamic finance and conventional sustainable investing is very possible.[13]

By sukuk issuances taking place in this market space, this could broaden out the range of investors attracted to this model and thereby further embed and strengthen the position of Islamic finance in the global economy.

Climate Change: Potential Opportunities for Islamic Finance

The concept of humanity having a trusteeship role in protecting the planet is an important tenet within Islam and this key principle can inform the Islamic finance industry of the opportunities and responsibilities to address the challenge of climate change.

This is not to deny the central importance of the environment in the world's other great religions. In Hinduism, the river Ganges is seen as a personification of the goddess Ganga. Protection of the environment is at the core of Jainism:

> One who neglects or disregards the existence of earth, air, fire, water and vegetation disregards his own existence which is entwined with them.[14]

The Jain concept of Ahimsa (non-violence) is linked to the protection of the environment. This leads to Jain monks and nuns acting in a scrupulous manner so that the environment is not harmed such as monks walking in the street and sweeping the ground with the utmost care to avoid accidentally crushing insects and monks wearing muslin cloths over their mouths to ensure they do not swallow any flies.

Concern for the environment is also reflected in the Yazidi religion which is followed by around 1 million people. In Lalish in Iraq, believers gain spiritual strength by being blessed at the sacred spring—a spiritual practice that has added contemporary resonance following the sufferings of the Yazidis at the hands of so-called Islamic State who invaded Sinjar province in 2014. The atrocities has been defined by the United Nations as genocide.

In Islam, the concept of vice-regency or khalifah places the environment as a core concern of the faith. As discussed in chapter five, the concept places humanity in a trusteeship role on Earth. Haneef argued that Islam is particularly well suited to address environmental concerns:

> The general public should know that they, as viceregents of God, are obligated (is wajib to them) to support any project that is undertaken for environmental protectionism. Because as God's viceregents they are answerable to God to maintain their environment.[15]

This is further exemplified when, in the Qur'ran, the need to protect environmental resources are stipulated:

> O Children of Adam! Eat and drink but waste not by excess, for God loveth not the wasters.[16]

The Prophet spoke of the need for water conservation:

> Do not waste even if performing ablution on the bank of a fast-flowing large river.[17]

These tenets link to the practical actions which could be adopted to protect the environment especially when the challenge for adapting and responding to climate change requires long-term financing.

Thomas Friedman has argued that patient capital is the ideal vehicle to help address climate change:

> Patient capital has all the discipline of venture capital — demanding a return, and therefore rigor in how it is deployed — but expecting a return that is more in the 5 to 10 percent range, rather than the 35 percent that venture capitalists look for, and with a longer payback period.[18]

However, as we have discovered, most countries have a patient capital gap which is shaped by low historical returns on certain forms of investment. Despite performance improvements in the clean tech sector over the past decade, institutional investors remain wary and have not developed the expertise and adopted the scale required to successfully capture attractive returns.

There is also a debate about the ideal place for these sources of investment to emerge from. As the level of environmental degradation initially emerged from the industrialisation of what are now developed countries, particularly from the nineteenth century, there is a global debate as to whether these developed nations should take the lead in addressing climate change. Whilst, as we will soon discover, actions are being taken by the European Union to address climate change, the scale of the problem would need developed nations to consider other options to further tackle this pressing issue.

The Chief Executive Officer of HSBC Amanah, Arsalaan Ahmed, reflected this viewpoint when discussing the need for the Islamic banking sector to address environmental objectives. The focus on the environment in developed countries, he said, does not reflect the immediate financial pressures of people living in emerging markets or, as Arsalaan Ahmed put it "*developed markets ideals meets emerging markets reality*".[19]

This is not to say that there is not a shift taking place within Islamic banking to address environmental concerns. HSBC Amanah, for instance, launched the world's first United Nations (UN) Sustainable Development Goals (SDGs) Sukuk in September 2018. It was described as "*the world's first ever benchmark sustainable sukuk issuance by a financial institution referencing the UN SDGs as use of proceeds*" with a value of RM500 million (US$12 million). This followed a US$1 billion SDG Sukuk issued by the same Islamic finance window in 2017.[20]

It is understandable that social concerns would take priority in emerging markets and it should be emphasised that environmental, social and governance (ESG), objectives which are being embraced by conventional banks and corporates, is also about addressing social issues, such as improving workers' pay levels, as was discussed in chapter four. It should be recognised, though, that in the Islamic finance markets of Malaysia and Indonesia poverty and health levels are interlinked with the issue of environmental degradation.

South East Asia suffers from bouts of haze pollution caused by the burning of forests either for timber, from large logging companies, or from people who need a living to survive by seeking new farmland In 1997/9, haze pollution in the region led to the hospitalisation of 40,000 people. In 2005 and 2006 haze incidents led to the Malaysian Government calling a state of emergency and ordering the closure of schools. In June 2012 even the iconic Petronas Towers in Kuala Lumpur was hidden from view by the denseness of the haze. In 2019, haze pollution continued from February to September.

As a consequence, there has been a debate as to whether the Governments of Malaysia and Indonesia are taking on board their khalifah responsibilities despite both countries incorporating aspects of Islamic economics within their political economy models. As one non-governmental organisation has argued, all responsible authorities should take on board their responsibilities to protect the environment:

> Malaysian and Singaporean companies in Indonesia also have to bear the responsibility of slashing and burning that is happening within their estate territories. It is the respective governments' responsibilities to take them to task. Just because they operate in a foreign country, they can't wash their hands and say it does not affect us when it actually does.[21]

Indonesia had been focusing on timber products as a key export earner:

> Indonesia has perhaps been reluctant to implement counter-measures that may compromise the objectives of national economic development. For example, cracking down on illegal logging practices in its rainforests would reduce the country's scope for generating timber export earnings and realising other economic benefits.[22]

Following the forest fires of 2015, the Indonesian Government did introduce regulations to protect peatlands to help prevent outbreaks of fire and haze. However, in April 2019, the Indonesian Environment Ministry issued a new regulation limiting the protection to peat domes thereby leaving three metre and biodiversity peat areas open once more for exploitation.

In May 2020, the problem of forest fires in the country led to a new regional haze incident which complicated the responses of regional public health authorities as they had to deal with respiratory illnesses caused by the haze and, separately, respiratory illness caused by the COVID-19 virus.

Therefore, the challenge going forward is whether sovereign Sukuks issued in Malaysia and Indonesia could address the shared issues of poverty alleviation and protecting, as well as enhancing, the environment.

The United Nations' International Panel on Climate Change (IPCC) has decreed that the scientific consensus is that human activity is leading to an unsustainable rise in carbon emissions which is harming the global ecosystem.

The World Bank found that if global temperatures were 4°C warmer than the pre-industrial period then the worldwide consequences would include:

> unprecedented heat waves, severe drought, and major floods in many regions with serious impacts on human systems, ecosystems and associated services.[23]

Lord Stern, the author of the groundbreaking 2006 *Stern Review* which considered the global economic consequences of unmitigated climate change, later went further than his initial report to illustrate the implications a lack of action could lead to:

> History indicates that vast movements of populations could involve severe, widespread and extended conflict, particularly where migration is across country borders.[24]

The Potential for Shari'a Compliant Emissions Trading

In 2015, nations came together and agreed in Paris to reduce carbon emissions by keeping a global temperature rise this century well below 2°C above pre-industrial levels and to pursue efforts to limit the temperature increase even further to 1.5°C. It was also agreed that various actions would be taken by developed countries to assist developing nations in meeting climate change targets.

In response to the Paris Agreement, the European Union stepped up its emissions trading scheme (which began in 2005). Under the scheme a cap is set on the total amount of certain greenhouse gases that can be emitted by installations covered by the programme. The cap is reduced over time so that total emissions fall.

Within the cap, companies receive or buy emission allowances, which they can trade with one another as needed. They can also buy limited amounts of international credits from emission-saving projects around the world. The limit on the total number of allowances available ensures that they have a value.

Each year a company must surrender enough allowances to cover all its emissions, otherwise heavy fines are imposed. If a company reduces its emissions, it can keep the spare allowances to cover its future needs or else sell them to another company that is short of allowances.

It is intended that trading enables emissions to be reduced where it costs least to do so. A robust carbon price also promotes investment in clean, low-carbon technologies.

Islamic finance would seem to be a good fit for emissions trading as realisable income projections can be discerned and the commodity being priced can be measured as well as meeting ethical standards.

Disappointingly, an Islamic finance emissions trading scheme has not been fully developed. Dr Naila Nazir of the University of Peshawar has argued against Islamic finance emissions trading as she stated in 2012 that carbon emissions was an artificial commodity and consequently was not asset based.

Ivano Iannelli, Chief Executive Officer of the Dubai Carbon Centre of Excellence has explained that emissions trading does fall within the framework of Islamic finance:

> CO2 *(carbon dioxide)* credits are a commodity based on adding value to existing project resources, and not a standalone intangible asset. Just like currencies which are backed by bank guarantees, CO2 credits are permits backed by an economic value given to specific commodities (i.e. power, water, fuel). As such, we strongly support Islamic banking compliance towards UN and government-backed CO2 emission reduction permits. Although we cannot foresee compliance in the voluntary market... the general consensus from all Shariah boards and scholars we have spoken with is that carbon credits should be Shariah compliant.[25]

However, Mufti Aziz ur Rehman, a religious scholar who has extensive expertise and experience in Islamic finance, was initially cautious about this field, whilst noting growing investor interest in this field within the UAE:

> The main question with regards to carbon trading is what is required to make what appears to be an artificial commodity trade into a real trade. My general opinion on the field and from my experiences in the discussions I have had with the companies, I feel the area is a totally new market and needs a lot of research and review.[26]

Nonetheless, the scientific consensus as to how carbon emissions can be measured and traded is comprehensive and so this should not be a hindrance in developing the Islamic finance side of this market.

The Iranian Government did consider shari'a compliant emissions trading in 2014. However, a 2019 University of Tehran study has found that with an increase in US sanctions being imposed on Iran, after the United States left the Joint Comprehensive Plan of Action[27] in 2018, this had affected policy priorities being set in Tehran.

The study also found "*a drastic increase in total CO2 emissions. Iran has become one of the most CO2 emitting countries after the revolution in 1979*".

With the Iranian authorities focusing on immediate economic imperatives, the report found that:

> future studies need to concentrate on development of carbon tax systems, diversification of net income, optimal privatization path, renewable energies, and CO2 capture technologies to shape more pragmatic scenarios in order to alleviate climate-change-related problems in this country.[28]

There is evidence of growing activity within the United Arab Emirates with emissions trading. However, the fact that this sector of Islamic finance has not grown exponentially may indicate the continuing reservations within the industry to embrace new market opportunities based, to some extent, upon the permissive investment culture which is prevalent in the industry.

Environmental Goals

The need for patient capital to address climate change has been given added weight by the insights of Fouquet and Pearson. Their findings concluded that it has historically taken between twenty-five to thirty years to move from one energy transition to another:

> The fastest historical sector-specific energy transitions observed here was thirty years. However, full energy transitions, involving all sectors and services, have taken much longer. Ultimately, the price of energy services played a crucial role in creating the incentives to stimulate energy transitions, but energy price shocks may have acted as a catalyst for stimulating processes that led to certain energy transitions. An additional key factor is whether the new technology offers new characteristics of value to the consumer, which can help create a market even when the initial price is higher. A crucial factor that can delay a transition is the reaction of the incumbent and declining industries.[29]

However, the urgency of climate change means we do not have thirty years to adapt to more renewable forms of energy. In 2008, the IPCC declared that global temperatures needed to be kept at around 1.5°C from pre-industrial levels by 2030.[30]

Then in 2020, IPCC commissioned research found that the failure of nations to limit global temperatures from rising over 1.5°C than they were in the pre-industrial era could cost the world economy more than US$600 trillion. However, the global economy could gain US$336—422 trillion by 2100, if action is rapidly taken to keep global temperature increases to between 2 and 1.5°C.[31]

However, as Fouquet has identified, incumbent energy providers may be resistant to this change. Stern, in turn, argued that traditional investment models is not sufficient to meet the climate change challenge and instead he called for "*risk sharing*". Stern added:

> Investors and entrepreneurs will create new business models in the context of the investment climate and opportunities that develop from the move to a low carbon economy - for example, different models of asset ownership such as leasing for rooftop solar panels.[32]

From this statement, it may be surmised that Stern is unaware that "*new business models*" to meet the specific issue of leasing for rooftop solar panels already exists in Islamic finance.

As discussed in chapter three, the concept of ijara being used to help finance solar panels has already been explored. We also discussed in chapter three that istisn'a is a good project financing tool that provides greater surety for investors as compared to conventional finance models.

An implementation of shari'a compliant investment programmes to meet environmental objectives is beginning to be implemented in the United Arab Emirates, especially in Abu Dhabi.

As part of the Abu Dhabi Vision 2030 strategy, the Abu Dhabi Government aims to have non-oil business sectors make up 64% of its overall economy by 2030—a very significant shift for the oil rich emirate. Abu Dhabi is also trying to source renewable energy via the Shams 1 Solar Plant which is one of the world's parabolic trough concentrated solar power energy bases.

The Abu Dhabi Government, as part of this 2030 strategy, wants to enlarge the Islamic finance base in the emirate and thereby explore how sukuks can be issued to help attain these ambitious environmental targets.[33]

The need for patient capital to protect the environment and so improve farming practices has also been highlighted by Friedman:

> A good example of what happens when you combine patient capital, talent and innovation in Africa is the Kenyan company Advanced Bio-Extracts (ABE), headed by Patrick Henfrey. He and his partners put together a fascinating group of both white and black African farmers and scientists to build the first company in Africa to cultivate the green leafy plant artemisia, often called sweet wormwood, and transform it into pharmaceutical grade artemisinin — a botanical extract that is the key ingredient in a new generation of low-cost, effective malaria treatments commonly known as artemisinin-based combination therapies (ACTs). Malaria still kills nearly one million people in Africa every year.[34]

The need for such long-term change to enhance yields in agriculture has also been studied by Yujiro Hayami and Vernon Ruttan. In 1971, Hayami and Ruttan produced a paper that considered the concept of Induced Innovation Theory within the context of agricultural development. This theory considered how changes in governance and institutions was required to ensure greater yields could be gained in agriculture.

In a subsequent paper produced in the 1980s, Hayami and Ruttan spoke of how:

> … the demand for institutional innovation can be satisfied by the development of new forms of property rights or more efficient market institutions …[35]

Hayami and Ruttan later added:

> We also insist on the potential significance of cultural endowments, including the factors that economists typically conceal under the rubric of tastes and that political scientists include under ideology.

The very changes that Hayami and Ruttan were calling for are inherent within Islamic finance—an ethical basis for change combined with practical contract models which provides surety for investors, positive market signals for future investment and helps ensure that sustainable development is at the heart of economic growth.

There is some resistance within the Islamic finance industry to move from a permissive investment culture towards a more proactive investment profile whereby these kinds of environmental objectives and other social goods can be targeted with the use of Islamic finance.

Stella Cox CBE, the Managing Director of the shari'a compliant firm, DDCAP, has described how some clients responded negatively to the idea of embedding environmental and socially responsible investment criteria within legal documentation:

> I can't tell you we haven't got pushback and when DDCAP suddenly starts to include impact related language, environmental considerations in its contractual arrangements, we do get the odd lawyer that comes back – let alone the odd client – that says 'Woah, lets just take a breather on this'.[36]

Whilst companies like DDCAP take the lead with the development of investment criteria for environmental and social objectives, it is not surprising that businesses who were used to the old permissive culture within the Islamic finance sector may resist this transitional period towards a more proactive investment regime within the industry.

However, with the Islamic Development Bank having successfully issued a US$1.5 billion Sukuk in June 2020 to help OIC countries recover from the coronavirus pandemic—with a focus on investing in the provision of essential public services and access to finance for small and medium sized businesses—we could be entering a new proactive investment era where the reticence of many participants in the Islamic finance industry may be finally coming to an end.

Islamic Microfinance: Models for Growth

Ahmed Al-Najjar was not a politician and he was not a religious scholar.

From the little that we know about Al-Najjar, we understand that he studied economics and he admired the German model of regional banks which had helped provide much needed finance to small and medium sized enterprises (SMEs) in West Germany's post-war reconstruction.

It was Ahmed Al-Najjar who—arguably—formed the first Islamic finance institution in the twentieth century. Though some analysts claim that interest free banking in the last century began in Hyderabad and Pakistan, it was the exemplar that was the Mit Ghamr bank in Egypt from 1963 which helped inspire many people as to what was practically possible.

What was striking about this institution was that this Islamic finance institution focused on microfinance. This contrasts with the contemporary

Islamic finance industry which has been accused of focusing too much on short term financing such as Murabaha, Ijarah and Salam.

One of the key figures in the development of the twentieth-century Islamic finance industry, Iqbal Khan (who is now the Chief Executive Officer of Fijr Capital) has argued that debt based models, such as murabaha, was initially preferred as the compliance and transparency infrastructure was not in place for the full-scale development of the Islamic finance industry. Khan added that for the 2020s, investment-based models such as mudaraba should now be in the forefront of the industry as the structures for openness and transparency are now in place. As Iqbal has commented "*Islamic finance was always a mudaraba based banking system*".[37]

Mit Ghamr did embrace a partnership approach towards investment whereby the bank became a partner in profit and loss depending on the amount of its contribution to capital. No covenant was asked for in order for loan arrangements to come into force. The bank was also involved in loans where repayments would take place without any form of mark-up or profit which is known as qard hasan. The bank is also believed to have had a fund to meet the needs of people enduring severe poverty.

In 1967 the bank's operations were transferred to larger commercial rivals. The reasons for the demise of Mit Ghamr is in dispute. It could have been a case of regulatory failure where Mit Ghamr had not properly registered with the Egyptian Central Bank. Other academics claim that the bank was closed down by the authorities as a successful Islamic financial institution would not have been in tune with Nasser's secular Arab nationalist vision.

What was clear, however, was that Islamic microfinance was a concept that worked. Since the Mit Ghamr experience, though, the most well-known microfinance operation is Dr Muhammad Yunus' Grameen microfinance programme which has transformed the lives of millions of people in Bangladesh. Yunus, when he was an economics professor at the University of Chittagong, witnessed the devastating famine which inflicted Bangladesh in 1974. The relief efforts at that time was struggling to keep people alive:

> ... perpetually hungry people survive solely on Government dole. Even the ration available in the kitchens is less than a marginal diet. Each of the 1,000 or more people who crowd around a feeding centre once a day

> is served one roti (unleavened bread) or four ounces of a porridge made from rice and lentils.[38]

One academic estimated that around 1.5 million people may have died from this famine.[39]

Yunus believed he could do something to help to help address desperate poverty and, in 1983, he formed Grameen Bank. The bank provided loans for people in Bangladesh who had no security to offer. The average loan amount offered was the equivalent of US$100. The bank's ethos was that people, however desperately poor, can manage their own financial affairs.

Grameen was such a success in changing lives for the better that, in 2006, Dr Muhammed Yunus was awarded the Nobel Peace Prize. By that time, more than seven million people had received loans. There is no doubt that Grameen is a microfinance exemplar. It is not, though, Islamic microfinance.

Grameen charge interest on their loans—though the interest rate is exceptionally low. To reduce the risk of adverse arrears rates, Grameen Bank ensures that should a borrower be unable to repay their loan, then the client would have to quit their membership of the bank as would the other group members that the client may have joined with as part of a loan arrangement. This approach seems to have been successful in mitigating against defaults.

The advantage of Islamic microfinance is that without the interest rate component, loans can be provided in an accessible way that enables microfinance to allow small business ventures to grow over time:

> … the persistence of high interest rates, even in highly active and competitive markets such as Bangladesh, has led policymakers especially to question whether the price of financial services for the poor is too high.[40]

However, concerns have been expressed that some of the contract types in Islamic finance may need additional support services for these models to be directly applicable to microfinance

Badawi and Grais considered the applicability of each contract type and how it related to microfinance. For instance, the risk sharing model of musharaka was considered:

> In practice, an Islamic microfinance provider would need to offer business development and capacity building services through a separate window than that of the financial transaction. Some conventional microfinance providers do offer training and other services to their clients. In many cases, however, these services rely on donor funds or cross subsidisation from other segments of a microfinance provider's business.

Badawi and Grais also considered the applicability of murabaha and ijara for microfinance. As discussed in chapter three, murabaha is a mark-up model whilst ijara is a leasing contract:

> The client in such a transaction benefits from competition on the wholesale market, but the costs to a microfinance provider associated with purchasing, maintaining, selling or leasing and then tracking a commodity raise questions about the efficiency of a murabaha or ijara transaction. Will these added costs, though perhaps improving the transparency, actually result in higher prices for microfinance clients?

However, it was considered that as this form of microfinance is commodity based, it had some distinct advantages:

> By emphasising materiality, murabaha and ijara instruments offer the potential to bank the poor through highly transparent transactions that leverage the economies of scale of wholesale markets.[41]

There are additional Islamic microfinance models that could prove to be particularly effective which includes the wakala model.

Wilson argued that the cooperative principles of takaful Islamic insurance with the delivery of microfinance services via a bank using the wakala (agency) model could be particularly effective in delivering microfinance services.

Under this wakala model, the Islamic microfinance institution could act as an agent whereby the microfinance fund could be provided from a zakat fund or donor agency. The microfinance institution would be paid a management fee. This helps to avoid conflict of interest problems from occurring.

As with a credit union, the clients could draw disbursements from the fund. As not all participants can withdraw funds a rationing mechanism would be necessary to meet demand when required (Fig. 7.1).[42]

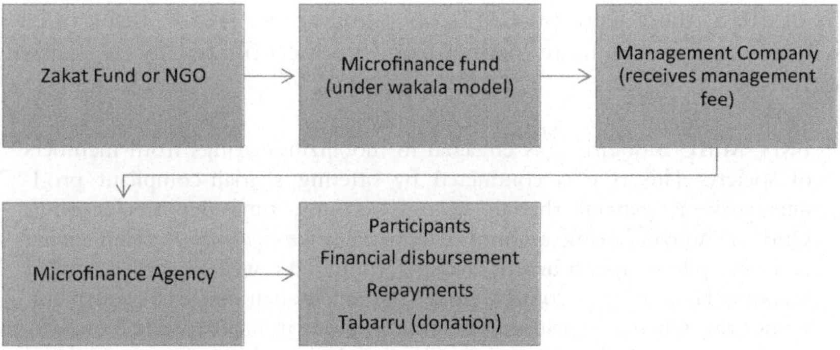

Fig. 7.1 Wakaful microfinance model

Indonesia: Baitul Maal Wat Tamwil

There is an Indonesian microfinance institution which has developed its own shari'a compliance mechanism and its origin and operations have arisen from the local community rather than from aid agencies, multilateral institutions, politicians or scholars.

Founded in 1997, Baitul Maal wat Tamwil (BMT) is a cooperative ensuring that those members of the community who pay into the fund are also decision-makers with the running of the fund. BMT was initially established in Sidogiri in east Java.

The concept of cooperatives as a financial model exits in Islamic insurance and is also based on the Indonesian concept of utilising the cooperative model to establish educational institutions. The concept of cooperation was stipulated within the 1949 version of the Indonesian constitution.[43]

Initially the BMT had a small number of contributors to the cooperative:

> People who contributed to the establishment of BMT MMU Sidogiri were: Hadlori Abd. Karim as the Chairman of Miftahul Ulum Islamic elementary school; Dumairi Noor as the Vice Chairman of Miftahul Ulum Islamic elementary school; Baihaqi Ustman as an Administrator Purser of Miftahul Ulum Islamic elementary school; Mahmud Ali Zain as a Chairman of cooperative of Sidogiri Islamic boarding school; and Muna'i Achmad as the Vice Chairman of Miftahul Ulum Islamic elementary school.[45]

As of 2015, there were 60 BMTs operating across Java.[45] BMT offers a suite of services which are distinct from products offered by the banking sector:

> BMT MMU Sidogiri ... is engaged in mobilizing savings from members of society. This role is conducted by offering shariah-compliant products such as general shariah savings account, time deposits account, Qurban/Aqiqah saving account *(children's savings account)*, Hajj saving account, pilgrimage/tourism saving account and wedding party saving account. Hajj saving account is under the mudarabah mode of investment. Under this scheme, a customer wishing to perform hajj deposits money by instalments to this fund over a specific period to be able to bear hajj related expenses when the fund is matured. The accrued dividend is distributed among the participating members for the whole period of investment.
>
> The BMT deposit products have some strength such as the duration of deposits which can be extended as the customers want; the customers will get an adequate profit sharing calculated on daily mechanism; mudarabah deposits that have been blocked cannot be released but still get profit sharing; investment is channelled to halal enterprises only; and the deposits can be used as a collateral of financing.
>
> Furthermore, to avoid the overlapping of job description between BMT and Islamic banks, BMT MMU Sidogiri only offers financing around Rp. 1 until 10 million.[46]

Other services offered includes:

- Mudarabah and Musharakah financing
- Murabahah financing
- Bai'Bitsamanil Ajil (deferred payment sale) financing
- Qard Hasan (benevolence/no interest loan)
- Pawnbroking (rahn)

The BMTs have been seen by most commentators as a great success:

> BMTs not only have a crucial role in reducing poverty and fostering local economic development but also in alleviating the scope and prevalence of illegal moneylenders trapping the poor. Using qard hasan scheme, BMTs succeed in eliminating the number of moneylenders as well as educating people regarding the jeopardy of riba.
>
> Poverty alleviation will be successful if Islamic financing institutions such as BMTs are massively conducted in many areas. So, given the important

role of BMTs in combating poverty, it is expected that the Indonesian Government, local as well as international Islamic organisations have intensified support for BMTs. The government can channel a proportion of public budget through BMTs which will then administer and manage funds for the appropriate clients. The two largest Islamic communities in Indonesia such as Nahdhatul Ulama and Muhammadiah also can maximise the role of BMTs to help the ummah, as the majority are still poor. The role of BMTs could be maximised when governments and Muslim communities are collaborating well.[47]

Dian Andari has also praised BMT for being accessible for poor people in Indonesia and as a convenient vehicle that can assist individuals who have decided to leave the rural villages to find work in the cities, often without much success:

As a microfinance institution, the BMT may provide better outreach as it is more accessible to the poorest people. The small amount of credit may encourage them to engage in financing activity. In addition, BMT as community-based cooperatives incorporate local wisdom and culture and can hence attract more participation of people, especially in rural areas where poverty is higher compared to urban areas.

More and more villagers move to cities to work. However, urbanization increases competition. People who fail in the tight competition will find more difficulties given higher living cost in the cities. Thus, to empower local communities and control hyper-urbanization, the BMT as an accessible institution for the poor has good potential in raising awareness and literacy in finance and the economy.[48]

However, Dian Andari did identify issues with financial sustainability and organisational capacity to meet the significant demand across Indonesia.[49] An Indonesian academic study into the effectiveness of BMTs reached similar conclusions:

… limitation of capital, human resources and the ability to understand the functions and programs that can be run by BMT. Therefore, the dimension of the activities that can be carried out by BMT covered only the narrow scope …[50]

BMT builds on other forms of microfinance which exists in Indonesia. Arisan is a microfinance format where, at social gatherings which take place at fixed times throughout the year, a member of the fund would receive an interest free loan by the drawing of lots. This is intended to be an equitable system where scarce funds in poor communities can be equally shared out to all members of the community.

Ericsson's Head of Marketing in Indonesia, Hardyana Syintawati, described her experiences as a child with the arisan format:

> When I was about ten years old, I thought that it was high time for me to have my own bike rather than sharing one with my sister. And so I asked my mom for one. She shook her head and told me: "I am sorry, dear, but I have no money to buy you a bicycle." But then she smiled and continued, "But I will have an arisan coming up. I can ask my friend if I can have the turn so that we can use the arisan money to buy you a bike!"[51]

These forms of microfinance are said to have their genesis in the communal societies of Indonesia and in the decision of the Dutch colonial authorities in the nineteenth century to import the Volkscredietwezen or credit system into Java.

Forms of microfinance were given a boost during the 'Green Revolution' when new agricultural techniques to increase yields was introduced into Indonesia from the mid-1960s. With the purchase of fertilisers being a key prerequisite to achieve increased harvests, microfinance was used to help farmers gain the upfront funds for the acquisition of these fertilisers.

Under Suharto's New Order regime, banks were encouraged, from 1983, to ensure there was microfinance provision. It was, though, the 1997 Asian Financial Crisis which led to a proliferation of microfinance schemes as the collapse in the value of the currency and asset prices hit the very poorest in Indonesian society.

Today, BMT is a trusted institution which has helped people to avoid the depredations of the money lenders who visit communities and charge high interest rates. BMT has not only helped people survive but has enabled individuals to put aside as much as they can reasonably afford in savings accounts.

Despite the criticisms regarding the lack of capacity, the very nature of BMT as a ground up initiative provides it with the strength and credibility to undertake its good work.

As ever with microfinance schemes, the issue is whether demand will outstrip the supply of funds. Potentially, the nature of this cooperative model with funds, however small, being topped up by individuals to the BMT will help this model continue to reach some form of sustainability.

Microfinance: The Role of the Islamic Development Bank

The Islamic Development Bank (IsDB) was one of a number of institutions which were founded in the 1970s and has since helped to shape the operation and practices of the contemporary Islamic finance industry.

The IsDB operates under the aegis of the Organisation of Islamic Co-operation (OIC). It was Malaysia's first Prime Minister, Tunku Abdul Rahman, who played a leading role in establishing the IsDB with the IsDB having been formally opened in October 1975. Rahman saw the IsDB as a key vehicle to engender a sense of global Muslim solidarity:

> After a time, I decided to win greater popularity for our movement by forming the Islamic Development Bank to give financial help to member countries, to make them feel they were taken care of by their richer Muslim brothers.[52]

Today, the IsDB serves the 57 member states of the OIC and Muslim communities in non-OIC countries. Its overall budget was US$7.8 billion in 2018.[53]

Alongside funding development projects, the IsDB promotes the concepts of Islamic finance and Islamic economics:

> As there is growing realization of the essence of Islamic finance, the IsDB considers its strategic advantage in knowledge of Islamic economics and finance as useful in shaping new frontiers for achieving sustainable development.[54]

The IsDB has, therefore, invested in the growth of the Islamic financial services market:

> In line with its core mandate, the IsDB has since inception been undertaking various activities to support the development of the Islamic Financial Services Industry (IFSI). Over the past 40 years, the IsDB Group has supported the development of IFSI through various initiatives, such as
>
> i. equity investments in Islamic financial institutions;
> ii. technical assistance activities for capacity building;
> iii. establishment of Islamic infrastructure institutions;
> iv. development of financial products/funds; and

v. the joint development of the "Ten-Year Framework for Developing the IFSI.[55]

As for its core development work, this has included support for microfinance projects:

> … the IsDB has been achieving encouraging development impacts through 56 active Islamic microfinance projects with a total approval of US$466.72 million. The portfolio is segmented into 17 standalone projects (US$333.14 million) and 39 agriculture projects with a microfinance component (US$133.58 million). The significance of the impacts of Islamic microfinance projects is illustrated with the recently completed Youth Employment Support project in Egypt and the Rural Income and Employment Enhancement Project in Uganda. The first project has created 20,257 jobs for the youths to date. The second has provided financing to 458,956 rural individuals and created employment opportunities for 1.2 million people throughout the country. In order to further enhance Islamic microfinance, knowledge dissemination activities on Islamic microfinance were undertaken. For instance, a workshop was organised on "Value Chain Financing at the Heart of Microfinance: How to do it and How to Measure its Impact". In addition, Islamic Microfinance for Women's Financial Inclusion Report and Toolkit was launched to provide mechanisms for financial inclusion through Islamic microfinance.[56]

There appears to be a focus from the Bank for utilising the Murabaha model for use in Islamic microfinance programmes. Impressive though this work clearly is, it should also be noted that the $466.72 million allocated for microfinance is out of a budget of nearly $8 billion. Admittedly, there are many calls on the IsDB funds including funding capital investment programmes so that the infrastructure in developing countries can support sustainable economic growth.

It is, though, the promise of microfinance that enables hope to be engendered that the poverty cycle can be broken. There is a specific hadith which recalls the words of the Prophet on this very subject:

> A man of the Ansar came to the Prophet (peace be upon him) and begged from him.
>
> The Prophet asked: Have you nothing in your house? He replied: Yes, a piece of cloth, a part of which we wear and a part of which we spread (on the ground), and a wooden bowl from which we drink water.

He said: Bring them to me. He then brought these articles to him and the Prophet took them in his hands and asked: Who will buy these? A man said: I shall buy them for one dirham. He said twice or thrice: Who will offer more than one dirham? A man said: I shall buy them for two dirhams.

He gave these to him and took the two dirhams and, giving them to the Ansari, he said: Buy food with one of them and hand it to your family, and buy an axe and bring it to me. He then brought it to him. The Apostle of Allah (peace be upon him) fixed a handle on it with his own hands and said: Go, gather firewood and sell it, and do not let me see you for a fortnight. The man went away and gathered firewood and sold it. When he had earned ten dirhams, he came to him and bought a garment with some of them and food with the others.

The Apostle of Allah (peace be upon him) then said: This is better for you than that begging should come as a spot on your face on the Day of Judgment. Begging is right only for three people: one who is in grinding poverty, one who is seriously in debt, or one who is responsible for compensation and finds it difficult to pay.[57]

With the exception of the poor man using his coins as seed money, this hadith is a description of the operation of microfinance. Whilst international development policy from a number of donor countries in recent years has moved towards this self-sustainability model, it is microfinance with its bottom up approach that is particularly well suited to address systemic solutions when meeting the objective of poverty alleviation.

The issuance of Sukuks could be a way forward to consider widening the funding base of the financing of Islamic microfinance. An under standing of the role of bond financing in supporting microfinance work can be seen with the work of the Grameen Foundation. In 2004 it issued a microfinance conventional bond in the United States which raised $40 million which was partly underwritten.

The Grameen Foundation had also established a $60 million Growth Guarantee Programme which was organised with Citibank. The programme included a 25% financial commitment to Citibank. In return Citibank issued a letter of credit to a financial institution which could loan funds to a microfinance institution.

It is these kinds of precedents which could be considered by the IsDB and other donor countries engaged in supporting microfinance in order to widen the pool of microfinance projects in developing countries.

As a consequence of the 2020 COVID-19 crisis, the President of the Islamic Development Bank Group, Dr Bandar Hajjar, has said the crisis could be a pivotal moment to help reshape the global economy:

> I believe this is an opportunity to shift towards actively shaping and creating markets that deliver sustainable and inclusive growth, rather than continue limiting our role at the government and international community level to reacting to market failures. We can proactively invest in creating and strengthening institutions that prevent crisis. We can coordinate scientific and technological responses, and research and development activities steering them towards public good. We can forge Public-Private-Philanthropic-People-Partnerships to ensure both citizens and economies are going to benefit.[58]

Further IsDB support for microfinance could help realise this vision.

Microfinance and Self-Sufficiency

Islamic microfinance can do more than simply address immediate needs. The Muslim Fund Najibabad in the Indian province of Uttar Pradesh is one example of the empowering capacity of such schemes.

The Fund, which is estimated to be worth US$18 million in deposits, was instigated by Izfarul Haq Zaki (also known as Qaziji) in 1972. Zaki recalls the day that he came home from his degree graduation ceremony to see moneylenders at the door of his home harassing his family for payment of loans—that had been accrued to pay for Zaki's education:

> My family had suffered badly at the hands of moneylenders. Since then I have promised myself never to let anyone from my community fall prey to them.[59]

Not only can microfinance free people from desperate poverty and away from the grasp of moneylenders but Islamic microfinance can help engender a savings culture which can ensure a growing asset base for a family and a community. In essence, micro savings can be seen as the flip side of microfinance loan provision.

Once immediate needs are addressed by a loan, the next step would be to engender a savings culture that is directly attributable to the individual ability to save. Nisar and Rahman have examined the operation of micro savings in India. At the very least, it was found to help sustain a base for forward loan provision:

> Micro savings have the crucial advantages of satisfying the demand for savings products from clients and mobilising large amounts of funds at low financial costs. Low financial costs, which in turn reduces the rate of lending for borrowers can be viewed as a society subsidising credit for needy members by demanding a low rate of returns on its capital.

This approach also has wider implications:

> …. savings have strong macroeconomic implications. Savings strengthen the process of development in societies and for the poor savings act as an insurance policy.[60]

Choudhury has analysed the interrelationship between Islamic microfinance and engendering a savings culture in Bangladesh and describes how Islamic banks provide loans which are tied to the Bai-Muajjal ('Sale and Purchase') concept. Similar to the salam model, Bai-Muajjal stipulates how the seller sells goods to the buyer at an agreed price payable at a fixed future date in lump sum or within a period of agreed instalments. The seller may also sell the goods purchased as per the order and specification of the buyer.

A bank would treat Bai-Muajjal as a contract between the bank and the client under which the bank sells the goods to the client at an agreed price payable at any fixed future date in a lump sum or within a defined period of agreed instalments. Therefore, the ownership of the goods is transferred by the bank to the client but the payment of the sale price by the client is deferred for an agreed period.

Choudhury states this loan provision is predicated upon Bangladeshi Islamic banks encouraging customers to begin to save according to their ability to do so:

> Senior bank staff members are trained in such a way as to motivate customers to improve their saving habits and also to give them moral teachings.[61]

Shari'a compliant microfinance schemes are operating across the developing world. It has distinct advantages over conventional microfinance as the interest rate component, even at a very low level, can be a significant hurdle for individuals and families when considering the options before them in enable them to move past surviving towards thriving.

Whilst for small and medium sized businesses, mudaraba and musharaka contract types are suitable for medium to long-term financing, the immediate needs to be met in developing countries would require murabaha and ijara contract types to be considered. The lessons of cooperative takaful Islamic insurance can also be applied to Islamic microfinance with the wakala model whilst the community led shari'a compliant schemes in Indonesia are an inspiring example as to how local people, battling against the odds, can improve the lives of their friends and neighbours.

The potential for the growth of shari'a compliant microfinance can be seen in a range of countries such as Nigeria. Around half of the Nigerian population (102,125,917 people) live in extreme poverty.[62] At the same time, the demand for shari'a complaint microfinance schemes in the country may exist due to this severe deprivation and because 51.6% of the population identify themselves as Muslim.[63]

However, a 2016 study found that:

> Despite the popularity of Islamic microfinance among Islamic banks in other countries like Bangladesh, Malaysia, Pakistan, and Sudan, none of the Islamic banks in Nigeria has come forward with a Sharī'ah compliant microfinance scheme as a way of contributing to the improvement of standard of living among the less privileged citizens of Nigeria.[64]

The potential for the growth of the shari'a compliant microfinance sector is there.

With the International Monetary Fund predicting, in April 2020, that by the end of 2020, the global economy would contract by—3%,[65] the demand for shari'a compliant microfinance could grow exponentially.

Microfinance and Developed Countries

So far, we have considered Islamic microfinance from the perspective of assisting poor communities in developing countries—but microfinance also operates in developed nations.

These schemes are not based on shari'a compliance. Instead, the programmes are managed by a Christian charity which operates the zero interest microfinance schemes in Australia and New Zealand.

Despite Australia being a wealthy country, one Australian charity which provides food banks for Australian households, stated in 2020 that 5 million Australians experienced food insecurity in the last 12 months, which included 1 in 4 Australian women experiencing food insecurity. In addition, "*at least once a week, 3 in 10 food insecure Australians go a whole day without eating*".[66] The Christian support organisation, the Salvation Army, has also reported incidents of food hunger in New Zealand.[67]

A Christian charity, Good Shepherd Sisters, which was instigated in 1863 in Melbourne by Saint Mary Euphrasia Pelletier, is pioneering zero interest rate loans across Australia and New Zealand. From 2012, the No Interest Loan Scheme (NILS) is said to have benefited more than 400,000 people.[68]

The British Government seemed intrigued by the NILS scheme and it therefore commissioned a consultancy to ascertain if such a project could operate in the United Kingdom. Poverty is an issue in the UK with the World Bank estimating that around 2 million people in the country suffer from some form of malnutrition[56] whilst a United Nations report from April 2019 stated that 1.5 million people suffered from destitution in the United Kingdom.[69]

In its report to the British Government, which was published in August 2019, the consultancy firm, London Economics, stated that not only was a NILS programme required, it would also reach a larger number of people compared to low interest loan schemes:

> This analysis suggests that, for a £500 loan repaid over 1 year, around 274 thousand people would be able to afford to repay a no-interest loan but not to repay a loan carrying interest at the CDFI average rate of 7.2%.[70]

The concept of interest inhibiting escape routes from poverty is now being embraced by NGOs and Governments in developed nations. This provides a space for shari'a forms of microfinance to enter this space. Not only can such an opportunity assist families who are facing hardship but it can be a gateway for new customers to consider and later access commercial Islamic finance services.

At a time when the idea of zero interest ideas is taking hold, the Islamic finance industry could consider how its concepts and products can be harnessed to engage with this emerging zeitgeist in developed nations.

Social Impact Bonds

Islamic finance could embrace social impact bonds. Unlike traditional bonds, social impact bonds are not affected by variables such as interest rate risk, reinvestment risk or market risk. They are still subject to default and inflation risk.

Investors gain a return on their investment by the number of social outcomes that had been attained. For instance, it could relate to the record of a substance abuse recovery charity and the investor could receive a return that is linked to the number of people who were imbibing alcohol and/or drugs but had since ceased doing so due to the actions of the charity.

It has been defined by a British NGO as:

> a financial mechanism in which investors pay for a set of interventions to improve a social outcome that is of financial interest to a government commissioner. If the social outcome improves, the government commissioner repays the investors for their initial investment plus a return for the financial risks they took. If the social outcomes do not improve above an agreed threshold, the investors stand to lose their investment.[71]

In 2011, Peterborough Prison in the UK issued a social impact bond which raised £5 million from seventeen social investors to fund a pilot project with the objective of reducing the re-offending rates of short-term prisoners. The relapse or re-conviction rates of prisoners released from Peterborough was compared with the relapse rates of a control group of prisoners over six years.

If Peterborough's re-conviction rates were at least 7.5% below the rates of the control group of prisoners, investors received an increased return that was directly proportional to the difference in relapse rates between the two groups and this was capped at 13% annually over an eight-year period.

Other examples include, in the United States, the New York City Social Impact Bond, launched in 2012, which raised $9.6 million to finance a programme aimed at reducing reoffending among young offenders at a correctional facility.

In Australia, the Newpin Social Benefit Bond, launched in New South Wales in 2013, raised AU$7 million capital for a parenting programme to return children from the care system to their families whilst also preventing children deemed to be at risk from entering the care system.

The social impact bonds model could be seen as equivalent to Hibat al-thawab (gift with expected compensation) with a verse in the Qur'ran that seems to relate to this structure:

> Whatever you lend out in interest to gain value through other people's wealth will not increase in Allah's sight, but whatever you claim in charity, in your desire for Allah's approval, will earn multiple rewards.[72]

Mezzanine Finance and Islamic Finance: A Comparative Analysis

As part of regular conventional financing functions, mezzanine finance can be considered by businesses. Mezzanine financing is a hybrid of debt and equity financing that gives the lender the rights to convert to an ownership or equity stake in the company in case of a default.

Mezzanine financing, which can be completed with little due diligence on the part of the lender and with little or no collateral on the part of the borrower, is treated like equity on a company's balance sheet.

Companies appreciate mezzanine capital, because the mezzanine investor provides subordinated financing without expecting to have the rights that a shareholder possesses.

Banks appreciate mezzanine financing, as it is subordinated to their bank loans and does not give the mezzanine investors any rights to participate, when in case of default the collaterals are sold and the recovery revenues are distributed. Mezzanine investors prefer companies with predictable cash flow, being able to cover the debt service for principal and interest payments.

Mezzanine investors do not favour small volume financing. US$11 million and more per company is an attractive size from the view of a commercial mezzanine investor. $3 million is often the lower limit for a commercial mezzanine investor.

Islamic finance compares favourably to conventional mezzanine financing. Islamic finance has some in-built advantages which would provide some support for technology businesses who are concerned at the defined timeframes for returns, the level of returns that are expected and the fear that accessing conventional funds could mean losing control of your own start-up business. With the risk sharing model combined with the stage by stage project funding approach of the istisn'a model, the opportunities for the Islamic finance industry in this field could be immense.

Risk sharing models in Islamic finance is ideal for long-term investment whilst murabaha and salam are good vehicles for short-term finance. It could be argued that the models which exist in Islamic finance can also be adopted for medium term financing. Such an approach would enable the Islamic finance sector to grow further by encroaching upon the space currently occupied by mezzanine finance providers.

Crowdfunding and Islamic Finance

Crowdfunding is a way of raising finance by asking a large number of people to contribute individually a small amount of money to support a business venture. Traditionally, financing a business project would have involved asking a few people to provide large sums of money.

Crowdfunding switches this idea around, using the internet to talk to thousands—if not millions—of potential funders. Typically, those seeking funds will set up a profile of their project on a website combined with the use of social media.

The first online crowdfunded project is thought to have occurred in 1997. Rock band Marillion were unable to afford to tour after the release of their seventh album so American fans used the then fledgling internet to raise $60,000 so they could play in the US.

With debt crowdfunding, investors receive their money back with interest. Also called Peer-to-Peer (p2p) lending, it allows for the lending of money while bypassing traditional banks. With equity crowdfunding, people invest in a venture in exchange for equity. Money is exchanged for shares or a small stake in the business or venture.

Within Islamic finance, crowdfunding is beginning to make itself felt. Yomken was formed in Egypt just one year after the 2011 Arab Spring when real change and reform across the Arab world seemed to be close at hand. The business was supported by the World Bank and it aimed to support micro and small enterprises (MSEs). Yomken had two key programmes:

An **open-innovation platform** for low-tech MSEs or NGOs working with these MSEs to post the challenges they face (publicly or anonymously) and then link them to creative solutions provided using the "wisdom of the crowd". These challenges can vary from product development, production process optimization, usage of alternative raw material, etc. This matchmaking process is fully compliant with the standards of transparency and intellectual rights protection, as described in the platform's Terms & Conditions.

A **marketplace** where innovators and creative people can post their innovative projects, patents and market researches to be linked with financial vehicles (e.g. VCs, Crowdfunding platforms and others) to get support and/or investment, as well as, other collaborators and knowledgeable people to assist in further developing their projects.[73]

Whilst the platform is not formally part of the Islamic finance sector, the company describes itself as "*shari'a friendly*" and it does not charge interest for its services.

Another Egyptian start-up was Shekwa. It describes itself as shari'a compliant and it aims to bring businesses and investors together for shari'a based investment opportunities.

Whilst Yomken and Shekwa are trailblazers, the lack of significant growth for Islamic finance in this space does indicate real potential which has yet to be realised.

As has been discussed elsewhere in this book, the permissive approach to investment strategy (as discussed in chapter four) may be a factor in not considering these new opportunities whilst the focus on sukuks from many in the investor community may mean that crowdfunding and other investment vehicles are being neglected as a consequence.

Nonetheless, shari'a complaint fintechs are slowly making their presence felt. These include Blossom Finance in Indonesia, Kestrl in the United Kingdom and Insha in Germany. It is the success or otherwise of shari'a compliant fintechs that will indicate whether the Islamic finance industry as a whole is more open to proactive investment strategies.

Impact Investing: Is Islamic Finance Being Ignored?

The synergies between Islamic finance and the concept of impact investing are strong.

Impact investments are defined as investments made with the intention to generate positive, measurable social and environmental impact alongside a financial return. Impact investments can be made in both emerging and developed markets and target a range of returns from below market to market rate.

The growing impact investment market provides capital to address systemic concerns such as sustainable agriculture, renewable energy, conservation, microfinance, and affordable access to basic services such as housing, healthcare, and education.

According to the Global Impact Investment Network, as of December 2018, the global size of the impact investment network was US$502 billion.[74] According to this report, 58% of impact investment funds are based in the United States and Canada and 21% of impact investment funds are based in Europe.

However, a closer look at these figures reveal some very surprising results. Only 1% of impact investment funds are located in the Middle East and North Africa, only 3% of impact investment funds are located in South Asia and only 2% of impact investment funds are located in South East Asia. However, how can this be so, when the Middle East and North Africa, South Asia and South East Asia are the global centres for Islamic finance where ethics and good investment practices are integral to Islam?

It could be that Islamic finance is not recognised for its ethos of impact investment and this is a perception issue which the industry needs to change. Whilst a significant proportion of Islamic finance is linked to trade finance and mortgages, the size of the Sukuk market is considerable and ethical values are key to choosing investments as part of the decision-making processes in connection with these issuances. Therefore, many of these Sukuks could be classed as impact investment.

As has been discussed earlier in this chapter, the permissive approach to investment when deciding which firms to invest in, rather than a more proactive investment strategy based on ethics, may be a factor as to why the Global Impact Investment Network (GIIN) believes there is such a low number of impact investment activity taking place in the regions of the world which contains significant Islamic finance operations.

As was discussed in chapter four, the decision of the Malaysian Central Bank to encourage Islamic financial institutions, via its Value Based Intermediation guidance, to consider proactive ethical investment strategies would tend to suggest that the GIIN may not have fully considered the role of at least a number of Islamic finance vehicles which operate in the impact investment space.

Family Offices and Islamic Finance

Family offices are also playing an active role in impact investments. A family office performs centralised management or oversight of investments, tax planning, estate planning, and philanthropic planning for a family which contains high net-worth individuals. GIIN have argued that a number of family offices:

> … belong to wealthy entrepreneurs, often those who have made their money in technology, which means, unsurprisingly, many impact investing projects involve tech solutions.[75]

Family offices can include charitable foundations such as the foundation set up by the Hong Kong businessman, Li Ka-shing, or the foundation set up by the founder of Alibaba, Jack Ma.

The combination of impact investment, philanthropy and family offices is becoming a global trend which is being felt in the Persian Gulf region. Arnaud Leclercq, head of new markets for Swiss private bank Lombard Odier has said that some of the bank's ultra-high-net worth and family office clients in the member states of the Gulf Cooperation Council require up to 100% of their portfolio to be shari'a compliant. This trend prompted the bank to expand its Islamic banking segment in 2012.[76]

Zaim Hajdari, who has an "InvestHalal" financial planning platform that screens financial assets to ensure shari'a-compliance, has argued that there is a potential for further family offices to be established in the United States to tap into shari'a compliant investments:

> … a fifth of American Muslims earn more than $1 million, 81% of them are aged between 18 and 49, 65% have a college or post-graduation degree, and 69% pray at least once a day.
>
> We feel that there is a high degree of probability that the same people who choose to live, eat and drink Halal …would also choose to invest Halal given the opportunity to do so.[77]

CSR Law in India: What Are the Implications for Islamic Economics?

Islamic finance could be impacted by the passage of the Corporate Social Responsibility (CSR) Law in India. India is the only country in the world which has bespoke legislation for CSR.

Following a change in company law in April 2014, businesses with annual revenues of more than 10 billion rupees (US$132 million) must give away 2% of their net profit to charity. Areas where this money can be invested include education, poverty alleviation, gender equality and food programmes.

A survey by accountancy firm KPMG found that 52 of the country's largest 100 companies failed to spend the required 2% in 2016. A smaller proportion has gone further, according to an Economic Times investigation, allegedly cheating the system by giving donations to their own charitable foundations minus a commission. One sustainability director was quoted to have said "*charitable giving used to be a big reputation builder for us, now it's just about legal compliance*".

Azim Premji, head of the Information Technology services firm Wipro has also expressed disquiet at the law:

> Spending 2% on CSR is a lot, especially for companies that are trying to scale up in these difficult times.

Indian Prime Minister, Narendra Modi, though, has been clear that the law in this area is required:

> I have requested the corporates to evolve plans under corporate social responsibility to build clean toilets, especially for girl students in schools. India should learn from foreign countries, where people are disciplined and do not litter in public spaces.

Despite the concerns of business, Mitra and Chatterjee have argued that the law is needed to address the excessive wealth inequalities within India:

> … India is home to the sixth largest super-rich population (billionaires) in the world. The total billionaire wealth was estimated to be $180 billion bringing India's billionaire population to 103. Therefore, the population is divided between the haves and the have-nots. The country has urban India on one side and rural Bharat on the other. Thus, under these circumstances, it is imperative that the national agenda should focus on empowering 'the poor and the deprived section of the society to achieve significant and sustainable human development and to bring about inclusive growth.[78]

Consequently, the ethical aspects of Islamic economics, particularly through its philanthropy activities such as via the payment of zakat, can be effectively utilised in the Indian context because of this legislative framework.

However, in December 2019, the Indian Parliament approved the Citizenship Bill, as tabled by the Hindu nationalist Bharatiya Janata Party (Indian People's Party—BJP), which—in effect—grants Indian citizenship to people who may originate from Pakistan, Bangladesh and Afghanistan unless they are Muslim. The passage of the law later led to rioting and ethnic tensions in Delhi.

Therefore the consequences for Islamic economics to express its ethical credentials via India's CSR legislative framework may be difficult within the wider Indian political context at the time of writing (2020) where there is evidence of a significant level of Islamophobia being expressed in parts of the country. On the other hand, the engagement of the values of Islamic economics via the processes as decreed by the CSR Law could be a useful contribution to begin to address communal tensions where they exist.

Islamic Finance: What Is Holding the Industry Back?

With Islamic finance structured for long-term investment patterns, questions have been asked by scholars and market participants as to why there has not been a step change in the stance of the industry in meeting these market opportunities.

Irfan, for example, has implied that greed combined with the chase for short-term profits is the underlying reason for the hesitancy of the Islamic finance industry to explore new revenue streams:

> What about taking up the mantle on ethical finance? Instead of financing the purchase of English Premier League football clubs – complete with pork pie stalls and bars serving alcohol, cleverly 'structured' out of the deal via a wrapper – perhaps Islamic institutions should take a greater role in championing employee rights and environmental concerns in the deals they finance – 'Sharia based' not just 'Sharia compliant'. Perhaps the types of assets they should be looking to finance should be the lifeblood of a real economy, the small and medium enterprises, rather than trophy assets for the personal enjoyment of ultra-high net worth princes.[79]

With the legal structures being identified with the ethical branding of Islamic finance combined with the sector taking greater advantage of patient finance opportunities, this could be a win-win scenario; good for gaining decent returns for investors and good for meeting the aims of attaining sustainable growth. Islamic financial institutions such as Al Rayan Bank in the UK, already cite ethics when promoting its mission to retail customers.[80]

One of the factors inhibiting growth relate to the negative permissions culture where the focus is on what not to invest in rather than proactively seeking new market opportunities.

Therefore, though behavioural factors could be inhibiting the industry's development, as Irfan implies, such inhibitions may also be linked towards the institutional culture of the sector itself.

In chapter four, we considered negative screening where people could invest in confidence knowing that their funds would be allocated on a shari'a basis by consulting the Dow Jones Islamic Markets Index (DJIMI).

Bennett and Iqbal studied the DJIMI and they argued in their 2013 study that Islamic finance relied heavily on negative screening.[79] Shari'a compliant equity funds have grown significantly through screening and filtering of shares according to a set of rules which screen out prohibited activities such as gambling and alcohol production.

Mohamed, Lehner and Khorshid have argued that the growth of the sector has been supply-side driven and so the customer demands that has been witnessed in conventional finance, which has led to a range of providers establishing ethical investment vehicles, has not been fully replicated in Islamic finance—even though Islamic finance is inherently ethically based. In Malaysia it was the Government rather than consumers that shaped the initial structure of the industry and this, consequently, influenced the product range that was introduced to the market.

Mohamed, Lehner and Khorshid argue that reference to historical precedents may lead to a more responsive Islamic finance sector going forward:

> The shift from the social sector to the government sector, by adding bureaucracy and removing the flexibility of the system, and the coming of colonial intervention in these Muslim countries contributed to the downfall of the zakat and waqf (charitable foundation) system world-wide. In some countries, like Turkey and Egypt vestiges of the old system continue to exist. And in countries like Malaysia and Singapore, there are attempts

at reviving the old system and using the concept to build more innovative ways to solve social issues.[81]

As we have seen in this chapter, there are many opportunities for Islamic finance to harness its USPs in terms of patient capital and its ethical framework by accessing new market opportunities. There have been some tentative steps taken by the industry in this direction such as the emergence of some vaccine sukuks, the establishment of some family offices in the Persian Gulf region and early discussions regarding shari'a compliant emissions trading.

Whilst the full potential of Islamic finance is yet to realised in the patient capital and ethical finance space, we have begun to discern synergies between Islamic finance concepts and conventional finance concepts such as social capital and impact investment.

As will be seen in the next chapter, the challenge is whether Islamic economics can now go beyond addressing micro economic themes, such as microfinance, to devising an Islamic monetary policy.

Looking forward to devising this policy framework has led to calls to look back to an asset that can support this form of macro-economics.

It is an asset that holds its lustre in all markets and cultures.

It is an asset that has driven people to profit and penury.

It is an asset that continues to excite the imagination.

That asset is gold.

Notes

1. As quoted in *Business Life*, British Airways, December 2018.
2. *Financial Times* (28 March 2018), Saudi Arabia Signs Soft Bank Deal to Invest $200bn in Solar.
3. *The Oxford Handbook of Business History*, page 516.
4. Invest Europe data.
5. Alex Lazarow (March 2020), *Beyond Silicon Valley*, Harvard Business Review.
6. *The Oxford Handbook of Business History*, page 208.
7. https://www.nbcnews.com/health/health-care/scientists-were-close-coronavirus-vaccine-years-ago-then-money-dried-n1150091.
8. Evidence to the US Congress, 4 March 2020.
9. https://medium.com/@aronsebastian/corporate-venture-capital-and-the-pharmaceutical-industry-52064fc5fb18.

10. Jack W Scannell, Alex Blanckley, Helen Boldon, Brian Warrington (March 2012), *Diagnosing the Decline in Pharmaceutical R&D*, Nature Reviews Drug Discovery.
11. Michael Bennett, *Vaccine Sukuks: Islamic Securities Deliver Economic and Social Returns*, World Bank blog (October 2015).
12. Mahavira.
13. Sayed Sikandar Shah Haneef (2002), Principles of Environmental Law in Islam, *Arab Law Quarterly*, vol. 17, no. 3, pp. 241–254.
14. Surah al Araaf, The Heights 7:31.
15. Al Thirmidhi.
16. Thomas Friedman, 'Patient' Capital for an Africa That Can't Wait, *New York Times*, 20 April 2007.
17. Islamic Markets webinar, 24 June 2020.
18. https://www.undp.org/content/undp/en/home/news-centre/news/2018/HSBC_Amanah_Malaysia_issues_worlds_first_United_Nations_Sustainable_Development_Goals_sukuk.html.
19. Anthony Tan, Centre for Environment, Technology and Development Malaysia as quoted in the Wall Street Journal, 20 June 2012.
20. Christopher Dent, *East Asian Regionalism*, page 267.
21. World Bank, June 2013.
22. Nicholas Stern, *Why Are We Waiting—The logic, Urgency and Promise of Tackling Climate Change*, pages 12–13.
23. Islamic Finance News, 15 May 2013.
24. This was an agreement signed by Iran, United States, China, United Kingdom, France, Germany, Russia, European Union in 2015 to ensure Iran would not acquire nuclear weapons. In 2018, the United States withdrew as a signatory to the agreement.
25. Seyed Mohsen Hosseini, Amirali Saifoddin, Reza Shirmohammadi, Alireza Aslani (February 2019), *Forecasting of CO_2 Emissions in Iran Based on Time Series and Regression Analysis*, University of Tehran.
26. Roger Fouquet (2016), Historical Energy Transitions: Speed, Prices and System Transformation, *Energy Research & Social Science*, vol. 22. pp. 7–12.
27. Ibid.
28. https://www.ipcc.ch/2018/10/08/summary-for-policymakers-of-ipcc-special-report-on-global-warming-of-1-5c-approved-by-governments/.
29. Yi-Ming Mei, Rong Han, Ce Wang, Qiao-Mei Lang, Xiao-Chen Yuan, Junjie Chang, Qingyu Zhao, Hua Liao, Baojun Tang, Jinyue Yang, Lijing Cheng, Zili Yang (April 2020), *Self Preservation Strategy for Approaching Global Warning Targets in the Post Paris Agreement Era*, Nature Communications.
30. Nicholas Stern, *What Are We Waiting?*, page 98.

31. Umar F Moghul, *A Socially Responsible Islamic Finance: Character and the Common Good* and Abu Dhabi Government *Vision 2030* documentation.
32. Thomas Friedman (20 April 2007), 'Patient' Capital for an Africa That Can't Wait, *New York Times*.
33. Vernon W Ruttan, Yujiro Hayami, *Can Economic Growth Be Sustained?*, pages 224–244.
34. Islamic Markets webinar, 10 June 2020.
35. *New York Times* (13 November 1974), Bangladesh Fears Thousands May Be Dead as Famine Spreads.
36. Islamic Markets Webinar, 12 August 2020.
37. Alamgir, M. (1980). Famine in South Asia: Political economy of mass starvation. Massachusetts: Oelgeschlager, Gunn & Hain.
38. Samer Badawi, Wafik Grais, 'Meeting the demand for sustainable shari'a compliant microfinance, *Shari'a-Compliant Microfinance*, pages 9–16.
39. Ibid.
40. Wilson, R. 2007. "Making Development Assistance Sustainable through Islamic Microfinance," *IIUM International Conference on Islamic Banking and Finance*. Kuala Lumpur.
41. The role of co-operatives within Islamic finance is discussed in chapter eight.
42. Muhammad Akhyar Adnam, Shochrul Rohmatul Ajija (2015), The Effectiveness of Baitul Maal wat Tamwill in Reducing Poverty, *Humanomics*, vol. 31, no. 2.
43. Ibid.
44. Ibid.
45. Ibid.
46. Dian Andari, Islamic Co-operatives Can Help Alleviate Poverty, *The Jakarta Post*, 8 August 2017.
47. Ibid.
48. A J W Mahri, S A Utami, Firmansyah, A Cakhyaneu (2015), *Baitul Maal Wat Tamwil as an Islamic Financial Inclusion Institution Model Towards Sustainable Development*, Universitas Pendidikan Indonesia.
49. Hardyana Syintawati, *Arisan and the Rise of M-Commerce in Indonesia* (22 September 2014), Ericsson blog.
50. Abdul Rahman, Putra Al-Haj (1983) Something to Remember (Selangor:Malaysia: Eastern Universities Press), p. 146.
51. IsDB Annual Report 2019.
52. Ibid.
53. Ibid.
54. Ibid.
55. *Sunan Abu-Dawud* [9:1637] Narrated Anas ibn Malik.
56. IsDB, 23 March 2020, https://www.isdb.org/news/president-of-the-islamic-development-bank-group-are-we-ready-for-the-post-covid-19-world.

57. As quoted in *Shari'a-compliant Microfinance*, Edited: S Nazim Ali, page 182.
58. Shariq Nisar, Syed Mizanur Rahman, 'Minority funds in India: Institutional mobilising of micro savings', *Shari'a-Compliant Microfinance*, pages 180–205.
59. Masudul Alam Choudhury, *Islamic Economics and Finance: An Epistemological Inquiry*, page 227.
60. World Data Lab—https://worldpoverty.io/headline/.
61. Central Intelligence Agency (2019), *The World Factbook.*
62. Dr AbdulRazzaq A Alaro, Abdulrahman H Alalubosa (2016), *Potential of Shari'ah Compliant Microfinance in Alleviating Poverty in Nigeria: A Lesson from Bangladesh, Proceeding of the 3rd International Conference on Islamic Banking & Finance*, jointly organized by IRTI-IDB, Jeddah and IIIBF, Bayero University, Kano.
63. https://www.imf.org/en/Publications/WEO/Issues/2020/04/14/weo-april-2020.
64. https://www.foodbank.org.au/hunger-in-australia/the-facts/?state=au.
65. https://www.nzherald.co.nz/hawkes-baytoday/news/article.cfm?c_id=1503462&objectid=11271828.
66. Good Shepherds Sisters website (2020).
67. https://data.worldbank.org/indicator/SN.ITK.DEFC.ZS?locations=GB.
68. https://undocs.org/A/HRC/41/39/Add.1.
69. https://londoneconomics.co.uk/wp-content/uploads/2020/03/NILS-feasibility-study-report.pdf. CDFI stands for Community Development Finance Institution.
70. Social Finance UK (2016).
71. Qur'ran, 30:39.
72. Yomken website (2020).
73. *Sizing the Impact Investing Market* (April 2019), Global Impact Investment Network.
74. FT Wealth, October 2015.
75. Global Ethical Banking (24 May 2019), *Rise of Islamic Finance Helps Muslim Family Offices Makes Investments True to Faith.*
76. Ibid.
77. Edited by Nayan Mitra, Rene Schmidpeter, *Mandated Corporate Social Responsibility: Evidence from India*, page 12.
78. Harris Irfan, *Heaven's Bankers: Inside the Hidden World of Islamic Finance*, page 145.
79. Al Rayan Bank describes its objectives as follows—"To be the leading provider of ethical, Sharia compliant retail banking services in the UK, delivering long term value for customers, staff and shareholders".
80. Michael Bennett, Zamir Iqbal (August 2013), How Socially Responsible Investing Can Help Bridge the Gap Between Islamic and Conventional

Financial Products, *International Journal of Islamic and Middle Eastern Finance and Management*.

81. Saadiah Mohamad, Othmar Lehner, Aly Khorshid (2016), A Case for an Islamic Social Impact Bond, *ACRN Oxford Journal of Finance and Risk Perspectives*, vol. 5, no. 2, pp. 65–74. The Dow Jones screening process is also discussed in chapter four.

CHAPTER 8

Can There Be an Islamic Monetary Policy?

Speculation and Interest Rates

In a shock move in January 2015, the Swiss central bank decided to decouple the Swiss franc from the Euro currency. The cap had been in place since 2011 and had essentially pinned the currency at 1.20 francs per euro.

The value of the euro collapsed by as much as 30% versus the franc and inflicted pain on many banks, traders and investors.

Analysing the event which surprised the US$5.1 trillion-a-day foreign exchange market, Bank of England researchers stated in February 2018 that traders "*withdrew liquidity and generated uninformative volatility*" and contributed to a "*decline*" in market quality of the euro and the dollar against the franc.

They singled out trades by bank algorithms for contributing to "*non-informative*" volatility in the rate of the euro to the franc.

This is an extreme example as to how currency movements which impact upon businesses and livelihoods have no relation to the real economy. This incident supports the core beliefs within Islamic economics that interest and speculation should be prohibited due to the damage caused to the real economy.

J. S. Watkins, *Islamic Finance and Global Capitalism*,
https://doi.org/10.1007/978-3-030-59840-2_8

Whilst speculation on currency markets is not allowed within Islamic finance, Islamic scholars have also argued that as fluctuations of currencies can unfairly damage livelihoods this demonstrates the need for a new international monetary order to be adopted.

The question is whether such an Islamic theory of monetary policy can be fully developed.

Many of you reading this book may think the world—even without Islamic economics—has already entered into a new monetary paradigm. At the time of writing (2020), the European Central Bank and the Bank of Japan had negative interest rates with investors effectively paying the central bank for their funds to be secured during tumultuous times.

In May 2020, the £3.8 billion gilt auction by the UK's Debt Management Office sold three-year government bonds with a negative interest yield of −0.003% whilst in September 2019, before the impact of the COVID-19 outbreak was felt, then US President Donald Trump tweeted that the US Federal Reserve should institute negative interest rates:

> Germany, and so many other countries have negative interest rates, "they get paid for loaning money," and our Federal Reserve fails to act! Remember, these are also our weak currency competitors![1]

Whilst the perspective put forward by Islamic scholars against interest rates has rarely occurred in a negative interest rate environment, the overriding principle that the concept of interest rates unfairly distorts the operation of the real economy remains the same.

Islamic scholars have been debating the pros and cons of the concept of interest for centuries. As we discovered in Chapter 3, the debate within Islam as to whether or not interest should be banned continues to flare up from time to time.

However, for supporters of Islamic economics, the need to develop an Islamic monetary policy goes beyond religious concepts and relates directly to economic necessity.

Tarek El Diwany argued that interest via discounted cash flow (a method of valuing a project, company or asset using the concepts of the time value of money) has manipulated the real economy and has hindered economic growth:

> Discounted cash-flow decision criteria encourage resource depletion and declines in product quality because distant consequences of current actions

> are undervalued by the discounting analysis. Yet discounted cash-flow analysis is forced upon entrepreneurs because most of the money that is used to finance projects is loaned into existence by the banking system at interest. Projects undertaken with borrowed money must therefore take into account the strictures of interest and thus the shadow of interest falls upon society.[2]

It is not just advocates of Islamic economics who argue that interest rates distort the workings of the real economy. Bannerjee illustrated the distorting role of interest rates within the context of attempts to lever in much needed investment in developing countries:

> An increase in wealth inequality would typically imply that there are more people who cannot invest as much as they want to, say, because they do not have enough credit or insurance. To compensate for the lack of investment demand from the poor, the rich, who are already in a position to invest as much as they want, would have to demand more capital. But this would happen only if the interest rate were lower, and a lower interest rate tends to discourage saving and thus investment.

Bannerjee later added that if the distortions of the interest rate mechanism combined with the widening income gap are considered then:

> ... it is not true that there is no need to worry about the rich getting richer as long as the poor are also getting richer. The point is that the rich and the poor compete for resources, including capital, and when the rich become richer it is harder for the poor to compete with them.[3]

However, economists from both the left and right of the political spectrum have argued that far from the interest rate mechanism distorting the real economy it is, in fact, a reflection of the real economy. On the right of politics, the UK's Adam Smith Institute has argued that interest rates are fine—as long as Governments are kept out of the way:

> ... a more sophisticated point to be made about interest rates ... is that they also express the extent to which people are willing to forgo something now for the prospect of a greater reward in future. In economic jargon, it's called time preference, and it tells entrepreneurs whether they should be investing in capital goods (that is, in things which are used to produce other goods), in 'durable consumer goods' (things like cars, fridges, even

> houses), or in goods for immediate consumption. Again, when governments mess around with interest rates, they distort the allocation of capital – investment goes to the wrong stages of production, and the wrong goods are produced. Supply and demand, once again, does not meet up.[4]

Whilst from the left, Thomas Picketty has also spoken about the necessity of the interest rate concept. Picketty, who has been associated with the socialist British politician, John McDonnell (McDonnell cited his hobby in *Who's Who as "generally fermenting the overthrow of capitalism"*), argued that when governments tried to ban interest it had led to the domination of the state at the expense of the people:

> Unfortunately for the people caught up in these totalitarian experiments, the problem was that private property and the market economy do not serve solely to ensure the domination of capital over those who have nothing to sell but their labour power. They also play a useful role in coordinating the actions of millions of individuals, and it is not so easy to do without them. The human disasters caused by Soviet style centralised planning illustrate this quite clearly.[5]

This is not to say that economists who believe interest rates are essential do not have different perspectives as to the role and purpose of the mechanism. For instance, the Austrian economist, Eugen Ritter von Böhm-Bawerk (1851–1914) argued that interest was connected to the time consuming process of production whereby "*the fruits of these time-consuming production processes exceed in value alternative rewards available to these resource owners through immediate exchanges in today's spot markets*".[6]

However, the Austrian School economist, Ludwig von Mises (1881–1973) dismissed Böhm-Bawerk's analysis and demonstrated that interest was not tied to time consuming production processes:

> If a tree is expected today to produce a steady annual stream of fruit in future years, this productivity will be entirely reflected in the tree's current market value. If a capital good can, through its investment today in a time consuming process of production, generate a high valued stream of output in the future, the value of that output will tend to be fully anticipated in today's market value of that capital good. This value will, in the absence of other causes for an interest phenomenon, rise to the point where the physical productivity of the capital good will be utterly unable

> to provide any flow of value return like the kind that we find in the real world phenomenon of interest.[7]

Nonetheless, von Mises strongly believed the interest rate mechanism was essential and, like Picketty decades later, feared the economic upheaval to the trade cycle if this mechanism was removed. Instead, von Mises argued, interest was required as it served as the standard of valuation regarding present goods versus future goods:

> If he (*the consumer*) were not to prefer satisfaction in a nearer period of the future to that in a remoter period, he would never consume and so satisfy wants. He would always accumulate, he would never consume and enjoy. He would not consume today, but he would not consume tomorrow either, as the tomorrow would confront him with the same alternative.[8]

In effect, von Mises was reflecting the view of the economist, Carl Menger (1840–1921) who argued that interest was pivotal for people to plan their future requirements as well as meeting their immediate needs:

> Human life is a process in which the course of future development is always influenced by previous development. It is a process that cannot be continued once it has been interrupted, and that cannot be completely rehabilitated once it has become seriously disordered. A necessary prerequisite of our provision for the maintenance of our lives and for our development in future periods is a concern for the preceding periods of our lives. Setting aside the irregularities of economic activity, we can conclude that economising men generally endeavour to ensure the satisfaction of needs of the immediate future first, and that only after this has been done, do they attempt to ensure the satisfaction of needs of more distant periods, in accordance with their remoteness in time.[9]

Economists who present ideas relating to an Islamic monetary policy would dispute the analysis of Menger and von Mises as the interest rate mechanism, far from helping people plan in advance, in fact leads to hoarding and a corresponding reduction of investment in the operation of the real economy. As we shall see later on in this chapter, it is not just advocates of an Islamic monetary system who take this line.

Do Interest Rates Reflect the Real Economy?

Nonetheless, interest rates continue to be seen by many economists as a reflection of the real economy as understood, in part, by the process of business cycles. Neoclassical theories would attribute the business cycle to the expansion and contraction of money and credit.

Keynesian theories attribute such fluctuations to the economic system itself. It is contended that the macro economy is prone to extended business cycles, with high levels of unemployed resources for long periods of time. Consequently, Keynesians argue, there are moments when the government can stimulate the economy. We will return to this analysis later in this chapter.

The primary interpretation of business cycles looks to changes in aggregate demand (AD). There is a correlation between changes in AD and interest rates. Theories which relate to changes in AD can be classified into two categories:

- The external theories find the root of the business cycles in the fluctuations of something outside the economic system (wars, revolutions, elections, economic policy, migrations, discoveries of resources).
- The internal theories look for the mechanism within the economic system itself (self-generating business cycles).

In considering the relationship between interest rates and business cycles, it is necessary to consider how business cycles generally occur as a direct consequence of shifts in AD. Decline in the AD lowers output and as a result of the downward shift in the AD curve, the gap between actual and potential GDP becomes greater during a recession (Figs. 8.1 and 8.2).

In this chart, the characteristics of a recession can be observed:

- Consumer purchases decline and businesses react by holding back production capacity.
- Real GDP falls.
- Business investment falls.
- The demand for labour falls.
- The prices of many commodities fall.
- Wages are less likely to decline, but they tend to rise less rapidly.

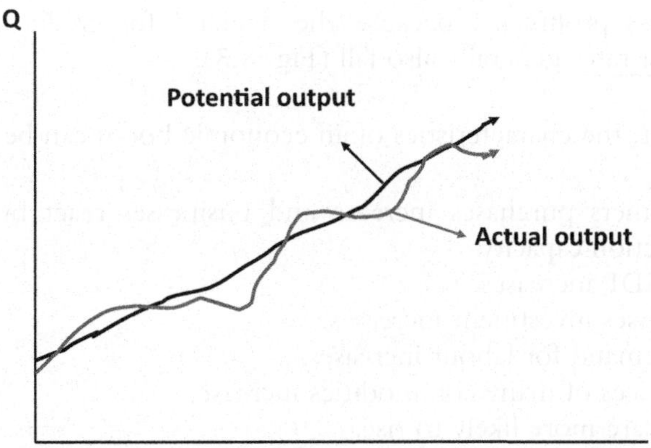

Fig. 8.1 Business cycle

Fig. 8.2 Business cycles as shifts in aggregate demand: Recession

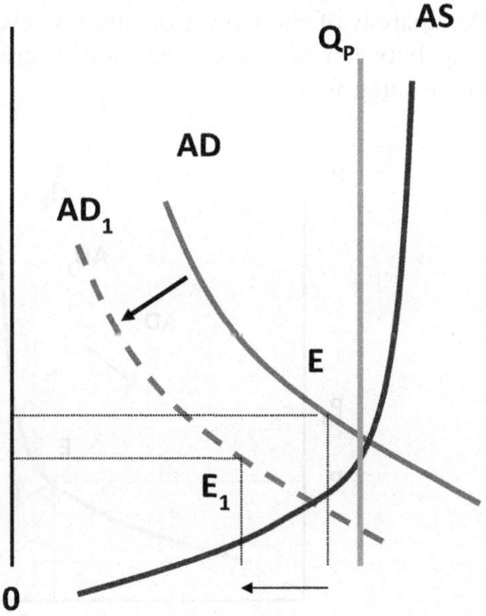

- Business profits fall because the demand for credit falls and so interest rates generally also fall (Fig. 8.3).

In this chart, the characteristics of an economic boom can be observed:

- Consumers purchases increase and businesses react by increasing production capacity.
- Real GDP increases.
- Businesses investment increases.
- The demand for labour increases.
- The prices of many commodities increase.
- Wages are more likely to rise.
- Business profit increases because the demand for credit also goes up and so interest rates generally increase as well.

An analysis of the length of business cycles and the consequent relationship between business cycles and interest rates has led to the following three categories:

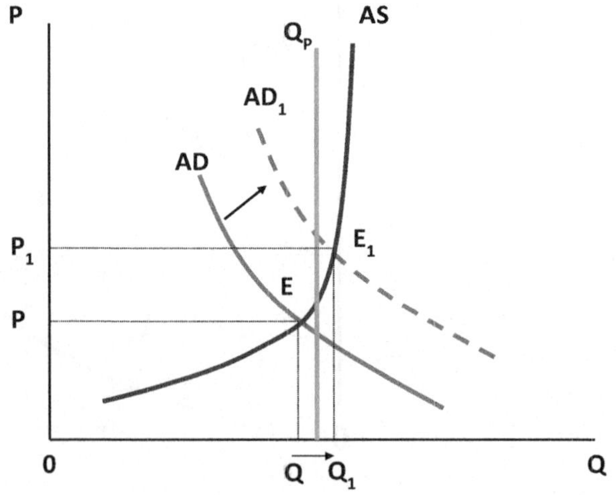

Fig. 8.3 Business cycles as shifts in AD: Economic boom

- Short-term (Kitchin) cycle: from 2 to 4 years. Consequences linked to changes in business inventories.
- Medium-term (Jouglar) cycle: from 7 to 11 years. Consequences linked to new business investment.
- Long-term (Kondratiev) cycle: from 30 to 50 years. Consequences linked to gains arising from technological innovation.

Therefore, this very brief overview of the relationship between the operation of business cycles and the interconnectedness between business cycles and interest rates would seem to contradict claims by Islamic scholars that the principle of interest rates is an artificial construct. Through the prism of conventional economic analysis, the interrelationship between AD, business cycles and interest rates would indicate that the interest rate mechanism does, in fact, help reflect the real economy.

Further support for the concept that interest rates support the workings of the macro economy can be found by citing the example of post war Italy. This was a country which used bureaucratic means to control the economy rather than adopting a primary focus upon the use of interest rates.

The medium cycle period of 1973–1993 was characterised by divergent fiscal and monetary policies. On the one hand, the nominal income grew, pulled by public spending, consumption and inflation; on the other hand, monetary policy, using the intermediate target of the total domestic credit, became restrictive. In a context of wage indexation to prices and a strong depreciation of the lira, successive governments were consistent in creating budget deficits which pushed up consumption and inflation.

In this period, monetary policy was not independent from fiscal policy. The creation of the monetary base through the Italian Finance Ministry generated high inflationary pressures and a further weakening of the currency. To cope with the external balance equilibrium, monetary authorities decided to resort to administrative controls—rather than adopt a focus upon the use of interest rates—in order to limit credit expansion (credit ceilings) and thereby control inflation and stabilise the exchange rate.

These administrative measures had the direct consequence of reducing loans to the private sector. Whilst real interest rates were negative for most of the 1970s, the subscription of government bonds was guaranteed only through administrative measures by compelling banks to hold these bonds in their portfolios.

Therefore, in this example, without the use of the interest rate mechanism to address inflationary pressures, limits on credit expansion led directly to additional financial burdens being placed upon business who had great difficulty in accessing credit.

The citing of this Italian experience demonstrates how, when interest rates are not used by monetary authorities, imbalances in an economy can still occur. This perspective would seemingly contradict the line held by advocates of Islamic economics that it is the inclusion of the interest rate mechanism which is the primary distorting factor within the setting of monetary policy.

Whilst the Italian example is also an example of fiscal and monetary policies being out of kilter with each other, any discussion of an Islamic monetary policy needs to consider scenario planning where such disconnects in public policy can occur and where the onus upon an Islamic monetary system to balance the economy could be all the greater without the support provided by the interest rate mechanism.

Islamic Economics: Lessons from the Wall Street Crash

So far the evidence that has been presented would support the concept of interest rates being essential to balance the operation of an economy by guarding against inflationary risks and by tying the operation of the interest rate mechanism to the concept of business cycles.

If we look at the 1929 Wall Street Crash, however, a different conclusion may be reached.

In this analysis interest rates were linked to the operation of the money markets. The money markets operated on the basis of speculation. The speculative bubble, that was not soundly based on the operation of the real economy, burst and the interest rate mechanism failed to mitigate the damage from the crash. As Islamic economics prohibits riba and maysir, the 1929 Wall Street Crash would seem to be a textbook illustration for Islamic economics scholars as to how not to run an economy.

If we explore this theme further, we can observe the interrelationship between interest rates and speculation. Cogley's analysis highlighted this symbiotic relationship. Cogley noted the situation in 1928:

> Motivated by a concern about speculation in the stock market, the Fed responded aggressively. Between January and July 1928 the Fed raised the

discount rate from 3.5% to 5%. Because nominal prices were falling, the latter translated into a real discount rate of 6%, which is quite high in a year following a recession. At the same time, the Fed engaged in extensive open market operations to drain reserves from the banking system.

Cogley argued that the US Federal Reserve was in a bind in 1928/9 and the immediate solutions to try to pre-empt the crash would also have caused severe damage to the real economy:

> If one grants that a speculative bubble existed at the beginning of 1928, when the Fed began to tighten, then stocks must have still been overvalued in the aftermath of the crash. After all, price-dividend ratios were about the same in the dark days of November 1929 as at the beginning of 1928, and fundamentals must surely have taken a turn for the worse. If equities were still overvalued, it follows that a further dose of contractionary monetary policy was needed to purge speculative elements from the market. Perhaps this is what motivated the famous advice of Treasury Secretary Andrew Mellon to President Herbert Hoover, to "liquidate labor, liquidate stocks, liquidate the farmers, liquidate real estate." To argue that the actions of 1928-1930 were stabilizing, one must adopt the liquidationist position.[10]

As the operation of the contemporary global economy is mediated by the use of the interest rate mechanism and speculation should we consider such events as the 1929 Wall Street Crash or the 2008 Global Financial Crisis as outliers which do not undermine the concepts of interest rates and speculation?

The work of Robert Schiller would indicate that the distorting effect of interest and speculation goes beyond bouts of financial crises as there is a systemic disconnect between the markets and the real economy.

Schiller, in his book, *Irrational Exuberance*, examined the theme of this disconnect and concluded that a more detached view of the markets was required:

> ... the stock market has not come down to historical levels: the price-earnings ratio as I define it in this book is still, at this writing (*2005*), in the mid-20s, far higher than the historical average. ... People still place too much confidence in the markets and have too strong a belief that paying attention to the gyrations in their investments will someday make them rich, and so they do not make conservative preparations for possible bad outcomes.[11]

Schiller analysed how market valuations raced ahead of company earnings at times of severe economic uncertainty such as the period leading up to Black Tuesday with the 1929 Wall Street Crash or the period leading up to Black Monday with the eventual 1987 stock markets crash and the 2001 dot com bubble.

The similarities between this analysis and the ethos of Islamic finance in avoiding gharar, maysir and riba in order for business operations to be based upon real world conditions is striking.

Interestingly, in the United States in particular, there is a debate taking place that is challenging the twin concepts of interest rates and speculation that is not related in any way to Islamic economics.

Indeed, there is now a resurgence in this US debate as to whether interest rates are needed or desirable. This has stemmed from the concept of Modern Monetary Theory (MMT).

Modern Monetary Theory posits the idea that some economies can print fiat currencies and not be too concerned about the inflationary consequences. This aspect of Modern Monetary Theory would not be supported by many Islamic scholars who believe some form of gold standard is required to support currencies, as we will soon discover in this chapter.

The focus on not having a limit on the production of fiat currencies seems designed to address the needs of the political economies of the United States and other developed nations. It is not clear from advocates of Modern Monetary Theory how such a policy would work for middle income and developing countries.

It is in the area of interest rates that Modern Monetary Theory and Islamic economics share similar ideas. Stephanie Kelton, who was the economics adviser to Senator Bernie Sanders (who unsuccessfully sought the Democratic Party nomination for the US Presidency in 2016 and 2020) argued that interest rates should be kept as near zero as possible in order to support the operation of the real economy.

Kelton has referred to the stance of the US Federal Reserve on interest rates:

> It is true that the Fed can pursue any rate policy it desires. It does not follow, however, that cutting interest rates will work to induce enough spending to maintain full employment. You can't simply assume borrowers will always have the appetite for more private debt, even if you make it really cheap to borrow. Businesses borrow and invest when they're

> swamped with customers (or expect to be). They don't passively take on more debt simply because the central bank has dangled cheaper credit before them.
>
> The evidence suggests that interest rates don't matter much at all when it comes to private investment .... It is even possible, as MMT has shown, that cutting rates could further slow the economy because lowering rates cuts government expenditures (interest payments), thereby exacerbating contractionary fiscal policy.
>
> This is in fact what modern monetary theory suggested when the European Central Bank went to negative rates, which MMT sees as a contractionary tax. But MMT recognizes that raising rates could offset contractionary fiscal policy, though in a highly regressive manner as the interest paid by the government tends to go to those with the highest incomes.[12]

With Kelton reportedly advising US President Joe Biden on economic policy and Senator Sanders and Congresswoman Alexandra Ocasio-Cortez expressing an interest in MMT, we are slowly seeing the idea of a world permanently having zero interest rates becoming part of the mainstream political debate in the United States. This is an intriguing prospect for advocates of Islamic economics to advance their own perspective on the interest rate question.

There are, though, two other sources of support for zero interest rates who arrived at this conclusion from completely different standpoints. Their perspectives would not be in accord with Islamic economics.

So—who were these individuals who wanted a complete reappraisal of the concept of interest rates?

Karl Marx—and Milton Friedman.

Karl Marx and Interest Rates

Marx argued that the interest rate was a construct for profit to be derived from the real wealth creators—the proletariat:

> Since interest is merely a part of profit paid, according to our earlier assumption, by the industrial capitalist to the money-capitalist, the maximum limit of interest is the profit itself, in which case the portion pocketed by the productive capitalist would 0. Aside from exceptional cases, in which interest might actually be larger than profit, but then could not be paid out of the profit, one might consider as the maximum limit

of interest the total profit minus the portion (to be subsequently analysed) which resolves itself into wages of superintendence.[13]

This analysis does bear some analogy to Islamic economic thinking where the interest rate is seen to be artificially contrived to inflate profits. El Diwany clearly spells out what he sees as the economic iniquities of the interest rate system which, he states, serves a minority of people to the disadvantage of wider society—and the planet:

> Given that aggregate debt under a fractional reserve banking system tends to grow in accordance with the rate of interest that is applied to it, society is forced into a continual expansion of its borrowing. New borrowing tends to imply the implementation of new commercial projects hence it can be said that economic growth is forced upon society. This concept has been largely ignored by mainstream economists. Its origin is within the monetary system and its impact is now becoming felt globally (damage to the ozone layer, global warming, resource depletion, congestion).[14]

The synergies between Marx and Islamic economics continue when we consider Marx's analysis at the role of interest in commercial transactions:

> Let us first assume that there is a fixed relation between the total profit and that part of it which has to be paid as interest to the money-capitalist. It is then clear that the interest will rise or fall with the total profit, and the latter is determined by the general rate of profit and its fluctuations. For instance, if the average rate of profit were = 20% and the interest = ¼ of the profit, the rate of interest would = 5%; if the average rate of profit were = 16%, the rate of interest would = 4%. With the rate of profit at 20%, the rate of interest might rise to 8%, and the industrial capitalist would still make the same profit as he would at a rate of profit = 16% and a rate of interest = 4%, namely 12%. Should interest rise only to 6% or 7%, he would still keep a larger share of the profit. If the interest amounted to a constant quota of the average profit, it would follow that the higher the general rate of profit, the greater the absolute difference between the total profit and the interest, and the greater the portion of the total profit pocketed by the productive capitalist, and vice versa. Take it that interest = 1/5 of the average profit. One-fifth of 10 is 2; the difference between total profit and interest = 8. One-fifth of 20 = 4; difference = 20-4 = 16; 1/5 of 25 = 5; difference = 25-5 = 20; 1/5 of 30 = 6; difference = 30-6 = 24; 1/5 of 35 = 7; difference = 35-7 = 28. The different rates of interest of 4, 5, 6, 7% would here always represent no more than 1/5, or 20%

> of the total profit. If the rates of profit are different, therefore, different rates of interest may represent the same aliquot parts of the total profit, or the same percentage of the total profit. With such constant proportions of interest, the industrial profit (the difference between the total profit and the interest) would rise proportionately to the general rate of profit, and conversely.[15]

Marx, therefore, saw interest as a profit-making mechanism. This was why Marx ridiculed what he saw as obtuse discussions which belied the real motivations behind the concept of interest rates:

> Nothing is more amusing in the reports of Parliament for 1857 and 1858 concerning bank legislation and commercial crises than to hear of "the real rate produced" as the directors of the Bank of England, London bankers, country bankers, and professional theorists chatter back and forth, never getting beyond such commonplaces as that "the price paid for the use of loanable capital should vary with the supply of such capital," that "a high rate and a low profit cannot permanently exist," and similar specious platitudes. Customs, juristic tradition, etc., have as much to do with determining the average rate of interest as competition itself, in so far as it exists not merely as an average, but rather as actual magnitude.[16]

Marx encapsulates his stance by arguing that the artificiality of the interest rate is because money had been transformed from a means of transaction to a commodity:

> These are some of the reasons why the general rate of profit appears blurred and hazy alongside the definite interest rate, which may fluctuate in magnitude, but always confronts borrowers as given and fixed because it varies uniformly for all of them. Just as variations in the value of money do not prevent it from having the same value vis-à-vis all commodities. Just as the daily fluctuations in market-prices of commodities do not prevent them from being daily reported in the papers. So the rate of interest is regularly reported as "the price of money." It is so, because capital itself is being offered here in the form of money as a commodity. The fixation of its price is thus a fixation of its market-price, as with all other commodities.[17]

This analysis chimes with the Islamic economic perspective that money should not be viewed as a commodity. As we discussed in Chapter 3, there are verses in the Qur'ran and the hadiths of the Prophet that also speak of the dangers—from an economic and moral perspective—as to the dangers of treating money as a commodity. The commonality of views between Marx and Islamic economics on the key issues of interest rates and the role of money is stark.

Milton Friedman

Whilst analogies between Communist thought and Islamic economics has been made on a number of occasions (also discussed in Chapter 9), it may seem odd to pray in aid the support of one aspect of Islamic economics from the Chicago School economist who is sometimes dubbed the 'Father of Monetarism', Milton Friedman.

Friedman clearly believed in laissez faire economics, in free markets and in warning against the dangers of Government intervention in the economy as to the consequences it may have for inflation. Friedman's belief in a natural rate of unemployment for the good operation of the markets does not find any synergies with Islamic economics.

Friedman, though, had his own concerns about interest rates and the preferability to keep rates to zero as much as possible. In his 1987 work, *Quantity Theory of Money*, he began his analysis by first quoting the Scottish Enlightenment thinker, David Hume, as to the ideal that should be reached for in terms of the price of money:

> [T]hough the high price of commodities be a necessary consequence of the increase of gold and silver, yet it follows not immediately upon that increase; but some time is required before the money circulates through the whole state.... In my opinion, it is only in this interval of intermediate situation, between the acquisition of money and rise of prices, that the increasing quantity of gold and silver is favourable to industry.... [W]e may conclude that it is of no manner of consequence, with regard to the domestic happiness of a state, whether money be in greater or less quantity. The good policy of the magistrate consists only in keeping it, if possible, still increasing ... (David Hume, 1752).

By quoting Hume, Friedman was arguing that the focus on the interest rate is not the key issue. Instead, what was important, was the overriding concern, as he saw it, of the free, open and transparent operation of commercial activities which can be addressed, in part, by money supply:

> The important consideration for monetary theory and policy is whether the demand for money can be treated as a reasonably stable function of a fairly

small number of variables and whether this function can be empirically verified with reasonable accuracy. Whether one important argument of the function is an interest rate or set of interest rates is much less important.[18]

As with Islamic economics, Friedman argued it was the price mechanism and how it operated to regulate the wider economy which was the prime consideration:

> One man can reduce his nominal money balances only by persuading someone else to increase his. The community as a whole cannot in general spend more than it receives; it is playing a game of musical chairs.
>
> The attempt to dispose of excess balances will nonetheless have important effects. If prices and incomes are free to change, the attempt to spend more will raise total spending and receipts, expressed in nominal units, which will lead to a bidding up of prices and perhaps also to an increase in output. If prices are fixed by custom or by government edict, the attempt to spend more will either be matched by an increase in goods and services or produce "shortages" and "queues". These in turn will raise the effective price and are likely sooner or later to force changes in customary or official prices.[19]

This insight enabled Friedman to consider how the concept of interest rates can impinge upon the free flow of the capital markets:

> The interest rate has received special attention in monetary analysis because, without quite realizing it, fractional reserve banks have created part of the stock of money in the course of serving as an intermediary between borrowers and lenders. Hence changes in the quantity of money have frequently occurred through the credit markets, in the process producing important transitory effects on interest rates.[20]

As we will see later in this chapter, this led Friedman to ponder as to whether the unintentional iniquities in interest rates linked, in part, to the conflicting demands of savers and borrowers, can be assuaged by currencies being underpinned by a standard respected across the world—the gold standard. A significant number of Islamic scholars also called for a gold standard to underpin currencies.

However, before we explore the issue of gold further, there was one other free market economist who also had concerns about the operation of interest rates.

Arthur Pigou

Arthur Pigou disagreed profoundly with Keynes as to how Keynes saw the operation of interest rates and Keynes' analysis of the 'liquidity trap'—which will be considered further in this chapter.

Pigou, though, did believe in the role of governments to intercede in the economy in defined circumstances. In his work, *The Economics of Welfare* (1928) he advocated government action when there are negative '*externalities*' such as a company's operations leading to a local river being polluted with waste. In such circumstances, Pigou argued that welfare economics can lead to governments taking action including in terms of charging additional taxes on firms causing negative externalities.

It was his 1943 work, *The Classical Stationary State*, where he analysed how the price mechanism can balance an economy without recourse to the use of interest rates. This became known as the Pigou Effect. According to the theory, price levels and employment fall, and unemployment rises. As price levels decline, real balances increase and, by the Pigou Effect, consumption in the economy is stimulated. Consequently, the economy attains full employment equilibrium. Pigou's conclusion was that the economy would operate on an equilibrium less than the full employment equilibrium only if prices and wages were constant.

The economist, Gottfried Haberler (1900–1995), endorsed the concept of the Pigou Effect enabling an economy to have some form of equilibrium:

> A banal confusion has marred discussion of the Pigou effect. No one has ever believed that a combination of deflation and an unchanged stock of base money would cause a recovery of demand in a high unemployment deflation. That straw man has unfortunately been the object of many "refutations". I should be clear, however, that as I am using the term, the "Pigou effect" does not assume that the stock of money is constant, and all the real wealth increase is due to deflation. The Pigou effect, as I am using the term, is simply the hypothesis that the real value of money rises under deflation, and an increase of real money balances under deflation – if sufficiently large – could cause higher demand growth.[21]

We can see, then, how a number of laissez-faire economists did not adopt an undue focus on interest rates but instead viewed the price mechanism and money supply combined with the good operation of free markets to be the determining factors when assessing the strength of an economy.

How, though, does the difference in perspective between monetarist thinkers and Keynes on the role of interest rates impact on ideas that are inherent in Islamic economics?

John Maynard Keynes

Chapter 12 of Keynes's groundbreaking work, *The General Theory of Employment, Interest and Money* (1936) began with an excoriating attack on the operation of contemporary capitalism:

> ...when the capital development of a country becomes a by-product of the activities of a casino, the job is likely to be ill-done.

Keynes also had serious reservations as to the concept of interest:

> The rate of interest is the 'price' which equilibrates the desire to hold wealth in the form of cash with the available quantity of cash.

Keynes went on to argue that savers wanted to hold cash for the benefit of interest rates and so this distorted the operation of the real economy. Therefore the 'speculative' motive for holding cash is the '*existence of uncertainty as to the future of the rate of interest*'.

Keynes attempted to evidence base this argument by stating that if this was not the case, investors who wanted to get out of equities would buy government debt. This, in turn, would drive up the price of bonds and lower the yield. Consequently, this would make the market more affordable for businesses to borrow for investment.

In fact, Keynes argued, when '*speculators*' consider the interest rate is too low, bonds are sold for cash, thereby stopping the fall in the interest rate. From these insights, Keynes argued that the desire to save gained stronger momentum than the need to spend in order to invest in business and to move towards gaining full employment. Keynes also argued that it was changes in output and employment—not interest rates—which enabled an economy to adjust to any '*shock*' to investment demand.

Is it any surprise that the 1930s academics from Osmania University in Hyderabad, as we will see in Chapter 10, argued that Keynes—without realising it—had vindicated the long-standing stance of Islamic economics that interest should be banned because of its corrupting influence on the real economy.

Keynes went on to argue that Government intervention was required at times of recessions to enable an economy to move forward and to seek to meet the goal of full employment. Keynes also made a wider point that Governments had a wider perspective to enable the good operation of economies and not leave matters solely in the hands of the free markets:

> …the powers of uninterrupted usury are too great. If the accretions of vested interests were to grow without mitigation for many generations, half the population would be no better than slaves to the other half.[22]

This, Keynes argued, was why the role of the State was sorely needed in the wider operation of the economy:

> …we are brought to my heresy – if it is a heresy. I bring in the State. I abandon laissez faire – not enthusiastically, not from contempt for that old good old doctrine, but because, whether we like it or not, the conditions for its success have disappeared.[23]

Whilst to this day, the monetarists and the Keynesians continue to debate the role of government in political economy, it is striking that both schools of thought shared reservations, in their different ways, as to the operation of the interest rate mechanism.

There remained, though, the relationship of the global economy with paper or fiat currencies which fluctuated in their value based upon trade flows, speculation and interest rate movements.

Islamic economists considered whether there was a way for currency operations to operate without gharar, maysir and riba.

An idea emerged that the answer was to ensure that all currencies were underpinned by the gold standard.

Gold Standard—Can It Really Work?

The 1997 Asian Financial Crisis was a shock to those south east Asian nations which the European media had styled as "*tigers*" with their rapacious growth rates and their pivotal role at the heart of global manufacturing.

A number of business and political leaders argued that the rout of south east Asian currencies on the global money markets, triggered by unease with the credentials of the Thai bhat, was unjustified.

It was from this crisis that modern calls for a gold standard emerged with the concept championed by the ever-energetic Mahathir Mohamad. The then Malaysian Prime Minister's demand stemmed from what he characterised as the unfairness of the markets:

> I am saying that currency trading is unnecessary, unproductive and immoral. It should be stopped. It should be made illegal.[24]

Mahathir's language was imbued with what can only be described as vile anti-Semitism. To take just one example, when Mahathir was speaking against speculation at the 1999 World Economic Forum in Davos it turned into an anti-Semitic rant by attacking an "*economic conspiracy in which some Jews are involved, and other Europeans*".[25]

It was not, though, just Mahathir who had concerns about the operation of the markets. There had, by then, been two other currency crises in the 1990s; the European Monetary System crisis in 1992/3 and the Mexican peso crisis of 1994/5.

Therefore, when Mahathir proposed, during the midst of the 1997 crisis, a gold payments system it received a positive response from many people including key decision makers who were becoming frustrated and anxious by the repeated currency crises of the time.

Mahathir spoke of a gold dinar to settle bilateral and multilateral trades amongst countries and so eliminate foreign exchange risk. Gold would be the medium of exchange and as a unit of account instead of using national currencies. Prices of exports and imports would be quoted in units of gold weight.

Central banks would ensure such a system worked by adopting "*gold accounting*" processes. As bilateral and multilateral trades were ongoing processes any gold that needed to be settled could be brought forward and used for future transactions and settlements. With the gold dinar concept, the hedging cost would be fixed against gold. There was still a risk with some currency fluctuations but, Mahathir argued, the support of the gold standard for this international payment system would work as gold had intrinsic value.

This was an innovative idea for it avoided the pitfalls of the gold standard supporting national currencies by focusing, instead, upon an international payments system. As we shall see later in this chapter, the idea of gold underpinning national currencies has been repeatedly discredited over time.

However, the concept of gold supporting trade and the use of the word 'dinar' also goes back to the early history of Islam where the Prophet himself spoke of the use of gold to facilitate trade deals.

Gold: Early Islamic History

> The Messenger of Allah (Peace Be Upon Him) said, 'Gold for gold, silver for silver, wheat for wheat, barley for barley, dates for dates, salt for salt, like for like, in equal weights, from hand to hand. If these species differ, then sell as you like, as long as it is from hand to hand'.[26]

This important hadith is often cited as one of the key sources for the prohibition of riba. However, the hadith also highlights how integral gold and the other commodities as cited, were in seventh-century Arabia to facilitate spot price transactions.

A verse in the Qur'ran also recognised the human desire to acquire gold:

> Mankind is tempted with love of delights such as women, children, heaps upon heaps of gold and silver, horses finely decked out, cattle and fertile land. All this is the infatuation of this present life, but with God is the fairest homecoming.[27]

The search for gold encouraged the development of trade routes between the caliphate and West Africa with key trading posts being established at Tunis, Fez and Marrakesh with gold fields having existed around Timbuktu.

Sijilmesa was located at the northern edge of the Sahara Desert. It was described as "*one of the greatest cities of North Africa and the most famous of the whole universe … whither traders take goods of no value and return with their camels laden with coarse gold*".[28]

Around 750 there was an attempt by the caliphate to invade West Africa to gain direct access to these gold reserves, but this attempt proved to be unsuccessful. European invaders also had gold in mind, amongst other motivations, with the invasion of the Levant during the Crusades (1095–1492).[29]

The importance of gold in the running of economies had been recorded by the Cairo based historian, Ahmad bin Abd al-Qader bin

Muhammad bin Ibrahim bin Tamin al-Bali al-Abidi al-Hsini also known as Taqi al-Din al-Maqrizi (1364–1441).

Al-Maqrizi saw how the malign influence of Governments can cause inflationary pressures which can lead to hardship and despair. Al-Maqrizi also condemned the internecine warfare that was an additional cause of deprivation alongside natural disasters:

> … when the hawadith (*emergency*) occur in 806 hijrah (*1403/4 CE*), the fall in the river Nile coupled with attacks by Timurlank on Blad-al-sham (*Syria*) and the high increases in prices in Egypt, the inflation multiplied over a long time, the destruction of money, political instability and internal conflicts, the destruction of Sa'id followed by migration of the people of Sa'id. People fall in utter poverty while government uses its power to confiscate private property. The government forced people to purchase goods at high prices. Thus, all of the above destroyed social and economic life of the people.[30]

It was Al-Maqrizi's analysis of the role of gold and silver in early Islamic history which contributes to our understanding as to how these precious metals were so highly valued and mirrored the desire for gold in Europe during the Middle Ages:

> The currency that was in circulation among the Arabs in pre-Islamic times consisted of gold and silver only. From other countries, the Arabs received gold dinars, among which were the imperial dinars from the Byzantine Empire. The dinar was called a dinar because of its weight, but it was also a coin. When God sent forth his Prophet Muhammad, the Prophet confirmed all these weights used by the inhabitants of Mecca and said: 'The weight is that of Mecca' and according to another version he said 'The weight is that of Medina'. The Messenger of God prescribed the Zakat on money accordingly: for every five uqiyahs of pure and unadulterated silver he imposed a zakat of five dirhams, i.e. equivalent to one nawat and every twenty dinars he imposed half a dinar. This system was adopted without the slightest alteration by Abu Bakr during his tenure as caliph, following the death of the Messenger of God. When Umar ibn Khattab became caliph, he kept the currencies as they were and did not alter them until the year 18 (*639-40 CE*) during the sixth year of his caliphate.[31]

Al-Maqrizi's praise for gold and silver in transnational business transactions contrasted with his view of copper coins known as fulus. Al-Maqrizi described how fulus was introduced during the rule of Sultan Barkuk in around 1382 to 1399 (the Mamluk period):

> During the time of Barquq, his wazir (*senior official*) increases the quantity of fulus. Traders from western Europe brought red copper to Cairo to sell them to the government to make profit. The minting of fulus in large quantities continued for many years. These firanj (*foreigners*) took away silver dirhams from Egypt to their countries. The people of Egypt converted silver dirham into decorations and utensils for both personal and business purposes. These incidents continued until it is rare and difficult to find silver. Meantime, fulus is found in abundance and serve as money and the measure of value.[32]

The story continues with Al-Maqrizi claiming that the over-abundance of fulus with inherently little value, combined with natural disasters, led to runaway inflation:

> Wheat prices remained at this level (seventy dirhams) until the Nile failed to reach its plenitude in 806 (*1403/4 CE*). This led to calamity: prices soured so high that the price of one irdabb (*Egyptian measure of grain at that time which is equivalent to around 70kg*) of wheat exceeded four hundred dirham of accounts. Prices of commodities such as foodstuffs, drink and clothing followed a similar trend, thus causing an increase unheard of in recent times in the wages of such persons as construction workers, labourers, craftsmen and artisans.[33]

After these experiences, Al-Maqrizi had discerned three core lessons for monetary reform. The first lesson was gold and silver were the essential commodities to be used as money:

> … the currencies that are legally, logically and customarily acceptable are only those of gold and silver and that many other metals are unsuitable as a currency. By the same token, the situation of the people cannot be sound unless they are obliged to follow the natural and legal course in this regard, namely that they should deal exclusively with gold and silver for pricing goods and estimating labour costs.[34]

The second lesson was that currencies must never be debased:

> If God would guide those whom He has entrusted with the welfare of His servants to reinstate gold as the exclusive basis for transactions as it

> was previously – to link the value of goods and the costs of labour – this would lead to the succour of the community, the amelioration of the general situation and the checking of the decay that heralds destruction.[35]

The third and final key lesson for Al-Maqrizi was that fulus should only be used for buying inexpensive items such as food and related daily household expenditure items:

> One mithqal (*a unit of mass which is equal to 4.25 grams*) of gold will be exchanged for 24 silver dirham coins. 24 dirham coins is equivalent to a weight of 140 dirhams in fulus, which will be spent for purchasing insignificant goods and for daily household transactions. This will greatly benefit the population and cause prices to drop.[36]

The concerns about debased currencies continued over the centuries. The Hanafi fiqh scholar, Ibn Abidin (1784–1836) argued that debased coinage meant that "*in our time, there is frequent rise and fall in their values as well*".[37]

The question, though, is whether these historical monetary developments have a bearing in shaping a contemporary Islamic monetary system.

Gold: The Lessons from the 1930s

> Hate scourged the land as the victims of the depression turned on those more fortunate than themselves. Shopkeepers driven out of business cursed the great stores; the millions of unemployed envied those with jobs and hated the 'bosses'; thousands of university graduates found the future barred to them and turned their despair on the establishment … Peasants, burdened with taxes and faced with low prices, despised city people while the masses of white collar unemployed envied the peasants their crops.[38]

This was Germany in the early 1930s following the impact of the 1929 Wall Street Crash. The economic turmoil and suffering endured across Germany contributed towards people seeking an alternative to their hardship. The economic trauma helped ensure the election of Adolf Hitler as Chancellor—and the rest, as they say, really is history.

It was, though, arguments about the role of gold which aggravated the crisis following the initial collapse in share prices.

Once the impact of the crisis hit Europe, the arguments over gold began. This was the era when gold supported the underlying strength of national currencies. In May 1931, Austria's largest commercial bank, Creditanstalt, collapsed. This led to a run on the Austrian schilling.

The Bank of France refused to offer loan facilities to Austria unless it renounced plans for a customs union with its old enemy, Germany. Austria did not accept these conditions. Around the same time, the Bank of France was substituting gold for foreign deposits and acquired US$539 million worth of gold—a huge figure at that time.

The German Chancellor, Heinrich Bruning, tried to stem the crisis and engender market confidence by cutting government spending but this contributed to additional mass unemployment and corresponding deflationary pressures. Bruning then said that because of the crisis, reparations imposed on Germany for the costs of World War One would cease. This led to a run on the Reichsmark.

Though there was an attempt by US President Herbert Hoover to relieve the pressure on Germany, the loss of gold and foreign exchange reserves from Germany and the imposition of credit controls meant that, by 1932, for all intents and purposes, Germany was no longer on the gold standard.

The United Kingdom was next to tumble out of the gold standard. A Treasury report published on 30 July 1931 projected that the deficit for 1932 would be £170 million which was £50 million above the previous estimate. With confidence falling in the pound, British gold reserves were being depleted.

In August 1931, a National Government—effectively a coalition government of the major political parties—was formed to address this existential crisis for the British economy. It implemented severe cuts in government spending which, as Keynes predicted, aggravated the crisis with the rise in unemployment and market confidence remaining at a low ebb.

The Bank of England, in the end, declared it was not feasible to convert the pound into gold as its reserves were perilously low. On 21 September 1931, the United Kingdom left the gold standard. Following this step 24 of the 47 countries who were on the gold standard decided that the currency link to gold had to end.

The implications of the 1929 Wall Street Crash had not been the first time that doubts were raised as to the efficacy of maintaining a gold standard. In fact, Fraser has argued that the very existence of the gold standard in the nineteenth century led money markets to be resistant to change in order to maintain their pre-eminent role in the economy:

> Due in part to their holdings in government bonds and to the nation's reliance on British gold reserves to finance its international trade, the great Wall Street banks were unshakably wedded to the gold standard and opposed to all forms of monetary inflation. Add to this a predilection for gilded opulence amidst chronic privation, and, under duress, this triangulation of the economy by Wall Street's strategic control over credit and transportation was bound to provoke.[39]

This series of incidents would seem to contradict the claims by some Islamic scholars that gold is a trusted medium of exchange which can support international currencies. However, the disparities in exchange rates for fiat or paper currencies are seen by some Islamic scholars to be more insidious in its manipulation of the real economy than the twentieth century gold standard:

> Paper and gold combined in a single system has allowed the misuse and manipulation of the exchange system. The paper as more is produced (i.e. manipulated) devalues against the gold. This caused some countries to drop the gold standard altogether.[40]

As we are about to discover, some Islamic scholars argue that you can have the best of both worlds—a gold standard currency—with limits on speculation.

Gold Dinar: Can It Work?

Some scholars argue that to avoid gold being moved around the world for currencies to avoid devaluations, a 'gold dinar' currency would be structured differently as compared to the debased gold backed currencies of the 1930s:

> 1. The Gold dinar should only be used for the exchange of goods or services. No paper money should be available for exchanges. This will cause the gold to float rather than be hoarded
> 2. The monetary value of the Gold dinar should be above its intrinsic value. This is to avoid the Gold dinar being exported to the countries which do not subscribe to it. Thus it can be of benefit to the participating countries;

> 3. Utilise Central gold bank - wakala system – (*wakala is an agency contract within Islamic finance*) for controlling and registering the amount of Gold dinar in existence and in circulation. In this way, the flow of Gold dinar can be controlled. For countries which adopt this system, the higher monetary value provides incentives to register and use the Gold dinar.[41]

A number of concerns can be applied to this model. In essence, the gold dinar would act as a single currency for a wide range of nations that may share similar values. However, countries in the Middle East do not share the same business cycles and so to maintain a single currency with a single central bank may not be realistic.

Some Islamic advocates of a non-interest-based monetary system argue that it needs to operate across a wide geographical area to ensure such a system is stable and mitigates against the risk of speculation unsettling the value of the currency.

It would, though, be difficult to discern as to how a common monetary area could operate across the Middle East. With the Gulf Co-operation Council having worked towards a regional common market modus vivendi and the framework of the Greater Arab Free Trade Area being in place, ideas as to the concept of a common monetary area continue to be mooted. A key requirement in the optimum currency area (OCA) theory is the business cycle symmetry amongst currency union members. There does not, though, appear to be a high degree of business cycle synchronisation in the Middle East. A 2013 study identified significant variables across the region:

> The range for the duration of recessions is about one year, while it is about three years for expansions. Algeria, Bahrain, Bangladesh, Egypt, and Morocco stand out with long periods of expansions, while Kuwait, Pakistan, and Turkey are marked with very short periods of expansions. The countries with longer (shorter) periods of expansions are not the countries with longer (shorter) periods of recessions. Iraq and Oman stand out with shortest duration of recessions while Saudi Arabia has the longest recession duration. The reported coefficients of variation indicate that expansions are more variable than recessions.[42]

The contrary argument is that the European single currency—the euro—does operate across Europe where different business cycles operate alongside the establishment of the European Central Bank.

For some countries, it can be argued that the euro has been a success, but the implications of the 2008 financial crisis also demonstrated the weaknesses in the euro structure.

All members of the single currency had to meet the following criteria:

1. Inflation shall be no higher than 1.5% of the Consumer Price Index
2. Ratio of annual Government deficit relative to GDP must not exceed 3% at the end of the preceding fiscal year
3. Government debt to GDP ratio must not exceed 60%
4. Countries should have been first members of the Exchange Rate Mechanism before joining the euro
5. Long-term interest rates should be no more than 2% of the average interest rate across the EU

In practice, these criteria were not fully met before 2008 which was already leading to questions marks as to the future of the euro. The impact of the 2008 crisis led these questions marks to morph into an existential crisis for the single currency.

The European banks affected by the crisis were bailed out in 2009 following the conclusions reached at the G20 summit in London. However, with sovereign debt already high in a number of eurozone countries, particularly in southern Europe, finance became unsustainable and markets, consequently, began to lose confidence.

Leaders during this period, such as the then Italian Prime Minister, Matteo Renzi, called for a Keynesian approach to tackle the crisis with a stimulus to the European economy whilst other leaders, in particular, German Chancellor, Angela Merkel, called for a neoliberal approach with debt being paid off first before stimulus measures could be considered. As the example of Greece during this crisis demonstrates, the Merkel position won out.

Admittedly, the euro is today one of the world's leading currencies but it is this set of monetary dilemmas that would need to be tackled in a gold dinar single currency.

Other criticisms could include how any mechanism could exist to ensure the monetary value of the gold dinar was always above its intrinsic value.

However, Milton Friedman looked back fondly to when the gold standard underpinned currencies:

> Under the current international fiat standard, the quantity of high-powered money is determined solely by the monetary authorities, consisting in most countries of a central bank plus the fiscal authorities. What happens to the quantity of high-powered money depends on their objectives, on the institutional and political arrangements under which they operate, and the operating procedures they adopt. These are likely to vary considerably from country to country. Some countries (e.g., Hong Kong, Panama) have chosen to link their currencies rigidly to some other currency by pegging the exchange rate. For them, the amount of high-powered money is determined in the same way as under an international commodity standard – by the balance of payments.
>
> The current system is so new that it must be regarded as in a state of transition. Some substitute is almost sure to emerge to replace the supply of specie as a long-term anchor for the price level, but it is not yet clear what that substitute will be.[43]

Friedman's penchant for the gold standard was also revealed in a 1960 letter to the then Republican Party candidate for US President, Senator Barry Goldwater:

> There are only two resolutions of the gold drain that are consistent with a free society. One is a full-fledged Gold Standard which would involve submitting our internal monetary policy to its discipline, including following a policy of internal deflation if that be required. This would be an excellent solution if followed by the major Western countries. But we do not now have such a system. And given the kind of political interventionism rife in the rest of the Western world, it would be undesirable for the US alone to act as if we did.[44]

Friedrick Hayek (1899–1992)—the leading figure in the development of laissez economics changed his stance on the gold standard. Initially he supported the gold standard. Other economists such as Irving Fisher, Gustav Cassel and Ralph Hawtrey supported the gold standard as they believed a stabilisation policy could work in the context of the unwillingness of many nations to establish exchange rates that reflected the impact of money printing during World War I.

Hayek's views began to change from 1935 and he abandoned his support for the gold standard and instead focused on the theoretical underpinnings for systems that would promote the same sort of stability and predictability that the gold standard had been designed to provide.

Support for fiat currencies was not a new phenomenon. One of the most powerful advocates for fiat currencies rather than gold currencies was Henry Thornton (1760–1815):

> A paper medium ... has been ... quite as convenient an instrument in settling accounts as the gold which it has displaced ... To reproach it with being a merely fictitious thing because it possesses not the intrinsic value of gold, is to quarrel with it on account of that quality which is the very ground of its merit. Its merit consists in the circumstances of its costing almost nothing.[45]

Thornton argued that the substitution of expensive gold with cheaper paper led to the employment of more productive capital. Banks, Thornton believed, acquired liquid assets to support the operation of paper money (more than one bank in the United Kingdom at that time could issue paper notes).

Thornton also repudiated the views of Adam Smith (1723–1790) that gold was a surer currency as compared to fiat currency:

> One of the consequences of Dr Smith's mode of treating the subject, is that the reader is led into the error of thinking, that when, through an excessive issue of paper, gold has been made to flow away from us, the expense of restoring it consists merely in the charge of collecting it and transporting it ... It follows, on the contrary, from the principles which I have laid down, that, in order to bring back gold, the expense not only of importing it may be incurred, but also that of purchasing it at a loss, and at a loss which may be either more or less considerable: a circumstance of great importance in the question. If this loss should ever become extremely great, the difficulties of restoring the value of our paper might easily be surmounted, and a current discount or difference between the coin and paper of the country would scarcely be avoidable.[46]

Thornton, then, addressed the arguments which are also put forward today by some Islamic scholars who support some form of gold standard. It was Thornton's analysis that gold standard supporters were looking at the monetisation of gold one dimensionally. When the role of fiat currencies was fully considered, Thornton declared, these currencies were more cost effective than a gold-based currency.

Mahathir, Keynes and the Gold Standard: Could It Work?

If we go back to Mahathir's concept in 1997, the then Malaysian Prime Minister was not arguing for a gold-based currency which, as we have discovered, a number of Islamic scholars continue to call for.

Instead he was calling for an international payments system that would be underpinned by gold but where national currencies would also operate. Iqbal argued that this payments structure would meet the needs of wider society:

> In my opinion, the gold dinar if implemented is similar to the forward contract but with its problems of "barter", speculative and arbitrage elements removed; and are also a superior tool for managing foreign exchange risk compared to the futures and option contracts. The gold dinar is likely to reduce transaction costs too, since only accounting record need to be kept. Transactions can be executed by means of electronic media with minimal cost. Hence, for international trades in this system, one no longer needs to open a letter of credit with a bank, incur exchange rate transaction costs (that is, the different buying and selling rates for currencies) or even face exchange rate risk.
>
> The gold dinar system also reduces the need to create large amounts of national currencies through multiple deposit creation in the banking sector. This therefore reduces the possibility of excessive speculation and future attacks on the Ringgit (*Malaysian currency*) like the one in 1997. The banking sector can compensate for this "implied" loss by viewing the gold dinar system as an opportunity and thereby providing the necessary services in collaboration with the central bank.[47]

As Iqbal acknowledges, speculation could still occur due to the continued existence of national currencies but that the risks should be lowered so that "*excessive*" speculation would be prevented. How the term 'excessive' could be defined in this context is harder to judge.

In order to fully consider Mahathir's concept, we should consider a very similar scheme that was put forward around 60 years earlier—by John Maynard Keynes.

During 1941, when the Second World War hung in the balance, Keynes was working on proposals for a post-war international payments system. Keynes' ideas later developed as the basis for the British negotiating position for a new international monetary settlement in advance of talks at the New Hampshire location of Bretton Woods.

Whilst Keynes' ideas were not accepted by the US negotiators, Keynes' ideas have some relevance if an Islamic monetary system based on the gold standard is to be given further serious consideration.

Keynes first argued that the flow of gold did not preserve equilibrium in the balance of payments except for the British silver inflation period of the sixteenth century and the British gold standard period of the late nineteenth century. The gold standard had failed as adjustment was "*compulsory for the debtor and voluntary for the creditor*"[48]

Instead, Keynes proposed an International Currency Union that was intended "*to secure creditor adjustment without renouncing debtor discipline*"[49]

All residual international transactions would give rise to surpluses and deficits in the balance of payments position would be settled through clearing accounts held by member central banks in an International Clearing Bank. This would enable member central banks to buy and sell their own currencies against debits and credits to their clearing accounts.

Keynes stated that these balances would be held in '*bank money*' which he termed '*bancor*'. Each member central bank would have an overdraft facility on the basis that it could access bancor which would be equal to half the average value of its country's total trade for the last five pre-war years.

Each national currency would have a fixed relation to a unit of bancor which was expressed in terms of a unit of gold. However, this proposal was not the same as the gold standard (where gold could be bought and sold) as though bancor could be bought for gold it could not be sold for gold.

The aim of Keynes was to have some standard to provide some surety to the payments system but to remove the incentive to hoard gold. In addition, the proposal had the added advantage, from the British perspective, that a neutral world currency can be relied upon instead of having to rely on the US dollar as the primary reserve currency.

Keynes' ideas were rejected by the lead American negotiator, Harry Dexter White, in the Bretton Woods talks:

> A 'trade dollar' or 'Demos' or 'Victor' or 'what-have-you' unit of currency supplementing the United States dollar, whether of the same or different value would no more help foreign trade than would the adoption of a new flag ...The specific nature of the new currency is never described nor are

> the gains that are presumed to result from such a currency ever started in meaningful language.[50]

The 1944 Bretton Woods settlement led to the formation of the World Bank, International Monetary Fund and a link between the US dollar and gold; the dollar's connection to a gold standard continued until 1971 when a small group of advisers huddled around President Richard Nixon at Camp David made the fateful decision for the dollar to float on world markets.

The similarity between Keynes' concept and Mahathir's championing of a gold dinar payments system is worthy of note. Both schemes aimed to reduce foreign exchange risk. Both proposals saw gold as a medium of exchange and as a unit of account. Both proposals would see central banks operate "*gold accounting*" processes—though admittedly in slightly different ways from each other. Both proposals wanted to avoid the hoarding of gold.

However, the fate of the Keynes' concept would indicate that without buy-in from the world's largest economic players, such as the United States, it is hard to see how such a scheme could be viable.

At a time when an increasing—though still relatively small—number of countries are beginning to use the Chinese renminbi as a reserve currency, then the incentives for China and the United States to engage in an Islamic style monetary system, which would place less emphasis on their respective currencies, seems limited.

However, that is not to say that such proposals are not worthy of further study and consideration and for the debate to continue to advocate for a more equitable monetary system.

The Islamic scholar, Mahmud Abu Saud (1911–1993) argued that the aim of standardisation of money needed to be reached:

> Unless we standardise our money and stabilise its value, by letting the value of our measured objects fluctuate no economy can be held in a sound and wholesome state, and nobody can rightly claim that money is the standard of value or the real unit of account.[51]

Rab, whilst calling for some form of gold standard, also seemed to recognise that this objective may not be feasible in the context of the strength of key fiat currencies such as the US dollar:

> Recently there have been efforts to revert back to gold standard. It is why the greedy capitalists (bankers, multinationals combine) that have succeeded in vesting control over major part of the resources of the world and are colluding to ensure that the gold prices fall or at least fail to rise with respect of US dollar/Euro etc. Such fraudulent activities provide undue gain to their perpetrators.[52]

Rab's words, whilst provocative in making accusations of a conspiratorial nature rather than considering the systematic workings of the money markets, does reflect the frustration as expressed by some scholars as to whether a gold dinar can ever be realised in contemporary macroeconomic conditions.

There is, though, one option that could be based on the operation of the real economy, is not as prone as gold is to speculation and could—theoretically—underpin an Islamic monetary system.

This potential solution could be an Islamic cryptocurrency.

Is There a Role for an Islamic Cryptocurrency?

Over the course of recent decades, the role of gold is no longer seen, by a significant number of market participants, as the essential asset that it once was.

In 1964, the whole premise of the *Goldfinger* movie was for James Bond to protect the gold bars at Fort Knox thereby stopping the collapse of the global economy. By 1971, this film was already out of date when President Nixon finally broke the link between the price of gold and the value of the dollar.

However, could an Islamic cryptocurrency provide the surety of support for an Islamic monetary system to operate?

Cryptocurrencies work on the basis of blockchain technology. Blockchain is a digital, decentralised ledger which keeps a record of all transactions that take place across a peer-to-peer network. The major innovation is that the technology allows market participants to electronically transfer assets without the need for a centralised third party.

Collaborative technology, such as blockchain, promises the ability to improve the business processes which occur between companies thereby lowering costs. Financial institutions are exploring how they could also use blockchain technology to upend everything from clearing and settlement to insurance.

A cryptocurrency has been defined as:

1. A currency system that does not require a central authority as the value of the currency is maintained through distributed consensus;
2. The system keeps an overview of cryptocurrency units and their ownership;
3. The system defines whether new cryptocurrency units can be created. If new cryptocurrency units can be created, the system defines the circumstances of their origin and how to determine the ownership of these new units;
4. Ownership of cryptocurrency units can be proved exclusively via cryptography;
5. The system allows transactions to be performed in which ownership of the cryptographic units is changed.[53]

A number of cryptocurrencies now exists which claim to be halal.

OneGram designed a cryptocurrency known as OGC or OneGram Coin which is backed by at least one gram of gold per coin.

In May 2018, the Halal Chain cryptocurrency was launched in Dubai. The Managing Director of Halal Chain, Abdullah Han, argued that his cryptocurrency was halal as the value of the currency was based on a basket of halal industries:

> HalalChain is a comprehensive ecosystem where the Islamic economy and the digital economy complement each other. However, the use of HalalChain is not only limited to the Halal industry, it can be used to bring transparency to food label claims such as organic, non-GMO, and gluten-free.[54]

The directors of the company cleverly branded their cryptocurrency by linking it to the UAE's Blockchain Strategy to encourage the growth of fintech across the emirates.

However, opinion is divided as to whether cryptocurrencies can be shari'a compliant. Evans, referring to a popular cryptocurrency brand, Bitcoin, argued that until the international monetary system changes to allow some kind of gold standard to exist, Bitcoin could be the next best option:

> In an ideal world, Bitcoin would not be necessary, and Islamic banks could transact in gold. However, doing so could isolate a gold bank from the global banking system within a financial sandbox and 'virtual gold' has been created by several groups of entrepreneurs since the 1990s with dubious results. Bitcoin, on the other hand, does not require vaults, guards, custodians and other very expensive points of failure based on trusted individuals one does not know. Also, if one wants to transact using gold across national borders, transportation and security can be prohibitively expensive. If one resorts to hawala (*the money is paid to an agent who then instructs an associate in the relevant country or area to pay the final recipient*) style networks with trusted agents at each end, then one winds up where we are today. At the other extreme, one can use the status quo banking system and fiat, which are founded in principles that violate shari'a. While Bitcoin might not be perfect, one could argue that it is less bad than current alternatives.[55]

Citing Bitcoin as shari'a compliant is a contentious judgement. The founder of Bitcoin remains a mystery despite protestations that the person who devised this cryptocurrency has been located. More importantly, from an Islamic finance perspective, there are wild fluctuations in the value of Bitcoin. This would resemble gharar. This was certainly the view of the Grand Mufti of Egypt, Dr Shawqi Alam, in January 2018:

> One of the most important features of the e-currency exchange market that distinguishes it from other financial markets is that it is the most risky of these markets. The risk is high in transactions that go up which makes it difficult if not impossible to predict their price and value. As it is left to factors that are not controlled or stable, such as consumer tastes and moods, this makes them very volatile and - very mysteriously - high and low.
>
> These unexpected fluctuations are in the prices of these electronic currencies. Although this market is the most risky of all financial markets, it is also the highest in profit rates, and this feature is used by brokers and their agents to attract dealers and investors to use these currencies, which weakens the ability of countries to maintain their local currency and control the movement of cash circulation. Its stability and viability is questionable as well as significantly and adversely affecting countries' fiscal policies and the size of expected tax revenues, while opening the way to tax evasion.[56]

Alongside this fatwa, an adviser to the Grand Mufti, Magdy Ashour, said that Bitcoin was "*used to fund terrorists*".[57] This was probably a reference to an incident in December 2017 (which would have been fresh in the minds of the Mufti and his advisers when drafting the fatwa) of an American citizen who was charged in New York, in December 2017, with fraud and money laundering by using Bitcoin, to help fund so-called Islamic State.[58] The Mufti's concerns were also shared by the Central Bank of India which prohibited the use of Bitcoin in April 2018.

One of the most prominent scholars engaged in Islamic finance, Sheikh Dr Abdul Sattar Abu Ghuddah, has expressed concerns about cryptocurrencies arguing that currency issuance is a matter for nation states and the fluctuations of some of these cryptocurrencies can cause harm at a national level and for individuals.[59]

The OIC's Fiqh Academy reserved its position on cryptocurrencies when it ruled on this matter in November 2019:

> The Synod decided to postpone the decision on the subject until holding a symposium on smart contracts, and after deciding on the issue of encoded currencies (coded) in order to study all aspects of smart contracts ...[60]

Whilst, in theory, cryptocurrencies could be seen as some form of surety for the operation of an Islamic monetary system, the leading scholars in Islamic finance have expressed understandable reservations due to excessive gharar and maysir in some forms of cryptocurrencies, such as the eponymous Bitcoin.

If, though, the emerging self-styled halal cryptocurrencies took off, this may change the nature and context of this debate. Would, though, governments in south east Asia and the Persian Gulf—who have taken a lead in Islamic finance—want to cede some of their influence in this market by their respective currencies having less of an influence in the sector compared to an emerging shari'a compliant cryptocurrency.

It seems very unlikely that such a scenario could be envisaged and if the view amongst some leading scholars that currency issuance is primarily a matter for Governments is maintained then the concept of shari'a compliant cryptocurrencies may never get off the ground.

Is There a Future for an Islamic Monetary Policy?

Our discussion as to the practicality of an Islamic monetary system has shown that the argument that interest rates distorts the real economy has real validity and goes beyond the bounds of theological debates.

Instead we have seen how diverse thinkers, from Marx to Friedman, either expressed outright hostility towards the concept of interest rates or, instead, expressed caution as to the operation of interest rates to moderate an economy rather than consideration of other mechanisms such as the use of money supply.

Keynes' analysis of interest rates accords with a number of Islamic scholars though John Maynard Keynes did not go so far as advocate the prohibition of interest rates. However, Keynes' ideas of a payments system partly based on gold has distinct similarities to Mahathir's concept of a shari'a compliant international payments system based on gold.

However, as we explored whether gold really was the best asset for an Islamic monetary system to exist, we came across the downsides to reinstituting this asset as a gold standard. Instead we explored whether a shari'a compliant cryptocurrency could be the basis for some form of Islamic monetary system. We saw how Islamic scholars expressed legitimate concerns as to whether cryptocurrencies are as open and transparent a financial vehicle as some cryptocurrency advocates suggest.

Whilst the US dollar remains the world's reserve currency and the Chinese renminbi is seen by others as a potential reserve currency of the future, it is difficult to envisage circumstances where an effective and practical Islamic monetary system could emerge on a global basis. For all countries need to operate within a global financial system which may not fully align with Islamic economics.

However, at a time where the concept of interest rates is being questioned separately from Islamic economic concepts, such as with the emergence of Modern Monetary Theory, this is the time for Islamic scholars to shape the monetary debates now in order to develop a more equitable global monetary system for the future.

In the meantime, there is a corresponding challenge for Islamic economics—whether a shari'a compliant international trade policy could emerge. That is why, in the next section of this chapter, we turn to the halal industries being developed in Indonesia.

Indonesia: An Islamic Trade Policy?

An Islamic monetary policy could have a bearing on shaping the wider political economy and this, in turn, could influence the direction of trade policy.

Political economic models already shape trade policy. This was seen in 2019/20 with the trade tensions between China and the United States related, in part, to the concept of free markets in connection with US style laissez-faire capitalism and the state capitalism model in China where the Chinese state maintains a stake in key industrial businesses such as the telecommunications company, Huawei.

Differentiations can be discerned between political economic models which use rational choice approaches to model the interaction between protectionist and liberal sectors of the economy whilst other models may consider the interplay between broader political and commercial interests at the systemic level, particularly within a domestic context.

As Heydon and Woolcock have observed:

> The wider political economy approaches to the analysis of preferential trade agreements also seek to include a range of institutional and systemic/international factors as well as societal (i.e. interest group) factors. The domestic societal factors are essentially the same as the sector interests included in the political economic models, but inclusion of institutional elements enables such factors as the relationship between economic (and political) reform and trade agreements to be addressed.[61]

How, then, would an Islamic political economic model impact on trade policy?

At the very least we can see early signs, in Indonesia, of a rebranding of key business sectors, termed as halal, and linking this rebranding with the concept and practice of the Islamic finance industry. These developments may, in time, inform a wider debate as to how trade policy should be conducted.

In November 2018, the Indonesian Government launched its *Islamic Economic Masterplan 2019–2024*. The document demonstrated the Indonesian Government's ambition to place the concept of Islamic economics at the heart of its political economic model.

This shift in emphasis reflects the influence of its neighbour, Malaysia, in successfully championing the Islamic finance model and thereby influencing the debate as to the nature and construct of the wider South East

Asian political economic model. There has been a disconnect between the development of halal industries and the emergence of Islamic finance. The Group CEO of Maybank, Dato' Mohamed Rafique Mericana, has mentioned how the certification of halal processes did not initially include the role of Islamic finance.[62]

Nonetheless, the focus on an "*Islamic Economic Masterplan*" reflects the changing domestic political phases which Indonesia has been through. Indonesia, as a political construct, is itself directly linked to the legacy of European imperialism in South East Asia. Before the intervention of European powers in the region, what became Indonesia was a collection of territorial states. These states did not exist in the sense of being established upon politically determined boundaries but instead upon rulers having spheres of influence.

It was the concept of gotong royong which is acknowledged to have had a direct bearing on the political structures of Indonesia and Malaysia. Gotong royong is a form of mutual aid. As Geertz described it:

> An enormous inventory of highly specific and often quite intricate institutions for effecting the cooperation in work, politics and personal relations alike, vaguely gathered under culturally charged and fairly well indefinable value images – rukun (mutual adjustment), gotong royong (joint bearing of burdens), tolong menolong (reciprocal assistance) governs social interaction with a force as sovereign as it is subdued.[63]

Islam is the dominant religion in both Malaysia and Indonesia and this may have some bearing on the ethos of maqasid al sharia'a (as discussed in Chapter 6) along with the mutual aid ethos of gotong royong.

It was these related concepts combined with European intellectual influences that led Sukarno, the first President of Indonesia, to develop Pancasila which are the principles governing the conduct of the State:

> The state of Indonesia which we are to establish should be a state of mutual co-operation. How fine that is. A gotong royong state.[64]

Therefore, in advance of the Japanese invasion of Indonesia in 1942 and the conflicts with British and Dutch forces from 1945, the impact of colonialism combined with indigenous patterns of thought and conduct had engendered a nationalist spirit across a wide geographical area which, in earlier centuries, had not been identified as one central state.

Indonesia tilted to the left and developed close links with China under Sukarno (1901–1970), whereas his anti-Communist successor Suharto (1921–2008) subsequently froze diplomatic ties with China and cooperated closely with the United States.

Suharto and his New Order regime came to power in 1966 in the wake of an abortive coup attempt the year before when six army generals were murdered. In a nation-wide purge from October 1965 to March 1966, an estimated 500,000 real and imagined Communists were killed following outbreaks of violence at a community level. This violence was fuelled by the Government's campaign against the Partai Komunis Indonesia (PKI—Indonesian Communist Party).

From 1969 to 1994 GDP growth averaged 6.8%. Poverty was reduced from almost 60%of the population when Suharto took office in 1968 to 13% by the time of the onset of the 1997 Asian Financial Crisis. From the early 1970s up to 1997 this positive track record of economic development formed the basis for the regime's main claim to legitimacy.

However, there were persistent public concerns that corruption and nepotism blighted the operation of the economy. Indonesia benefited from the increase in oil prices from the mid-1970s following the 1973 Yom Kippur War[65] and from global manufacturing supply chains being largely based in East Asia.

In 1990 President Suharto formed the Ikatan Cendekiawan Muslimin se-Indonesia (Association of Indonesian Muslim Intellectuals—ICMI) which was intended to be a further base of support for the regime. Around the same time, Abdurrahman Wahid, chairman of Nahdlatul Ulama (Rise of the Islamic Scholars) emerged as a critic of the government whilst calling for democracy and religious toleration. With growing opposition from within the Muslim community as well as opposition efforts led by Sukarnoputri Megawati in addition to disputed election results in 1997, the fuse was lit for the end of the Suharto regime.

However, it was the 1997 Asian Financial Crisis that finally changed the political and economic direction of Indonesia. In early August the Indonesian rupiah came under increasing pressure from the markets and on 14 August 1997 the central bank allowed the currency to float, resulting in a devaluation from around 2,600 to nearly 3,000 rupiah against the US dollar.

Throughout September 1997 the rupiah continued to depreciate, driven by high demand for US dollars from domestic businesses. The rupiah's fall was also triggered by domestic capital flight. The neoliberal approach of the International Monetary Fund package for Indonesia, which included fiscal reductions and structural reforms, combined with the Asian Financial Crisis impacting on South Korea led to a significant increase in unemployment levels amongst Indonesians.

The combination of a deteriorating economy with popular pressure for change and tensions within the political elite forced Suharto to resign from the Presidency on 21 May 1998.

How, though, has the Indonesian political economic model changed from clientelism and a form of neo-liberalism, under Suharto, to the Indonesian state promoting Islamic economics as part of its core governing platform?

Islamic finance had begun slowly in the country with the first Islamic cooperatives established in 1990 followed by Islamic rural banks in 1991 and the first Islamic commercial bank being established in 1992. In 1998 the central bank gave official recognition to the existence of a dual banking system with Islamic and conventional banking.

However, the primary reason for the shift towards a more forceful approach towards an Islamic economic system may be linked to electoral politics. For instance, the Partai Keadilan Sejahtera (PKS—Prosperous Justice Party) has grown in popularity. The party's vision states that the PKS "*strives for Islam as the solution for the problems in the national and state life*" whilst its policy programme states that Islam should be placed "*within the context of the unitary state of Indonesia which is based on Pancasila*".

Therefore, this adherence to constitutionalism recognises the domestic political context that the PKS operates within. Some critics accused the Indonesian Government of pandering to populism by bringing in the draft criminal code which, amongst other matters, would have outlawed adultery, effectively prohibit gay sex, result in women who have had unlawful abortions being jailed for four years, and would expand the remit of the country's blasphemy law.

The code would also have criminalised people who insulted the president or the Indonesian state. However, President Joko Widoko, also known as Jokowi, decided to postpone the implementation of the law in September 2019 after widespread civil unrest against these proposals.

Whilst President Jokowi has spoken of his admiration of the political economic models of Germany and China, especially in respect of industrialisation[66] the focus on an Islamic Economic Masterplan also reflects the influence of its next door neighbour, Malaysia, whose success in levering in Islamic finance revenue streams since the early 1980s, is now being emulated in Indonesia.

However, the masterplan—whilst referring to Islamic finance—has a different emphasis on Islamic economics as compared to Malaysia:

> Reinforcement of Halal Value Chain is the main strategy that accelerates the Islamic economic growth. With the real sector as a driving force, the resulting multiplier effect is more optimal. The main sectors that are the focus of strengthening the Halal Value Chain includes halal food and beverage clusters, Muslim fashion, halal tourism, halal media and recreation as well as halal pharmaceuticals and cosmetics. To obtain maximum results, the development of various clusters are also accompanied by the strengthening of Islamic finance, MSMEs (*Micro, small and medium enterprises*) and the digital economy.[67]

Halal products would include cosmetics that do not include ingredients that would not be allowed within Islam such as any animals that are forbidden for Muslims to consume or that are not slaughtered according to shari'a law; anything decreed as najs which is defined as filth, including ingredients that are themselves not permissible such as pigs and their derivatives, blood and carrion, fluids or objects discharged from humans' or animals' bodies, such as urine, excrements, blood, vomit and pus; alcohol from alcoholic drinks; contamination from najs during preparation, processing, manufacturing or storage.

The focus on the Halal Value Chain reflects the focus of President Jokowi (who was re-elected for a second term which is due to end in 2024) on manufacturing and agriculture which are seen as key drivers to help improve the productivity of the country beyond Java in an attempt to spread prosperity to Borneo and the 17,506 other islands in Indonesia. Therefore, it is no surprise that food and drink is emphasised as Jokowi wants to increase employment in the agricultural sector.

As part of this strategy, Halal Valley has been established. It is a 500-hectare industrial park which contains a number of halal businesses located in the Moderncikande Industrial Estate in Cikande (Banten), 52 kilometres from Jakarta. Pascall Wilson, who has played a key role in establishing Halal Valley, has argued that it will help Indonesia access new markets with "*new OIC halal* brands".[68]

Four Islamic banks—Bank Mandiri Syariah, BRI Syariah, BNI Syariah and Bank Muamalat Indonesia—are involved in financing this development. This reflects the ambition of the masterplan to marry Islamic finance with halal-based production. Indonesia's neighbour, Malaysia, is also beginning to adapt by developing its own halal industries with the Malaysian Halal Development Corporation, in September 2020, urging Japanese businesses to invest in Malaysian halal markets.

Indonesia, however, remains an intriguing example as to an economy that uses Islamic finance as a stepping stone towards embedding the concept of Islamic economics in its production processes. This, in turn, could impact on trade policy such as negotiating trade access that may impinge on Intellectual Property Rights (IPR) or research and development (R&D) in halal pharmaceutical products. The discussion of such issues—in particular to protect the halal brand—could be a feature of future multilateral trade talks.

However, only time will tell how the Islamic Economic Masterplan will impact upon the Indonesian political economic model. President Jokowi also wants to lever in foreign direct investment from countries beyond the OIC by relaxing labour laws and making it easier for foreign firms to gain permits to trade.

Nonetheless, we can see how Islamic finance is beginning to shape the wider economy beyond financial services. With the Maybank Group CEO predicting that the growing synergies between Islamic finance and halal industries will "*link ASEAN and GCC through the halal economy*"[69] this trend may very well accelerate with other OIC countries, besides Malaysia, potentially following the Indonesian lead in halal production in the years ahead.

Notes

1. Twitter personal account of US President Donald Trump, 3 September 2019.
2. Tarek El Diwany (2002), *History of Banking: An Analysis*, as cited in *Viability of the Islamic Dinar.*
3. Abhijit V. Bannerjee (2010), *Investment Efficiency and the Distribution of Wealth* as contained in the World Bank/International Bank of Reconstruction and Development report, *Equity and Growth in a Globalising World.*
4. Adam SmithInstitute, *Interest Rates and the Price System*, https://www.adamsmith.org/blog/tax-spending/interest-rates-and-the-price-system.

5. Thomas Picketty, *Capital in the Twenty First Century*, page 687.
6. Israel M. Kirzner, *Ludwig von Mises*, page 150.
7. Ibid., page 151.
8. Ludwig von Mises (1966), *Human Action*, 3rd rev. ed. (Chicago: Henry Regnery), page 484.
9. Carl Menger (1976), *Principles of Economics* (New York: New York University Press), page 154.
10. Timothy Cogley (26 March 1999), *Monetary Policy and the Great Crash of 1929: A Bursting Bubble or Collapsing Fundamentals?* Federal Reserve Bank of San Francisco.
11. Robert Schiller (2005), *Irrational Exuberance*.
12. https://stephaniekelton.com/paul-krugman-asked-me-about-modern-monetary-theory-here-are-4-answers/.
13. Karl Marx, Chapter 22—*Division of Profit. Rate of Interest. Natural Rate of Interest.* Das Kapital.
14. Tarek El Diwany, *History of Banking: An Analysis*, Proceedings of the 2002 International Conference on Stable and Just Global Monetary System (Kuala Lumpur).
15. Karl Marx, Chapter 22—*Division of Profit. Rate of Interest. Natural Rate of Interest.* Das Kapital.
16. Ibid.
17. Ibid.
18. Milton Friedman (1966), Interest Rates and the Demand for Money, *The Journal of Law & Economics*, vol. 9, pp. 71–85.
19. Milton Friedman (1987), "Quantity Theory of Money" by Milton Friedman In *The New Palgrave: A Dictionary of Economics*, edited by John Eatwell, Murray Milgate, and Peter Newman, vol. 4, pp. 3–20. New York: Stockton Press; and London: Macmillan.
20. Ibid.
21. As quoted by Eric Lonergan, *Money* (Routledge).
22. John Maynard Keynes, *Tract on Monetary Reform*, page 56.
23. John Maynard Keynes (7 June 1924), A Drastic Remedy for Unemployment—A Reply to Critics, *The Nation*, vol. xxxv, no. 10, p. 312.
24. Mahathir Attacks Speculation And Soros, Who Returns Fire (22 September 1997), *Wall Street Journal.*
25. *Mahathir Blasts Speculators* (30 January 1999), CNN.
26. Hadith narrated by Ubida ibn al-Samit and reported by the Hadith narrator Muslim in the book of transaction.
27. Qur'ran, 3:14.
28. Vilar, 1976, page 46.
29. According to Professor Andrew Watson as recorded in a 1967 paper for the Economic History Society.
30. Al-Maqrizi, Ighatat al-Ummah bi-kashf al-ghummah.

31. Ibid.
32. Al-Maqrizi, Shothur-al-‘ugood fi thiker al-Nuqud
33. Ibid.
34. Al Maqrizi, Ighatat al-Ummah bi-kashf al-ghummah.
35. Ibid.
36. Ibid.
37. Ibn-Abidin, *Majmū‘ah Rasā’il Ibn ‘Abidin*, 62.
38. John Toland, *Hitler*, page 252.
39. Steven Fraser, *Wall Street: A Cultural History*, pages 99–100.
40. Hafiz Majdi Ab Rashid, Dodik Siswantoro, John A Brozovsky, *The Stability of the Gold Dinar and Accounting Implications: An Empirical Study*, paper presented to the 2002 International Conference on Stable and Just Global Monetary System (Kuala Lumpur).
41. Ibid.
42. Dr. Mehmet Balcılar, Dr. Nezahat Küçük (2013), *Features of Business Cycles across the Middle East and North Africa: A Nonparametric Analysis* (Eastern Mediterranean University, Cyprus)
43. Milton Friedman (1987), "Quantity Theory of Money" by Milton Friedman In The New Palgrave: A Dictionary of Economics, edited by John Eatwell, Murray Milgate, and Peter Newman, vol. 4, pp. 3–20. New York: Stockton Press; and London: Macmillan
44. Letter dated 13 December 1960. Box 27. Folder 24. Friedman Papers.
45. Henry Thornton, *Paper Credit*, pages 178–179.
46. Ibid., page 205.
47. Dr Jacquir Iqbal, *Islamic financial management: Volume 1*, pages 163–164.
48. As quoted by Robert Skidelsky, *John Maynard Keynes*, page 676.
49. Ibid.
50. White Archives (March 1942), *United Nations Stabilisation Fund.*
51. Abu Saud, supra., at 63.
52. Hifzur Rab, *Problems Created by the Fiat Money, Islamic Dinar and Other Available Alternatives.* Paper presented to the 2002 International Conference on Stable and Just Global Monetary System (Kuala Lumpur).
53. Jan Lansky (January 2018), Possible State Approaches to Cryptocurrencies, *Journal of Systems Integration*, vol. 9, no. 1, pp. 19–31.
54. https://medium.com/@QitmeerChain/blockchain-powered-halal-chain-launched-in-dubai-will-revolutionize-halal-products-compliance-9436b2299ae5.
55. Charles W. Evans (June 2015), Bitcoin in Islamic Banking and Finance, *Journal of Islamic Banking and Finance.*
56. Ahram (Egyptian newspaper), 1 January 2018.
57. *Egypt Today*, 31 December 2017.

58. *US Woman used Bitcoin to Move Cash to Islamic State, Police Say* (15 December 2017), BBC, 15 December 2017.
59. Abdul Sattar Abu Ghaddah (2018), *al Nuqud al Raqamiyah al Ru'yah al Syar'iyyah wal Athar al Iqtisodiyah* (Doha) 24–25.
60. Resolution No 230 (1/24), Fiqh Academy, 15 November 2019.
61. Kenneth Heydon, Stephen Woolcock, *The Rise of Bilateralism: Comparing American, European and Asian Approaches to Preferential Trade Agreements*, page 219.
62. Islamic Markets webinar, 1 September 2020.
63. C. Geertz, *Local Knowledge: Fact and Law in Comparative Perspective*, page 167.
64. Indonesia Government website.
65. The implications of the 1973 Yom Kippur War on the development of the Islamic finance industry is discussed in Chapter 10.
66. Bloomberg television interview, October 2019.
67. Indonesian Government, *Islamic Economic Masterplan 2019–2024.*
68. https://halalfocus.net/malaysia-halal-cluster-network-with-halal-clusters-in-indonesia-malaysia-and-spain/.
69. Islamic Markets webinar, 1 September 2020.

CHAPTER 9

Varieties of Capitalism and Islamic Finance: A Comparative Study

Islamic Finance, Socialism and the Profit Motive

> In my youth I was groping in search of an ideology and a life mission. The choice was between socialism, which had glamour for the youth at that time, or going back to my roots, Islam.[1]

This was the dilemma facing Khurshid Ahmad. Today, Ahmad is a shari'a scholar of renowned repute who has played a seminal role in the Islamic finance industry in Pakistan, Saudi Arabia and the United Kingdom.

Ahmad's youthful ruminations relate to a trend where leading scholars and politicians identified a commonality of interests between Islam and left-wing economics even if some of these scholars later rejected left-wing thought for what was seen as the denial of spirituality.

In fact, whilst Communism wholeheartedly rejected the concept of religion this was not the case with a number of socialist schools of thought. The British socialist thinker, R H Tawney (1880–1962) wrote of a symbiotic relationship between socialism and Christianity:

> … in order to believe in human equality it is necessary to believe in God. It is only when one contemplates the infinitely great that human differences appear so infinitely small as to be negligible … What is wrong with the modern world is that having ceased to believe in the greatness of God,

J. S. Watkins, *Islamic Finance and Global Capitalism*,
https://doi.org/10.1007/978-3-030-59840-2_9

> and therefore the infinite smallness (or greatness – the same thing!) of man, it has to invent or emphasise distinctions between men.[2]

R H Tawney's argument reflects the views of some writers in the Islamist tradition that postmodernism was responsible for a lack of spirituality and a corresponding rise in societal discord, as discussed in Chapter 6. R H Tawney's argument of the belief in God contributing to the well running of society had synergies with the work of Al-Farabi (872–950) whose writings influenced the leader of the 1979 Iranian Revolution, Ayatollah Khomeini, to try and aim for a more perfect state with the establishment of a theocratic government in Iran.

Al Farabi wrote of the ideal of a "*virtuous city*" where his description of the running of the city happened to have parallels with contemporary mutual models of capitalism:

> … is the one in which there is mutual assistance for earning what is necessary to constitute and safeguard bodies. …. Among the necessary cities, there may be some that bring together all of the arts that procure what is necessary. Their ruler is the one who has fine governance and excellent stratagems for using [the citizens] so that they gain the necessary things and fine governance in preserving these things for them or who bestows these things on them from what he has.[3]

The concept of mutual assistance, areas of responsibility and citizens working together for a shared collective endeavour are the characteristics we see in mutual organisations and cooperatives. The aim of these cooperatives to not only meet commercial targets but also to help cooperative members to realise their full potential can also be related to a concept in Islam known as Ihsan.

Ihsan exemplifies the link between spiritual fulfillness and addressing daily issues such as finance and working within an economy:

> Ihsan is the final destination of the true believer. It is that state of human existence and experience where the here and now begins to merge with the hereafter. It is sometimes that fleeting moment when time becomes still and the believer has this profound experience that brings with it a sense of awe, amazement and fulfilment. Such moments are rare and only very few fortunate individuals experience it, and even fewer able to record and describe it for others. It is also a state of being when one is at peace with oneself and with the circumstances of one's existence. One is neither

> insecure about the future nor one grieves the past. Life itself becomes a reward, a beautiful fulfilment. This is Ihsan, the final destiny of the true believer, the more fortunate of them experience it here, and others will know it hereafter.[4]

How would this spiritual concept relate to economics and mutualism?

> To me, Ihsan is about doing beautiful things in difficult circumstances. It is engaging with the world in pursuit of social justice and not remaining silent in the face of oppression.[5]

Therefore, we can identify this link between contemporary political and economic struggles and spiritual fulfilment as a core theme within Islam. It should be also recognised that Ihsan is also associated with the spiritual practices associated with the Sufi movement within Islam.

The concept of Ihsan has some parallels with the work of Jonathan Edwards (1703–1758). Edwards was part of the religious movement known as the Great Awakening which shaped American practices of Christianity and contributed towards the formation of an American national identity in advance of the War of Independence. Edwards wrote that religion can detect "*divine things*" by "*the beauty of their moral excellency*" and by "*the sense of spiritual beauty ... all true experimental knowledge of religion*" and "*a whole new world of knowledge*" can be discerned.[6]

These theological insights help to illuminate the synergies between left-wing politics, Islamic finance and Christian socialist movements. Tawney, for one, wrote of the ethical issues which needed to be addressed within capitalism:

> A society in which some groups do much of what they please, while others can do little of what they ought, may have virtues of its own: but freedom is not one of them. It is free in so far, and only in so far, as all the elements composing it are able in fact, not merely in theory, to make the most of their powers, to grow to their full stature, to do what they conceive to be their duty and – since liberty should not be too austere – to have their fling when they feel like it.[7]

This reflects the thinking within Islam that laissez-faire capitalism inhibits a person's ability to fulfil their spiritual-self whilst capital owners dominate the means of exchange within an economic system and so inhibit the space for such self-realisation to take place.

It is the writings of the British socialist and artist, John Ruskin (1819 – 1900) which particularly resonates with Islamic thought:

> It is impossible to conclude, of any given mass of acquired wealth, merely by the fact of its existence, whether it signifies good or evil to the nation in the midst of which it exists. Its real value depends on the moral sign attached to it, just as strictly as that of a mathematical quantity depends on the algebraic sign attached to it. Any given accumulation of commercial wealth may be indicative, on the one hand, of faithful industries, progressive energies and productive ingenuities: or, on the other, it may be indicative of mortal luxury, merciless tyranny, ruinous chicanery.[8]

Ruskin's description of the moral implications of wealth creation chimes with Islamic thinking and helps illustrate how over many years linkages have been discerned between Islamic thought and socialism.

Zulfikar Ali Bhutto (1928–1979) used the formation of the Pakistan People's Party (PPP) in December 1967 to equate left-wing politics with Islam. One of the PPP's Foundation Documents referred to the struggle against "*oppression, exploitation and slavery*" and called on "*the masses of Pakistan to unite ... until this land brightens up with the divine light of God*".[9]

Michel Aflaq (1910–1989) was a leading figure with the formation of the Baath (Renaissance) Party. Whilst the Baath Party is now associated with the sadistic dictatorship of Saddam Hussein (1937–2006) in Iraq and the current brutal regime of Bashar Al-Assad in Syria, the Baath Party was initially founded with a left-wing prospectus in mind. There was a belief that was expounded by Aflaq in the 1950s that left-wing politics was in line with the beliefs of Islam:

> The power of Islam has revived to appear in our days under a new form, Arab nationalism.[10]

Akram al-Hourani (1912–1996), who also played a role in supporting the formation of the Baath Party in Syria, spoke of the influence of his family's Sufi teaching on his thinking for rural economic reform. Thompson argued that despite Hourani's association with Syrian military rule, he was really a middle of the road social democrat:

> In another time and place, Hourani's efforts might have produced a Scandinavian style social welfare state. But conditions inside and outside of 1950s Syria did not favour such a democratic transition.[11]

Muammar Gaddafi (1942–2011) gained power in Libya via a military coup in 1969. To consolidate his rule, Gaddafi issued the *Green Book* which described an ideal society which would be governed on a linear basis based on Islam and which included socialist ideas:

> The ultimate solution lies in abolishing the wage-system, emancipating people from its bondage and reverting to the natural laws which defined relationships before the emergence of classes, forms of government and man-made laws. These natural rules are the only measures that ought to govern human relations. These natural rules have produced natural socialism based on equality among the components of economic production and have maintained public consumption almost equal to natural production among individuals.

However, in 2008, Gaddafi praised capitalism and promised to institute economic reforms. In reality it was crony capitalism that was prevalent within the Libyan political economic model, with Gaddafi and his sons creaming off state money to fund their luxury lifestyles whilst most citizens in the oil endowed country were suffering from deprivation. This divide was further exposed in 2011 when the Gaddafi regime finally collapsed with citizens plundering the palaces of the regime.

The seminal British Liberal economist, John Maynard Keynes (1883–1946) went further and instead of comparing Islam to socialism he, instead, compared the religion to Communism. However, the comparison was intended to damn both Communism and Islam:

> My feelings about Das Kapital are the same as my feelings about the Koran. I know that it is historically important and I know that many people, not all of whom are idiots, find it a sort of Rock of Ages and containing inspiration. Yet when I look into it, it is to me inexplicable that it can have this effect. Its dreary, out of date, academic controversialising *(sic)* seems so extraordinarily unsuitable as material for the purpose. But then, as I have said, I feel just the same about the Koran. How could either of these books carry fire and sword round half the world? It beats me.

Keynes made this statement in a private letter to his friend, the Irish playwright, George Bernard Shaw, in December 1934 so this could have been an attempt at facetiousness. The disdain directed towards Islam could, in addition, have been a reflection of British imperialist attitudes of that era. It is of note, however, that Keynes felt it was natural to draw an analogy between Communism and Islam. It demonstrates how this line of thought persisted for many decades.

Indeed, it was during the 1920s, 1930s and 1940s that Muslim academics and Muslim politicians in British controlled India were considering whether there were similarities and differences between Islam and Communism.

This was a period when growing anti-colonial feelings was being expressed and the 1917 Russian Revolution was seen as a fresh experiment in challenging the old guard of capitalism and imperialism. After all it was Lenin who described imperialism as the highest form of capitalist exploitation.

To understand this period and how it relates to our own time, we should recall that some thinkers during this period used the terms 'socialism' and 'communism' interchangeably without discerning the difference between the two concepts. Nonetheless, the ideas of socialism and communism did play their part in the early history of Islamic finance.

Moshir Hosain Kidawi was an elected politician who advocated change in society. In his book, *Islam and Socialism* (1912), Kidawi saw advantages in socialism where equality of opportunity could be attained. Kidawi saw parallels between socialist ideas and the early Muslim community of the Prophet with riba being outlawed, zakat being instituted and an open governance system being established. However, he believed that the forms of socialism prevalent in the early twentieth century did not recognise the spiritual dimension and it operated within bureaucratic systems which were counter-intuitive to engaging with wider society.

Kidawi did believe that "*true socialism*" could be achieved in Asia rather than Europe to enable the spiritual dimension in socialist thought to be embedded. Kidawi argued that this objective was best achieved within the culture of religiosity as practiced in Asia compared to what he perceived to be a secular Europe. When Kidawi spoke of advancing socialism with an understanding of spirituality, this was not an exclusionist doctrine as he argued that many Hindus and Buddhists would also support this policy direction.

This inclusive approach was a key theme in Kidawi's thought. Kidawi rejected the idea, for example, that the concept of Pan-Islamism would not be respectful of other faiths. In his book, *Pan-Islamism* (1908), Kidawi described how in history it has been forces who advocated Christianity which tried to suppress religious diversity and this was not the case under the caliphate. Kidawi argued that Pan-Islamism would respect ethnic and religious diversity.

Abdul Hafiz Mohamed Barakatullah (1854–1927), like Kidawi, advocated change via the adoption of Pan-Islamism. Barakatullah also saw the linkages between Communism and Islam and called on:

> ... the Muhammadans of the world and Asiatic nations to understand the noble principles of Russian Socialism and to embrace it seriously and enthusiastically.[12]

Once Pakistan gained independence in 1947, debate continued as to the parallels between Communism and Islam. Ishtiaq Hussain Qureshi (1903–1981) used his academic credentials to test Islamic concepts in the "*crucible*" of day to day life. Qureshi also advocated participatory democracy within Pakistan. As far as the links with Communist thought was concerned, Qureshi wrote that the Soviet Union was a model for social justice but that its "*materialist dialectics*" should be rejected.[13]

However, equating Islamic finance with left-wing politics (or the espousal of socialism) may not be altogether fair. As we discussed in Chapter 2, in respect of prices and competition policy, Islamic finance has a number of synergies with laissez-faire economics. The communitarian approach of Islamic finance is, though, distinctive as compared with conventional finance.

Conventional finance has often been equated with a laser like focus on monetary rewards at the expense of wider social and environmental requirements. A legal precedent in the United Kingdom would, at first glance, seem to bear this stereotype out.

The High Court of England and Wales considered, in the early 1980s, the demand of the trustees who were responsible for the coal miners' pension fund. Some of the trustees, who had been appointed by the National Union of Mineworkers (NUM), argued for moral considerations to be taken into consideration when investment policies for the pension fund were being considered.

In a 1985 judgement (the same year that the NUM was comprehensively defeated following a year-long strike in opposition to Margaret Thatcher's Government) the High Court ruled that financial considerations took precedence when investment decisions were being considered:

> Trustees cannot be criticised for failing to make a particular investment for social or political reasons, such as in South African stock for example, but may be held liable for investing in assets which yield a poor return or for disinvesting in stock at inappropriate times for non-financial criteria.[14]

Whilst legal experts have since argued whether the judgement really did mean that ethical issues would always be trumped by financial concerns when investment decisions were being made, it is a judgement that is often cited as an example of the overriding desire for profit inherent within Western capitalism.

However, as we discussed in Chapter 5, conventional finance institutions are now encouraged to consider wider social and environmental objectives and it would be wrong to stereotypically equate all of Western capitalism with a sole obsession for wealth accumulation.[15]

Indeed, the desire for wealth was seen as a means to an end—not an end in and of itself—for some of the leading European merchants of the nineteenth century. To demonstrate this point, we can look at the City of Birmingham in the United Kingdom.

Nineteenth-Century British Capitalism and the Work Ethic in Islamic Finance

From where I am typing this book I am just ten minutes away from Birmingham Council House—a building which reflects the philanthropic tendencies of nineteenth-century capitalism. Technically, it is a just a building which houses the offices of the locally elected councillors and the senior municipal officers but, in reality, it is much more than that.

It is a grandiose structure with Romanesque ornamentation, decorated columns and detailed carving which is rich in symbolism. It projects civic pride with elaborate decoration, buttresses and gold leaf. Within the building is an elaborate staircase leading to the wood panelled debating chamber and a grand hall which is still used for civic receptions.

Towards the top of the building is an image of a muse, representing the city, bestowing justice on the city's citizens. On the other side of the square is the Town Hall—which is intended to be the exact copy of the Parthenon.

This is how nineteenth-century business leaders saw themselves—as creators of wealth and benefactors to the nation. They thought they were the inheritors of a new world where they would be the patrons of culture and munificence with analogies to the Roman senate and, even further back, to the demos of ancient Athens.

Instead of the landed aristocrats leading the way as had been the practice for much of British history, it was now the entrepreneurs and the merchant class that was in the vanguard of the nation. With the square named after the eponymous Queen Victoria, this small locale is a microcosm of the Victorian attitudes prevalent amongst the business elite.

However, whilst advances were made by Birmingham's civic leaders by clearing the slums and improving the living conditions of working people, the suffering and urban plight that impacted the vast majority of the population on a day-to-day basis was said to be so severe that legend has it when Queen Victoria travelled through the area she closed the curtains of her carriage to avoid casting her eyes on the blighted industrial landscape.

It has been argued that an anti-entrepreneurial culture in Britain emerged in the later nineteenth century and early twentieth century which Wiener and others have argued, hindered future growth. This attitude reached such a level of intensity that Stanley Baldwin, the UK Prime Minister in the 1920s and 1930s described the country as "*the tinkle of the hammer of the anvil in the country smithy, the corncrake on a dewy morning, the sound of the scythe against the whetstone and the sight of the plough team coming over the brow of the hill*" when it was, in fact, one of the most industrialised countries in the world.[16]

Nonetheless, the business culture that was engendered in this era was a mix of entrepreneurship and exploitation combined with civic endowments to improve the daily lives of workers whilst focusing on short term returns in a business environment that was greatly aided for the business owners by the spoils of the British Empire.

It is argued by advocates of laissez-faire capitalism that modern business corporations are also inherently based on morality. Rebutting the claims by some on the Left, as well as by some Islamic scholars, that capitalism ignores moral teaching in the blind pursuit of profit, Lord Griffiths of Florestfach, who was a policy adviser to the UK Prime Minister,

Margaret Thatcher, has argued that the modern corporation represents a "*moral community*":

> The question of what should be included in a company's moral standard and the way in which it is expressed will vary from company to company. But in examining the statements of a variety of companies there are recurring themes: the need for integrity, transparency, honesty and telling the truth; a respect for the individual person because of his or her innate dignity as a fellow human being; a sense of fairness in the way people are treated; the ideal of service, especially in relation to customers but also in the style of leadership shown by executives; the value of teamwork; the responsibility of the corporation to respect the environment; and a commitment to support those communities in which the corporation has facilities. In fact, these themes appear so frequently in different sectors, different countries, different continents and different cultures, that they become less a collection of disparate values chosen by individual companies and more and more a set of universals.[17]

Whilst nineteenth-century British entrepreneurs were inspired by history and their philanthropic desires, Griffiths argues that the modern incarnation of a business corporation also reflects these core moral values.

This interesting analysis may be contentious for some who may point to recent financial scandals where this level of morality was not in evidence though Griffiths would argue that the very failure of businesses who do not embrace such a moral standard epitomises the need for some form of morality to operate within an enterprise.

Whilst Griffiths refers to morality in laissez-faire capitalism, the moral driving force behind the nineteenth-century British entrepreneurs can be seen, in part, with the motivations of some of the participants in the Malaysian Islamic finance industry. As the business culture changed Victorian Britain in its own way, the concept of Islamic economics was also beginning to shape contemporary business culture.

Patricia Sloane-White's work has found that business culture was being shaped by Malaysian firms who engaged with Islamic finance.

Sloane-White discussed managers and business owners who "*work in Islamic banks and insurance companies and the companies that service them, such as human resources and training consultancies, and accountancies and auditing firms whose owners and directors have fully embraced the Islamic economic model*".

As in nineteenth-century Britain, Sloane-White found that Malaysian managers in the Islamic finance sector were proud to be seen as merchants though, in the Islamic context, this was linked to the profession of the Prophet who, before receiving the revelation, was a trader.

Sloane-White also found, when engaging with a cohort of Malaysian managers, that the concept of trade being in the "*genes*" was a constant refrain:

> He explained that when Islam first came to the Malay Peninsula in the thirteenth century via Muslim traders who then intermarried with the Malays, the Malays "inherited" their capacity for both piety and trade. Another businessman, an Islamic banker, believed, too, that trade was a "recessive gene" in his blood. Malaysia, once a crucial stop on Islam's ancient trade routes but eclipsed by colonialism, the Chinese, and the West, will rise again on a new (and virtual) "Silk Road", trading such things as the global sovereign sukuk funds and other innovative Islamic financial instruments now in development by Malaysia's innovative "sharia entrepreneurs".

This could be viewed as a continuation of the national identity question that has constantly hovered over Malaysian society and politics. As will be discussed in Chapter 10, the formation of the Malaysian state was dominated by the need to develop a sense of national consciousness in a nation whose borders were designated as a consequence of the legacy of competition between British and Dutch colonialists. The early period of the Malaysian state was dominated by the concept of identity and the initial need for separate political parties to represent the Malay, Chinese heritage and Indian heritage communities.

Therefore, this determination, as expressed within Sloane-White's study, to associate religious identity with the history of Malaysia before the era of British imperialism, resonates with this wider identity debate. However, when Sloane-White approached the issue of ethnic identities in Malaysia, the response she received was robust:

> ... all of the men in my study described themselves as Muslim businessmen, sharply distinguishing themselves from those they called "Malay" or "bumiputra businessmen" born of NEP[18] economic programmes. They characterized the entire previous generation of bumiputra businessmen, as well as many of their contemporaries, as cronies and clients of corrupt Malay politicians, men whose interests lay merely in the accumulation of wealth. A bumiputra businessman, one company director said dismissively,

> "sits at the feet of his political masters, makes himself a slave to money, and puts avarice before religious duty while all along claiming to be religious".

These reactions chime with the nineteenth-century British merchants who looked down with disdain at the perceived corrupt practices of the landed aristocracy of their era. However, these comments also demonstrate how Islamic finance, by becoming an intrinsic part of the Malaysian political economic model, is also having an impact on the psyche of a number of Malaysian market participants. The rise of religious identity in Malaysia is discussed in more detail in Chapter 10.

Sloane-White elaborated on this ethnic—religious identity point by referring to how the managers she surveyed used the word 'barakah' meaning blessing:

> I heard the word barakah countless times in the offices and conference rooms in which I interviewed highly placed figures in the Islamic economy — the corporate leaders who have, by virtue of their corporate positions, many resources and many blessings at their disposal. But it is a term of relatively new provenance in Malay-Muslim corporate circles, replacing, I think, among the men I spoke to, a different term that justified rewards for other Malay-Muslims: bumiputra.[19]

In Chapter 6, we considered how the concept of vice-regency or trusteeship of humanity on Earth (khalifah) had shaped the underlying philosophical basis of the Islamic finance industry. As was also considered in Chapter 7, this very concept lends Islamic finance the ability to address environmental concerns.

However, there could be a more insidious side to this concept for Sloane-White discovered that khalifah was cited by some employers in Malaysia as a rationale to know the private lives of their employees. Khalifah was cited by one employer, for example, as to how he approached HR management within the firm:

> We want to know everything about them. We ask questions about their wife or husband and the children. We ask and we watch — is this a good family, a pious family? Is everyone in this family fulfilling their duties? Is the employee managing his or her family well? This tells us how they will perform their job. If we see flaws at home or at work, we will guide and coach them towards a more Islamic lifestyle. Long after their probation ends, at company events and family days, spouses and children will

> continue to be observed. There is no "faking it" in this organisation, and those who cannot comply leave on their own accord.

There is a danger of reading too much into this finding for HR management systems that vary around the world and leaders throughout East Asia have referred to the close bonds between employers and employees as reflective of "Asian values"—a concept that will be explored in greater depth in this chapter.

The Sloane-White study is just one example of considering how Islamic finance is shaping business culture. This subject is worthy of further empirical research to ascertain the varieties of business cultures being potentially impacted by ideas around Islamic economics and how this may or may not relate to enhanced commercial performance and wider societal consequences.

Varieties of Capitalism

Sayyid Qutb (1906–1966) was a leading Muslim Brotherhood figure in Egypt who spoke of an Islamic alternative to laissez-faire capitalism. Qutb was eventually imprisoned and executed by the Egyptian authorities. The description of capitalism which Qutb adopted was scathing:

> self-indulgent, individualistic, crime-infested, and oppressive social order ruled by tyrants who brutally abuse their subjects and unjustly govern according to their own whims and self-interests.[20]

Whilst Qutb eventually saw himself as part of an ideological struggle against what he perceived as secular Arab nationalism as represented by Gamal Abdul Nasser, this concept of capitalism in all parts of the world representing a nihilist tyranny is clearly far from the mark—though for some people living under colonialism there may have been an element of sympathy with this description.

Another figure from this era took a contrary approach to Qutb and claimed that any talk of capitalism was already old fashioned and did not relate to the post-war world. Anthony Crosland was a leading Labour Party politician who eventually became British Foreign Secretary before unexpectedly dying from a stroke when he was just 58.

In 1956, Crosland's seminal work, *The Future of Socialism*, was published. The book changed British politics with the Labour Party moving towards a more social democratic approach with Crosland laying out a road-map for Labour to attain electoral success.

Reading the book now, its whole approach is very parochial. There is hardly any mention about the UK's economic place in the world despite the fact that the United Kingdom was then part of a grand alliance in the Cold War, that British forces were based in Germany whilst UK troops were fighting rebels in the Malay Peninsula and the Mau Mau group in Kenya.

This was also the era of the Korean War (which again involved British troops). Shortly after the book was published, the United Kingdom was involved in the Suez crisis which quickly led to a retreat of British forces as a direct consequence of American economic pressure. The United Kingdom was also still paying off its wartime debts to the United States (which was only finally cleared in 2006).

Crosland argued that the United Kingdom was a post capitalist state—but not in the Communist sense:

> As for the dogma of the 'invisible hand', and the belief that private gain must always lead to the public good, these failed entirely to survive the Great Depression; and even Conservatives and businessmen now subscribe to the doctrine of collective government responsibility for the state of the economy.[21]

Crosland claimed that a new name was required for the model of the political economy which Britain then had:

> I once rashly joined in the search for a suitable name, and in New Fabian Essays called the new society 'statism'. But it was, on reflection, a bad choice. It has come to be widely used, especially in the U.S.A., but as a synonym for 'collectivism', which was not the connotation intended. Having had no better idea since then, I have no intention of trying again. Nevertheless, I believe that our present society is sufficiently defined, and distinct from classical capitalism, to require a different name.

Whilst the former Oxford don was perplexed by terminology, this post war consensus in Britain may, in hindsight, have been more attuned to Keynesian economics. Whatever the case may have been, the declaration of capitalism having been surpassed by a new economic model at that time turned out to be a false dawn.

However, Crosland was right to discern that there are differences in capitalist political economic models and the stereotype of capitalism as articulated by Qutb and others was not valid.

What are these varieties of capitalism?

Hall and Soskice pioneered this study of differences in capitalism—but they began their study from one key underlying assumption:

> The varieties of capitalism approach can … be useful for understanding political economies that do not correspond to the ideal type of a liberal or coordinated market economy.[22]

Hall and Soskice identified distinctions between American capitalism and European capitalism. Market liberal capitalism in the United States was defined as being based upon an individualist value-system with ideals of personal liberty. This was combined with a minimalist state role providing basic public goods and the protection of property rights.

In turn this corresponded with a deregulated, privatised, liberalised and low tax market economy. The emphasis of this form of political economy was upon the objective of shareholder value in order to attain profit maximisation. This corresponded with the need for managerial incentive-structures which are capital market-based such as bonuses based on share price performance whilst labour market 'flexibility' was a key corrective to balance the overall economy.

This contrasted sharply with European social market capitalism. In this political economic model there is a corporatist, regulatory state which aimed to address market failure whilst institutionalising market order. There was a mixed economy with strong regulatory structures and systems.

The focus of this model was upon stakeholder value which was based on communitarian ideals of participation which would include workers, consumers and the local community. Production is said to be more aligned with finance with an emphasis on long-term R&D investment rather than short-term profit. Social solidarity in labour relations is, arguably, a key principle within social market capitalism which engenders higher wages combined with the aim of high productivity.

The differences between these two models are exemplified by two very different economists—Wilhelm Ropke (1899–1966) and Milton Friedman (1912–2006).

Ropke can be seen to represent the social market political economy. Instrumental in the reconstruction of West Germany following the end of the Second World War, he admired the Swiss model of government of decentralisation with decision-making being devolved to grassroots communities. Ropke argued that support for farmers, shop keepers and industrial workers was required under certain circumstances to maintain a functioning economy. Ropke's ideas were dubbed by the then German Finance Minister, Ludwig Erhard (later West German Chancellor) as the "*social market economy*".

Friedman's ideas were embraced by US President Ronald Reagan during the 1980s. Friedman argued that a natural rate of unemployment was inevitable in a well-functioning market economy when the economic concept of supply and demand was in force. Government intervention, Friedman believed, can cause inflation to accelerate and so the best way to control inflation was via the use of money supply. Friedman's ideas in respect of the interest rate mechanism is discussed in Chapter 8.

In the twenty-first century, the concerns regarding the operation of capitalism in Europe and North America further to the 2008 global financial crisis and the ability of capitalism to adapt to the consequences of the 2020 COVID-19 crisis, has fuelled the debate as to the future role of capitalism.

Much of the contemporary debate concerning political economy had related to the competing models of laissez-faire capitalism as championed by the United States and state capitalism as exemplified in China. State capitalism can be defined as combining statism with the strategies of private multinational companies. In other words, it is:

> a theory of state guided globalisation that conceptualises the state as an active agent in guiding the process of integration within the global political economy at both the macro and micro levels.[23]

As Wilson has argued, the powers of the Chinese state in guiding economic development can only go so far as international institutions and multinational enterprises also directly influence and shape the nature of the Chinese capitalist system:

> Chinese officials cannot fully control the actions of foreign investors, local actors, and international organisations that bring pressure to bear on reformers. In this sense, China is best described as pursuing state-guided

> globalisation, a term that reflects state efforts to harness global forces that it cannot fully control in order to advance its long-term development strategy and short-term goals.[24]

This does not mean that state capitalism equates to liberalisation:

> Since the present Chinese leadership took power, market orientated liberalisation has been minor. And as such policies have wound down, they have been supplanted by renewed state intervention: price controls, the reversal of privatisation, the rollback of measures encouraging competition, and new barriers to investment.[25]

The influence of officials in directing investment towards key businesses can also lead to stresses and strains within the Chinese capitalist system. As Carney has pointed out, there is intense competition amongst Communist Party officials to gain promotion. Such a system can lead to negative economic costs accruing:

> Local officials have an incentive to encourage over-lending and over-borrowing for the benefit of their local jurisdiction while passing the costs off onto the broader Chinese society. Because state owned enterprises and banks can be confident of being rescued, firms become uncompetitive and unprofitable over time, and banks accumulate non-performing loans.[26]

Does the political economic model as represented by the manifestation of the Islamic finance market offer an alternative to these two competing visions?

It can be argued that Islamic economics does indeed offer a new approach by enabling entrepreneurs to flourish but ensuring these same business people operate within an ethical framework that has buy-in from wider civil society.

This perspective of Islamic finance can be viewed from the concept of iqtisad which indicates an intermediate or medium course to take in life. The word is based on the Arabic term which can be translated as economy. It is derived from the root, qasada, which conveys the notion of being moderate, frugal, thrifty and provident. However, the verb iqtasada also relates to adopting a middle course.

This analysis is complicated by the fact that state capitalism is not just a phenomenon in China as this concept is alive and well amongst the monarchical states of the Persian Gulf who have incorporated some form of Islamic economics within its governance operating model.

Kurlantzick, for example, has argued that state capitalism in Qatar has been particularly effective:

> … its autocratic government has used its resource wealth to build internationally competitive companies in gas related industries like petrochemicals and fertiliser, as well as to help create other globally competitive firms, like media giant Al Jazeera. Still, even in Qatar the competitive companies that have been created depend heavily on expatriate management and expertise.[27]

Consequently, the interplay between state capitalism and the encouragement of Islamic finance in some of these nations can be seen to be intrinsically linked.

As Islamic finance and Islamic economics is based on communitarian approaches then the form of state capitalism in the Gulf would not equate precisely to the statist style of state capitalism in China.

There is a form of capitalist political economy which does equate to the communitarian principles within Islamic economics and that is East Asian developmental capitalism.

Islamic Finance and East Asian Developmental Capitalism

Islamic economics is not the only approach within the field of political economy which claims to have found a middle way between the perceived rapaciousness of capitalism and the bureaucracy of socialism.

Julius Nyerere, the President of Tanzania from the early 1960s to 1985, once said:

> The foundation and objective of African socialism is the extended family … 'ujamaa', then or 'familyhood' describes our socialism. It is opposed to capitalism, which seeks to build a happy society on the basis of the exploitation of man by man; and it is equally opposed to doctrinaire socialism which seeks to build a happy society on a philosophy of inevitable conflict between man and man.[28]

Despite Nyerere's claims, the reality of the political economic model for Tanzania was a country riven by divisions with the formal and informal economies operating side by side:

> The economic trajectory of post-independence Tanzania is painfully familiar. A poor choice of economic policies led to economic decline, which manifested itself in growing and acute scarcities of essential goods and services. Pervasive scarcities, in turn, gave rise to the rapid spread of parallel markets, which gradually came to provide a larger and larger proportion of what ordinary Tanzanians consumed on a day-to-day basis. Tanzania developed a binary economic system.[29]

Tanzania's oligarchic approach to governance combined with geopolitical risk demonstrated that any claim of a middle way between capitalism and socialism was just political rhetoric:

> Despite desperate economic conditions, Tanzania did not initiate an economic reform program until summer 1986, nearly seven years after the end of the Ugandan War. If the famine conditions that prevailed during summer and fall 1974 are taken as Tanzania's low point, twelve years elapsed before the 1986 IMF agreement, which most observers view as the beginning of the transition to a market economy. During all that time, Tanzania managed to limp along with only minor changes in its policies: the pattern of poor policy choices leading to poor economic conditions persisted.[30]

There is, though, a political economy model that is not linked to religion or socialism and which also has synergies with forms of state capitalism with Islamic finance characteristics. It also claims to have found a middle way between laissez faire capitalism and a range of socialist ideas.

This is the developmental state model that has proven to be such a success in East Asia, enabling trans-Pacific trade to overtake trans-Atlantic trade from 1982.[31]

South East Asia has witnessed this emergence of developmental capitalism. The region is home to two of the largest Muslim populated states in the world—Indonesia and Malaysia as well as the Muslim majority monarchical state of Brunei Darussalam. In addition, the region is also home to Thailand, with a strong Buddhist heritage and Singapore—a vibrant and entrepreneurial city state. These and other nations form the nexus of the East Asian economy.

The capitalist models across East Asia vary—from historic trends in Japan, South Korea and Taiwan of active state interventionism in the market economy through to state guided capitalism in China, efforts by the Malaysian Government to influence the capitalist system to favour the Malay ethnic group and onto personal elite relationships shaping capitalist development in the Philippines.

However, there is a common theme that runs through different strands of East Asian capitalism which is the role of the developmental state. Unlike in the United States and, to a lesser extent in Australia and New Zealand where market forces are seen as the primary driver of the capitalist system, East Asian nations—in very different forms—see the role of the State as integral with market forces to develop the economy, thereby enhancing the prospects of the nation state.

Walter and Zhang have identified four features of East Asian capitalism[32]:

- Co-governed: State guided but with business influence
- State led: Heavily state controlled
- Networked: State influenced but significant business inputs and influences
- Personalised: State controlled but heavy private influence

The critical role of the State in these differing forms of capitalism has been linked by some commentators to the perspectives from the former Malaysian Prime Minister, Mahathir Mohamad and the founding Prime Minister of Singapore, Lew Kuan Yew (1923 – 2015) who, in the 1990s, referred to "*Asian values*" and how a strong State can lead to a strong economy.

Thompson claimed that this approach was designed to marry authoritarian government rule with populist support:

> These dictatorships set standards of rapid economic development against which future regimes would be judged. While organised labour was demobilised and industrialists made dependent on the state, the middle classes acquired a sense of entitlement.[33]

Asian values were cited by various south east Asian countries to justify not just their economic models but also their governance structures:

> In Indonesia 'Asian values' were invoked as a form of developmentalism, with the claim that, until prosperity is achieved, democracy remains an unaffordable luxury. This Protestant-ethic-like form of 'Asian values' attributed high growth rates to hard work, frugality, discipline and teamwork which only a 'disciplined' (i.e. authoritarian) regime could provide during the early stages of development. Indonesia's strongman Suharto's 'New Order' government emphasised deliberation (musyawarah) instead of opposition in order to reach consensus (mufakat), excluding the masses from politics except during brief 'election' campaigns through the 'floating mass principle' .... In Malaysia and Singapore, by contrast, the 'Asian values' discourse was an attempt to justify authoritarianism after economic development to help co-opt their large middle classes.[34]

However, is Thompson right to assume that talk of 'Asian values' was a PR ruse to impose authoritarianism or was there really a difference in capitalist practices?

East Asian 'developmental' capitalism can be defined as a 'developmental partnership' between governments and business which is underpinned by a civil society which supports this overall economic approach.

This model was particularly effective for '*Late industrialisation*'—in other words the industrialisation of economies following the industrialisation which had occurred in North America, Europe and, to some extent, Japan.

With governments providing guidance to domestic business actors this was said to have enabled long-term transformative economic objectives to be attained. From a societal perspective, developmental capitalism is based on the concept of group ethic principles, stakeholder capitalism and growth with equity.

When seen within this context, the developmental capitalist model and the general concept of 'Asian values' is not too far away from the holistic approach of Islamic finance with contract models and an underlying ethos based on long-term growth, communitarian relationships—not just the needs and/or wants of shareholders—and how societies are integrated to meet the needs of the public weal.

This is also relevant when we consider the prominent role of Islamic finance in Malaysia. As Malaysia is integrated in the wider east Asian economic ecosystem, the impact of Islamic finance in Malaysia is therefore felt across the wider region.

Mahathir was instrumental to the role that Islamic finance now plays in the Malaysian economy. A range of factors played a part in Mahathir's thinking when in his first term as Prime Minister (1981–2003), he revitalised the economy:

> Mahathir's vision of economic and enterprise development for Malaysia was … just as inspired by neo-liberalism, including its active promotion of privatisation. Mahathir appeared above all enamoured with the stock market, an instrument which he felt has been effectively fostered by businesspeople in the United States to rapidly create huge firms …. The active deployment of privatisation and the stock market, pivotal features of a neo-liberal state, to cultivate big business had an immense impact on the pattern of publicly listed firms in Malaysia.[35]

As Gomez described it, Malaysia saw "*the simultaneous implementation of the developmental state and neo-liberal models*".[36]

This change undertaken by Mahathir was around the same time that Mahathir encouraged elements of Islamic economics to be part of the body politic of Malaysia for Mahathir could also see the synergies between contemporary practices of Islamic finance and the concept of developmental capitalism.

Mahathir has spoken of his pragmatic approach towards Islamic finance:

> Some people think we should totally replace conventional banking with Islamic banking. That disturbs the whole financial business. By leaving the conventional banking in place and introducing Islamic banking, people have a choice. I don't think that it would ever be a complete Islamic system because conventional banking is very powerful and it's difficult to displace it completely.[37]

This pragmatism is tied to the marriage of 'Asian values' with Islamic finance:

> Asian values, he says, are mostly compatible with Islamic values, and so his governments have been built on the fusion of these. So with government imbued with both Asian and Islamic values, regulation is designed to protect the good of the many. He explains, "Government is there to serve the people and maintain peace. Islam is about peace. All these things match. Islam doesn't tell you to kill people. No, it's a crime to kill, steal, and be corrupt. So the values are the same, except for one thing—we believe in the welfare of the majority, the community, the ummah. The West believes in the rights of one person, where one person exercises his

right and at the same time he undermines the right of the community. They want to tolerate it, but we say no. Even if it's your right but if you take away the rights of the community, then it's wrong".[38]

1997Asian Financial Crisis and Its Implications for Islamic Finance

The claim of a communitarian approach within the twin constructs of East Asian politics and economics faced a severe test following the shock of the 1997 Asian Financial Crisis. This crisis also was a further spur for the development of the Islamic finance market in the region.

The crisis began in July 1997 when the markets signaled their lack of confidence in the Thai baht currency. Thailand de-pegged its currency from the US dollar in 1997. This led to global markets selling the baht and leading to a loss of investor confidence in other South East Asian economies:

> The chain of events exposed both the extent of regional financial market interdependence and also the relative weakness of existing regional co-operative mechanisms to deal with a crisis of this scale.[39]

With a domino effect, markets began to question the very basis of currencies across all south east Asian nations and this had knock-on impacts with sharp drops in values for property and other asset markers.

At the time it was the biggest economic shock in the region since the end of the Second World War and it led some commentators in North America and Europe to then speculate whether this was the end of the region's '*economic miracle*':

> Region-wide boom was followed by a regional economic crisis. Nothing shows the extent of capitalist networks better than their failure. A currency crisis in insignificant Bangkok had no business causing economic havoc from Jakarta to Seoul. But the ties that bind in good times can rebound during the bad patches. Having lost its Cold War significance, the Pacific Asian financial situation was not saved by a Washington-led financial posse as had been the case for neighbouring Mexico in the mid-1990s. Instead, one country after another regardless of whether it ran budget deficits or had a 'bubble economy' succumbed to the regional snowball effect. Because they perceived their investments to be within a common region,

> foreign investors withdrew their money regionally, even if the crisis had originally been localised.[40]

The currency crisis led to the collapse of the Suharto regime in Indonesia with a more open and democratic governance structure emerging in its stead—as well as contributing towards the difficult birth of East Timor as an independent nation.

The concept of laissez-faire economics took a knock as far as many East Asian governments were concerned because of the stance as adopted by the International Monetary Fund (IMF) in response to the Asian Financial Crisis.[41] As Stedman Jones argued:

> This colonisation of international institutions by neoliberal ideas carried with it the logic of Milton Friedman's claims about the link between economic and political freedom.[42]

Therefore, when the Asian Financial Crisis (AFC) occurred the IMF offered help on a neoliberal basis rather than from a Keynesian perspective. Keynes argued that in times of severe economic downturns, a Government could pump prime the economy to restore economic stability. This approach was an anathema to neoliberal thinkers who argued that reducing the size of fiscal deficits and creating incentives for additional private sector investment was the key to economic recovery. Therefore, in response to the AFC, the IMF proposed fiscal retrenchment in return for financial help.

As Khatkhate stated:

> By placing the structural reforms enabling foreign ownership of domestic firms in the East Asian countries ahead of liquidity relieving measures, the Fund played into the hands of its detractors that this advice was not dispassionate and it had its own hidden agenda.[43]

Consequently, neighbouring countries that had seen themselves as competitors for attracting international capital now saw themselves as allies to support their brand of capitalism. Combined with the support of the powers in the region—China and Japan—this also encouraged further articulation of "*Asian values*" distinguishing east Asian capitalism from other models.[44]

Openness to trade was critical for South East Asian countries' economic development in the period up to the 1997/98 crisis and it was this process that led to inherent economic weaknesses being exposed in the global marketplace:

> Many of its countries have followed a similar path to development, moving in the space of a generation from inward looking economies dominated by agricultural production to industrialised, outward looking, market orientated economies, open to trade and capital flows. With this openness has come severe vulnerability, exposed during the Asian financial crisis of 1997/98, but also rapid development.[45]

However, this précis belies a wider truth as to the period of South East Asian economic development in advance of the 1997/98 financial crisis. It can also be propositioned that East Asian nations were adopting a "nation first" approach towards economic development which placed economic primacy with the immediate needs of the nation state rather than with the region as a whole. This was not an illogical stance for the East Asian nations to take at the time:

> These 'developing countries' were doing precisely what the United States had done when it was a developing country and had erected steep tariff walls and provided lavish state subsidies for railroads and other vital infrastructure.[46]

It was not just South East Asia that was prone to the contagion of financial instability:

> The Asian Financial Crisis exposed Japanese financial institutions to increased risk to the extent that they had loans directly or indirectly tied to the rest of Asia. The crisis heightened the sense of unease and rendered financial markets more susceptible to any shock.[47]

Therefore, the crisis contributed to a greater realisation that enhanced economic co-operation was sorely required:

> The 1997–98 crisis opened a new chapter in the process of regional integration: that of monetary and financial co-operation. The devastating financial hurricane highlighted a number of shortcomings in the Asian model, including the risks of over investment, the dangers of over rapid

> financial liberalisation for emerging countries and the fragility of the previous regional integration model.[48]

Japan led the coordinating response towards regional economic co-operation and recovery in the form of the Chiang Mai Initiative. In 2000 it was agreed that a regionwide network of bilateral currency swap agreements would be available. In 2003 a revamped Association of South East Asian Nations (ASEAN) Swap Agreement facility strengthened the arrangements that came out of the Chiang Mai Initiative:

> An important factor here was the widely held view amongst East Asia's policy elites that the IMF had failed the region on many accounts, and some level of regional self reliance was required, especially as East Asia possessed the world's largest financial reserves.[49]

Other factors soon impinged upon East Asian nations to encourage greater economic co-operation:

> With the 1997 Asian economic crisis as a turning point, intra ASEAN economic co-operation entered a new phase because the structures of the world economy and the East Asian economy surrounding ASEAN had changed to a great extent. The first change was China's rapid growth and its expanding influence.... The second change was the stagnation of worldwide trade liberalisation by the World Trade Organisation (WTO) and the evolution of Free Trade Agreements. The third change was the increased interdependency throughout East Asia, including China, and the development of the foundation for economic cooperation throughout East Asia.[50]

The Asian currency crisis of 1997/98 was a turning point for regional cooperation and the longer term trends for such cooperation to continue was established with the economic rise of China and the impact China has upon the complex supply chains of South East Asia.

These trends were beneficial for the Islamic finance industry in the region. Indonesia followed the lead of Malaysia in establishing an Islamic finance market and, as discussed in Chapter 8, has made some significant steps forward in engendering a halal industry covering products from cosmetics to pharmaceuticals. Brunei Darussalam has also made great strides with establishing a domestic Islamic finance industry.

Beyond Muslim majority countries in the region, other neighbouring countries began to consider the role of Islamic finance in their economies. Islamic finance existed in Thailand in a very limited way with the Pattani Islamic Saving Cooperative. By 2001, four other Islamic savings cooperatives had been introduced in Thailand; Ibnu Affan Saving Cooperative, As-Siddiq Saving Cooperative, Saqaff ah Islam Saving Cooperative and Al- Islamiah Saving Cooperative.

The Government Savings Bank utilised an Islamic window to provide Islamic banking products and services for the country's four million Muslims (approximately 6% out of a total population of 66.8 million population), along with the Bank for Agriculture and Agricultural Cooperatives. In 2001, KrungThai Bank opened an Islamic branch just prior to the introduction of the Islamic Bank of Thailand Act which was passed in 2002, paving the way for the establishment of the state-owned Islamic Bank of Thailand. In 2010, the Thai government announced a Trust Act would be enacted to issue a Sukuk.

The first tentative steps was taken in the Philippines to establish Islamic banking when in August 2019 the Republic Act No. 11439 ("Islamic Banking Act") was signed into law which provided for the organisation, regulation and powers of Islamic banks to be established in the Philippines.

In the powerhouse economy that is Japan, many banks are now engaged in Islamic finance and in 2015 the Japan Institute of Islamic Finance was established in Tokyo to help train finance professionals.

The economic integration of the region after the 1997 Asian Financial Crisis has contributed towards Islamic finance becoming a more accepted part of the regional financial services landscape.

The greater financial firepower of the region, due to the established position of the Islamic finance industry in Malaysia, Indonesia and Brunei, as well as the contribution of investors from outside the region, enabled new shari'a compliant investment instruments to contribute to the wider economic development of East Asia which is, thanks to its role in manufacturing, the pivotal region for the global economy.

As Mahathir has argued, the linkages between Islamic finance and East Asian developmental capitalism do exist and therefore the Islamic finance industry is a natural fit between its values, strategy and product lines with East Asian concepts of communitarianism.

At the same time, the marriage of state capitalism and Islamic finance within the political economic models of the Gulf states has synergies with the enlarged role of the State encouraging the growth of private enterprise in East Asia. The potential for Islamic finance to further embed itself in the region, including within nations with non-majority Muslim populations such as Thailand, due to these synergies, could be significant in the years ahead.

What is striking, though, is that the Malaysian experience of bringing together 'Asian values' with Islamic finance is being emulated beyond South East Asia and is now felt in Kazakhstan at the very heart of the Caucuses.

Varieties of Capitalism Case Study: Kazakhstan and Islamic Finance

Kazakhstan is an interesting example of a nation whose identity and political economy is being influenced by a range of outside factors, one of which is Islamic finance.

Gallo argued that whilst recent academic literature on the region has focused upon filial linkages as to how the Kazakh state has operated, there has been a lack of attention as to how global economic trends has interacted with local societal conditions to shape the contemporary shape of Kazakhstan's political economy:

> The privatisations of state-owned assets have empowered, not weakened, familism and patronalism, with their corollary of cronyism and corruption. Kazakhstan's patronal system, rather than representing the outcome of a traditional political culture, has to a large extent re-emerged as a rational adaptation to the challenges of globalisation.[51]

Kazakhstan is close to Russia and the position of Russian policy as it concerns foreign and security policy also reflects, to some extent, the Kazakh stance. It should be remembered that Russian President, Vladimir Putin, has concerns as to the actions of near neighbours and how it may impact upon Russian sovereignty.

As Dmitri Trenin, Director of the Carnegie Centre in Moscow has commented, President Putin "*watched, in amazement, the United States pulling the plug on their Egyptian ally, Hosni Mubarak, after a week of mass protests in Cairo's Tahrir Square, and then putting up with Muslim Brotherhood Islamists in power. Sparks from Arab revolutions could ignite Russia's geopolitical underbelly*".[52]

Putin has wanted to maintain a sphere of influence on Russia's borders following what he perceived as the disaster of the collapse of the Soviet Union:

> Above all, we should acknowledge that the collapse of the Soviet Union was a major geopolitical disaster of the century. As for the Russian nation, it became a genuine drama. Tens of millions of our co-citizens and co-patriots found themselves outside Russian territory. Moreover, the epidemic of disintegration infected Russia itself.[53]

Nonetheless the example of Expo 2017, which was held in Astana, was an indication that Kazakhstan, whilst maintaining close ties with Russia, is also developing a nuanced economic and foreign policy programme which is opening up the nation to a range of influences beyond its near neighbour.

Despite Kazakhstan opening itself up to global influences, the familial based nature of domestic politics has continued to stymie the country's economic performance. The country is dependent on oil production and the fluctuations of the oil price during the 2010s did not ensure economic sustainability was attained.

This, combined with the devaluation of the tenge in 2015/16, has hit the Kazakh economy. After the 2008 global financial crisis, the banking sector was re-nationalised which deterred global banking groups from entering the Kazakh market. Therefore, Kazakhstan tried to maintain elite structures in the country's body politic whilst also undertaking a delicate balancing act in maintaining close ties to Russia whilst opening up the Kazakh economy to global investment:

> ... multi-ethnic Kazakhstan soon opted for both neoliberal and developmental paradigms as ways to reinforce its economic elite and avoid potential dependence on neighbouring Russia and China. In the 1990s, with about a third of its population Russian native speakers, Kazakhstan felt it necessary to open to Russia and the world and espouse a Eurasian and internationalist rhetoric. Nevertheless, several factors—Russia's post-2014 economic woes, the drop in the price of oil, China's weakening demand for energy—may jeopardise the solid economic conditions that have supported Kazakhstan since independence.[54]

It was within this context, that Islamic finance begun to make itself felt within Kazakhstan's political economy. In 2010 the then President,

Nursultan Nazarbayev, declared his intention to make Kazakhstan the regional hub for Islamic finance. The Government announced a 41-point plan setting targets for enticing and creating new Islamic banks. In July 2012, the Development Bank of Kazakhstan issued a Sukuk which raised US$75 million. A branch of Al Hilal Islamic Bank (a subsidiary of Al Hilal Abu Dubai) also opened in the country.

The Kazakh Government also declared it wanted to follow the Malaysian model of engendering an Islamic finance market:

> Both have a multi-ethnic population, a strong government and a pervasive crony culture that extends into the financial markets. Despite the privatization that Malaysia undertook following the crisis, government participation in Malaysian capitalism remained extensive, with rent-seeking persisting in the market. This ability of the state to remain present in the market while moving to a capital market-based financial system has not passed unnoticed by President Nazarbayev. Similarly, in Malaysia the market was initially the development project of political and business elites, a point of clear interest to similar groups in Kazakhstan.[55]

Hoggarth argued that the development of the Islamic finance sector helped the nation find its identity after Kazakhstan was thrust into independence following the final precipitous collapse of the Soviet Union in 1991:

> Conveniently, Islamic finance reconnects Kazakhstan to its pre-Soviet identity as part of the state's post-colonial identity building; but, rather than creating the image of a 'backward facing' society, it simultaneously projects a desire to be a dynamic market leader in the modern global economy via Islamic finance which is empathetic to the values of the nation.[56]

The positioning of Kazakhstan in the Islamic finance market space may also impact upon the political economies of its neighbours:

> When Kazakhstan adopted comprehensive legislation to form the basis for the introduction of Islamic banking and finance to the country, the legislation also attempted to create a "level playing field" in which Islamic products could operate in a clearly-defined legal framework, without advantages or disadvantages in such key areas as civil, banking, tax, and securities law. Islamic banking legislation has also been adopted in Kyrgyzstan and it could spread to other Central Asian countries. Although, in the short run,

> Islamic banking and finance may play a small role, Kazakhstan's legislation may serve as a model for legislation of neighbouring countries. In particular, if there appear to be profits to be made from Islamic banking, there will be pressure to adopt enabling legislation in Russia.[57]

Kazakhstan is a good example of a nation that is still in the throes of developing its national identity. Learning from the Malaysian experience enables Kazakhstan to utilise its cultural and religious heritage to develop a market that demonstrates it is outward looking whilst connecting the development of the economy to historical precedents.

Kazakhstan's experience demonstrates how a country can balance its immediate domestic and foreign policy needs whilst embracing Islamic finance for wider economic and national identity objectives.

Whether, in the long run, Islamic finance can succeed in advancing an economy that is predicated upon oligarchic relationships is another matter. The country has severe deprivation levels amongst its population despite its oil wealth. These problems were aggravated at times of crisis such as when, in April and May 2020, due to lockdown restrictions in an effort to limit the spread of the COVID-19 virus, more than 4 million Kazakhs lost their sources of income.[58]

Public discontent in Kazakhstan indicates that it is the restructuring of governance that will be the key to unlocking the nation's economic growth.

The banner from one disgruntled demonstrator in Almaty really said it all:

> Why are people poor in a country rich with oil and gas?[59]

Utopian Visions and Mutualism

Six miles from where I am working on this book is Bournville. Though a suburb of the UK city of Birmingham, it looks like a quaint English village with its artisan houses, its manicured lawns and its community centre. This was the settlement which George Cadbury established in 1893 so that workers in his world famous chocolate factory did not need to live too far away.

However, Cadbury's vision went beyond the utility of his business. From a Christian Quaker background, George Cadbury also wanted the residents of Bournville to have the space and time to enjoy the arts, to exercise as well as to work. This was Cadbury's idea of a Utopia coming alive in the Birmingham suburbs.

Islamic economics is based, in part, upon a utopian ideal where an equitable business and economic system helps ensure social justice and freedoms for individuals living in a society. These ideals were reflected in other environments such as Bournville.

Robert Owen (1771–1858) also experimented with the ideal of creating a new kind of Utopia via the utilisation of ethical business practices. When Owen took over the cotton mill at New Lanark by Scotland's River Clyde he spoke of how he helped create a happy and regulated society where crime went down and happiness levels across the population of 2000 people went up.

Owen looked at the management of the cotton mill before he took over the reins:

> It is not to be supposed that children so young could remain, with the intervals of meals only, from six in the morning until seven in the evening, in constant employment, on their feet, within cotton mills, and afterwards acquire much proficiency in education. And so it proved; for many of them became dwarfs in body and mind, and some of them were deformed. Their labour through the day and their education at night became so irksome, that numbers of them continually ran away, and almost all looked forward with impatience and anxiety to the expiration of their apprenticeship of seven, eight, and nine years, which generally expired when they were from thirteen to fifteen years old.[60]

Along with Owen's leadership of the cotton mill was an emphasis upon education of the workforce. He claimed that his example of New Lanark could be applied to public policy which would be to the benefit of wider society:

> Say not, my countrymen, that such an event is impracticable; for, by adopting the evident means to form a rational character in man, there is a plain and direct road opened, which, if pursued, will render its accomplishment not only possible but certain. That road, too, will be found the most safe and pleasant that human beings have ever yet travelled. It leads direct to intelligence and true knowledge, and will show the boasted acquirements of Greece, of Rome, and of all antiquity, to be the mere weakness of mental infancy.[61]

Ironically the cotton that Owen's mill was processing had originated from the labours of people who had been bound into slavery in the British colonies in the Caribbean and from plantations in the southern United States. Therefore, his espousal of the creation of a perfect society in New Lanark does sound hollow within this context. Owen also did not address how financing can be equitable for this perfect society to be formed—a theme which Islamic finance concepts goes out of its way to address.

Another example of where business practices are said to have contributed to a more equal society is the kibbutz model in Israel. The first kibbutz was formed by the Sea of Galilee in 1909 and today there are around 270 kibbutzim across Israel where, on average each kibbutz has a population of around 600 people:

> The kibbutz functions as a direct democracy. The general assembly of all its members formulates policy, elects officers, authorizes the kibbutz budget and approves new members. It serves not only as a decision-making body but also as a forum where members may express their opinions and views. Day-to-day affairs are handled by elected committees, which deal with areas such as housing, finance, production planning, health, and culture. The chairpersons of some of these committees, together with the secretary (who holds the top position in the kibbutz) form the kibbutz executive. The positions of secretary, treasurer and work coordinator are, as a rule, full-time, while other members serve on committees in addition to their regular jobs.[62]

The kibbutz model is more than an economic unit which encourages cooperative working. It also signals a distinct form of socialism which aims to challenge laissez-faire capitalism:

> The kibbutz makes a contribution of prime importance to the Israeli working class struggle to replace capitalism with socialism, by providing a prototype of future Israeli socialist society and by concretising – not in drawing plans but in everyday life – the ways to a solution and the possibility of a solution of the fundamental problems of every co-operative society, questions that are still subject to prejudice, doubts and suspicions. The implications and importance of the superiority and greater efficiency of the collective method of production over capitalist private enterprise go far beyond the agricultural sector. The kibbutz movement that is preserving its collectivist principles and, at the same time, prospering economically, is thereby dealing a heavy blow to the prestige of the 'irreplaceability' of

> private initiative and, therefore, contributes greatly to the socialist education of the Israeli working class – in the Histadrut,[63] parties and youth movements.[64]

Despite the kibbutz challenge to laissez-faire capitalism, the movement has other connotations with Palestinians due to the "Tower and Stockade" establishment of 52 kibbutz settlements during the period of the 1936–39 Arab Revolt. The revolt represented opposition to the British Mandate in Palestine and to land being granted to Jewish settlers.

From a political economy perspective, the kibbutz movement was an attempt to embed cooperative principles within the political economy of a nation state. However, this model—like Owen's and Cadbury's—does not fully address the financial side of a business and as to how the financing of the operations of an economy can fully meet the needs of attaining an equitable society.

Cooperative values, though, as expressed through the medium of Islamic insurance, aims to address a community approach to financing and which goes beyond the profit and loss sharing contract models which we discussed in Chapter 4.

It is the cooperative values within the Islamic finance form of insurance—known as takaful—which resonates with wider cooperative forms of economic governance. Whilst, as we are about to discover, there are some gory origins to takaful, the contemporary cooperative values of takaful is a direct link between the mutualism of the cooperative movement and the communitarian values of Islamic finance.

Takaful: Islamic Insurance and the Principle of Cooperative Economics

How can insurance ever be allowed from an Islamic perspective?

Gaining or making money based on uncertainty is prohibited and speculation is prohibited whilst conventional insurance can be seen to be based on uncertainty and speculation.

From a shari'a perspective, conventional life insurance can be seen as the ultimate gamble for insurance companies. After all conventional insurance companies work out premiums based on the expectations of a person's lifespan when that could be seen as gambling on a person's health.

The conventional life insurance industry would clearly not agree. In fact, they would argue that assessments of a person's health at any given point can provide a fair assessment of a person's future lifespan.

Contemplating your own death is never ideal at the best of times. From a shari'a perspective, contemplating a death for the calculation of premiums based on a series of imponderables and where protection of life is key to Islamic concepts of justice would be haram.

However, consumer support for the concept of life insurance exists because many people see this form of insurance as one of the most responsible acts any person can do to protect the financial well-being of their family if tragedy struck.

How, then, can insurance be shari'a compliant?

Islamic insurance is based upon cooperative principles whereby members of a community invest for the common good and is used as a mutual fund when problems occur in that community.

It is from this concept that Islamic insurance known as takaful has emerged. The derivation of the word 'takaful' comes from the Arabic word, Ta'mein' which means to safeguard and reassure. It is argued that takaful embodies the concept of Tawakkul where a person would strive to mitigate any risk during their life. One hadith is often highlighted to demonstrate this concept:

> ... the Holy Prophet told a Bedouin Arab who left his camel untied trusting to the will of Allah; "Tie the camel first and then leave it to Allah ...[65]

The Qur'ran refers to the principle of co-operation:

> And co-operate ye one another in righteousness and piety ...[66]

Beyond the religious texts, the precedent described by jurists to support the practice of takaful seems, at first glance, to be a long way from the ideals of co-operation as it involves the graphic notion of 'blood money'.

The concept of 'Aqilah existed in seventh-century Arabia where if a member of a tribe was killed by a person from another tribe, the heir of the victim would be paid compensation, or 'blood money, by the close relatives of the perpetrator. These close relatives would be described by the Arabic term 'Aqilah. This may not seem to resemble cooperative ideals but, upon closer examination, we can see cooperative principles are, in fact, at play:

> Readiness of the ancient Arabs at that time to pay compensation to the heir of the victim denoted a kind of insurance practice and such compensation seemed to be a kind of financial protection for the heir of the deceased against the unexpected death of the victim.[67]

There is also a less dramatic precedent which jurists have pointed to which refers to the cooperative principle of a mutual fund to provide money for people at times of trouble. Waqf, meaning endowment, is either a property or an endowment fund which can be for the benefit of the wider community. Precedents for this concept exist from the very early period of Islam.

When Abu Bakr became the Caliph following the death of the Prophet, he reasoned that the physical assets of the Prophet were there for the whole community. Consequently, these assets were endowed to the office of the Caliph, rather than to the person of the Caliph, to help meet the government's duties in serving the early Muslim community. Abu Bakr also created a family trust comprising of assets he had accumulated.

The successor to Abu Bakr as Caliph, Umar, having completed the conquest of Egypt, vested the assets gained in a waqf for the service of the umma (Muslim community). In fourteenth century Egypt, most of the agricultural land within the valley of the River Nile was vested in waqfs.[68]

As can happen in any financial arrangement, corruption and mismanagement occasionally occurred and this included a time when a mutawalli (trustee of a waqf) in Fez speculated in the grain markets and squandered the entire endowment when the market turned sour.[69]

Ibn Abidin (1784–1836), a Hanafi jurist based in Damascus, was one of the key figures whose scholarly work led to today's takaful industry. In his study of insurance, though Ibn Abidin was aware of the precedents for Islamic insurance, he was surprised that further developments in marine insurance had not been made over the years:

> … it is hard to believe that Muslims did not practise *(marine)* insurance before the nineteenth century. Muslims were involved in marine activities in the Mediterranean and the Indian Ocean from the seventh century on. Contacts between Islam and Christianity existed in Spain, Sicily, Italy,

> Cyprus and Malta. Thus, Muslims must have been exposed at least to the European marine insurance (if not to other types of insurance) which was part of the usual conduct of trade in the Middle Ages.[70]

Ibn Abidin argued that insurance could be allowed within Islam under certain conditions:

> If something is lost from his possession without his fault and it was also not possible for him to protect it from accidents such as fire, sinking, robbers and attackers, then it is agreed upon opinion that he should not be held responsible. However, since he has collected rent for protection and stipulated guarantee, his position is like a person to whom something has been deposited for protection on rent, so that if it is lost, he would be the guarantor.[71]

As with most Islamic finance developments, the first step change in formally establishing a takaful market began in the 1970s. In 1979 the Islamic Insurance Company in Sudan, the Islamic-Arab Insurance Company in Dubai and the National Company for Cooperative Insurance in Saudi Arabia were established.

The contemporary development of the Islamic finance market, as we will discover further in Chapter 10, were linked to debates about national identity and the interplay with religious identity. This was viewed within the context of decolonialisation and the rising income of the Persian Gulf monarchies in the 1970s with the utilisation of oil and gas fields and the significant increase in the oil price following the 1973 Yom Kippur War.[72]

The stance against conventional insurance was confirmed by the OIC's Fiqh Academy in December 1985:

> The commercial insurance contract, with a fixed insurance premium, as practiced by commercial insurance companies, contains substantial gharar, which renders the contract defective. Consequently, it is legally forbidden.[73]

This judgement spurred on the establishment of the takaful market and as of 2019 this sector was valued at US$23.7 billion.[74]

In the contemporary takaful industry there are several models used. Wakala describes an agency or a delegated authority where a muwakkil (principal) appoints the wakil (agent) to carry out specific work on behalf of the muwakkil. The takaful company acts as the agent on behalf of the participants to run the takaful fund. All risks are borne by the fund and any surplus profits belong to the participants. There is a management fee included in this model which can include a performance-related bonus which would be predicated on the investment profile of the underlying fund.

With the Mudaraba model the takaful company acts as the Mudarib (entrepreneur) and the participants act as the Rab al Mal (capital providers). The contract specifies how the investment profit or loss will be shared out. The Mudarib does not gain a fee if the participants suffer a loss. The underwriting fee takes the form of a management charge.

The combined model brings together elements of the Wakala and Mudaraba models. As with the Wakala model, there is a fixed fee for management purposes. The Mudarib would also receive a percentage of the investment fund depending upon performance of the underlying fund.

There is a controversial model used in takaful which is the tabarru model. Tabarru means donation. Under this model, a participant agrees to donate a predetermined percentage of their financial contribution to a Takaful fund to provide assistance of joint guarantee and mutual help should another participant in the fund suffer a loss.

Though the tabarru model has been approved by eminent scholars, doubts remain. For example, is the donation really a donation?

> First, donation (tabarru') implies that the thing donated cannot return, in whole or part, to the donor. Once one donates something it departs one's ownership and becomes the property of the beneficiary. However, the donor in Takaful will practically get his donation back when the loss befalls him, since he gets an unallocated amount from the Takaful fund.
>
> Second, the intention of the participants is not practically that of donation. In fact, all policy holders contribute their premiums only to cover themselves, and they have no intention whatsoever of donating their premiums to any party. Third, a donation is not a donation if it is in exchange of another donation, like "I donate to you if you donate to me", and this is the case with the existing models of Takaful where we have mutual commitments of donations; one from the policy holders and the other from the Takaful fund.[75]

Then the level of uncertainty (gharar) seems to be a significant factor in the tabarru model:

> Inherent excessive gharar: In the absence of any specific contract and lack of proper disclosure with regard to the amount of donation and treatment in case of possible early termination ... there is inherent gharar that may render the arrangement Sharīʿah non-compliant as it affects the rights and the liabilities of the parties.[76]

Putting aside the controversies which beset the tabarru model of takaful, the overall takaful market is predicated on cooperative principles of shared responsibility, investing in a fund for the good of the wider community as well as for people who are pitching in with funds and maintaining the Islamic finance principle of the underlying fund investing in the real economy.

The takaful model, then, is a demonstration of cooperative economic values in action.

The question for the Islamic finance industry as a whole is whether this principle of co-operation can move beyond takaful to other product areas where investment in the real economy can be called for.

Cooperative Economics: Lessons for the Islamic Finance Industry?

Cooperatives have proven to be a highly successful model of business ownership and for generating finance. These businesses are owned and run jointly by its members who also share in the profits.

In Europe, the beginnings of the cooperative movement are identified with Germany when Franz Hermann Schulze-Delltzsch set up a cooperative bank in 1852. Friedrich Wilhelm Raiffeisen developed the movement and by the time of his death in 1888, credit unions had spread to Italy, France, the Netherlands and Austria.

The cooperative movement in the United Kingdom began in Rochdale in Lancashire in the mid-nineteenth century. The “Rochdale Pioneers”, as they came to be known, wanted to sell “pure” food at “full weight and measure” at a time during the Industrial Revolution when these items were not guaranteed at shops. By retailers coming together this meant they could combine their buying power and control quality. The Cooperative Wholesale Society was formed in 1863 and is now the Cooperative Group.

It is in Spain where cooperative businesses have been particularly successful. There are around 18,000 workers’ cooperatives in Spain which employs around 300,000 people. This includes 800 cooperatives in the Basque Country and over 5000 cooperatives in Catalonia.

It is Mondragon which has shown the way in realising the commercial potential of co-operation. Based in the Basque region, it is the tenth largest business in the country. Having started in white goods manufacturing, Mondragon is now engaged in bicycle production and lift manufacture. Mondragon also has major interests in retailing and in education, where it operates schools, technical colleges and a cooperative university. It also has fourteen research and development centres.

Mondragon's retail arm, Eroski is jointly run by representatives of consumers and employees. Its schools and universities enable formal governance roles for staff, students and other stakeholders such as other co-ops and local authorities. Mondragon also operates a bank, an insurance company and other cooperatives which are active in financial services.

It is in Indonesia where cooperatives, including cooperative financial institutions, are identified with the values of Islam. It was Mohammad Hatta (1902–1980) who played the critical role in advancing the concept of co-operation in Indonesia. Co-operation was even cited in Article 38 of the 1949 version of the constitution.

As the first Vice President of an independent Indonesia, Hatta ensured the Ministry of Economic Affairs had an Office for Cooperative Services solely devoted to encouraging co-operation within the Indonesian political economic model.

Hatta along with Sukarno, who became the first President of an independent Indonesia, co-operated with the Japanese occupation forces when Dutch colonial troops surrendered in 1942. Hatta, who was a cautious politician, only declared Indonesian independence in 1945 when he and Sukarno were kidnapped by university students.

In his book, *The Cooperative Movement in Indonesia* (1957), Hatta condemned the Japanese occupation forces for having manipulated cooperatives to expropriate resources on the cheap. It was in independent Indonesia, Hatta claimed, that there was now a resurgence in cooperative activity:

> Everywhere one notices co-operative activity. Suspicion of co-operation, which became prevalent when the Japanese occupied our country, is beginning to disappear. Confidence in co-operation is coming back to life! Areas that used to be unfavourable for co-operatives because of the

> highly individualistic spirit of the people are now becoming accessible to co-operatives.[77]

Hatta's attack on individualism reflected his belief that cooperative values, within the Indonesian context, was based on the South East Asian communal ethos of Gotong-royong and the teachings of Islam. Hatta did believe in individuality rather than individualism and this differentiation was connected to his view of co-operation in society:

> ... that individuality should not be confused with individualism. Individualism is an understanding or philosophy of living which places the individual before society as we find in the economic teachings of Adam Smith. Individuality is the nature of an individual who is conscious of self-respect and has faith in himself.[78]

As we can see from his dismissal of Smithian economics, Hatta saw the cooperative movement as an alternative to laissez-faire capitalism. In addition, Hatta argued that not only were cooperative values in sync with the governing Pancasila ideology, which was intended to engender a sense of Indonesian nationhood, but it was directly linked to the teachings of Islam:

> In realising our national ideal that 'the economy should be organised on a co-operative basis', we should not forget that our state is based on moral principles, which are embodied in the Pancasila, the five principles: Divine Omnipotence, humanity, national consciousness, democracy and social justice.[79]

Cooperative values were also essential, according to Roesli Rahim who served under Hatta as an official in the Ministry of Economic Affairs, in order to counteract the crop purchasers who took advantage of poor farmers. This was when, during the 1950s, Indonesia was a largely an agrarian economy:

> This chronic need for credit all too often causes the peasant to borrow money on unfavourable terms from speculative crops purchasers, who grant such credits without many formalities in order to secure his agricultural produce under profitable conditions.[80]

The cooperative movement was a popular cause in the first part of the twentieth century when Muslim traders promoted co-operation—but there was a backlash to these early efforts:

> Since this association had Islam as its basis, it became highly popular with the people. Stimulated by its propaganda, hundreds of co-operative shops sprang up all over the country, most of which had little success. This failure shocked people's confidence in co-operation so much that the mere mention of the word 'co-operation' was repugnant to them.[81]

Legislation under the Dutch colonial authorities in 1915 and 1927 began to embed the statutory framework for co-operation. The whole concept of co-operation, which was already associated with Islam and Gotong-royong, was now being associated with nationalism and an end to colonialism when nationalists helped organise the Cooperative Congress in Jakarta in 1929.

Following the formal announcement of Indonesian independence in 1949, a range of cooperatives were established which included:

- Credit unions;
- Consumption cooperatives (purchasing products);
- Processing cooperatives (acquiring and using machinery to process agricultural products);
- Marketing cooperatives (marketing the products of copra, rubber, pepper and tea).

Hatta became disenchanted with the growing role of private enterprise in the Indonesian economy at the expense of his cooperative ideals and in 1955 he resigned as Vice President. Hatta had begun to see his position as being without any real influence whilst he grew increasingly concerned at the autocratic tendencies of Sukarno who advocated 'guided democracy'.

Hatta's legacy, though, has embedded co-operation in the body politic of Indonesia. As of 2016, there were 212,135 cooperatives in the country with a total membership which amounted to 15% of the population.[82] This included the Islamic Boarding School Cooperatives (Kopontren).

The cooperative movement has also influenced the growth of the sector in neighbouring Malaysia. As of November 2019, the top Malaysian cooperatives had combined assets totalling RM123.24 billion (US$29 billion), according to the Malaysia Cooperative Societies Commission.

Despite the strength of cooperatives in Indonesia and Malaysia, combined with the corresponding strength of the Islamic finance market in both countries, there continued to be a disconnect between the majority of the product range offered by the Islamic finance industry and the role and focus of the cooperative movement.

This is due to the products offered by the global Islamic finance sector being geared towards forms of trade finance and to meet the needs of institutional investors in the capital markets. Important as these activities are to the health of the Islamic finance market and the propagation of the values of the sector in the global money markets, the fact that a disconnect has grown between Islamic finance and co-operation—when both models share the same values—indicate a lost opportunity by the Islamic finance industry to reach out to new consumers and to tackle the problem of financial exclusion.

This is especially so in Indonesia where the cooperative movement was based, to a large extent, on Islamic values and where, as discussed in Chapter 7, a community led initiative in Java has led to new forms of shari'a compliant microfinance.

Al-Muhurraimi and Hardy, in a 2013 study, also explored the connections and differences between the cooperative movement—specifically cooperative banks—with Islamic finance.

It found there were some operational differences between the two models:

> Islamic banks and cooperatives—especially credit unions—differ in some of their main business lines. An Islamic bank has to act somewhat in an investment bank-like manner, taking outright ownership or shares in commodities, products, and firms. Even if it specializes in household finance—perhaps the financing of auto purchases and housing—it will have to own and to some extent manage an inventory of cars, apartments, and houses. In contrast, the typical cooperative bank or credit union would own very little non-financial assets beside what it uses for its own operations and collateral seized from defaulted loans, which the credit union would normally try to dispose of quickly. Thus, the distribution of returns will differ even when financing otherwise similar projects and enterprises.[83]

When it came to the relationship between Islamic finance and cooperative credit unions, greater affinity between the two models was identified:

> Nonetheless, there is a certain affinity between the guiding principles of Islamic finance and cooperative banks and especially credit unions, namely, in their emphasis on solidarity between all those involved and a rejection of usurious or unfair financing conditions. Credit unions are expressly built on the notion of community and sharing of burdens and rewards.

The authors wondered why there were no Islamic cooperative banks:

> It seems at least possible for an Islamic bank to be organised along cooperative and in particular credit union lines, and such a structure could be both beneficial and highly consistent with the principles of Islamic finance. Such a structure would enhance mutuality in business dealing, as emphasized in Islamic jurisprudence, where obligations to various stakeholders have long been recognised. There would be greater equality among the parties and more need to respect diverse interests, while risk sharing and the avoidance of predetermined returns would be at least as comprehensive.

The paper concluded with this defining statement:

> … it seems that an institution with ownership and governance according to cooperative bank and especially credit union principles could operate according to Islamic principles, and there may be advantages in doing so: a mutualist structure would be very much in keeping with Islamic precepts about inclusiveness and risk-sharing, but it would also strengthen incentives to ensure that savers' interests are fully taken into account when deciding how much risk to bear. At the same time, greater risk sharing across the community making up a cooperative bank's member-owners, and especially the availability of savings products that participate in the upside and downside risk to which the bank is exposed, would make the institution more resilient, and also perhaps strengthen incentives for its good governance.

The principles set by the practice of co-operation within takaful is already a precedent which can be taken forward in order for the Islamic principle of co-operation to embrace the wider cooperative movement.

Imagine, then, the potential growth prospects for the Islamic finance industry if the synergies between cooperative forms of ownership and enterprise combined with Islamic finance concepts of equity and risk sharing was finally brought together on a large-scale basis.

The implications for the Islamic finance industry to recognise related sectors, such as the cooperative movement, and then move the industry forward in a proactive way by enticing an ever increasing number of consumers into its orbit is an opportunity not to be missed.

There are some scholars who argue that the Islamic finance industry comparing itself to conventional finance is the real problem in holding back the sector in terms of fully realising its values. Masudul Alam Choudhury stated:

> The Qur'ran and the Sunnah together taken up as the Islamic fundamental epistemology present the unified worldview of conscious oneness in unequivocal terms. But Muslims have missed this scholarship that stems from the universal worldview. Contrarily, much of Islamic economics, finance, science and society have imitated the neoliberal paradigms to construct a perception without true Islamic foundation. This kind of Islamic scholarship now merely shines like the lurid moon glimmering in her borrowed light.[84]

In fact, it could be argued that far from the Islamic finance industry trying to copy conventional finance, it has taken a cautious and permissive approach that has precluded consideration of new opportunities which are already present in the market place. This caution is understandable for the industry, by historical standards, is very new and the focus on shari'a compliance—fundamental though this is—has engendered a permissive culture in the industry.

There is also a bias in the Islamic finance industry to focus on tried and tested products such as mortgages, trade finance and shari'a compliant capital market instruments. Instead a horizon scanning approach to consider new market opportunities should be adopted which can include the marrying of Islamic and cooperative structures to enhance market share.

This is especially the case in the 2020s where Islamic finance and economics could receive a variable reception beyond its core markets due to the growing popularity of 'doughnut economics'.

Doughnut Economics, the Circular Economy and Islamic Finance

Doughnuts, in popular culture, are emblematic of a consumerist society due to the cartoon character, Homer Simpson, having a sweet tooth for the delicacy. However, doughnuts now have a competing connotation.

In 2012, the British economist, Kate Raworth, advanced doughnut economics theory in order to develop a model which would lead towards economic and environmental sustainability. Raworth argued that the current global economic trends were a cause for concern especially when there are increasing global temperatures due to carbon emissions.

Raworth stated that as countries, such as China and India, reach developed nation status then consumer demands for the good things in life, such as the use of cars, could further increase carbon emissions making the current trajectory for the planet unsustainable.

However, to tackle extreme poverty, the level of changes that needed to be made could be limited if viewed within a global context:

> Food: Providing the additional calories needed by the 13 per cent of the world's population facing hunger would require just 1 per cent of the current global food supply.
> Energy: Bringing electricity to the 19 per cent of the world's population who currently lack it could be achieved with less than a 1 per cent increase in global CO_2 emissions.
> Income: Ending income poverty for the 21 per cent of the global population who live on less than $1.25 a day would require just 0.2 per cent of global income.[85]

To further develop the theory, Raworth stated there were nine environmental themes that needed to be addressed for sustainable living and a sustainable economy to be attained:

- Climate Change
- Rate of biodiversity loss
- Nitrogen cycle
- Phosphorus cycle
- Stratospheric ozone depletion
- Ocean acidification
- Global freshwater use
- Change in land use
- Atmospheric aerosol loading
- Chemical pollution

In addition, Raworth identified human rights and social targets to assess economic sustainability models for the planet. Ultimately, Raworth proposed a happy medium for a sustainable economic model to be achieved which was called '*living within the doughnut*':

> ... (it is) clear that moving into the safe and just space for humanity demands far greater equity in the distribution of incomes and resource use, within and between countries, as well as far greater efficiency in how resources are used. The over-riding aim of global economic development must be to enable humanity to thrive in the safe and just space, ending deprivation and keeping within sustainable limits of natural resource use. Traditional economic growth policies have largely failed to deliver on both accounts: far too few benefits of economic growth have gone to people living in poverty, and far too much of GDP's rise has been at the cost of degrading natural resources. The critical economic question is whether or not global GDP growth can be harnessed as a tool for moving into the doughnut – or whether a different approach to economic development is needed.[86]

To explain further the doughnut analogy, the inner ring of the doughnut is the minimum standards required to survive as defined by the United Nations Sustainable Development Goals. The outer ring of the doughnut represents the environmental pre-requisites for human survival on Earth. Between the two rings is the dough where the sustainable targets can be met which marries poverty alleviation with environmental sustainability.

In 2017, Raworth developed this concept further with her book, *Doughnut Economics: Seven Ways to Think Like a 21st-Century Economist*, which was praised by, amongst others, the British environmental campaigner, George Monbiot who called it a "*breakthrough alternative to growth economics*".

In April 2020, Amsterdam City Council adopted doughnut economics as its governing principle for the running of the city which could even impact upon the operation of one of Europe's busiest ports:

> The port of Amsterdam is the world's single largest importer of cocoa beans, mostly from west Africa, where the labour is often highly exploitative.
>
> As an independent private company, it could reject such products and take the economic hit, but at the same time almost one in five households in Amsterdam qualify for social benefits due to low incomes and savings.
>
> Van Doorninck *(Deputy Mayor of Amsterdam, Marieke Van Doorninck)* says the port is looking at how it moves on from dependence on fossil fuels

> as part of the city's new vision, and she expects that to naturally evolve into a wider debate over other pressing dilemmas brought to the forefront by the doughnut model.
>
> "It gives space to talk about whether you want to be the place where products are being stored that are produced by child labour or by other forms of labour exploitation," she says.[87]

Doughnut economics can be related to Islamic finance and Islamic economics such as the environmental guardianship concept of khalifah (which is discussed in Chapter 6).

The RFI Foundation, in their 2018 report, *Environmental Impact in Islamic Finance*, advocated the linkage between Islamic finance and doughnut economics. However, instead of referring to the khalifah concept, it emphasised wasatiyyah. Wasatiyyah refers to the concept of moderation and sustainability. One verse from the Qur'ran reads:

> And thus have We willed you to be a community of the middle way (ummatan wasatan), so that you might bear witness to the truth before all mankind, and that the Apostle might bear witness to it before you ...[88]

RFI Foundation argued that wasatiyyah, if understood correctly, has strong connotations with doughnut economics:

> Wasatiyyah within the context of Islamic sustainable business would suggest that investments ought to meet people's needs while operating within the boundaries of sustainability and an efficient economic system.

The report added:

> The concept of wasatiyyah resonates in the proposals of Oxford scholar Kate Raworth in her book Doughnut Economics. This work proposes that economics should be redefined to address the equilibrium in efficiently utilising depleting natural resources while meeting the social needs of all people. She identified an ecological outer circle consisting of nine "planetary boundaries" proposed in an earlier work of Johan Rockström and colleagues. These boundaries must not be violated.

The core concept of maqasid al-sharia'a (discussed in Chapter 6), was also cited by the RFI Foundation for marrying doughnut economics with Islamic finance:

> The maqasid al-Shari'ah (higher objectives of Islamic law) – which also contribute to the fundamentals of a sustainable Islamic banking system – are primarily oriented towards the protection and preservation of five essential values (daruriyyat); namely faith, life, intellect, family, and property. These must be protected as a matter of priority and promoting and enhancing them by all suitable means is also a priority commitment of Muslim authorities and in Muslim majority countries where the principles of Shari'ah influence public policy. Muslim jurists have discussed the five daruriyyat in detail. Preservation of wealth (maqasid hifz al-mal), which mainly addresses the Shari'ah objectives relevant to an Islamic financial system, are generally proclaimed on the premise that wealth should not remain idle and non-productive, but must be circulated, capitalised and sustained through growth and development.

There is a corresponding concept to doughnut economics which also has synergies with Islamic thought. The circular economy can be defined as an alternative to a traditional linear economy where waste in resource production and consumption is accepted. Within the circular economy, resources are kept in use for as long as possible, extracting the maximum value from them whilst in use, then recover and regenerate products and materials at the end of each service life.

Walter Stahel and Genevieve Reday first explored the concept in a 1976 paper for the European Commission. A number of large corporate businesses now claim that circular economy concepts are integrated within their day to day management of business operations.

The Ellen MacArthur Foundation has argued that the regulatory, environmental and resource pressures on business means that the circular economy should be embraced. The difference, the Foundation argued, is that when in the past the price mechanism was the spur to business innovation this cannot be relied upon in an era where climate change is taking place. The costs of environmental degradation cannot always be mirrored within the price mechanism:

> ... these dynamics present a major challenge for the current 'take-make-dispose' system. While this system, too, will respond to price signals, these signals are incomplete and distorted. We therefore believe that under a business-as-usual scenario the market will not overcome the lock-in effect of existing production economics, regulations, and mindsets and will therefore not address the large and continued imbalances described here quickly and extensively enough to be able to keep meeting future demand.[89]

The circular economy has been formally endorsed by the Chinese Government. In 2006, in its 11th Five Year Plan, the circular economy was a dominant theme for China's economic development:

> Circular-economy cities and provinces involve four systems: the industrial system, the infrastructure, the cultural setting, and social consumption; the infrastructure serves as the basis for the rest, with the industrial system affecting social consumption, and social consumption affecting the human habitation environment. Thus the four systems together constitute a larger complex system.
>
> First, there is a need to build a circular economy based industrial system featuring industrial symbiosis and material circulation. In such a system people use resources from the ecological system to manufacture, distribute, and deliver products. The system provides material and funding support for regional development with its production functions, covering primary, secondary, and tertiary industries.
>
> Second, infrastructure development is indispensable. This includes the building of water-recycling systems, clean energy systems, and clean mass transit systems. A sound urban infrastructure guarantees circular economic development. A circular economy-oriented urban infrastructure is based on circulation of materials, efficient use of energy, and information sharing within the system, on integration of clean production, eco industry and eco-agriculture, and on formulation of a holistic strategy.
>
> Third, a commitment to "green" planning, landscaping, and architecture is also needed. An eco-friendly human habitation environment helps to restore the ecosystem in cities and boost the quality of life. To sustain the long-term health of ecosystems requires that resource use, production, and waste disposal be conducted below the ecological threshold.
>
> Fourth, green distribution and consumption should be encouraged and practiced. Within the framework of a circular economy, consumption should be based on harmony between humanity and nature, ensuring that consumption by current and future generations can move from simple to sophisticated levels. Consumer preferences, behaviour, and patterns should be oriented toward environmental protection, ecological balance, and sustainable social development, with governments adopting policy measures to ensure the formation of a circular consumption mechanism. In this way, human demand for materials, ecological health, and mental health can be satisfied while establishing a virtuous cycle in the environment and in the social consumption system, thus enriching the content of circular economy practice.[90]

These groundbreaking plans for China, the start of efforts by some corporate businesses to embrace circular economy concepts and even the linkage made by environmental campaigners between the circular economy and the 2015 Paris Agreement to reduce carbon emissions have made this theory a popular talking point in socially responsible investment (SRI) circles.

Therefore, why has the circular economy not been picked up by Islamic finance practitioners? According to Youssef Aboul-Naja, it is the institutional structure of Islamic finance which prevents these circular economy concepts from being embraced:

> Maybe the problem is not with Islamic finance, nor the Islamic banks, but with the way we perceive our products. 'Sometimes a change in perspective is all it takes to see the light' (Dan Brown).[91]

It is these different perspectives within Islamic finance and Islamic economics which has profoundly shaped the direction of political economic models in core Islamic finance markets in south Asia, east Asia, Africa and the Middle East. The existence of Islamic finance is also shifting the tectonic plates beneath the Russian body politic.

As we will see in the next chapter, the success of Islamic finance is profoundly changing the political and social dynamics of a range of countries that are at the heart of the global Islamic finance market. Whilst many of these countries have authoritarian regimes, the open and inclusive nature of Islamic finance are contributing towards enabling these nations to be open to a broad range of societal influences. It is this relationship between Islamic economics and political economy which we shall turn to next.

Notes

1. As quoted by Emmy Abdul Alim, *Global Leaders in Islamic Finance*, page 20.
2. Diary entry for 6 March 1913 as quoted in J M Winter and D M Joslin (eds), *R H Tawney's Common Place Book*, page 54.
3. Al Farabi, *Political Regime* C, 2, 94: 77.
4. Muqtedar Khan, *Islam and Good Governance: A Political Philosophy of Ihsan*, page 77.
5. Ibid., page 248.
6. Jonathan Edwards (1746), *A Treatise Concerning the Religious Affections*.

7. R H Tawney, *We Mean Freedom* (1944).
8. John Ruskin (1860), *Unto This Last*.
9. Pakistan People's Party Foundation Document 7 (1967).
10. John F Devlin, *The Baath Party: A History from Its Origins to 1966*, page 25.
11. Elizabeth F Thompson, *Justice Interrupted: The Struggle for Constitutional Government in the Middle East*, page 205.
12. English translation of the pamphlet, Bolshevism and the Islamic Body-Politic, preserved in the UK archives, IOR/L/PS/10/836.
13. Ishtiaq Hussain Qureshi, *The Future Development of Islamic Polity* (1946), page 23.
14. *Cowan v Scargill* [1985] Ch 270. The reference to South Africa was the growing movement in the UK and elsewhere for sanctions to be imposed against South Africa because of its apartheid regime. The UK Government, at that time, opposed sanctions against South Africa.
15. John Maynard Keynes also expressed frustrations concerning laissez faire capitalism where he ridiculed the laser like focus on profit during a speech in Dublin in 1933: "We destroy the beauty of the countryside because the unappropriated splendours of nature have no economic value. We are capable of shutting off the sun and the stars because they do not pay a dividend. London is one of the richest cities in the history of civilisation, but it cannot 'afford' the highest standards of achievement of which its own living citizens are capable, because they do not 'pay'".
16. Cited Bunce 1994: 33. John Major, UK Prime Minister from 1991 to 1997, also offered a similarly bucolic description of the United Kingdom on 22 April 1993 when he described the largely urban and services based society in the following terms—"Fifty years on from now, Britain will still be the country of long shadows on county (cricket) grounds, warm beer, invincible green suburbs and – as George Orwell said – old maids bicycling to Holy Communion through the morning mist".
17. Lord Griffiths (2001), *Capitalism, Morality and Markets* (Institute of Economic Affairs).
18. NEP stands for the New Economic Policy that lasted from 1971 to 1991. It was designed, in part, to provide economic opportunities for the indigenous Malay—or bumiputra—population which could either be viewed as discriminatory for Chinese origin or Indian origin communities or as a form of positive discrimination to level up economic opportunities across all communities.
19. Patricia Sloane-White (2011), Working in the Islamic Economy: Sharia-ization and the Malaysian Workplace, *Journal of Social Issues in South East Asia*, vol. 26, no. 2, pp. 304–334.
20. Jeffrey Halverson et al. (2011), *Master Narratives of Islamist Extremism*, page 42.

21. Anthony Crosland (1956), *The Future of Socialism.*
22. Peter A Hall, David Soskice (2001), *Varieties of Capitalism: The Institutional Foundation of Comparative Advantage*, page 35.
23. *Remade in China, Scott Wilson*, page 16.
24. Ibid., page 43.
25. Derek Scissors, *Deng Undone* article in *Foreign Affairs* (May 2009), page 24.
26. Richard W Carney, *East Asian Capitalism*, page 161.
27. Joshua Kurlantzick, *State Capitalism: How the Return of Statism Is Transforming The world*, page 41.
28. Julius Nyerere (1962), *Freedom and Unity: Uhuru na Umoja.*
29. Michael F Lofchie (2014)*The Political Economy of Tanzania: Decline and Recovery* (University of Pennsylvania Press), page 27.
30. Ibid., page 94.
31. *Cambridge Yearbook of European Legal Studies*, vol. 3, edited by Alan Dashwood, J R Spencer, Christophe Hillion, Angela Ward (2000), page 510.
32. Andrew Walker, Xiaoke Zhang, *East Asian Capitalism*, page 17.
33. Mark R Thompson (2004), Pacific Asia After 'Asian Values', *Third World Quarterly*, p. 1084.
34. Ibid.
35. Edmund Terence Gomez, as quoted in *East Asian Capitalism: Diversity, Continuity and Change* (2012), page 71.
36. Ibid., page 72.
37. As quoted by Emmy Abdul Alim, *Global Leaders in Islamic Finance*, page 97.
38. Ibid., page 110.
39. Christopher M Dent, Organising the Wider East Asia Region, ADB Working Paper, Christopher M Dent, page 9.
40. Mark R. Thompson (2004), Pacific Asia After 'Asian Values': Authoritarianism, Democracy, and 'Good Governance', *Third World Quarterly*, vol. 25, no. 6, pp. 1079–1095.
41. Chinese, Thai and Malaysian leaders stated the IMF response was harming livelihoods in the region at the Association of South East Asian Nations (ASEAN) summit in December 1997. ASEAN Foreign Ministers hinted at their concern with the IMF's actions at its summit in July 1998.
42. Daniel Stedman Jones, *Masters of the Universe*, page 332.
43. *East Asian Financial Crisis and the IMF*, Economic and Political Weekly, 25 April 1998, Page 965.
44. China and Japan were competitors for regional leadership in their different approaches to support the south east Asian economies in the late 1990s.
45. Jon Lunn, Gavin Thompson (December 2011), South East Asia, House of Commons Library.

46. Steve Fraser, *Wall Street*, pages 531–532.
47. Thomas F Cargill, Takayuki Sakamoto, *Japan Since 1980*, page 112.
48. Claude Meyer, *China or Japan*, page 86.
49. Christopher M Dent, Organising the Wider East Asia Region, ADB Working Paper, page 11.
50. Ibid.
51. Ernesto Gallo (May 2020), Globalisation, Authoritarianism and the Post-Soviet State in Kazakhstan and Uzbekistan, *Europe-Asia Studies.*
52. Carnegie Centre, November 2017.
53. Vladimir Putin, April 2005.
54. Ernesto Gallo (May 2020), Globalisation, Authoritarianism and the Post-Soviet State in Kazakhstan and Uzbekistan, *Europe-Asia Studies.*
55. Davinia Hoggarth (2016), The Rise of Islamic Finance: Post-colonial Market-Building in Central Asia and Russia, *International Affairs.*
56. Ibid.
57. Peter B Maggs (2011), Islamic Banking in Kazakhstan Law, *Review of Central and Eastern European Law*, vol. 36.
58. Reuters (6 June 2020), *Kazakh Police Detain Dozens of Anti-government Protesters.*
59. Ibid.
60. Robert Owen, *A New View of Society*, Second Essay.
61. Ibid.
62. Jewish Library website.
63. The reference to Histadrut is an Israeli trade union which is also an economic in the Israeli co-operative movement.
64. Peretz Merhav (1980), *The Israeli Left: History, Problems, Documents*, page 155.
65. *Kitab – ui Sifatul Qiyamah wa ar-Rakaik al Warah*, Bab 20, No. 2517, at 668.
66. Qur'ran, 5:2.
67. Mohd. Masum Billah (1998), *Islamic Insurance: Its Origins and Development. Arab Law Quarterly*, vol. 13, no. 4, pp. 386–422.
68. Benedikt Koehler, *Early Islam and the Birth of Capitalism*, page 121.
69. Timur Kuran, *The Long Divergence.*
70. Vardit Rispler-Chaim (1991), Insurance and Semi-Insurance Transactions in Islamic History Until the 19th Century, *Journal of the Economic and Social History of the Orient*, vol. 34, no. 3, p. 143.
71. Ibn Abidin, Majmū'ah, 2:178.
72. These trends are discussed in more detail in Chapter 10.
73. El-Gamal, Islamic Finance, 2006: page 147.
74. IMARC, *Takaful Market: Global Industry Trends, Share, Size, Growth, Opportunity and Forecast 2020–2025.*

75. Abdulazeem Abozaid (2016), *A Critical Shariah View of Takaful Structures*, Munich Personal RePEc Archive.
76. Dr Abu Umar Faruq Ahmad (January 2015), *The Search for an Alternative to Tabarru' in Takaful Models*, Bloomberg/International Shari'ah Research Academy for Islamic Finance.
77. Mohammed Hatta (1957), *The Co-operative Movement in Indonesia*, page 53.
78. As quoted by Benjamin Higgins (1958), Hatta and Co-operatives: The Middle Way for Indonesia? *The Annals of the American Academy of Political and Social Science*, vol. 318, pp. 49–57.
79. Ibid.
80. Mohammed Hatta (1957), *The Co-operative Movement in Indonesia*, page xvii.
81. Ibid., page xxi.
82. G Azhari, M N Syechalad, I Hasan, M S A Majid, (2017), The Role of Cooperative in the Indonesian Economy, *International Journal of Humanities and Social Science Invention (IJHSSI)*, vol. 6, no. 10, pp. 43–46.
83. Saeed Al-Muhurraimi, Daniel C Hardy (August 2013), *Cooperative and Islamic Banks: What Can They Learn from Each Other?*, International Monetary Fund Working Paper.
84. Masudul Alam Choudhury, *Islamic Economics and Finance: An Epistemological Inquiry*, page 169.
85. Kate Raworth (February 2012), *A Safe and Just Space for Humanity: Can We Live Within the Doughnut?* (Oxfam).
86. Ibid.
87. Guardian (8 April 2020), *Amsterdam to Embrace 'Doughnut' Model to Mend Post-coronavirus Economy*.
88. Qur'ran, 2:143.
89. Ellen MacArthur Foundation (2013), *Towards the Circular Economy*.
90. Feng Zhijun, Yan Nailng (June 2006), *Putting a Circular Economy into Practice in China*, Integrated Research System for Sustainability Science and Springer.
91. Youssef Aboul-Naja, *Circular Economy and Islamic Finance: An Ijarah Way Forward*, Islamic Finance News, 16 September 2015.

CHAPTER 10

Islamic Economics and Political Economy

The Emergence of the Islamic Finance Industry in the Twentieth Century

Whilst the ideas, values and even some of the practices of the contemporary Islamic finance industry stem from religion, the concept of a truly separate Islamic finance model only really came into its own in the twentieth century.

Some researchers have argued that the practical application of Islamic finance in the modern era began in the 1890s with an interest-free loan facility in southern India whilst in 1923 an interest-free credit society was established in Hyderabad.[1] Mit Ghamr in Egypt from 1963 is credited by many in the Islamic finance industry for being the very first Islamic financial institution of the modern era.[2]

The emergence of the Islamic finance industry was shaped by the struggle against colonialism with the corresponding interface with evolving ideas around the concept of national identities combined with the expression of religious identity. Globalisation and changes in technology were also transforming economic relations within societies:

> Islamic finance is a post-colonial project born of the desire to create a system of capital movement that complies with a set of values distinct from the so-called western tradition.[3]

J. S. Watkins, *Islamic Finance and Global Capitalism*,
https://doi.org/10.1007/978-3-030-59840-2_10

In this chapter, we will look at several key regions which were integral to the development of the industry during the twentieth century:

- Pakistan
- Saudi Arabia, United Arab Emirates, Iran and the wider Middle East
- Malaysia
- Sudan

By the end of this chapter we will look at the next phase of the Islamic finance story where the industry was impacting on disparate countries such as the Republic of Ireland and the United Kingdom and changing the political direction of the Russian Orthodox Church and its influence on wider Russian society.

There were some commonalities amongst the core nations which played integral roles in the emergence of the Islamic finance industry.

These countries, in different ways, were part of the anti-colonial movement and the subsequent development of national identities. The very idea, for example of an Indonesian nation or a Malaysian nation, was in response to the campaign to free peoples from European colonialism.

Before the nineteenth century, the concept of independent nation states in east Asia had not taken hold. Instead the wider south east Asian region was a fluid trading bloc with allegiances not necessarily defined to specific international borders. Therefore, the struggle against colonialism led to an emerging sense of national identity which was also linked, in some instances, to identities being based upon faith.

The evolving concept of defined national borders did not just reflect changing political realities for south east Asia. As Chua Beng Huat has argued:

> … nationalism as a relatively 'modern' sentiment (means) much of Southeast Asia is still embedded in local traditions, which are often anti-individualistic.[4]

As we saw in Chapter 9, the concept of gotong royong (communal work) and shared ideas regarding religious identity contributed to Mohammad Hatta, the first Vice President of Indonesia, to speak of the need to roil back against individualism in the 1950s whilst Mahathir Mohamed, when Prime Minister of Malaysia during the 1997 Asian Financial Crisis, stressed the communal nature of regional politics with his espousal of 'Asian values'.

If we consider the Persian Gulf region we can see that in the nineteenth century, Manasir peoples depended on date farming, fishing, pearling and tending livestock. This required extensive migration from al-Hasa in modern day Saudi Arabia to the Hajar Range in modern day Oman. Therefore Manasir peoples' allegiances to territorially based rulers was conditional and the concept of national borders was not immediately accepted within the region.

Prince Mohammed Al Faisal Al Saud of Saudi Arabia, who has played a pivotal role from the 1970s onwards with the development of the Islamic finance industry, identified the concept of the nation state as being detrimental to the Middle East - and to Islam:

> It is no longer possible to have the caliphate today, it is no longer viable today. Unfortunately it is because of the development of the idea of the nation-state, which the West has imposed on the rest of the world. For me as a Muslim, the nation-state is one of the most pernicious ideas that has come about. That idea fractured the world and made you different from me and me from you.[5]

The Prince, in these comments, was also reflecting the Salafist[6] perspective in Islam, which reflected an opinion which had been held by the governing Al Saud family that national borders had compromised the central role of Arabia in the Middle East. In 1966, King Faisal of Saudi Arabia had said:

> We do not need to import foreign traditions. We have a history and a glorious past. We led the Arabs and the world .... With what did we lead them? The word of one God and the shari'a of His Prophet.[7]

We will come back to this theme later in this chapter in our discussion of the role of Saudi Arabia in the formation of the Islamic finance industry.

The nineteenth and twentieth centuries were also periods when national economies were becoming more interconnected in a phenomenon which is now termed as globalisation.

Colonial authorities created its own set of dynamics with the emergence of class based economies where trained indigenous individuals would meet some of the technical needs of a developing global economy whose overriding purpose was to extract resources for export.

Inevitably, there was also a backlash in colonial territories against economic expropriation by European Governments and also cultural expropriation with fears that cultural and faith-based identities were being diluted by a combination of colonialism and globalisation.

This complex interplay of disparate factors can be seen in south Asia where the period leading up to the partition of India and Pakistan in 1947 shaped the emerging polemics calling for an Islamic economic system to be instituted.

From Partition to the Political Economy of Pakistan

Pakistan has been described as "*an intriguing paradox*".[8]

A superficial analysis of the economic opportunities which exist within Pakistan would suggest that the nation should look forward to a time when there will be high growth rates with a concomitant increase in living standards.

Pakistan has a growing skilled workforce whose expertise is valued across the world. It was the beneficiary of funding from the United States when Pakistan was identified as a US ally during the Cold War. The country is now being courted by China as part of its Belt and Road Initiative.[9]

In addition:

> Pakistan is blessed with fertile cropland watered by rivers that flow down from the Himalayas; it inherited the world's largest irrigation system from the British at independence.[10]

However, according to the Asian Development Bank, 24.3% of people live below the national poverty line (2015), 2.3% of the population live below US$1.90 per day (2019) and infant deaths is 69 per 1000 live births (2018).

Pakistan was one of a handful of nations which instituted Islamic economics as an intrinsic part of its political economic model. It is not, though, the failure of Islamic economics which contributed to Pakistan's economic difficulties.

Easterly has argued that, instead, the fault lies with the realisation of elite theory, where a limited number of people control the levers of power and the distribution of resources, which has led to systemic inequalities:

> There were some attempts to co-opt the masses in the populist governments of Z.A. Bhutto and Benazir Bhutto, which we could think of as one section of the elite using the poor majority as a weapon against another section of the elite. However, the powerful position of the army and the landlords has prevented any passing of decision-making to the illiterate majority. Each segment of the elite is powerful enough by itself to exclude the majority from power, even when it is feuding with another segment.[11]

In the 2018 Pakistan General Election, Imran Khan—who became Prime Minister—also argued that "*Pakistan has elite capture*"—a view he reiterated in government whilst advocating reforms.

Nonetheless, the emergence of Pakistan led to new thinking about Islamic economics and, at one time, enabled, ostensibly, an Islamic political economic structure being instituted following a military coup. Therefore, to understand where the Islamic finance industry is now, we need to first consider how the impact of the struggle for Indian independence and the establishment of Pakistan shaped the contemporary industry.

In 1914 Gandhi left South Africa to return to India to campaign for an eventual end to British rule. During this same period there was also a demand for a new Muslim independent state to be established in the north west of the then British Raj.

One of the early leaders calling for the creation of this state was Allama Muhammad Iqbal (1876–1938). Iqbal's poetry was much admired and in 1922 the British State recognised his artistry by awarding him a knighthood. Iqbal, who is now known as the 'Spiritual Father of the Nation' gave a powerful rallying call in the now famous Allahabad Address of 1930:

> The principle of European democracy cannot be applied to India without recognising the fact of communal groups. The Muslim demand for the creation of a Muslim India within India is, therefore, perfectly justified. The resolution of the All-Parties Muslim Conference at Delhi is, to my mind, wholly inspired by this noble ideal of a harmonious whole which, instead of stifling the respective individualities of its component wholes,

affords them chances of fully working out the possibilities that may be latent in them.

Earlier in Iqbal's career, his work *Ilmul Iqstiad* (The Science of Economics) was published in 1903. This book did not explore in detail the concept of Islamic finance but it did cover a range of economic themes and it referenced the need for some form of ethical structure in economics:

> The question has arisen in the present age whether poverty is also a necessary element in the global system. Is it not possible that every individual is free from the suffering of poverty? Can it not be that the heart-rending calls of those quietly groaning all over the place silence forever and the sad spectacle of poverty that frightens a caring heart, disappear from the face of the earth like a blot on the landscape?[12]

Iqbal spoke of the artificiality between the division of secular and spiritual objectives. Taking this conclusion one step further, he argued that economic relations had to factor in the needs of wider human society—a theme that scholars working within Islamic finance has articulated ever since:

> ... matter is spirit in space – time reference ... The spirit finds its opportunities in the natural, the material, the secular. All that is secular is therefore sacred in the roots of its being.[13]

It was three academics from Osmania University in Hyderabad who did so much to establish Islamic economics as an area of academic study and who were pioneers in the early history of the industry. These academics shared the vision of Iqbal as to how Islamic concepts can reshape society.

Muhammed Hamidullah (1908–2002) was one of these academics who condemned laissez-faire capitalism for causing "*poverty like a tragic spectre has haunted the ceaselessly toiling humanity*".[14] Hamidullah went on to write of the partnership contract model to share risks in a business venture—now a key component within Islamic finance.

Manazir Ahsan Gilani (1892–1956) popularised the concept of Islamic economics with his book, *Islami Ma'ashiyyat* (Islamic Economics) in the mid -1940s. In 1945, Gilani wrote that interest could be accepted by Muslims when working or living in countries that did not have Islamic institutions or structures to ensure "*they will be protected from being gobbled up by different communities when they enter into the international struggles of the financial world*".[15]

It was Anwar Iqbal Qureshi who made a seminal contribution to the establishment of Islamic economics as an academic discipline. In his 1946 work, *Islam and the Theory of Interest*, Qureshi argued that the work of John Maynard Keynes had led to the insight that the amount of individual savings was largely determined by fluctuations in income and not connected to interest rates.

Qureshi also noted that Keynes had argued that excessive savings distorted the workings of an economy. Consequently, Qureshi concluded that the cultural milieu of upper class society within Britain had inhibited Keynes from reaching the obvious conclusion, drawn from Keynes's own analysis, that the concept of interest was a hindrance to the proper workings of the real economy.[16]

Sheikh Mahmud Ahmad made a very similar point in his 1952 book, *Economics of Islam* whilst also envisaging the establishment of Islamic banks on the basis of a joint-stock company model with limited liability.

Though there was a short-lived Islamic finance experiment in Pakistan in the late 1950s when rural landlords set up interest-free loan facilities,[17] it was the rhetoric of a controversial political activist in the period immediately leading to partition who moved the Islamic finance agenda forward.

Abdul Ala Maududi (1903–1979) founded Jamaat-e-Islami (Assembly of Islam) in 1941. Maududi took a hardline approach on a whole range of issues such as the role of women in society:

> he saw "women's visibility" in the bazaar, colleges, theatres, restaurants "as the greatest threat to morality. Art, literature, music, film, dance, use of makeup by women: all were shrieking signs of immorality"[18]

Maududi even claimed music was an evil that was linked to non-Islamic economics:

> For them ("rich people") music was a regular need to satisfy which another army had to be secured of musicians, dancing girls, drum-beaters and manufacturers of musical instruments.[19]

These constant references to the denigration of women in society was, according to Ahmed, reflective of the sexual mores of that time:

> This aspect of Maududi's theory reproduces contemporaneous notions of the male libido as a rapacious and irrepressible force next to which female sexuality is cast in a passive and inferior role. Amongst Indian Muslims of Maududi's generation, the assumption is taken from popular psychoanalytic theories of the early twentieth century and is linked, retrospectively, to Islam's sacred and classical legal sources.[20]

It has also been argued that this fundamentalist standpoint stemmed from the changing social situation impacting Muslims in northern India at the turn of the twentieth century where the status of the community was said to have declined amidst a rise in communal tensions between the Muslim and Hindu communities. During this same period, the standing of the wider ummah was seen to be questioned as a consequence of the weakness of the Ottoman Caliphate in the wake of the First World War.

In any case, Louer argued, Jamaat-e-Islami was not popular and this lack of support was utilised by this group as a strength:

> Rather than pursue large-scale recruitment, it sought to create an elite characterised by moral rectitude, discipline and total commitment to the cause. It was fiercely criticised by the ulama who had organised themselves into other movements to fight colonialism. In their view, Maududi, who did not belong to their world, was in no position to legitimately speak on behalf of Islam.[21]

Supporters of Maududi would argue that the ulama did not recognise that Maududi was close to or was a Mujaddid—a key historical figure who was reviving adherence to the faith. Whilst Maududi was speaking of the need for Islamic economics, he was also presenting a wider perspective that would lead to a debate within contemporary Islam as to the direction of the religion; a debate which continues to intrude at different stages during the history of Islamic finance:

> Maududi, in the modern era, was the principle reviver of the idea of 'the reviver' and in the process made the entire tradition of revival and reform (Tajid was Islah) in Islam, the Islamic justification for contemporary revivalist movements which needed Islamic justification for their break from traditional Islam without inviting the often fatal accusation of innovation (bid'a).[22]

Whilst there were early attempts to legislate for measures that were congruent with an Islamic economy in the final years of the British Raj and the early years of Pakistani independence, it was Maududi's aim of cultivating an elite to move his agenda forward which was initially successful—with the coming to power of General Zia.

General Muhammed Zia-ul-Haq led a military coup which deposed the civilian Government in 1977. Zia remained the leader of Pakistan until his untimely death in 1988.

Zia changed the direction of Pakistan from the path as indicated by Pakistan's founder, Muhammed Ali Jinnah (1876–1948). Jinnah saw the formation of Pakistan as a refuge for Muslims to find their faith free from, as he saw it, Hindu domination. Jinnah was from a Shi'a family and the Prime Minster of Pakistan, at the time of the 1977 coup, Zulfikar Ali Bhutto, also had Shi'a decendents.

However, under Zia, there was a policy of Sharization (Islamisation) of society which was, in part, inspired by Jamaat-e-Islami. In addition, Zia's ideas may have been shaped by the Barelvi legacy.[23]

Other influences on Zia included the Deobandi school which emerged from Deoband near Delhi in the nineteenth century. This school opposed any idea of modernising religious teaching based on European models, opposed Sufi (Islamic spiritual movement) practices and opposed Shi'a thought.[24]

The measures that Zia enacted included, for instance, declaring that women who became pregnant due to being raped could face a potential criminal charge of adultery.[25] Sharization also led to a revised economic system being introduced in Pakistan.

Tentative steps to embrace Islamic finance had, though, already been taken by the previous administration which Zia had overthrown. In 1974, the Organisation of Islamic Co-operation held its summit in Lahore where there was support from the leaders of Muslim majority countries for the establishment of the Islamic Development Bank. In 1979, Zulfiqar Ali Bhutto's government announced plans for banking within the nation to be interest free within three years.

Zia, though, ostentatiously, declared that the institution of Islamic economic practices as a key priority for his government. In banking, interest was outlawed and a profit and loss system was introduced in 1980. However, the ban on interest was more apparent than real.

A World Bank report highlighted, for instance, that in 1980—1981, farmers in the Chambhar area in Sindh province were obliged to seek funds from 60 money lenders who were offering loans at 78.5% interest whilst banks in the region were offering loans at 10% interest:

> The borrowing rate also varied enormously across borrowers: the standard deviation of the interest rate 38.14 per cent, compared with an average lending rate of 78.5 per cent. In other words, an interest rate of 2 per cent and an interest rate of 150 per cent are both within two standard deviations of the mean.[26]

It was the Zakat and Ushr Ordinance that led to a step change in transforming the Pakistani economy. Enacted in 1980, the ordinance meant that a tax would be deducted each year from bank accounts holding 3000 rupees or more whilst for people who held land or cultivated crops, cash or crops would be levied at 10% of the land's yield.

In response to this change in tax policy, Shi'a groups objected as they argued Jafari fiqh required Shi'a Muslims to pay zakat directly to poor people of their choice and not to the State. There were also concerns that zakat paid to the Government was being directed towards Sunni educational networks.[27] Following a large Shi'a demonstration in Islamabad in 1980, the Government decided Shi'a Muslims would be exempt from the zakat tax. Bouts of sectarian violence between the Sunni and Shi'a community has remained an issue for the nation.

As far as the popularity of Jamaat-e-Islami was concerned, it struggled to gain electoral traction when Zia eventually allowed elections in 1985. The group only gained 10 of the 68 National Assembly seats it contested and won just 13 seats in the various provincial assemblies.

In 1988, Zia died in an unexplained plane crash and bouts of civilian rule followed which was combined with the active political engagement of the military.

Observers of Pakistan expressed doubts that the country's economic leaders had really taken to heart the adoption of Islamic finance. One secret US diplomatic cable stated:

> Due to the high level of complexity for structuring and monitoring Islamic finance, its growth in Pakistan will likely be slow, despite growing consumer interest in the concept.[28]

In 1999 the Shari'at Appellate Bench of the Supreme Court ordered the Pakistani Government to eliminate all interest-based banking by

2001. However, as Professor Ahmad Khurshid has noted (who worked with Zia on reforms to the economy and was integral to the 1976 Mecca Conference on Islamic economics) the judgement was not fully implemented:

> After that things began to change slightly but again because of the lack of political will, the entire report could not be implemented. But somehow the central bank started to move in that direction and that is how, from 2002 onwards, Islamic banks or banks which would have totally self-contained Islamic units came into existence.[29]

The formal position of the central bank of Pakistan was made clear in a filing to the Shari'at Appellate Bench of the Supreme Court of Pakistan in 2002:

> … it is the State Bank of Pakistan's considered judgement that a parallel approach will be in the best interests of the country. This means that Islamic banking is introduced as a parallel system of which a beginning has already been made, it is provided a level playing field vis a vis the existing conventional banks, and its further growth and development is supported by Government and State Bank of Pakistan through appropriate actions. This approach will eliminate the risk of any major costs/damage to the economy, give a fair chance to Islamic banks to develop alongside the conventional banks, and will provide a choice to the people of Pakistan, and the foreigners doing business in/with Pakistan, to use either of the two systems.[30]

The Pakistani Government was not as diplomatic as the central bank in its submission to the Court. It rejected the idea that the nation should only have an Islamic banking structure by stating that it was:

> … not practical or feasible and if attempted will pose a high degree of risk to the economic stability and security of Pakistan.[31]

As of December 2018, the Islamic banking share of overall Pakistani banking assets was at 12.9% and constituted 14.8% of all total bank deposits in the country.[32]

In addition, the association of Islamic finance with Maududi has contributed to the sector being classified as a "*fundamentalist doctrine*".[33] These connotations are not helpful for the growth prospects of the industry.

Maybe a more fundamental issue is why Islamic economics was never firmly established in Pakistan.

Stephens argued that the bureaucratic structures that the State had inherited from the colonial era and its internal political contradictions had inhibited fundamental change:

> … Muslim leaders equated political power, whether as a community or as a nation, with the ability to project a unified religious identity – an emphasis that made tackling socio-economic divisions ill advised. Their focus on Muslim consensus mirrored the unitary forms of sovereignty that undergirded secular legal governance under the British. Without challenging these underlying political forms, attempt to rethink the relationship between Islam and the economy faltered, revealing the entrenched legacy of colonial government. Today, however with post-colonial states more firmly established, there might be opportunities to return to early twentieth century visions of Islamic social justice – particularly their emphasis on rethinking basic structures of governance.[34]

Saudi Arabia and the Religious Drive for Islamic Finance

King Faisal and the development of the Saudi Islamic finance industry

Saudi Arabia is the largest economic power amongst the Persian Gulf monarchical states. The nearly US$800 billion-dollar economy[35] is also a global leader in Islamic finance. The Saudi drive to lead in this field is not purely down to economics.

The primacy of Saudi Arabia goes beyond its significant oil resources and relates to its positioning at the heart of the Middle East—and of Islam. The King of Saudi Arabia is known as the Custodian of the Two Holy Mosques referring to the holy cities of Mecca and Medina (this epithet has been used by a series of Muslim leaders over the centuries).

One of the five pillars of Islam is the annual Hajj pilgrimage which is obligatory for Muslims to perform at least once in their life if they have the capacity to do so. Consequently, the Saudi state has a special responsibility to safeguard Mecca (which is the intrinsic heart of the Hajj) and Medina (which is not part of Hajj but is visiting by pilgrims). Medina is home to the Masjid Al Nabawi (Prophet's Mosque) and includes the burial sites of the Prophet and the first two caliphs, Abu Bakr and Umar.[36]

It was King Faisal who not only took decisive steps to engender an Islamic finance industry but, on a broader scale, led efforts to establish a global pan-Islamic community where Muslim values could be advanced. It was Faisal's vision, particularly during the 1960s and 1970s, shaped by his devout beliefs, which began to change the contours of the contemporary Saudi state, as well as the future direction of the Islamic finance industry.

The vision seemed to stall when, in 1975, King Faisal was murdered by a disgruntled nephew. However subsequent developments, such as the seminal 1976 Islamic Economics conference, were examples of the continuation of Faisal's legacy.

The changes that Faisal saw during his lifetime were extraordinary. His father, King Abdulaziz bin Abdul Rahman (1875–1953) brought the modern Saudi state into being after dealing with family and tribal rivals with tact—and sometimes with force —which included encouraging the religious Ikhwan community to join forces with him.

At the same time, King Abdulaziz bin Abdul Rahman was adroit in dealing with powerful outside powers to maintain and enhance his territorial control—whether that was the Ottoman Empire, the British Empire or, subsequently, the United States. It was, though, the discovery of oil which began to transform the economic life chances of Saudi citizens.

By the time that King Faisal came to the throne the country was being transformed with major urban planning projects, international investment and a stronger profile in foreign affairs. One of the core issues which preoccupied King Faisal was the Arab nationalist position of the then Egyptian leader, Gamal Abdul Nasser. Nasser had finally gained power in 1954 following an earlier military coup in 1952.

Clearly King Faisal would not have welcomed the idea of the institution of the Egyptian monarchy being abolished. It was hardly a good precedent for the future prospects of his Al Saud family.

However, it was the nationalist rhetoric of Nasser which also disturbed the King. Not only was Nasser's stance seen as a threat to the very existence of the Saudi state but Faisal, a devout man, put greater store in the vision of Muslim unity as an objective that should be attained rather than ambitions regarding regional Arab unity.

It was in this context that Faisal was advancing a system of Islamic economics to be embraced across the Muslim world. Nasser, on the other hand, saw Faisal as wrecking Arab unity. Consequently, Nasser called

Faisal "*a traitor to the Arab cause*" and that the concept of Muslim solidarity was really "*an American - British conspiracy*" to divide the Arab world.[37]

This was, of course, the time of the Cold War and due to a series of missteps by the United States and outright hostility from the UK and France towards Egypt (as was shown by the failed military intervention with the 1956 Suez Crisis) Egypt became more closely aligned with the Soviet Union for economic and security support. King Faisal was a passionate anti-communist who saw this political model as a direct threat to Islam. As this anecdote shows, Faisal saw no hope for Egypt as long as Nasser stayed on this nationalist course:

> Murad Ghalib, an Egyptian politician and diplomat, used to say that on one visit to Saudi Arabia he told Faisal of his intention to perform the Hajj umra, the latter was surprised: "Do you really believe in God?".[38]

The growing animosity between Egypt and Saudi Arabia led to a proxy war in Yemen with each power supporting opposing forces (arguably similar, at the time of writing in 2020, to Saudi Arabia and Iran backing opposing military forces in Yemen).

It was within this context that King Faisal's aim for Muslim unity and his efforts to head off communist and Arab nationalist ambitions, led to a series of moves which contributed to the advancement of the Islamic finance industry.

Unexpectedly, the emerging Islamic finance sector was given a boost via a crisis outside Saudi borders. Whilst King Faisal took seriously his custodian responsibilities for Mecca and Medina, he also felt a religious responsibility for a holy city that was not within his kingdom. Jerusalem was where the Prophet was spiritually transcended to heaven. It was Faisal's desire that one day he would visit Jerusalem when the city would be governed by a Muslim government.

Therefore, it was a shock for Faisal and other leaders when, in August 1969, the Al-Aqsa Mosque in Jerusalem was damaged by fire caused by a Christian extremist. The arson destroyed part of the roof and the 800-year-old pulpit of Salahuddin (remembered for his role in fighting against the European forces in the Crusades which included the recapturing of Jerusalem from the Crusaders in 1187).

The outcry at this desecration technically led to the formation of the Organisation of the Islamic Conference (now renamed as the Organisation of Islamic Co-operation—OIC) at the instigation of the Grand Mufti of Jerusalem, Amin al-Husseini[39] with the Mufti declaring that this was the moment for Muslim nations to come together in solidarity.

However, it was the work of King Faisal who had spent much time in preparing the ground for such an organisation to be established which was the real catalyst for the formation of the OIC. Faisal saw Communist nations and the establishment of the Israeli state as the primary motivations for Muslim states to work more closely together to advance, what he believed, were shared values.

Though there were some tensions between Saudi Arabia—as a majority Sunni state and Iran—as a majority Shi'a state, the work of intermediaries such as King Hussein of Jordan and Kamel Mroueh, owner of the Lebanese newspaper *Al Hayat*, enabled some form of modus vivendi between Saudi and Iran. The dynamics of this relationship, and consequently the impact this had on the Islamic finance industry, changed after the 1979 Iranian Revolution, as will be discussed later in this chapter.

Over time the OIC[40] began to address issues of common Muslim values thereby helping to realise the vision of King Faisal. This included, in 1983, the establishment of the Fiqh Academy. Fiqh refers to Islamic jurisprudence and the academy is now housed in the Saudi Arabian city of Jeddah. The terms of reference for the Academy are:

> To achieve the theoretical and practical unity of the Islamic Ummah (community) by striving to have Man conform his conduct to the principles of the Islamic Sharia at the individual, social as well as international levels.
>
> To strengthen the link of the Muslim community with the Islamic faith.
>
> To draw inspiration from the Islamic Sharia, to study contemporary problems from the Sharia point of view and to try to find the solutions in conformity with the Sharia through an authentic interpretation of its content.[41]

Consequently, the judgements reached by the Academy have significant influence in terms of the shape and conduct of the Islamic finance industry. One very consequential resolution was the ban on excess profits which the Academy reached in 1985:

> Any excess or profit on a loan for a deferred payment when the borrower is unable to repay it after the fixed period and similarly any excess or profit on a loan at the time of contract are both forbidden as riba in the Shari' ah.

This significant judgement has enhanced the credibility of Islamic finance. When the concept of profits is not tied to the initial value of the loan this theoretically makes loan financing more affordable for customers who may be reassured that they do not need to worry about hidden costs. However, how the word "*excess*" could be interpreted remains a matter of debate. At the very least, some framework exists for the criteria of loan affordability to be assessed.

The influence of Saudi Arabia in Islamic finance reflects the perspective of the country being steeped in the Hanbalite theological school which has a literalist approach towards Islamic theology compared to the more interpretative fiqh schools such as Hanafi and Shafi'i as well as the recourse to intellect (aqd) in Shi'a Jafari thought.

Consequently, Hanbalite understanding of Islamic finance had some form of dominance in the industry due to the OIC and the International Islamic Fiqh Academy both being based in Jeddah.

After the assassination of King Faisal in 1975, his successor, King Khalid, carried on many of the initiatives that had begun under Faisal's reign. This included the inauguration of the OIC's Islamic Bank for Development in Jeddah in 1975.

King Khalid, on the occasion of the opening of the bank, spoke of the need to continue Faisal's work whilst using the event to reiterate Saudi opposition to the establishment of the state of Israel—a reminder that the early history of Islamic finance was imbued with geopolitics:

> The best way to honour the memory of Faisal is for all of us to accomplish his goal to ensure the solidarity and unity of all Muslims, and to strive to achieve the greatness of the Muslim umma. Above all, it is to realise his greatest hope to pray, by God's grace and will, in al-Aqsa mosque, the first of the two qiblahs (*the direction used by Muslims to pray towards Mecca*) and the third holiest shrine, with Jerusalem once again Arab, free and dedicated to the service of God and His religion.[42]

Wahhabism and Islamic Finance

One of the most important figures in Islamic finance, Prince Mohammed Al Faisal Al Saud, has described himself as a salafist—a belief system which some politicians in Europe and North America would describe as being equated with terrorism.

The Prince's work has included the establishment of the Faisal Bank of Egypt and the Faisal Bank of Sudan. Prince Mohammed would reject the stereotyping of his beliefs and has, instead, pithily summed up his influences:

> Mohamed ibn Abdullah (pbuh); Mohamed Al Saud, my great-great-great-grandfather; and Mohamed Abd Al Wahhab, who is the reformer in Saudi Arabia. To me, that is Salafism.[43]

The first of these is the Prophet. The next two men cited by the Prince has shaped modern Saudi Arabia—and consequently the impact the country has had on the Islamic finance industry.

The development of the Saudi state was a confluence of religion and politics. For both Mohamed Al Saud and Mohamed Abd Al-Wahhab saw advantages in a shared alliance which changed the religious and political direction of Arabia.

During the eighteenth century, there were political rivalries between differing tribal leaders. However, when Mohamed Al Saud delivered his partnership with the religious leader, Mohamed Abd Al-Wahhab, the rivalries between tribal leaders took on a new dimension:

> The pact had the effect of converting skirmishes between minor Arabian powers into an expansionist jihad (struggle) in the path of God against the forces of idolatry.[44]

Wahhabism is a popular Sunni movement instigated by the theologian, Muhammad ibn Abd al-Wahhab (1703–1792) from Najd. Al-Wahhab's teachings is now the dominant form of Islam within Saudi Arabia.

Ibn Abd-al-Wahhab said he relied on the Qur'ran and the hadiths without the need for speculative philosophy in order to embrace the practices as set by the early Muslims known as the Salaf.

Later Wahhabism became associated with a range of beliefs known as Salafism whereby believers argue that Islam had been distorted by accretions of other philosophical and cultural influences and so a focus on "original" Islam was required. This underlying thought was linked to Al-Wahhab's view of perceived moral decline and political weakness in the Arabian Peninsula.

The tensions between Wahhabism, which is linked to Hanbalite fiqh, with Hanafi fiqh, was exemplified by the condemnation of Wahhabism by the Hanafi jurist, Ibn Abidin (1784–1836). Ibn Abidin was from Damascus and felt the defeat of the Ottoman Empire, the military success of the Al Saud tribe in Arabia and their subsequent defeat in 1818. In his work, *Hashiya Radd al-Muhtar*, Ibn Abidin wrote:

> His words and who consider the Companions of our Prophet (Allah bless him and give him peace) to be disbelievers are not a condition for someone to be a Kharijite,[45] but rather are a mere clarification of what those who revolted against 'Ali (Allah Most High be well pleased with him) in fact did. Otherwise, it is enough to be convinced of the unbelief of those they fight against, as happened in our own times with the followers of 'Abd al-Wahhab, who came out of the Najd in revolt, and took over the sanctuaries of Mecca and Medina. They followed the Hanbali madhhab (fiqh), but believed that they were the Muslims, and that those who believed differently than they did were polytheists. On this basis, they held it lawful to kill Sunni Muslims and their religious scholars, until Allah Most High dispelled their forces, and the armies of the Muslims attacked their strongholds and subdued them in 1233 A.H. (1818 CE).[46]

This harsh language, whilst redolent of the era, has some echoes in the differences which continue to exist between different schools of fiqh. It is also a demonstration that the current debate within Islam as to its future direction is not a new phenomenon.

Whilst Wahhabism has been described by some politicians and newspaper leader writers as an insular and narrow form of Islam this does not chime with the stance as adopted by King Faisal. Instead, Faisal's literalist approach towards religion inspired him to work for pan-Islamic unity via dialogue and to engage positively with outside powers who shared similar values. Consequently, the early steps in the formation of the Islamic finance industry was outward looking. As these steps originated, in part, from Saudi Arabia, it should be recognised that Wahhabi thought would have played a role in these developments.

This openness to other Islamic ideas beyond Wahhabism was seen in 1976 with the first international Islamic economics conference held in Mecca. This was a turning point in Islamic finance. It established on a firmer footing the contemporary academic study of Islamic finance and it enabled further logistical steps to be followed which has helped the industry become the US$2.05 trillion sector it is today.[47]

> However valuable the contributions made by some scholars in their individual capacities, they could not provide the thrust needed to establish the separate identity of the subject. It was the First International Conference on Islamic Economics held at Makkah in February 1976 which served as a catalyst at an international level and led to an exponential growth of literature on the subject.[48]

In one of the papers presented to the conference, Khurshid Ahmad, who was influenced by the thinking of Abul A'la Maududi,[49] declared that Islamic finance and economics was a new approach in political economy:

> Contemporary Islamic finance is neither a transient political articulation of militant Islam nor simply an angry outburst against western nations. On the contrary, it heralds the Muslims' positive and creative response to the ideological challenge of Western civilisation. For the Muslim world it is an attempt to try to reconstruct society and the economy by drawing primarily upon its own rich but neglected religio-cultural sources.[50]

Ijaz Shafl Gilani in his paper to the conference went further in defining Islamic economics and Islamic finance:

> As Muslims we adhere to certain values dealing with economic issues and relations. These values are related to production, distribution and consumption of wealth. The pursuit of these values is supposed to achieve two goals: prosperity in our individual and group lives and prosperity in the world hereafter. The goal of prosperity in this world is broken down into sub goals such as group solidarity as a means to achieve the goal of prosperity. Similarly, there are other sub goals such as the higher rate of economic growth, higher standards of living etc.[51]

Gilani argued that Islamic economics was linked but divided between the "*High Road*" (values) and the "*Low Road*" (economic objectives). This is a particular perspective in Islam which would not be shared by other scholars from other fiqh schools who would argue that values and the economy are part of a holistic whole which is required to achieve moral and community objectives.

Gilani's insight, though, has echoes of Karl Polanyi's work, *The Great Transformation* (1944) where the theory of embeddedness reflects the concept that individuals and the economy cannot be fully understood without considering other societal factors, such as religion. Polanyi analysed the effort to create an economic sphere increasingly separate from non-economic institutions that would function only to maximise profit—thereby embedding society in the market—instead of the market being embedded in society. Polanyi argued that such an effort was bound to fail and this could bring in its wake dangerous societal reactions such as fascism.

Economic thinkers from the Scottish Enlightenment, such as Adam Smith and David Hume, would also dispute the contention that working towards economic objectives is distinctly different from meeting spiritual needs whilst Max Weber spoke of the ethos of Protestanism being essential to the advancement of capitalism.[52]

Nonetheless, it was partly within Hanbalite thought that the conference agreed on a number of seminal objectives which had profound consequences for the future direction of the Islamic finance industry. This ranged from strategic objectives such as "*calling on Muslim Governments to bolster the existing Islamic banks and propagate and extend the scope of interest free banking*"[53] through to the detailed work of structuring legal definitions which, in many ways, has shaped the practical day-to-day implementation of Islamic finance processes ("*Formation of a Committee to compile a dictionary of Islamic Economics terminology in different languages*"[54]).

Fundamentally, the conference decided that the future operation of Islamic economics and Islamic finance should be predicated on the following philosophical principles:

> The belief that the universe belongs to Allah and that all wealth belongs to Allah.
>
> That Man is a trustee of what he possesses of the bounties of God.
>
> That private ownership approved by Islam is within the framework of the proper means of earning and spending and satisfaction of the obligations on wealth.
>
> The economic system of Islam achieves social equilibrium and solidarity.[55]

We should consider this final point for it is a dividing line between Islamic economics and some laissez-faire economists. To demonstrate this difference, we can consider the work of the laissez-faire British economist, Arthur Seldon (1916–2005). Seldon argued:

> The virtue of capitalism is that it ... does not require good men and women. The virtue of socialism is that men and women who may start with good intentions, but who are skilled in acquiring coercive power, can use it to do harm.[56]

Seldon later added:

> The market discovers and ejects its bad people sooner than politics.[57]

Though this is a comparison between capitalism and socialism, one suspects Seldon would have felt the same about any economic model that was predicated on a set of moral beliefs rather than upon the free operation of the market.

Seldon put great store in the price mechanism which, in turn, could lead to moral outcomes whilst objecting to the concept of charitable giving directed to poor people:

> You have never been poor. I have. The poor do not thank those who bring them gifts in kind which question their capacity and affront their dignity. Cash gives the power of choice; care, service in kind, denies choice. But much more than that; the poor who are given care or kind will never learn choice, judgement, discrimination, responsibility. To give cash is to take risks but they are the risks the child takes when he learns to walk.[58]

It was this thinking which was adopted by key politicians in the United Kingdom and the United States, particularly during the 1980s, with the concept of "*trickle-down economics*" where, eventually, the benefits of a competitive system would trickle down the supply chain to support workers in a range of vocations.

Whilst we can debate the efficacy or otherwise of trickle-down economics it is an interesting counterpoint that at the very same time when Islamic economics was coming into its own and promoting concepts of solidarity, laissez-faire economic thinkers in the US and the UK were reaching opposite conclusions based on the values of competition and consumer choice.

Therefore from 1976 with the development of Islamic economics and the practice of Islamic finance combined with the liberalisation of social norms and the development of the economy in Saudi Arabia, this was the moment when, potentially, at an early stage in the history of Islamic finance, this model could have been embraced beyond OIC nations.

However, just ten years after the fire that damaged the Al-Aqsa mosque in Jerusalem, there was a dramatic siege in the holy city of Mecca which reset Saudi politics for decades and arguably impinged upon the very development of the Islamic finance industry itself.

The Siege of Mecca and the Aftermath: The Impact on the Islamic Finance Industry

In 1979, a group of pilgrims who were worshipping by the Kaa'ba in Mecca unexpectedly displayed guns and declared that the Mahdi was amongst them.

In the hadiths, the coming of the divinely guided one—the Mahdi—is foretold where the redeemer of Islam would rid the world of evil before the Day of Judgement. This concept is not directly cited within the Qur'ran.

There has been much academic analysis regarding the immediate and indirect causes of this insurrection. Reasons cited has included the income gap widening in Saudi Arabia with oil income transforming the nation and the fast pace of cultural changes changing day-to-day life. Comparisons have been made between the failed uprising in Mecca and the success of the 1979 Iranian Revolution in overthrowing a monarch who was out of touch and running a corrupt rentier economy.

After the initial shock of the siege wore off, Saudi forces eventually regained control of Mecca with the advice of French special forces. This siege happened in the same year where there was a Shi'a uprising in the Eastern Province of Saudi Arabia and where a Shi'a led revolution led to a theocratic government in Iran.

It was the siege of Mecca that had the greatest psychological shock on the Saudi regime. With the reputation of the King of Saudi Arabia as the Custodian of the Two Holy Places being undermined with the siege and the subsequent loss of life, it effectively stymied efforts by Crown Prince Fahd to liberalise the state which would have included plans for direct elections. King Khalid declared "*the solution to the religious upheaval was simple: more religion*".[59]

Women were no longer featured in the media and cinemas closed down whilst religious teaching in schools was enhanced and the security forces were invasive in everyday life.

Consequently, the ability to link the concept of Islamic finance with liberalisation was missed and this has contributed to a number of commentators, such as Timur Kuran, categorising Islamic finance as indelibly linked to fundamentalism. However, as we discovered in Chapters 2 and 9, Islamic finance shares features with laissez-faire economics and with social democracy and this stereotyping of Islamic finance is not justified when we take a holistic view of the industry.

Tensions Within Wahabbism

The 1979 insurrection demonstrated tensions within Wahhabi thought for whilst it inspired King Faisal to be open to dialogue, this same school of thought was associated with fundamentalism.

The influence of Wahhabi ideas led the Saudi Government to allocate at least US$87 billion for the overseas promotion of Wahhabism from 1973 to 2003.[60] This funding was highlighted repeatedly following the 11 September 2001 terrorist atrocities in the United States. The majority of the terrorists responsible for these acts had been Saudi citizens. This was how one American Senator viewed the consequences of the financial support for Wahhabism:

> The problem we are looking at today is the State-sponsored doctrine and funding of an extremist ideology that provides the recruiting grounds, support infrastructure and monetary life blood of today's international terrorists. The extremist ideology is Wahhabism, a major force behind terrorist groups, like al Qaeda, a group that, according to the FBI, and I am quoting, is the "number one terrorist threat to the U.S. today".[61]

This view was refuted by the Saudi Government and by some commentators such as Mohammed Alyahya, Fellow of the US think tank, the Atlantic Council:

> Blaming Wahhabism or Salafism for violent radicalism is not merely an intellectual slip or an injustice to Salafis, it is a distortion that stands to obstruct fighting violent radicalism and understanding its causes. Any religious ideology adopted by radicals is often a mask for other issues. Blaming or even destroying an ideology like Salafism will not end radicalism.[62]

We will consider further how the 9/11 tragedy directly impinged upon the Islamic finance industry in Chapter 11. However, we can say at this point in our discussion that a tension existed within Wahhabism as the path of dialogue and debate, as exemplified by King Faisal with the formation of the OIC, and others within this tradition which saw Islam within an exclusionary context where Muslim countries should be completely divorced from non-Muslim states.

One of those people who adopted the latter approach was Hamid al-'Ali. Born in 1960 in Saudi Arabia, he received his Masters degree in Qur'anic Sciences from the University of Medina. After moving to Kuwait, he became the Secretary General of the Kuwaiti Salafi Movement from 1997–2000, a professor of Islamic culture at the College of Islamic Education, and an Imam in Kuwait City.

In 2003, he received a two-year suspended prison sentence for publicly opposing Kuwait's stance on the Iraq war and he was later released in November 2005. In December 2005, he was acquitted by a Kuwaiti judge of conspiracy charges against the Kuwaiti government.

In 2012 Al-'Ali delivered a sermon at a mosque in Doha after being accused of being linked to a terrorist group—a step which led one British newspaper to condemn the Qatari Government for not taking action against Al-'Ali.[63]

When it came to Islamic finance, Al-'Ali called for an Islamic finance system to be separated from countries which did not adhere to Islam as the sole principle of government in order for "*the liberation of economics from its enslavement to non-Muslims*".[64]

Consequently, Al-'Ali proposed the following steps for Islamic finance:

- Banking Transactions: Establish Islamic banks in Muslim countries to promote banking transactions between Muslims, support investment in domestic projects that would benefit Muslim young people and open lines of credit specifically for Muslims.
- Monetary Policy: Establish an Islamic currency standard that would rival or exceed the international strength of the US dollar.
- Capital Investment: Keep capital inside Muslim countries, invest in Muslim projects and ensure capital is administered "*by Muslim hands.*"[65]

Admittedly, Al-'Ali's ideas are held by a minority of people and, ironically, these concepts would stop Islamic ideas as expressed within Islamic finance and Islamic economics from shaping the future direction of the key global challenges facing all of us such as the need to alleviate poverty, to tackle climate change and to work towards a more peaceful world.

Nonetheless, it would be wrong not to recognise the debate regarding Islamic finance within Wahabbi thought and how such controversies impact upon the perception and direction of the industry.

It is significant that the shocks of 1979 fundamentally changed the direction of Saudi society. The current Saudi Crown Prince, Mohammed bin Salman said, in March 2018 that before 1979, "*We were living a normal life like the rest of the Gulf countries, women were driving cars, there were movie theatres in Saudi Arabia*".[66]

> It is the Crown Prince who is now committed to changing Saudi society for the better including ensuring an enhanced role for Islamic finance within the domestic economy. However, internal Saudi politics may again impinge upon the Islamic finance industry.

Crown Prince Mohammed Bin Salman and Islamic Finance

> Lush with 600-year-old olive trees, landscaped gardens and swaying palms, the Ritz-Carlton, Riyadh is one of those Saudi Arabia luxury hotels that completely envelopes its discerning guests in majestic surroundings and discreet, attentive service.

So reads the website for the Ritz-Carlton Hotel. However, the service that was provided to guests in November 2017 was of a very different character. Crown Prince Mohammed bin Salman ordered many of the members of the governing Al Saud family to be imprisoned in the five-star hotel in what was described as an anti-corruption drive.

Notable detainees included Prince Alwaleed bin Talal, whose US$17 billion fortune had regularly placed the Prince in *Forbes* magazine's *Rich List*.

This was not the first time that corruption was allegedly said to be part and parcel of the Saudi economic model. Prince Bandar bin Sultan Al Saud seemed to condone corruption in a 2001 American television interview:

> Now, if you tell me that building this whole country and spending $350 billion out of $400 billion, that we had misused or got corrupted with $50 billion, I'll tell you 'Yes' but I'll take that anytime. But more important, who are you to tell me this? I mean, I see every time all the scandals here or in England or in Europe. What I'm trying to tell you is, so what? We did not invent corruption. This happened since Adam and Eve. I mean Adam and Eve were in heaven and they had hanky-panky and they had to go down to Earth. So, I mean this – this is human nature. But we are not as bad as you think.[67]

Critics of the Crown Prince, though, argued that this time the anti-corruption drive was a ruse to strengthen his position and weaken the influence of relatives linked to the late King Abdullah, who had died in 2015:

> Until a few days ago, Saudi was essentially a one-party state. The vast Al Saud family was deeply and broadly institutionalised, with members holding numerous levers of power. Now we're seeing a power-shift towards a narrow subset of the royal family.[68]

In letters that were circulated amongst some members of the royal family, one of the princes called on the remaining sons of Ibn Saud to unite in order to depose the Crown Prince:

> How can we accept that our fate is hostage to the whims of adolescents and the yearnings of impatient men.[69]

An American think tank noted that 2017 was the year when Saudi foreign and domestic policy took a decisive pivot away from the "safety first" approach which had marked, to varying degrees, the style of government adopted by rulers such as King Abdullah (1924–2015) and King Fahd (1921–2005):

> 2017 turned out to be an extraordinarily pivotal year for Saudi Arabia, including hosting President Trump on his first trip abroad as President, leading a blockade of rival Qatar, MBS's palace coup to become Crown Prince, the continued devastation of the Saudi-led coalitions war in Yemen, and MBS's detention of political rivals, just to name a few of the major developments in Saudi Arabia's domestic and foreign policies.

This same think tank also reported that the Kingdom used American lobbying firms to maintain its influence in the United States, especially when support for Saudi Arabia in Washington DC soured following the 2018 murder of Saudi journalist, Jamal Khashoggi at the Saudi consulate in Istanbul.[70]

However, whilst these actions were taking place, the Crown Prince was also leading the largest economic transformation of the country's economy since the discovery of oil in the 1930s with the Vision 2030 Strategy. Former CIA Director, David Patraeus, described Vision 2030 as a "*revolution .... not a transition*".[71]

This strategy included the initial public offering of Saudi Aramco in December 2019 which valued the oil firm at US$1.7 trillion. Later, in April 2020, the Saudi Government announced plans for a major privatisation programme.[72]

One of the key elements of the 2030 Strategy is to further embed the Islamic finance industry within the political economy of the nation:

> Enhancing the Islamic finance offerings in the Kingdom is among the key objectives of the program. The program considered two options to achieve this goal: an explicit initiative focusing solely on Islamic finance vs. relevant initiatives focusing on enhancing right Shari'ah compliant products within their domain. The program decided to go with the second option. Initiatives focusing on enhancing the current product offering (e.g., debt capital markets, savings products) will define right mechanisms to provide the necessary Shari'ah compliant offerings. This will enable the correct specialization within each domain and avoid overlap/cannibalization with conventional products that will be offered.[73]

Vision 2030 also emphasised the need for financial services cooperation to be widened across the Gulf Cooperation Council (GCC—which covers Saudi Arabia, United Arab Emirates, Kuwait, Bahrain, Qatar and Oman). With Saudi Arabia being the largest economy within the GCC the potential for a further step change with the development of the Islamic finance sector remained a tangible possibility.

The focus of Islamic finance within Vision 2030 is also linked to three other issues which the strategy has identified—the need for Saudi Arabia to strengthen its capital markets capability, the limited loan provision to small and medium sized enterprises (SMEs), the need to improve bank account provision for all Saudi citizens and to improve the savings rate for consumers.

The decision to list the IPO for Saudi Aramco with the Saudi stock exchange, Tadawul, when the listing was expected to be held in either London or New York, indicated a conscious decision by the Saudi Government to focus on capital markets enhancements within the kingdom—which could have a direct bearing on the provision of a range of Islamic finance models designed for business investment via Tadawul.

Vision 2030 has also identified that a significant proportion of the population does not hold bank accounts which is an unusual feature to observe within a developed economy. Only 74% of adults hold a bank account and the figure is even lower for women with only 61% of women holding bank accounts. In addition, Vision 2030 has identified that only 2% of SMEs gain commercial loans whilst the household savings ratio for Saudi citizens is only 2.4%.[74]

With Islamic finance having a prominent position within the Vision 2030 strategy, each of these issues could be addressed with the greater provision of Islamic finance bank accounts, enhancing savings products using Islamic finance investment models and by using key Islamic finance models to help diversify the Saudi economy away from its reliance on energy markets by strengthening domestic demand with a widening of the SME market base.

However, the prospects for the Islamic finance sector's development was not helped by the initial reaction of investors to the Ritz-Carlton detentions:

> "Half my Rolodex is in the Ritz right now. And they want me to invest there now? No way. The wall of money that was going to be deployed into the kingdom is falling apart" said one investor whilst another investor commented "One day we are sleeping at the Ritz-Carlton, excited about a new era. The next day they have turned the hotel into a prison — what sort of message does this send us? We some need stability." A banker is quoted to have said "The boss came back enthused. Now he's just wondering what the hell is going on there".[75]

It was expected that this incident could have been a short term blip with market confidence in the kingdom returning over time but, in September 2019, the Crown Prince told US media that the 2018 murder of Mr Khashoggi had involved Saudi officials as the perpetrators. Though Mohammed bin Salman denied personal involvement in the murder he did say "*I get all the responsibility because it happened under my watch*".[76]

The impact of the murder did affect markets and continued uncertainty with Saudi politics may impinge on market confidence which could hinder the significant growth potential of the Islamic finance sector in the kingdom and across the Gulf. However, an even more significant event has impacted the Saudi economy.

Saudi Arabia and the Gulf Monarchial States: Islamic Finance and Global Markets

On Monday 20 April 2020, the United States WTI oil price closed at—(minus) $37.63 per barrel.[77]

The next morning, Brent crude, the benchmark for global oil prices, fell below $20 a barrel—a drop of more than 20%—as concerns grew that global storage space was running out.

For Saudi Arabia, this was a worrying time for though the country was known to have the lowest costs in the world for oil production, it can only turn in a profit when the price of oil was above $20 a barrel and around 50% of Saudi Arabia's GDP was linked to oil revenues.[78]

Such a crash in oil prices shocked markets where it was getting to the state where, for a very short time, American producers were, in effect, paying purchasers to buy their oil.

The global economic lockdown caused by the COVID-19 outbreak was making itself felt in the corporate boardrooms of the major oil companies which led Fatih Birol of the International Energy Authority to declare that "*this will go down in history as Black April*".[79] Whilst this price drop was exceptional, it seemed to auger a period where there would be a decline in demand for oil stocks over the medium term.

The implications for Saudi Arabia was not lost on commentators:

> Saudi Arabia needs an US$80-per-barrel price to balance its budget, realize its plans to diversify its economy and sustain a heavily subsidized economy. In the balance is the stability of both the Russian and Saudi Arabian political systems and current regimes.[80]

This historic moment was blamed on the coronavirus contagion but this negative news for oil producers came on top of a warning from the International Monetary Fund (IMF) in February 2020 for the Persian Gulf region.

At a time when many global decision makers were still only dimly aware of the lives being lost to the virus in Wuhan, the IMF warned that Saudi Arabia and other Gulf Cooperation Council (GCC) oil producing countries had to speed up their response towards diversifying their economies.

With teenage Swedish climate change activist, Greta Thunberg, providing renewed momentum to the campaign for Governments to switch to renewable energy sources and, at the same time, an increase in oil production in the United States combined with an oil price spat between Saudi Arabia and Russia this was proving to be a heady mix for the Gulf—even before the coronavirus outbreak.

In its report, the IMF warned:

> In the context of broader goals of sustainability and sharing of exhaustible oil wealth with future generations, all GCC countries have recognized the lasting nature of their challenge and are already planning continued fiscal adjustment in the context of their broader strategic long-term visions. However, the expected speed and size of these consolidations in most countries may not be sufficient to stabilize their wealth. These adjustments need to be accelerated and sustained over a long period of time, in line with the expected path of hydrocarbon revenue. In illustrative simulations, long-term fiscal sustainability in the GCC requires the average non-oil primary fiscal deficit to decline from the present level of 44 percent of non-oil GDP to mid-single digits by 2060.[81]

Therefore, tough choices would have to be made sooner rather than later:

> Continued economic diversification will be important but would not suffice on its own. Countries will also need to step up their efforts to raise non-oil fiscal revenue, reduce government expenditure, and prioritize financial saving when economic returns on additional public investment are low. While fiscal starting positions are still strong in a global context in four of the six GCC countries, the longer-term fiscal challenges are substantial. The intergenerational distribution of wealth would be helped by an early start. Gradual fiscal adjustment would ease the burden on the current generation, but the size of required fiscal consolidation would be made larger and its burden transferred onto future generations who would inherit a lower stock of wealth.[82]

Such warnings had been made years before. In 2009, the UK Liberal Democrat politician, Vince Cable, argued that oil prices and the peg to the US dollar made Gulf nations particularly vulnerable to systemic risks:

> The Gulf states ... peg their currencies to the dollar, with consequences similar to China – not least growing inflation as a consequence of, in effect, adopting US monetary policy. But they are also different from China in that foreign assets are often privately owned and hidden. They differ, too, in that their economies depend upon oil exports, and the collapse in oil prices that we have seen in the latter part of 2008 may make their surplus savings short-lived.[83]

With the IMF warning that the region had 15 years to adjust, the regional newspaper, *Gulf News,* tried to reassure their readers in February 2020 with the headline "*Gulf states must not overreact on IMF report*".[84] Just a few months later the newspaper featured an altogether different headline for their worried subscribers, "*COVID-19: How to cope with debt in UAE after a pay cut*".[85]

However, the Gulf has proven to be an innovative and resilient region. Dubai was transformed into a major international financial hub in just a few decades and Qatar (admittedly with very large gas reserves) is on the verge of hosting the 2022 FIFA football World Cup whilst Manama is a thriving business centre.

The GCC nations of Saudi Arabia, United Arab Emirates, Qatar, Bahrain, Oman and Kuwait had been working, in advance of the 2020 crisis, to diversify their economies with some considerable success. A GCC common market had been achieved from 2008 and there had been discussions about a GCC single currency.

All this regional cooperation changed when, in 2017, Saudi Arabia led a multinational embargo against Qatar due to allegations that Qatar was backing terrorist groups. Qatar argued that it was merely expressing its own foreign policy which was more open to opposition groups in the Arab world, such as the Muslim Brotherhood—a stance which Saudi Arabia would not tolerate.

However, despite the ongoing tensions within the GCC (at the time of writing in 2020), there is one economic theme which does unite GCC nations—and that is Islamic finance. In slightly different ways each GCC nation has focused on Islamic finance as one of the key vehicles which will help drive the economic diversification of the regional economy.

It is, indeed, a feature of the political economic model of the Gulf. With the potential of a global decline in oil usage in the first half of the 2020s, following the pandemic, the focus on Islamic finance as a key driver for economic diversification may increase.

In addition, it is the engagement of Gulf investors in Islamic finance which helped entice London to market itself as a centre of Islamic finance expertise. In October 2013, the then UK Prime Minister, David Cameron, told an international Islamic finance conference in London:

> I don't just want London to be a great capital of Islamic finance in the Western world, I want London to stand alongside Dubai and Kuala Lumpur as one of the great capitals of Islamic finance anywhere in the world.

As for Saudi Arabia, some commentators argue that the kingdom could do even more to embrace Islamic finance to help the nation through this transitional period from a reliance on oil and gas. An indication that the Saudi Government was taking action to further utilise Islamic finance as a key vehicle for transforming the economy came in June 2020.

In that month, two Saudi Islamic banks, the National Commercial Bank and Samba Financial Group announced that they were engaged in their first tentative steps to finalise a merger.

This new merged bank would have assets of 802 billion riyals (US$214 billion). As the Saudi sovereign wealth fund were significant stakeholders in both banks, this is seen as an attempt by the Saudi state to create one of the largest Islamic banks in the world. Such a development would help position Saudi Arabia as one of the world's leading providers of Islamic finance products and services.

However, in May 2020, it was announced that 8.5% of Saudi reserves, which equated to US$40 billion, had been transferred to Saudi's sovereign wealth fund. This fund then used these monies to take advantage of the economic downturn in the United States, caused by the COVID-19 crisis, to buy shares in Disney, Facebook, Starbucks, Bank of America, Qualcomm, Berkshire Hathaway, Uber, Live Nation (events company), Carnival Corp (cruise liners) amongst other US stocks.

Tarek Fadlallah of Nomura Asset Management implied that this investment strategy was not the right course for Saudi Arabia to take in order to meet its on-coming domestic economic challenges. Fadlallah argued that the sovereign wealth fund was there for a "*rainy day*" and with the

COVID-19 crisis, "*this is clearly a rainy day*". Instead, Fadlallah argued, the sovereign wealth fund should be engaged in a "*programme of buying sukuks for companies who do not have assets for the capital market*".[86]

If Fadlallah's advice was ever followed, the impact of Islamic finance in terms of widening access to entrepreneurial finance for medium and large businesses in Saudi Arabia and across the region could prove to be transformational in embedding a robust and diverse business base which could innovate for the long term due to Islamic finance's risk sharing model.

In the future, when we consider Islamic finance's place in the global political economy, the diversification of the Gulf economies from a reliance on fossil fuel income streams to the provision of finance, services, tourism and manufacturing will be the key consideration.

United Arab Emirates and the Gulf States: Crossing the Finishing Line

An early misty spring morning in the Suffolk countryside is a moment to relish. The fresh breeze combined with the sound of galloping hooves is not an uncommon experience when horses are exercised by their trainers and stable hands.

Newmarket, a beautiful British country town, is just 65 miles from London and the history of the area included the visits of King Charles I (1600–1649) whose belief that he was chosen by God to lead the kingdom meant he was never going to compromise with the equally hard-nosed Parliamentarian, Oliver Cromwell—leading to the inevitability of the English Civil War.

Today, Newmarket owes its economic prosperity, in large part, to two contemporary monarchs. Queen Elizabeth II is passionate about horse racing and has visited the town on a regular basis to see her horses being trained.

Then there is Sheikh Mohammed bin Rashid Al Maktoum, the ruler of Dubai and the Vice President of the United Arab Emirates (UAE).

Sheikh Mohammed's interest in horse racing started from an early age:

> As a young man, Sheikh Mohammed was captivated by the power, elegance, speed and grace of horses and he rode bareback races with his friends on the sands of Jumeirah Beach.[87]

Whilst studying English in Cambridge, the Sheikh and Sheikh Hamdan Bin Rashid Al Maktoum, now the deputy ruler of Dubai and UAE Finance Minister, went to the 2000 Guineas race meeting in Newmarket.

Then, when he was in his 20s, Sheikh Mohammed bin Rashid Al Maktoum saw his horse, Hatta, win at Brighton by the Sussex coast. The Sheikh's commitment to British horse racing has grown ever since and now the town of Newmarket and the British horse racing industry's very prosperity is indelibly linked to the UAE Vice President.

One of the highlights of the Sheikh's horse racing career was in 2018 when on a sunny June day, Masar won the Derby at Epsom in Surrey. It was an impressive win (I was avidly watching the race on television ensconced on my mother's sofa) and I remember how the crowds roared and the television interviewer excitedly welcomed the Sheikh to the winning enclosure.

Today, Sheikh Mohammed is responsible for the Godolphin Stables at Newmarket and the Darley Stud thoroughbred management and breeding operation. Sheikh Mohammad also sponsors the annual Godolphin Stud and Stable Staff Awards, which celebrates the role of stud and stable staff around the UK and is organised by the British Horseracing Authority in conjunction with the *Racing Post* newspaper.

Sheikh Hamdan has also invested in both racing and breeding when he acquired significant operations in the UK and the Republic of Ireland. Over the decades, the Godolphin operation, with its signature sky blue colour, has spread beyond the UK to a stable in the Republic of Ireland, two stables in Dubai, three stables in Australia, three stables in the United States and a stable in Japan.

The horse racing industry is based on thoroughbreds from the Middle East including the Darley Arabia horse that was bought by Thomas Darley in Aleppo in 1704. It is these bloodlines that has aided the success of the Godolphin brand.

As Sheikh Mohammed has said:

> In the race for excellence there is no finish line.[88]

Amidst this success, some critics have argued that the sponsorship of horse racing promotes gambling which is against the strictures of Islam. Sheikh Mohammed has strongly denied he is involved in gambling and won damages from the British newspaper, the *Daily Mail*, in 2001 when the paper falsely claimed that the sheikh had personally gambled by laying a wager with a bookmaker.

The journalist, Robin Cherry, vividly described how the ban on gambling and the celebration of horse racing is combined during the classic Dubai Gold Cup meeting:

> Islam forbids gambling, of course, but all race attendees received a free "Pick Seven" ballot that they could use to choose their horses—and win up to $15,000 of prize money. Admission to the lawn was free. Between races, children played soccer. Some men unrolled mats on the grass and then settled to their knees, praying southwest toward Mecca before heading for the rail. Then the starting bell would ring, and the magnificent Arabian purebreds would barrel down the track, the thundering of their hooves mixing with the cheers of the crowd.[89]

It was no coincidence that the investment in horse racing and the rise of Islamic banking both began in the 1970s. This period witnessed a very high rise in the oil price and this increased wealth contributed towards the economic transformation of the Persian Gulf monarchical states.

The immediate trigger for this oil wealth was the 1973 Yom Kippur War which is also dubbed as the Ramadan War. In an attempt to regain territories lost in the Six Day War in 1967, Egyptian and Syrian forces launched a surprise attack against Israel on the Day of Atonement—Yom Kippur—the holiest day in the Jewish calendar. At a time when there was a lack of activity within Israel at this moment of reflection, invading forces struck and made significant gains.

Eventually, following the initial shock of the attack, Israeli forces counterattacked and made deep inroads in Egypt and Syria where Israeli forces were closing in on Cairo and Damascus. Eventually, mediation by the United States led to the withdrawal of the Israeli forces. Syria failed to regain the Golan Heights whilst Egypt did eventually regain the Sinai Peninsula, after the war, as the consequence of a peace treaty between Israel and Egypt as mediated by the United States.

It was at this time that the oil wealth of the Middle East increased. In response to the United States supplying defence equipment to Israel during the war, Iran, Iraq, Saudi Arabia, Qatar, Kuwait and the United Arab Emirates decided on 16 October 1973 to unilaterally increase the price of oil from $3.01 to $5.12 per barrel—a 70% increase. Then, on the very next day, these same nations announced that oil exports to the

United States and other countries supporting Israel would be reduced by 5% each month and there would be subsequent 5% cuts each month until support for Israel ceased.

In response, on 19 October 1973, US President Richard Nixon announced a $2.2 billion military and financial aid package for Israel. Within the next two days from this announcement, the decision to reduce oil exports led, instead, to an outright oil embargo of the United States and other countries supporting Israel ranging from apartheid South Africa to the Netherlands.

The steps taken by these nations can be seen, from one perspective, as part of a shift in the balance of power between the oil companies and the oil producing nations. In January 1973, oil prices were already on the rise when the posted price of Saudi Arabian light oil was $2.59 a barrel and by July 1973 it had increased to $2.95 a barrel. In 1970, Libya, Iran and Kuwait had won significant concessions from the oil companies.

However, it would be unfair to argue that the tactics of the oil exporting countries was primarily driven by the desire to increase income streams. As the then US Ambassador to Saudi Arabia, James Akins, had put it, King Faisal felt the embargo was inevitable:

> He *(Faisal)* was not happy he had to do it but there was never any question about it. It was never debated. In fact, Faisal told me at one time that if he hadn't imposed the embargo the Saudi people would have strongly objected. Faisal made several statements about this. He said, we are producing more oil than we need. We cannot rationally absorb the income we have from this oil production. We're only doing this because you've asked us to. And we will not continue unless there is some progress in restoring Arab lands. He made that point over and over again. They were sorry to have had to impose the embargo but we were sending arms to Israel during the war. We were flying planes from Germany straight into the occupied Sinai with military equipment. This was considered a hostile act against the Arabs. Then Congress voted for a massive increase of aid to Israel and that was the last straw. It made the embargo inevitable.[90]

On 22 October 1973 the United Nations brokered a ceasefire which went into effect three days later. However, on 22 December 1973, an Organisation of the Petroleum Exporting Countries (OPEC) meeting set the oil price at $11.65 a barrel. The increased income was consequential for in 1970 oil exports generated $7.7 billion for OPEC members and by 1974 this revenue had increased to $88.8 billion.

In March 1974, OPEC ended the embargo against the United States and in June 1974 the embargo against the other nations supporting Israel was also lifted thereby restoring exports to September 1973 levels.

Alongside the increase in oil revenue, which drove forward the establishment of Islamic banking, was the culmination of British decolonisation. After much toing and froing in London, the UK Government announced in 1968 that its colonial role and its stationing of naval forces in the Persian Gulf would cease in 1971.

With international boundaries in flux and the concern from the Gulf monarchies that part or all of their territories could be picked off by larger neighbouring countries, such as Iran, during the power vacuum left by Britain there was a push to form a federation of monarchical states.

Whilst the effort was not altogether successful, it did lead to the formation of the United Arab Emirates (UAE) bringing together Dubai, Abu Dhabi, Ajman, Fujairah, Ras al Khaimah, Sharjah and Umm al Quwain. This was, by no means, an easy process, as Sheikh Mohammed bin Rashid Al Maktoum saw for himself, with his father, as the leader of Dubai, striving to develop a strategic alliance with the ruler of Abu Dhabi:

> There were so many obstacles that faced the Union. In the end they came out for noon prayers and after that they went back for a long discussion. And I heard them as I was near to them. I heard Rashid say to Zayed "With God's blessing, you are the President" and Zayed said "With God's blessing, we lay the foundation stone and the wall will be built, God willing".[91]

The formation of the UAE and the other Gulf monarchical states with, at the same time, a large increase in oil revenue, led to a re-evaluation within the elites of the region as to the role, purpose and status of the Gulf within geopolitics and the global economy. It was at that moment that Islamic banking was formally born.

In 1975, the Dubai Islamic Bank (DIB) was established followed shortly thereafter, in 1977, by the formation of the Faisal Islamic Bank of Egypt, the Faisal Islamic Bank of Sudan, the Kuwait Finance House and the Jordan Islamic Bank. Then in 1979 the Bahrain Islamic Bank was founded.

Further Islamic banks were formed with Islami Bank Bangladesh and Tadamon Islamic Bank Sudan in 1983 and Albaraka Islamic Investment Bank in 1984. UAE investment was crucial to the success of these banks.

Analysts of the region often define the Gulf monarchical nations as rentier states where wealth is generated by the possession of a natural resource which is produced and sold with relatively minimal productive activity by a small number of workers.

Such a characterisation is understandable when, at first glance, we consider the formation of the UAE. For despite a coup in Sharjah in 1972 and continued political instability in this emirate in 1987 and 1990 combined with the initial reluctance of Ras al Khaimah to join the United Arab Emirates for fear that it may be dominated by Abu Dhabi and Dubai, the UAE held together. It was the oil wealth of Abu Dhabi that helped solidify this new political nation.

However, it would not be fair to completely define the region by using the prism of rentier state analysis. The then ruler of Dubai, Sheikh Rashid bin Saeed Al Maktoum (Sheikh Mohammed's father) aimed to diversify the economy of Dubai so that his emirate did not just focus on its port but also upon financial services and tourism. This was a further impetus to drive forward the Islamic finance industry.

Saeed bin Ahmed Al Lootah, the founder of DIB has said it was his religious principles which inspired him to form the bank:

> I was raised on Islamic teachings and these say that *riba* cannot be touched. Travelling to many countries I saw how people transacted with banks and did their business and trading. Over here in Dubai there were also these riba banks. And nobody said anything, nobody objected. That made me think: Why do we have to accept their banking and financial system? Why don't we use Islamic principles? People can buy and sell and do financing, all of that without using riba.[92]

However, Al Lootah also stated that he sought guidance from Sheikh Rashid bin Saeed Al Maktoum who advised Al Lootah to work out the details of the proposal and subsequently, after detailed work had been undertaken, the UAE Currency Board approved the formation of the DIB.

In 1979, Dubai hosted the world's first ever Islamic banking conference. It was at this event that scholars approved the use of murabaha—one of the most important contract models in Islamic finance.[93]

Over the years, the other Gulf monarchical states have developed their own Islamic finance industries. The largest Islamic bank operating in Bahrain is the Saudi led Al-Baraka Bank Group which had assets of

US$24.6 billion as of the first half of 2018. Shares in this group were floated on the Bahraini stock exchange.

Also in the Bahraini market space is Ithmaar Bank, which held assets of BD3.25bn (US$8.6bn) as of the second half of 2018. Again in Bahrain is the Al Salam Bank, with assets of BD1.62bn (US$4.3bn). Its shares are also traded on the Bahrain stock exchange. Then, in 2017, the Central Bank of Bahrain established an online regulatory sandbox. This is a virtual space which facilitates the development of fintech through safe testing of innovative products, services, business models and delivery mechanisms, without the automatic application of regulatory and financial consequences.

In other words, financial products and services based on new technologies, or modifications of existing technologies, are tested in the sandbox without the burden of time-consuming regulations and licencing requirements. Saudi Arabia adopted a similar sandbox approach from 2008.

In 2019, Kuwait also decided to innovate to encourage the growth of fintech in its kingdom whilst Qatar had also been developing its own regulatory approach which caused some upset amongst market participants.[94]

However, it is Dubai that has been particularly active in attempting to keep its competitive edge in fintech and the Islamic finance market. Commins argue that one of the motivations for Dubai's efforts in the 2000s related to the internal tensions which continued to linger within the UAE:

> Dubai emerged from relative obscurity to become known as a glitzy city-state perched on the edge of Arabia. Slender skyscrapers, man-made residential islands in the shape of palm trees and indoor ski slopes made Dubai a global brand for conspicuous consumption and leisure. The whimsical image was part of a serious strategy to wean the emirate from dependence on oil by developing heavy industry using cheap energy and seeking overseas investment opportunities. Dubai's Al Maktoum rulers were determined to develop an economic foundation that would enable them to keep Abu Dhabi at arm's length.[95]

The population of the UAE has risen by over 10,000% since the 1960s with Dubai having more skyscrapers per square mile than anywhere else on Earth, having the world's largest shopping mall, hosting the world's biggest water show and is home to the world's tallest tower—the Burj Khalifa.

It was in this context that Dubai decided that the World Expo, which was to be held in its emirate in 2020, would feature an Islamic finance conference thereby heralding the role of the sector as a key part of the global political economy. As one of the sponsors put it:

> Emirates Islamic is proud to be the Official Islamic Banking Partner for Expo 2020 Dubai. Aligned with Expo 2020 Dubai's theme of 'Connecting Minds, Creating the Future', Emirates Islamic is dedicated to providing innovative Islamic banking products and services and to create sustainable solutions for our customers.[96]

However, this forward-looking approach as adopted by the Dubai Government had to be seen against growing concerns as to the actions of the UAE Government within the nation and in terms of its foreign policy. In reference to the murder of the Saudi journalist, Jamal Khashoggi, in the Saudi consulate in Istanbul in 2018, one US think tank cast aspersions against the UAE's recent actions:

> While the Emiratis had nothing to do with Khashoggi's murder, they've worked hand-in-hand with the Saudis in the devastating war in Yemen. Emirati involvement in Yemen—including funding a targeted assassination program there—has contributed to the war there becoming the world's worst humanitarian crisis. And, the UAE, just like Saudi Arabia, has an abhorrent human rights record—arbitrarily detaining and disappearing its own citizens, and unlawfully imprisoning Western academics.[97]

This same think tank claimed that the UAE was actively lobbying in Washington DC to maintain its credentials as a reliable ally of the United States despite growing criticism that the country was receiving from some quarters. This lobbying is said to include the:

> considerable influence that Abu Dhabi Crown Prince Mohammed bin Zayed appears to hold within the Trump administration and the sway of the UAE's Yousef al Otabia, who has been called "Washington's most powerful ambassador," due in no small part to his notoriously lavish parties.[98]

In 2019, UAE withdrew its forces from Yemen as it began to focus attention on the World Expo in Dubai. However, the COVID-19 outbreak delayed the start of the Expo to October 2021. The UAE continued to develop its own distinct foreign policy when it made the historic decision, via the offices of US President Donald Trump, to establish diplomatic relations with Israel in August 2020. Later that year Bahrain also announced its intentions to ensure the nation had diplomatic ties with Israel.

Whilst international attention in the first half of 2020 was naturally focused on the public health and economic implications of the novel coronavirus, Dubai heralded the start of the holy month of Ramadan to announce a new initiative to enhance its reputation as the leading international centre for Islamic finance—the unified global legal and legislative framework for the Islamic finance sector.

In May 2020, the UAE Ministry of Finance, the Islamic Development Bank (IsDB) and the Dubai Islamic Economy Development Centre (DIEDC) announced plans for a global legislative framework in order to attain improved standardisation within the sector.

A memorandum of understanding was signed between DIEDC and the Accounting and Auditing Organisation for Islamic Financial Institutions (AAOIFI), enabling DIEDC to use AAOIFI's standards as a reference in building the international legal framework with the guidance of the Ministry of Finance and IsDB.

The international legal firm, Norton Rose Fulbright, whose expertise in Islamic finance is well known within the industry, were appointed to help draft the code. The ambitions of this project were made clear by the UAE Economy Minister and DIEDC Chairman, Sultan bin Saeed Al Mansouri:

> The legislative framework for Islamic economy will lead to a vertical and horizontal expansion of the sector globally due to the number of member countries in the Islamic Development Bank. This will serve as a crucial factor in triggering the steady and rapid growth of Islamic finance. Enabling and standardising legislations provides the guarantees and trust needed to build smoother and stronger business relations. New courts are expected to be established worldwide to settle Islamic financial disputes according to the new unified legislative framework.[99]

This is yet another indication that the Islamic finance industry, whilst still in its formative stage, may be coming of age and, as a consequence, its role in the political economy of a range of nations around the world could prove to be particularly consequential.

The impact that this announcement may have on shaping the role of Islamic finance within the wider global political economy could be immense. Instead of the sector being seen as an interesting niche area for academic study, Islamic finance, once the complex compliance issues were finally dealt with[100] could be seen as a more significant model which would play a key part in the operation of the global economy alongside the concepts of Keynesianism and monetarism.

However, before we get carried away, this is also an audacious attempt by the UAE, and Dubai in particular, to lead developments within the sector outside of the established multilateral organisations such as AAOIFI. Whilst a memorandum of understanding with AAOIFI has been agreed for this work to take place, Dubai's deputy ruler, Sheikh Hamdan bin Rashid Al Maktoum, has acknowledged that the proposed draft framework would have to be approved by the multilateral institutions before it could come into force.

The question is whether Malaysia, which is also a leader in Islamic finance, would want to cede its leadership role and defer to a UAE led initiative which may enhance the UAE's position in Islamic finance at the expense of Malaysia. As Saudi Arabia has made much of the running in the industry, will the kingdom see this move as potentially weakening its leadership role which has been demonstrated time and again including with the influential work of the OIC's Fiqh Academy based in Saudi Arabia.[101]

As for the multilateral institutions themselves, will they feel bounced by the UAE initiative to accept the framework and how will the framework reconcile the different Sunni fiqh schools?

These are very difficult questions which lies at the heart of this new initiative and the risk for Dubai in taking on this challenge, if it fails, is clear for its reputation as the self-styled "*capital*" of Islamic finance.

However, this bold approach reflects the attitude of Sheikh Mohammed bin Rashid Al Maktoum:

> To ensure success, we have to join the race and win. After all, no-one ever remembers who came second – not even the second man to climb Everest or to walk on the moon![102]

Only time will tell whether the decision to announce plans for a unified global framework for Islamic finance will be as successful in being finalised and crossing the finishing line as Sheikh Mohammed's horses have been at winning races.

Iran

The global Islamic finance industry is predicated upon Sunni concepts.

It is Sunni fiqh schools which scholars in the industry refer to when reaching judgements on new product lines.

It is Sunni ideas which influence thinking at the primary Islamic finance multilateral institutions such as the OIC's Fiqh Academy based in Jeddah, the Islamic Financial Services Board based in Kuala Lumpur or the Auditing and Accounting Organisation for Islamic Financial Institutions (AAOIFI) based in Manama.[103]

The Islamic finance industry is geared towards meeting the needs of Sunni Muslims in core markets such as Turkey, Saudi Arabia, UAE, Kuwait, Qatar, Egypt, Sudan, Pakistan, Bangladesh, Malaysia, Indonesia and Brunei Darussalam.

It is Iran with a majority Shi'a Muslim population which sees and implements Islamic finance practices from a purely Shi'a perspective. As we discussed in Chapter 2, Jafari fiqh is distinct from Sunni fiqh as it recognises rational intellect or reasoning (aql) as a source of reaching judgements under shari'a law. Aql is a concept that is viewed as being capable of inferring judgments drawn from both pure and practical reason. Whatever is judged necessary by reason is also judged necessary by revelation.

Ali Shariati

The link between Islam and economics was made most forcefully in Iran by an academic who had no sympathy with the religious establishment. Ali Shariati (1933–1977) was an academic who returned time and again to the iniquities of capitalism and spoke of the promise of Islam to provide spiritual growth and fulfilment.

Unlike the approach adopted within Sunni Islam, he would not defer to religious scholars but he also believed in individuals gaining a greater understanding of the spiritual plane without any mediation from Shi'a religious figures.

Shariati often referred to Abu Zarr, one of the earliest Muslims, who had personally heard the Prophet speak of the revelation. There is a difference of view between Sunni and Shi'a Islam as to the role and actions of Abu Zarr. Shariati drew on the Shi'a perspective on the story of Abu Zarr and connected this to a critique of 1970s Iran.

Shariati described Abu Zarr as saying:

> I am perplexed by a person who finds no bread in his house. How is it that he does not rise against the people with his sword unsheathed.[104]

Such comments drew a parallel with the opulence which surrounded the Shah of Iran with the decline in living standards for the majority of the Iranian people. Shariati, though, continued to cite the narrative of Abu Zarr who objected to the financial grandeur which was accrued by Caliph Uthman (this is the view of Shi'a Islam where a very different view of these events is recorded within Sunni Islam).

In a play under Shariati's direction, the character of Abu Zarr proclaimed that all property belongs to God's subjects—an interpretation which was condemned by both Sunni scholars and Shi'a religious leaders.

Shariati gave his description as to how Abu Zarr viewed Uthman:

> The humiliated working masses and the helpless were suppressed under the heels of usurers, slave merchants, the wealthy and aristocrats.

This could be seen as more of a critique against the Shah's regime rather than an analysis of early Islamic history. However, this next passage, where Abu Zarr is accusing Uthman of breaching the code of Islamic justice, also reflects Shariati's perspective as to how Islam could inform the constructs of the political economy:

> This capital, wealth, gold and silver which you have hoarded must be equally divided among all Muslims. In Islam's economic and ethical system, everyone must share in the others' benefits and in all blessings of life.[105]

It is the story of Cain and Abel where Shariati drew direct comparisons to late twentieth century capitalism. Cain and Abel were the sons of Adam and Eve. Cain, who was the first born, was a farmer whilst Abel was a shepherd. Both brothers gave their offerings to God and God preferred the offering from Abel. In a fit of jealous rage, Cain murdered Abel. God sent Cain on a life of wandering in penance for his sins.

This account, which is shared by Judaism and Christianity as well as Islam, was used by Shariati as a parable against capitalism. Cain is viewed as the capitalist landowner and subsequent generations of capitalists who were subjugating the heirs of Abel. These heirs wanted to share private property. The heirs of Cain wanted to gobble up private property:

> It is the responsibility of every individual in every age to determine his stance in the constant struggle between the two wings we have described and not to remain a spectator. The end of time will come when Cain dies and the system of Abel is established anew.[106]

Despite this visionary depiction, Shariati's zeal for change did not include a role for the Shi'a religious leaders:

> Our mosques, the revolutionary left and our preachers work for the benefit of the deprived people and are against the lavish and lush. But our jurists who teach jurisprudence and giver verdicts are right wingers, capitalists and conservative. In short our fiqh works for capitalism.[107]

Shariati fled Iran to escape from the Shah's security forces and sought sanctuary in the port city of Southampton in the United Kingdom. Tragedy struck when, at the age of just 41, Shariati died from a heart attack.

By the time of his death, Shariati had helped prepare the ground for what became the 1979 Iranian Revolution. Shariati's ideals of Islam shaping a new economic system was supported across the nation. However, despite his fierce anti-clericalism, it was the Shi'a religious establishment who successfully promoted an Islamic economic system across Iran.

Mohammed Baqir al-Sadr

Whilst Shariati regaled against the clerics, it was a senior Iraqi Shi'a cleric who had significant influence over the future leader of Iran, Ayatollah Ruhollah Khomeini.

Mohammed Baqir al-Sadr (1935–1980) was from a prestigious clerical family. His father was Grand Ayatollah Haydar al-Sadr (1891–1937). It is said that al-Sadr's lineage went back to the seventh Imam of Shi'a Islam, Musa ibn Ja'far al-Kadhim (745–799).

Though a number of people would argue that al-Sadr was always committed towards political struggle, this is not a unanimous view:

> As a religious jurist, he was constrained to side with those people who needed his guidance and demanded his leadership against tyranny. He was probably never consulted by the leaders in Iran or those of the Islamic movement in Iraq.[108]

Al Sadr was a highly respected figure in Shi'a Islam. It was Al-Sadr who wanted to improve the training of religious scholars and, to this end, he designed text books for different ages and levels of understanding. It was his leadership of the Iraqi Da'wa Party[109] that led him into conflict with the largely secular Ba'athist regime.[110]

By the 1970s, the Ba'ath Party in Iraq was running a security state and the military tenor of state institutions led to fierce reprisals against anyone who showed any form of dissent. At first, the Ba'ath Party was reticent to act against senior Shi'a clerics due to the public backlash against the regime that such actions could cause.

The success of Khomeini in establishing a theocracy in Iran in 1979, however, changed the calculus of Saddam Hussein, who had gained power following a videotaped purge of officials which he had presided over at a party gathering earlier that year.

In 1980, Saddam Hussein ordered the execution of al-Sadr and his sister, Sayyidah Bint al-Huda, who was also at the forefront of anti-Baathist protests in Iraq.

Al-Sadr continues to be remembered with much solemnity where his struggle is linked to contemporary events. For example, thousands of mourners gathered at a bridge in the Iraqi city of Basra, with the bridge now known as the Shaheed Mohammed Baqir al-Sadr Bridge, in January 2019, to pay respects to the body of Abu Mahdi al-Muhandis, the slain leader of Hashed al-Shaabi, an Iraqi paramilitary force which had close ties to Iran.

Iranian media outlets continue to recall the deaths of Mohammed Baqir al-Sadr and Sayyidah Bint al-Huda whilst the *Tehran Times* went out of its way to note that the day in 2003 when US forces tore down the 16 foot statue of Saddam Hussein in Firdaus Square in Baghdad happened to be the same day as the 1980 executions.[111]

It was al-Sadr's contribution to Islamic economic theory which has had a significant impact in shaping the fiscal and monetary policies of the Islamic Republic of Iran. A reading of al-Sadr's detailed Iqistiduna (Our Economy) offers a critique of laissez-faire capitalism and Communism. It is al-Sadr's perspective on Islamic economics which had some synergies with social democratic thought.

Al-Sadr presented the analysis that the concept of khalifah or vice-regency (as discussed in Chapter 6) directs how capitalism is viewed within an Islamic context:

> The Islamic doctrinal belief that human society has passed from (the instinctive and natural stage to) the stage of reason and reflection ruled, expresses the Islamic concept of human society. The Islamic doctrinal belief that the ownership of goods and property is not the personal right of man but devolves upon him by virtue of the process of his appointment to the vicegerency of God reflects the specific Islamic concept about a definite legislation the establishment of the institution of private property, according to the Islamic conception the goods and property are the goods and property of Allāh in their entirety and God appoints sometimes individuals as His vice regents for the management of the goods and property. The conception expresses by this that man's right to property is a right which he holds by virtue of a legislative act which appoints him to the viceregency of God in respect of it (that is he holds it as trust from God).[112]

Al-Sadr also provided an interesting analysis as to how the nature of Islamic economics provides some form of certainty in business affairs. This point is elucidated upon by consideration that the means of production is not about the production of assets but, instead, the production of utility to serve wider business cycle objectives:

> The other conception, borrowed in advance by us from the future discussion is the view of Islam concerning exchange as one of the phenomena of economic life. According to it, the exchange by its original nature constitutes a branch of production and for when a merchant sells the products of another person he thereby shares in the process of production. Production is always a production of utility and service not a production of matter. Material or substance, cannot be created anew for the commodity produced and the preparation of it for the delivery of it to the hands of consumers, realize anew rather a commodity has no utility vis-à-vis the consumers without this preparation of it. Every tendency of exchange,

> which time distances it far from its true occurrence and renders it an intrusive operation meant only for the beneficiary and results in the lengthening of the distance between the commodity and its consumers, is an anomalous tendency differing from the nature of the function of the exchange.[113]

Al-Sadr was not doctrinaire in his economic beliefs. In fact, he adopted an agile approach within the framework of Islamic economics, where the operation of economic policy could take account of contemporary conditions without recourse to the socio-economic environment which existed at the time of the Prophet. From that point alone, such a stance is distinct from Sunni salafist thought (as discussed earlier in this chapter). To reach this conclusion, he considered the role of Muhammed as the Prophet separately from his role as Caliph:

> The Prophet did not issue them (decisions) in his capacity, as the promulgator of the permanently established injunctions (which admit no alteration, change or modification) but in the sense of his being a ruler and guardian of the Muslims. Then as such they cannot be considered a permanent part of the economic doctrine of Islam.[114]

Al-Sadr also argued for reasoning or ijtihad to be considered when defining economic thought as compared to qiyas (analogy) or other uṣūl al-fiqh (methodologies) used in fiqh whilst emphasising, again, the need to be agile in assessing economic policy:

> The form of the economic doctrine which we will create since it depends upon the Islamic (economic) rules and Islamic (economic) conceptions and inasmuch as these rules and conceptions depend upon a form of result of a particular ijtihād in the understanding of the text which comprise these rules and conception and the method of arranging these text and bringing them together, will be a reflection of a definite ijtihād it cannot be decided with a finality that the form is an actual form of Islamic economic doctrine (system) since error in ijtihād is possible so on account of that it is possible that different mujtahid (one who exercises ijtihād that is consensus and independent nature of opinion and judgement) might present different forms of Islamic economic doctrine (system) in accordance with their diverse ijtihād. All these forms will be considered as forms of Islamic economic doctrine (system) because they represent exercise of the process of ijtihād allowed and acknowledged by Islam and patterns and norms (rules) of which it has formed.[115]

Al-Sadr also challenged the starting point for the consideration of economic policy. In an analysis of capitalist models and Communist thought, the emphasis is placed upon the means of production. The argument goes that once a full understanding of the means of production has been assessed then the issue of how wealth is distributed can be considered as a pivotal but second order issue as the means of production creates the wealth in the first place.

Lord Jones, the former head of the British business lobby group, the Confederation of British Industry (CBI), often cites how production processes are the "*wealth creators*" and Government should recognise what he sees as a fact before other policy considerations are factored in:

> So, at the CBI, I would get onto the shop floor of a manufacturing facility and shout out loud 'this is where money is made – making things!' .... It forged in me a deep respect for their efforts, and I also wanted the politicians and civil servants who imposed the festoons of red tape around these creative risk takers to understand how easy it is to strangle our wealth creators and cut off the very lifeblood of our country.[116]

Al-Sadr argued that, in fact, it is the distribution of incomes and resources that comes before production as this is the distribution which makes production possible. Therefore, far from other considerations, such as aiming for the economy to tackle social ills, being distinct from wealth creation, it is the very basis of preparing the ground for production to take place in the first place:

> ... the distribution became the starting point or first stage in the Islamic system of economy instead of production as is done in the traditional political economy for the very distribution of the sources takes place before the operation of the production and every organization which is connected with the operation of production itself is reduced to the second stage.[117]

Whilst it is very fair to say that there is not much in common between Jones and Al-Sadr in terms of the milieus which they operated within and the differences between their formative experiences, it is worth seeing this distinction between the two as the different concepts do have some bearing on the contemporary differences between some forms of capitalism and some contemporary concepts which exists in Shi'a economic thought.

Al-Sadr also took an approach to tackling poverty which has some connection with social democratic thought. Al-Sadr argued that the State helping to alleviate poverty in one country would not be on a par with poverty alleviation in another country as there would be different expectations as to what is or is not poverty depending upon the state of development inherent in each country:

> … we learn that Islam has not accorded an absolute sense and fixed implication to all cases and circumstances of poverty. For instance, it cannot be held that inability of satisfying simple basic need constitutes poverty. But it has rendered manner of living not of reaching up to the living standard of people a meaning of poverty and the actual purport of poverty will be enlarged commensurate with what raises the standard of living, for, in such a case, lagging behind the pace of this rise of the standard of living would constitute poverty, if, for instance, people are accustomed to have an independent house of their own as a result of the expansion of civilization and the flourishing condition of the country a family's not having an independent house of their own in that country would constitute a kind of poverty while in a country which has not reached such a standard of ease and comfort of life, a family's want of an independent house of its own would not constitute to be poverty.[118]

As it happens, this reflects the view by some academics that so-called 'generous' welfare systems can contribute to wider macroeconomic enhancements:

> We might ask the—maybe naïve—question: If it was true that receiving generous benefits from the state keeps unemployed people from looking for a job, why does a country with generous benefits such as Denmark not have dramatically higher unemployment levels than a country with stingy benefits such as the United Sates? The answer, as some research suggests, is that rather than only providing disincentives to work, benefits can also help unemployed people find a better job. This happens in two ways. First, having a financial buffer for themselves and their families enables jobseekers to wait for a job offer that matches their skills and requirements instead of having to take the first offer that comes their way. Eventually that means that jobs and employees have a better fit, which reduces the likelihood of quick employee turnover. Second, benefits provide jobseekers with the time and means to invest in their human capital. This increases their skill level and their employability which again will enable them to find a good job that they can and will keep for a longer time. Through these mechanisms,

> the safety net of the welfare state thus can be seen to work as a trampoline rather than a hammock.[119]

This is not to say that al-Sadr was a social democrat—far from it. Al Sadr praised the establishment of a theocratic government in Iran. When it came to economic policy, Al-Sadr took a nuanced approach. Consequently, Al-Sadr backed the risk sharing model of Islamic finance as represented within the global Islamic finance industry industry by the mudaraba and musharaka contract models.

Whilst Al-Sadr influenced the leader of the Iranian Revolution, Ruhollah Khomeini, on economics, he also influenced the Iranian Revolution with his ideas as to the ideal form of theocratic government. It was this concept, through the Guardian of the Jurist principle that was to shape modern Iran—and establish a shari'a compliant banking system across the country.

Wilāyat al-Faqīh—Guardianship of the Jurist

> The only thing I have sought in my life is to make the establishment of an Islamic government on earth possible. Since it has been formed in Iran under the leadership of Imam (Khomeini) it makes no difference to me whether I am alive or dead because the dream I wanted to attain and the hope I wanted to achieve have come true, thanks to God.[120]

These were the defiant words of al Sadr to his Iraqi interrogators in the period leading up to his execution.

This belief in theocracy stems from the differences in Shi'a Twelver Islam as compared to Sunni Islam, where religious guidance is required before the arrival of the hidden Iman. This reflects the consideration of spiritual concepts in Shi'a Islam which do not bear exact parallels with Sunni Islam.

This division is not altogether clear cut as in 2014 Abu Bakr al-Baghdadi (1971–2019) declared himself in a quasi-religious role as a 'caliph' when so-called Islamic State seized areas of Syria and Iraq which have since been reconquered. Al-Baghdadi identified his relatively small group of followers as 'true' Sunni believers.

How did Ayatollah Ruhollah Khomeini (1902–1989) view economic policy in Iran through the prism of Wilāyat al-Faqīh?

In the period leading up to the 1979 revolution, there was uncertainty inside and outside Iran as to what kind of governance would be introduced by a Khomeini shaped administration.

The US administration of President Jimmy Carter were blindsided by the fall of the Shah and was surprised by the taking of American hostages from the US Embassy (the crisis began in 1979 and ended with the release of the hostages ending in January 1981 during the inauguration of Carter's successor as President—Ronald Reagan).

The then CIA Director, Stansfield Turner, later explained the lack of preparedness on the American side:

> We let him *(President Carter)* down badly with respect to our coverage of the Iranian scene. We had not appreciated how shaky the Shah's political foundation was; did not know that the Shah was terminally ill; did not understand who Khomeini was and the support his movement had; did not have a clue as to who the hostage-takers were or what their objective was; and could not pinpoint within the embassy where the hostages were being held and under what conditions. As far as our failure to judge the Shah's position more accurately, we were just plain asleep.[121]

As it happened, some of Khomeini's closest associates were also unaware of their leader's plans. Abolhassan Bani-Sadr was the first President of the newly installed Islamic Republic of Iran before he was obliged to flee the country when Khomeini and his allies turned against him. Bani-Sadr, who wanted to introduce Islamic economics as the governing principle of the Iranian Government, spoke of the policy stance of the Ayatollah when Khomeini was in exile in France:

> France was the crossroads of ideas and information, which is why he picked it after Kuwait refused to take him. When he was in France he was on the side of freedom. He was scared that the movement wouldn't reach its conclusion and he'd be forced to stay there.

However, Bani-Sadr spoke of his shock when he recalled a conversation the two men had in Qom, shortly after Khomeini's return to Iran:

> (Khomeini) told me he had said things in France that were convenient, but that he was not locked into everything he had said there and that if he felt it necessary to say the opposite he would. For me it was a very, very bitter moment.[122]

The concept of guardianship of the jurist was justified by Khomeini by the period before the appearance of the Hidden Imam and also the khalifah or trusteeship role of humanity on Earth. At the same time, Khomeini seemed to place some limits upon the exact roles of jurists in such a system of governance:

> When we say that after the Occultation, the just faqih (jurist) has the same authority that the Most Noble Messenger and the Imams had, do not imagine that the status of the faqih is identical to that of the Imams and the Prophet. For here we are not speaking of status, but rather of function. By "authority" we mean government, the administration of the country, and the implementation of the sacred laws of the shari'a.
>
> The spiritual status of the Imam is the universal divine viceregency that is sometimes mentioned by the Imams (peace be upon them). It is a viceregency pertaining to the whole of creation, by virtue of which all the atoms in the universe humble themselves before the holder of authority. It is one of the essential beliefs of our Shi'i school that no one can attain the spiritual status of the Imams, not even the cherubim or the prophets.[123]

In practice, the Supreme Leader oversaw the governance of the country.

There are elections for the Presidency and for Parliamentarians but individuals are vetted before they can become candidates. Nonetheless, there is a form of hybrid democracy within Iran, though the threats by the successor to Khomeini as Supreme Leader, Ali Khamenei, in 2009 to Mir-Hossein Mousavi and his supporters to cease uttering their vote rigging allegations concerning for the Presidential election of that year indicates the significant powers the Supreme Leader has.

However other analysts have argued that the system of government is more nuanced than this characterisation would give credit for. For instance, when Mahmoud Ahmadinejad was President from 2005 to 2013, he was described by some commentators as a puppet of Ayatollah Khamenei. The truth was rather more nuanced than that:

> He is even the president who has taken on the Supreme Leader. Despite his failure to take control of the Ministry of Intelligence, Ahmadinejad has pressed his claim for executive authority, not through a direct challenge to Khamenei, but through a series of administrative and political manoeuvres.[124]

It is this form of court politics which, as we shall see, has had a knock-on impact on the nature and form of Islamic economic policy in Iran.

Nonetheless, it is clear that Wilāyat al-Faqīh does impact on the construct of Islamic finance in Iran due to the constitutional role of the Supreme Leader in overseeing economic affairs.

This does not mean that this form of Wilāyat al-Faqīh is not without controversy in Shi'a Islam. There have been a number of Shi'a jurists who did not view the concept of the guardianship of the jurist in the same way as Khomeini. This included Ayatollah Hussein-Ali Montazeri (1922–2009) who was expected to succeed Khomeini as Supreme Leader until he was demoted just months before Khomeini's death. Montazeri once remarked of the Supreme Leader, Ali Khamenei:

> You are not of the rank and stature of a highest religious authority.[125]

Iran backed Hezbollah (Party of God) in Lebanon has also adopted the Wilāyat al-Faqīh concept but has adapted it to take account of the religious and ethnic diversity in Lebanon.

In February 1985, Hezbollah published an open letter which differentiated Wilāyat al-Faqīh from the Iranian Government position. Hezbollah stated in its Open Letter that its aims included:

> ... adopting a system that the people establish of their own free will and choice.[126]

Unlike Hezbollah, it is the uncompromising version of Wilāyat al-Faqīh which is on display in Iran.

How, then, does the Islamic economic policy of Iran work in practice?

The Concept of Interest in Foreign Transactions and Monetary Policy

In 1983, the Majles or Iranian Consultative Assembly approved the Free Banking Operations Act. Banks were nationalised and interest was prohibited across the Iranian banking system. This was a seismic step in finally outlawing riba from the operation of the Iranian economy.

When it came to engaging with other countries or foreign businesses, the ban on riba was not so clear cut. The dilemma as to whether interest should be allowed when dealing with foreign entities emerged in the very early years of the Islamic Republic.

Just before the revolution, the Government of the Shah had agreed, in 1975, to provide loan financing to the French Atomic Energy Commissariat with an interest rate on the loan of 8.75%. However, when the loan was being repaid to the new theocratic government in Iran, the French Government tried to be cute and said the repayments would not include interest as, under the new Iranian constitution, interest was prohibited in all financial transactions.

Maybe not surprisingly, the Iranian Government rejected the French position and demanded the interest payments well as payment of the capital. Whilst the financial inducements were clear from the perspective of Iran to receive these interest payments, on what legal basis could interest payments be accepted?

After all, riba is prohibited under Articles 43 and 49 of the constitution. In fact, Article 49 provided the State with the powers to take money earned by individuals which had been gained by interest and from other activities deemed to be prohibited within Islam.

This very question was asked by the executive branch of the Iranian Government to the Council of Guardians in 1987. The Council of Guardians has significant powers in the Iranian constitution as stipulated under Article 98:

> The interpretation of the constitution is the responsibility of the Guardian Council. This is determined with the approval of three-fourths of its members.

The 12-member panel, made up of senior clerics and jurists, considered the following policy question as presented by the executive branch:

> Whether or not the taking of interest and late payment damages by the Iranian Government, enterprises and companies from foreign governments, enterprises and companies which have been stipulated in the contracts concluded between them … and in accordance with what the Iranian side investigates and finds, that the foreign sides and foreign authorities from the viewpoint of their religious beliefs and convictions do not consider the charge of these funds as illegal, and they even regard them as legal, is inconsistent with the rules and precepts of the sacred religion of Islam and the provisions of the Constitution.[127]

The reply from the Council of Guardians was short and to the point:

> The taking of interest and damages due to late payment from foreign governments, enterprises, companies and foreign nationals who in terms of their religious beliefs do not regard them as unlawful, from the point of view of Islam is permissible. Therefore, claiming such funds is not inconsistent with the Constitution and Articles 43 and 49 of the Constitution are not applicable to this case.[128]

How can this be so?

One analysis of this ruling is that the Council of Guardians may have prayed in aid the Shi'a concept of Ilzam. Derived from the fifth Imam, Muhammad al-Baqir (677–733) it puts forward the perspective that if a practice is accepted in a non-Shi'a jurisdiction as legal whilst in a Shi'a jurisdiction, the same practice would be illegal, then the Shi'a jurisdiction can obligate the non-Shi'a jurisdiction to fulfil a commitment by meeting the legal necessity to adhere to an agreement—even though the same practice in a Shi'a jurisdiction would be prohibited.

To explain further, if we consider the French Government stance in trying to avoid paying interest on the Iranian loan, as the agreement had been made and as interest is a perfectly legal practice in France, then interest payments should be paid to Iran. When later in the 1980s there were loan disputes between Iran and the United States, Iran insisted on the interest element of loans being paid.

However, when an Iranian loan to Pakistan, which had been agreed in 1976, was due to be repaid, the Majles and Council of Guardians agreed, in 1981, that interest should not be charged. This would have been in accordance with Ilzam as Pakistan also, ostensibly, had an interest-free banking system. So, under Ilzam, as interest was banned in Iran and Pakistan, the interest payment obligation could be removed from the loan agreement.

Whilst the Ilzam concept is logical and understandable, the fact that al-Sadr spent so much time denigrating the riba concept and describing how interest distorts the real economy, shows that there is a tension between these two positions. In this context, it is no surprise that the executive branch of the government sought guidance from the Council of Guardians.

However, whilst some form of riba was accepted in foreign transactions, can we say with confidence that interest is banned in the domestic banking system?

Whilst interest was formally banned in the banking sector, when it came to monetary policy that was a different matter as the approach adopted by Mohsen Nourbakhsh demonstrated.

Mohsen Nourbakhsh was the Governor of the Central Bank of Iran and was later Finance Minister where, in this latter role, he pushed through free market reforms under the business-friendly President, Akbar Hashemi Rafsanjani (1934–2017). Due to deflationary pressures, the Majles forced the resignation of Nourbakhsh as Finance Minister in 1986. From 1989 until his death in 2003, Nourbakhsh served again as Governor of the Central Bank. From 2008, there was an additional push by the Iranian Government to liberalise the economy.

In his role at the Central Bank, Nourbakhsh continuously used the interest rate mechanism to control inflation. In fact, when Nourbakhsh spoke of the use of interest rates this was seen as unremarkable by the Iranian media. When Nourbakhsh, spoke of interest being charged on loans, this was reported in the Iranian media without comment:

> He said that Iranian banks are studying applications from the private sector seeking loans from the special reserve account for the projects to be carried out. The interest rate for the loans will be in concord with the international interest rates which are between seven to 8.5 percent, Nourbakhsh said.[129]

When Nourbakhsh unexpectedly died from a heart attack in 2003, the official tributes were fulsome in their praise. Then President Mohammad Khatami, described Nourbakhsh as a "*very sincere, intelligent and capable serviceman*". The Council of Ministers also praised his accomplishments for having played:

> … a key role in putting shape into the monetary policies of the country by unifying the Iranian currency and establishing a reserve fund (for the surplus oil revenues) as well as (helping with the) eye-catching rise of the Central Bank's reserves.[130]

Geopolitics and the Iranian Banking System

Had the concept of interest become normalised in Iran?

The Iranian Government would argue that since the foundation of the Islamic Republic, it had faced economic sanctions from its near neighbours such as Saudi Arabia, as well as from the United States. Therefore, it had to be agile in its international business transactions and in monetary policy to grow the economy in the face of such intense hostility.

Whilst it is beyond the purview of this book to detail the different manifestations of Iran—Saudi tensions, it is worth noting that Shi'a Iran and Sunni Saudi Arabia were allies, when these countries cooperated with other nations to increase the price of oil during the 1973 Yom Kippur War.

Grievances emerged after the 1979 Revolution. The Islamic Republic complained that the tomb of the Prophet's daughter, Fatima and the tombs of the four Imams, Hassan al-Mujtaba, Ali Zayn al-Abidin, Muhammad al-Baqir and Ja'far al-Sadiq, had been attacked in the al-Baqi' cemetery in Medina. Iran disapproved of Wahhabism and Saudi Arabia was concerned that Iran wanted to export its revolution to its Shi'a majority Eastern Province and to Shi'a majority Bahrain which is governed by the Sunni Khalifa royal family.

It should be noted that there was a rapprochement in 1994 when diplomatic relations were restored between Iran and Saudi Arabia. However, in January 2002, in the aftermath of the 9/11 atrocities, US President George W Bush identified Iran as part of the "*axis of evil*" in reference to Iranian support to militias such as Hezbollah.

Then, in 2003, the United States led invasion of Iraq led to concerns amongst the Sunni monarchies in the region that Iran could benefit from the invasion by increasing its influence amongst the Shi'a community in Iraq. King Abdullah of Jordan infamously encapsulated this perspective in December 2004:

> If pro Iran parties or politicians dominate the new Iraqi Government, a new 'crescent' of dominant Shi'a movements or governments stretching from Iran into Iraq, Syria and Lebanon could emerge.[131]

Against this backdrop, the agility of the Iranian authorities to reassess the role of interest in international trade and monetary policy when it was facing economic sanctions may not be too surprising.

How, though, was interest viewed within the domestic banking system?

Whilst it is correct to state that interest is banned in Iran, commercial transactions are linked to Mobadala which can be described as provisional profit. Deposit bank rates are notionally linked to the performance of the bank whilst fees are charged against loans. However, these rates remain static and the deposit rate does not seem to change whatever the performance of a bank may be.

The rates do change subject to action by the Iranian authorities which takes account of wider economic considerations. This has led critics of the Iranian economic system to claim that Mobadala, to all intent and purposes, equates to interest rates.

When the cap on lending was reduced by the authorities this was, naturally, reported by media outlets as a change in interest rates:

> The regulator lowered the cap on interest rates offered by banks, in a bid to boost business lending. After being pushed by various groups to increase business financing, the Money and Credit Council reduced the cap on one-year deposit interest rates by 200 basis points to 20 percent. The decision will be binding for all commercial banks from May 3. The council, in charge of setting monetary policy, announced its decision to ease monetary policy after a much anticipated meeting on Tuesday. The MCC is headed by the governor of the central bank, but the minister of economy and lawmakers are also members. Monetary officials hope the nine percent drop in the cap will reduce borrowing rates and help dissipate the credit crunch that pundits say is suffocating business performance.[132]

However, before the conclusion is definitively reached that interest rates are effectively hidden within the concept of Mobadala, Iranian Islamic contract options do provide the facility of interest-free loans in the form of gharzul-hasaneh.

The application of a number of the Islamic finance structures in Iran has some differences with the contract types discussed throughout this book. As was considered in the first half of this book, the global Islamic finance industry has been informed by Sunni norms and concepts.

The Islamic finance structures in the Iranian banking system are:

Gharzul-hasaneh: An interest-free, non-profit loan extended by a bank for a defined period of time. A service charge is incurred. It is believed that the first gharzul-hasaneh was registered in Tehran in 1969.

Joalah: The undertaking by one party (the jael—normally a bank) to pay a specified amount of money (the joal) to another party in return for rendering a specified service in accordance with the terms of the contract. The party rendering the service shall be called Amel (Agent or Contractor).

Mosaqat: A contract between the owner of an orchard or garden with another party (the Amel) for the purpose of gathering the harvest of the orchard or garden and dividing it, in a specified ratio, between the two parties.

Mozaraah: A contract where the bank turns over a specified plot of land for a specified period of time to another party for the purpose of farming the land and dividing the harvest between the two parties at a specified ratio.

Mozarebe: A contract where the bank undertakes to provide the capital and the other party undertakes to use the capital for commercial purposes and divide the profit at a specified ratio between the two parties at the end of the term of the contract.

Mozarebe has synergies with the musharaka contract model as discussed in Chapter 4.

As for Gharzul-hasaneh, Sadr has argued that this contract type can induce competition which, in turn, can reduce costs for consumers:

> Clearly, applicants always prefer Gharzul-hasaneh loans to other types of finance for financing their activities. Given such state of demand on one side and preferences of suppliers to offer Gharzul-hasaneh loans on the other side, there will be room for intermediaries to be formed and lower the contract cost between the two sides. In fact, Gharzul-hasaneh funds (GHF) and organizations were established in Iran to fulfil this purpose.

Sadr pointed out that the demand for the loan to be repaid can be brought forward:

> Gharzul-hasaneh contracts entail features which make them very desirable for offering loans, despite their zero rate of return. The fact that lender has the right to have the principal paid back at any time that he asks for it, make it a very secure loan. Therefore, the supplier may treat his Gharzul-hasaneh loans as liquid assets in his portfolio. This feature may lead further to substitution of these loans for money, when they are held for precautionary purposes.[133]

It could be argued that the ability by the lender to demand repayment of the loan at any time does provide an element of uncertainty or gharar for the borrower which could be seen as a condition which is prohibited in Islamic finance. On the other hand, gharzul-hasaneh does provide an interest-free loan option to consumers which is similar to the qard hasan (interest free loan) which notionally exists—but is not often utilised—in the global Islamic finance industry.

Informal Economy

A significant proportion of commercial activity in Iran is related to the informal economy. The concept of the informal economy has been defined as "*a process of income generation characterized by one central feature: it is unregulated by the institutions of society, in a legal and social environment in which similar activities are regulated*".[134]

The Peruvian economist, Hernando de Soto, has argued that the informal economy is vibrant entrepreneurialism in action and it is the bureaucracy and complexities of the State that drive such innovative businesses to operate illegally. De Soto had drawn on his own experiences in Peru:

> When I saw the poverty in Peru with all those people working on the streets, in 1979, I said to myself, "if Peruvians are working very hard what is the cause of the poverty?" I saw people on the pavements, I saw them in the "Young Villages", as we call the miserable neighbourhoods surrounding Lima, building, labouring, showing enterprise and diversifying their client base…Why do they always achieve levels that are so low, despite all this?

After much analysis, De Soto concluded:

> … in the case of Peruvians at least, and we imagine this is true of the other Latin American countries too, it is not a question of things being done illegally due to a vocation for illegality, but because the law itself was extremely costly for them. So, one of us, who had read the liberal classics, found a solution: get rid of all law and regulations and move to a situation of total liberty so that Peru could start to produce.[135]

In the case of Iran, it is a combination of state actors as well as societal factors beyond the structures of the state that has engendered a significant informal economy sector. There are different perspectives as to the size of the informal economy:

> Although … informal activity is found throughout the world, partly as a result of money laundering and tax avoidance, the size of the informal

economy in Iran is thought to be particularly large, perhaps accounting for most of non-oil GDP.[136]

The Iranian Government has suggested that around six million people earn a living within the informal economy and it seems to have concurred with De Soto's analysis that excessive bureaucracy has helped ensure the burgeoning of this sector. The Deputy Minister for Co-operatives, Labour and Social Welfare, Ahmad Meydari stated in 2017:

> One solution is to cut bureaucracy and the restrictive rules and regulations of the Cooperatives Ministry. If employers must pay high payroll taxes or pension contributions for workers, they may prefer to employ fewer people. In fact, the rise in the cost of employing workers in the formal economy leads to reduced hiring of workforce and, consequently, a fraction of the workforce misses the chance of working in the formal economy. The chances of these people falling into poverty are much greater since they don't have insurance coverage and cannot access banking facilities.[137]

It has also been argued that the commercial operations of the bazaar is contributing to the continuation of money lending outside of the formal banking sector. A 1962 analysis considered the attraction of money lenders operating in Iranian community markets or bazaars as compared to the loan facilities offered by banks:

> Bazaar moneylenders, taking advantage of banks' indifference to loan purposes, discount their own (or someone else's) paper at 8 to 12 per cent and relend at about triple the rate. Since bank deposits pay 2 to 6 per cent, savings are also drawn to the bazaar. Merchants with surplus cash temporarily released from inventories turn to moneylending as an alternative earning possibility for liquid funds; in fact, most large bazaar moneylenders are also merchants – the borderline is essentially indistinguishable.[138]

A 1998 study demonstrated that the essential role of moneylending in the bazaar format had continued and that there were linkages between formal and informal money lending:

> … the survey of the operation of the informal credit markets revealed the presence of linkages between the formal and informal sectors. The new institutional economics complementarity hypothesis explains the existence of links by suggesting that the formal and informal sectors, due to

> their differential comparative cost advantages, essentially cater to different segments of the financial markets. The presence of linkages between the two sectors, in turn, explains the resiliency of the informal credit markets in the bazaar. In sum, consistent with the new institutional economics, this study suggest that these categories fit the reality in the case of Iran.[139]

Whilst the role of informal moneylenders in the Iranian national economy requires further study, there is every reason to suggest that such interest-bearing activities continues to some extent.

It is the role of state actors in the informal and formal economy that is having a particular impact as to how the concept of Islamic economic policy is shaping Iran.

State Actors

The Sepah or Iranian Revolutionary Guard has a powerful political, security—and economic—role in national life.

The Revolutionary Guards—or to give them their full title, the Guards Corps of the Islamic Revolution (Sepah-e Pasdaran-e Enqelab-e Eslami) is an intrinsic part of the Iranian state.

The role of Sepah in the affairs of other countries is reflected within the relevant text of the Iranian Constitution:

> With respect to the Islamic content of the Iranian Revolution, which was a movement for the victory of all the oppressed people over their oppressors, the constitution prepares the ground for continuing this revolution at home and abroad. Specifically, it strives to expand international relations with other Islamic movements and people in order to pave the way for the formation of a single, universal community, in accordance with the Qur'anic verse, "Verily, this Brotherhood of yours is a single Brotherhood, and I am your Lord and Cherisher: therefore Serve Me (and no other)" (21: 92), to also assure that the continuous struggle for the emancipation of the deprived and oppressed nations of the world is strengthened.

This became the basis for operations conducted by the unit of the Sepah known as the Qods (Jerusalem) Force. The name alludes to the opposition of Iran to the existence of the State of Israel. The Qods Force may have been formed around the time of the Israeli invasion of Lebanon in 1982 when Sepah personnel went to Lebanon to assist Shi'a groups.

The reputation of Sepah as a fighting force was valued by many Iranians following the devastating Iran–Iraq War (1980–1988) where an estimated 1 million people died on the Iranian side and 250,000 to 500,000 people died on the Iraqi side.[140]

The role of Sepah in supporting aligned groups outside its borders included its assistance to Hezbollah when Israeli forces crossed into Lebanon in 2006 and the active role of Sepah to support President Bashir al-Assad during the ongoing Syrian War (at the time of writing—2020).

The US assassination of Qods commander, Qasem Soleimani, in January 2020, in Baghdad and the military response from Iran against American bases in Iraq demonstrated the key security and political role which Sepah has within the public life of Iran.

It is the economic role of Sepah that has had an impact on domestic Iranian life. The Sepah has major interests in construction and civil engineering (notably through the Khatam al-Anbia organisation), in the oil industry and in telecommunications. Sepah also has close relations with several Bonyads—tax-exempt charitable foundations—the most important of which has been the Bonyad-e Mostazafan va Janbazan (Foundation for the Oppressed and War Veterans) and the the Bonyad Shahid va Omur-e Janbazan (Foundation of Martyrs and Veterans Affairs). These bonyards have been involved in a wide range of sectors, from shipping to chemicals, retail and tourism.

It is the involvement of Sepah in the informal economy that has concerned many people, including a member of the Majles, Ali Ghanbari:

> Unfortunately, one third of the imported goods are delivered through the black market, underground economy, and illegal jetties. Appointed institutions that don't obey the government and have control over the means of power; institutions that are mainly military, are responsible.[141]

Another Majles member claimed that Sepah informal market activities could be valued at US$12 billion per year whilst another elected politician stated that "*invisible jetties ... and the invisible hand of the mafia control 68 percent of Iran's entire exports*".[142]

This, alongside Sepah's role in the formal economy, makes the organisation a powerful domestic economic actor. It should be noted that the example of the military being a key economic participant is not an unusual factor when analysing national political economic structures. The active commercial role of the military forces in the economic life of Egypt or, for that matter, Myanmar, are just two of the many examples of such practices which could be cited around the world.

In the Iranian space, however, Sepah can be a key determining force in shaping the future direction of the country's self-declared Islamic economic policy.

How Sepah will evolve in this sphere will depend, in part, on whether the sanctions regime against Iran will continue or be lessened in the future.

Future Direction of the Iranian Islamic Finance Industry

Iran has been severely affected by economic sanctions with the oil rich nation having been in recession even before the onset of the 2020 COVID-19 outbreak impacted the country's public health and economy.

When President Donald Trump announced that the United States would withdraw from the Joint Comprehensive Plan of Action, which was intended to stop Iran acquiring nuclear weapons, this led to a reinstatement of US sanctions in 2018.

In 2019, the US ended sanctions exemptions for entities that were trading with Iran. Consequently, combined with earlier economic pressures, the GDP of Iran contracted by an estimated 4.8% in 2018 and was forecast to shrink another 9.5% in 2019, according to the International Monetary Fund. The unemployment rate rose from 14.5% in 2018 to 16.8% in 2019.

Therefore, the potential for the Iranian Islamic financial industry, which has had 40 years of consistent development, to contribute to Iranian economic well-being by competing in international markets, is being denied by the ongoing sanctions regime.

Whilst critics of the structure of the Iranian economy could argue that the prohibition of interest is a misnomer due to the Mobadala concept, the provision and popularity of interest-free loans in the form of gharzul-hasaneh should not be ignored when considering the extent of interest-free loan provision across the country.

Nonetheless, due to external pressures combined with internal pressures such the role of informal moneylenders and state actors involved in the informal economy, it would be fair to state that the ambitions of Shariati and Al-Sadr who, in their very different ways, were calling for an equitable Islamic political economy, have not been realised.

That is not to say that Shariati and, in particular, Al-Sadr have not influenced the direction of the Iranian economy. The official prohibition on interest, the usul al-fiqh or principles of Islamic jurisprudence adopted in Iran to assess financial policy and the provision of interest-free loans is indicative of this influence.

In practice, against the backdrop of public unease against economic conditions, which was partly reflected in the public discontent following the disputed 2009 Presidential election, and subsequent bouts of unrest, such as demonstrations in November 2019 in protest against fuel price increases, it has been the pragmatic approach of the late Mohsen Nourbakhsh which has won out.

The potential for the Iranian Islamic finance sector to be one of the major global players in the industry is immense. The country is at the crossroads of the Middle East, it has huge economic potential in the form of a skilled workforce, a growing middle class and oil and gas wealth. Iran has had over 40 years of experience with the development of Islamic finance institutions.

However, until economic issues take precedence over geopolitical considerations, the full potential for the Iranian Islamic finance industry to play its full part in global markets will not be realised.

Malaysia and the Heart of the Global Economy

Malaysia and International Supply Chains

The centre of global manufacturing is East Asia.

International Production Networks (IPNs) has ensured the region is at the centre of manufacturing with most consumer products sold in global markets being sourced from the region.

Until the 2020 COVID-19 crisis occurred, it was expected that this pattern would continue for the foreseeable future. However, from the first half of 2020, politicians in the United States and within the European Union called for manufacturing to be based nearer to their consumers after problems were experienced with supply chains during the pandemic.

In 2019, before the pandemic struck, south east Asia was growing at 9.4% per annum—an incredible growth rate.[143]

At the heart of the south east Asian region are Malaysia, Indonesia and Brunei Darussalam. These nations, to different degrees, contain Muslim majority populations where the Indonesian Muslim population are primarily located on the islands of Java, Sumatra, Kalimantan and Sulewesi whilst the Malaysian Muslim population are mostly located on the Malay Peninsula.

It is in Malaysia that the Islamic finance market is a core feature of the national economy but, until the 2010s, there was not a significant Islamic finance presence in Indonesia. Ariff was derogatory towards the strength of the faith in Java when he tried to explain why the sector had not developed at an earlier stage in Indonesia.

Ariff claimed that the Indonesian *Pancasila* doctrine is secular and does not encourage faith-based economic policies.[144] Pancasilia is a doctrine that is intended to bring the peoples of the nation together under some common values. Contrary to Ariff's assertion, the concept of belief in God is part of Pancasilia-Ketuhanan Yang Maha Esa (Belief in Almighty God).[145]

In Malaysia, however, a conscious political decision was made in the 1980s to place Islamic finance at the heart of the political economy of the nation. This strategic positioning helped position Malaysia as a leading country within the Organisation of Islamic Co-operation (OIC) and the Islamic Financial Services Board (one of Islamic finance's multilateral organisations) is located in Kuala Lumpur.

An illustration of the pervasiveness of Islamic finance in Malaysia has been provided by Rudnyckyj with this vivid snapshot of life in the Malaysian capital:

> Today, in the streets and public spaces of Malaysia's larger cities, the ubiquity of Islamic finance cannot be missed .... Along Kuala Lumpur's main arteries, advertisements seek to lure customers with the Bank Islam credit card that provides 'free takaful coverage, low fees and no compounding finance charges'. Inside the city's ultra-modern train station and on the streets outside, eye catching advertisements for Al-Rajhi Bank, a Saudi Arabian firm that claims to be the world's largest Islamic bank, encourage potential customers to 'Get There Fast' with 'Al Rajhi Personal Financing'. On the other side of the station, a branch of Kuwait Finance House does brisk business.[146]

The implications of Islamic finance being part of the political economy of Malaysia for the wider East Asian region is significant. For Malaysia has become the gateway for Islamic finance to access markets in the world's most economically dynamic region.

Unlike in the Middle East where geopolitical rivalries, such as between Iran and Saudi Arabia or the ongoing Israeli-Palestinian conflict, can cloud a range of economic issues, Malaysia has the benefit of being part of the Association of South East Asian Nations (ASEAN) which has developed close economic, education and cultural links within the region and which has enhanced the diplomatic influence of its member states, particularly in relation to China, Japan and the United States.

The decision of President Barack Obama in 2012 for the United States to "*pivot*" towards East Asia, in preference to Europe and the Middle East was short-lived and has been superseded by President Donald Trump's economic nationalism of "*America First*". That moment, though, did exemplify the dominant role the region now plays in the global economy.

Consequently, the political decision to incorporate Islamic finance in the Malaysian economic model has the tangible potential for this market to grow and prosper beyond its borders.

To consider the role of Islamic finance in Malaysia, we need to step back and take an overview of the factors that led to the formation of Malaysia—for these factors have a direct bearing as to how Islamic finance has prospered across the nation.

When the nation of Malaysia was being formed at the tail end of British colonialism, the debate was centred as to how to engender a sense of nationhood amongst peoples that were brought together by historical accidents such as British colonialism, Japanese occupation, Dutch occupation in neighbouring islands that became Indonesia, the Malay 'Emergency' against the Malay Communist Party forces and rivalries between elites that led to the initial ambition of a Greater Indonesia being stymied:

> The fall of Japan came when many societies were at their lowest ebb: battle scarred, battle hardened, at war with one another. But as the Malay radical, Mustapha Hussain, had earlier reflected, 'although the Japanese Occupation was described as one of severe hardship and brutality, it left something positive, a sweet fruit to be plucked and enjoyed only after the surrender'. Now history seemed open, at a juncture when the peoples of colonial Asia could shape their own future as they had not been able to do within living memory.[147]

Colonialism could be seen as helping to engender the forceful expression of national identity. This self-expression had added resonance when the control mechanisms used by the European powers failed when Japan invaded these same countries in the early 1940s. The concept of the inevitability of European rule ended at that moment and contributed to the rise of nationalism which saw its full expression after the defeat of Japan in 1945.

At first, the focus on forming a sense of national identity was centred upon reconciling ethnic identities rather than factoring in religion. However, from the 1980s, debate in Malaysia began to shift towards religious identity and this trend contributed to the concurrent debate as to the emergence and development of the Malaysian Islamic finance market.

The struggle over ethnic identities was part of the formative experience of Malaysia. This included the debate as to whether the Chinese heritage majority population of Singapore could be part of a country where the majority of the population on the Peninsula was Malay.

These ethnic tensions had their basis, to some extent, with the operation of British colonial policy which enabled a divide and rule approach to be adopted and included the powers of patronage of the British Crown to be awarded to different ethnic groups in terms of economic opportunities.

Once Malaysia was declared independent from British rule in 1963, the governing coalition of the Alliance consisted of separate political parties for the Malay, Chinese and Indian communities. How to hold the country together was a natural pre-occupation of Malaysia's first Prime Minister, Tunku Abdul Rahman, who even chose a popular cabaret song to be the country's national anthem, over the objections of many of his Cabinet Ministers, as it would be recognisable across the nation and could help bring differing communities together.

The Singapore leader, Lee Kuan Yew, in the months leading up to the 1965 expulsion of Singapore from Malaysia, was hopeful that the country could move beyond ethnic tensions. Referring to Tunku Abdul Rahman, Lee told Singaporean television:

> We both want to get a Malaysian Malaysia, but we propose route 'A', direct from many States together into one federation, from many groups together into a multiracial party, towards a multiracial, united Malaysia.[148]

A truly multiethnic Malaysian identity was, arguably, only attained to some extent in the twenty first century though, as we shall see, the domestic debate over religious identity is far from being resolved.

Former Malaysian Deputy Prime Minister, Anwar Ibrahim, argued in 1996 that the Muslim communities across south east Asia had an open approach to outside influences, implying that Islamic culture in the region should not be confused with Islamic culture in the Middle East (though, like Ariff, he also seemed dismissive as to the strength of Islam in Java). Implying that the region was open for business as compared to the fractious Middle East, Anwar Ibrahim wrote:

> This peaceful and gradual Islamisation has moulded the South East Asian Muslim psyche into one which is cosmopolitan, open minded, tolerant and amenable to cultural diversity. Of course, their outlook is also fashioned by the strong presence of people of other faiths who reciprocate Muslim tolerance. Unlike other non-Muslims in the West, their perception of Islam is not distorted by the prism of the Crusades.[149]

The rivalry between Anwar Ibrahim and Mahathir Mohammed was not a good example of such tolerance with the animosities between the two men poisoning Malaysian politics for decades. Whilst, though, it was domestic politics which placed a premium on placing Islamic finance within the political economy of Malaysia, the inspiration for this movement was found in academia.

The Legacy of Ungku Aziz

Ungku Aziz was born in 1922. His father was a Malayan Prince. However, it was Aziz as an economist and academic that helped shape the early years of the Malaysian state. Aziz was associated with the New Economic Policy which argued for positive discrimination for the Malays at the expense of the Chinese and Indian heritage populations who were perceived to have gained economic advantages over the indigenous population. Such attitudes aggravated ethnic tensions in the country for many years.

However, it is in the field of Islamic finance, that Ungku Aziz had a huge impact in the formative years of the industry. Aziz questioned why pilgrims going on Hajj would not be able to undertake this important duty in a shari'a compliant way—specifically whether the role of usury, when pilgrims sought funds for the pilgrimage, could be removed.

Aziz's paper titled *Rancangan Membaiki Ekonomi Bakal-bakal Haji* (Programmes to help prospective hajj pilgrims improve their economic conditions) in 1959 became the basis for the foundation of Perbadanan Wang Simpanan Bakal-bakal Haji (Trust fund for prospective hajj pilgrims) in 1962. Tabung Haji (Hajj Trust Fund) was a product of a merger between this organisation and Pejabat Urusan Hal Ehwal Haji (the office of Hajj Affairs) in 1969.

Muslims in rural areas across Malaysia sold surplus rice to purchase buffaloes which were then sold to acquire land. Those farmers with endowments would then sell land to raise funds to perform the Hajj:

> Ungku Aziz concluded that such a practice was inefficient, fraught with risks and unsuitable in a modern economy. In the process of buying and selling buffaloes, farmers could incur losses and in obtaining and holding land as a form of savings can be perilous in case of high rents, sub-division and fragmented farms due to the law of inheritance. In addition, although savings in the form of cash was desirable, savings within a formal corporation insured against loss, fire or theft compared with keeping cash at home. The alternative method of savings with conventional financial institutions was not palatable to rural Malays as interest payments or usury is prohibited in the execution of the Hajj.[150]

So, in 1962, the Pilgrims Savings Corporation was formed. In 1969, the Pilgrims Management and Fund Board or Tabung Haji was established. Mudarabah, Musharaka and ijara was used to help pilgrims access the funds that were required to go on pilgrimage.

The precedent Ungku Aziz achieved was a milestone in the history of Islamic finance. For Ungku Aziz had developed an inclusive and engaging form of Islamic finance, which was not linked to political or theological debates around the direction of Islam, but was purely directed to enable disadvantaged people to maintain some standard of living and—at the same time—fulfil their religious duties.

The contract models that Ungku Aziz piloted in the early 1960s are, at heart, the same structures (with modifications) which are used day in and day out in the contemporary Islamic finance industry. The legacy of Ungku Aziz should not be underestimated as we consider the whole story of the early history of Islamic finance.

This savings and investment model, with mutual risk sharing at its heart, is the very model of Islamic finance seen today in Dubai, London, Kuala Lumpur, Paris, New York, Tokyo and around the world:

> Overall, Tabung Haji has become a renowned Islamic financial institution that has enabled the realisation for many pilgrims to perform the Hajj successfully supplanting the previously and traditionally unreliable and inefficient methods. Tabung Haji provides evidence that Malaysian Muslims,

> especially from the rural community, have been able to perform the Hajj in less time while at the same time insuring against physical losses; additionally the savings have helped build domestic capital for national economic development.

In fact, these collective funds are now a key element of the Kuala Lumpur Stock Exchange further helping to embed Islamic finance in the mainstream of Malaysian society.

Whilst Ungku Aziz was a pioneer in Islamic finance, this was only part of the story in Malaysia which led Islamic finance to have such a prominent role in the contemporary political economy of the country. Internal politics and a regional financial crisis both played their part in elevating Islamic finance within the body politic of Malaysia.

Domestic Politics

In May 1969, the Parliamentary elections were a setback for the established parties in the governing Alliance. When opposition supporters celebrated in the streets of Kuala Lumpur, this riled Government supporters and violent clashes ensued. At least 196 people died, many of which were of Chinese heritage, though some academics claim the number of people killed were much higher. Yet again, ethnic differences were at the core of Malaysian politics.

In response to the violence, the Government suspended Parliament and instituted emergency rule. This was the start of a renewed process to heal the ethnic tensions. In January 1970, the Malaysian Government convened the National Consultative Council. Its terms of reference read that its aim was to:

> … establish positive and practical guidelines for inter-racial co-operation and social integration for the growth of the Malaysian national identity.

On Independence Day—31 August 1970—the Government declared the Rukunegara (Articles of Faith of the State) which proclaimed the ideology that citizens of Malaysia were told to adhere to:

> Our nation, Malaysia, being dedicated to achieving a greater unity of all her peoples; to maintaining a democratic way of life; to creating a just society in which the wealth of the nation shall be equitably shared; to

> ensuring a liberal approach to her rich and diverse cultural traditions; to building a progressive society which shall be orientated to modern science and technology.
>
> We her people, pledge our united effort to attain those ends guided by these principles:
>
> Belief in God
> Loyalty to King and Country
> Sanctity of the Constitution
> Rule of Law
> Good Behaviour and Morality

It was against this backdrop that one politician used incendiary language which seemed designed to inflame tensions.

Mahathir Mohamad had fallen out with his Party—the United Malay National Organisation (UMNO). He wrote a book that was chock a block full with racist stereotypes in order to justify a policy of positive discrimination for the benefit of the Malay indigenous population.

But the author of this book went on to lead Malaysia into the twenty first country as a vibrant multicultural democracy with a vast improvement in the standard of living—and ensured Islamic finance was part of the political economy of Malaysia.

Mahathir Mohamad, in his 1970 book, *The Malay Dilemma*, was deliberately courting controversy. In one passage, Mahathir wrote:

> The Malays are spiritually inclined, tolerant and easy-going. The non-Malays, and especially the Chinese, are materialistic, aggressive and have an appetite for work.

Racist stereotypes were cited throughout *The Malay Dilemma:*

> The Chinese and Indians coming from countries with vast populations are less concerned about good behaviour and manners. In their lives, nobility, which is always associated with breeding, was totally absent. Age and riches are the only things they defer to.

Anti semitic comments can also be found in its pages. There is a reference to the place of Islam in society where, in reference to the Malays, he wrote that they had "*the fatality of people of the Islamic faith*" later adding that "*a Malay, by definition, is one who professes the Islamic faith*".

The book was banned by the Malaysian Government which was only lifted in 1981—when Mahathir became Prime Minister.

The track record of Mahathir as Prime Minister did not fit with the racist stereotypes of his 1970 book for he worked with all communities and made strenuous efforts to build a genuine multicultural society.

However, the book was a success in raising Mahathir's profile and it indicated how debates about ethnic identity would morph over the years into debate about religious identity.

Following the 1969 riots, the Government instituted the New Economic Policy (NEP). As well as advancing the economic prospects of the nation, it had a stated aim of levelling up the economic opportunities for the indigenous Malay population. Whilst debates continued as to the effectiveness of the NEP, a new Malay middle class emerged whilst urbanisation transformed the nation with Kuala Lumpur becoming an international metropolis.

In 1981 Mahathir became Prime Minister at a time when his UMNO party was facing a growing electoral threat from the Parti Islam Se-Malaysia (PAS—Malaysian Islamic Party). PAS argued for a stronger sense of Islamic identity within Malaysia even though around 40% of the population were not Muslims. The UMNO felt it had to stave off this electoral challenge.

Consequently, the Government placed Islam at the heart of everyday Government actions which included making religious education mandatory at schools, funding the building of mosques, establishing the International Islamic University—and taking central government action to establish an Islamic finance market.

Mahathir credits Prince Mohammed Al Faisal Al Saud of Saudi Arabia for approaching him with the idea of establishing an Islamic finance institution.[151] However, the steps taken to establish an Islamic bank, establish a regulatory structure for Islamic finance, to encourage a vibrant Islamic finance market and to be the first country in the world to issue a Sukuk were significant achievements in and of themselves. It married the need to garner the support of a growing Malay and Muslim middle class with the UMNO whilst staving off the electoral threat of the PAS.

This embrace of Islamic identity also impacted on Malaysia's foreign policy with the nation playing an active role in the Organisation of Islamic Co-operation (OIC). However, the electoral success of PAS continued to concern UMNO and in 1990 an opposition alliance which included the

PAS won the state and federal seats in Kelantan and PAS took over the Kelantan state government.

This may have been an additional spur for Mahathir to announce in, 1991, his Vision 2020—for Malaysia to be a developed nation by 2020. It had nine aims:

- A unified nation of one Malaysian people
- A society that is psychologically liberated, secure and developed;
- A mature democratic society;
- A moral and ethical society;
- A liberal and tolerant society;
- A scientific and progressive society;
- A caring society;
- An economically just society with equitable wealth distribution;
- A prosperous society with an economy that is fully competitive, dynamic, robust and resilient.

This strategy again impacted on the Islamic finance industry. In 1993 the Islamic Banking Scheme effectively instigated Malaysia's development as a dual banking system, where the conventional interest-based system and the Islamic system would function alongside each other.

In 1994, the Islamic Inter Bank Money Market was set up to ensure borrowing between banks could occur without the use of the interest principle. This was a shari'a compliant version of the London Inter Bank Offered Rate (LIBOR) which is responsible for lending between conventional banks.

In 1997, the National Shari'a Advisory Council within the country's central bank was established to ensure compliance with Islamic banking and takaful standards. In 2002, the Islamic Financial Services Board, one of the industry's multilateral organisations, was firmly established in Kuala Lumpur.

Malaysia had already made history when the world's very first Sukuk was issued in the country in 1990. In 2002, the world's first sovereign Sukuk was issued in Malaysia which effectively kick started the world's multimillion-dollar Sukuk market.

Islamic Finance and the Religious Identity Debate

As was discussed in Chapter 8, the 1997 Asian Financial Crisis was an additional spur for the Government to embrace Islamic finance with Mahathir condemning the neoliberal economic remedies that were then being foisted on the region by the International Monetary Fund.

As Professor Abbas Mirakhor, who became the first Chair of Islamic finance at the Kuala Lumpur based Global University of Islamic Finance (INCEIF), has argued, it is the stance of the Malaysian Government, that has transformed the Islamic finance market in Malaysia and, to some extent, across South East Asia:

> One of the reasons why I'm here is because the country has established a unique paradigm for development and progress of Islamic finance. The most important element of this paradigm is the top-down commitment of the authorities toward this objective ..... It is the commitment of the governor of Bank Negara Malaysia, the central bank, and the government of Malaysia that generate the hope that as this paradigm progresses toward full fruition, the constraints mentioned earlier could be removed first in Malaysia. Other countries can then reduce the learning cost of establishing a full-fledged risk-sharing system leveraging on Malaysia's experience. As part of the commitment of the central bank to the strengthening of Islamic finance, the INCEIF has been established as the only institution of higher education fully dedicated to Islamic finance.[152]

Whilst Malaysia's Islamic finance market is now world leading, some critics argue that this focus on faith is leading to new forms of discrimination in Malaysia:

> ... Indians and Chinese have had to go to court seeking the return of the bodies of their husbands or fathers who had supposedly converted to Islam, without the knowledge of family members. They have invariably lost their case to the Muslim religious authorities. The same holds true for non-Muslim women, who have fought for custody of their children in cases of divorce from converted husbands. Another religious issue is the destruction of Indian Hindu temples, allegedly erected on public land, without regard for local sentiment.[153]

There is also a debate as to how equitable the economic development policies have really been:

> … the NEP has proved to be a corrupt instrument for wealth creation for only an elite class of favoured Malay individuals, making them very wealthy. After three decades of such corruption and the intensification of income inequalities brought about by the globalisation of capitalism, the NEP has become intolerable for the majority of the population, including many Malays.[154]

The Malaysian scholar and professor of sociology at the National University of Singapore, Syed Farid Alata also referred to corruption when he was analysing the role of Islamic finance within the wider Malaysian economy:

> In Malaysia and Indonesia we have the ersatz form of capitalism, due to the peculiar nature of state involvement in development. Ersatz capitalism is capitalism that is based on state patronage, and the investment of transnational corporations and their technology…. The focus on ersatz capitalism leads to a consideration of patronage and related phenomena such as rent seeking and corruption. Capitalists are dependent on the state for assistance in order to be successful. Kleptocrats or corruptors extend various forms of favours to private capitalists, that encompass incentives, licensing, protectionism, low-interest loans from state banks, concessions, and joint ventures. The relationship between kleptocrat and capitalist is one of patron and client. This is a special relation between a politically powerful patron and a client who needs his/her protection due to the inadequacies of formal economic institutions. Therefore, the role that state officials play in advancing their private material interests takes its toll on economic development. Here we are referring to the activities of corrupt state officials.[155]

These harsh judgements were made before the 1MDB affair became an international scandal. In July 2020, Najib Razak, was found guilty of syphoning off RM 2.67 billion (US$700 million) via a national investment vehicle when he was Prime Minister. The scandal was so far-reaching that investigations were ongoing in the United States, United Kingdom, United Arab Emirates, Switzerland, Singapore, Seychelles, Luxembourg, Indonesia, Kuwait, Hong Kong and Australia.

During the trial of Najib Razak for graft, the prosecution authorities alleged that Najib asked the UAE Crown Prince Sheikh Mohammed bin Zayed al Nahyen to help him cover up the alleged fraud whist in May 2020, the Kuwaiti authorities began to investigate as to what role their country may have had in this affair.

As for Vision 2020, Malaysia just missed out on advanced country status as defined by the World Bank but the gross national income per person, as of 2019, was US$11,40 whilst the target was US$12,376. As for equality targets:

> ... Malaysia's Gini coefficient score (0.41), about the same as the United States (0.415) means that its social equality is still nothing to be proud of.[156]

Whilst the rough and tumble of Malaysian domestic politics continues, the economic transformation of the nation has changed the long-standing social enmities between differing ethnic groups.

However, the focus on religious identity is a revised form of identity politics and this debate regarding religious and ethnic discrimination could impact on the scope and range of the Islamic finance market as its very flourishing is directly linked to Government actions which relate to identity politics.

However, as we saw in Chapter 9, the very success of the Malaysian Islamic finance market is now linked to the regional concept of "Asian Values"—a construct that has helped the industry prosper across south east Asia.

Sudan

Until 2019, the Sudanese Government had claimed that its political economy was solely based upon Islamic economics since 1984. It was claimed that Sudan had a fully shari'a compliant economic model which was meeting the needs of its people.

In 2016, a Sudanese Government backed promotional brochure spoke of the economic benefits of Islamic finance within a stable nation:

> A fully Shariah-compliant system following Shariah standards in all aspects, Sudan is considered one of the rich countries in North Africa, with fertile lands, abundant natural resources of livestock, crops and manufacturing. The economic stability of Sudan, as measured by Gross Domestic Product (GDP), shows favourable trends and the republic's economy is expected to gradually moderate in 2016 ....[157]

This rosy picture was far from reality. Instead of Sudan being economically "*stable*" the nation fitted the very definition of crony capitalism.

It is significant that for many decades, Sudan was held up by the Islamic Development Bank and Saudi Arabia as an example of a nation whose underlying political economic structure was premised upon Islamic economic thought. In reality, the role of Islamic finance was used as a political cover to address the fluid nature of domestic Sudanese politics and as a revenue stream which related to the geopolitical relationship between Sudan and Saudi Arabia.

The scale of the nation's economic woes was finally revealed for all to see when President Omar al-Bashir was toppled from power in 2019. The end of the Bashir regime, which began in 1989, was due to a combination of popular protests, declining economic indicators and the eventual decision of the military to end Bashir's rule.

In late 2019, the Sudanese transitional government backed a report produced by the UK think tank, the Royal Institute of International Affairs. The findings of the report showed up the severe challenges faced by the authorities:

> Sudan's former leaders indulged in heavy off-budget spending, which needs to be accounted for and ended. The budget, which has long been heavily weighted towards subsidies, state transfers and security expenditure, needs to be restructured to prioritise health, education and social welfare.

It had been the power of patronage that had led to endemic corruption which contributed to the crippling of the economy:

> The biggest challenge facing the government over the medium to long term will be to dismantle the entrenched patronage networks that came to control all institutions and key sectors of the Sudanese economy under President Bashir, including businesses owned by the military-security apparatus.

The practice of al-tajneed was widespread. This can be defined as setting aside part of the state institutions' revenues which were generated from bribes. These bribes were from citizens who needed normal administrative functions to be processed. In turn, these funds were not included in the state's general budget.

The Royal Institute of International Affairs, also known as Chatham House, concluded that Sudan required US$8 billion in foreign financial assistance over the next two years plus an immediate need of US$2 billion to support the value of the currency.

Debt was estimated to be between US$50 billion to US$60 billion. Only 10% of farming land used modern irrigation systems and it was estimated that 75% of the gold mined in Sudan was being smuggled out of the country. Sudan had already lost 75% of its oil income when South Sudan formally seceded and became the world's newest nation state in 2011.

It is beyond the purview of this book to consider the ramifications of the two civil wars which blighted the country once it gained independence from British colonial rule in 1956, the impact of the horrific massacres in Darfur which has led to Bashir being indicted for war crimes by the International Criminal Court and as to how war with neighbouring Chad in 2005 further weakened the nation state.

It is striking that against this track record, Sudan maintained the fiction that its economic model was based on Islamic finance. In this context it is useful to consider the fourteenth century scholar, Ibn Khaldun, who studied the role of internal competition within political elites and how this related to national cycles of decay and renewal. Khaldun commented that poor governance created a cycle of decay whilst competition within political elites remained high:

> Do not think that injustice consists in only taking money or property from its owner without compensation or cause, even though this is what is commonly understood. Injustice is more comprehensive than this. Anyone who confiscates the property of someone or forces him to work for him, or presses an unjustified claim against him, or imposes on him a duty not required by the Shariah, has committed injustice. Collection of unjustified taxes is also injustice; transgression on another's property or taking it away by force or theft constitutes injustice; denying other people their rights is also injustice.[158]

This pattern was reflected, until recently, in Sudan but the ability to brand the country as an exemplar for Islamic economic ideas did assist with the geostrategic positioning of the country in respect of Sudan's relations with Persian Gulf nations. In large measure this shift in positioning can be attributed to Hasan al-Turabi (1932–2016).

For many people, Al-Turabi will be remembered for enabling Sudan to provide sanctuary to the al-Qaeda leader, Osama bin Laden from

1990 to 1996, where Al-Turabi's activities is said to have contributed to the United States designating Sudan as a "*state sponsor of terrorism*" and when, in 1995, Al-Turabi was implicated in an assassination attempt against the then Egyptian President, Hosni Mubarak. Others recall Turabi's active role in military dictatorships which led to anyone being seen as a political dissident being imprisoned and tortured.

However, Al-Turabi's reputation as a fundamentalist was contradicted by other stances that he adopted at other stages in his career. Al-Turabi was accused by US intelligence agencies of being close to Osama bin Laden but in 1996, Sudan expelled the Al-Qaeda leader from the country. In 1994, Illrich Ramirez Sanchez, popularly known as Carlos, was extradited to France for terrorist offences. Whilst in 1992, Al-Turabi visited Washington DC:

> There he tried to put the best face (or mask) on the Islamic movement – one that would resemble Eastern Europe's democracy movements.[159]

In 2006, he said drinking alcohol could be allowed in certain circumstances—a view that is not generally accepted by Islamic scholars. Turabi later spoke of women's rights and how the first person to accept the revelation as revealed by the Prophet was a woman and how the Prophet sought the counsel of women and men.

For some American news outlets, this transformation of Turabi's views in the 2000s was hard to take in:

> Imagine if a conservative American religious leader—say, the Rev. Pat Robertson or the late Rev. Jerry Falwell—suddenly started promoting feminism, became a champion of affirmative action, or started hanging out with Snoop Dogg.
>
> Now, imagine the shock many Sudanese felt when the nation's top Islamic scholar, Hassan al-Turabi, publicly stated in 2006 that Muslim women didn't need to cover their hair with a veil. Or when he advocated the use of traditional music and dance for Islamic worship. Or when he encouraged the people of Darfur to oppose the government of President Omar al-Bashir.[160]

Berridge has argued that it was Turabi's pragmatism in the face of a fluid domestic political scene which led to these political zig-zags:

> An opposition leader remarked of al-Turabi in 1995 that one of his distinguishing features was his acceptance of the need to 'swim with the current even if it goes against his wishes'. This recognition signals the relevance of the local political context to the political form that Islamism took in Sudan. Al-Turabi's Islamist experiment was shaped by the fluid and unstable character of the Sudanese state, His power was not so much a product of personal charisma, significant as this was, as his ability to adapt to Sudan's highly fluid political environment by repeatedly reconfiguring the network of alliances that held the formal government, the shadow government and the security apparatus together.[161]

Turabi led the Sudanese section of the Muslim Brotherhood in the 1960s[162] and he was close to the business, political and military elite in Khartoum. However, when Turabi did contest elections, when they were held, the level of support he received was limited. This may be due to the Wahhabi approach to Islam[163] which Turabi adopted which resonated amongst the Sudanese elite but did not fully connect with the spiritual Sufi tradition that was prevalent in the rest of the country.

Turabi was close to two Sudanese leaders who gained power via military coups—Jaafar Nimeriy and Omar al-Bashir. In 1969, Nimeriy gained power by overturning a civilian government in a military coup. Despite his success, Nimeriy's base of support was limited. Consequently, he reached out to Turabi and other religious leaders to strengthen his position. It was during this period that an Islamic finance institution was said to have been used to help buttress the new President's position.

The Faisal Islamic Bank of Sudan was, according to Berridge, used to support the regime with the bank's founder, Saudi Prince Mohamed Al Faisal Al Saud having acted as one of the mediators in the "1977 Reconciliation" between Nimeriy and religious leaders. These actions:

> … transformed the higher echelons of the Islamic Movement into a 'corporation', empowering a small elite of financiers and officials whose links to the Islamic banking system enabled them to accrue power and influence in both the public and private sectors.[164]

It has been argued that Saudi Arabia wanted to ensure Sudan remained within its sphere of influence—and Islamic banking may have helped to attain this strategic objective:

> It was Islamists with strong connections in Saudi Arabia, notably Ali Abdalla Yacub and Abd al-Rahim Hamdi, who first established the relationship with al-Faisal and procured the capital used to fund the emergence of Islamic banking in Sudan. Thus, al-Turabi's movement in cash-strapped Sudan became beholden to Saudi financial institutions and pious foundations, many of which identified with a Salafi brand of Islam quite distinct from his own.[165]

In 1984, Al-Turabi as Attorney-General under President Nimeriy decreed that conventional banking would cease and only Islamic finance would be allowed. As a consequence, Al-Turabi said that Sudan's Central Bank "*must find another role to play*" which indicated either a lack of interest as to the role of a central bank in a purely Islamic economy or he was not keen on the supervisory role the Central Bank could adopt to ensure banking due diligence was adhered to.[166]

Whatever was the reason, the neglected role of the central bank has made the institution a centre for reform under the transitional government from 2019.

Whilst these political shenanigans were taking place, the needs of the Sudanese people were not being addressed. There was a need to invest in agriculture to improve daily life but an analysis of conventional and Islamic banking during the period of civilian government before Nimeriy, during Numeriy's presidency and then during the Bashir regime from 1989 found that the funding needs of farmers was being ignored.

Instead, exploitative lending practices at a village level continued whilst funds from the banking sector focused on the security apparatus and related businesses:

> The village crop buyer in rural Sudan combines this function with trading consumer goods by allowing farmers to barter some of their crop before harvesting for consumer goods at a reduced price agreed in advance in an informal contract known as the shiel system. As a result of the lack of loanable funds, the shiel system has dominated traditional agriculture and is characterised as being very exploitative.[167]

As noted by Ibrahim:

Traditional agriculture, crafts and small-scale industries are dominant in Darfur and Kordofan regions in which the degree of bank concentration is very poor … the *FIB (Faisal Islamic Bank of Sudan)* has mainly concentrated on traditional commercial banking activities.

Ibrahim added:

In Sudan, development effort was - and still is - concentrated in Khartoum and the Central Region. All other regions are backward, with slight variations. Darfur, Kordofan and the Southern regions are the most backward areas in terms of development projects, per capita income and standard of living. The new branches have been located in areas that already had banking facilities, hence they have made little contribution to rural development and a balanced distribution of investment throughout the country.[168]

The transitional government is now focusing on reform plans that will also aid the process towards an elected civilian government whilst the former President is on trial for embezzlement.

In August 2019, Bashir was charged with hoarding US$90 million that he had received from the late King Abdullah of Saudi Arabia and current Saudi Crown Prince Mohammed bin Salman, with some of these funds ($25 million) found in the former President's home. The defence legal team for Bashir claimed the funds were received in a personal capacity.

Now that the Bashir regime is over, Saudi Arabia and the United Arab Emirates decided, in April 2019, to offer US$3 billion of support to maintain stability in Sudan—though the journalist, Nesrine Malik, claimed it was really an attempt to maintain the Gulf's sphere of influence in Sudan.[169]

In the meantime, the Sudanese transitional Prime Minister, Dr Abdalla Hamdok, in October 2019, called for wholesale reform of the economy:

Achieving a successful democratic transition will be contingent on addressing serious economic challenges, with deep reforms needed to stabilize the economy and implement structural transformation in the coming years. Wide-ranging political and economic reforms, correctly formulated and applied, must create the conditions for assured growth, development and prosperity in the long term.[170]

Then in September 2020, Hamdok and Abdel-Azizi al Hilu of the Sudan People's Liberation Movement formally agreed to separate religion from the state—thereby ending any special recognition of shari'a within Sudanese law.

The Islamic economic model of Sudan, then, is over.

Except, of course, it never really existed in the first place as crony capitalism was the real model of the Sudanese economy.

The issue for the Islamic finance industry is whether the branding of Islamic finance as it related to decades of poor governance in Sudan will negatively impact the wider global perception of the sector. As for Sudan itself, only time will tell if the positive models of Islamic finance will, at last, be applied to the reconstruction of the nation.

The Russian Orthodox Church and Islamic Finance

The emergence of Islamic finance has had an influence for a range of nations that were not intimately involved in the formation and development of the industry.

This later stage in the history of Islamic finance is impacting upon geopolitics and how other faiths are responding to the ideas and efficacy of Islamic finance.

Russia is an interesting case study in this respect for, until recently, Russia was not seen as a key market for Islamic finance despite the fact that 10% of the Russian population (14,220,000 people) are Muslims who may be interested in this market.[171]

In fact, Russian President, Vladimir Putin, seemed hostile to Islam in the first half of the 2000s.

At that time, Russian forces were fighting separatists in the Russian province of Chechnya in what became known as the Second Chechen War (1999–2009). According to Taus Dzhabrailov, who was the head of Chechnya's then interim Parliament, between 150,000 to 160,000 people were killed during the First Chechen War (1994–1996) and the Second Chechen War.[172]

During a press conference with then German Chancellor, Gerhard Schroder, in 2002, Putin made a bizarre comment about Islam and circumcision when a *Le Monde* journalist challenged the Russian President on the use of fragmentation bombs in Chechnya.

Later in this same press conference, when again answering a question on the war against Chechen separatists, Putin said "*You are in danger if you decide to become a Muslim. It is not going to save you anyway because they believe traditional Islam is hostile to their goals*". The remarks were condemned by the European Commission as "*entirely inappropriate*".[173]

However, in November 2019, President Putin was full of praise as to the values of Islam. Speaking at a religious conference in Kyrgyzstan, Putin said "*Islam and Orthodox Christianity, just like other world religions, are based on fundamental humanistic values that are of enduring importance — on mercy and love for one ... justice and respect for human beings*".[174]

What can account for this change in perspective?

Geopolitical considerations are a key concern as Russia's position in the world has shifted over the first two decades of the twenty first century. Boris Yeltsin and his successor, Vladimir Putin, made strenuous efforts to build positive relationships with the United States and the European Union. Later, though, Russian forces directly intervened in the Syrian civil war whilst there were allegations in June 2020 of Russian mercenaries engaged on one side of the Libyan civil war. As Dmitri Trenin of the Carnegie Centre in Moscow argued:

> Russia's military engagement in Syria was not only, or even primarily about Syria or even the Middle East. Moscow was seeking a comeback to the global arena as a great power.[175]

Russia was also seeking allies further to EU and US sanctions after Russian forces annexed Crimea from Ukraine in 2014. The Russian economy has been severely impacted by sanctions where the political economic model of the nation was seen as flailing from the actions taken in 1991 following the end of the Cold War:

> The problem was not that the young reformers were too radical, but that they were too fanatical. They sought to impose capitalism with the same fervour as their ancestors had fought for communism or defended autocracy. And they made the classic mistakes of all fanatics. They thought their own small band of revolutionaries could transform Russia without grassroots support – and they found themselves without a political powerbase. They thought the central tenet of their faith, private property, was ultimately all that mattered – and watched helplessly as corruption, a weak state and ineffective laws made private ownership close to irrelevant. They made a Faustian bargain with the oligarchs which forever corrupted their revolution.[176]

It is within this context that Islamic finance was seen as a new opportunity for Russia to access finance. The state development bank, Vnesheconombank, established trade delegations to the Middle East to gain an understanding of Islamic finance. Further trade delegations to learn about Islamic finance came from the Moscow Industrial Bank, SME Bank and the Russian Direct Investment Fund.

However, in 2009, Igor Shuvalov, First Deputy Prime Minister of Russia, stated during the *Russia-Arabic World Business Dialogue* that Russia was not seeking investment in the banking sector from the Gulf:

> Lately many countries, and even Western governments, look at the Arabic world as a donor community. We are not one of them.[177]

The emergence of Islamic finance in Russia has not been plain sailing. The Badr-Forte Bank was licenced in 1991 and became fully operational in 1997 but in 2006 it lost its banking licence for non-compliance with anti-money laundering regulations. Other Islamic finance operations have been closed by the authorities such as Amal Financial House, a subsidiary of Bulgar Bank in Yaroslavl in 2017, Ellips Bank in Nizhniy Novgorod and Express Bank in Dagestan in 2013.

This may be no reflection on Islamic finance per se but the consequences of the decisions of the head of the Russian Central bank, Elvira Nabiullina, to finally tackle corruption across the whole of the Russian banking sector. At least 293 banks lost their licences, some of which included large institutions such as Vneshprombank and Intercommerzbank.[178]

This confusing picture may also indicate the internal tensions within the Russian political system combined with a tendency by some in the Russian elite to prioritise geopolitical matters before other considerations.

However, Islamic finance has made itself felt in Russia by the response of the Russian Orthodox Church. In June 2015, the Russian Orthodox Church called on the Duma (Russian Parliament) to pass legislation to allow shari'a compliant banking to take place.

Hoggarth argued that the stance of the Church was intended to help Russia access new sources of funding to combat sanctions. This analysis presumably relates to the close links between the hierarchy of the Russian Orthodox Church and the Presidency.[179]

In fact, I would contend the actual reason for the Church's stance is more innovative than this rationale would suppose.

The Russian Orthodox Church wants to establish its own finance system to rival laissez-faire capitalism and it has been inspired by the role and growth of Islamic finance. Far from seeing Islamic finance as a rival system, the Russian Orthodox Church sees Islamic finance as a model it can learn from. As will be discussed in Chapter 11 a similar perspective has been adopted by the Church of England.

Dmitri Lubomudrov, a legal adviser to the Russian Orthodox Church, stated that an Orthodox financial system was needed more than ever:

> We realised we couldn't stay dependent on the Western financial system but must develop our own. As with the Islamic system, the Orthodox one will be based not just on legislation, but on Orthodox morality as well, and will be an invitation to businessmen seeking security at a time of crisis.[180]

At the launch of the Orthodox financial system in January 2015, Russian Orthodox Church officials referenced the commercial success of Islamic finance to justify their venture. This initiative was inspired by theological motives. One of the key drivers of the initiative, senior Orthodox cleric, Vsevolod Chaplin, had condemned Western style capitalism for corrupting morals.

Under the system that was unveiled in 2015, there would be a similar permissive approach to investment strategy as seen in Islamic finance where sectors, such as gambling, are excluded from receiving funds. However, the Orthodox system does allow interest in loan repayments—but at a very low level which would not be comparable to a market rate.

The Russian Orthodox Church was also adopting a similar approach to currency exchange rate fluctuations as adopted in Islamic finance where futures trading on an intangible asset, such as money, is prohibited. The head of the Church, Patriarch Krill of Moscow, told Rossiya-1 TV in January 2015 that exchange rate fluctuations did not reflect the real economy—a stance that is generally shared by Islamic scholars:

> There's no need to dramatise this sudden change in the exchange rate - it cannot radically impact on the welfare of most citizens. Without it, we wouldn't have switched to diversifying our economy. But it's time now to create a real economy, producing value through a genuine consolidation of our country's economic power.[181]

Despite the backing of the Patriarch the establishment of the Russian Orthodox Church financial system was not meant to be—for now.

The Church established Peresvet Bank which traded as the Commercial Bank for Charity and Spiritual Development of the Fatherland.

In 2016, the central bank put Peresvet under "*temporary administration*" following an inspection. In April 2017, the central bank lent 66.7 billion roubles (US$1.9 billion) to keep the bank afloat. Later that year the Russian Regional Development Bank owned by oil producer Rosneft took over Peresvet which continued to require further central bank financial support in 2018.

Whilst the ambitions of the Russian Orthodox Church became embroiled within the endemic problems of the Russian banking system, the whole episode demonstrated how Islamic finance was changing ideas from people of other faiths as to the meaning and contribution of Islam towards meeting social and equitable objectives.

That is one of the singular achievements of Islamic finance in changing hearts and minds as to the values and vision of Islam for the wider world.

Egypt

The future direction of the Islamic finance industry is not as linear as some commentators would suppose. It has been envisaged that Islamic finance would appeal to countries with majority Muslim populations and this would be the core market for the industry.

However, as discussed in Chapter 9, the widening of the Islamic finance market between Malaysia, Indonesia and Brunei Darussalam to other nations across South East Asia such as Thailand, with a majority Buddhist population, and the economic powerhouse which is Japan, are indicators that this form of finance has attractions for a wider consumer base due to its agile contract structures and its ethical framework for investment.

This is not to ignore the fact that Islamic finance providers were also trying to appeal to Muslim minority populations in various East Asian countries but the interest in the model is growing beyond this core consumer base.

Beyond East Asia, we can test the hypothesis that Islamic finance will always have a strong presence in countries with large Muslim populations. That has not proved to be the case in Egypt and Lebanon.

As of 2017 in Egypt, there were three Islamic finance institutions and there were around twelve Islamic finance 'windows'—conventional banks who operate separate Islamic finance operations.

Islamic finance assets were valued at 226 billion Egyptian pounds in 2017 (US$12.8 billion) which was an increase of 10.24% as of 2016 but, overall, Islamic finance made up 6% of the Egyptian banking sector.[182] This is in a country with the largest population in the Arab world (98.42 million).[183]

The rule of Gamal Abdul Nasser from the early 1950s was prone towards nationalisation and maintaining the dominant role of the State within the economy. This was a reaction to the colonial diktats of the British whose expropriation of Egyptian resources marred the development of the Egyptian economy.

In 1956, the UK and France, with the support of Israel, tried to regain control of the Suez Canal. Nasser's success in not succumbing to these military advances (aided by US President Dwight Eisenhower putting economic pressure on the UK, France and Israel to withdraw their troops) strengthened Nasser's political standing.

From an economic perspective, this also led Nasser to impose import controls and to continue the nationalisation of foreign-owned assets. As Nasser advanced the cause of Arab nationalism, he was coaxed by the Soviet Union who began to provide military supplies to Egypt.

Falling within the Soviet sphere of influence may have been an additional factor for Egypt to continue its nationalisation drive. In the 1960s, Nationalisation Laws 117 and 118 were passed enabling the state to be part of the means of production. The 1962 National Charter gave the State the power to nationalise any company that was owned jointly with the private sector.

However, the failure of Egyptian forces in the 1967 Six Day War against Israel not only shook the confidence of the Egyptian state but it began to change the economic direction of Egypt.

Nasser offered his resignation as President in a dramatic broadcast to the Egyptian people. There were demonstrations for Nasser to remain in post and when, in September 1970, Nasser died from a heart attack, the streets of Cairo were filled with thousands of mourners paying tribute to the departed leader.

It was during the period of Nasser's rule that—arguably—the first ever Islamic financial institution was formed in Egypt during the 1960s. The short-lived bank was not even called Islamic but this could have been out of deference to the ruling authorities whose primary ideological driver was Arab nationalism as opposed to the goal of Muslim unity as propagated by King Faisal of Saudi Arabia (the experience of Mit Ghamr is discussed in detail in Chapter 6).

The accession of Anwar Sadat to the Presidency heralded the era of infitah or economic openness. This was a significant pivot away from the socialist policies of Nasser towards opening up international trade. This policy direction was before the establishment of the first Islamic banks in Saudi Arabia and the UAE.

Foreign capital was invited into Egypt and joint banking ventures between Egyptian and European banking entities were formed. The oil price rise in 1971, at the instigation of the members of the Organisation for Petroleum Exporting Countries (OPEC) also had a knock-on impact in assisting Egyptian economic growth.

In 1973, Egyptian and Syrian forces attacked Israel in the Yom Kippur War (also known as the Ramadan War). Whilst the attacking forces were not successful, the initial gains made in the campaign, strengthened Sadat's position with other Arab governments. With these improved relations with its neighbours, the decision was made by Prince Mohammed al Faisal al Saud to open the Faisal Islamic Bank of Egypt with the institution first opening its doors in 1979.

A further economic consequence of the Yom Kippur War was that Egypt was able to gain financial support from its neighbours but concerns grew as to the amount of funds Egypt was seeking:

> A new wariness had crept into the relations between Egypt and its Arab creditors. On the one hand Saudi Arabia and Kuwait came to the conclusion that what they were providing was essentially balance of payments support to sustain a way of life, based on consumer subsidies, that Egypt could not afford.[184]

It was political concerns which began to upset Sadat's economic policies. In 1979, US President Jimmy Carter finally brokered an agreement between Sadat and Israeli Prime Minister, Menachem Begin that led to the return of the Sinai to Egypt. This was seen as a betrayal of the Palestinian cause and so later that year the Arab League expelled Egypt as a member under pressure from the Palestine Liberation Organisation leader, Yasser Arafat.

In 1981, Sadat was assassinated by a soldier during a military parade who was associated with Gama'a Islamiyya (Islamic Group). The assassination led to Hosni Mubarak becoming President.

The shock of the murder of Sadat contributed towards Mubarak having concerns about Islamic banking—for could this form of finance contribute to the rise of Islamist movements who were resorting more and more to violence in their advocacy of their vision of an Islamic society?

This concern was amplified when the Egyptian academic, Farag Foda was assassinated by Gama'a Islamiyya in 1992. Foda's critique of Islamist movements included his concerns as to the implications of Islamic banking in the public realm:

> Moneyed Islam flaunted its wealth to promote new, supposedly more righteous ways: introducing Islamic banking and then demanding that female employees wear the veil.[185]

During the funeral, thousands of people paid tribute to Foda including representatives of the Egyptian Government.

The influential scholar, Sheikh Muhammad Metwalli al-Sha'rawi (1911–1998) was said to be interested in Islamic banking but Mubarak did not encourage the growth of the industry.

As was discussed in Chapter 6, the Muslim Brotherhood had, over time, formulated a position that Islamic economic structures needed to be instituted. The advocacy of this stance by the Muslim Brotherhood may have further deterred Mubarak from taking seriously this model of finance when it was associated with a group that yearned for his downfall.

The rise of Islamist sentiment was an issue which Mubarak constantly dealt with. Therefore, when Gad al-Haq, the Grand Imam of Al-Azhar (one of the senior positions in Sunni Islamic jurisprudence) issued a fatwa supporting Islamic banking and also a fatwa supporting the horrific practice of female genital mutilation, this rang alarm bells for Mubarak. In 1996, Gad al-Haq died and Mubarak ensured he was replaced by Sheikh Muhammad Sayyid Tantawi.

As we discussed in Chapter 3, it was Tantawi who issued the controversial fatwa which stated that interest rates were allowed under shari'a law. Public support for Islamic finance in Egypt was also not helped when, in the 1990s, a series of so-called Islamic financial institutions turned out to be pyramid selling or ponzi schemes with investors losing their money in the ensuing scandal (this is discussed further in Chapter 5).

By the time of the 2011 Arab Spring, it was believed that the military was content with the economic status quo with estimates ranging between 5 to 40% of the economy being directly linked to the military and the International Monetary Fund stating that around half of Egyptian manufacturing was controlled by the military.[186]

After the short-lived Presidency of Mohammed Morsi of the Muslim Brotherhood, Abdel Fattah el-Sisi gained power and led an economic reform programme from 2016. With the backing of a $12 billion loan from the International Monetary Fund (IMF), the Government moved towards floating exchange rates, the introduction of value added tax, reforming energy subsistence and poverty alleviation programmes and improving access to finance for small and medium sized businesses.

In June 2020, in response to the economic pressure that the country was enduring because of the implications of the COVID-19 pandemic, the IMF agreed to a $5.2 billion standby arrangement for Egypt.

The reticence that held back Mubarak in embracing Islamic finance is a perspective that Sisi seems to agree with. Though President Sisi and Crown Prince Mohammed bin Salman of Saudi Arabia have developed a close working relationship on a wide range of subjects—from the 2017 economic blockade of Qatar to the Libyan civil war—there is no evidence to suggest that this has also led to the Egyptian Government being more open about Islamic finance.

Whilst it remains the view amongst key Egyptian decision makers that Islamist movements and Islamic finance are connected in some way, the potential for movement in embracing Islamic finance may continue to be very limited.

So far, there has been some cautious movement in allowing some Islamic finance activity to take place. As we saw in Chapter 7, this includes Islamic crowdfunding operations in Cairo.

Time will tell whether this gradual trend towards opening up to the opportunities offered by Islamic finance will continue.

Lebanon

Beirut was described as the Paris of the Mediterranean. With its café culture and bohemian culture, Beirut was viewed as the cultural capital of the Middle East bringing together an eclectic mix of views and culture. It was also a centre for international trade and finance.

However, the rise of Islamic banking in the 1970s coincided with the devastating Lebanese civil war which lasted from 1975 to 1990. 150,000 Lebanese and non-Lebanese people were killed and at least a further 100,000 people suffered severe injuries.

What began as a serious clash between Maronite Christian militias against a coalition of Palestinian, Sunni and Druze groups escalated when, from 1976, Syrian forces entered Lebanon on the pretext of keeping the peace whilst using force to maintain and expand its sphere of influence.

In 1989 the Arab League sponsored the Taif Accords which eventually brought peace and a new constitutional settlement for the country. It was agreed that in order to reflect the religious diversity of Lebanon, the President must be a Maronite Christian, the Prime Minister must be a Sunni Muslim, and the Speaker of the National Assembly must be a Shi'a Muslim.

This arrangement stemmed from the "National Pact", an unwritten agreement which was established in 1943 during meetings between Lebanon‘s first president (a Maronite) and its first prime minister (a Sunni). This arrangement was formalised in 1990 with the drafting of the Constitution following the Taif Accords. The Lebanese Parliament also has seats allocated for elected politicians from differing Christian and Muslim groups.

It was Rafiq Hariri, a successful businessman who had made his money in Saudi Arabia during the civil war, who was able to take hold of the political initiative and lead the reconstruction of the country as Prime Minister from 1992 to 1998 and from 2000 to 2004. Whilst other countries in the region were considering the role of Islamic finance within their political economic structures, Hariri focused on adopting a form of developmental capitalism—with the State guiding development—to transform the prospects of the nation.

The Council for Development and Reconstruction was established to oversee the reconstruction. Solidere was a company listed on the Beirut stock exchange which owned the property rights for central Beirut. These two entities were key in levering in funds from Gulf investors. The Lebanese currency was also anchored to the US dollar. The central bank took an active role to maintain high interest rates to sustain investors' interest in buying Lebanese treasury bills. The whole economic effort was backed by the World Bank and the International Monetary Fund.

Baumann argued that all was not as it seemed:

> Rafiq Hariri and his technocrats were defending their policies with liberal rhetoric. Growth was to be private sector driven; macro-economic stability was to attract foreign investors; the state acted not as a producer or wealth redistributor but a facilitator in creating a business-friendly environment—not least through providing world-class infrastructure.
>
> Yet Hariri's policies and the way they were realised through the takeover of key economic institutions by the Hariri network made Lebanon less liberal. The establishment of Solidere rode roughshod over the rights of property owners. Lebanon had maintained a free-floating exchange rate even in the darkest days of currency collapse in the 1980s, but under Hariri's watch the exchange rate regime was altered into a highly managed—and highly costly—dollar peg. Both policies clearly benefited Hariri personally, via his share in Solidere and ownership of Banque Mediterranee.[187]

For many Lebanese citizens, the sight of construction work taking place across the nation was what really mattered. It gave many people renewed hope that the country was pivoting away from war, sectarian division and destruction towards a brighter future. It led some people to call Rafiq Hariri "*Mr Lebanon*". It also meant that the economic strategy—whilst utilising investment from the Gulf—included little space for Islamic finance to operate within.

In February 2005, Rafiq Hariri was assassinated when his car exploded—caused by a bomb which also killed an additional 21 people (a member of Hezbollah was later found guilty of conspiracy in these murders by a United Nations tribunal in August 2020). The Syrian Government denied they were responsible but public opinion reacted with shock and condemnation of Syria as Hariri was a critic of the continuing Syrian military presence in the country as well as being concerned at the role of the Syrian and Iranian backed Hezbollah militia in southern Lebanon.

Later that month, over 70,000 people demonstrated in Beirut's Martyrs Square against the Syrian military presence. In March 2005, between 200,000 to 500,000 supporters of Hezbollah demonstrated in support of the Syrian presence. In response, 1 million people packed into Martyrs Square later that same month demanding an end to Syrian troops being stationed in the country. The public pressure and the changing political dynamics proved too much for the Syrian Government and in April 2005, Syrian forces finally left Lebanon.

With war, political upheaval and the original economic approach adopted for reconstruction, Lebanon has not had the time—compared to other Middle Eastern countries—to embrace Islamic finance. This political turmoil erupted again in 2017 when the son of Rafiq Hariri, Saad Hariri—who was, by then, Prime Minister, resigned from his post whilst visiting Saudi Arabia.

Allegations swirled that the Saudi authorities were holding Saad Hariri against his will. The direct intervention of French President, Emmanuel Macron, seemed to take the heat out of the crisis with Saad Hariri remaining in post until he was forced to resign in January 2020 due to the economic crisis. Then in August 2020, there was an explosion at the port of Beirut. It emerged the devastation and loss of life was caused by the negligent storage of ammonium nitrate. In response to public pressure, the Lebanese Government resigned.

As of July 2018, there were five Islamic banks in the country.[188] Adnan Youssef of the Al-Baraka Group noted that it may take some considerable time for Islamic finance to bed in within Lebanon:

> Even in the Gulf region where Islamic finance is booming, it took a lot of time for people to invest in the industry. Islamic banks were not available in Saudi Arabia, Qatar and Oman 15 years ago, for instance, and they went into full gear only a short time ago.[189]

From 2019, the Lebanese economy went into freefall which was later aggravated by the COVID-19 pandemic and the explosion at the Port of Beirut:

> To keep those investments coming, the central bank offered ever-higher interest rates for large deposits, whose yields could be covered only by newer deposits at even higher rates.
>
> That strategy, which analysts have likened to a state-sponsored Ponzi scheme, ran out of gas last year when new depositors suspected the policy was unsustainable and stopped coming. Soon, the real dollars in the bank were far short of the theoretical dollars that had been earned in interest on previous deposits.[190]

With the economic crisis having morphed into a political crisis, it seems the time has never been quite right for Islamic finance to be firmly established in a stable Lebanon.

Republic of Ireland and the United Kingdom

The rolling lush green hills of County Kildare and County Limerick may not automatically be associated with Islamic finance.

The Republic of Ireland, though, is quietly positioning itself as a European centre for Islamic finance. If successful, this would be a significant economic achievement.

How has Ireland begun to position itself as an Islamic finance hub?

France had the opportunity to be the leading European centre for Islamic finance. As we shall see in the next chapter, France did not fully embrace this market.

Then along came Brexit.

Before the decision was made for the UK to leave the European Union, the United Kingdom had been one of the most successful countries—with a non-Muslim majority population—to lever in Islamic finance investments.

The London Stock Exchange met the needs of Islamic finance investors and the UK Government had been adept in adapting tax laws to ensure that ijara mortgages did not incur two sets of stamp duty when title of ownership of a property was transferred.

As discussed in Chapter 4, the UK also pioneered sovereign Sukuk issuances in the European market space.

There are three substantial reasons for the Islamic finance market having succeeded so well in the UK. The first relates to the primacy of London as one of the top two money markets in the world. With some reticence from the United States to engage fully with Islamic finance (as will be discussed in Chapters 11 and 12), this has left the space open for London to realise these opportunities.

Despite fierce party political competition in the UK, growing the Islamic finance market has gained cross party consensus—despite the occasional Islamophobic headline in some British newspapers.

The UK also has a significant Muslim population (2.5 million)[191] which enables a core market to develop and grow. This had contributed to Birmingham and Leeds also becoming European centres of Islamic finance.

Finally, the UK has been successful for many years in levering in investment from the Gulf, particularly from Qatar. The Qatar Investment Fund (QIA) has significant investments in the United Kingdom. Sheikh Hamad bin Jassim bin Jaber Al-Thani, the former head of the QIA was quoted in

2016 as stating that the total value of Qatari investment into the UK was £30 billion.[192]

QIA holdings in the UK include:

> 879 commercial and residential properties in London, including the Canary Warf Group, Chelsea Barracks, the Shard tower, the HSBC Tower and Harrods; the QIA also has a stake in the Savoy Hotel, while another unit of the QIA, Qatar Holdings, owns Claridge's Hotel, the Berkeley and the Connaught Hotels, with an additional stake in the Intercontinental Hotel, Park Lane.
> 22% of Sainsbury's (convenience chain stores)
> 20% of London Heathrow airport. Qatar Airways also has a 20% stake in IAG, owner of British Airways
> 6% of Barclays Bank.[193]

Whilst Islamic banking began in the UK in 1985 with Murabaha financing, it was the initiative of Qatari investors to recognise the UK as the place for the development of Islamic retail banking. The UK's first Islamic retail bank, Islamic Bank of Britain (IBB), was formed in 2004. In 2014, the bank was taken over by the Qatari bank, Masraf Al Rayan and IBB was renamed Al Rayan Bank.

Not all banks have maintained their Islamic finance operations in the UK. HSBC had an Islamic retail finance window in the UK—HSBC Amanah. It has since ceased operations in Britain whilst HSBC Amanah continues to grow from strength to strength in Malaysia.

In terms of the financial institutions involved in Islamic wholesale or investment banking in the UK, these include:

- United Bank UK
- Standard Chartered
- HSBC
- Al Rayan Bank
- Rosette Merchant Bank
- Barclays Capital
- Royal Bank of Scotland
- Gatehouse Bank
- QIB UK
- European Islamic Investment Bank

- Bank of London and the Middle East

However, these bright prospects for the continued growth of the industry in Britain dimmed due to the outcome of a referendum on whether or not the UK would remain a member of the European Union.

On 23 June 2016, 51.89% of people (17,410,742) who voted in the referendum decided to leave compared to 48.11% who voted to remain (16,141,241).

This provided a tremendous opportunity for the Republic of Ireland to lever in Islamic finance funds from the UK as it would remain in the world's largest single market—the European Union (EU).

The commercial advantages of EU membership included the 1987 Single European Act (SEA). With its economic provisions, the SEA instigated the world's largest trading area. It did so by permitting the free movement of goods, capital, labour and services amongst and between member states.

There is also the EU's Services Directive. With the directive having been agreed to by EU member states in 2006, its objective was to make progress towards a genuine Single Market in Services by simplifying administrative procedures, removing obstacles for services activities and enhancing trust between EU member states and the confidence of providers and consumers in the Single Market. Whilst this specific directive did not include banking, it enabled subsidiary support services for banking to be provided on a cross European basis.

In May 2020, the European Union agreed for a renewed push to complete the Capital Markets Union. If attained, this will make it even easier for banks based in any member state to provide services to businesses across Europe. The European Banking Authority also provides a single rulebook for banking operations to take place across the EU.

In January 2020, the UK formally left the European Union but the UK remained in a transitional phase until the end of December 2020 when EU single market rules would still have applied.

During this period, the British Government was negotiating with the EU's European Commission for the financial services industry in the UK to be treated as equivalent to EU based banks so that access to the single market would continue. However, on 30 June 2020, Michel Barnier, the lead EU negotiator in the talks with the British Government, made it clear that the UK Government's objective would not be achieved:

> I know that many hope our equivalence decisions will provide continuity. Many believe that 'responsible politicians' on both sides of the Channel should make this happen but things have to change. The UK and the EU will be two separate markets, two jurisdictions. And the EU must ensure that important risks to our financial stability are managed within the framework of our single market.[194]

Whether by chance or design, the Irish Government had positioned itself to be in a good position to take advantage of Brexit when it came to Islamic finance.

The Republic of Ireland was not going to leave the EU and during the first stage of Brexit talks, the EU institutions had firmly supported the Irish Government over the controversial issue of trade passing across the Republic of Ireland/Northern Ireland (UK) border.

In addition, as an English-speaking jurisdiction, this enabled the transfer of operations to Ireland from the UK to be that much easier. Ireland had already been successful in attracting major tech firms such as Facebook and Alphabet (parent company of Google) to the country—though the EU later complained that business tax rates for these firms were too low.

The Irish Government had also prepared the ground for attracting Islamic finance businesses. In October 2009, the Irish Revenue Commissioners published a Tax Briefing which clarified the taxation of several Islamic finance products, without amending any provisions of Irish law. It confirmed that three Islamic finance products —takaful, ijara and Islamic investment funds—would be taxed just like conventional insurance, leasing and investment funds.

The Finance Act 2010 later amended provisions of Ireland's tax laws to "*extend tax treatment applicable to conventional finance transactions to … Islamic financial products which achieve the same economic result in substance as comparable conventional products*".

These 2010 changes would prove to be particularly helpful for Sukuk issuances and ijara financing.

In 2012, the then Taoiseach (Irish Prime Minister), Enda Kenny, spoke of Dublin being a hub for Islamic finance whilst the then Tánaiste (Irish Deputy Prime Minister), Eamon Gilmore, declared that Ireland was a "*good fit*" for Islamic finance adding:

> We have to think of Ireland, in the words of President Clinton, not just as a gateway to Europe, but as a gateway to the world.[195]

A 2019 KPMG report found that "*approximately 20% of the Islamic funds market outside the Middle East are located in Ireland*".[196]

In 2016, Saudi Arabia issued a US$17.5 billion sovereign Sukuk on the Irish Stock Exchange.

In 2017, the Irish Stock Exchange listed a Sukuk issuance which raised US$9 billion. The Irish Stock Exchange also had sovereign Sukuk listings from Kuwait, Jordan, Oman and Bahrain.

In 2018, a subsidiary of Abu Dhabi Islamic Bank listed a US$750 million Sukuk facility on the Irish Stock Exchange. Other Sukuk issuers on the Irish Stock Exchange included Saudi Electricity Company, Emirates, Kuwait Energy, Ruwais Power Company and Emirates Telecommunications Corporation.

Ireland has a small Muslim population of around 50,000 people in a country whose total population is 4.9 million.[197] Whilst Islamic retail banking could be marketed to the Irish Muslim community, it is the investment side of Islamic finance—and Ireland's access to the world's largest single market (especially after Brexit)—which may continue to attract interest from the Gulf to Ireland.

After the 2019 Irish General Election, the largest opposition party was Sinn Fein. The party is well known for having been the political wing of the Irish Republican Army (IRA).

During the period of the "Troubles" between 1968 and 1998, violence between republicans, including the IRA, and loyalist militias combined with the role of the UK security forces, contributed to the deaths of at least 3500 people in Northern Ireland.

There is another side to Sinn Fein, though. From 1908 to 1921, Sinn Fein ran a co-operative bank whose operations had synergies with some of the contemporary practices of the Islamic finance industry.

Therefore this legacy of cooperative finance from Ireland's main opposition party combined with the support for Islamic finance from the two main political parties, Fianna Fail and Fianna Gael, who formed a coalition government with the Green Party in June 2020, means that political support for the continued development of the Islamic finance industry in the Republic of Ireland is likely to remain robust.

Political Economy and Islamic Finance

Far from Islamic finance being a niche product, it is now part of the mainstream financial services products being offered in south east Asia and the Middle East. This is changing the political economy of these regions where issues to do with equity, social justice and fairness are part of the everyday discourse in respect of the operation of a household or a country.

This is not to say that Islamic finance has engendered in and of itself a fairer society. Concerns about endemic corruption in Malaysia or human rights abuses in the UAE still exist. What has changed, however, is how Islamic finance is altering the framework of the debate where ethical considerations has to be factored alongside competing societal forces.

At the same time, Islamic finance can be entwined with identity politics. We see that clearly in Malaysia where faith-based identities is beginning to take some precedence within the domestic political discourse as compared to debates about ethnic identity politics.

For Saudi Arabia, which is home to the holy cities of Mecca and Medina, Islamic finance and its self-identification with adherence towards Islam means that the elevation of Islamic finance within the body politic is a powerful statement as to the projection of its values beyond its borders.

However, when Islamic finance is associated with extremism and violence, as we discussed in respect of Egypt, then the progress of this industry can be stymied. In this scenario, identity politics is acting against the development of the industry in the Arab world's most populous country.

Beyond Muslim majority countries, we can see how the ethos and values of Islamic finance is beginning to shape society such as in Russia with the positive stance of the Russian Orthodox Church towards Islamic finance. In practice, we can see that Islamic finance is being used as a proxy to condemn the secular and laissez-faire capitalist approach within Russia and to demonstrate to citizens that a faith-based financial system is not just desirable but practical as well.

As we will see in the next chapter, it is no surprise that the Church of England also cites shari'a law and Islamic finance in a positive vein to counteract the dominant secular and free market narrative that is prevalent in the United Kingdom.

It is, though, the example and effectiveness of Islamic finance which is probably having the greater impact in the UK in shaping domestic debates as to the shape of an ideal political economic system whilst in the Republic of Ireland, Islamic finance is being seen as a good fit for the nation economically but also in line with the ethical framework of the country which was based, to some extent, upon Catholicism.

However, as we are about to discover in the next chapter, some countries that seem ideally suited to embrace Islamic finance, such as France and the United States, are not doing so to a sufficient degree. We will discover whether one of the major hurdles holding back the further growth of Islamic finance across the world is not issues inherent within the industry but rather the broader matter of Islamophobia itself.

Could Islamophobia be deterring key decision makers from even considering the benefits of Islamic finance in the first place and—if this is so—what can be done by the industry to tackle this form of bigotry?

Notes

1. Amit K Kashyap, Anjani Singh Tomar (2016), *Financial Market Regulations and Legal Challenges in South Asia*, page 264.
2. Mit Ghamr is discussed in Chapter 7.
3. Davinia Hoggarth (2016), The Rise of Islamic Finance: Post-Colonial Market Building in Central Asia and Russia, *International Affairs*, vol. 92, no. 1.
4. Edited by Mark Beeson, *Contemporary Southeast Asia*, page 118.
5. As quoted by Emmy Abdul Alim, *Global Leaders in Islamic Finance*, page 70.
6. Salafist thinking reflects a revivalist branch of thought within Islam.
7. *Umm al-Qura*, 8 April 1966.
8. William Easterly (June 2001), *The Political Economy of Growth Without Development: A Case Study of Pakistan*, World Bank.
9. The Belt and Road Initiative is a global development strategy as developed by the Chinese Government in 2013 involving infrastructure development and investments in around 70 countries.
10. William Easterly (June 2001), *The Political Economy of Growth without Development: A Case Study of Pakistan*, World Bank.
11. Ibid.
12. Quoted by Pervez Tahir (January 2002), Introducing Iqbal the Economist, *The Pakistan Development Review*.
13. Mohammad Iqbal (2013), *The Reconstruction of Religious Thought in Islam*, pages 122–123.
14. M Hamidullah (April 1936), Islam's Solution to the Basic Economic Problems, Islamic Culture.

15. Sayyid Manazar Ahsan Gilani, Masalah yi Sod Muslim aur Harbimen, Maqalat-Gilani, page 152.
16. Keynes' ideas on the role of interest rates is discussed in Chapter 8.
17. Aurangzeb Mehmood (2002), Islamisation of Economy in Pakistan: Past, Present and Future, *Islamic Studies,* vol. 41, no. 4, pp. 675–704. Islamic Research Institute, Islamabad.
18. Irfan Ahmad (2013), *Islamic Reform in South Asia*, edited by Filippo Osella and Caroline Osella (Cambridge University Press), page 322.
19. Abul Ala Maududi, *Economic System of Islam*, page 25.
20. Safdar Ahmed, *Reform and Modernity in Islam.*
21. Laurence Louer, *Sunnis and Shi'a: A Political History.*
22. Muqtedar Khan, *Islam and Good Governance: A Political Philosophy of Ihsan*, page 44.
23. Syed Ahmad Barelvi (1786–1831) was from the Indian state of Awadh (now within the Indian state of Uttar Pradesh) who had used violence to oppose the Shi'a criticism of the first three caliphs.
24. Jamaat-e-Islami, the Barelvi legacy and the Deobandi school continues to have some relevancy in contemporary Pakistani religious and political discourse.
25. James Wynbrandt (2009), *A Brief History of Pakistan* (Facts on File). pages 216–217.
26. Abhijit V Banerjee (2010), *Investment Efficiency and the Distribution* as cited in *Equity and Growth in a Globalising World* (World Bank).
27. Ahmed, *Sectarian War*, page 29.
28. US diplomatic cable released via Wikileaks. Date of the cable was 14 January 2008.
29. As quoted in *Global Leaders in Islamic finance*, edited by Emmy Abdul Alim, page 30.
30. Review Judgement on Ribā: The Supreme Court of Pakistan (Sharī'at Appellate Bench), *Islamic Studies*, vol. 41, no. 4, 2002, pp. 705–724.
31. Ibid.
32. Central Bank of Pakistan, *22 Banks in Pakistan Offering Islamic Banking with 22% Annual Growth,* 12 December 2018.
33. Timur Kuran, *Islam & Mammon*, page 2.
34. Julia Stephens, *Governing Islam, Law, Empire and Secularism in Modern South Asia*, page 195.
35. World Economic Outlook Database, October 2019, *IMF.org*. International Monetary Fund.
36. Shi'a Islam has a different perspective on the order of the caliphs as discussed in Chapter 2.
37. Alexei Vassiliev, *King Faisal of Saudi Arabia*, page 341.
38. Ibid., page 290.

39. Amin al-Husseini has gone down in history as the man who, for a time, negotiated with Adolf Hitler in order to establish a Palestinian state.
40. The OIC today brings together 57 nations with a combined population of around 1.8 billion people.
41. OIC website (2020).
42. *Umm al Qura*, 18 July 1975.
43. As quoted in *Global Leaders in Islamic Finance*, edited by Emmy Abdul Alim, page 71.
44. David Commins, *The Gulf States—A Modern History*, page 63.
45. This is a reference to Muslims who rebelled against the third and fourth caliphs, Uthman and Ali, and the rulers of the Umayyad and Abbasid caliphates (Shi'a Islam has a different view on the order of the caliphs as discussed in Chapter 2).
46. Ibn Abidin, *Hashiya Radd al-Muhtar, 4.262.*
47. Figure as of 2017 as cited in *Mordor Intelligence, Global Islamic Finance Market Growth, Trends, and Forecast (2018–2024), June 2019.*
48. Muhammad Umer Chapra (1996), "What Is Islamic Economics?" Islamic Development Bank, Islamic Research and Training Institute, page. 45.
49. Maududi's role in the emergence of Islamic finance is discussed in the first part of this chapter.
50. Khurshid Ahmad's introduction paper to the First International Islamic Economics Conference (1976).
51. Ijaz Shafi Gilani (1976), *The Political Context to Islamic Economics: High and Low Road Strategies,* First International Islamic Economics Conference.
52. Weber's ideas are discussed further in Chapter 6.
53. Communique, First International Islamic Economics Conference, 1976.
54. Ibid.
55. Ibid.
56. Arthur Seldon, *Capitalism*, page 334.
57. Ibid., page 335.
58. Institute of Economic Affairs (IEA—British think tank) archive.
59. Robert Lacey (2009), *Inside the Kingdom: Kings, Clerics, Modernists, Terrorists, and the Struggle for Saudi Arabia* (Viking), page 48.
60. Lowry Institute for International Policy (2011), *The Future State of the World: What It Means for Australia's Foreign Aid Program.*
61. US Senator Jon Kyl during hearing before the sub-committee on terrorism, technology and homeland security of the Committee on the Judiciary of the US Senate investigating *Terrorism: Growing Wahhabi influence in the United States,* 26 June 2003.
62. https://www.telegraph.co.uk/news/worldnews/middleeast/qatar/11125897/The-Club-Med-for-terrorists.html.

63. Hamid al-'Ali (23 May 2002), Khasa'is al-Iqfisad al-Islami (Principles of Islamic Economics).
64. Hamid al-'Ali (2002), al-Banuk al-Islamiya.
65. In 2019, King Salman decreed that women could drive cars. However, some of the women activists who campaigned for this decree have been imprisoned. At the time of writing (2020) the imprisoned activists included Loujain al-Hathloul, Samir Badawi, Nassima al-Sadah, Nouf Abdelaziz, Shedan al-Anezi.
66. PBS, *Frontline* (2001).
67. Jim Krane (November 2017), Fellow in Energy Studies, Rice University's Baker Institute, Houston.
68. *The Economist magazine*, 5 October 2015.
69. Ibid.
70. Ben Freeman (October 2018), Center for International Policy, *The Saudi Lobby: How the Kingdom Wins in Washington.*
71. As cited in an interview for the BBC TV series, *House of Saud* (2018).
72. Saudi Government statement as reported by Saudi state news agency, SPA, 1 April 2020.
73. Saudi Government, *Financial Sector Development Program Charter—Delivery Plan 2020.*
74. Ibid.
75. *Financial Times*, 17 November 2017, *Saudi Investors Check Out After Hotel Turned into Luxury Prison.*
76. PBS *Frontline* documentary, 1 October 2019.
77. West Texas intermediate is a grade of crude oil used as a benchmark in oil pricing. This grade is described as light crude oil because of its relatively low density, and sweet because of its low sulfur content.
78. Professor Atif Kurbursi, 21 April 2020. https://theconversation.com/oil-crash-explained-how-are-negative-oil-prices-even-possible-136829.
79. Bloombery Television interview, 22 April 2020.
80. Ibid.
81. International Monetary Fund (February 2020), *The Future of Oil and Fiscal Sustainability in the GCC Region.*
82. Ibid.
83. Vince Cable, *The Storm: The World Economic Crisis and What It Means*, page 107.
84. https://gulfnews.com/business/analysis/gulf-states-must-not-over-react-on-imf-report-1.69793158.
85. https://gulfnews.com/uae/coronavirus-how-to-cope-with-debt-in-uae-after-a-lay-off-pay-cut-1.71073638.
86. Bloomberg Television, 19 May 2020.
87. Godolphin website (2020).
88. Ibid.

89. *The Atlantic* (April 2010), *All the Sheikh's Horses* (April 2010).
90. J Robinson (1988), page 83.
91. HE Sheikh Mohammed bin Rashid Al Maktoum, *Spirit of the Union.*
92. As quoted by Emmy Abdul Alim, *Global Leaders in Islamic Finance,* page 38.
93. Murabaha is explained in Chapter 4.
94. The controversial decision of the Qatar Central Bank in 2011 to ban conventional banks from establishing Islamic finance windows in its territory is explored in Chapter 11.
95. David Commins, *The Gulf States: A Modern History*, page 188.
96. https://www.emiratesislamic.ae/eng/expo-2020/.
97. Ben Freeman (October 2019), *The Emirati Lobby: How the UAE Wins in Washington*, Center for International Policy
98. Ibid.
99. UAE Ministry of Finance media release, 7 May 2020.
100. Compliance is discussed in further detail in Chapter 5.
101. OIC's Fiqh Academy is explored in Chapter 5.
102. HE Sheikh Mohammed bin Rashid Al Maktoum, *My Vision*, page 17.
103. The governing Khalifa royal family in Bahrain are Sunni Muslims whilst the majority of the Bahraini population are Shi'a Muslims.
104. Ali Shariati (2003), *Religion vs Religion,* translated by Laleh Bakhtiar, page 60.
105. Ali Shariati, translation, *And Once Again Abu Dharr Part 1.*
106. Ali Shariati (1968), *Islamology.*
107. Ali Shariati, *Jahatgiri-ye Tabaqati-e Islam*, vol. 10, pages 37–38.
108. *T M* Aziz (1993), The Role of Muhammad Baqir Al-Sadr in Shii Political Activism in Iraq from 1958 to 1980. *International Journal of Middle East Studies*, vol. 25, no. 2, pp. 207–222.
109. Da'wa refers to prosleytising the faith of Islam.
110. Baath literally means renaissance.
111. Tehran Times (10 April 2018), *The ninth of April, the martyrdom of the Sadrs*, 10 April 2018
112. Mohammed Baqir al-Sadr, *Iqistiduna*, Volume 2, Part One (Iranian Government translation).
113. Ibid.
114. Ibid.
115. Ibid.
116. Digby Jones, *Fixing Britain: The Business of Reshaping Our Nation.*
117. Mohammed Baqir al-Sadr, *Iqistiduna*, Volume 2, Part One (Iranian Government translation).
118. Mohammed Baqir al-Sadr, *Iqistiduna*, Volume 2, Part Two (Iranian Government translation).

119. Thomas Biegert, London School of Economics, LSE US Centre Blog, https://blogs.lse.ac.uk/usappblog/2017/10/03/a-generous-welfare-state-can-help-reduce-unemployment-if-there-are-good-job-opportuni ties-for-the-jobless/.
120. Al Nu'mani as quoted in al Ha'iri, Mabahith, 162–163.
121. Stansfield Turner (2005), page 180.
122. Reuters (4 February 2019), *Iran's First President Says Khomeini Betrayed 1979 Islamic Revolution,* 4 February 2019.
123. Khomeini, *Islam and Revolution*, page 64.
124. Scott Lucas, The US and Iran: Ahmadinejad, as cited in *Scripting Middle East Leaders*, page 223.
125. Charles Kurzman (2001), Critics Within: Islamic Scholars' Protest Against the Islamic State in Iran, *International Journal of Politics, Culture and Society*, vol. 15, No. 2, p. 347.
126. Hezbollah Open Letter, 16 February 1985.
127. Majmu'a Qawanin Sal-I 1366 (The Collection of Laws, 21 March 1987–20 March 1988), Iranian Ministry of Justice, page 912.
128. Ibid.
129. Nourbakhsh: Iranian Economy Has High Potential for Creating Jobs, *Tehran Times*, 17 April 2001.
130. Iran's Central Bank Governor Mohsen Nourbakhsh Dies of Heart Attack, *Iran News*, 23 March 2003.
131. Jordanian Government press conference, December 2004.
132. Drop in Deposit Rates, *Financial Tribune*, 29 April 2015.
133. Kazem Sadr (February 2008), 'Gharzul-hasaneh financing and institutions' as cited in *Islamic Finance for Micro and Medium Enterprises,* IRTI and Universiti Brunei Darussalam.
134. Castells and Portes, 1989, page 12.
135. Hernando de Soto, *Why Does the Informal Economy Matter? (*trans: Tim Ennis)
136. Rodney Wilson, *Islam and Economic Policy,* pages 117–118.
137. High Cost of Employment Boosting Informal Economy, *Financial Tribune*, 16 October 2017.
138. Richard E Benedick (1962), The Money Market In Iran, *The Pakistan Development Review*, vol. 2, no. 3, pp. 406–421.
139. Maryam Gahadassi (June 1998), *Informal Financial Institutions in Bazaar,* Cahiers d'etudes sur la Mediterranee orientale et le monde turco-iranien.
140. Guardian (23 September 2010), *Iran and Iraq Remember War That Cost More Than a Million Lives.*
141. Radiofarda (2006), "Sepah, Terrorism, and Militarism Irani dar meidan-e Jahani" (IRGC, Terrorism and Iranian Militarism in the globe), August 15, 2007b; Sazegara.

142. Open Source Center (2007), "Iran Economic Sanctions, Government Corruption 1–7 Nov 07," OSC Summary in Persian, IAP20071119306005, November 1–7, 2007d.
143. https://www.aseanstats.org/wp-content/uploads/2019/11/ASEAN_Stats_Leaflet_2019.pdf.
144. Mohamed Ariff (September 1988), Islamic Banking, *Asian-Pacific Economic Literature*, vol. 2, no. 2.
145. The role of Islamic finance in Indonesia is discussed further in Chapter 9.
146. Daromir Rudnyckyj (November 2013), From Wall Street to Halal Street, *The Journal of Asian Studies*, vol. 72, no. 4, pp. 831–848.
147. Christopher Bayly, *Forgotten Wars*, page 516.
148. Lee Kuan Yew comments on Television Singapura, 25 May 1965.
149. Anwar Ibrahim, *The Asian Renaissance*, page 112.
150. Rajah Rasiah, Norma Mansor, Chandran VGR (October 2015), Royal Professor Ungku Abdul Aziz: A Key Pillar in Malaysia's Development, *Institutions and Economies*, vol. 7, no. 3.
151. Emmy Abdul Alim, *Global Leaders in Islamic Finance*, page 125.
152. Ibid.
153. Chua Beng Huat (2010), within *East Asia's New Democracies*, page 238.
154. Ibid., page 237.
155. Syed Farid Alatas as contained in *The Blackwell Companion to Islamic Contemporary Thought*, page 596.
156. South China Morning Post, 3 January 2020.
157. General Council of Islamic Banks and Institutions/Islamic Research and Training Institute, *Sudan Islamic Finance 2016: Next Phase of Development.*
158. Ibn Khaldun, *Muqaddimah*, 288; R: II. 106–107.
159. Ami Ayalon (1992), *Middle East Contemporary Survey*, Volume Xvi, page 195.
160. Christian Science Monitor (13 July 2007), *Sudan's Legendary Islamist Take a Moderate View.*
161. W J Berridge, *Hasan al-Turabi: Islamist Politics and Democracy in Sudan*, page 80.
162. The role of the Muslim Brotherhood as it relates to Islamic finance is discussed further in Chapter 6.
163. The influence of Wahhabi thinking as it relates to Islamic finance is discussed earlier in this chapter.
164. W J Berridge, *Hasan al-Turabi: Islamist Politics and Democracy in Sudan*, page 80.
165. Ibid.
166. https://www.dabangasudan.org/en/all-news/article/op-ed-central-bank-essential-to-sudan-banking-reform.

167. Badr Al-Din Ibrahim, K. Raffer et al. (eds.), *The Least Developed and the Oil-Rich Arab Countries*, page 224.
168. Ibid.
169. https://www.theguardian.com/commentisfree/2019/may/05/saudi-arabia-sudan-uprising-omar-al-bashir.
170. Royal Institute of International Affairs (October 2019), *Sudanese Stakeholder Dialogues.*
171. US State Statement, 2017.
172. Chechen Official Puts Death Toll for 2 Wars at Up to 160,000, *New York Times*, 16 August 2005.
173. Putin Rejects Political Solution to Chechnya Conflict, *Independent*, 13 November 2002.
174. Islam and Orthodox Christianity Have the Same Values, Putin Says, *The Moscow Times*, 22 November 2019.
175. Carnegie Centre, November 2017.
176. Chrystia Freeland, *Sale of the Century: The Inside Story of the Second Russian Revolution,* page 349.
177. Why Islamic Banking Is Not Working in Russia, *Russia Beyond*, 29 March 2017.
178. Ibid.
179. Davina Hoggarth (2016), *The Rise of Islamic Finance: Post-Colonial Market Building in Central Asia and Russia,* International Affairs.
180. Russia's Orthodox Church Unveils Its Own Financial System, *The Tablet*, 15 January 2015.
181. Ibid.
182. Figures sourced from the Egyptian Islamic Finance Association.
183. World Bank. Population figures as of 2018.
184. John Waterbury, *The Egypt of Nasser and Sadat: The Political Economy of Two Regimes,* page 417.
185. Kim Ghattas (2020), *Black Wave*, page 188.
186. James L Gelvin, *The Arab Uprisings,* page 62.
187. Hannes Baumann, *Citizen Hariri*, page 85.
188. Hiyum Sujud, Boutheina Hachem (July 2018), Reality and Future of Islamic Banking in Lebanon, *European Journal of Scientific Research*, vol. 149, no. 4, pp. 410–422.
189. As quoted by Al Bawaba (6 January 2014), *Why Islamic Finance Is Failing in Lebanon.*
190. *New York Times* (10 May 2020), Lebanon's Economic Crisis Explodes Threatening Decades of Prosperity.
191. UK Census (2011).
192. Rhiannon Curry (17 March 2017), Qataris Own More of London Than the Queen, *Daily Telegraph.*

193. Jamie Robertson (9 June 2017), *Qatar: Buying Britain by the Pound*, BBC; Mohammed Sergie (11 January 2017), *The Tiny Gulf Country With a $335 Billion Global Empire*, Bloomberg.
194. Bloomberg (30 June 2020), *EU's Barnier Rejects UK Plans for Banking After Brexit.*
195. *The Journal* (12 May 2012), Ireland Is Becoming a Hub for Islamic Finance—But What Exactly Is It?
196. https://home.kpmg/i.e./en/home/insights/2019/05/islamic-finance-from-an-irish-perspective.html.
197. Eurostat (2019).

CHAPTER 11

Branding and Islamophobia

1990s and 9/11: Islamophobia

I remember the conversation so well.

In my then role as the Executive Director of an umbrella regional organisation, I recall outlining the benefits of Islamic finance to a representative of a Chamber of Commerce.

I spoke of the patient capital advantages and how the removal of the interest requirement enables repayment of loans based on the ability of the business to finance its liabilities rather than on an arbitrary figure linked to interest rates.

The Chamber of Commerce person was enthusiastic and wanted to know more until I told him that this financing model was called Islamic finance.

> James - you will have to change the name. That branding won't work around here.

This incident occurred in the 2000s when Islamophobia was openly expressed in the United Kingdom and countries around the world following the horrific terrorist attacks in the United States on 11 September 2001.[1]

Islamophobia was defined by the UK's Runnymede Trust, with its 1997 report, *Islamophobia: a challenge to us all*:

J. S. Watkins, *Islamic Finance and Global Capitalism*,
https://doi.org/10.1007/978-3-030-59840-2_11

> a useful shorthand way of referring to dread or fear of Islam – and therefore to fear or dislike of all or most Muslims.

Professor Tariq Modood of Bristol University has gone further and developed a wider definition of Islamophobia which attempts to address the range of motivations inherent with this prejudice:

> Islamophobia is the racialising of Muslims based on physical appearance or descent as members of a community and attributing to them cultural or religious characteristics to vilify, marginalise, discriminate or demand assimilation and thereby treat them as second-class citizens.[2]

Islamophobia clearly predated 9/11. Edward Said spoke of the 'otherness' that was viewed in some societies in respect of Islam and Islamic culture which, for the purposes of his book, he termed as Orientalism:

> a manner of regularised (or Orientalised) writing, vision and study dominated by imperatives, perspectives and ideological biases ostensibly suited to the Orient. The Orient has become a mirror image of what is the inferior and alien Other to the West.[3]

Interestingly, Said linked the phenomenon of Islamic fundamentalism with the concept of post-colonial thinking where the legacy of European dominance had contributed to the development of narrow ideological constructs as articulated by Maududi[4] amongst others.

The Islamic scholar, Ibrahim Abu-Rabi (1956–2011) argued that this form of fundamentalism "*is as strong a component ... in modern societies as the Quranic impact on the Arab mind*".[5] Part of the context of this insight reflects the perspective that fundamentalist violence contravenes the belief system of Islam.

There is a specific verse in the Qur'ran which condemns acts of violence:

> On that account: We ordained for the Children of Israel that if any one slew a person—unless it be for murder or for spreading mischief in the land—it would be as if he slew the whole people: and if any one saved a life, it would be as if he saved the life of the whole people.[6]

It is beyond the purview of this book to consider the socio-economic, political and religious factors that has contributed towards the emergence of Islamophobia and fundamentalism.

However, it is important to consider this issue from the perspective of Islamic finance as this form of prejudice has predisposed many people to be opposed to Islamic finance before knowing about the nature and content of this finance model.

Arguments regarding the rise of Islamophobia was particularly prevalent in the early 1990s. At that time there was renewed hope amongst policymakers in the United States that the end of the Cold War marked a new era of global cooperation and shared prosperity. Nowhere was this articulated so clearly than by Francis Fukuyama who declared that the early 1990s could be the "*end of history*":

> What we may be witnessing is not just the end of the Cold War, or the passing of a particular period of post-war history, but the end of history as such: that is, the end point of mankind's ideological evolution and the universalization of Western liberal democracy as the final form of human government.[7]

The optimism of Francis Fukuyama that the liberal economic model had prevailed was reflected by the comments of a range of European and North American decision makers during this era. US President George H W Bush prefigured this optimism just months before the end of the Cold War:

> I come before you and assume the Presidency at a moment rich with promise. We live in a peaceful, prosperous time, but we can make it better. For a new breeze is blowing, and a world refreshed by freedom seems reborn; for in man's heart, if not in fact, the day of the dictator is over. The totalitarian era is passing, its old ideas blown away like leaves from an ancient, lifeless tree. A new breeze is blowing, and a nation refreshed by freedom stands ready to push on. There is new ground to be broken, and new action to be taken. There are times when the future seems thick as a fog; you sit and wait, hoping the mists will lift and reveal the right path. But this is a time when the future seems a door you can walk right through into a room called tomorrow.[8]

The Cold War was over, Russia was now an ally of the United States and economic growth was going from strength to strength. Whilst the opening up of China since Deng Xiaoping came to power in 1978 had led to year on year increases as measured by GDP, the view from the United States in the early 1990s was that the world was entering an era of uni-multipolarity with the US as the sole superpower accompanied by a number of major powers.

The implications of this shift were expected to be a rise in instability in some parts of the world as the restraining influence of countries linked to various Cold War allies had been removed. Therefore, it was believed that there could be an increase in United Nations (UN) peacekeeping operations.

On the plus side, there would be a decline in the nuclear deterrence posture being adopted by various nations. Ultimately, the expectation was a rise of geo-economics or economic interdependence between various nations.

It was against this backdrop that a very different vision of the future was put forward by the US political scientist, Samuel Huntington. In a seminal 1993 article, Huntington claimed that with the end of the Cold War there would now be a "*clash of civilisations*". This narrative was based on a series of faulty assumptions. For instance, Huntington made the following claim:

> The people of different civilisations have different views on the relations between God and man, the individual and the group, the citizen and the state, parents and children, husband and wife, as well as differing views of the relative importance of rights and responsibilities, liberty and authority, equality and hierarchy.[9]

The flaws in this argument has already been referred to in Chapter 6 for there are differences within faiths and within nations on these very same topics. Weber spoke of the distinct differences of belief that shaped attitudes and behaviour within the one country of Germany. We have also seen how capitalism in Europe does not share all the same features as capitalism in the United States. However, Huntington was presenting a view of a fairly uniform approach within each "*civilisation*" which would lead to a "*clash of civilisations*". Within this argument is a series of non-sequiturs that were never adequately addressed by Huntington.

However, the most striking feature of this article was the claim that the West now had new opponents:

> Those countries that for reason of culture and power do not wish to, or cannot, join the West, compete with the West by developing their own economic, military and political power ... The most prominent form of this co-operation is the Confucian – Islamic connection that has emerged to challenge Western interests, values and power.[10]

There are so many confusing currents in this statement. It claims that a secular belief system such as Confucianism is mixed up with Islam—where Islam is not linked to Confucianism but instead is part of the Judeo-Christian credo. The idea of a conspiracy between "Confucian" powers and "Islamic" powers did not bear any scrutiny back in 1993 and with the suffering of the Muslim Uighur people in Xinjiang, particularly with the establishment of camps in the province from 2017, the idea of a special pact between "civilisations" clearly does not stand up today.

The former UK Liberal Democrat leader, Vince Cable saw such comments as revealing a racist streak—with an intriguing analogy to racism in British upper middle-class suburbs:

> There are those who derive some comfort from being members of relatively rich and predominantly (but decreasingly) white societies that have been able to look down with a mixture of pride and pity on those who are less materially fortunate. They fear that any fundamental change in the world order will be at their expense: that the global economy is a 'zero-sum game', in which new competitors subtract from the well-being of already developed nations. Just as the arrival of large, boisterous, upwardly mobile immigrant families in a prosperous neighbourhood creates a shudder of apprehension among the established residents, the arrival of (mainly Asian) nouveaux riches on the world stage is not universally welcomed.[11]

Despite the racist undertones in Huntington's article, it did resonate at the time amongst a proportion of the *Foreign Affairs* readership—maybe for the very reasons as cited by Cable.

Nonetheless there was one aspect of Huntington's thesis which did ring true which is that at the end of the Cold War, nationalist and ethnic issues, which were suppressed to some extent by the prevailing powers, came to the fore when ideological rivalry was no longer dominant.

Despite the flaws in the "clash of civilisations" argument, Huntington's thesis gained further traction following the tragedy of the 11 September 2001 terrorist attacks in the United States.

It was against this context that the Islamic finance industry was growing in size and in performance and where the industry was proving itself as a valid finance model in its own right.

Islamophobia and the Islamic Finance Industry

Muslims experienced significant levels of Islamophobia:

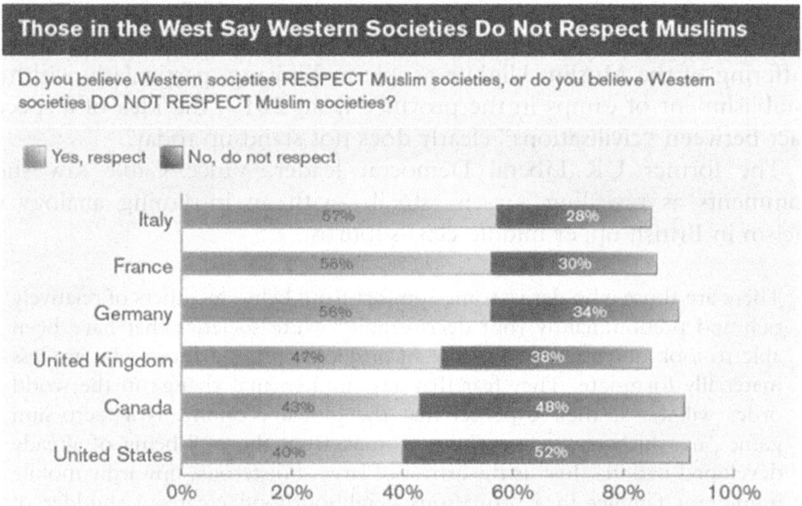

As this 2011 Gallup poll indicated, a significant proportion of Muslims in Europe and North America had experienced Islamophobia.

A Gallup poll in 2010 found that Americans from a range of faith groups were aware of Islamophobia in the United States:

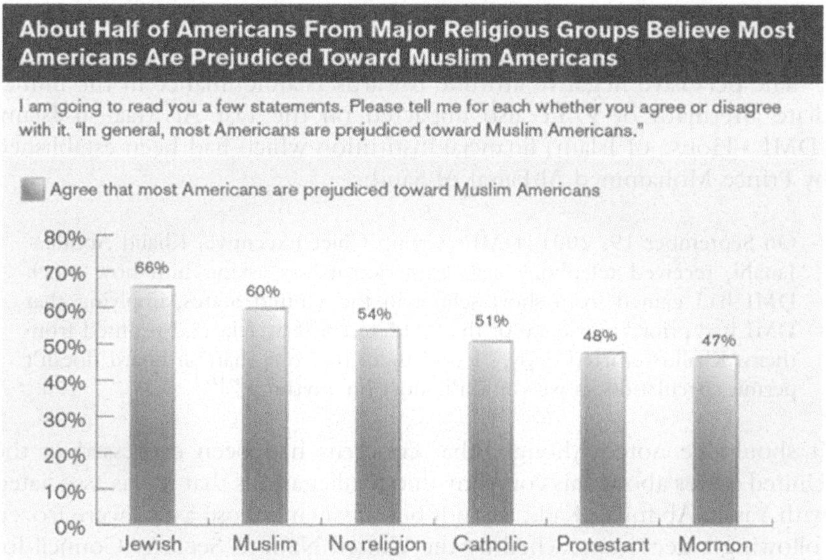

The terrorist atrocities led to suspicions being expressed by leading US Government officials that Al-Qaeda terrorist financing was being channelled via Islamic financial institutions.

The then US National Security Adviser, Sandy Berger, opined that terrorist money was "*hidden in underground, Islamic banking facilities*".[12] After this comment was made it was said to have taken six months for the then US Treasury Secretary, Paul O'Neill, to learn about Islamic finance following meetings held in Saudi Arabia, Kuwait and Bahrain.[13] As Warde observed:

> To those who were quick to associate anything Islamic with terrorism, Islamic banks and financial institutions provided a logical target. In a climate of generalised suspicion, Islamic banks – and more generally banks from the Islamic world – were considered guilty until proven innocent. Virtually every work in the 'secrets of terrorist financing' genre made such allegations.[14]

A 2016 study found there was no additional money laundering issues within Islamic banking as compared to conventional banking though it was recommended that volumes of funding linked to zakat should continue to be monitored and compliance requirements should remain under constant review.[15]

The pervasive negative attitude towards Islamic finance in the immediate aftermath of 9/11 also impacted on the Dar Al Maal al Islami (DMI—House of Islam) financial institution which had been established by Prince Mohammed Al Faisal Al Saud:

> On September 19, 2001, DMI's Group Chief Executive, Khalid Abdulla-Janahi, received telephone calls from journalists asking him how much DMI had gained from short selling in the United States, implying that DMI had prior knowledge of the 9/11 terrorist attacks and profited from them. Khalid retorted dryly, "I told them that our shari'ah board doesn't permit speculation so we couldn't short on anything."[16]

It should be noted, though, that concerns had been expressed in the United States about this company due to allegations that it was associated with Yassin Abdullah Kadi, a Saudi businessman whose assets were frozen following a decision reached by the United Nations Security Council for his alleged association with the Afghan Taliban and Osama bin Laden.

The founder of the Al-Baraka bank, Saleh Abdullah Kamal or Sheikh Saleh, also complained that Islamic finance was being unfairly targeted in the United States shortly after the 9/11 attacks. The bank was investigated for alleged money laundering activities linked to terrorism but action against this bank was dropped at the Federal Court of the Southern District of New York in December 2006.

As soon as the confirmation that investigations had ceased had been announced, Sheikh Saleh said, via his US lawyer, "*Where do I go to get my name and reputation back?*"[17]

During an Islamic banking conference held in Bahrain during November 2001, both Prince Mohammed Al Faisal Al Saud and Saleh Abdullah Kamal condemned the stereotypical depiction of Islamic finance as a harbinger for terrorism.[18] However, the horror of 9/11 has had a long-lasting effect with the rise of Islamophobia and in negatively harming the credibility of the industry.

Rushdi Siddiqui, who played an instrumental role in the development of the Dow Jones Islamic Markets Index[19] argued that the best way for the industry to respond to these perceptions was to be more sensitive to public attitudes in the United States, including with the views of Muslim communities in the US:

> People living in the Muslim world involved in Islamic finance have a disconnect with the Muslims living in America and the pressures they're going through post 9/11. They don't know because most of the Muslim world, to be honest, have not been to the States and they've not had a conversation with someone whose family was killed in 9/11.

Instead, Siddiqui argued, Islamic finance can be part of the bridge that can help overcome the animosities that immediately flowed out of 9/11:

> … I resolved to do whatever I can in my power so that Muslims and Islam are not remembered for that fiasco and catastrophe but instead for kindness and goodness. And if my vehicle and platform happen to be Islamic finance, so be it.

Nonetheless, Siddiqui observed, the tragedy of 9/11, as one of its by products, had put back the growth of the sector in the US by decades:

> Things were going nicely, then 9/11 happened. A lot of lives were affected, and it impacted on the psyche of the country. You don't recover in five or ten years. It would take a generation. But it doesn't mean you stop entirely doing what you do.[20]

Arguably an indication as to how Islamic finance continued to be clouded by cultural prejudices was discerned from a 2009 incident as recounted by Irfan.

Irfan recalled a time when a *New York Times* journalist questioning him regarding a potential Sukuk default pertaining to a major construction firm in Dubai (this account has been slightly amended from the original):

> From her office 11,000 km away, the reporter from the Times had only a sketchy understanding of the issues. 'Make it simple for me to understand. Talk to me as if I'm your mom in words of one syllable', she said. 'So what happens to the bond holders? Do they go to a Shariah court? Does an Imam decide on who gets paid what?' It became clear to me that she thought this complex sukuk documentation would be judged by a group of unkempt old mullahs in shalwar kameez, squatting in a circle on the floor of a stone mosque, like some Afghani jirga dispensing summary justice to the hapless investor. I asked myself in what context she would discuss Islamic transactions. Terrorist financing? The injustice of the Sharia and its incompatibility with Western standards of decency and transparency?[21]

As Irfan indicated in this account, the journalist, instead of reporting on a business event, had instead viewed the story as a cultural issue which would lead to a debate about ethical norms. This is a further example as to how the prevalence of Islamophobia pervaded too many debates regarding the future of the industry

Anecdotally, I can recall the visible reactions I received when I told people of my intention to write this book. A significant number of the comments I received was far from positive.

There does not seem to be statistical data which validates the concern that Islamophobia is holding back the growth of the sector. Inferences can be gained from general polling data which records the level of anti-Muslim feeling in different countries though this does not confirm a direct correlation between Islamophobia and the slow growth of the Islamic finance market.

Nonetheless, Professor Mohamed Ariff of Bond University in Queensland, Australia argued that Islamophobia was hindering the growth of the sector:

> It may take 50 years. We started in 1963 with opening the first bank, now we have around 500 institutions with 2-3 trillion dollars of assets. We will make this grow, but slowly.[22]

European Court of Human Rights: Has the Court Misunderstood Shari'a Law?

As was discussed in Chapter 2, shari'a law is the legal framework where legal rulings are defined. This includes fatwas pertaining to Islamic finance.

Negative feelings towards shari'a law has been expressed in many media outlets. Maybe more surprisingly, the European Court of Human Rights (ECHR) has also sharply criticised shari'a law.

The ECHR had been considering the actions of the Turkish Constitutional Court when, in 1997, it had dissolved the Refah (Welfare) Party. Refah had gained 35% of the votes cast in the 1996 Turkish local elections.

The decision to dissolve Refah was based on the individual statements of leading members of the Party. The Turkish Constitutional Court found that whatever may be in the policy platform of Refah, the individual comments revealed that Refah intended to set up a plurality of legal systems leading to discrimination based upon religious beliefs; that it intended to apply shari'a law which was said to be the antithesis of democracy and that some of the personal statements made reference to using force rather than adopting constitutional methods to evince change.

In 2003 the Grand Chamber of the ECHR concurred with the ruling of the Turkish Constitutional Court.

However, the ECHR went further and provided this negative critique of shari'a law:

> "... the court considers that Shari'a which faithfully reflects the dogmas and divine rules laid down by religion is stable and invariable. Principles such as pluralism in the political sphere or the constant evolution of public freedoms have no place in it. The court notes that when read together the offending statements which contain explicit references to the introduction of Shari'a are difficult to reconcile with the fundamental principles of democracy as conceived in the Convention *(European Convention of Human Rights)* taken as a whole. It is difficult to declare one's respect for democracy and human rights while at the same time supporting a regime based on Shari'a which clearly diverges from Convention values, particularly with regard to its criminal law and criminal procedure, its rules on the legal status of women and the way it intervenes in all spheres of private and public life in accordance with religious precepts. In the Court's view, a political party whose actions seem to be aimed at introducing Shari'a in a state party to the Convention can hardly be regarded as an association complying with the democratic ideal that underlies the whole of the Convention".[23]

This damning indictment implied that shari'a law was on a par with the common law in England and Wales or European law in the sense that it is codified. The judgement of the Court also stated that shari'a law was unchanging as it was based on divine precepts.

If we consider the ECHR's implication that shari'a is codified and that it contains detailed stipulations, as with other forms of jurisprudence, we find that this understanding is simply not correct.

Shari'a law provides a framework where detailed study can lead to differing interpretations depending upon which Islamic school and/or scholar is analysing any issue in any given context.

As Usmani observed:

> It must be understood that when we claim that Islam has a satisfactory solution for every problem emerging in any situation in all times to come, we do not mean that the Holy Quran and Sunnah of the Holy Prophet or the rulings of Islamic scholars provide a specific answer to each and every minute detail of our socioeconomic life. What we mean is that the Holy Quran and the Holy Sunnah of the Prophet have laid down the broad principles in the light of which the scholars of every time have deduced specific answers to the new situations arising in their age. Therefore, in order to reach a definite answer about a new situation the scholars of Shariah have to play a very important role. They have to analyse every question in light of the principles laid down by the Holy Quran and Sunnah as well as in the light of the standards set by earlier jurists enumerated in the books of Islamic jurisprudence. This exercise is called Istinbat or Ijtihad... [T]he ongoing process of Istinbat keeps injecting new ideas, concepts and rulings into the heritage of Islamic jurisprudence... [24]

The founder of the Shafi'i school of thought emphasised how shari'a law was a dynamic form of jurisprudence:

> 1323- He said: What is analogy (qiyās)? Is it the same as ijtihād (reasoning) or are they two separate notions?
> 1324- I (Al-Shāfi'ī) said: they are synonyms.
> 1325- He said: So what is in common between them?
> 1326- I said: Everything which was revealed for the Muslims contains either a binding command, or a legal proof upon which future rulings can be based to uphold Truth and Justice. Thus, if revelation gave us a direct ruling [regarding the matter at hand], Muslims must follow that ruling; and if revelation did not make a ruling on this specific matter, then a proof for the just and true ruling must be sought via ijtihād. And, ijtihād is qiyās.[25]

Dr Rowan Williams echoed this very point when he was the Archbishop of Canterbury (the most senior cleric in the world Anglican Christian community):

> so far from being a monolithic system of detailed enactments, shari'a designates primarily ... 'the expression of the universal principles of Islam and the framework and the thinking that makes for their actualisation in human history'. Universal principles: as any Muslim commentator will insist, what is in view is the eternal and absolute will of God for the universe and for its human inhabitants in particular; but also something that has to be

'actualised', not a ready-made system. If shar'ia designates the essence of the revealed law, shar'ia is the practice of actualising and applying it; while certain elements of the shari'a are specified fairly exactly in the Qur'ran and Sunna and in the hadith recognised as authoritative in this respect, there is no single code that can be identified as 'the' shari'a.[26]

How about the concerns expressed by the ECHR that shari'a law contradicts the liberal and democratic pluralist values of the European Convention of Human Rights?

Whilst shari'a law may be cited by some authoritarian regimes as an excuse to impinge upon civil liberties, this is a political judgement and is not based on the strictures of shari'a law.

When the Prophet left Mecca for Medina in 622, he established a constitution which recognised the religious and secular rights of peoples of all faiths in Medina.

When the Prophet died, the first Caliph of the Muslim community was Abu Bakr who said that he encouraged people to monitor and correct him wherever he went wrong.[27]

John Esposito and James Piscatori also examined the claim that shari'a law was inherently undemocratic:

In recent decades, many Muslims have indeed accepted the notion of democracy but differed as to its precise meaning. Muslim interpretations of democracy build on the well-established Qur'anic concept of shura (consultation), but place varying emphases on the extent to which 'the people' are able to exercise this duty. One school of thought argues that Islam is inherently democratic not only because of the principle of consultation, but also because of the concepts of ijtihad (independent reasoning) and ijma (consensus). It is argued that, just as Islamic law is rescued from the charge of inflexibility by the right of jurists in certain circumstances to employ independent judgement and to secure agreement among themselves, Islamic political thought is rescued from the charge of autocracy by the need of rulers to consult widely and to govern on the basis of consensus.[28]

The ECHR judgement claimed that shari'a law is not compatible with secular principles of jurisprudence. However, this is yet another misunderstanding reached by the Court.

Makdisi, in his study of shari'a law found that, in fact, it has a secular bias that is distinct from the commandments of the faith itself:

> The manner in which an act was qualified as morally good or bad in the spiritual domain of Islamic religion was quite different from the manner in which that same act was qualified as legally valid or invalid in the temporal domain of Islamic law. Islamic law was secular not canonical ... Thus, it was a system focused on ensuring that an individual received justice, not that one be a good person.[29]

It is the opinion of this author that the judgement reached by the ECHR was based on faulty premises. Whether it came to issues of legal precedence, whether the law is codified and its relationship to democracy, on every single matrix the ECHR judgement was factually incorrect.

It is fair to surmise that for such a respected Court to reach this judgement, it would negatively shape public opinion as to the concept of shari'a law and, therefore, of the Islamic finance industry itself which employs scholars who are knowledgeable in shari'a law.

The fact that the Church of England has been in the vanguard in rebutting inaccurate notions regarding shari'a demonstrates how Islam and, in turn, the Islamic finance industry is continuing to win over a broad section of society despite the prevalence of ill-informed opinion masquerading as value judgements.

Turkey: Branding and domestic politics

The issue of branding has bedevilled the Islamic finance industry from the very beginning. Whilst the model has enormous benefits for peoples of all faiths and none, the negative perception of Islam in some countries has led to some participants in the Islamic finance industry to consider whether renaming Islamic finance is necessary in order to reach a wider market.

Interestingly, either the first—or one of the first—Islamic financial institutions in the modern era did not use the word 'Islamic' in its brand name.

In 1963, an Islamic financial institution was formed by Ahmad Al-Najjar in the Mit Ghamr area of Egypt. Whilst there is still more to discover as to this historic development, what has emerged is that this institution avoided the use of the word "Islamic" in the name of the bank.

According to one analysis, this was because if the religious genesis of this finance model had been included in the bank's name, the Egyptian Government at that time would have taken a very dim view of the political implications of such a development. This was when Nasser was promoting the concept of pan Arab nationalism whilst King Faisal of Saudi Arabia was arguing that a pan-Islamic sense of identity should be engendered instead:

> Despite its Islamic orientation, the Mit Ghamr Bank could not operate openly under the Islamic banner due to the government's hostility toward Islamic movements. Najjar had to hide the Islamic identity of his project under slogans of socialism.[30]

The issue of branding also emerged in March 2009 when the official newspaper of the Vatican, *Osservatore Romano, backed Islamic finance as an ethical model which conventional banks should learn from. This led Haitham Abdou from the Kuwaiti based ITS Group to declare that this was an indication that* Islamic banking should be ready for a rebrand as ethical banking needed to reach out to new markets:

> Pope Benedict urged the western community to look at the Islamic banking model because of its ethical principles, to restore confidence amongst their clients at a time of global economic crisis. It was really quite shocking to me to read such a thing coming from the Pope, but that's what led me to believe that Islamic banking is crossing the religious boundaries and being seen as an ethical business model.[31]

Similar considerations may have been at play in Turkey where Islamic finance is known as participation banking. Participation banking began in the 1980s with Albaraka Turk becoming the first participation bank in 1984 followed shortly thereafter by Faisal Finance.

Turkey, having adopted a secular constitution, abolished the caliphate and the religious position of sheyh ül-islam under the direction of Mustafa Kemal Ataturk (1881–1938: Ataturk meaning Father of the Turks).

The idea of citing religion in financial affairs would not have fitted within the Turkish political context. This would particularly have been the case in the 1980s, when participation banking first emerged in Turkey, with the election of Turgut Ozal's Motherland Party as the governing party in the 1983 Turkish General Election.

Some political parties were beginning to advocate for some form of Islamic economic policy. In the 1970s, the National Salvation Party called for a "*Muslim common market*". In the 1990s, the Refah Party called for an Islamic style welfare state before the Turkish Constitutional Court outlawed the party for wanting to breach the secular constitution of the state—a ruling that was later endorsed by the European Court of Human Rights, as we discussed earlier in this chapter.

The former Turkish Prime Minister, Necmettin Erbakan (1926–2011) who helped to form the Refah Party, was part of the 'National Outlook' movement which criticised laissez-faire capitalism whilst calling for riba to be prohibited.

The religiously based Adalet Ve Kalkinma Partisi (AKP—Justice and Development Party) gained electoral dominance from 2002. It differentiated itself between the Motherland Party and the Refah Party—but, in fact, AKP incorporated policy ideas from both parties:

> The AKP is a party that rejects political Islamism as its ideological backbone yet is inspired by it, especially in its understanding of morality, which found its manifestation in the appellation that the party elite saw as appropriate for their ideological program: "conservative democracy". Inspired by Ozal's policies of free market and political liberalism, the AKP severed its ties with political Islamism and defined a new role for Islam that narrowed its political manifestations.[32]

Over time the AKP began to openly express the Islamic basis of participation banking but in a very cautious way. A leaked US diplomatic cable revealed that the AKP led Government had concerns as to whether the promotion of Islamic finance could annoy civil society and possibly the military who could see this promotion as another attempt to undo Ataturk's secular legacy.[33]

However, a failed military coup against the AKP in 2016 emboldened party leader, Recep Tayyip Erdogan. In 2017, Erdogan won a referendum giving him, as President, enhanced powers.

Under President Erdogan, it was announced in December 2019 that there would be new rules to regulate participation banking. The regulations now emphasise the Islamic basis of participation banking:

> An act against Islamic jurisprudence and rules cannot be considered legitimate even if it is legal and in accordance with the established practices of the market.

The regulations, in respect of auditors, state:

> The auditor should act with the fear of God, the Exalted and be constantly aware that God, the Exalted, is watching him.[34]

Orhan Kemal Cengiz, former president of the Human Rights Agenda Association, a Turkish non-governmental organisation, has argued that the religious language contained in the regulations is one of a number of indicators which demonstrates a continued policy shift by President Erdogan to gradually move Turkey from a secular constitution to a more religiously based society.[35]

Erdogan is positioning Turkey as a country that embraces the Islamic economic model. In a speech to an Islamic finance conference in June 2020, the Turkish President claimed that there was no option but to change the current economic system which was prevalent in much of the world. Erdogan added that Islamic economics was the key to "*getting out of the crisis*" which, he said, bedevilled the global economy:

> Over-financing has created a bloated economic model, which acts only over concern about unearned income, without considering social and human costs. Contrary to what has been promised, the distribution of income and wealth is gradually deteriorating all over the world, and the gap between the countries widened.[36]

With Erdogan stating that "*we aim to make Istanbul the centre of Islamic finance and economy*" it will be interesting to see whether this is just a branding exercise to attract Islamic finance investment, which would be an important step in and of itself. Alternatively, Turkey could begin to reposition its political economic structure to enable Islamic economics to become a key theme within the Turkish body politic.

If Turkey really does embed some form of Islamic economics in its policy direction in one of the most populous countries in the region (82 million people) at the crossroads of Asia and Europe, the impact that such a move would have on neighbouring countries, in possibly following the Turkish lead in adopting Islamic economic ideas, could be profound.

France—Is Prejudice Hindering the Growth of the Domestic Islamic Finance Industry?

It is in France that it would have been expected that Islamic finance would flourish.

As one of the key nations within the European Union and within the single currency eurozone, the country has many advantages to develop its Islamic finance market. This includes the very well developed links France has with many nations with significant Muslim populations which were once French colonies.

The FranceAfrique policy has been successful in maintaining close economic, security and political ties between France and its former colonies. Until May 2020, a currency link was maintained in these relationships. The CFA Franc (African Financial Community or Cooperation Franc) began in December 1945 and it was the common currency of fourteen nations in central and western Africa and the Comoros Islands. There were two monetary institutions for the two respective zones namely the Central Bank of Central African States (CEMAC) and the Central Bank of Western African States (UEMOA). Both were influenced by the Bank of France.[37]

Maybe the greatest advantage that France had to develop its own Islamic finance market is its significant Muslim population. A 2017 Pew Research report estimated the Muslim population of France to be 5,760,000 or 8.8% of the total population. This is the second largest Muslim minority population in Europe.

With these advantages, the French Government took some initial steps to develop the Islamic finance market following the 2008 financial crisis. Some legal measures to accommodate Islamic financial products within the French legal framework was adopted mitigating the tax friction with the implementation of Islamic finance products.

In December 2007, Paris EUROPLACE, the organisation which promotes the French capital's role as a financial centre, established the Islamic Finance Commission. Since then, the French financial markets regulator, the Autorité des marchés financiers (AMF), has issued two positions allowing shari'a compliant investment funds and Sukuk listings. The Bourse de Paris (Paris stock exchange) has created a Sukuk division and four tax regulations (relating to murabaha, sukuk, ijarah and istisn'a) have been published which confirm a parity of tax treatment with conventional financial products.

However, despite these initial efforts, the Islamic finance market in France did not really get off the ground. As Mohyedine Hajjar observed:

> The insufficient legal framework and the bad tax reputation caused the escape of the foreign Islamic investors and the immobility of the internal market. Despite the presence of the biggest Muslim community in Europe in France[38] and therefore a large potential for Islamic finance products, the French market is stagnant. The main French economic and financial

> actors prefer to stay in the shadows and the market is left to brokers and councils which affected public confidence....[39]

Hajjar added:

> The current situation of Islamic finance development in France is the result of private initiatives only, which provides a diversified supply of solutions in spite of the limited suitability of the French legal framework.[40]

Hajjar was unclear as to the reasons for this limited development of the sector, including why Islamic banks have not been established in France.

This situation seems, at first, to be very surprising as France has so many advantages to ensure the success of the Islamic finance market. Marie-Liesse de Luxembourg argued that the efforts of the French state to develop the Islamic finance market lost its impetus when Christine Lagarde left the role of Finance Minister in 2011.[41]

Lagarde had told the French Islamic Finance Forum organised by Secure Finance and the Franco-Arab Chamber of Commerce in November 2008 that "*La finance islamique présente avantages*" adding "*We are determined to make Paris a great centre for Islamic finance*".

However, is it as straightforward as a personnel change which meant progress has been stymied?

As the *Le Parisien* newspaper reported at the time of the 2008 conference, Islamophobia was the major hurdle hindering the growth of the industry:

> Hervé de Charette, president of the Franco-Arab Chamber of Commerce emphasizes that "importing Islamic banking into France would help the integration process". The main obstacle: "Islamic banking arouses fear because it is associated, wrongly, with religious fundamentalism, even with the financing of terrorism," deplores Elyès Jouini, professor of economics at the University of Paris.[42]

There is also a view amongst some decision makers in France that secularism or *laïcité* must be defended. *Laïcité is formally expressed in a 1905 French law which, under Article Two of this legislation, directs the State not to support or to fund any religion.*

Whilst other European countries are open about supporting religious diversity, the concept of secularism in France leads to a more nuanced debate as to the role of all religions in French society:

> In Paris, the political milieu and the media are split between partisans of a strict version of laïcité, thus incarnating the general will against all the particular wills, and partisans of an open version of laïcité, both liberal and libertarian, i.e. aligned with their time. The quarrel goes beyond the country's borders, and France is regularly accused of intolerance towards religions by part of the international community. In reality, these two debates merge into one: strict laïcité, i.e. French laïcité, vs open laïcité, i.e. Anglo-Saxon communitarianism.[43]

Nicolas Sarkozy reflected this strict secularist viewpoint as President when he declared to the National Assembly in June 2009:

> But I tell you, we must not be ashamed of our values. We must not be afraid of defending them.

It has been noted that in the same speech, Sarkozy also said:

> We must not fight the wrong battle. In the republic, the Muslim religion must be respected as much as other religions.

However, according to a 2007 US diplomatic cable which was leaked to Wikileaks, Sarkozy's position on Islam was also reflected in the debate, ongoing at that time, as to whether Turkey should be a member of the European Union:

> Whatever the ramifications of keeping Turkey out, he opposes bringing 70 million Muslims into Europe.

The debate in France regarding secularism and faith led to the ban, enacted from April 2011, which prohibits women wearing the face-covering veil or niqab, as well as stopping people wearing other masks in public spaces.

Horrific terrorist acts also impacted on French public opinion. These atrocities included, in November 2015, a series of venues in Paris being attacked which led to the deaths of 130 people as well as the deaths of the seven terrorists responsible for these crimes.

The *New York Times* commented on the changes in attitude amongst key decision makers in France shortly after these atrocities:

> It was largely unspoken but nevertheless clear: Secular France always had a complicated relationship with its Muslim community, but now it was tipping toward outright distrust, even hostility.[44]

Later, in 2016, with Sarkozy's renewed bid for the Presidency, he again referred to the debate between French secularism and faith:

> There can be no happy identity as long as we do not reaffirm that the French identity is not more important than particular identities.[45]

In response to this rhetoric, then French President, Francois Hollande said:

> no one doubts France has a problem with Islam.[46]

The political tempo of this debate increased during 2020 when President Macron announced plans to tackle religious "separatism" by, for example, monitoring activities within mosques, requiring imams to be trained and certified within France and ensuring Islamic organisations which receive public funding would need to adopt a "secular charter". Then in October 2020, Samuel Paty was murdered in a Parisian suburb by an extremist for teaching children about freedom of speech in a local school where references were made to controversial cartoons depicting the Prophet. This murder raised political tensions within France as to the role of Islam in society. It can be argued that with the active debate as to the nature of secularism and how it relates to faith, a concept such as Islamic finance may be caught up in this atmosphere and not be able to flourish as fully as it could, bearing in mind the advantages France has for this market to flourish.

Further study as to the relationship between Islamophobia and debates regarding secularisim and the development of the French Islamic finance market would be beneficial to ascertain the extent of this prejudice and debate in inhibiting the growth of this market.

Qatar Central Bank and the Islamic Finance Industry

So far in our discussion, we have witnessed how Islamophobia has hindered the growth of the industry and the emerging debate as to the very description and branding of Islamic finance.

There can, though, be decisions made within the industry which can also help to hold back the full potential of the industry. One example of an ill-judged decision was made by the Qatar Central Bank in 2011.

It decided that the operation of Islamic 'windows'—conventional banks operating separate Islamic banking operations—would be prohibited. This was a surprising decision at a time when the industry was beginning to reach out beyond its core consumer market to appeal to people of all faiths and none.

The Qatar Central Bank argued that due to the difficulties between separating income streams between conventional banking and Islamic banking that this decision had to be made.

However, from the perspective of developing a global Islamic finance brand, this action could be identified as a misstep as it provided a disincentive for global investment banks to fully engage in Islamic financing across the Gulf. Admittedly, Islamic finance 'windows' operate in other Gulf jurisdictions but it sent a message, however unintended it may have been, that conventional banking could not be trusted to follow shari'a compliant banking at a time when this brand of finance was being embraced by customers who felt more comfortable to accessing such services from 'windows' as they were already acquainted with these bank brands.

Irfan claims that the unexpected decision by the Qatar Central Bank was a direct consequence of behind the scenes discussions regarding the behaviour of some conventional banks:

> Unknown to most, regulators and scholars had been having closed door discussions in the lead up to the ban. The scholars were wising up to structured product platforms that gave the investor no legally enforceable security interest in the Islamic assets; or that allowed for the bank to reuse those assets for its own purposes without permission of the investor; or commodity murabaha transactions to finance real estate assets because the credit risk management departments of conventional banks couldn't envisage any financing that didn't look like, smell like and act like an interest-bearing loan; or products that engaged in non-compliant hedges

> on the other side of the trade, because the Islamic investor couldn't see the hedge; or, at its most basic, the simple co-mingling of Islamic depositors' funds in centralized pools of money where returns were smeared into one homogeneous whole.[47]

Whilst accepting that these concerns are valid, the solution—to ban conventional banks from engaging in Islamic finance via the use of 'windows'—rather than improving compliance requirements within Qatar—has created an unnecessary negative image to enable the popularity of Islamic finance to move beyond its core markets.

There was speculation at the time as to whether there were other reasons for this prohibition:

> Several reasons are given. First, it is believed that the CBQ's ban may hurt Shari'ah-compliance industry by reducing the market share of Islamic finance and discoursing further development of the industry. Second, some reports also indicated that a number of Shari'ah scholars expressed their concern over the decision as well. Third, some put forward political reasons for the decision arguing that the CBQ is in fact trying to help its Islamic banks whose market share is deteriorating due to competition from conventional counterparts.[48]

However, the face value reason for the prohibition, whilst understandable, meant that the ban had an impact on the Qatari Islamic finance industry. Instead of encouraging money flows into Qatari Islamic banks, the initial reaction seems to have been customers moving funds into conventional banking accounts due to brand loyalty:

> The figures suggest a sharp slowdown in growth: Islamic banking assets grew 20.9 percent in 2012 and 35.1 percent in 2011. Conventional lenders have experienced a similar trend, posting growth in assets of 17.9 percent in 2012 and 23.4 percent in 2011.
>
> Before the ban, Islamic windows captured 54.6 billion riyals of assets, according to the International Monetary Fund. Since Qatar's ban took effect at the end of 2011, Islamic banks have added 57.5 billion riyals of assets to their balance sheets.
>
> This suggests that if Islamic banks absorbed the assets from the Islamic windows in their entirety, their growth excluding this factor has been minimal.
>
> The data may also indicate that a significant proportion of money leaving the Islamic windows simply moved to the conventional sides of the

> same banks - implying that for many customers, brand loyalty or attractive financial terms were more important than the Islamic nature of the business.[49]

Whilst Qatari Islamic banks are doing well, it can be argued that the overall impact of this ban in terms of branding and the marketability of the wider Islamic finance industry has sent out unnecessarily negative messages about the industry when a focus on improving compliance in Islamic finance 'windows' may have been more beneficial for Qatar and the global Islamic finance industry.

Branding and the Future of the Islamic Finance Industry

There is much to learn from Islamic finance, whether or not individuals are of a faith or of no faith at all.

However, as I learnt from my own discussion with a Chamber of Commerce representative, the issue of Islamic finance branding opens up a wider debate regarding religion, identity and prejudice.

Even in Malaysia, which has one of the most successful Islamic finance markets in the world, there is a debate as to whether a change in branding would broaden the consumer base of this sector. As the former Malaysian Prime Minister, Mahathir Mohamed, has said:

> In a way, it (the Malaysian Islamic finance market) has succeeded more than I expected. But also it has not expanded to be accepted generally as a banking system. You see we are emphasising the religious and Islamic part of it. If you stress on not charging interest and not calling it Islamic banking, maybe it will expand much faster.[50]

The branding issue goes beyond the issue of Islamophobia, though the impact of this form of bigotry cannot be underestimated.

The branding debate also points to a wider truth as indicated by Mahathir. Islamic finance has so much to offer to a wide consumer base but for some markets, it continues to be seen as a niche product line.

Therefore, could the industry do more to promote its products in a more inclusive way which reaches out to new market players?

Rushdi Siddiqui certainly thinks so. Siddiqui was instrumental in developing the Dow Jones Islamic Markets Index in 1998 which transformed the industry from being seen as, primarily, a debt financing vehicle to being recognised as a capital investment structure:

> Unfortunately, most people think about Islamic finance in isolation. They don't understand the external environment of perceptions. We think that what we have is so great that we forget about the environment that it operates in. If that external environment isn't lobbied correctly then your idea remains in the ivory tower.[51]

To address this change of marketing direction would require a significant shift in resources which would take into consideration such corporate communications concepts such as framing theory and agenda setting theory.

It has been said that Islamic finance is a risk-averse industry and therefore such marketing considerations may not be embraced. Instead the industry could continue to rely on revenue streams from the mortgage market and takaful as well as enticing investors from the Persian Gulf region and Malaysia to invest in Sukuks.

However, the Islamic finance industry has taken risks to get to the stage it is at now. From innovative contract structures to meet real world business needs through to enticing global investment banks to engage in ethical investment structures to order to attract a new investor class.

These are very significant achievements in their own right.

Though market participants, such as Harris Irfan, express frustration at what he sees as the slow pace of change within the Islamic finance industry, I find it to be a remarkable achievement that Islamic finance concepts has been partially successful in persuading investment banks to think about long term and ethical financing.

This is an achievement that the Left in many European countries and in North America had been calling for with very limited success and where, despite the gains of the mutualism movement (as discussed in Chapter 9), it failed to significantly shift thinking in investment banking.

If we really want to change the world for the better, as Siddiqui indicates, we need to continue to reach out beyond the "*ivory tower*".

Therefore, whilst the industry has the opportunity to take the next steps in marketing itself, the hurdle of Islamophobia, which the industry is saddled with, remains.

How Islamic finance overcomes Islamophobia so that all societies benefit from this model will be one of the industry's key challenges in the years ahead.

Notes

1. University of California, https://belonging.berkeley.edu/global-justice/islamophobia/resource-pack-us/othering-discrimination-hate-crimes.
2. Evidence to the UK's House of Commons Home Affairs Select Committee, August 2019, http://data.parliament.uk/writtenevidence/committeeevidence.svc/evidencedocument/home-affairs-committee/islamophobia/written/104325.htmle.
3. Edward Said (1978), *Orientalism*, page 202.
4. The legacy of Maududi is discussed in Chapter 10.
5. As quoted by Berridge, *Hasan al-Turabi*, page 5.
6. Qur'an, Sura Al Ma'idah, Verse 32.
7. Francis Fukuyama (1992), *The End of History and the Last Man*.
8. US President George H W Bush, Inauguration speech, 20 January 1989.
9. Samuel P Huntington (1993), The Clash of Civilizations?, *Foreign Affairs*, vol. 72, no. 3, pp. 22–49.
10. Ibid.
11. Vince Cable, *The Storm: The World Economic Crisis and What It Means*, page 96.
12. Gene J. Koprowski (12 March 2002), Islamic Banking Is Not the Enemy, *Wall Street Journal*.
13. Ibrahim Warde, *The Price of Fear: The Truth Behind the Financial War on Terror*, page 74.
14. Ibid.
15. Nadim Kyriakos-Saad, Manuel Vasquez, Chady El Khoury, Arz El Murr (2016), *Islamic Finance and Anti Money Laundering and Combating the Financing of Terrorism*, International Monetary Fund working paper.
16. Emmy Abdul Alim, *Global Leaders in Islamic Finance*, page 71.
17. Barbara Ferguson (18 December 2006), US Court Throws Out Case Against Saleh Kamel, *Arab News*, http://www.arabnews.com/node/292445.
18. Ibrahim Warde, *The Price of Fear*, page 75.
19. The Dow Jones Islamic Markets Index is discussed in Chapters 5 and 7.
20. As quoted by Emmy Abdul Alim, *Global Leaders in Islamic Finance*, page 188.
21. Harris Irfan, *Heaven's Bankers: Inside the Hidden World of Islamic Finance*, page 110.
22. https://www.aa.com.tr/en/turkey/islamophobia-prevents-islamic-finance-expansion-malaysian-scholar/219396, 11 September 2013.

23. Refah Partisi and Others v Turkey (No. 2) (2003) 37 EHRR 1 (GC).
24. Usmani (1998, p. 237).
25. Al-Shafi'ī (1939, p. 477).
26. Lecture by the Archbishop of Canterbury, Dr Rowan Williams (7 February 2008), *Civil and Religious Law in England: A Religious Perspective*.
27. Shi'a Islam has a different view as to the order of the caliphs as discussed in Chapter 2.
28. Esposito and Piscatori, *Democratisation and Islam*, supra n 31, 434.
29. John Makdisi (1999), *The Islamic Origins of Common Law*, page 1704.
30. W S Hegazy (2007), Contemporary Islamic Finance: From Socioeconomic Idealism to Pure Legalism, *Chicago Journal of International Law*, vol. 7, no. 2, pp. 581–603.
31. Vatican Praises 'ethical' Sharia banking, *World Finance*, 4 January 2011.
32. Ahmet Yildiz as cited in *The Blackwell Companion to Contemporary Islamic Thought*, page 50.
33. The US diplomatic cable of 12 June 2009 which was released by Wikileaks read that a recent Islamic finance conference had shown that "*the Islamic rooted Justice and Development Party (AKP) is reluctant to propose pro-Islamic finance legislation, because of fears of a strong backlash from secularists deeply suspicious of the ruling party's motives*".
34. Turkish Official Gazette, 14 December 2019.
35. https://www.al-monitor.com/pulse/originals/2020/01/turkey-is-the-country-drifting-towards-sharia-rule.html#ixzz6IeqYz7rh, 14 January 2020.
36. *Turkey's Erdogan Says Islamic Economy Can Pull World 'Out of Crisis'*, TRT World, 14 June 2020.
37. The French Government ratified the end of the franc relationship with Francophone African countries on 21 May 2020. There was a transition to the new Eco currency for countries covered by the Economic Community of West African States (ECOWAS).
38. Germany has the largest Muslim community in Europe as of 2015.
39. Mohyedine Hajjar (2019), *Islamic Finance in Europe*.
40. Ibid.
41. Marie Liesse de Luxembourg (July 2016), *La finance islamique en France: que valent ces paroles?*, Archives de sciences sociales des religions.
42. Le Parisien, 27 November 2008.
43. Professor Anastasia Colosimo (2020), Institut Montaigne (French think tank) blog.
44. https://www.nytimes.com/2015/11/17/world/europe/after-paris-attacks-a-darker-mood-toward-islam-emerges-in-france.html.
45. Nicolas Sarkozy (2016), *Tout pour la France*.
46. Francois Hollande (2016), *A President Should Not Say That*.

47. Harris Irfan, *Heaven's Bankers: Inside the Hidden World of Islamic Finance*, page 125.
48. Saray Consultancy, https://saraycon.com/recent-fiasco-in-qatar-a-need-for-good-governance-shariah-governance/.
49. Reuters (20 March 2014), *Growth of Qatar's Islamic Banks Falls Near Conventional peers*.
50. Emmy Abdul Alim, *Global Leaders in Islamic Finance*.
51. Ibid.

CHAPTER 12

The Future of Islamic Finance

Binary choices are asked of us when the options being presented are, really, complex.

In 2016, the referendum in the United Kingdom on whether to remain or leave the European Union (EU) was presented to voters with a simple tick box A5 sheet of paper with "Remain" and "Leave" printed in bold font.

Behind this exercise were complex arguments as to where sovereignty lies, whether or not you can maintain democratic accountability on a national basis within a multinational institution and whether the concept of 'pooled sovereignty' can be justified with accountable institutions.

The difficult arguments continued when the economy was discussed. Would the nation have a greater voice in international trade without the UK's interests being mediated via a multilateral organisation? Or are global institutions like the International Monetary Fund so influential, the UK gains more influence on the world stage via the EU?

As it happened, I voted "Remain" and many people I talked to in the West Midlands voted "Leave" but however anyone voted, these were complex arguments narrowed down to binary choices which all of us in Britain were obliged to make on a single day in June.

Is it really fair for us in daily life to make decisions on binary choices? Most of us, I suspect, would say no as the choices before us as individuals

J. S. Watkins, *Islamic Finance and Global Capitalism*,
https://doi.org/10.1007/978-3-030-59840-2_12

or for our families, our community, our country or our world are so complex we need to develop tailor made and nuanced answers.

However, as with the 2016 referendum, we are sometimes asked to pick a side not on the merits of the case but on who is backing either side. During the referendum campaign, I heard Remain campaigners argue that their option was the only choice to make because otherwise you would be associated with the narrow nationalism of the anti-EU politician, Nigel Farage.

I also heard Leave campaigners say that their option was the only choice to make otherwise you would be associated with Tony Blair who brought the country to war in Iraq on a premise of the existence of Iraqi weapons of mass destruction which later proved to be incorrect.

In reality there were supporters of either option who came from a wide range of backgrounds and beliefs who may have had no truck with Nigel Farage or Tony Blair but still supported Leave or Remain.

This analogy helps us to consider the future of Islamic finance as for some commentators it is less about the merits of Islamic finance than who is backing the concept.

Timur Kuran argues that fundamentalist figures—such as Maududi or Yusuf al-Qaradawi who promote division and a "either you are with us or against us" stance to religion—are associated with Islamic finance.

It is implied that you should also oppose Islamic finance because these men support the idea of Islamic finance.

This, I would suggest to you, reader, is a non sequitur. It is again boiling down complex issues to a binary choice of who you want to be associated with.

Throughout this book, we have seen how the development of Islamic economics and Islamic finance is beginning to meet the objectives of the United Nations' Sustainable Development Goals, is providing a more sure footed basis for some of the poorest people to begin to improve their lives via Islamic microfinance and to develop new funding structures that can address the most significant long-term issue of all to impact our planet—climate change.

That is not to say the arguments put forward by Timur Kuran and others should not be addressed. As someone who would describe himself as a staunch supporter of liberal democracy, feminism and progressive politics—as well as being agnostic - it is clearly not comfortable for me to be reminded of the fact that the innovative concepts of Islamic finance which is giving new hope of an economic structure that can work for people of all faiths and none has developed, in part, from fundamentalist ideals.

But reminded I must be.

For if we are to see the full potential of Islamic finance for the global economy, we should understand, respect and appreciate how the Islamic finance concept has developed, the influences that has shaped Islamic finance to the stage it has reached thus far and how fundamentalist doctrines has the potential to continue to shape and reset ideas about Islamic finance and Islamic economics.

At the same time, we should also consider and respect how the very essence of Islam, as represented in the Qur'ran, sunna and hadiths has informed the ethical underpinning of Islamic finance. We have discussed how the oneness of God via the concept of Tawhid and the framework to live an ethical life via the concept of masaqid al shari'a has developed an open and honest approach towards financial relations which can contribute to realising peoples' potential—no matter what background a person may be from.

We have also considered how the thought of the four Sunni schools of jurisprudence, the reasoning of Jafari Shi'a thought and the insights of Al-Ghazali amongst others has contributed to the ethical underpinning of Islamic finance.

It was the polymath, Abu Yūsuf Ya'qūb ibn 'Isḥāq aṣ-Ṣabbāḥ al-Kindī (801–873) who said:

> We should not be ashamed to acknowledge truth and to assimilate it from whatever source it comes to us, even if it is brought to us by former generations and foreign peoples. For him who seeks the truth there is nothing of higher value than truth itself; it never cheapens or debases him who reaches for it but ennobles and honours him.

We have also seen how Islamophobia is holding back the growth of the Islamic finance industry. Attacks against Muslim communities and the stereotyping of Islam is, tragically, still a feature of modern life though solutions are being found within civil societies across the world to tackle this and other forms of bigotry.

In December 2015, Donald Trump uttered inflammatory comments during a campaign speech in South Carolina for the US Presidency:

> Donald J Trump is calling for a complete shutdown of Muslims entering the United States until our country's representatives can figure out what the hell is going on. *(Cheers)* Have no choice. We have no choice.

Schmid has argued that such comments and what seems to be the corresponding lack of action to encourage an Islamic finance market in the United States is not just harmful for holding back a growth sector within the US economy but can also be counter-intuitive to US aims to counter Islamic fundamentalism:

> Tied closely with "Islamic Law" (Sharia or Shariah), Islamic finance is subject to political risk in markets that lack understanding of its core principles. As one scholar noted, "For the purposes of public discussion, it was the word 'Shariah' that was radioactive." After September 11, U.S. officials ramped up their vigilance and targeting of transnational sources of terrorist funding. To what degree politics has influenced the development of Islamic finance is still unclear.
>
> Some would even argue that modern business practices serve as a moderating force: While Islamic bankers do not necessarily share any commitment to Western-style liberalism or democracy, their drive for markets and profits may indirectly contribute to a more competitive politics. Their economic success sets the stage for greater democracy by encouraging popular participation in financial activities, by shifting the political weight within popular Islamist movements in favour of "responsible" business elements ready to coexist with the capitalist order, and by accumulating finance capital, helping to consolidate the structural power of the commercial banking system and the autonomy of the private business sector.[1]

The wider implications of embracing Islamic finance from a patient capital, ethical investment and—as Schmid has put it—a geopolitical perspective could provide a win-win scenario for the global economy.

It was in that context that we considered the synergies which exist between Islamic finance and the communitarian politics and the developmental capitalism of east Asia and the mutual financial models prevalent in parts of Europe and south east Asia. This has given us an understanding as to how the future of Islamic finance can thrive in economic structures that is not directly linked to Islam due to the practical solutions to complex problems offered by Islamic economics.

As we have also identified, Islamic finance is now part of the political economy of Malaysia. Critics may argue this only happened because of a political decision in the 1980s for one Malaysian political party to electorally outflank another Malaysian political party.

Others may argue that the role of Islamic finance in the Malaysian political economy is linked to the history of ethnic tensions with the majority of the Malay ethnic population being associated with Islam. Whilst discerning the causes for this phenomenon is important, so is assessing the outcome of this model for the 2020s with Islamic finance now a key feature in a nation that is on the threshold of attaining developed nation status as defined by the World Bank.

Other examples of Islamic finance being incorporated in the political economy of a nation may point to less than happy conclusions. Sudan's economic model was said to be based on Islam. In fact, the model was a version of crony capitalism riven by corruption and, to some extent, ethnic tensions and whose leader, Omar al-Bashir, when toppled from power in 2019, refused to take responsibility of the violence meted out in Darfur or to the fact that millions of dollars was found in his home instead of in the Sudanese Finance Ministry. Such a record is not an indictment against Islamic finance but it is an indictment against those who use Islamic finance and Islamic economics for nefarious purposes.

The Malaysian scholar, Syed Farid Alatas, has expressed his concerns as to how the concept of Islamic economics can be abused for base political purposes:

> At best, under the guise of "Islamic economics" the neglect of issues that usually come under the purview of political economy such as the relationship between the state and the economy and corruption, are tantamount to the legitimation of the status quo, the very state of affairs that Islamic economics claims it wishes to eradicate. At worst, Islamic economics in its neo-classical versions actively promotes the type of economic system that it claims to criticise.[2]

There are, though, positive indications that the concepts of Islamic economics and Islamic finance is shaping positive ideas as to the future of the global economy.

Whilst the contemporary debate regarding political economy is often dominated by the championing of laissez-faire economics in the United States and the demonstration of state capitalism in China, Islamic finance provides a model, within a political economy perspective, where the freedoms of entrepreneurs to generate wealth within the framework of ethics as exemplified by Islamic finance, may provide some pointers towards attaining sustainable global growth rates in the future.

In the midst of the 2020 COVID-19 crisis and the growing tensions with the United States, Chinese President Xi Jinping declared:

> We've come to the understanding that we should not ignore the blindness of the market, nor should we return to the old path of a planned economy.[3]

Whilst it would be too much at this stage to expect the Chinese political model to embrace Islamic finance, this statement by Xi is an indication as to how the wider political community is open to new ideas about attaining sustainable development via innovative finance models.

Felipe Fernandez-Armesto sees religion as having less to do with doctrine and more to do with social norms:

> … most adherents of most systems, religion is not primarily a matter of belief: if it were, it would probably not be such a potent force in human affairs, with the energy to create misery and happiness, war and peace. Few people know the doctrines or dogmas of their faith and fewer really care about them … Religion shapes society not because it is about belief, but because it is about behaviour. Your religion is part of what you do, how you do it and whom you do it with.[4]

One of the Founding Fathers of the United States, Benjamin Franklin (1706–1790) saw religion as more of a social norm rather than as a system of thought:

> I think vital religion has always suffered when orthodoxy is more regarded than virtue; and the scriptures assure me that on the last day we shall be examined not on what we thought but on what we did; and our recommendation will be that we did good to our fellow creatures.[5]

For Islamic finance to be seen in these terms as for primarily serving the ummah, whilst laudable in and of itself, would miss the true potential of the sector to change for the better the financial services offered to people of all faiths and none in developed and developing countries.

As Dr Jemlah Mahmood, the special adviser to the Malaysian Prime Minister on Public Health, said at the height of the 2020 COVID-19 pandemic, Islamic finance, due to the very construct of this model, can do so much for the whole of humanity:

> There is a real opportunity for Islamic finance to offer solutions … as part of the need for longer term developments … to address the Sustainable Development Goals.[6]

However, the space race of the 2020s may indicate that the need for long-term patient capital to realise significant ambitions already exists in conventional finance without the recourse towards innovative models such as Islamic finance.

The Amazon shopping entrepreneur, Jeff Bezos, arguably the world's richest person, has invested millions of dollars in Blue Origin and is one of a handful of pioneering companies in developing reusable space vehicles. According to the New York Times, Bezos sells $1 billion of his Amazon stock each year to keep Blue Origin operational—and solvent. Bezos has said that his aim is to expand the horizons of humanity whilst maintaining life on Earth:

> We can harvest resources from asteroids, from Near Earth Objects and harvest solar energy from a much broader surface area – and continue to do amazing things.

Bezos went further and added that the colonisation of the solar system could support a trillion people:

> Then we would have 1000 Einsteins and 1000 Mozarts, how cool would that be?[7]

At the same time, Elon Musk, the CEO of the electric car company, Tesla, whose personal fortunes was transformed with the online payment platform, PayPal, is in charge of Space X—a company that proclaims on its website:

> SpaceX designs, manufactures and launches advanced rockets and spacecraft. The company was founded in 2002 to revolutionise space technology, with the ultimate goal of enabling people to live on other planets.

In May 2020, Space X became the first private company to transport astronauts into space and Musk is now exploring whether it may be possible to make Mars habitable for permanent human settlements.

These, literally, out of this world concepts—with the rivalry between Bezos and Musk on show—would seem to indicate that American style laissez-faire capitalism and the competitive spirit has the potential to deliver sustainable and long-term patient capital to reach for the stars.

However, whilst these examples are remarkable, they are outliers in terms of levering in capital for much needed investments. As was discussed in chapter six, the highly successful Silicon Valley model of finance has contributed to funding online platforms for a range of uses, from the acclaimed Uber platform to the much used Airbnb.

Gaining investment capital in Silicon Valley for non-online platform technologies such as climate change adaptability has proven to be a harder ask whilst we saw how the funding structure in the pharmaceutical sector does not always lead to solutions being explored for a range of public health contingencies.

Can Islamic finance rise to the challenge in providing the long-term investment that is needed for sustainable economic growth. In theory, the answer would seem to be yes—with its risk sharing models of finance such as musharaka and mudaraba and the project financing model of istisn'a.

However, it has been argued that the Islamic finance industry is too focused on short-term rewards:

> Change in a risk-averse industry, like the murabaha -centric Islamic banking, takes time. I think it has to go through a few market cycles and some external shocks before we can see to its stability. If after shocks the bandwidth of volatility is more narrow vis-à-vis it's conventional counterpart, then we know we're really onto something.[8]

This is the challenge that the Islamic finance industry now faces after the twin shocks of the 2008 and 2020 crises.

How does it transition from a permissive based funding platform to truly using the sophisticated contract models and ethical framework to promote a proactive investment strategy that will meet the funding needs required to sustain technological change?

The Islamic finance industry can learn lessons from the growth of the venture capital industry. The US venture capital industry only began in the 1960s:

> … in no small part because the formal institutional intermediaries in the country had largely given up on entrepreneurial finance.[9]

If the Islamic finance industry plays it right, it can be called upon in the 2020s to address patient finance in the same way that Venture Capital was called on in recent decades to address entrepreneurial finance.

There are many challenges facing the industry in the years ahead such as issues to do with branding, Islamophobia, compliance and much, much more.

However, in many ways, Islamic finance is ahead of its time. In the 1980s if it was suggested that there should be restrictions on speculation this would have been seen as a full-frontal attack on the freedom of the markets. Today, in the United States, the Volcker rule (named after the former US Federal Reserve Chairman, Paul Volcker—1927–2019) stops banks from using their accounts for short-term proprietary trading of securities, derivatives and commodity futures, as well as options on any of these instruments.

The rule also bans banks from acquiring or retaining ownership interests in hedge funds or private equity funds, subject to certain exemptions. The Volcker Rule relies on the premise that these speculative trading activities do not benefit the banks' customers. The Volcker Rule seems to justify many of the long-standing criticisms of speculative trading from Islamic scholars.

In the 1980s, a UK court ruled that gaining good returns was the overriding issue when making investment decisions. Today, conventional finance institutions are reassuring customers that they do have ethical values by embracing environmental, social and governance (ESG) key performance indicators (KPIs). This is another example where Islamic finance was ahead of its time and now, the conventional finance industry is catching up.

Therefore whilst it is easy to refer to challenges facing the Islamic finance industry, the fact that its ethical values and practical approaches has been vindicated by the actions of conventional finance actors and institutions, indicates that, whatever happens in the future, Islamic finance has proved itself and it has a robust structure to move forward.

The main challenge, though, is within the Islamic finance industry itself. Does it want to move past murabaha as one of its main product lines? Does the industry want to focus only on Sukuk rather than other forms of risk sharing as exemplified by the musharaka and mudaraba contract models?

In other words, does the industry want to move beyond the niche product lines it is so successful in to embrace the long-term risk sharing vision that some of the early thinkers in Islamic finance envisaged such as Unghu Aziz, Anwar Iqbal Qureshi and Ahmed Al Najjar?

Admittedly, all industries are influenced by the structures that they operate within and Islamic finance is clearly no different in that respect. A risk averse and permissive approach to investment strategy has engendered a modus operandi across the industry.

However, at a time when conventional finance has adopted ESG KPIs to meet changing consumer needs, this is an ideal opportunity for the Islamic finance industry to enter this space.

Whilst it is a positive development that ESG is becoming a kitemark for success in conventional finance, it is questionable as to whether the operational structures are there within conventional finance to meet the sustainable growth needs on a secure basis to really deliver change.

For Islamic finance, it has the values, the framework, the emerging compliance infrastructure, the contract models and the long-term ability to meet these financing requirements.

For some Islamic finance market participants, the turmoil caused by the 2020 COVID-19 crisis may be the time to consider afresh where the industry is going and to adapt to new market conditions that are likely to continue for some time as a new economic 'normal' takes hold across the global economy.

Sultan Hussan of CIMB Islamic Bank has said that the crisis means that the industry can enter into a "*new paradigm*".[10] Iqbal Khan of Fijr Capital has argued that the crisis means that it is time to look again at the Islamic banking model and move towards a greater emphasis on mudaraba based banking[11] whilst the credit ratings agency, Standard and Poor's predicted new opportunities for the sector:

> COVID – 19 offers an opportunity for more integrated and transformative growth with a higher degree of standardisation, stronger focus on the industry's social role and meaningful adoption of financial technology.[12]

Will the industry embrace new opportunities or will it stay within its comfort blanket of focusing on debt-based instruments? Will the industry move further to meet the global challenges of public health, climate change and poverty alleviation—or will the industry revert to the critics who argue that the Islamic finance participants just want to mirror conventional finance interest-based instruments in a shari'a context?

The values of Islamic finance mark out the industry for its ethics and the promise it holds for attaining a better world.

Abū-Muhammad Muslih al-Dīn bin Abdallāh Shīrāzī also known as Saadi (1210–1291 or 1292) was a poet who encapsulated the human condition.

One of his greatest works is now on display at the entrance of the United Nations headquarters in New York:

Human beings are members of a whole,
In creation of one essence and soul.

If one member is inflicted with pain
Other members uneasy will remain.

If you have no sympathy for human pain
The name of human you cannot retain.

This is, then, the challenge for the Islamic finance industry.

Can it embrace concepts that has synergies with the values and practices of Islamic finance so that this wider base of expertise can fully attain the full potential for the industry - and Islamic economic ideals—to fully shape the global economy of the future.

Will the Islamic finance industry adopt a stronger profile to meet the demand for long-term finance?

Will the Islamic finance industry become proactive with ethical investment strategies?

So—the question for the Islamic finance industry is simply this.

You have the opportunity to meet these emerging market needs.

Will you adapt your internal business culture to meet this challenge?

Notes

1. Todd J Schmid (May 2013), *The Real Shariah Risk: Why the United States Cannot Afford to Miss the Islamic Finance Moment*, University of Illinois Law Review.
2. Syed Farid Alatas, *Blackwell Companion to Contemporary Islamic Thought*, page 596.

3. Comments by President Xi to political advisers on the side lines of the National People's Congress as reported by Xinhua news agency, 24 May 2020.
4. Felipe Fernandez-Armesto, *Millennium: A History of Our Last Thousand Years*, page 273.
5. Quoted in A J Mapp (1987), *Thomas Jefferson: A Strange Case of Mistaken Identity*, page 410.
6. Islamic Markets webinar, 6 May 2020.
7. Comments made at NASA/Apollo 11 gala, 15 July 2017.
8. Rushdi Siddiqui as quoted by Emmy Abdul Alim, *Global Leaders in Islamic Finance*, page 183.
9. Geoffrey Jones, R Daniel Wadhwani, *Entrepreneurship* within *The Oxford Handbook of Business History*, page 519.
10. Islamic Markets webinar, 9 June 2020.
11. Islamic Markets webinar, 10 June 2020.
12. Standard and Poor's statement, 15 June 2020.

A Brief Literature Review

The literature review concerning Islamic finance and Islamic economics can often be defined as the consideration of the technical aspects as exemplified by *Understanding Islamic Finance* as authored by Muhammad Ayub or a consideration of the position of Islamic economics within the prism of religious thought. A good example of this latter form of analysis can be found with Masudul Alam Choudhury's work, *Islamic Economics and Finance: An Epistemological Inquiry* which majors on the philosophical and religious concepts which are integral to Islamic economics.

In respect of examining Islamic finance and Islamic economics literature from a political economy perspective, there are titles such as Timur Kuran's *Islam and Mammon* which considers the efficacy of this form of finance and its historical basis as it pertains to fundamentalist ideas. Rodney Wilson's *Islam and Economic Policy* provides a summary of some Islamic economic concepts and its applicability towards an analysis of the political economy.

In terms of the development of a holistic approach towards understanding the position of Islamic finance and Islamic economic concepts within the framework of political economic analysis, Ibrahim Warde's work, *Islamic Finance in the Global Economy* and Masudul Alam Choudhury's book, *Money in Islam: A Study in Islamic Political Economy* aims to provide such an approach.

J. S. Watkins, *Islamic Finance and Global Capitalism*,
https://doi.org/10.1007/978-3-030-59840-2

However, both Warde and Choudhury perceive the juxtaposition between Islamic economics and capitalism within a binary context where capitalism is defined as a laissez faire system. The idea of considering Islamic economics within the field of the Varieties of Capitalism (VoC) analytical framework is not fully considered by Warde and Choudhury.

Therefore for the preparation of this book, the literature review went beyond academic works which solely focused on Islamic economics and Islamic finance to also consider VoC literature such as *Varieties of Capitalism: The Institutional Foundations of Comparative Advantage* as edited by Peter A Hall and David Soskice.

Warde and Choudhury's work, though their analysis is of great merit, were published in the 2000s and so were not able to benefit from considering the significant advances of the Islamic finance industry during the 2010s. Therefore, for the preparation of this book various contemporary sources of information such as news outlets and webinars were also utilised.

As there was an examination of the interplay between Islamic finance within the political and economic constructs of various countries a wider analysis of political and economic works was undertaken in preparation for the development of this book. This included Joshua Kurlantzick's *State Capitalism: How the Return of Statism Is Transforming the World* and Elizabeth Thompson's *Justice Interrupted: The Struggle for Constitutional Government in the Middle East* amongst many other works.

The themes of this book included the study of:

- Religion
- History
- Politics
- Finance
- Business studies
- Economics
- Sociology
- Political economy

Therefore a wide range of literary sources were studied including works by Milton Friedman, Karl Marx, John Maynard Keynes and Arthur Pigou as well as specialist literature which considered the legacy of the Osmania

University academics from the early twentieth century and other Islamic finance pioneers such as Ahmad Al Najjar and Ungku Abdul Aziz.

This book has examined how Islamic finance and Islamic economic ideas are influencing the operation of the global markets and how these concepts are challenging the practices of the conventional finance industry. It has also explored how Islamic finance compares with a range of ethical finance and business finance practices. This has also led to an enlarged literature review to ascertain the precise details of these concepts for a full comparative analysis with Islamic finance and Islamic economics to be undertaken.

Consequently, this work has taken a holistic approach towards the interrelationship between Islamic finance and Islamic economics with the study of the political economy. It has considered how religious, economic, sociological and political concepts has helped—and hindered—the Islamic finance industry in various regions and nations of the world.

This has necessitated a wide study of academic literature and at the end of each chapter readers are referred to the academic sources that were used to consider each topic under discussion in this book.

Readers gain a good understanding of Islamic finance and Islamic economics and how this relates to political economic analysis with reference material provided for readers to undertake further research in specialist areas which may be of interest.

Index

J. S. Watkins, *Islamic Finance and Global Capitalism*,
https://doi.org/10.1007/978-3-030-59840-2

The manufacturer's authorised representative in the EU is Springer Nature Customer Service Centre GmbH, Europaplatz 3, 69115 Heidelberg, Germany. If you have any concerns regarding our products, please contact ProductSafety@springernature.com

Printed and bound by CPI Group (UK) Ltd, Croydon, CR0 4YY

30/09/2026

02225451-0019